G000058487

The

# *Complete*

# STRANGERS
# IN
# PARADISE

## VOLUME THREE

### Part Three

# The Complete Strangers In Paradise: Vol. III, *Part Three*

Story and Art by
## Terry Moore

Managing Editor
**Robyn Moore**

Color by
**Brian Miller, Hi-Fi Colour Design**
**Jessica Kindziersky Digital Chameleon,**

The Complete Strangers In Paradise: Volume Three *Part Three* is published by Abstract Studio, Inc., P. O. Box 271487, Houston, Texas 77277-1487, U.S.A.    All contents TM & ©2001 Terry Moore. The title, Strangers In Paradise, and the likenesses of its characters are trademarks of Terry Moore and their unauthorized use is prohibited by law. All inquiries or correspondence, Email: SIPnet@StrangersInParadise.com  Anataka suki desu..

www.StrangersInParadise.com.

Printed in Canada.                                                                              ISBN 1-892597-14-4

# CONTENTS

"Why do we do these things to each other? In the end, after all the reasons that seem to die with us, what's the point? I can't help feeling we're all being used. That somebody, somewhere, has set us all up and they're laughing at us as we fall, taking each other out, one by one... until there are none."

-Katchoo

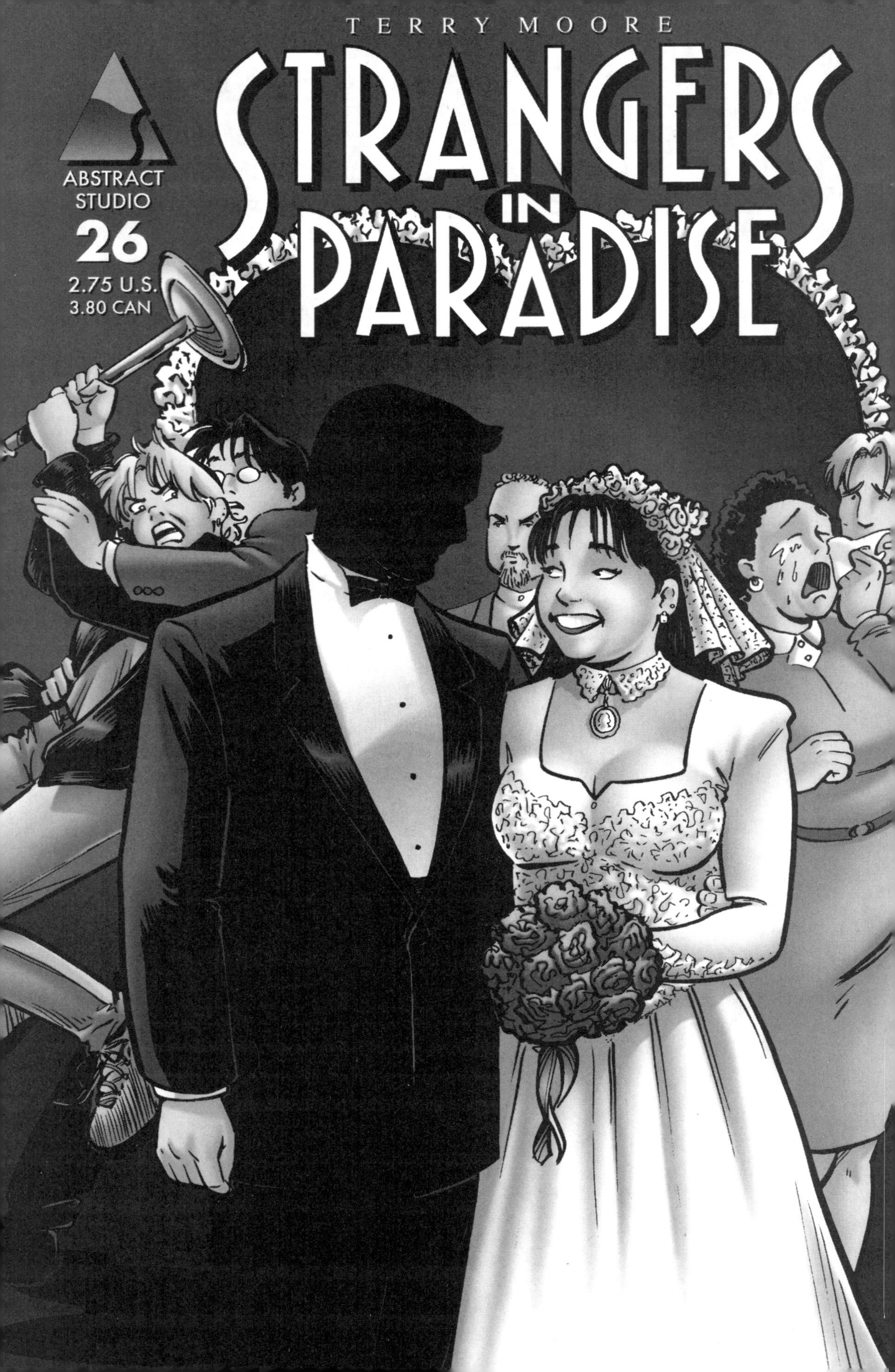
TERRY MOORE
STRANGERS IN PARADISE
ABSTRACT STUDIO
26
2.75 U.S.
3.80 CAN

I am waiting for you to see
What you do to me and to stop it
    Running late

I am waiting for you to love me
Please come and touch me
  I'll thank you
    Running late

Desperate running to
Catch you briefly to
Let you see me
When I can be wrong

Count the pennies you give to me
Days I dare to say what I'm thinking
    Running late

I hold wonders in dreams and slumbers
I work to want to release them
    Running late

Blazed and blasting they swear it's lasting to
Hear the footsteps behind me
    Running late

Desperate running to
Catch my dream globe I
See my heart in
The middle on fire

    Running late

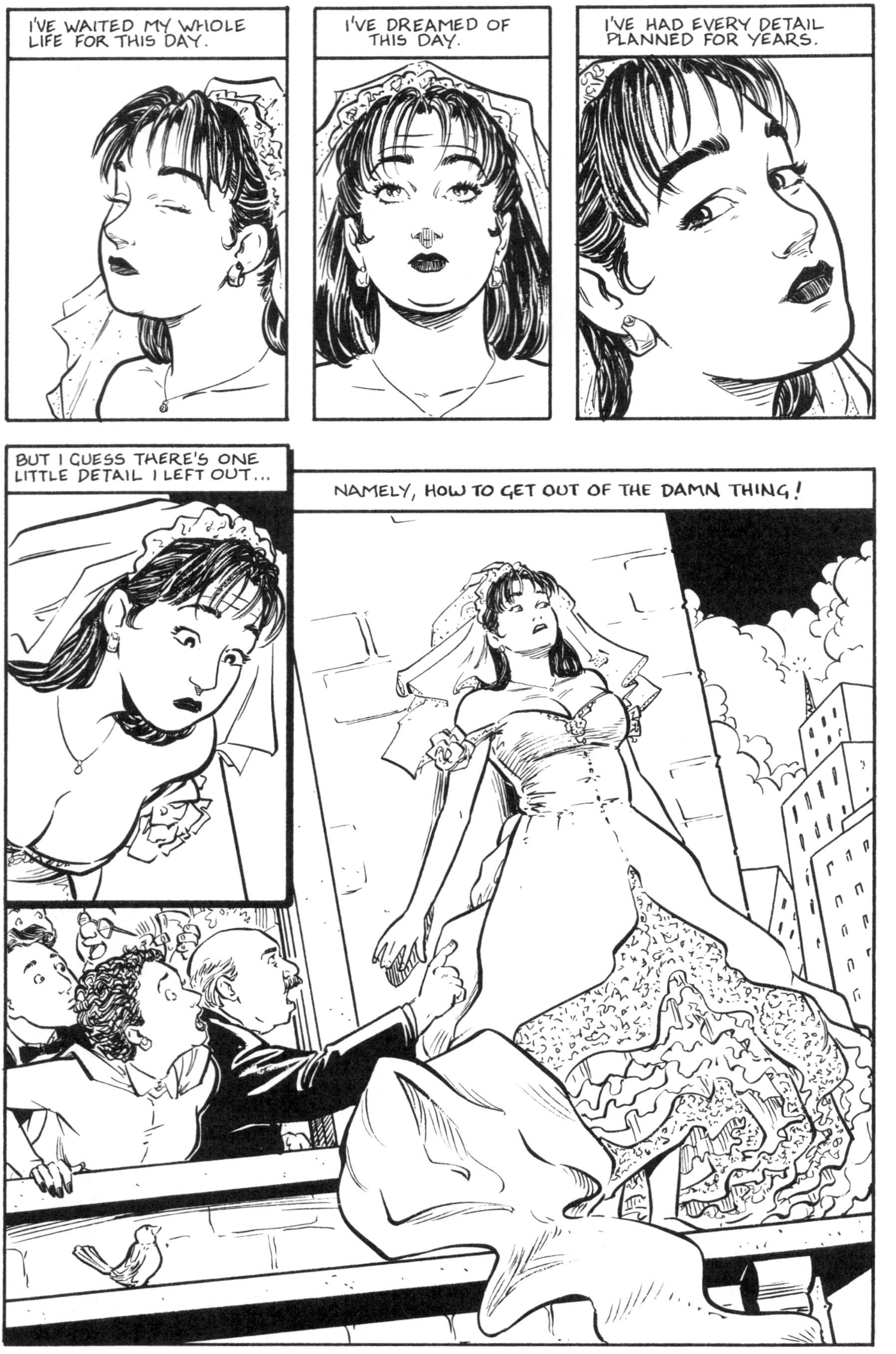
I'VE WAITED MY WHOLE LIFE FOR THIS DAY.
I'VE DREAMED OF THIS DAY.
I'VE HAD EVERY DETAIL PLANNED FOR YEARS.
BUT I GUESS THERE'S ONE LITTLE DETAIL I LEFT OUT...
NAMELY, HOW TO GET OUT OF THE DAMN THING!

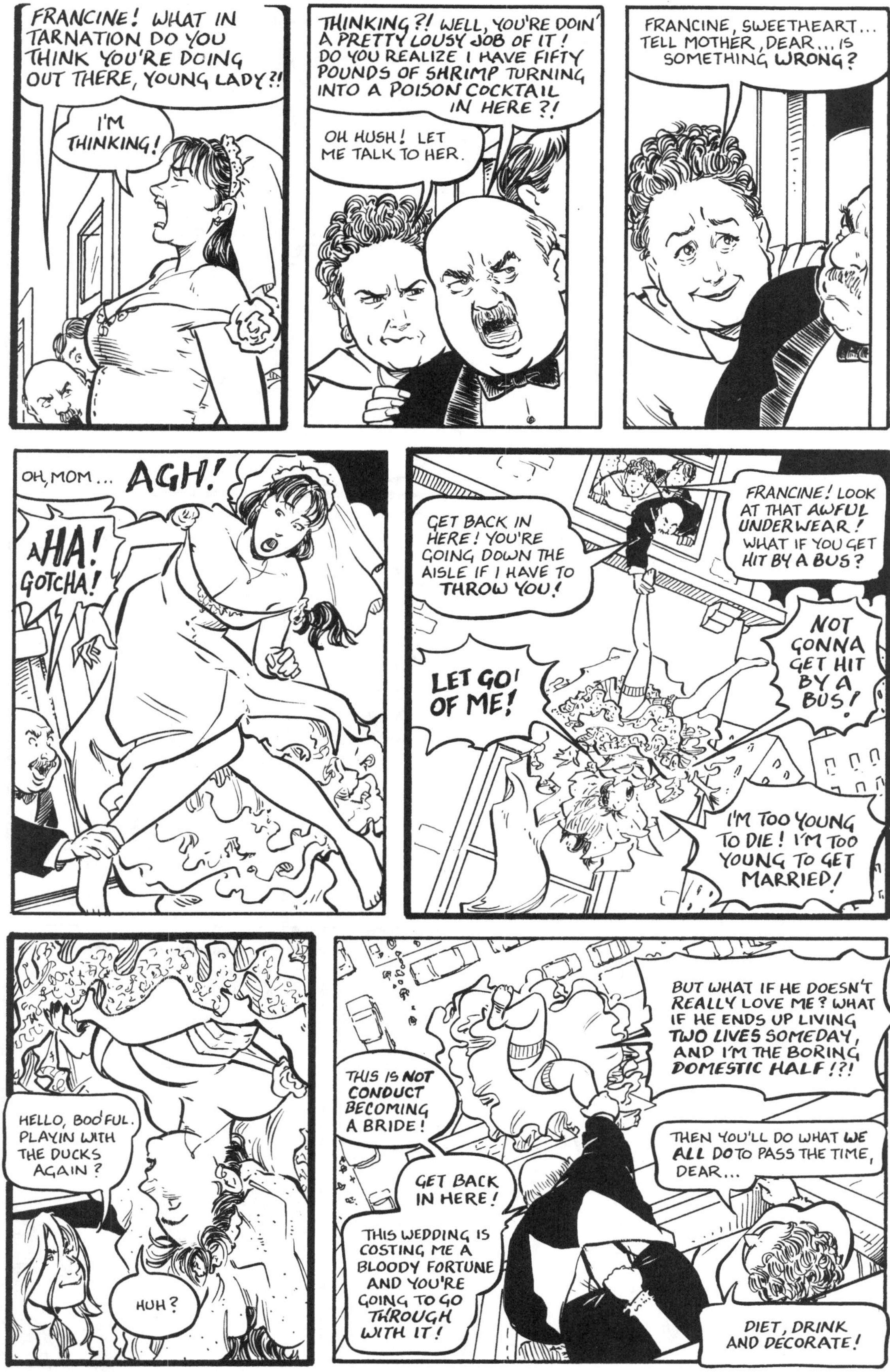
FRANCINE! WHAT IN TARNATION DO YOU THINK YOU'RE DOING OUT THERE, YOUNG LADY?!
I'M THINKING!
THINKING?! WELL, YOU'RE DOIN' A PRETTY LOUSY JOB OF IT! DO YOU REALIZE I HAVE FIFTY POUNDS OF SHRIMP TURNING INTO A POISON COCKTAIL IN HERE?!
OH HUSH! LET ME TALK TO HER.
FRANCINE, SWEETHEART... TELL MOTHER, DEAR... IS SOMETHING WRONG?
OH, MOM...
AGH!
AHA! GOTCHA!
GET BACK IN HERE! YOU'RE GOING DOWN THE AISLE IF I HAVE TO THROW YOU!
FRANCINE! LOOK AT THAT AWFUL UNDERWEAR! WHAT IF YOU GET HIT BY A BUS?
LET GO OF ME!
NOT GONNA GET HIT BY A BUS!
I'M TOO YOUNG TO DIE! I'M TOO YOUNG TO GET MARRIED!
HELLO, BOO'FUL. PLAYIN WITH THE DUCKS AGAIN?
HUH?
THIS IS NOT CONDUCT BECOMING A BRIDE!
BUT WHAT IF HE DOESN'T REALLY LOVE ME? WHAT IF HE ENDS UP LIVING TWO LIVES SOMEDAY, AND I'M THE BORING DOMESTIC HALF!?!
GET BACK IN HERE!
THIS WEDDING IS COSTING ME A BLOODY FORTUNE AND YOU'RE GOING TO GO THROUGH WITH IT!
THEN YOU'LL DO WHAT WE ALL DO TO PASS THE TIME, DEAR...
DIET, DRINK AND DECORATE!

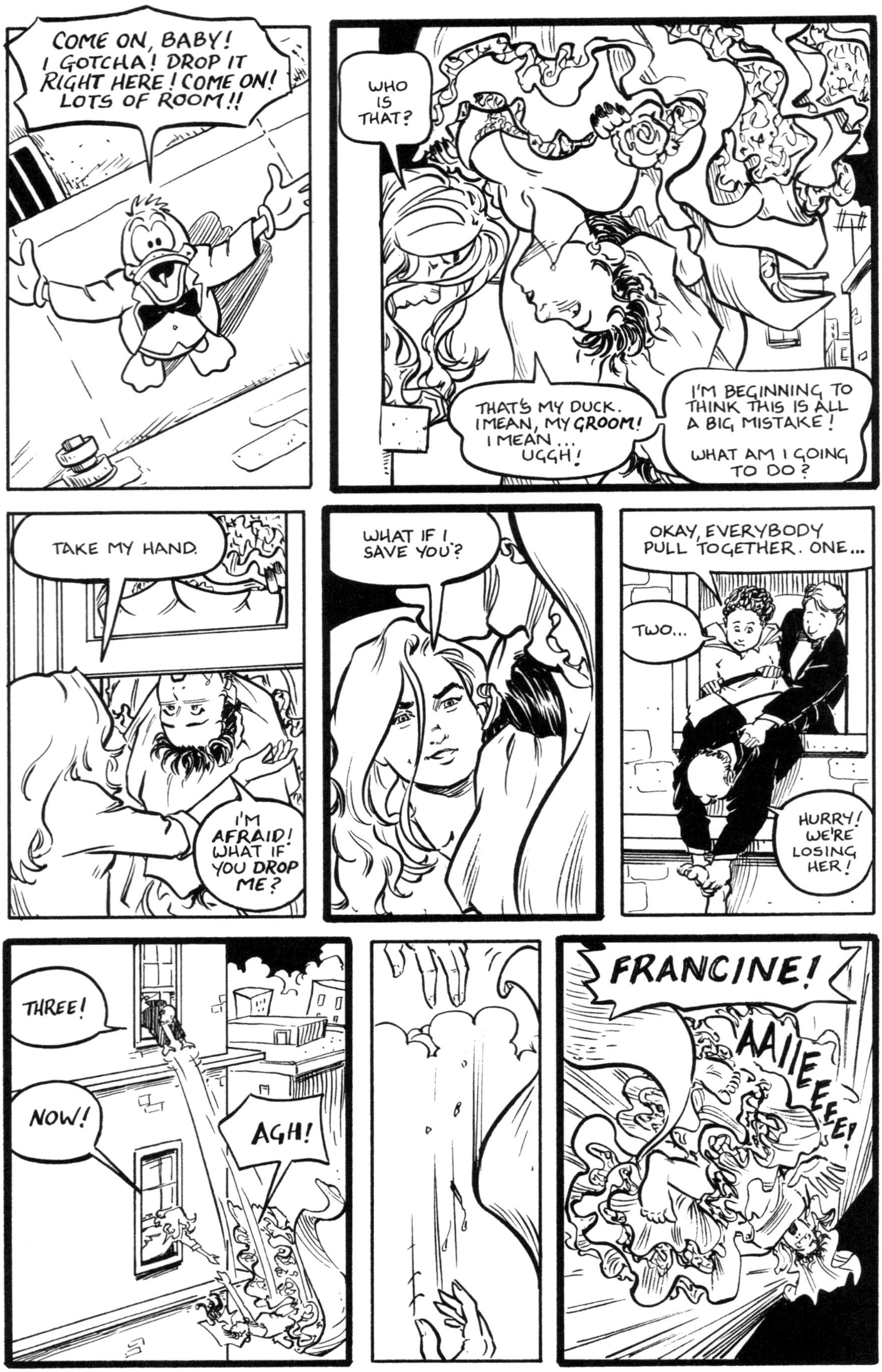
COME ON, BABY! I GOTCHA! DROP IT RIGHT HERE! COME ON! LOTS OF ROOM!!
WHO IS THAT?
THAT'S MY DUCK. I MEAN, MY GROOM! I MEAN... UGGH!
I'M BEGINNING TO THINK THIS IS ALL A BIG MISTAKE!
WHAT AM I GOING TO DO?
TAKE MY HAND.
I'M AFRAID! WHAT IF YOU DROP ME?
WHAT IF I SAVE YOU?
OKAY, EVERYBODY PULL TOGETHER. ONE...
TWO...
HURRY! WE'RE LOSING HER!
THREE!
NOW!
AGH!
FRANCINE!
AAIIEEEEE!

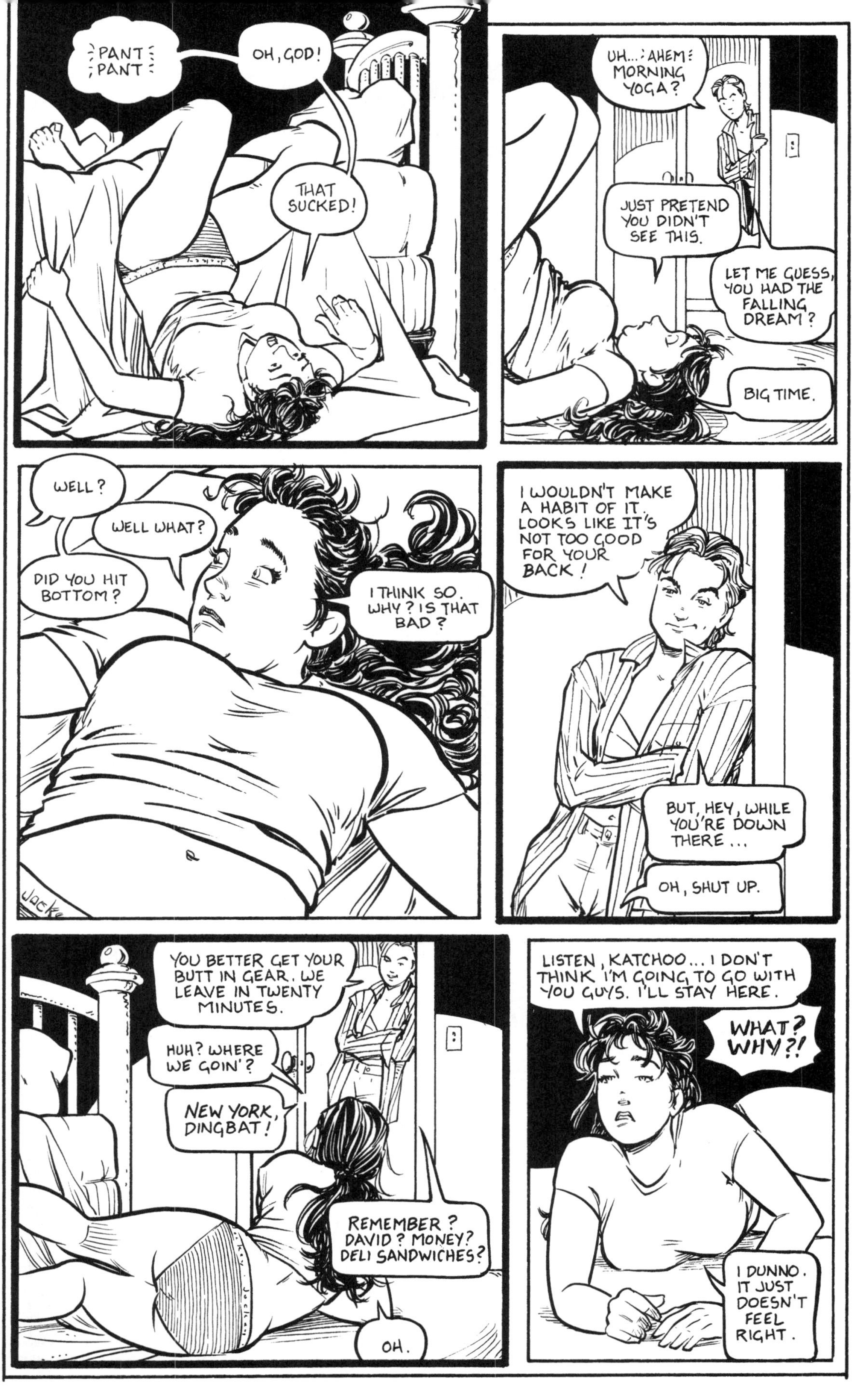
PANT PANT
OH, GOD!
THAT SUCKED!
UH... AHEM MORNING YOGA?
JUST PRETEND YOU DIDN'T SEE THIS.
LET ME GUESS, YOU HAD THE FALLING DREAM?
BIG TIME.
WELL?
WELL WHAT?
DID YOU HIT BOTTOM?
I THINK SO. WHY? IS THAT BAD?
I WOULDN'T MAKE A HABIT OF IT. LOOKS LIKE IT'S NOT TOO GOOD FOR YOUR BACK!
BUT, HEY, WHILE YOU'RE DOWN THERE ...
OH, SHUT UP.
YOU BETTER GET YOUR BUTT IN GEAR. WE LEAVE IN TWENTY MINUTES.
HUH? WHERE WE GOIN'?
NEW YORK, DINGBAT!
REMEMBER? DAVID? MONEY? DELI SANDWICHES?
OH.
LISTEN, KATCHOO... I DON'T THINK I'M GOING TO GO WITH YOU GUYS. I'LL STAY HERE.
WHAT? WHY?!
I DUNNO. IT JUST DOESN'T FEEL RIGHT.

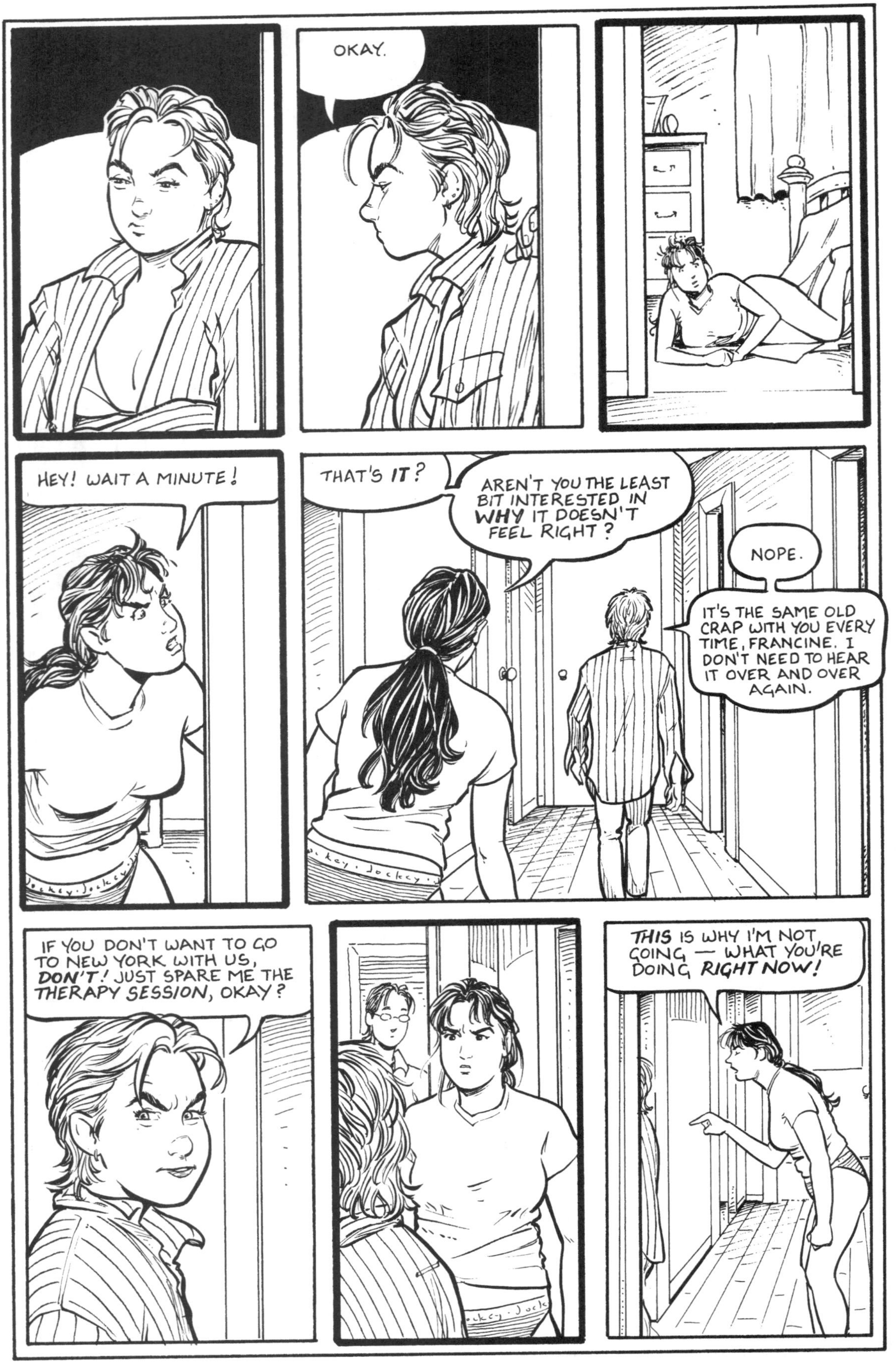
OKAY.
HEY! WAIT A MINUTE!
THAT'S IT?
AREN'T YOU THE LEAST BIT INTERESTED IN WHY IT DOESN'T FEEL RIGHT?
NOPE.
IT'S THE SAME OLD CRAP WITH YOU EVERY TIME, FRANCINE. I DON'T NEED TO HEAR IT OVER AND OVER AGAIN.
IF YOU DON'T WANT TO GO TO NEW YORK WITH US, DON'T! JUST SPARE ME THE THERAPY SESSION, OKAY?
THIS IS WHY I'M NOT GOING — WHAT YOU'RE DOING RIGHT NOW!

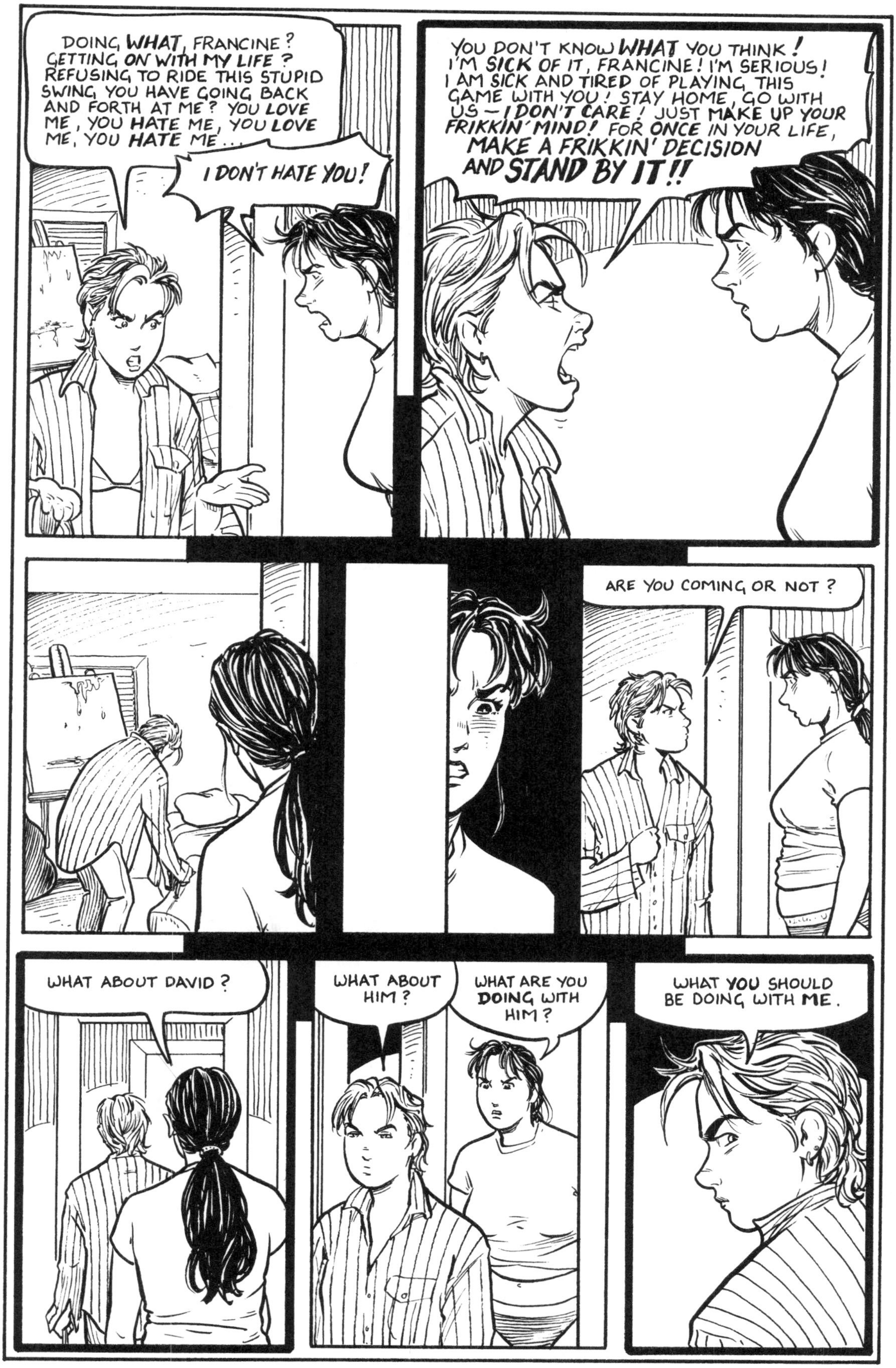
DOING WHAT, FRANCINE? GETTING ON WITH MY LIFE? REFUSING TO RIDE THIS STUPID SWING YOU HAVE GOING BACK AND FORTH AT ME? YOU LOVE ME, YOU HATE ME, YOU LOVE ME, YOU HATE ME...
I DON'T HATE YOU!
YOU DON'T KNOW WHAT YOU THINK! I'M SICK OF IT, FRANCINE! I'M SERIOUS! I AM SICK AND TIRED OF PLAYING THIS GAME WITH YOU! STAY HOME, GO WITH US — I DON'T CARE! JUST MAKE UP YOUR FRIKKIN' MIND! FOR ONCE IN YOUR LIFE, MAKE A FRIKKIN' DECISION AND STAND BY IT!!
ARE YOU COMING OR NOT?
WHAT ABOUT DAVID?
WHAT ABOUT HIM?
WHAT ARE YOU DOING WITH HIM?
WHAT YOU SHOULD BE DOING WITH ME.

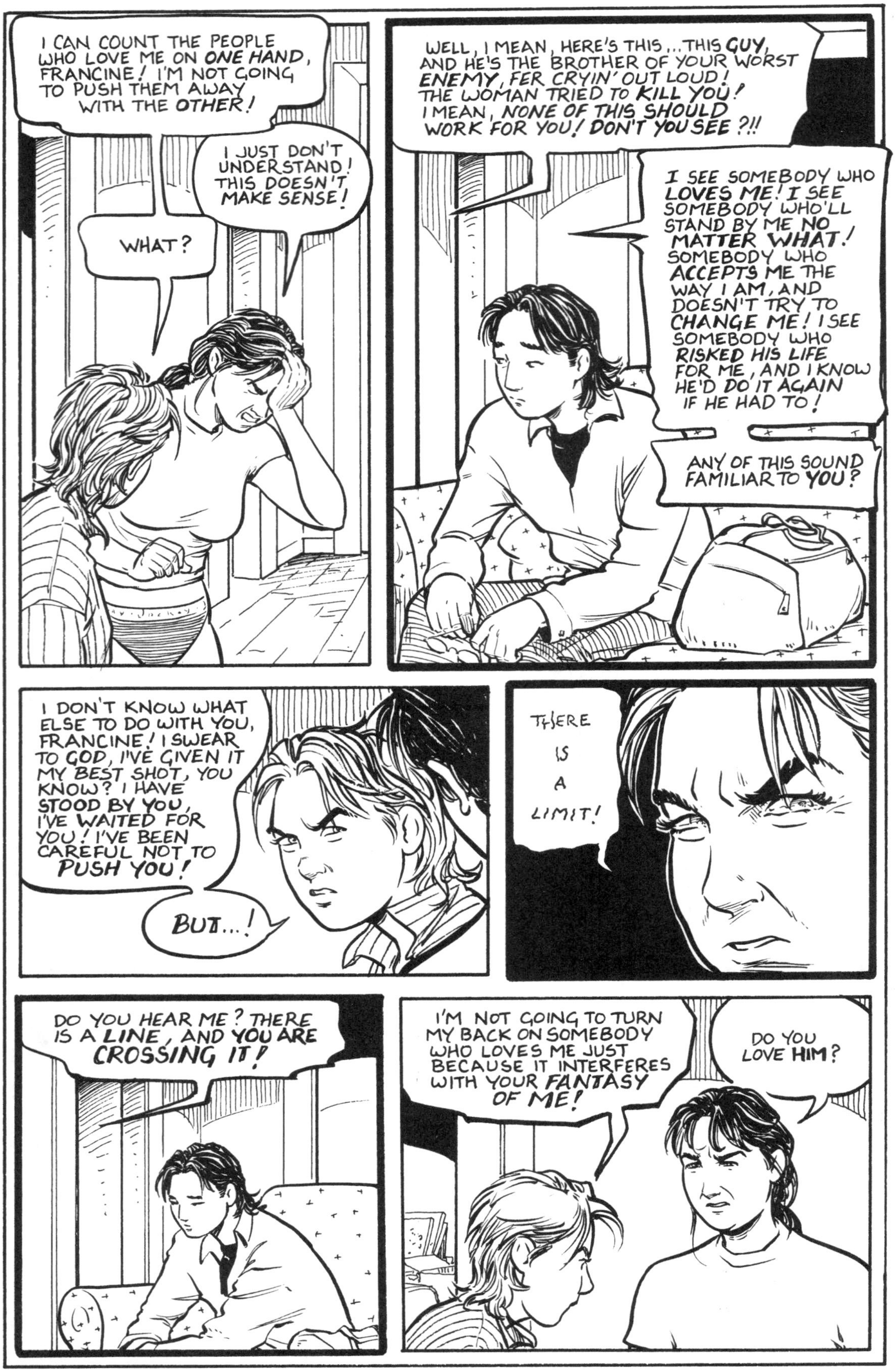
I CAN COUNT THE PEOPLE WHO LOVE ME ON ONE HAND, FRANCINE! I'M NOT GOING TO PUSH THEM AWAY WITH THE OTHER!
I JUST DON'T UNDERSTAND! THIS DOESN'T MAKE SENSE!
WHAT?
WELL, I MEAN, HERE'S THIS... THIS GUY, AND HE'S THE BROTHER OF YOUR WORST ENEMY, FER CRYIN' OUT LOUD! THE WOMAN TRIED TO KILL YOU! I MEAN, NONE OF THIS SHOULD WORK FOR YOU! DON'T YOU SEE ?!!
I SEE SOMEBODY WHO LOVES ME! I SEE SOMEBODY WHO'LL STAND BY ME NO MATTER WHAT! SOMEBODY WHO ACCEPTS ME THE WAY I AM, AND DOESN'T TRY TO CHANGE ME! I SEE SOMEBODY WHO RISKED HIS LIFE FOR ME, AND I KNOW HE'D DO IT AGAIN IF HE HAD TO!
ANY OF THIS SOUND FAMILIAR TO YOU?
I DON'T KNOW WHAT ELSE TO DO WITH YOU, FRANCINE! I SWEAR TO GOD, I'VE GIVEN IT MY BEST SHOT, YOU KNOW? I HAVE STOOD BY YOU, I'VE WAITED FOR YOU! I'VE BEEN CAREFUL NOT TO PUSH YOU!
BUT...!
THERE IS A LIMIT!
DO YOU HEAR ME? THERE IS A LINE, AND YOU ARE CROSSING IT!
I'M NOT GOING TO TURN MY BACK ON SOMEBODY WHO LOVES ME JUST BECAUSE IT INTERFERES WITH YOUR FANTASY OF ME!
DO YOU LOVE HIM?

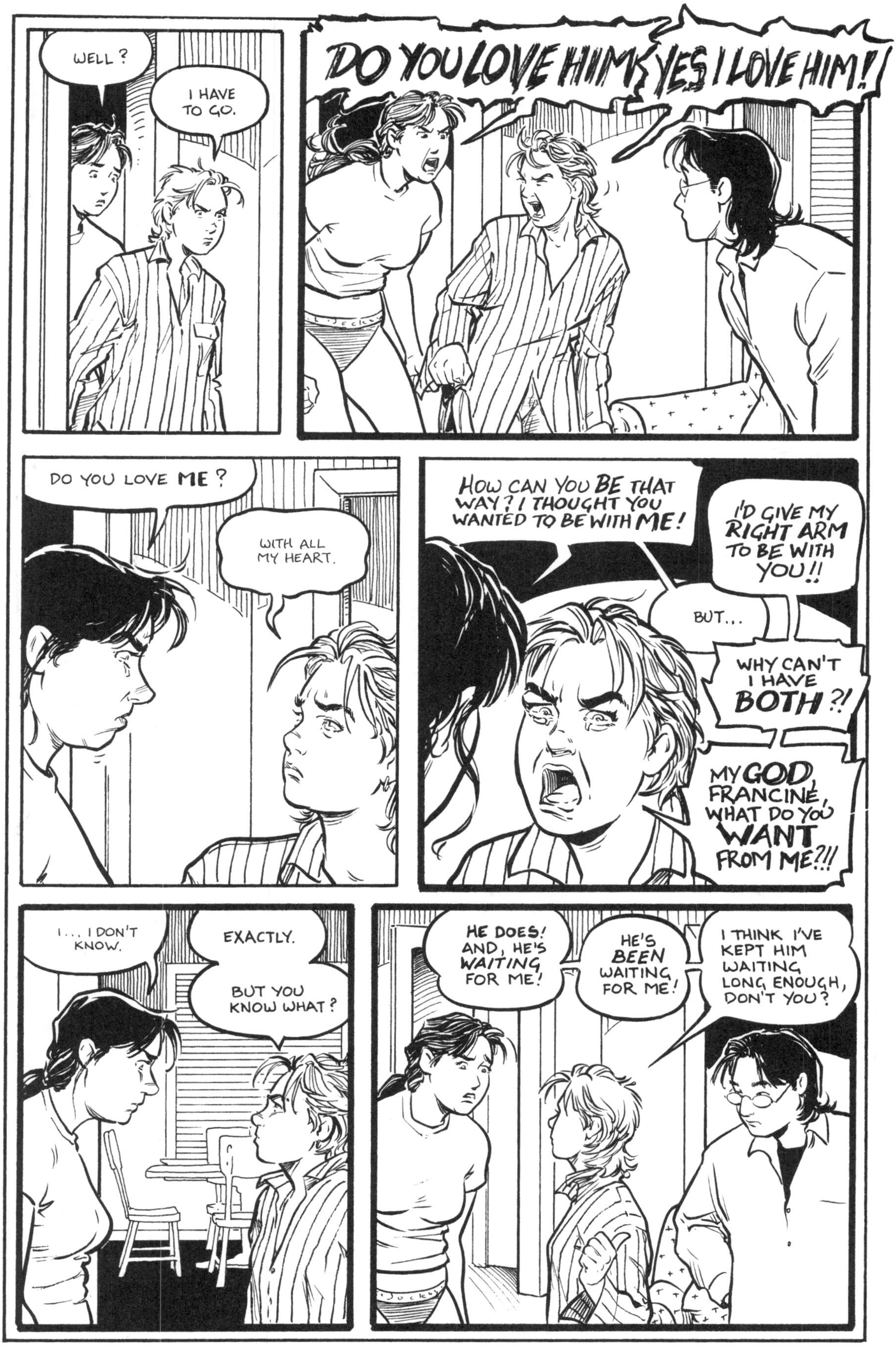
WELL?
I HAVE TO GO.
DO YOU LOVE HIM? YES I LOVE HIM!
DO YOU LOVE ME?
WITH ALL MY HEART.
HOW CAN YOU BE THAT WAY? I THOUGHT YOU WANTED TO BE WITH ME!
I'D GIVE MY RIGHT ARM TO BE WITH YOU!!
BUT...
WHY CAN'T I HAVE BOTH?!
MY GOD, FRANCINE, WHAT DO YOU WANT FROM ME?!!
I... I DON'T KNOW.
EXACTLY.
BUT YOU KNOW WHAT?
HE DOES! AND, HE'S WAITING FOR ME!
HE'S BEEN WAITING FOR ME!
I THINK I'VE KEPT HIM WAITING LONG ENOUGH, DON'T YOU?

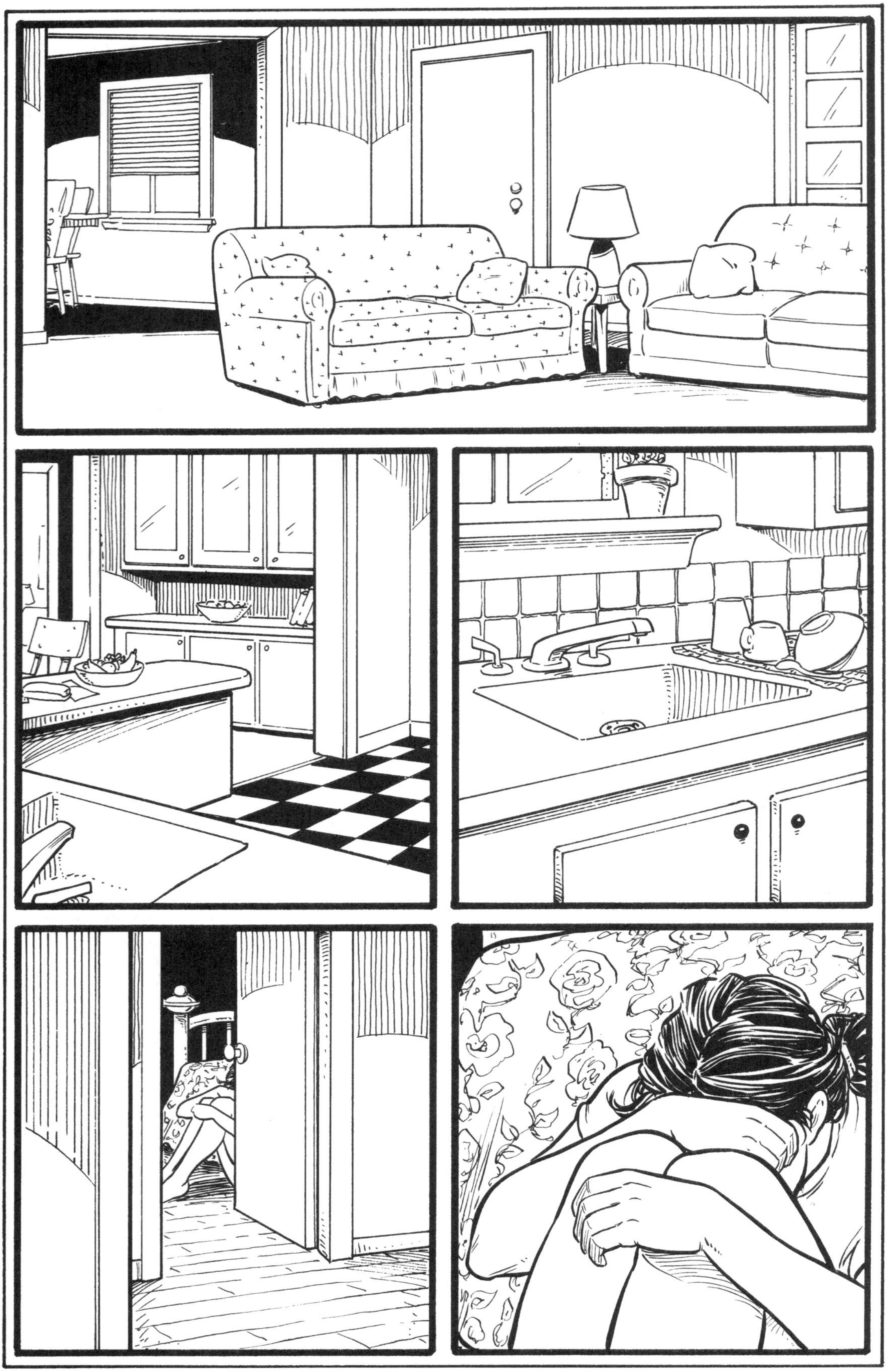

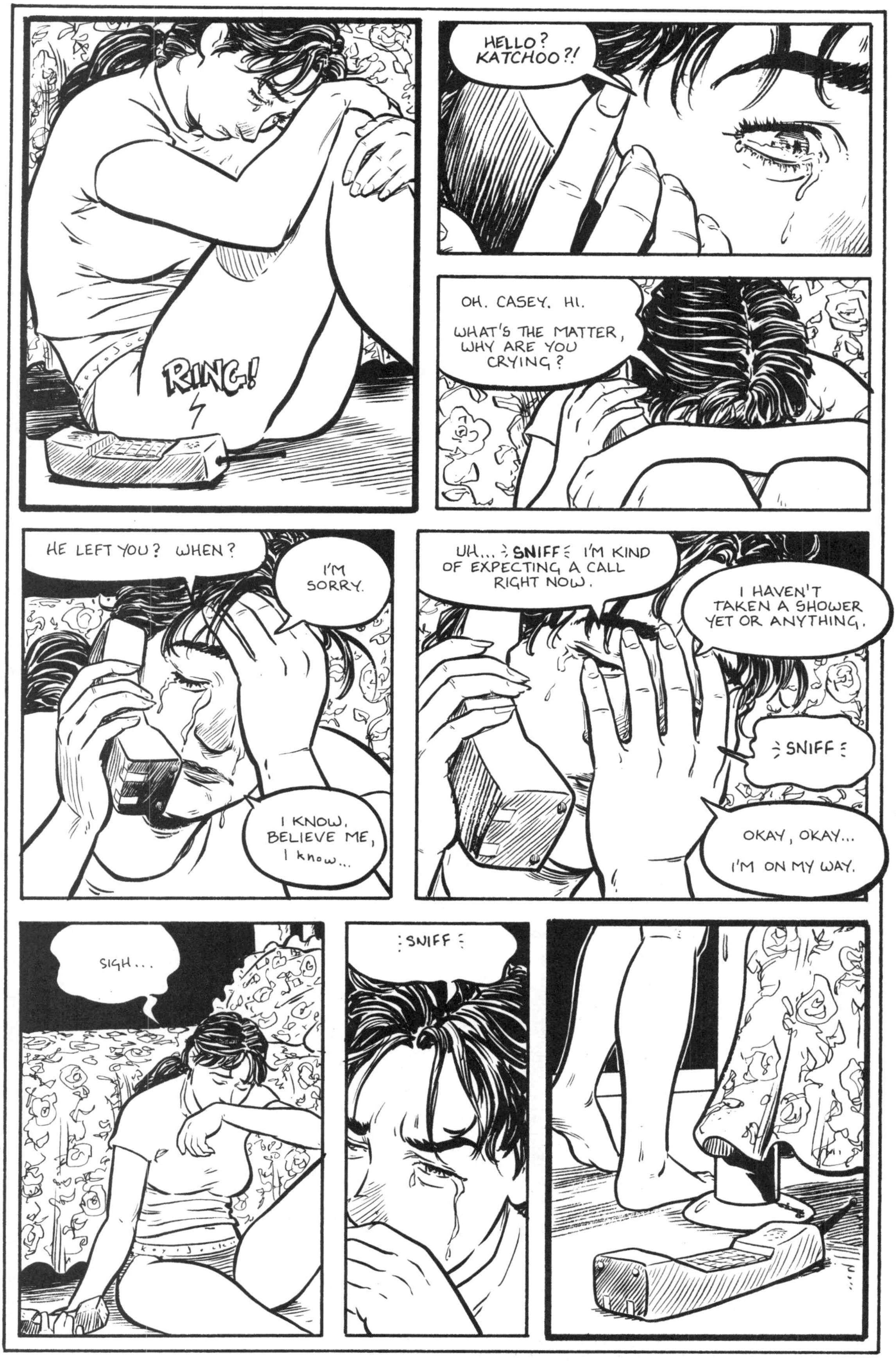
RING!
HELLO? KATCHOO?!
OH. CASEY. HI.
WHAT'S THE MATTER, WHY ARE YOU CRYING?
HE LEFT YOU? WHEN?
I'M SORRY.
I KNOW. BELIEVE ME, I know...
UH... SNIFF I'M KIND OF EXPECTING A CALL RIGHT NOW.
I HAVEN'T TAKEN A SHOWER YET OR ANYTHING.
SNIFF
OKAY, OKAY...
I'M ON MY WAY.
SIGH...
SNIFF

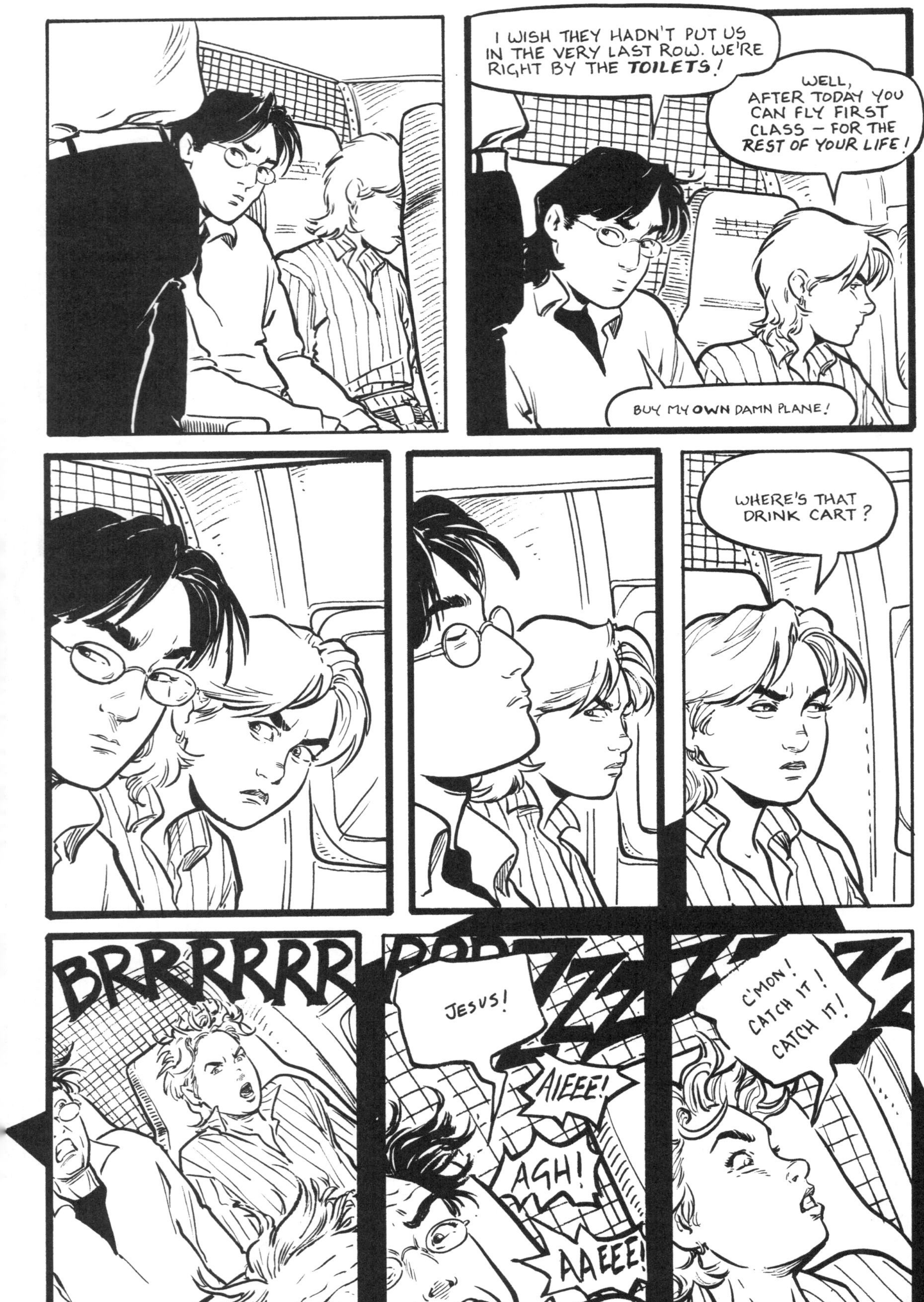

I WISH THEY HADN'T PUT US IN THE VERY LAST ROW. WE'RE RIGHT BY THE TOILETS!
WELL, AFTER TODAY YOU CAN FLY FIRST CLASS — FOR THE REST OF YOUR LIFE!
BUY MY OWN DAMN PLANE!
WHERE'S THAT DRINK CART?
BRRRRRRR
JESUS!
AIEEE!
AGH!
AAEEE!
C'MON! CATCH IT! CATCH IT!

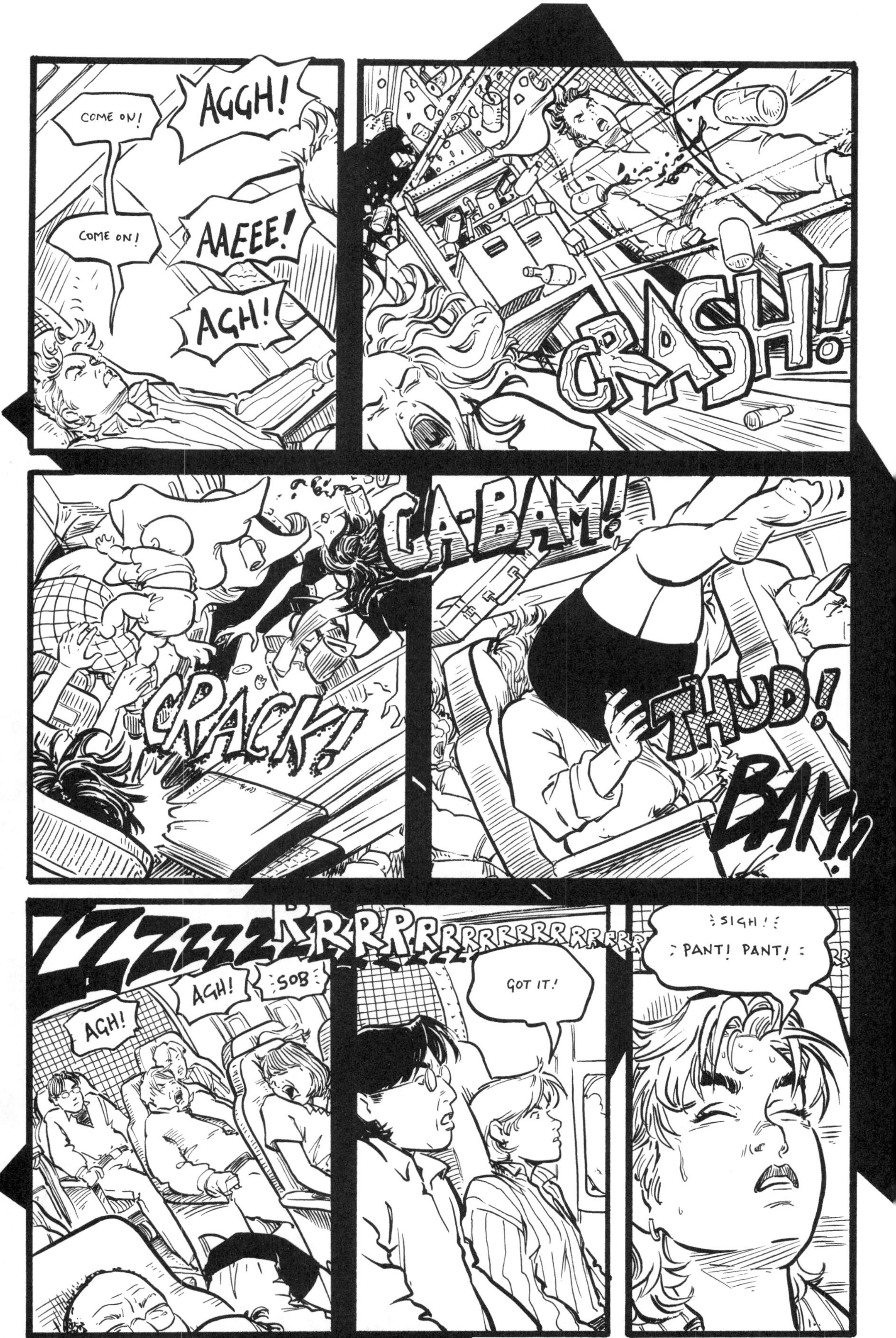
COME ON!
AGGH!
COME ON!
AAEEE!
AGH!
CRASH!
CA-BAM!
CRACK!
THUD!
BAM!!
ZZZZZZRRRRRRRRRRRRRRRRR
AGH!
AGH!
SOB
GOT IT!
SIGH!
PANT! PANT!

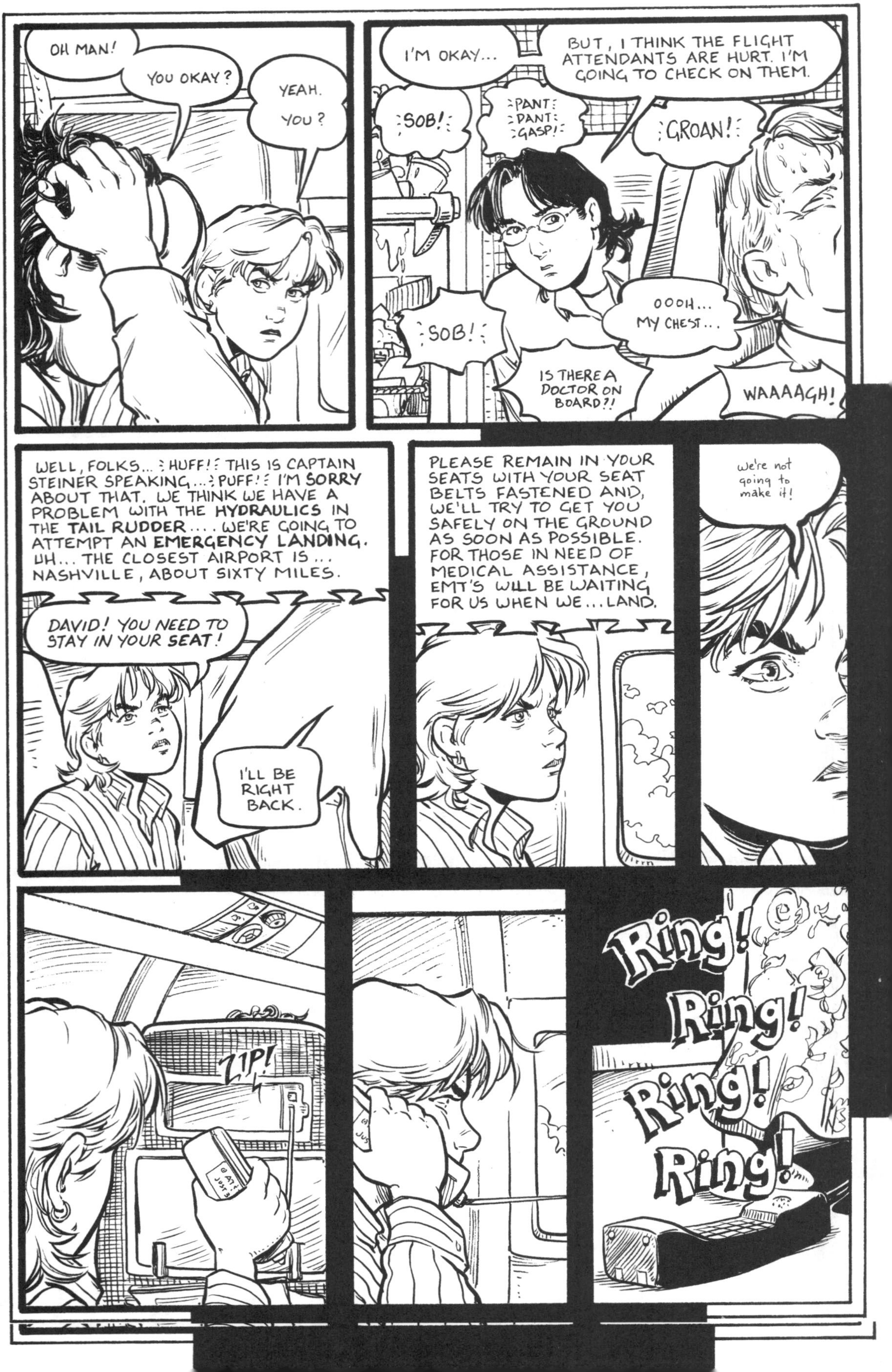
OH MAN!
YOU OKAY?
YEAH.
YOU?
I'M OKAY...
BUT, I THINK THE FLIGHT ATTENDANTS ARE HURT. I'M GOING TO CHECK ON THEM.
SOB!
PANT PANT GASP!
GROAN!
SOB!
OOOH... MY CHEST...
IS THERE A DOCTOR ON BOARD?!
WAAAAGH!
WELL, FOLKS... HUFF! THIS IS CAPTAIN STEINER SPEAKING... PUFF! I'M SORRY ABOUT THAT. WE THINK WE HAVE A PROBLEM WITH THE HYDRAULICS IN THE TAIL RUDDER.... WE'RE GOING TO ATTEMPT AN EMERGENCY LANDING. UH... THE CLOSEST AIRPORT IS... NASHVILLE, ABOUT SIXTY MILES.
DAVID! YOU NEED TO STAY IN YOUR SEAT!
I'LL BE RIGHT BACK.
PLEASE REMAIN IN YOUR SEATS WITH YOUR SEAT BELTS FASTENED AND, WE'LL TRY TO GET YOU SAFELY ON THE GROUND AS SOON AS POSSIBLE. FOR THOSE IN NEED OF MEDICAL ASSISTANCE, EMT'S WILL BE WAITING FOR US WHEN WE... LAND.
We're not going to make it!
ZIP!
Ring!
Ring!
Ring!
Ring!

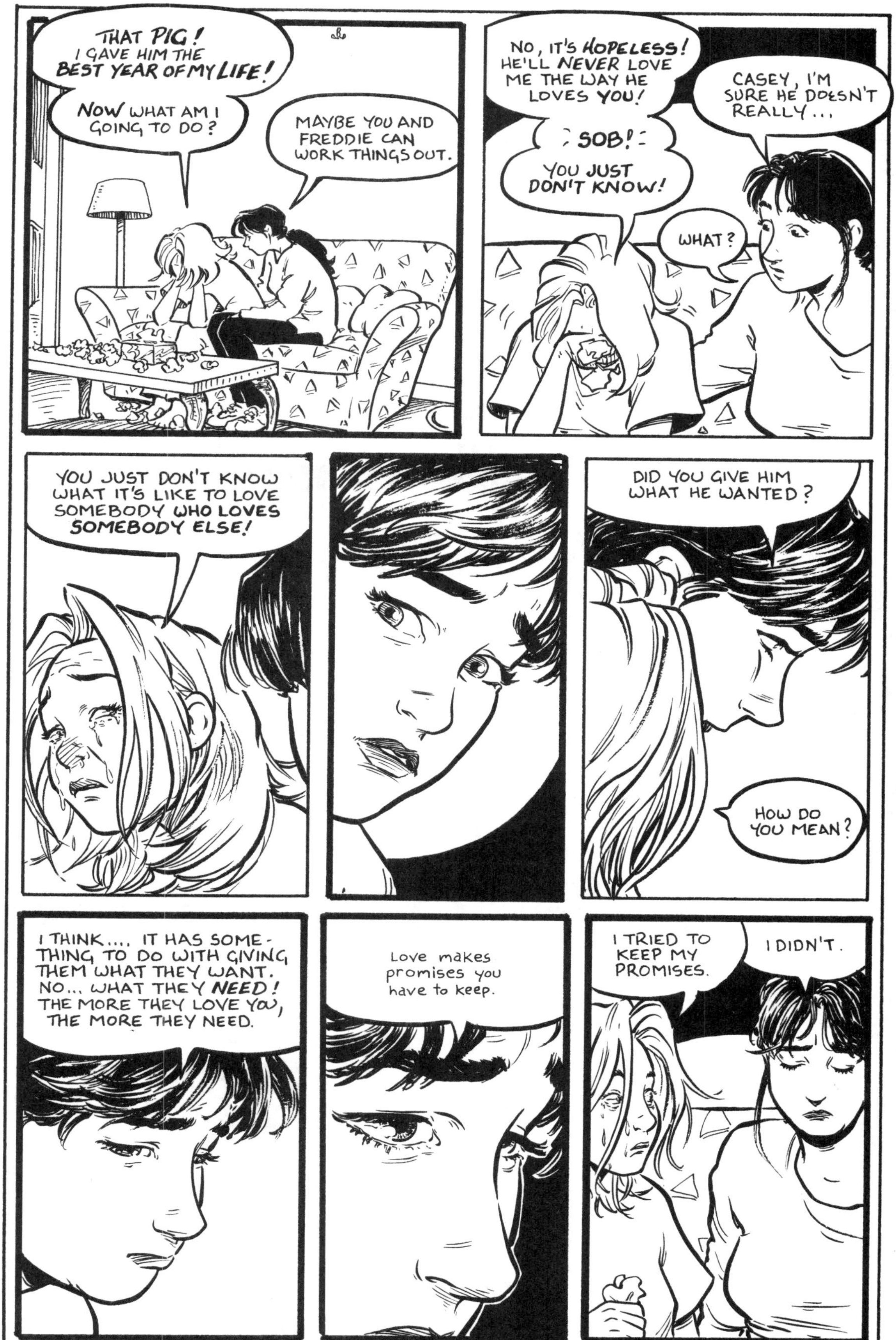

THAT PIG! I GAVE HIM THE BEST YEAR OF MY LIFE!
NOW WHAT AM I GOING TO DO?
MAYBE YOU AND FREDDIE CAN WORK THINGS OUT.
NO, IT'S HOPELESS! HE'LL NEVER LOVE ME THE WAY HE LOVES YOU!
SOB!
YOU JUST DON'T KNOW!
CASEY, I'M SURE HE DOESN'T REALLY...
WHAT?
YOU JUST DON'T KNOW WHAT IT'S LIKE TO LOVE SOMEBODY WHO LOVES SOMEBODY ELSE!
DID YOU GIVE HIM WHAT HE WANTED?
HOW DO YOU MEAN?
I THINK.... IT HAS SOMETHING TO DO WITH GIVING THEM WHAT THEY WANT. NO... WHAT THEY NEED! THE MORE THEY LOVE YOU, THE MORE THEY NEED.
Love makes promises you have to keep.
I TRIED TO KEEP MY PROMISES.
I DIDN'T.

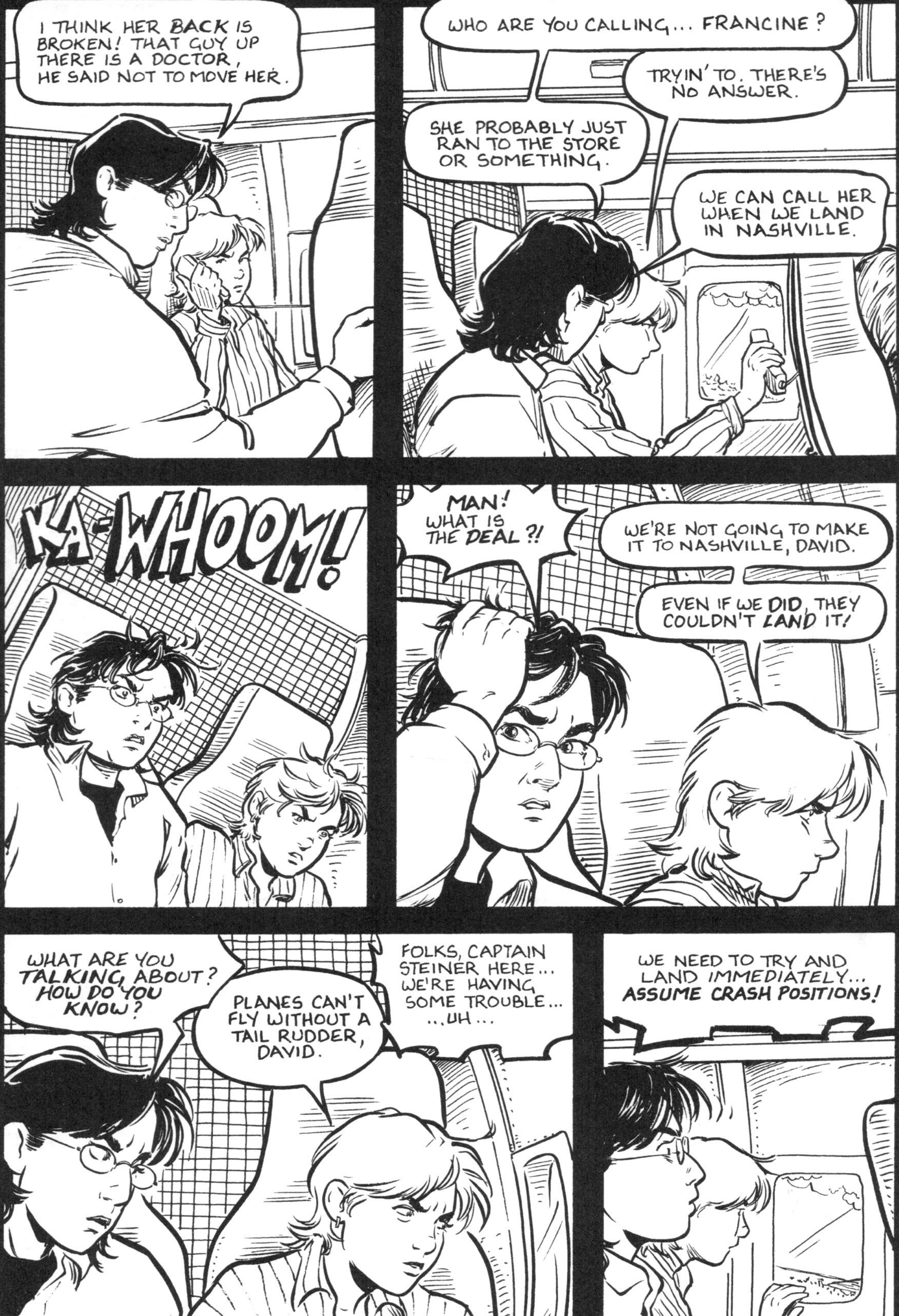

I THINK HER BACK IS BROKEN! THAT GUY UP THERE IS A DOCTOR, HE SAID NOT TO MOVE HER.
WHO ARE YOU CALLING... FRANCINE?
TRYIN' TO. THERE'S NO ANSWER.
SHE PROBABLY JUST RAN TO THE STORE OR SOMETHING.
WE CAN CALL HER WHEN WE LAND IN NASHVILLE.
KA-WHOOM!
MAN! WHAT IS THE DEAL?!
WE'RE NOT GOING TO MAKE IT TO NASHVILLE, DAVID.
EVEN IF WE DID, THEY COULDN'T LAND IT!
WHAT ARE YOU TALKING ABOUT? HOW DO YOU KNOW?
PLANES CAN'T FLY WITHOUT A TAIL RUDDER, DAVID.
FOLKS, CAPTAIN STEINER HERE... WE'RE HAVING SOME TROUBLE... ...UH...
WE NEED TO TRY AND LAND IMMEDIATELY... ASSUME CRASH POSITIONS!

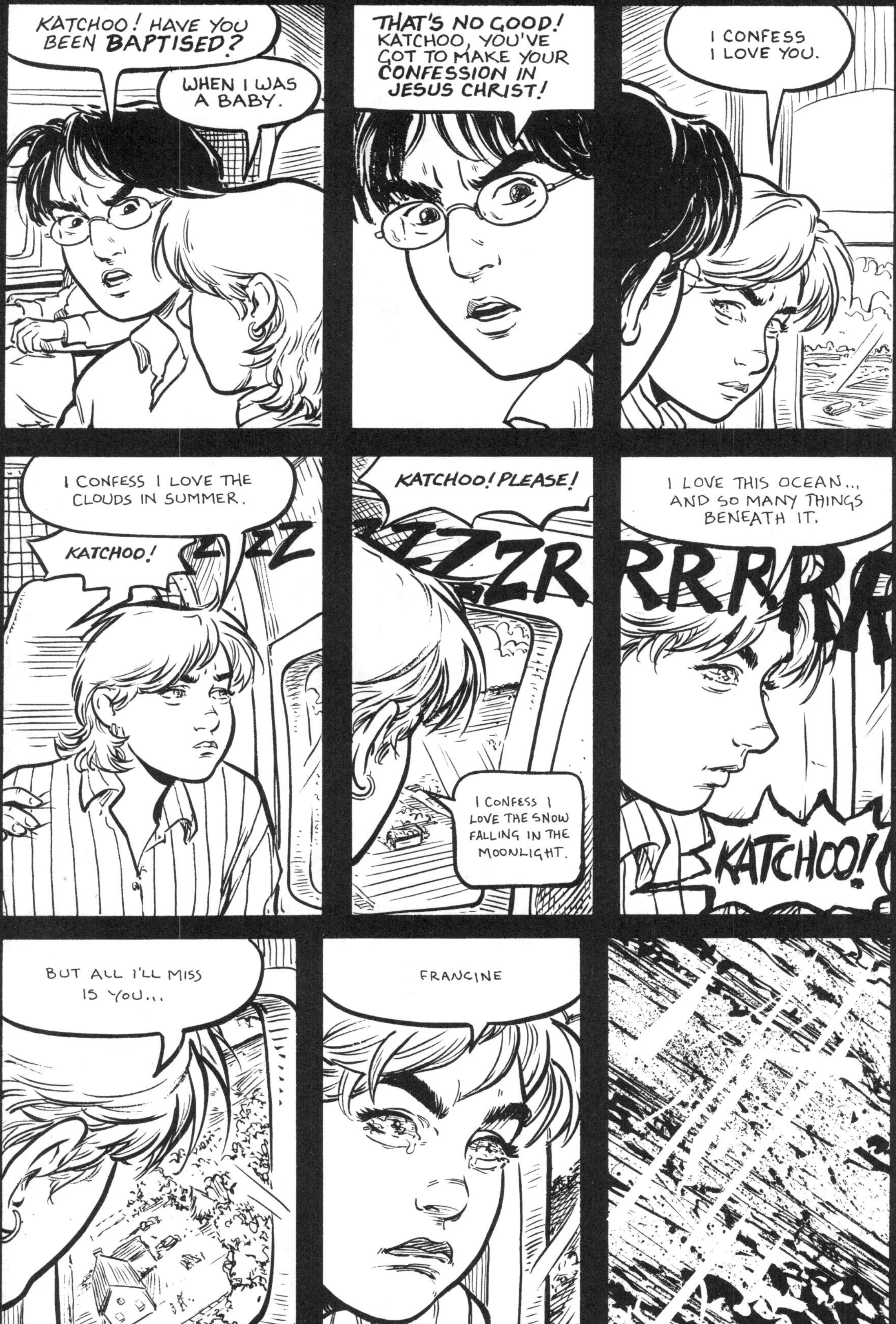
KATCHOO! HAVE YOU BEEN BAPTISED?
WHEN I WAS A BABY.
THAT'S NO GOOD! KATCHOO, YOU'VE GOT TO MAKE YOUR CONFESSION IN JESUS CHRIST!
I CONFESS I LOVE YOU.
I CONFESS I LOVE THE CLOUDS IN SUMMER.
KATCHOO!
KATCHOO! PLEASE!
ZZZZZZRRRRRRR
I CONFESS I LOVE THE SNOW FALLING IN THE MOONLIGHT.
I LOVE THIS OCEAN... AND SO MANY THINGS BENEATH IT.
KATCHOO!
BUT ALL I'LL MISS IS YOU...
FRANCINE

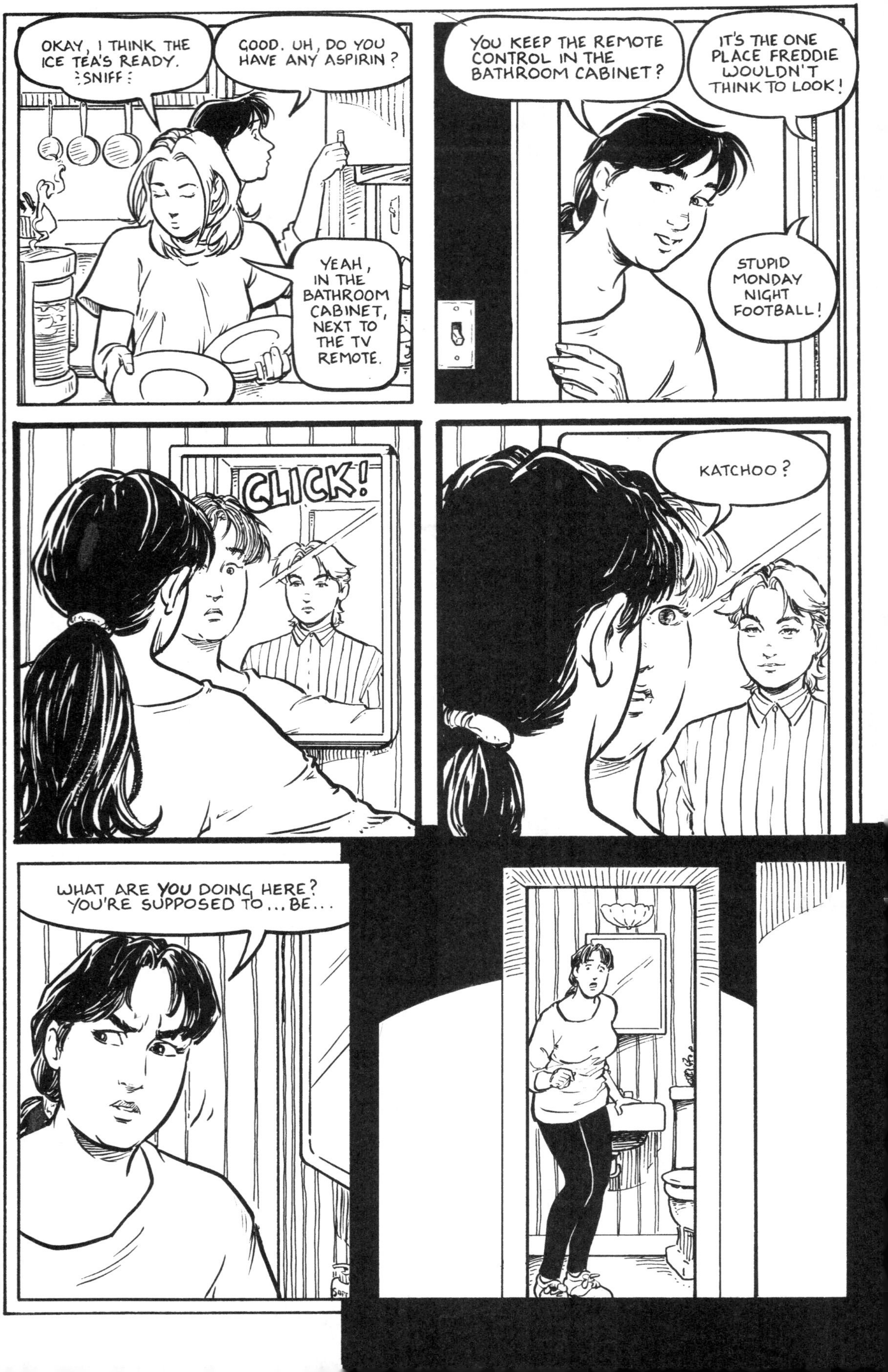
OKAY, I THINK THE ICE TEA'S READY. :SNIFF:
GOOD. UH, DO YOU HAVE ANY ASPIRIN?
YEAH, IN THE BATHROOM CABINET, NEXT TO THE TV REMOTE.
YOU KEEP THE REMOTE CONTROL IN THE BATHROOM CABINET?
IT'S THE ONE PLACE FREDDIE WOULDN'T THINK TO LOOK!
STUPID MONDAY NIGHT FOOTBALL!
CLICK!
KATCHOO?
WHAT ARE YOU DOING HERE? YOU'RE SUPPOSED TO... BE...

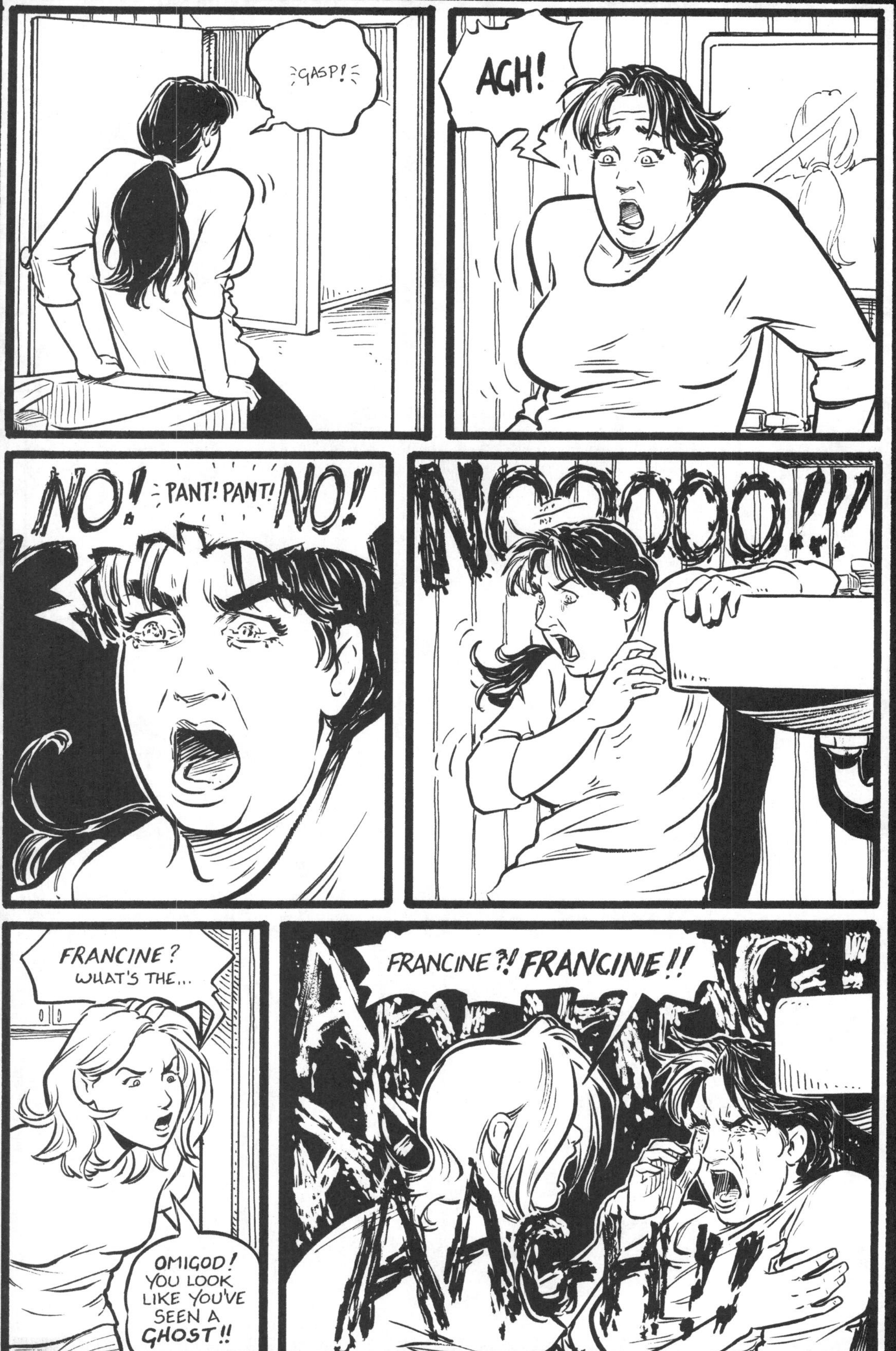
GASP!
AGH!
NO! PANT! PANT! NO!!
NOOOOOO!!!
FRANCINE? WHAT'S THE...
OMIGOD! YOU LOOK LIKE YOU'VE SEEN A GHOST!!
FRANCINE?! FRANCINE!!
AAGH!!

ABSTRACT
STUDIO
27

2.75 U.S.
3.80 CAN

# STRANGERS IN PARADISE

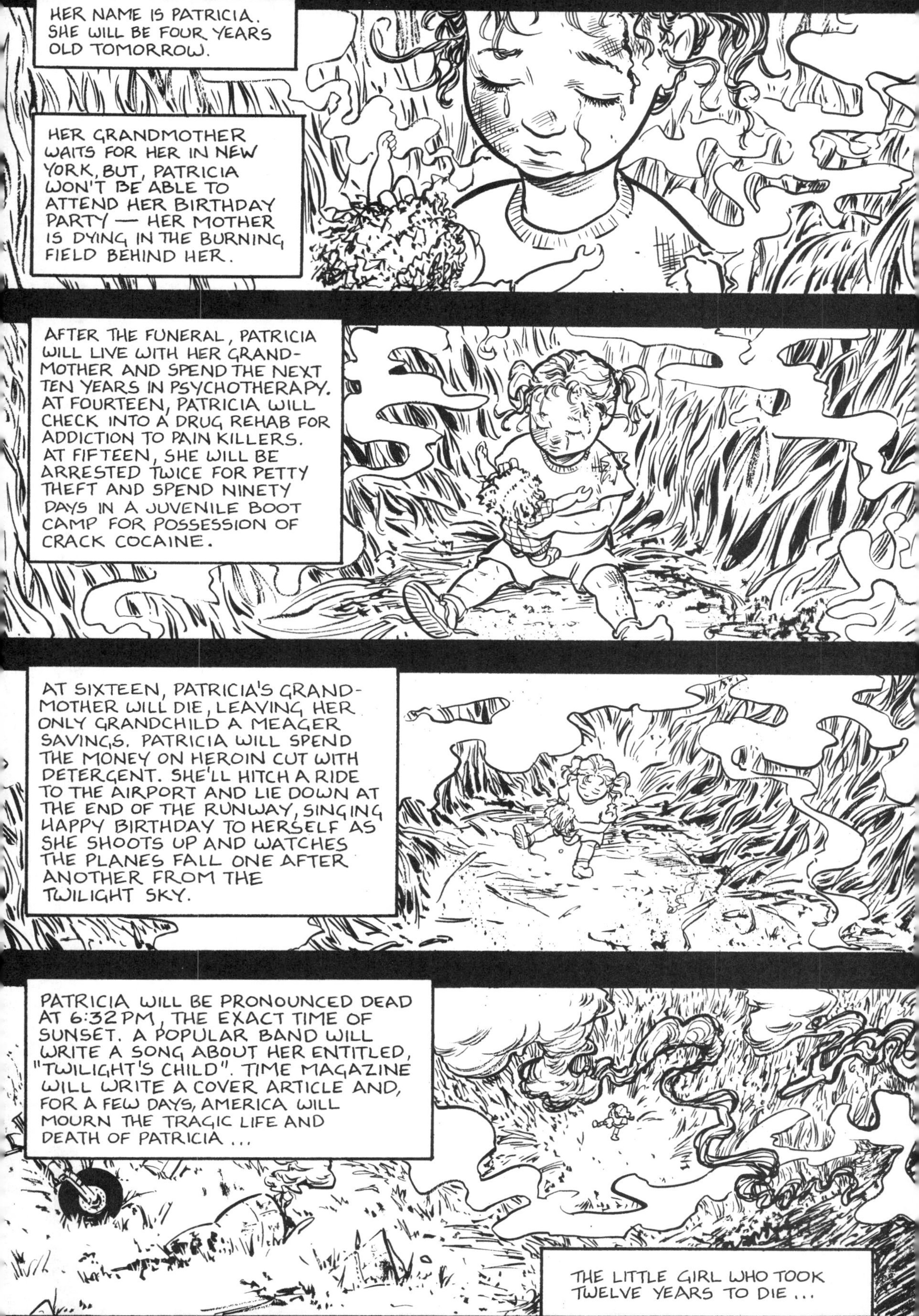
HER NAME IS PATRICIA. SHE WILL BE FOUR YEARS OLD TOMORROW.
HER GRANDMOTHER WAITS FOR HER IN NEW YORK, BUT, PATRICIA WON'T BE ABLE TO ATTEND HER BIRTHDAY PARTY — HER MOTHER IS DYING IN THE BURNING FIELD BEHIND HER.
AFTER THE FUNERAL, PATRICIA WILL LIVE WITH HER GRAND-MOTHER AND SPEND THE NEXT TEN YEARS IN PSYCHOTHERAPY. AT FOURTEEN, PATRICIA WILL CHECK INTO A DRUG REHAB FOR ADDICTION TO PAIN KILLERS. AT FIFTEEN, SHE WILL BE ARRESTED TWICE FOR PETTY THEFT AND SPEND NINETY DAYS IN A JUVENILE BOOT CAMP FOR POSSESSION OF CRACK COCAINE.
AT SIXTEEN, PATRICIA'S GRAND-MOTHER WILL DIE, LEAVING HER ONLY GRANDCHILD A MEAGER SAVINGS. PATRICIA WILL SPEND THE MONEY ON HEROIN CUT WITH DETERGENT. SHE'LL HITCH A RIDE TO THE AIRPORT AND LIE DOWN AT THE END OF THE RUNWAY, SINGING HAPPY BIRTHDAY TO HERSELF AS SHE SHOOTS UP AND WATCHES THE PLANES FALL ONE AFTER ANOTHER FROM THE TWILIGHT SKY.
PATRICIA WILL BE PRONOUNCED DEAD AT 6:32 PM, THE EXACT TIME OF SUNSET. A POPULAR BAND WILL WRITE A SONG ABOUT HER ENTITLED, "TWILIGHT'S CHILD". TIME MAGAZINE WILL WRITE A COVER ARTICLE AND, FOR A FEW DAYS, AMERICA WILL MOURN THE TRAGIC LIFE AND DEATH OF PATRICIA ...
THE LITTLE GIRL WHO TOOK TWELVE YEARS TO DIE ...

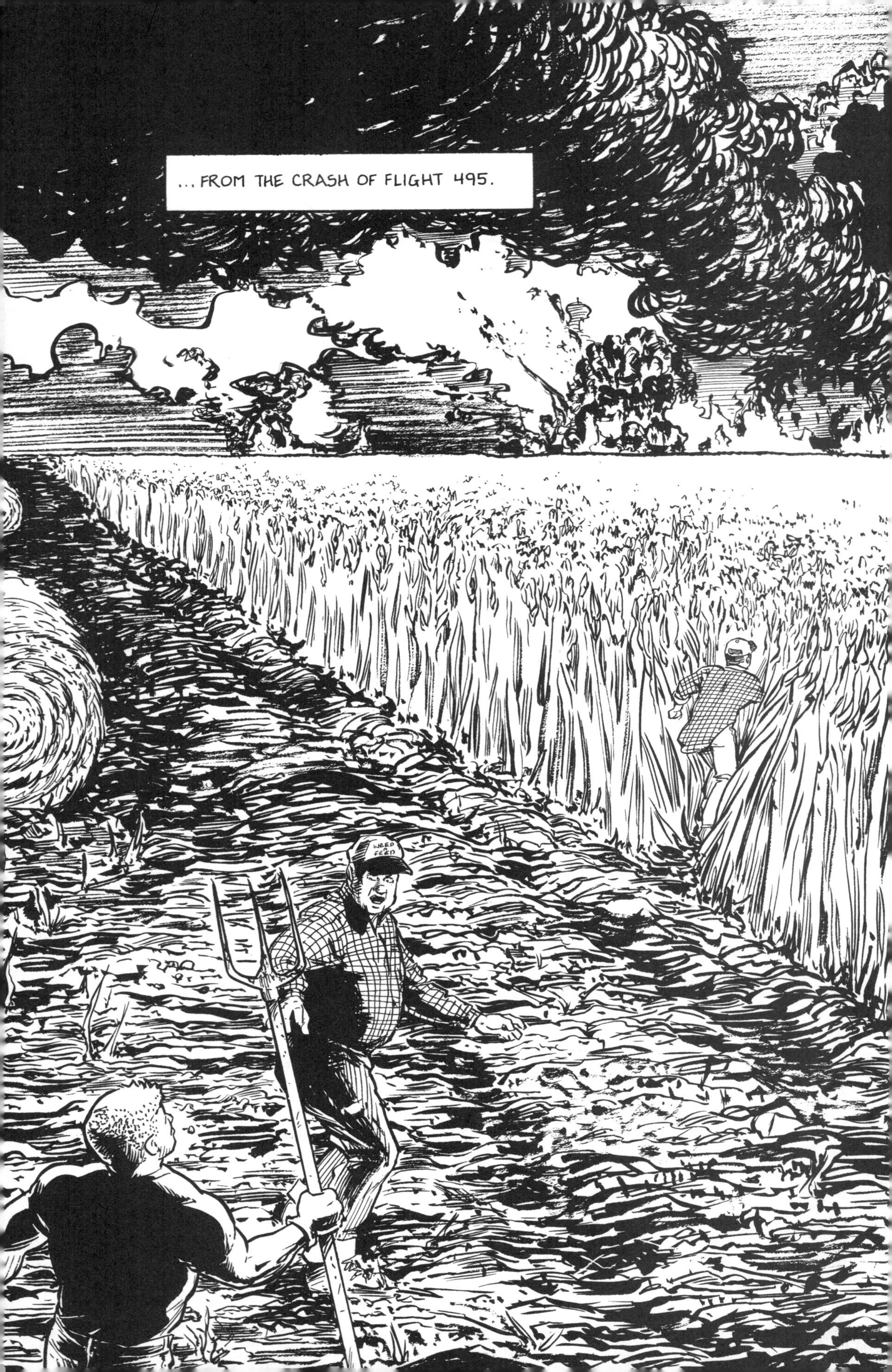
... FROM THE CRASH OF FLIGHT 495.
WEED N FEED

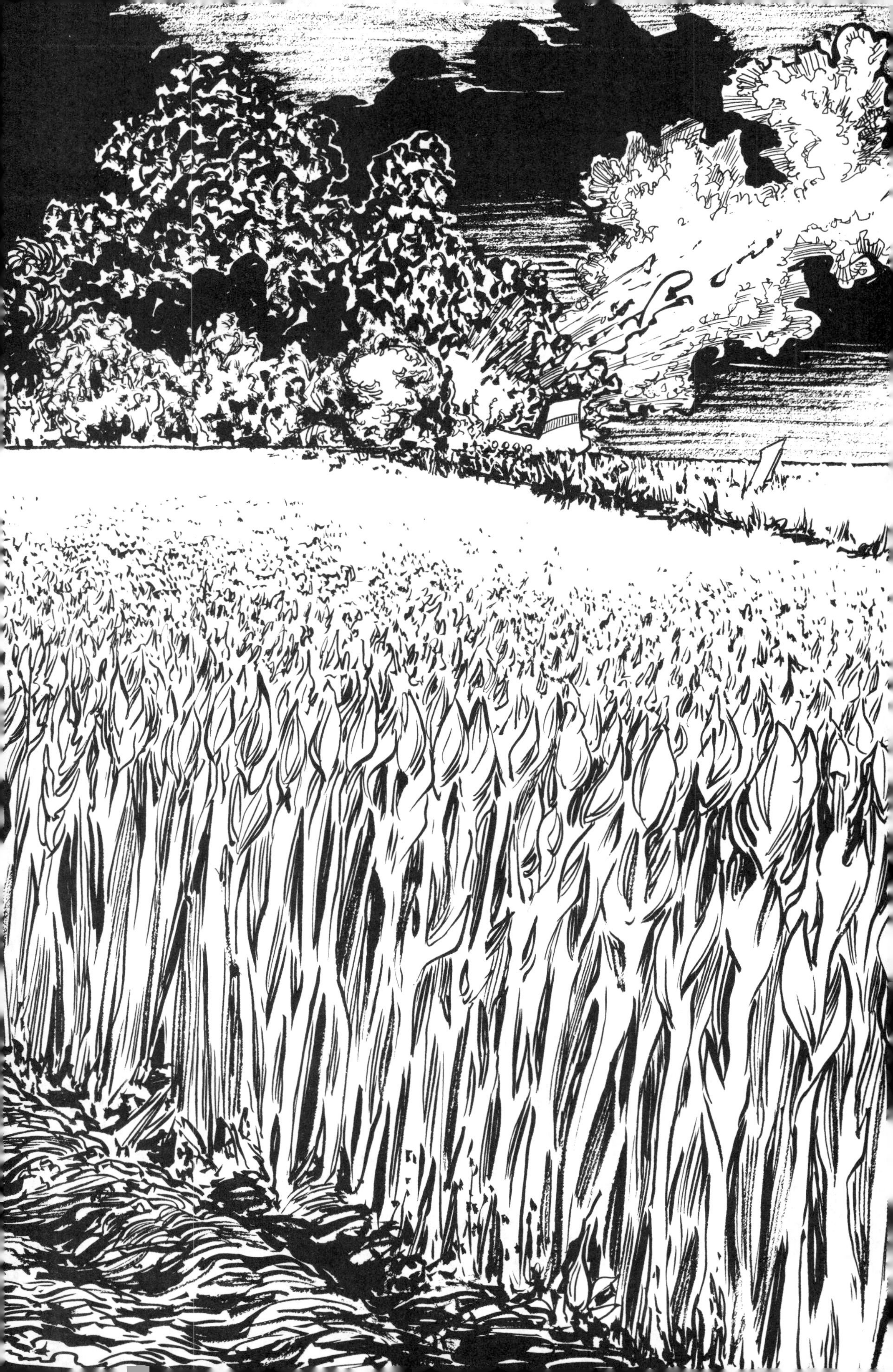

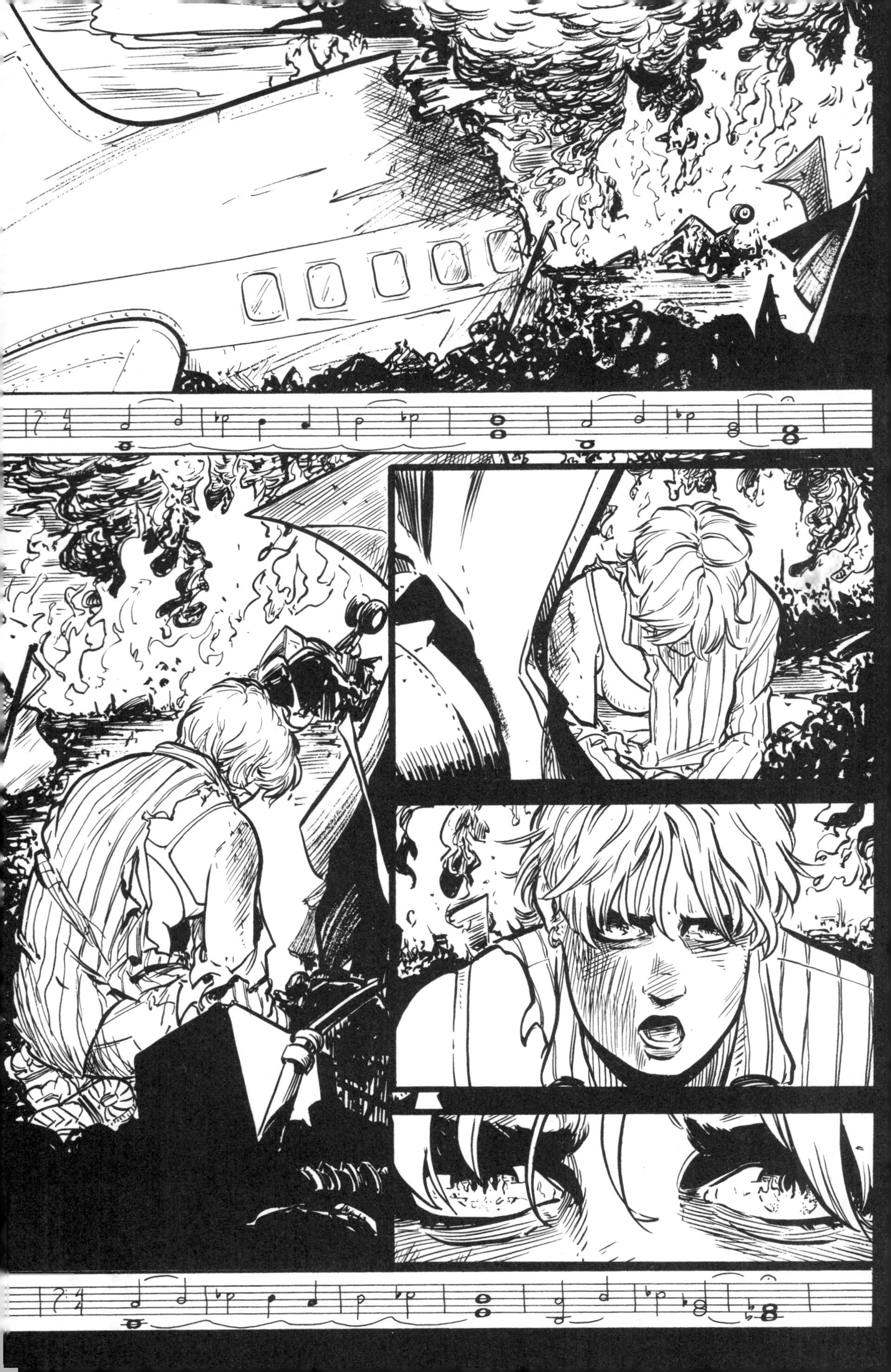

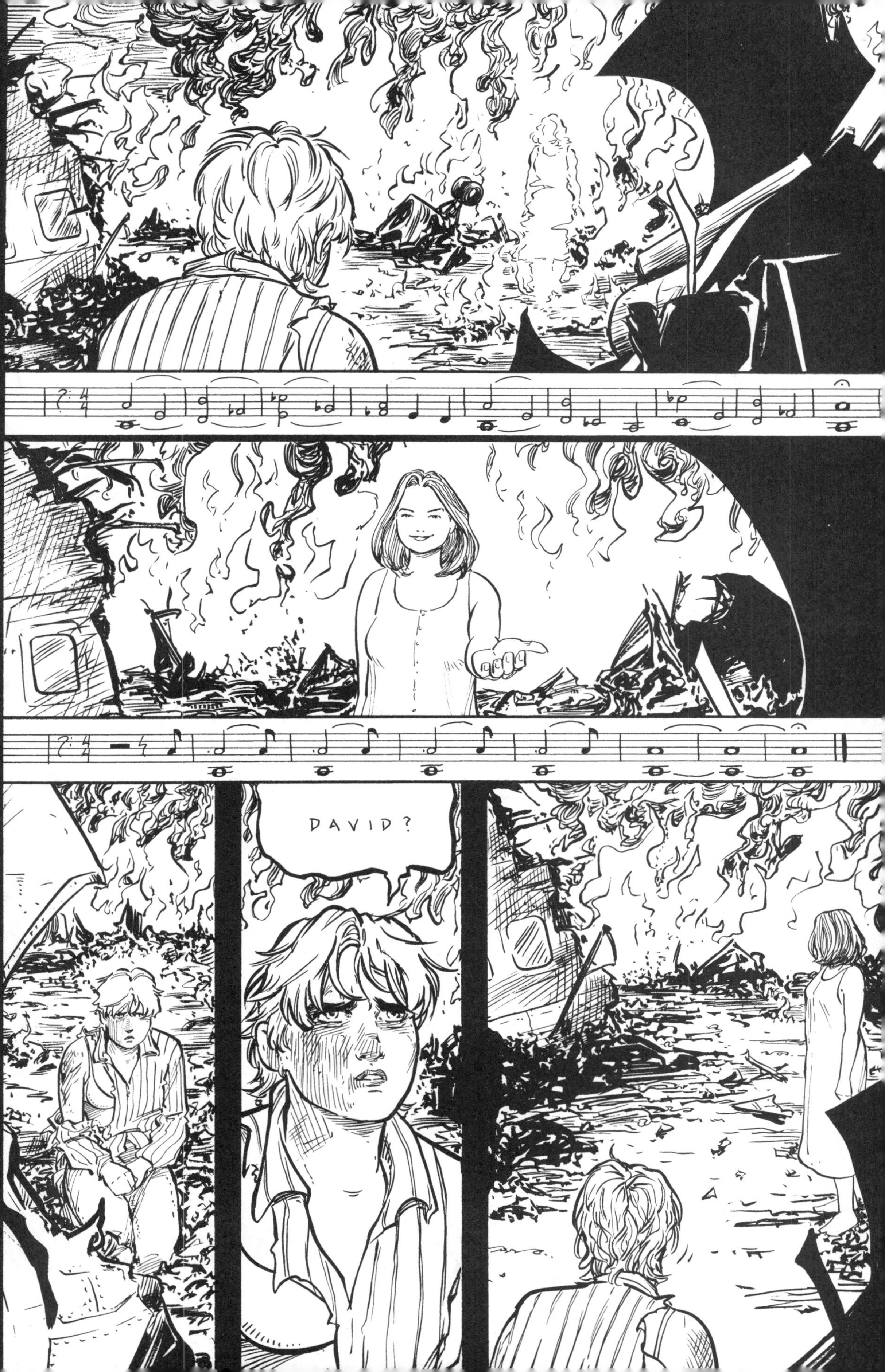
DAVID?

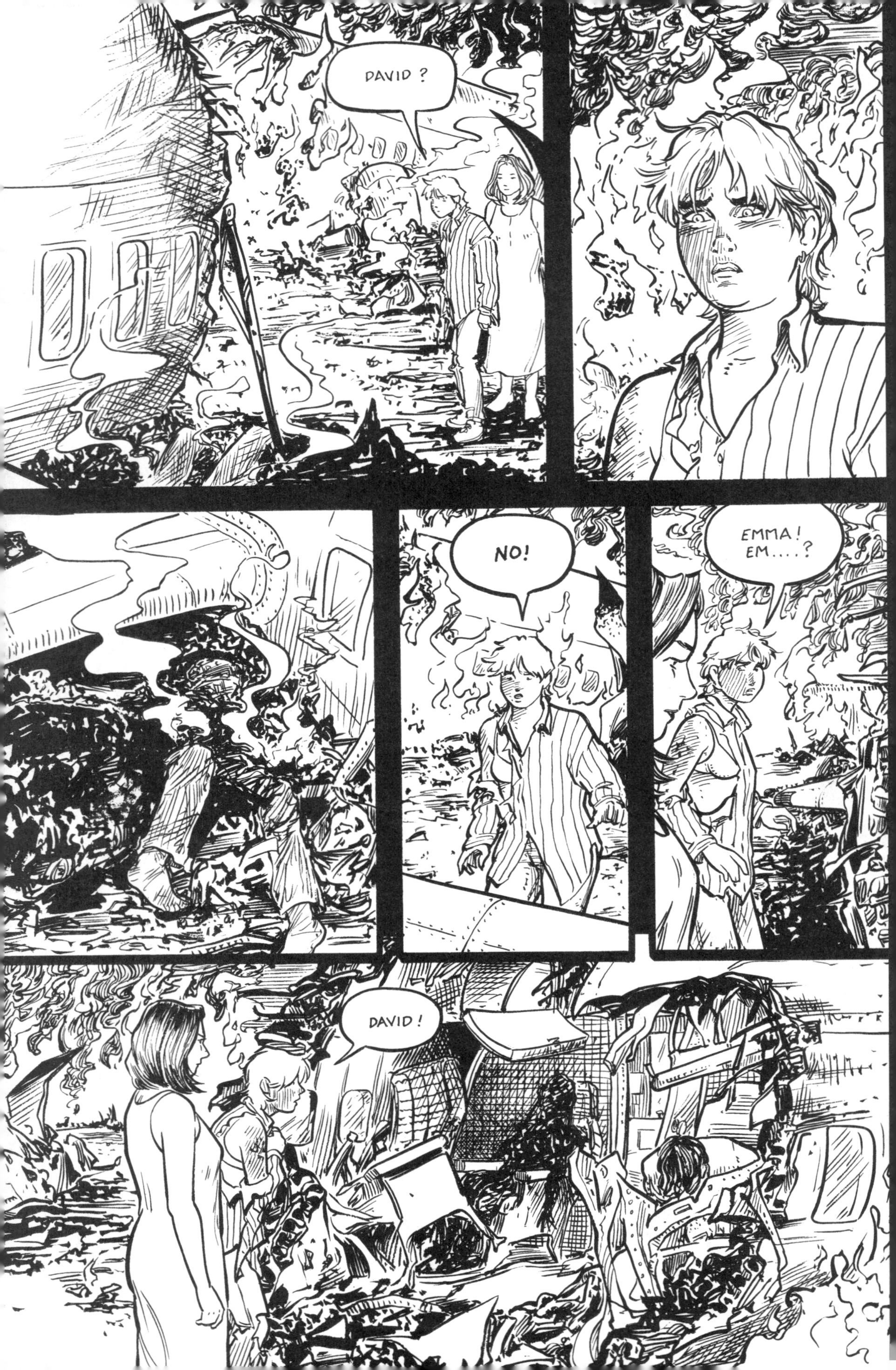
DAVID ?
NO!
EMMA! EM....?
DAVID!

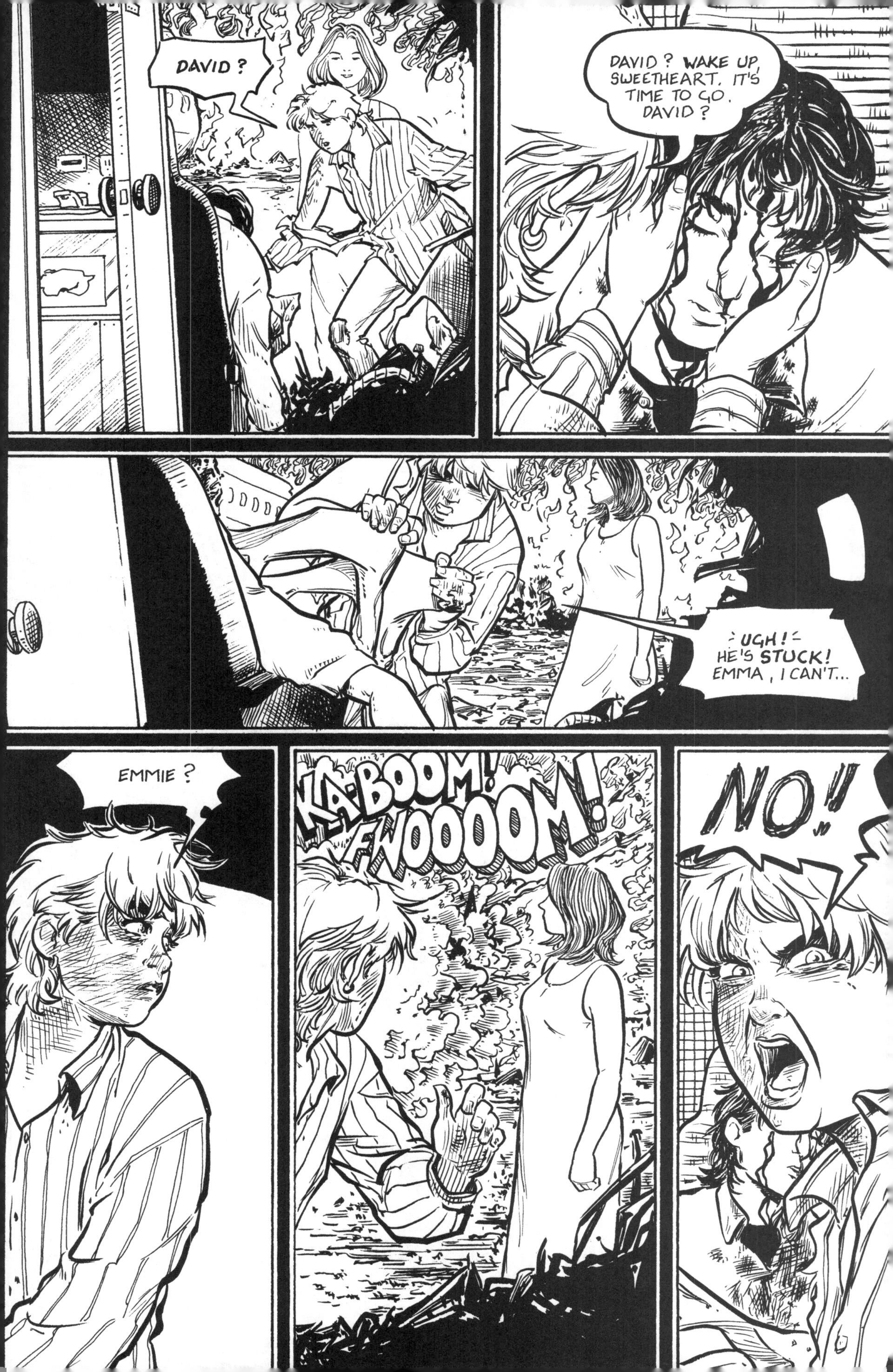
DAVID ?
DAVID ? WAKE UP, SWEETHEART. IT'S TIME TO GO. DAVID ?
UGH! HE'S STUCK! EMMA, I CAN'T...
EMMIE ?
KA-BOOM!
FWOOOOM!
NO!!

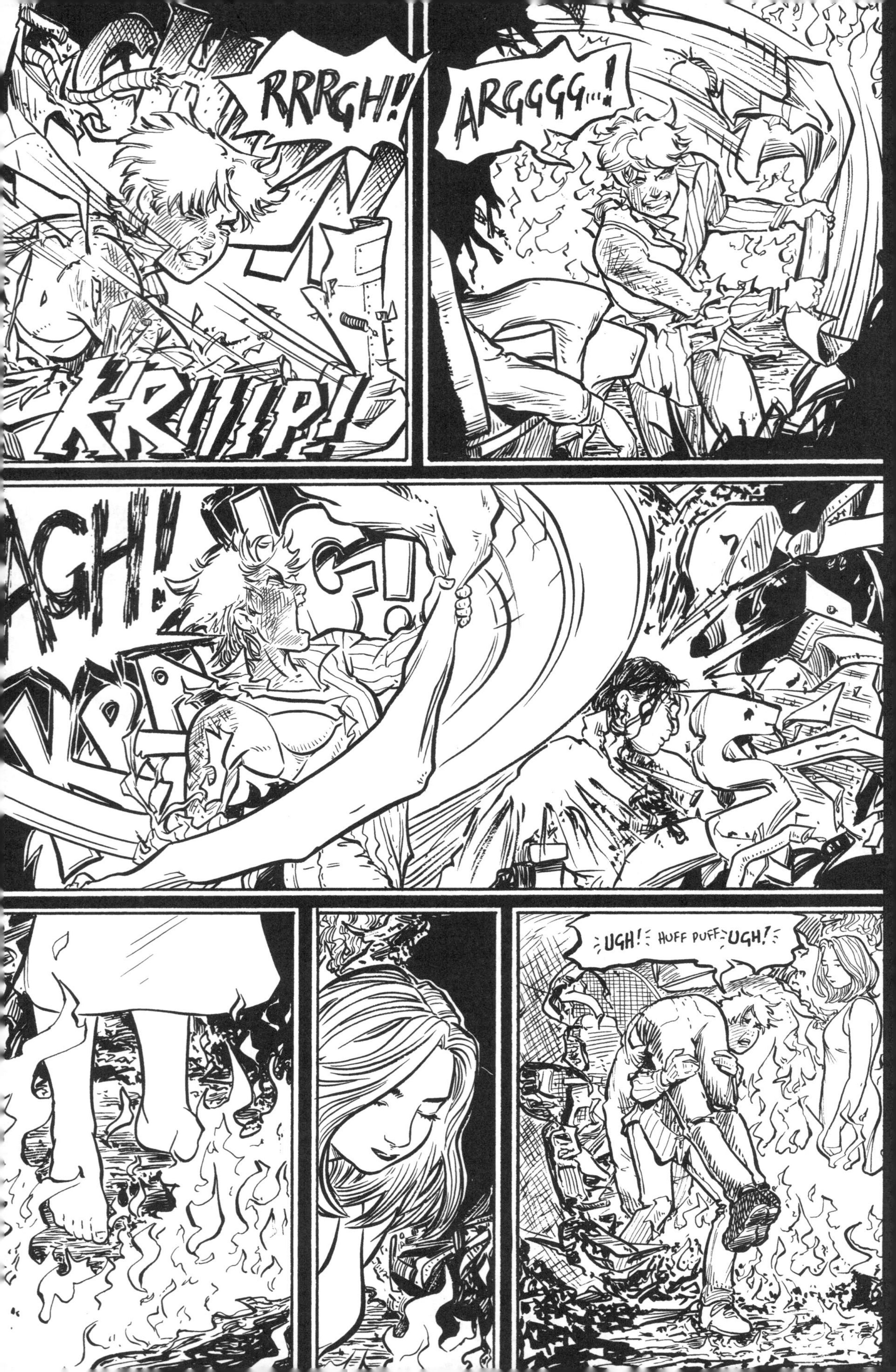
RRRGH!
KRIIIP!
ARGGGG...!
UGH! HUFF PUFF UGH!

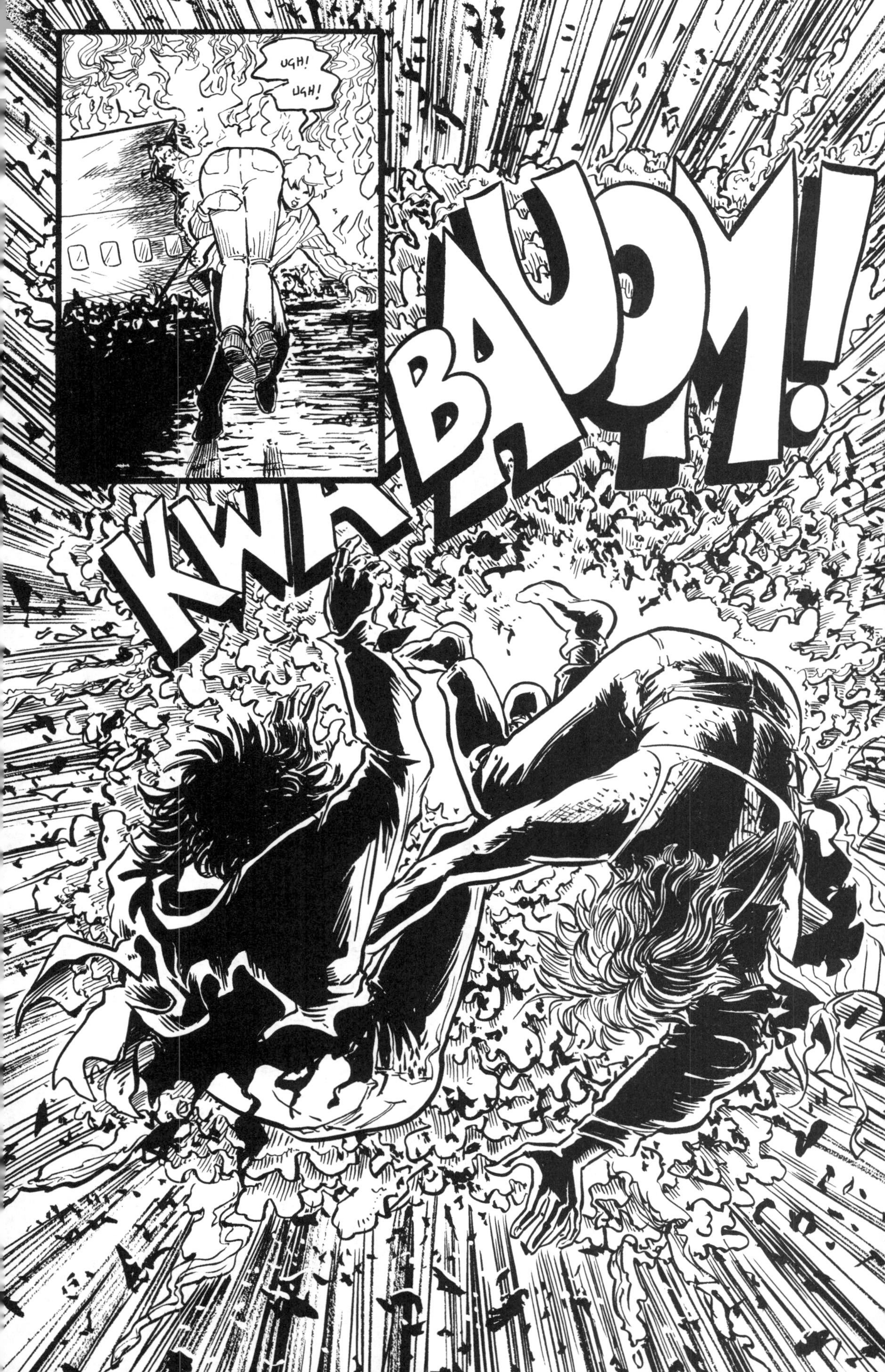
UGH!
UGH!
KWA-BAUOOM!

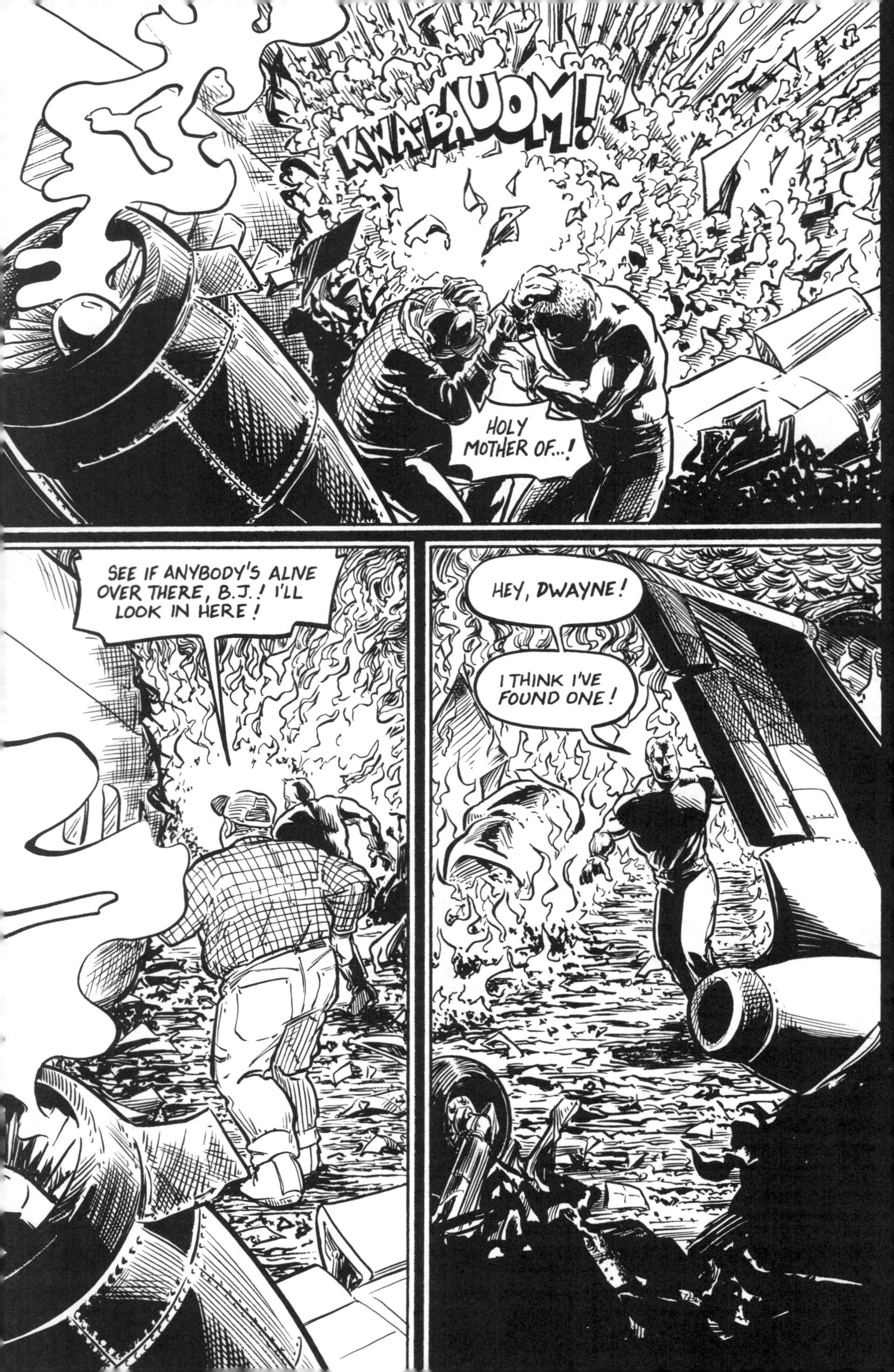
KWA-BAUOM!
HOLY MOTHER OF...!
SEE IF ANYBODY'S ALIVE OVER THERE, B.J.! I'LL LOOK IN HERE!
HEY, DWAYNE!
I THINK I'VE FOUND ONE!

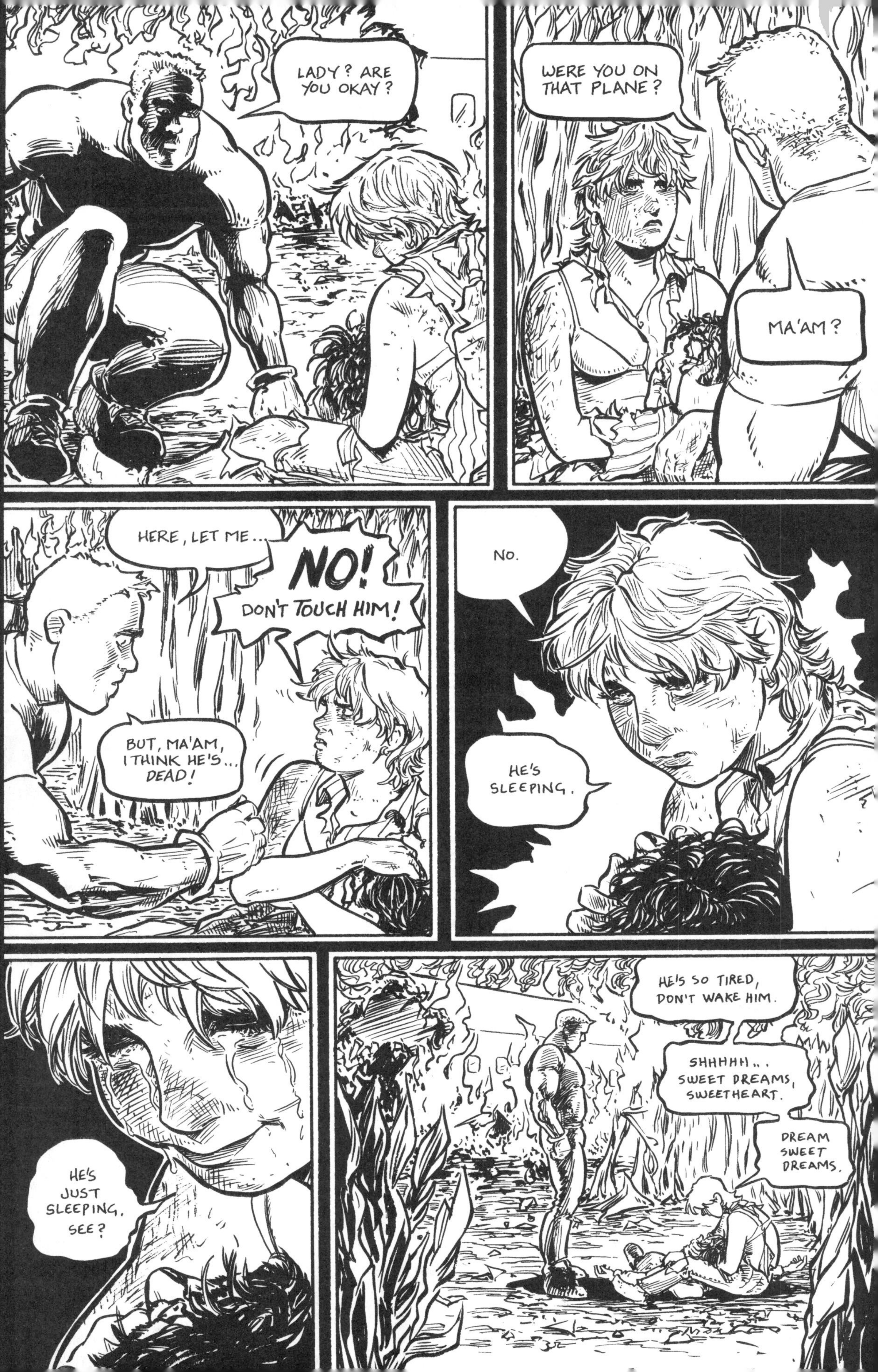
LADY? ARE YOU OKAY?
WERE YOU ON THAT PLANE?
MA'AM?
HERE, LET ME...
NO! DON'T TOUCH HIM!
BUT, MA'AM, I THINK HE'S... DEAD!
NO.
HE'S SLEEPING.
HE'S JUST SLEEPING, SEE?
HE'S SO TIRED, DON'T WAKE HIM.
SHHHHH... SWEET DREAMS, SWEETHEART.
DREAM SWEET DREAMS.

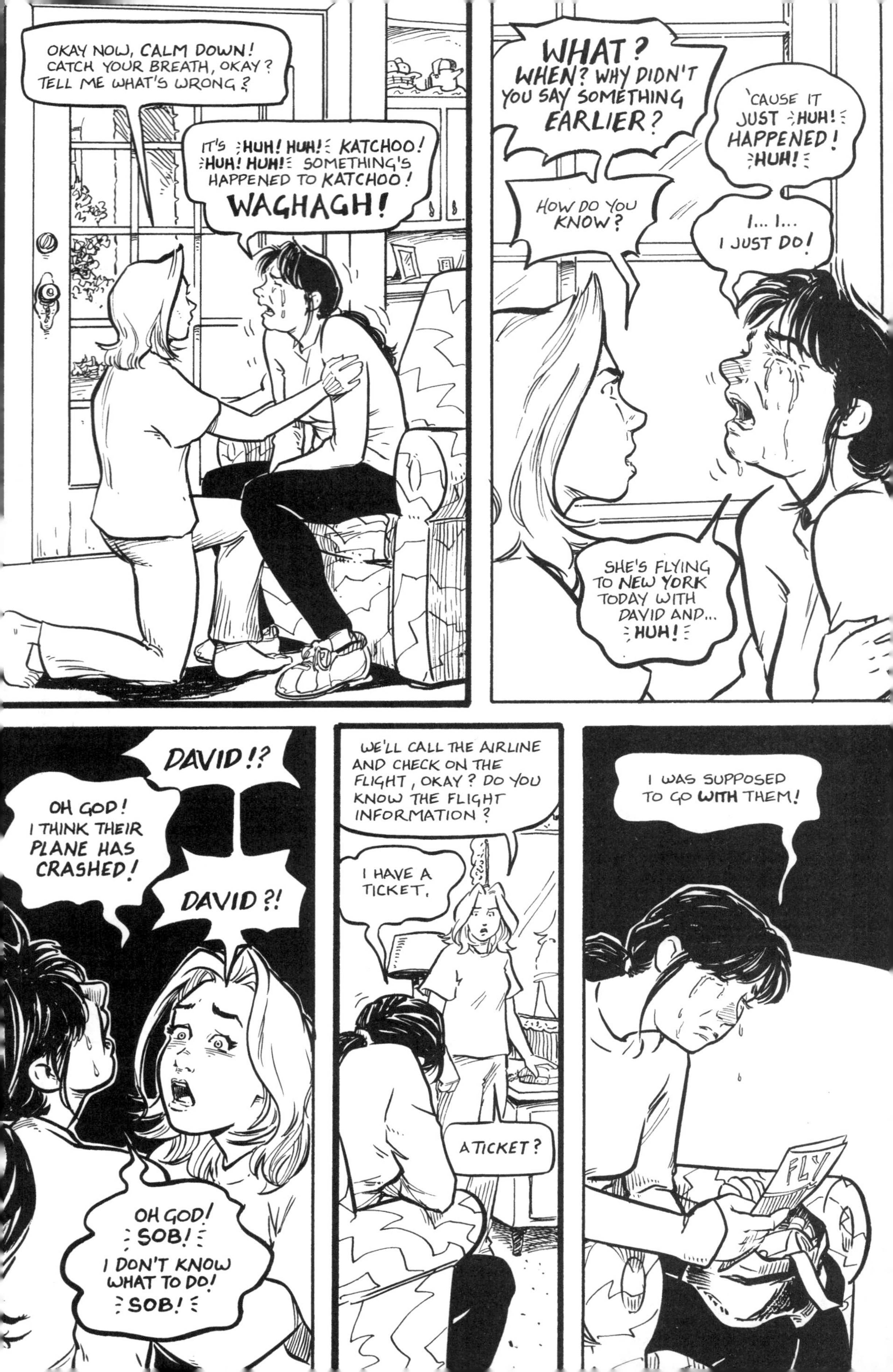
OKAY NOW, CALM DOWN! CATCH YOUR BREATH, OKAY? TELL ME WHAT'S WRONG?
IT'S HUH! HUH! KATCHOO! HUH! HUH! SOMETHING'S HAPPENED TO KATCHOO! WAGHAGH!
WHAT? WHEN? WHY DIDN'T YOU SAY SOMETHING EARLIER?
'CAUSE IT JUST HUH! HAPPENED! HUH!
HOW DO YOU KNOW?
I... I... I JUST DO!
SHE'S FLYING TO NEW YORK TODAY WITH DAVID AND... HUH!
DAVID!?
OH GOD! I THINK THEIR PLANE HAS CRASHED!
DAVID?!
OH GOD! SOB! I DON'T KNOW WHAT TO DO! SOB!
WE'LL CALL THE AIRLINE AND CHECK ON THE FLIGHT, OKAY? DO YOU KNOW THE FLIGHT INFORMATION?
I HAVE A TICKET.
A TICKET?
I WAS SUPPOSED TO GO WITH THEM!
FLY

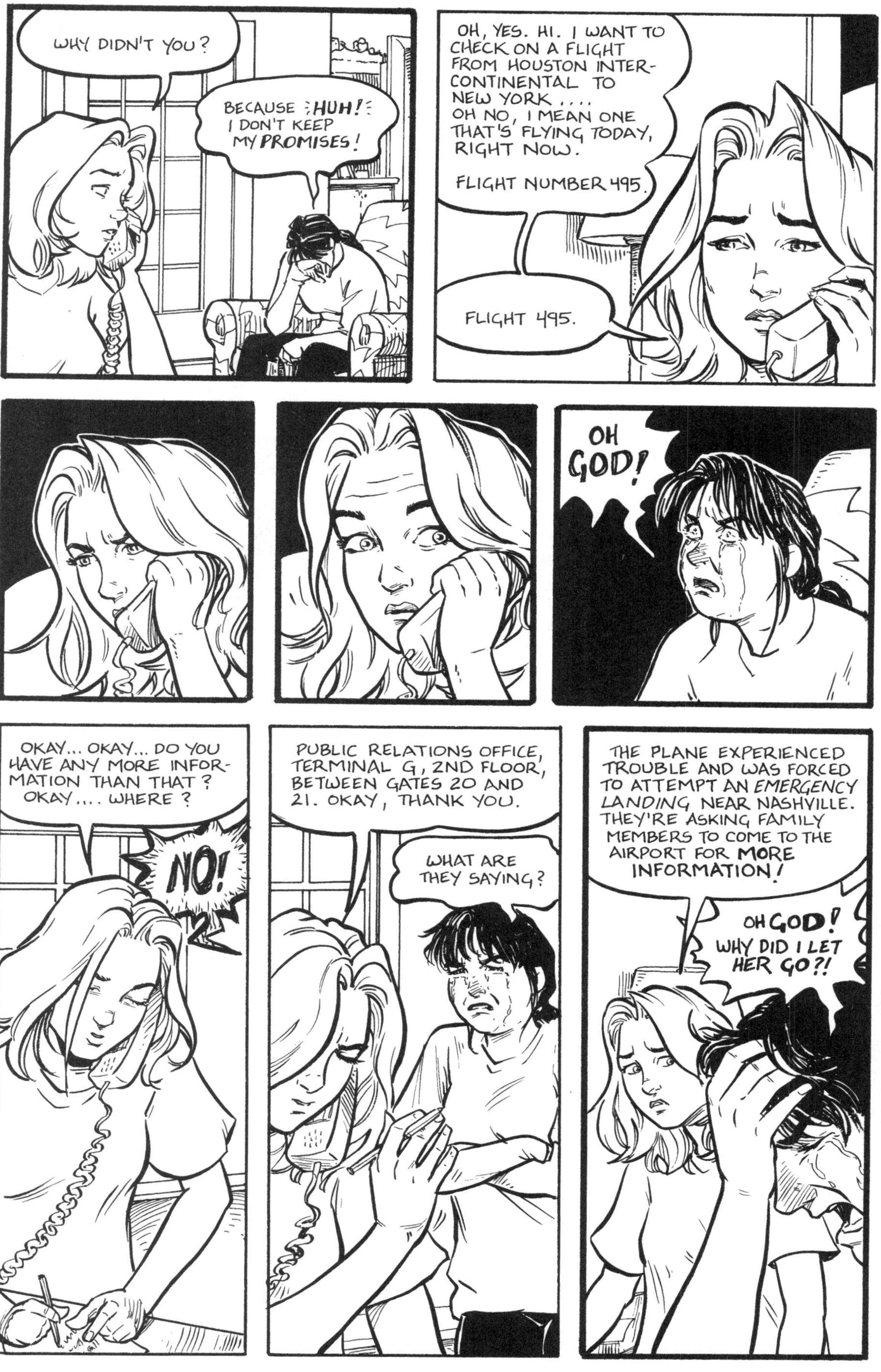
WHY DIDN'T YOU?
BECAUSE HUH! I DON'T KEEP MY PROMISES!
OH, YES. HI. I WANT TO CHECK ON A FLIGHT FROM HOUSTON INTER-CONTINENTAL TO NEW YORK.... OH NO, I MEAN ONE THAT'S FLYING TODAY, RIGHT NOW.
FLIGHT NUMBER 495.
FLIGHT 495.
OH GOD!
OKAY... OKAY... DO YOU HAVE ANY MORE INFOR-MATION THAN THAT? OKAY.... WHERE?
NO!
PUBLIC RELATIONS OFFICE, TERMINAL G, 2ND FLOOR, BETWEEN GATES 20 AND 21. OKAY, THANK YOU.
WHAT ARE THEY SAYING?
THE PLANE EXPERIENCED TROUBLE AND WAS FORCED TO ATTEMPT AN EMERGENCY LANDING NEAR NASHVILLE. THEY'RE ASKING FAMILY MEMBERS TO COME TO THE AIRPORT FOR MORE INFORMATION!
OH GOD! WHY DID I LET HER GO?!

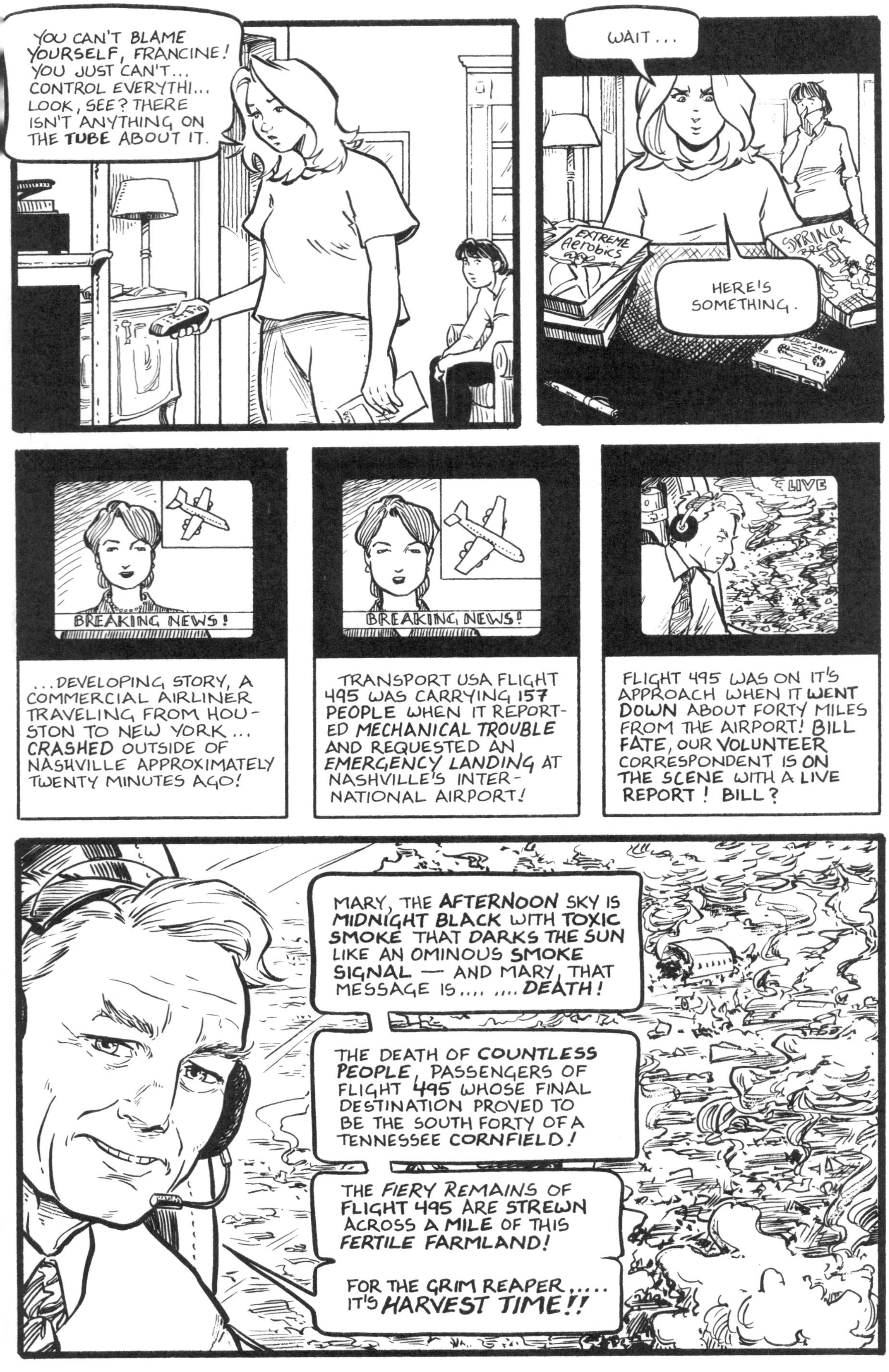

YOU CAN'T BLAME YOURSELF, FRANCINE! YOU JUST CAN'T... CONTROL EVERYTHI... LOOK, SEE? THERE ISN'T ANYTHING ON THE TUBE ABOUT IT.
WAIT...
EXTREME Aerobics
SPRING BREAK II
HERE'S SOMETHING.
BREAKING NEWS!
...DEVELOPING STORY, A COMMERCIAL AIRLINER TRAVELING FROM HOUSTON TO NEW YORK... CRASHED OUTSIDE OF NASHVILLE APPROXIMATELY TWENTY MINUTES AGO!
BREAKING NEWS!
TRANSPORT USA FLIGHT 495 WAS CARRYING 157 PEOPLE WHEN IT REPORTED MECHANICAL TROUBLE AND REQUESTED AN EMERGENCY LANDING AT NASHVILLE'S INTERNATIONAL AIRPORT!
LIVE
FLIGHT 495 WAS ON IT'S APPROACH WHEN IT WENT DOWN ABOUT FORTY MILES FROM THE AIRPORT! BILL FATE, OUR VOLUNTEER CORRESPONDENT IS ON THE SCENE WITH A LIVE REPORT! BILL?
MARY, THE AFTERNOON SKY IS MIDNIGHT BLACK WITH TOXIC SMOKE THAT DARKS THE SUN LIKE AN OMINOUS SMOKE SIGNAL — AND MARY, THAT MESSAGE IS.... ....DEATH!
THE DEATH OF COUNTLESS PEOPLE, PASSENGERS OF FLIGHT 495 WHOSE FINAL DESTINATION PROVED TO BE THE SOUTH FORTY OF A TENNESSEE CORNFIELD!
THE FIERY REMAINS OF FLIGHT 495 ARE STREWN ACROSS A MILE OF THIS FERTILE FARMLAND!
FOR THE GRIM REAPER..... IT'S HARVEST TIME!!

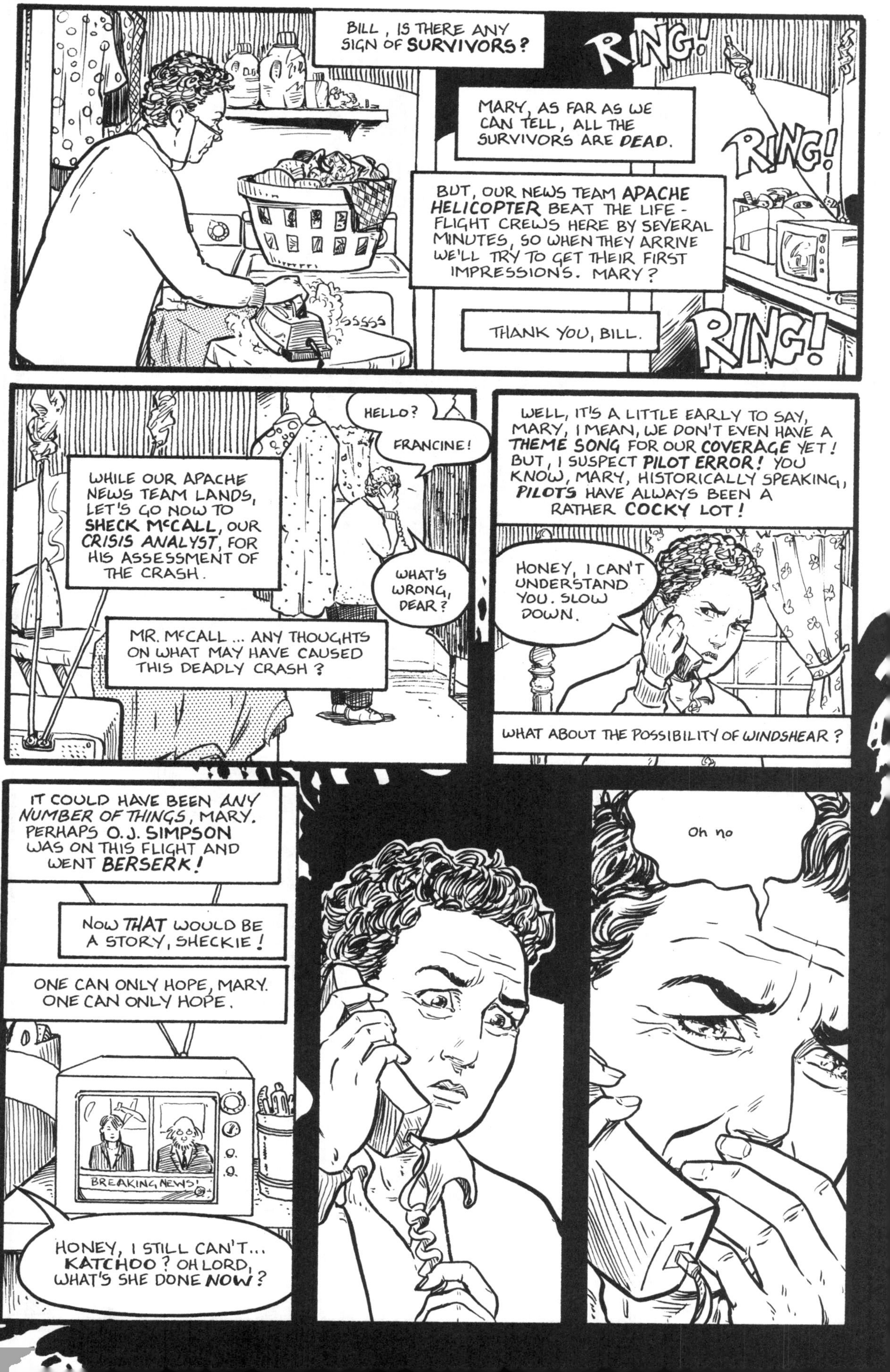

BILL, IS THERE ANY SIGN OF SURVIVORS?
RING!
MARY, AS FAR AS WE CAN TELL, ALL THE SURVIVORS ARE DEAD.
RING!
BUT, OUR NEWS TEAM APACHE HELICOPTER BEAT THE LIFE-FLIGHT CREWS HERE BY SEVERAL MINUTES, SO WHEN THEY ARRIVE WE'LL TRY TO GET THEIR FIRST IMPRESSIONS. MARY?
SSSSS
THANK YOU, BILL.
RING!
HELLO?
FRANCINE!
WHILE OUR APACHE NEWS TEAM LANDS, LET'S GO NOW TO SHECK McCALL, OUR CRISIS ANALYST, FOR HIS ASSESSMENT OF THE CRASH.
WHAT'S WRONG, DEAR?
MR. McCALL ... ANY THOUGHTS ON WHAT MAY HAVE CAUSED THIS DEADLY CRASH?
WELL, IT'S A LITTLE EARLY TO SAY, MARY, I MEAN, WE DON'T EVEN HAVE A THEME SONG FOR OUR COVERAGE YET! BUT, I SUSPECT PILOT ERROR! YOU KNOW, MARY, HISTORICALLY SPEAKING, PILOTS HAVE ALWAYS BEEN A RATHER COCKY LOT!
HONEY, I CAN'T UNDERSTAND YOU. SLOW DOWN.
WHAT ABOUT THE POSSIBILITY OF WINDSHEAR?
IT COULD HAVE BEEN ANY NUMBER OF THINGS, MARY. PERHAPS O.J. SIMPSON WAS ON THIS FLIGHT AND WENT BERSERK!
NOW THAT WOULD BE A STORY, SHECKIE!
ONE CAN ONLY HOPE, MARY. ONE CAN ONLY HOPE.
BREAKING NEWS!
HONEY, I STILL CAN'T... KATCHOO? OH LORD, WHAT'S SHE DONE NOW?
Oh no

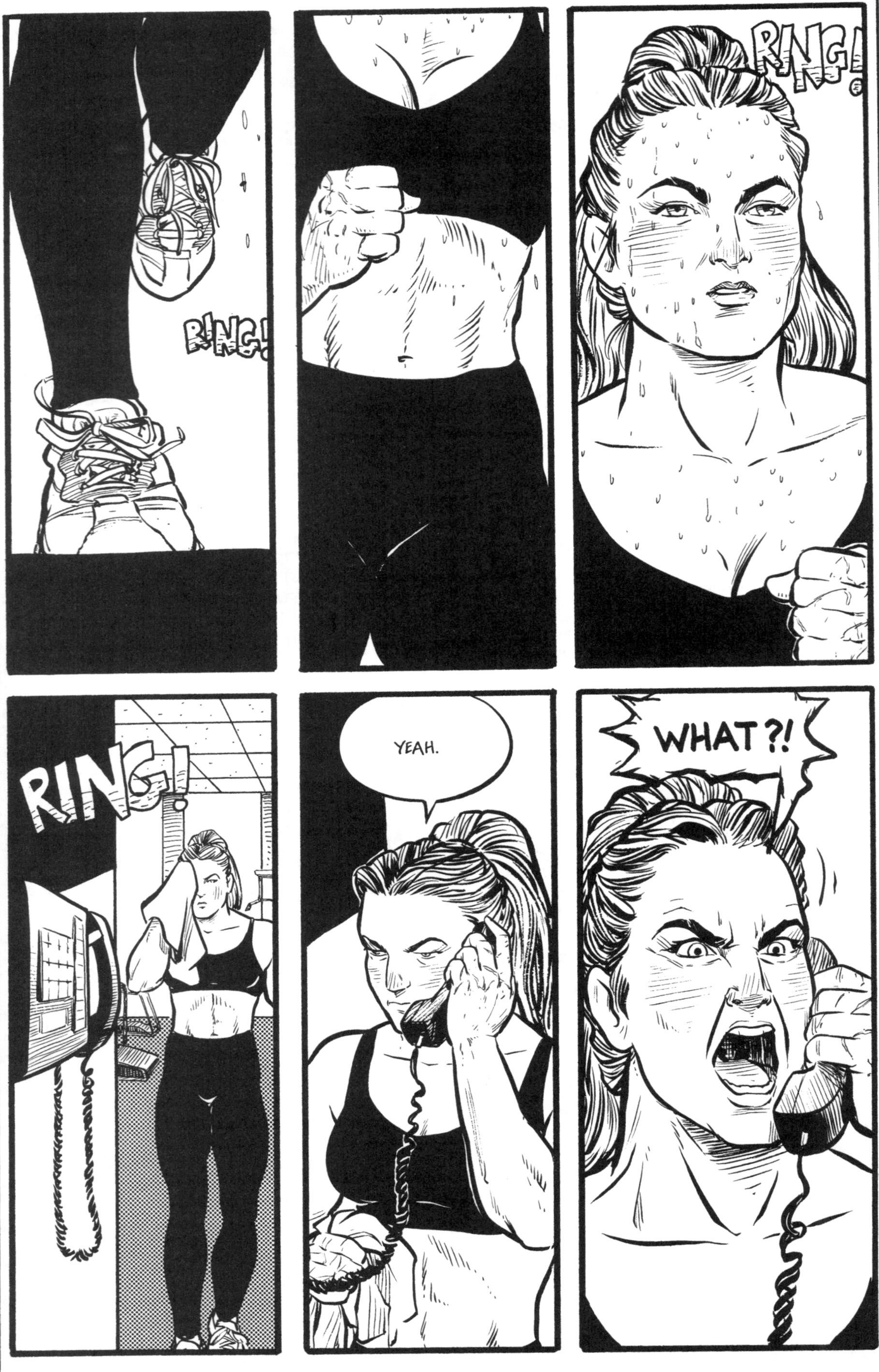

RING!
RING!
RING!
YEAH.
WHAT?!

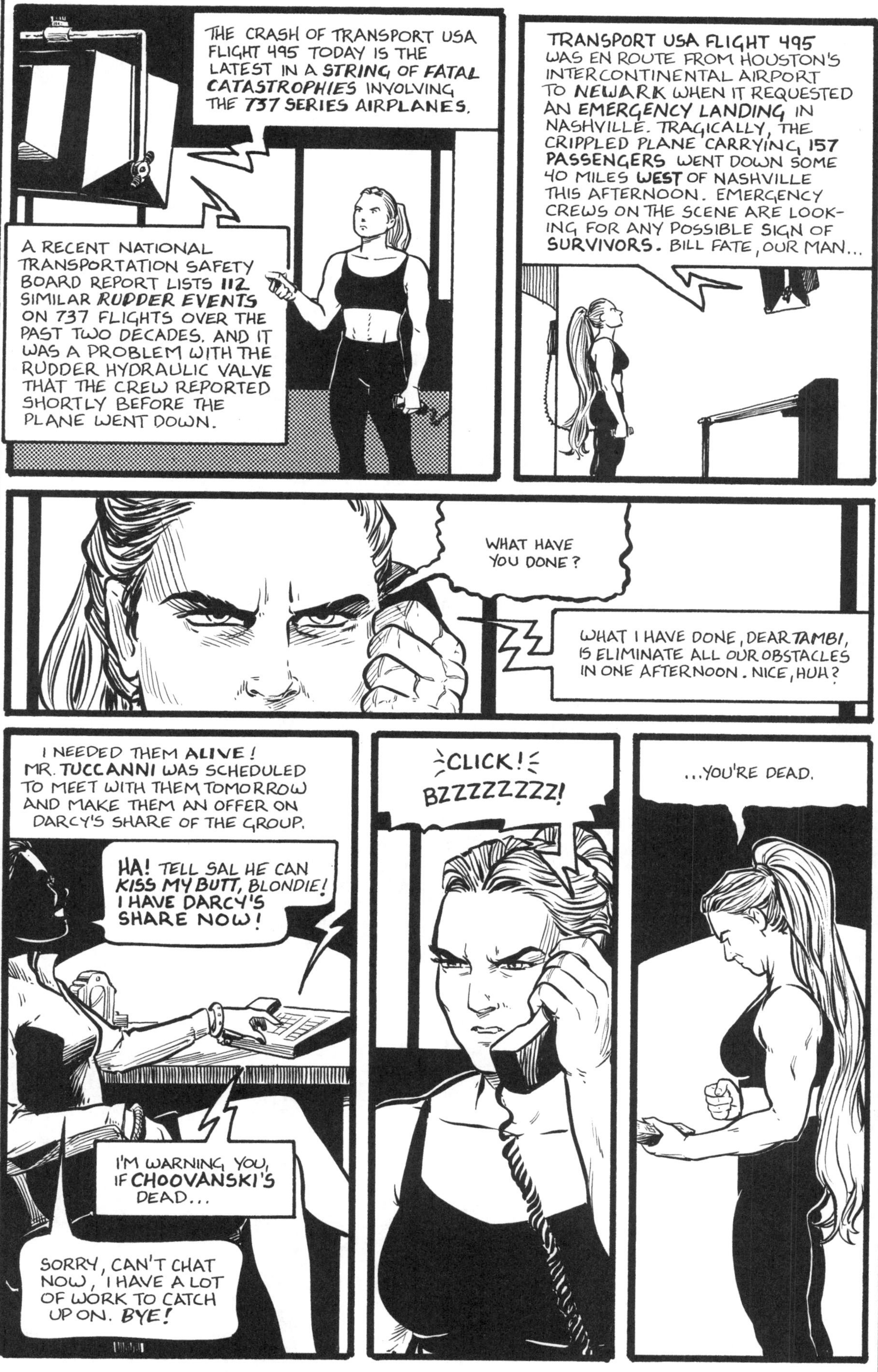
THE CRASH OF TRANSPORT USA FLIGHT 495 TODAY IS THE LATEST IN A STRING OF FATAL CATASTROPHIES INVOLVING THE 737 SERIES AIRPLANES.
A RECENT NATIONAL TRANSPORTATION SAFETY BOARD REPORT LISTS 112 SIMILAR RUDDER EVENTS ON 737 FLIGHTS OVER THE PAST TWO DECADES. AND IT WAS A PROBLEM WITH THE RUDDER HYDRAULIC VALVE THAT THE CREW REPORTED SHORTLY BEFORE THE PLANE WENT DOWN.
TRANSPORT USA FLIGHT 495 WAS EN ROUTE FROM HOUSTON'S INTERCONTINENTAL AIRPORT TO NEWARK WHEN IT REQUESTED AN EMERGENCY LANDING IN NASHVILLE. TRAGICALLY, THE CRIPPLED PLANE CARRYING 157 PASSENGERS WENT DOWN SOME 40 MILES WEST OF NASHVILLE THIS AFTERNOON. EMERGENCY CREWS ON THE SCENE ARE LOOKING FOR ANY POSSIBLE SIGN OF SURVIVORS. BILL FATE, OUR MAN...
WHAT HAVE YOU DONE?
WHAT I HAVE DONE, DEAR TAMBI, IS ELIMINATE ALL OUR OBSTACLES IN ONE AFTERNOON. NICE, HUH?
I NEEDED THEM ALIVE! MR. TUCCANNI WAS SCHEDULED TO MEET WITH THEM TOMORROW AND MAKE THEM AN OFFER ON DARCY'S SHARE OF THE GROUP.
HA! TELL SAL HE CAN KISS MY BUTT, BLONDIE! I HAVE DARCY'S SHARE NOW!
I'M WARNING YOU, IF CHOOVANSKI'S DEAD...
SORRY, CAN'T CHAT NOW, I HAVE A LOT OF WORK TO CATCH UP ON. BYE!
CLICK!
BZZZZZZZZ!
...YOU'RE DEAD.

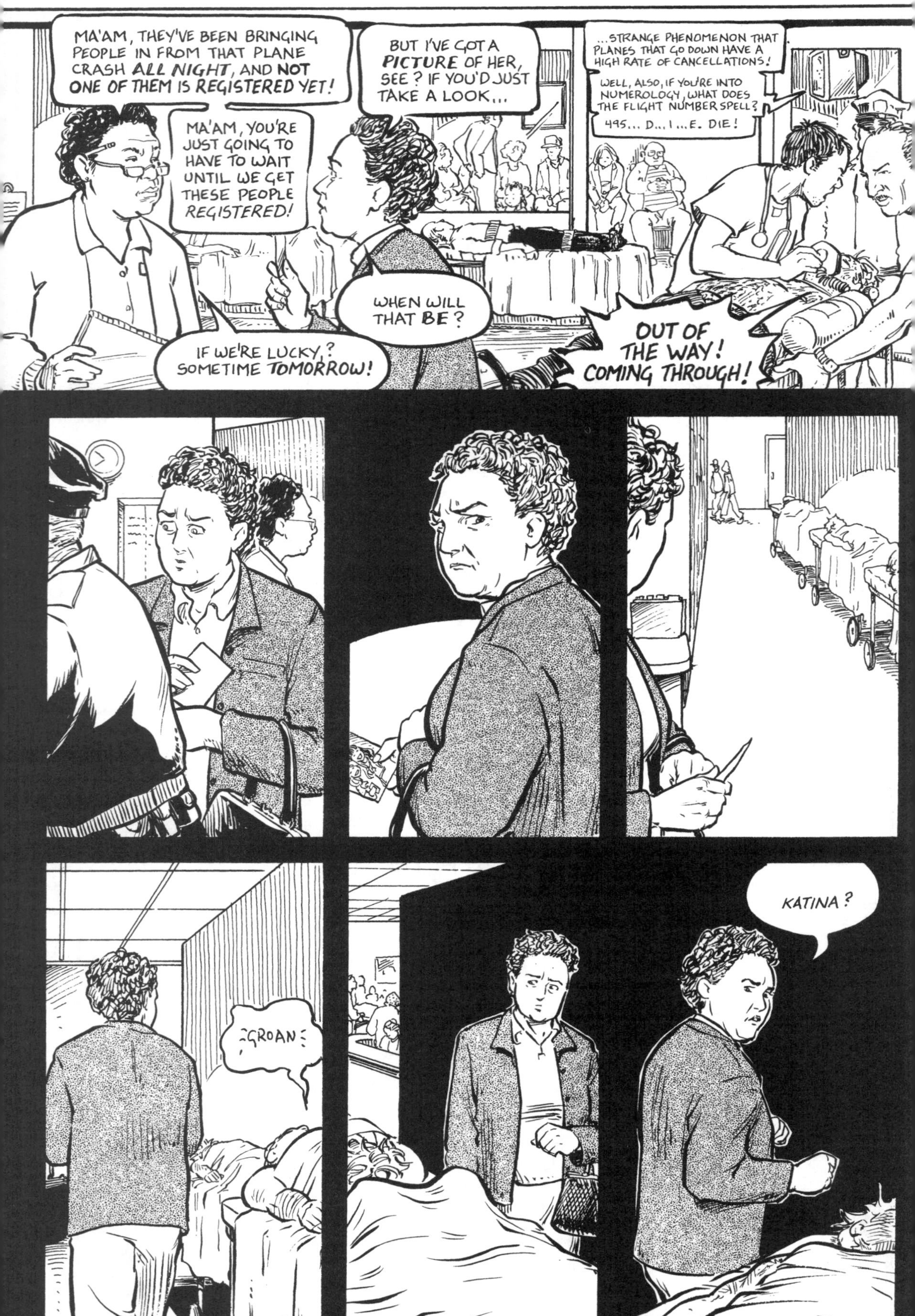
MA'AM, THEY'VE BEEN BRINGING PEOPLE IN FROM THAT PLANE CRASH ALL NIGHT, AND NOT ONE OF THEM IS REGISTERED YET!
MA'AM, YOU'RE JUST GOING TO HAVE TO WAIT UNTIL WE GET THESE PEOPLE REGISTERED!
BUT I'VE GOT A PICTURE OF HER, SEE? IF YOU'D JUST TAKE A LOOK...
WHEN WILL THAT BE?
IF WE'RE LUCKY, SOMETIME TOMORROW!
...STRANGE PHENOMENON THAT PLANES THAT GO DOWN HAVE A HIGH RATE OF CANCELLATIONS!
WELL, ALSO, IF YOU'RE INTO NUMEROLOGY, WHAT DOES THE FLIGHT NUMBER SPELL?
495... D... I... E. DIE!
OUT OF THE WAY! COMING THROUGH!
GROAN
KATINA?

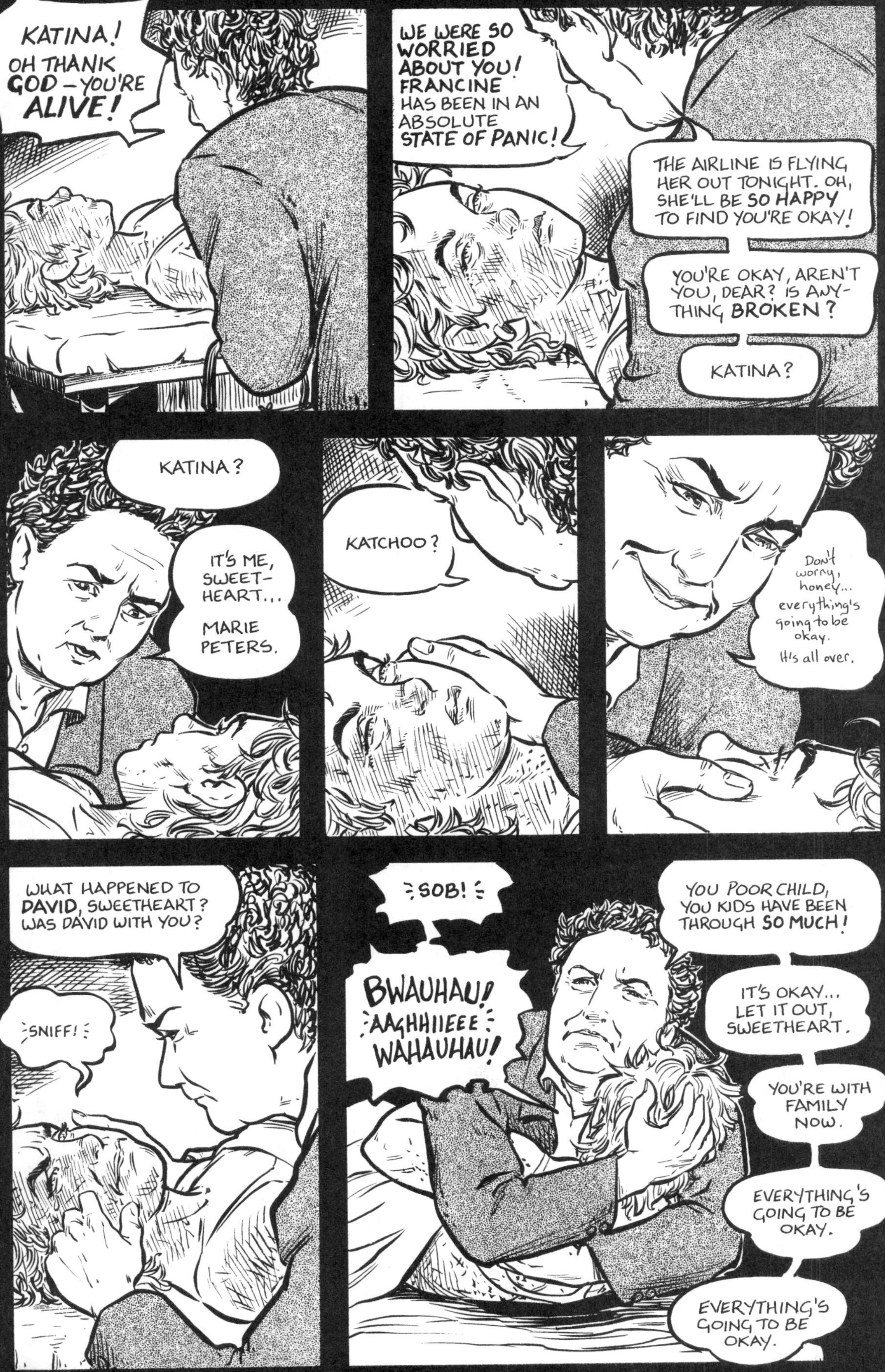
KATINA! OH THANK GOD — YOU'RE ALIVE!
WE WERE SO WORRIED ABOUT YOU! FRANCINE HAS BEEN IN AN ABSOLUTE STATE OF PANIC!
THE AIRLINE IS FLYING HER OUT TONIGHT. OH, SHE'LL BE SO HAPPY TO FIND YOU'RE OKAY!
YOU'RE OKAY, AREN'T YOU, DEAR? IS ANYTHING BROKEN?
KATINA?
KATINA?
IT'S ME, SWEETHEART...
MARIE PETERS.
KATCHOO?
Don't worry, honey... everything's going to be okay.
It's all over.
WHAT HAPPENED TO DAVID, SWEETHEART? WAS DAVID WITH YOU?
SNIFF!
SOB!
BWAUHAU! AAGHHIIEEE WAHAUHAU!
YOU POOR CHILD, YOU KIDS HAVE BEEN THROUGH SO MUCH!
IT'S OKAY... LET IT OUT, SWEETHEART.
YOU'RE WITH FAMILY NOW.
EVERYTHING'S GOING TO BE OKAY.
EVERYTHING'S GOING TO BE OKAY.

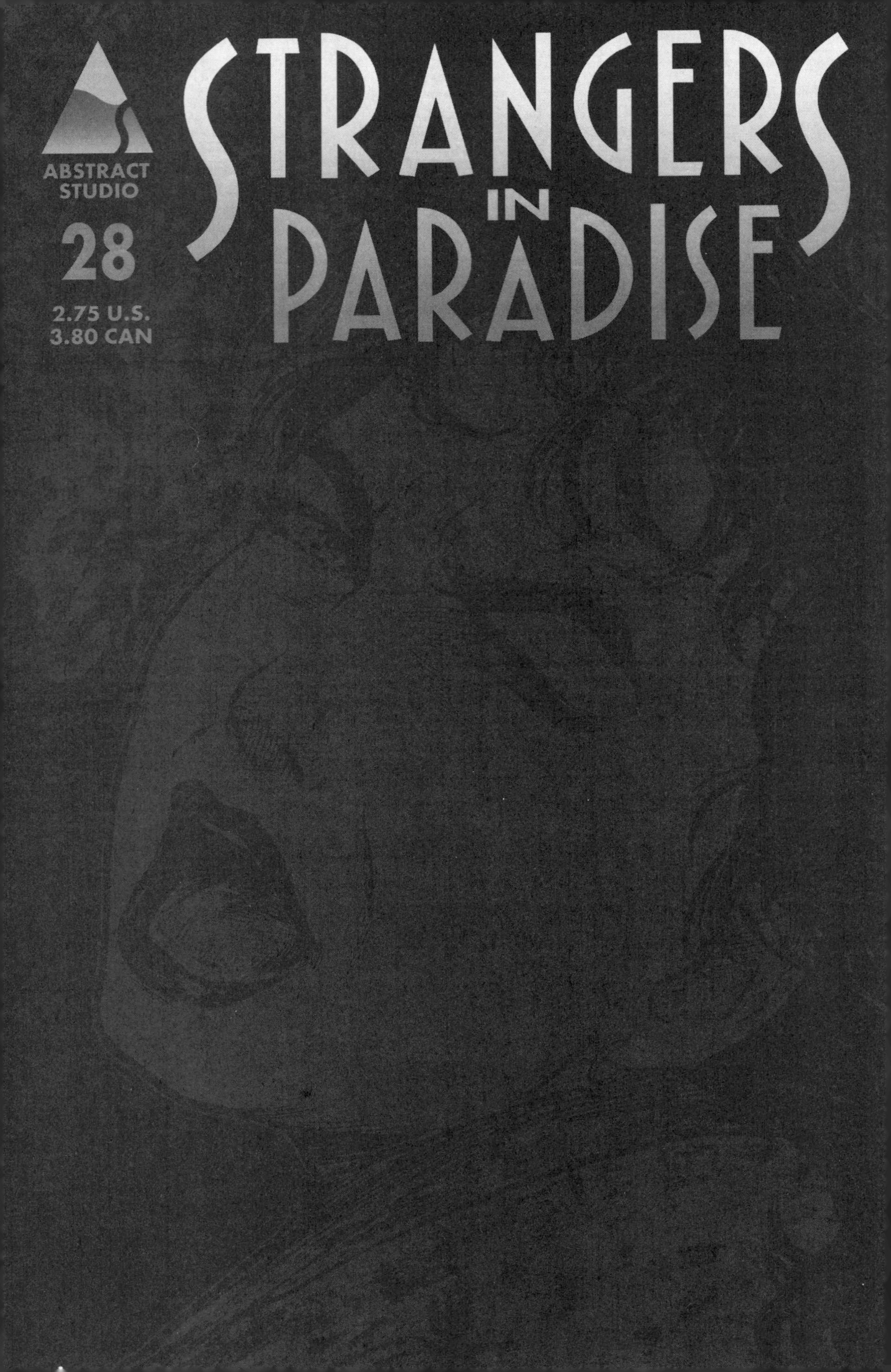
ABSTRACT STUDIO
28
2.75 U.S.
3.80 CAN
STRANGERS IN PARADISE

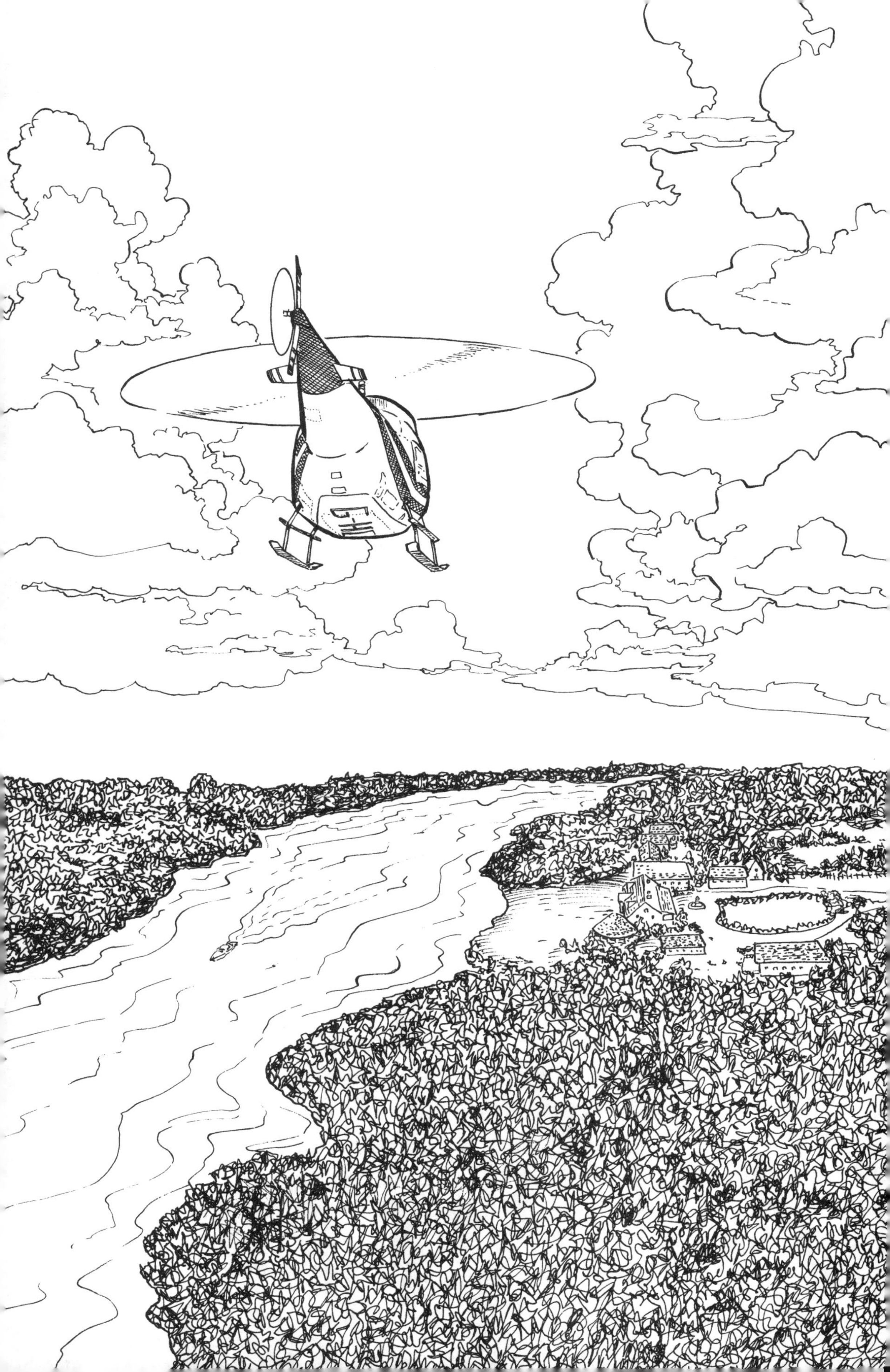

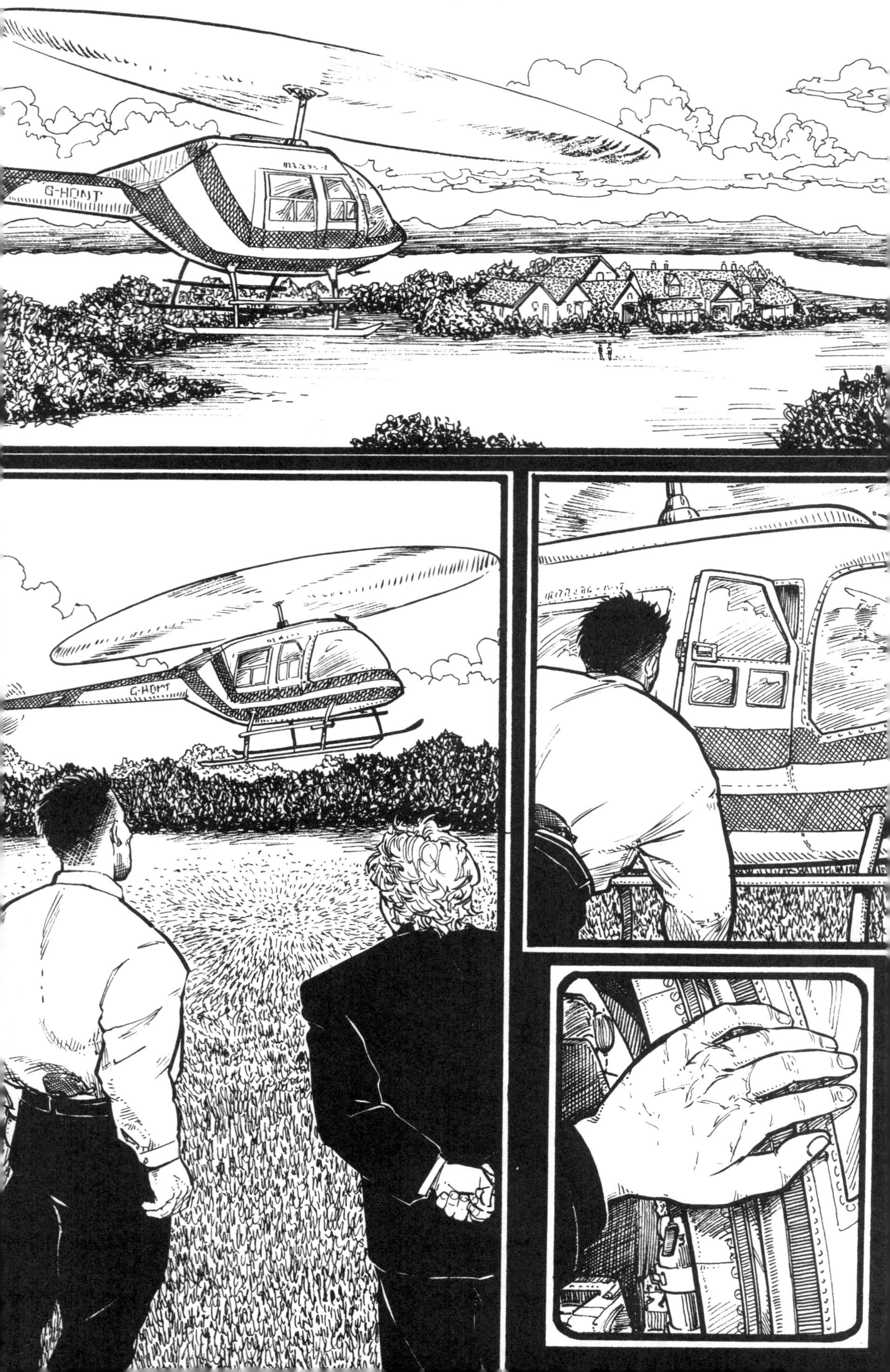
G-HONT
G-HONT

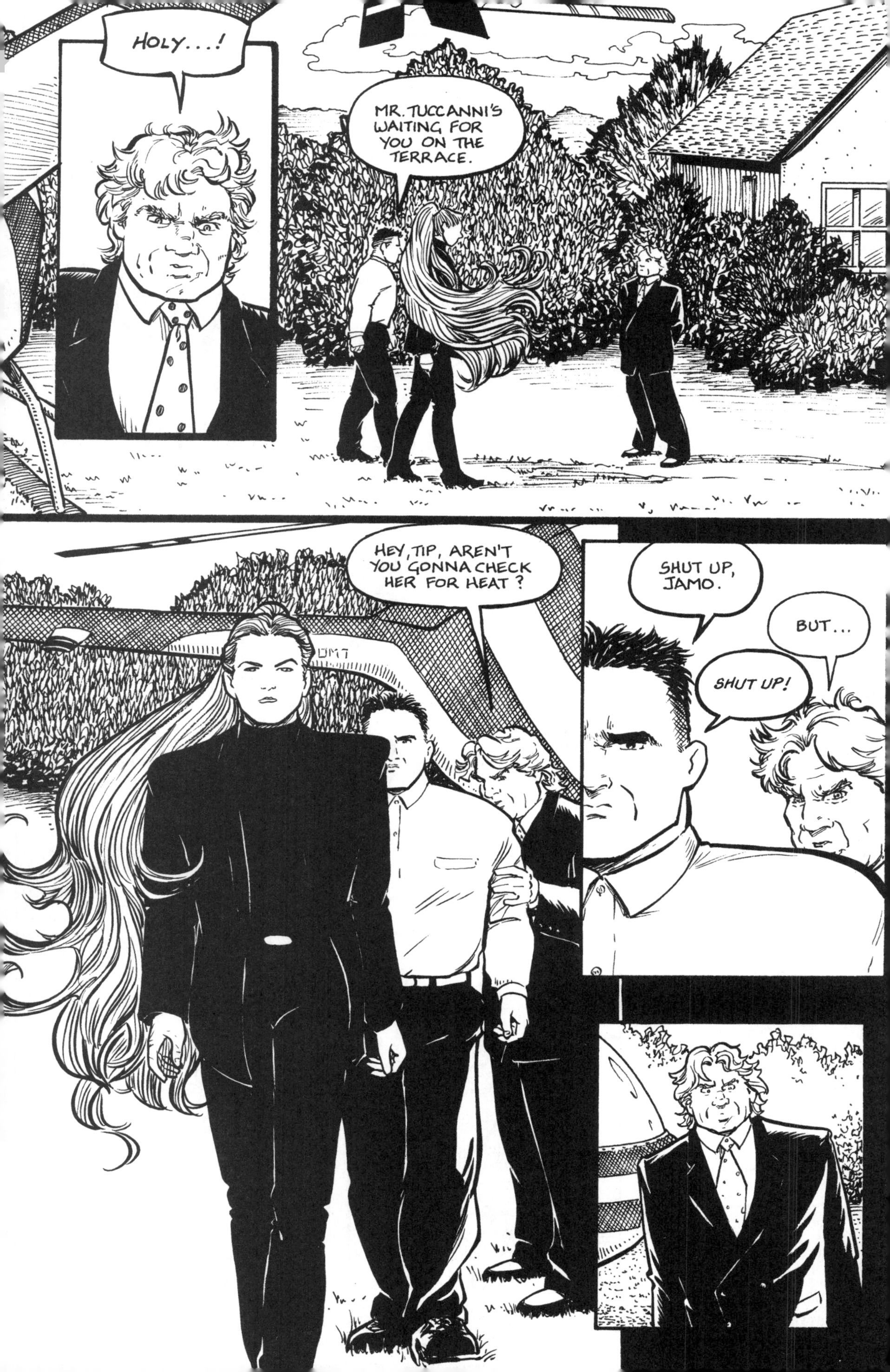
HOLY...!
MR. TUCCANNI'S WAITING FOR YOU ON THE TERRACE.
HEY, TIP, AREN'T YOU GONNA CHECK HER FOR HEAT?
SHUT UP, JAMO.
BUT...
SHUT UP!

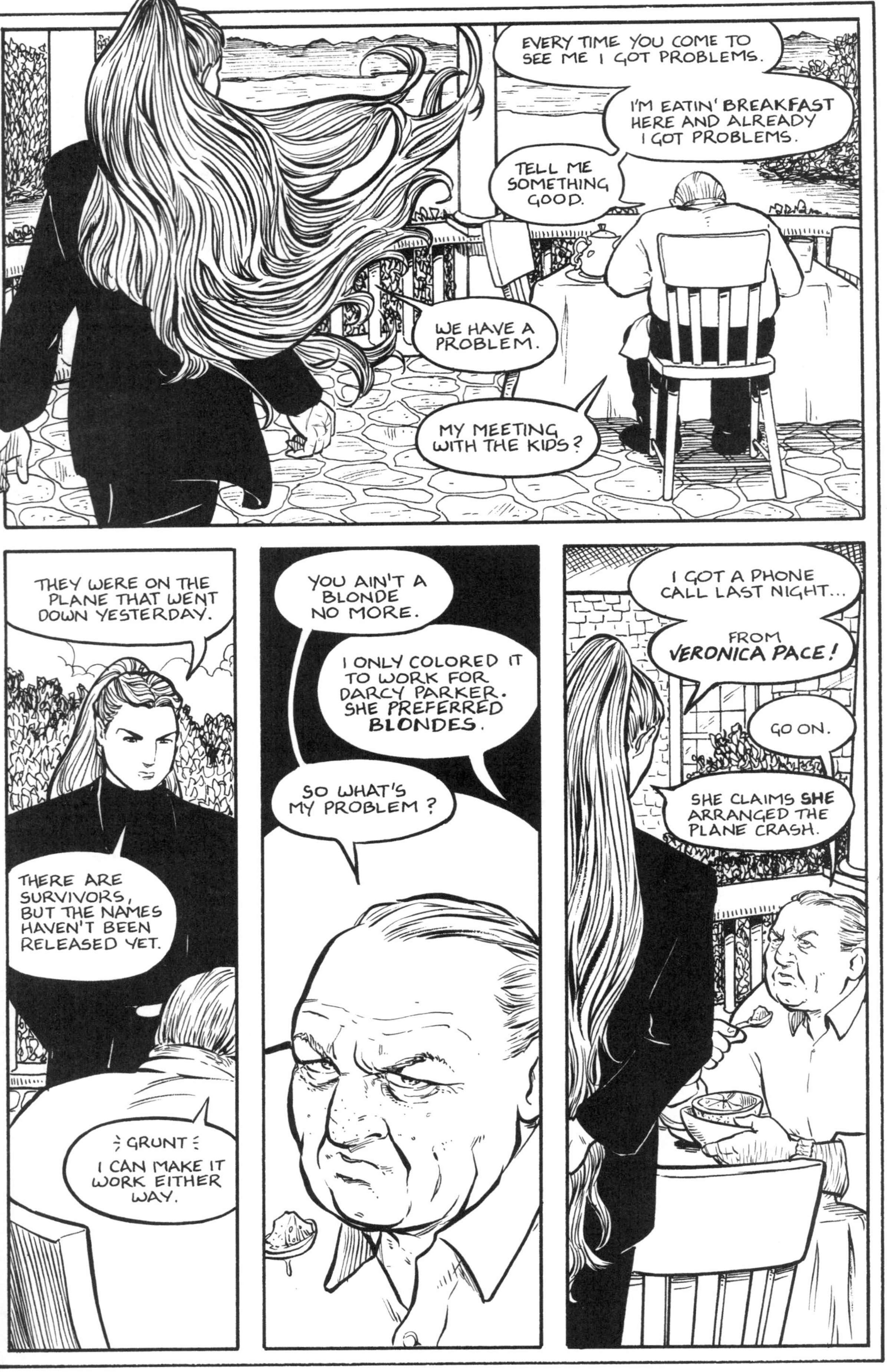

EVERY TIME YOU COME TO SEE ME I GOT PROBLEMS.
I'M EATIN' BREAKFAST HERE AND ALREADY I GOT PROBLEMS.
TELL ME SOMETHING GOOD.
WE HAVE A PROBLEM.
MY MEETING WITH THE KIDS?
THEY WERE ON THE PLANE THAT WENT DOWN YESTERDAY.
THERE ARE SURVIVORS, BUT THE NAMES HAVEN'T BEEN RELEASED YET.
GRUNT
I CAN MAKE IT WORK EITHER WAY.
YOU AIN'T A BLONDE NO MORE.
I ONLY COLORED IT TO WORK FOR DARCY PARKER. SHE PREFERRED BLONDES.
SO WHAT'S MY PROBLEM?
I GOT A PHONE CALL LAST NIGHT...
FROM VERONICA PACE!
GO ON.
SHE CLAIMS SHE ARRANGED THE PLANE CRASH.

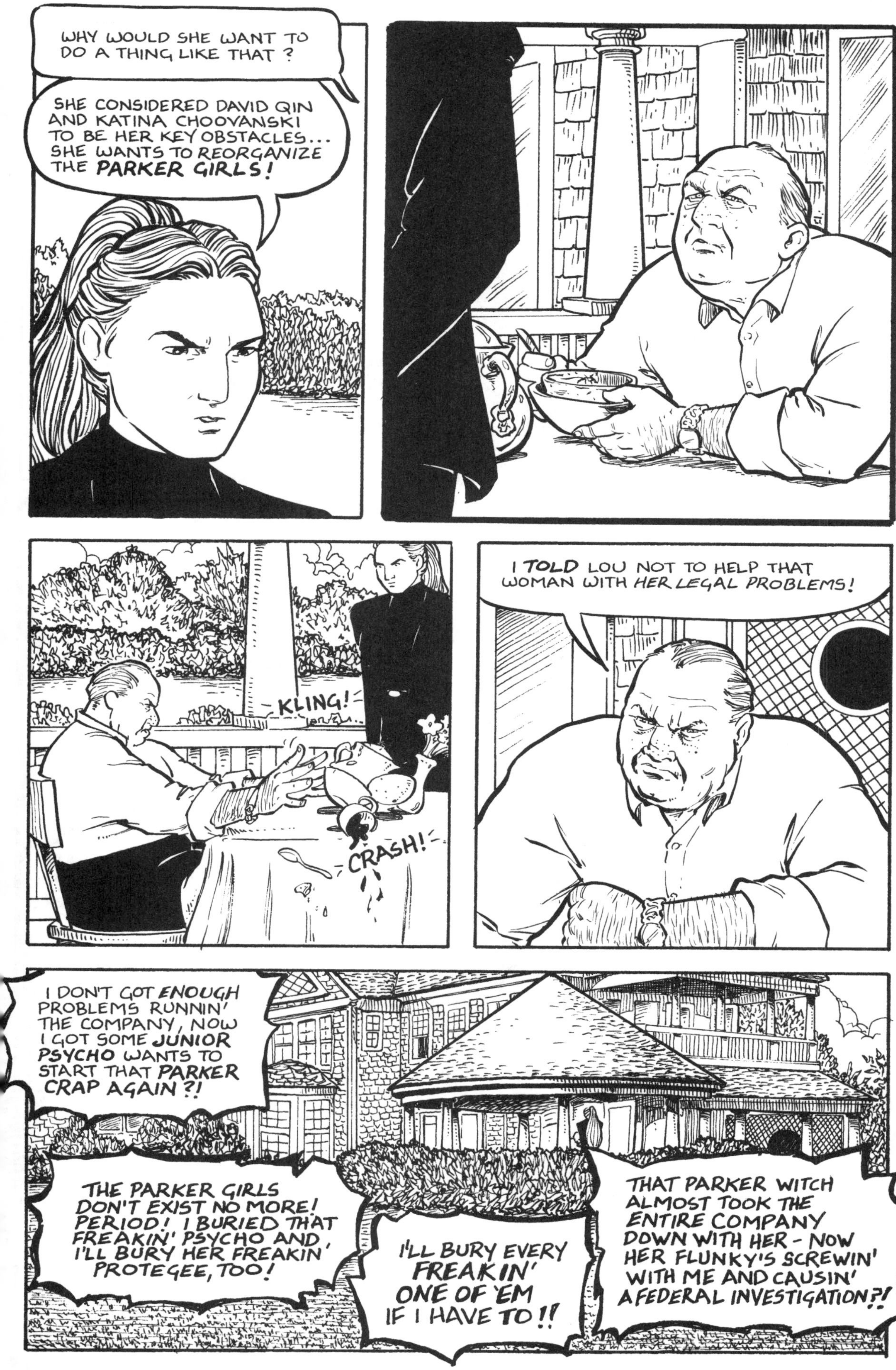
WHY WOULD SHE WANT TO DO A THING LIKE THAT ?
SHE CONSIDERED DAVID QIN AND KATINA CHOOVANSKI TO BE HER KEY OBSTACLES... SHE WANTS TO REORGANIZE THE PARKER GIRLS!
KLING!
CRASH!
I TOLD LOU NOT TO HELP THAT WOMAN WITH HER LEGAL PROBLEMS!
I DON'T GOT ENOUGH PROBLEMS RUNNIN' THE COMPANY, NOW I GOT SOME JUNIOR PSYCHO WANTS TO START THAT PARKER CRAP AGAIN ?!
THE PARKER GIRLS DON'T EXIST NO MORE! PERIOD! I BURIED THAT FREAKIN' PSYCHO AND I'LL BURY HER FREAKIN PROTEGEE, TOO!
I'LL BURY EVERY FREAKIN' ONE OF 'EM IF I HAVE TO!!
THAT PARKER WITCH ALMOST TOOK THE ENTIRE COMPANY DOWN WITH HER - NOW HER FLUNKY'S SCREWIN' WITH ME AND CAUSIN' A FEDERAL INVESTIGATION?!

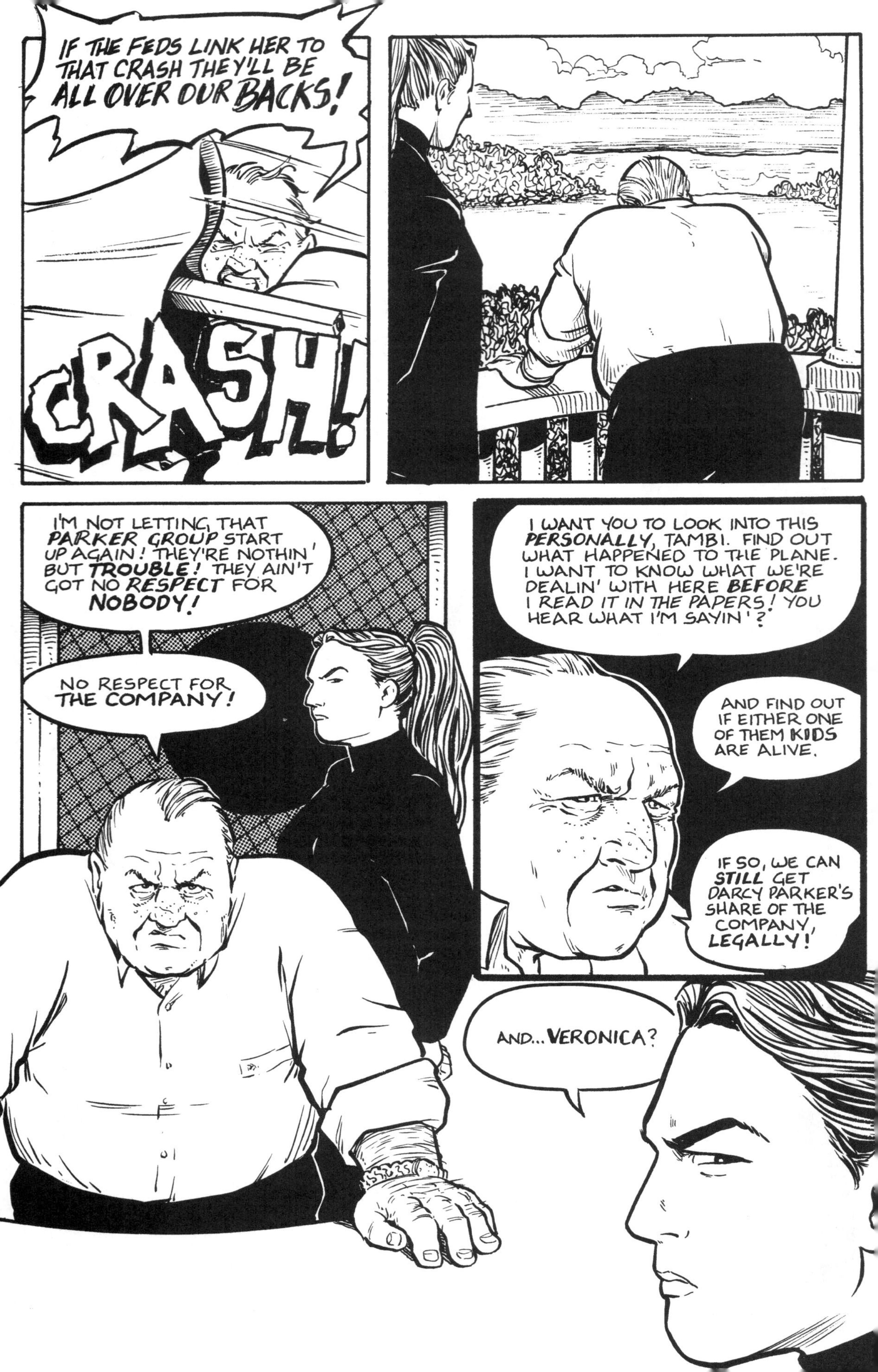
IF THE FEDS LINK HER TO THAT CRASH THEY'LL BE ALL OVER OUR BACKS!
CRASH!
I'M NOT LETTING THAT PARKER GROUP START UP AGAIN! THEY'RE NOTHIN' BUT TROUBLE! THEY AIN'T GOT NO RESPECT FOR NOBODY!
NO RESPECT FOR THE COMPANY!
I WANT YOU TO LOOK INTO THIS PERSONALLY, TAMBI. FIND OUT WHAT HAPPENED TO THE PLANE. I WANT TO KNOW WHAT WE'RE DEALIN' WITH HERE BEFORE I READ IT IN THE PAPERS! YOU HEAR WHAT I'M SAYIN'?
AND FIND OUT IF EITHER ONE OF THEM KIDS ARE ALIVE.
IF SO, WE CAN STILL GET DARCY PARKER'S SHARE OF THE COMPANY, LEGALLY!
AND... VERONICA?

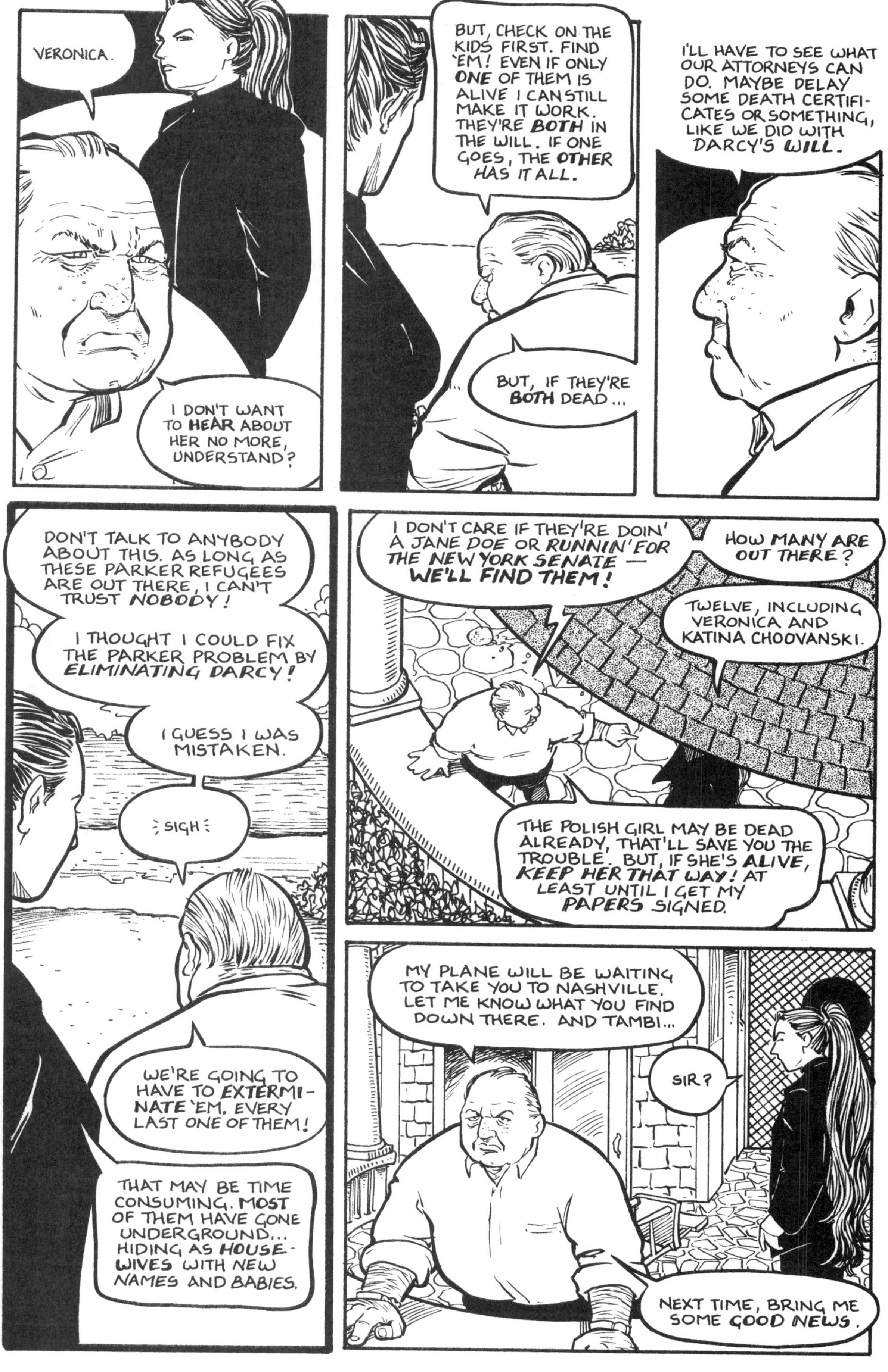
VERONICA.
I DON'T WANT TO HEAR ABOUT HER NO MORE, UNDERSTAND?
BUT, CHECK ON THE KIDS FIRST. FIND 'EM! EVEN IF ONLY ONE OF THEM IS ALIVE I CAN STILL MAKE IT WORK. THEY'RE BOTH IN THE WILL. IF ONE GOES, THE OTHER HAS IT ALL.
BUT, IF THEY'RE BOTH DEAD...
I'LL HAVE TO SEE WHAT OUR ATTORNEYS CAN DO. MAYBE DELAY SOME DEATH CERTIFICATES OR SOMETHING, LIKE WE DID WITH DARCY'S WILL.
DON'T TALK TO ANYBODY ABOUT THIS. AS LONG AS THESE PARKER REFUGEES ARE OUT THERE, I CAN'T TRUST NOBODY!
I THOUGHT I COULD FIX THE PARKER PROBLEM BY ELIMINATING DARCY!
I GUESS I WAS MISTAKEN.
SIGH
WE'RE GOING TO HAVE TO EXTERMINATE 'EM. EVERY LAST ONE OF THEM!
THAT MAY BE TIME CONSUMING. MOST OF THEM HAVE GONE UNDERGROUND... HIDING AS HOUSEWIVES WITH NEW NAMES AND BABIES.
I DON'T CARE IF THEY'RE DOIN' A JANE DOE OR RUNNIN' FOR THE NEW YORK SENATE — WE'LL FIND THEM!
HOW MANY ARE OUT THERE?
TWELVE, INCLUDING VERONICA AND KATINA CHOOVANSKI.
THE POLISH GIRL MAY BE DEAD ALREADY, THAT'LL SAVE YOU THE TROUBLE. BUT, IF SHE'S ALIVE, KEEP HER THAT WAY! AT LEAST UNTIL I GET MY PAPERS SIGNED.
MY PLANE WILL BE WAITING TO TAKE YOU TO NASHVILLE. LET ME KNOW WHAT YOU FIND DOWN THERE. AND TAMBI...
SIR?
NEXT TIME, BRING ME SOME GOOD NEWS.

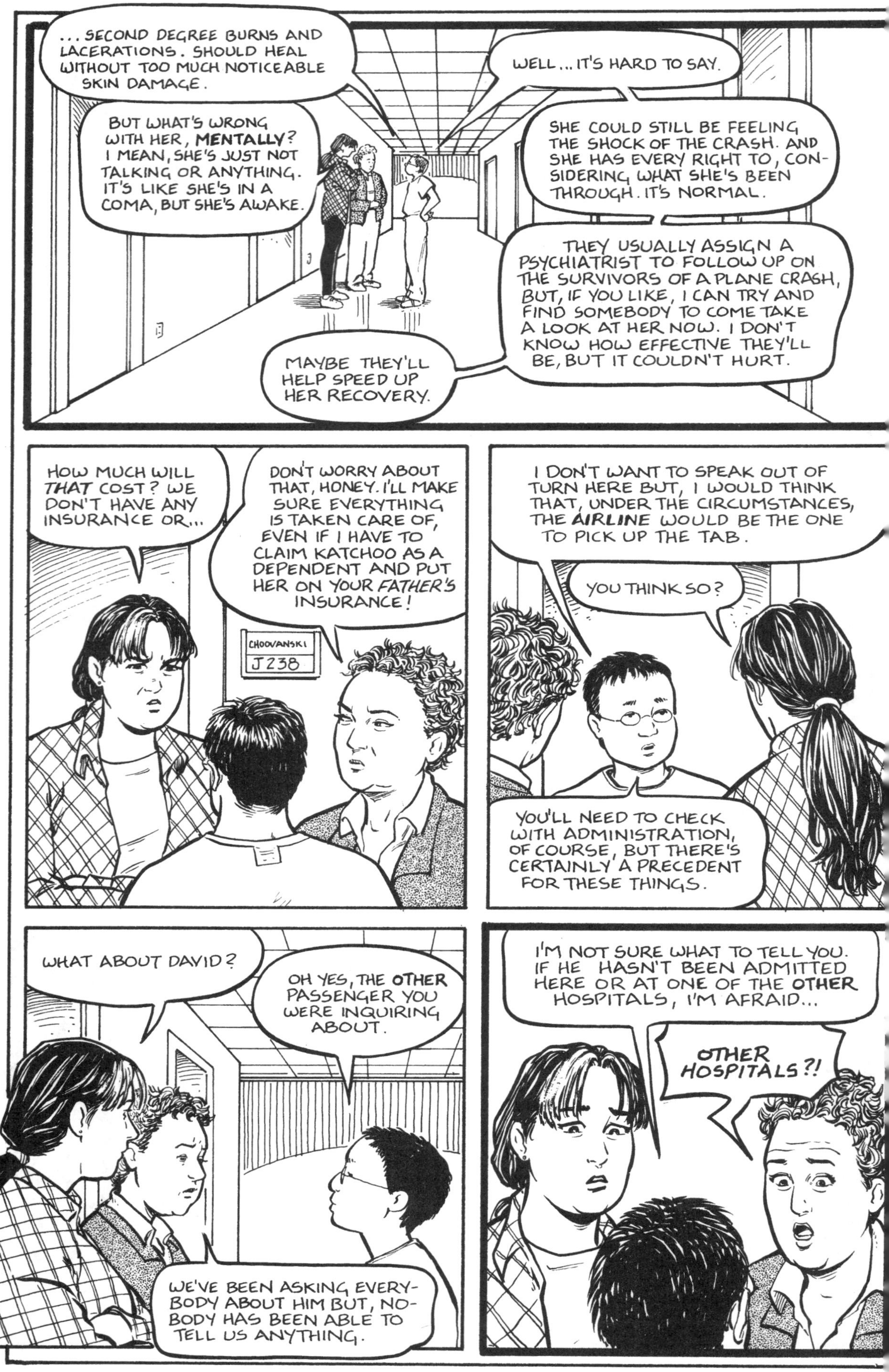
...SECOND DEGREE BURNS AND LACERATIONS. SHOULD HEAL WITHOUT TOO MUCH NOTICEABLE SKIN DAMAGE.
BUT WHAT'S WRONG WITH HER, **MENTALLY**? I MEAN, SHE'S JUST NOT TALKING OR ANYTHING. IT'S LIKE SHE'S IN A COMA, BUT SHE'S AWAKE.
WELL... IT'S HARD TO SAY.
SHE COULD STILL BE FEELING THE SHOCK OF THE CRASH. AND SHE HAS EVERY RIGHT TO, CONSIDERING WHAT SHE'S BEEN THROUGH. IT'S NORMAL.
THEY USUALLY ASSIGN A PSYCHIATRIST TO FOLLOW UP ON THE SURVIVORS OF A PLANE CRASH, BUT, IF YOU LIKE, I CAN TRY AND FIND SOMEBODY TO COME TAKE A LOOK AT HER NOW. I DON'T KNOW HOW EFFECTIVE THEY'LL BE, BUT IT COULDN'T HURT.
MAYBE THEY'LL HELP SPEED UP HER RECOVERY.
HOW MUCH WILL *THAT* COST? WE DON'T HAVE ANY INSURANCE OR...
DON'T WORRY ABOUT THAT, HONEY. I'LL MAKE SURE EVERYTHING IS TAKEN CARE OF, EVEN IF I HAVE TO CLAIM KATCHOO AS A DEPENDENT AND PUT HER ON YOUR *FATHER'S* INSURANCE!
CHOOVANSKI
J238
I DON'T WANT TO SPEAK OUT OF TURN HERE BUT, I WOULD THINK THAT, UNDER THE CIRCUMSTANCES, THE **AIRLINE** WOULD BE THE ONE TO PICK UP THE TAB.
YOU THINK SO?
YOU'LL NEED TO CHECK WITH ADMINISTRATION, OF COURSE, BUT THERE'S CERTAINLY A PRECEDENT FOR THESE THINGS.
WHAT ABOUT DAVID?
OH YES, THE **OTHER** PASSENGER YOU WERE INQUIRING ABOUT.
WE'VE BEEN ASKING EVERYBODY ABOUT HIM BUT, NOBODY HAS BEEN ABLE TO TELL US ANYTHING.
I'M NOT SURE WHAT TO TELL YOU. IF HE HASN'T BEEN ADMITTED HERE OR AT ONE OF THE **OTHER** HOSPITALS, I'M AFRAID...
**OTHER HOSPITALS?!**

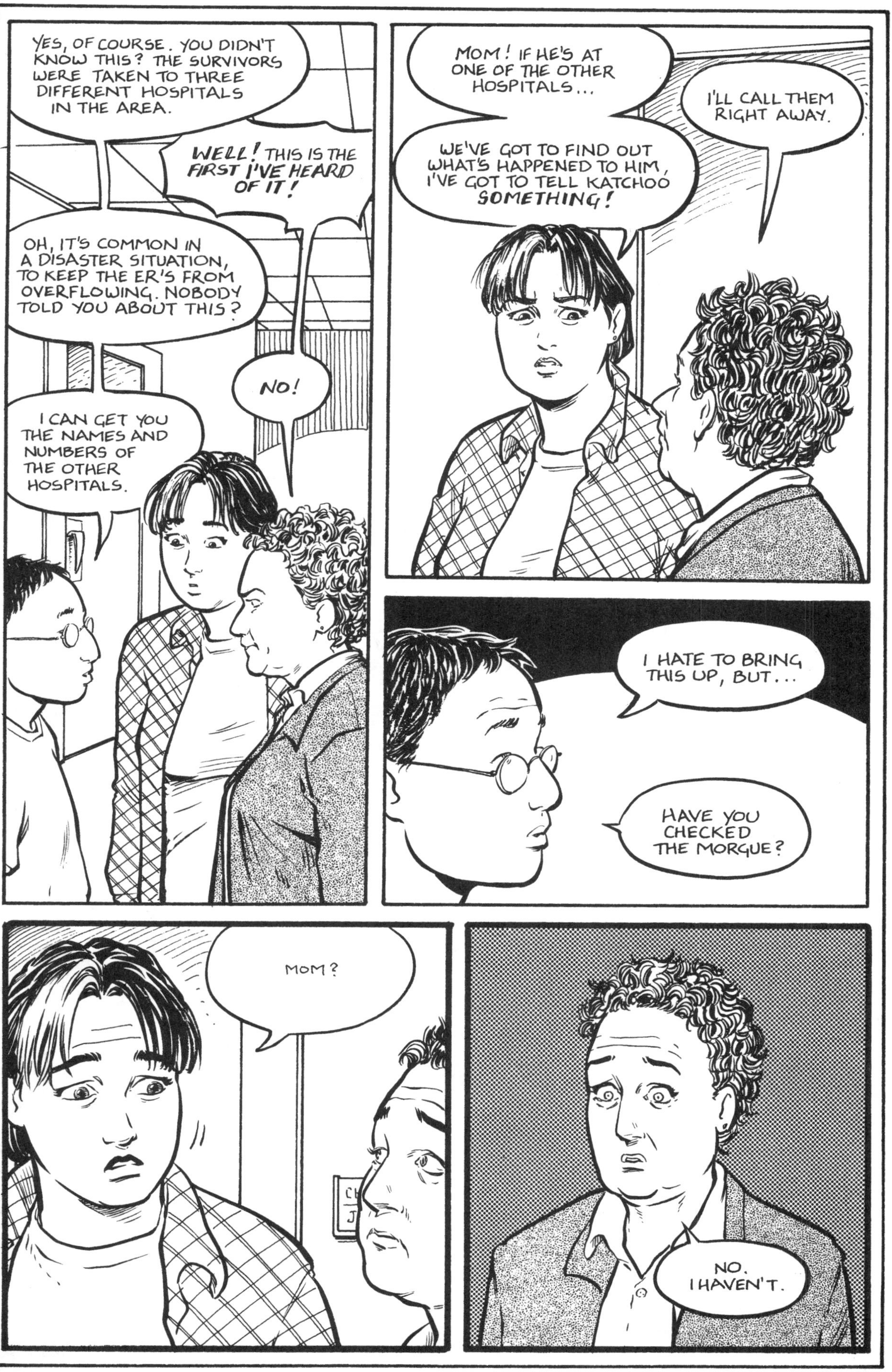
YES, OF COURSE. YOU DIDN'T KNOW THIS? THE SURVIVORS WERE TAKEN TO THREE DIFFERENT HOSPITALS IN THE AREA.
WELL! THIS IS THE FIRST I'VE HEARD OF IT!
OH, IT'S COMMON IN A DISASTER SITUATION, TO KEEP THE ER'S FROM OVERFLOWING. NOBODY TOLD YOU ABOUT THIS?
NO!
I CAN GET YOU THE NAMES AND NUMBERS OF THE OTHER HOSPITALS.
MOM! IF HE'S AT ONE OF THE OTHER HOSPITALS...
WE'VE GOT TO FIND OUT WHAT'S HAPPENED TO HIM, I'VE GOT TO TELL KATCHOO SOMETHING!
I'LL CALL THEM RIGHT AWAY.
I HATE TO BRING THIS UP, BUT...
HAVE YOU CHECKED THE MORGUE?
MOM?
NO. I HAVEN'T.

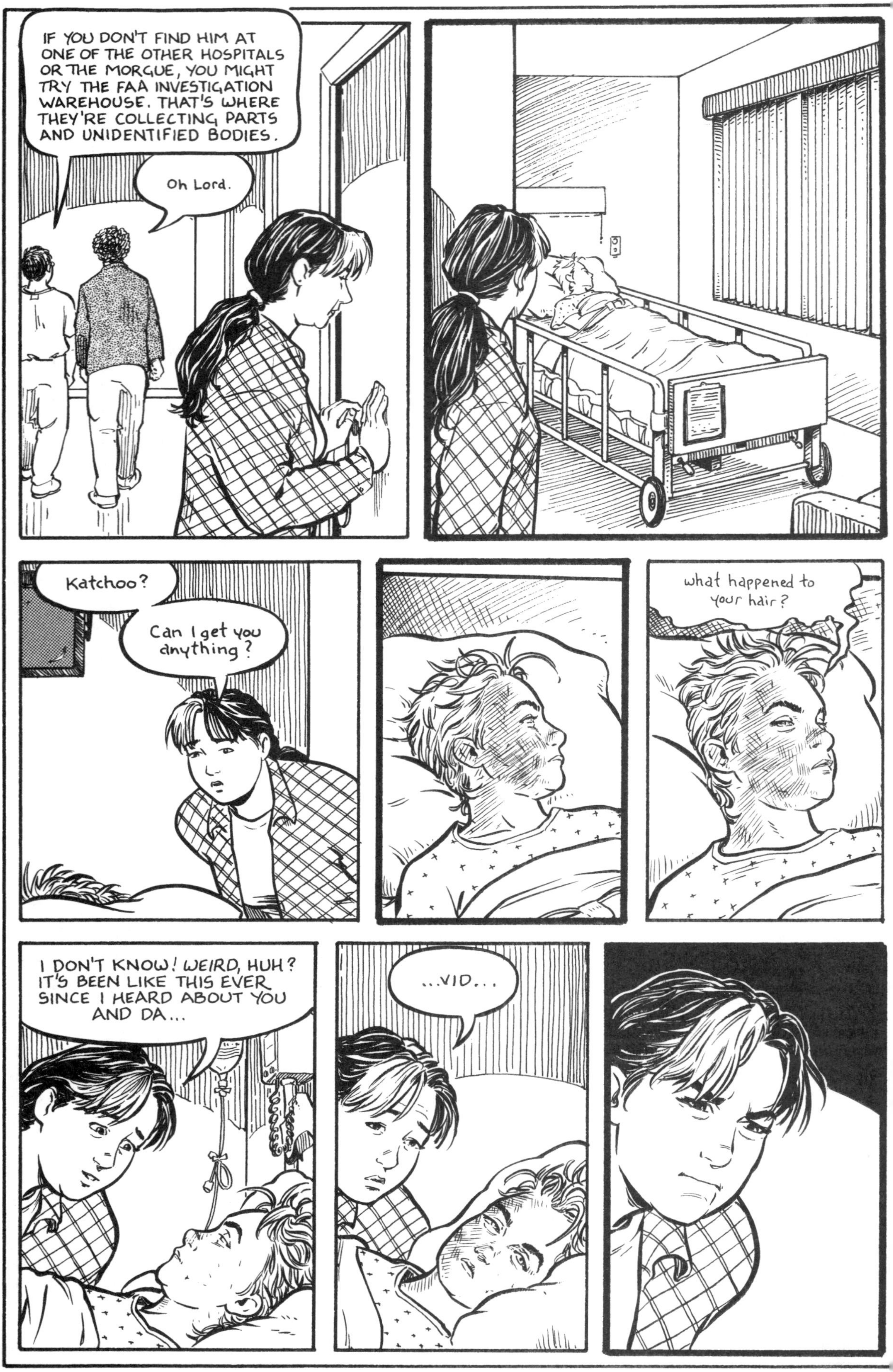
IF YOU DON'T FIND HIM AT ONE OF THE OTHER HOSPITALS OR THE MORGUE, YOU MIGHT TRY THE FAA INVESTIGATION WAREHOUSE. THAT'S WHERE THEY'RE COLLECTING PARTS AND UNIDENTIFIED BODIES.
Oh Lord.
Katchoo?
Can I get you anything?
what happened to your hair?
I DON'T KNOW! WEIRD, HUH? IT'S BEEN LIKE THIS EVER SINCE I HEARD ABOUT YOU AND DA...
...VID...

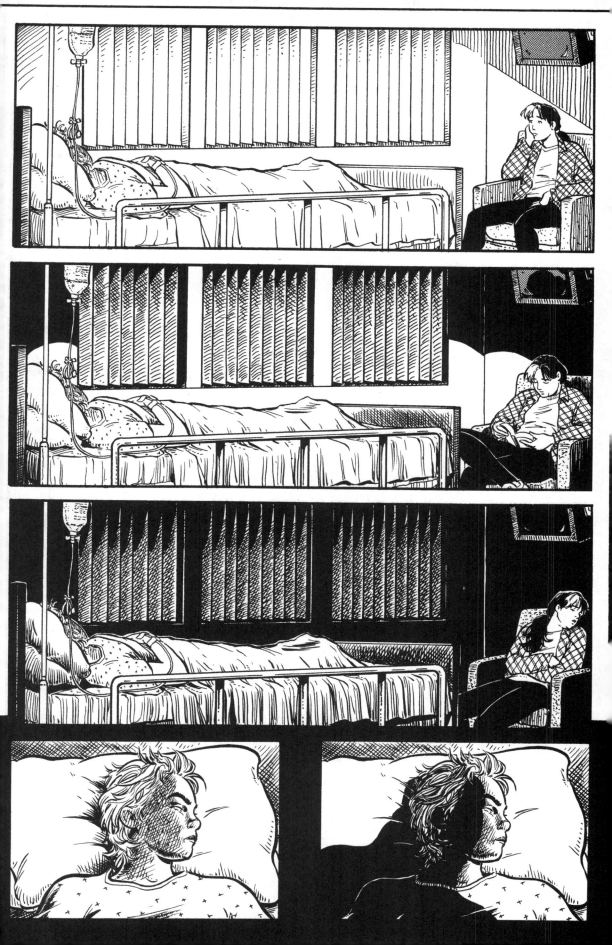

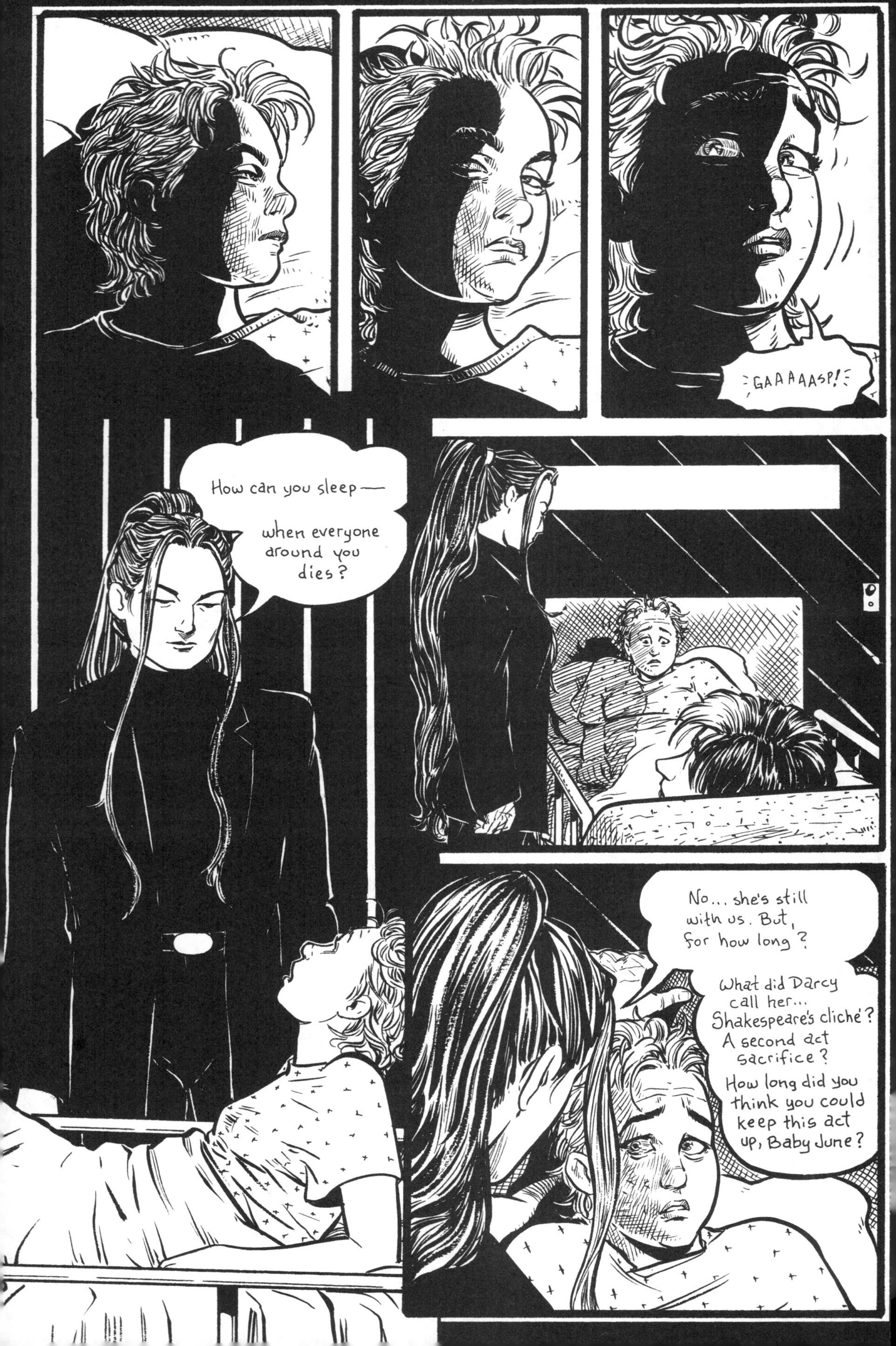
GAAAAASP!
How can you sleep—
when everyone around you dies?
No... she's still with us. But, for how long?
What did Darcy call her... Shakespeare's cliché? A second act sacrifice?
How long did you think you could keep this act up, Baby June?

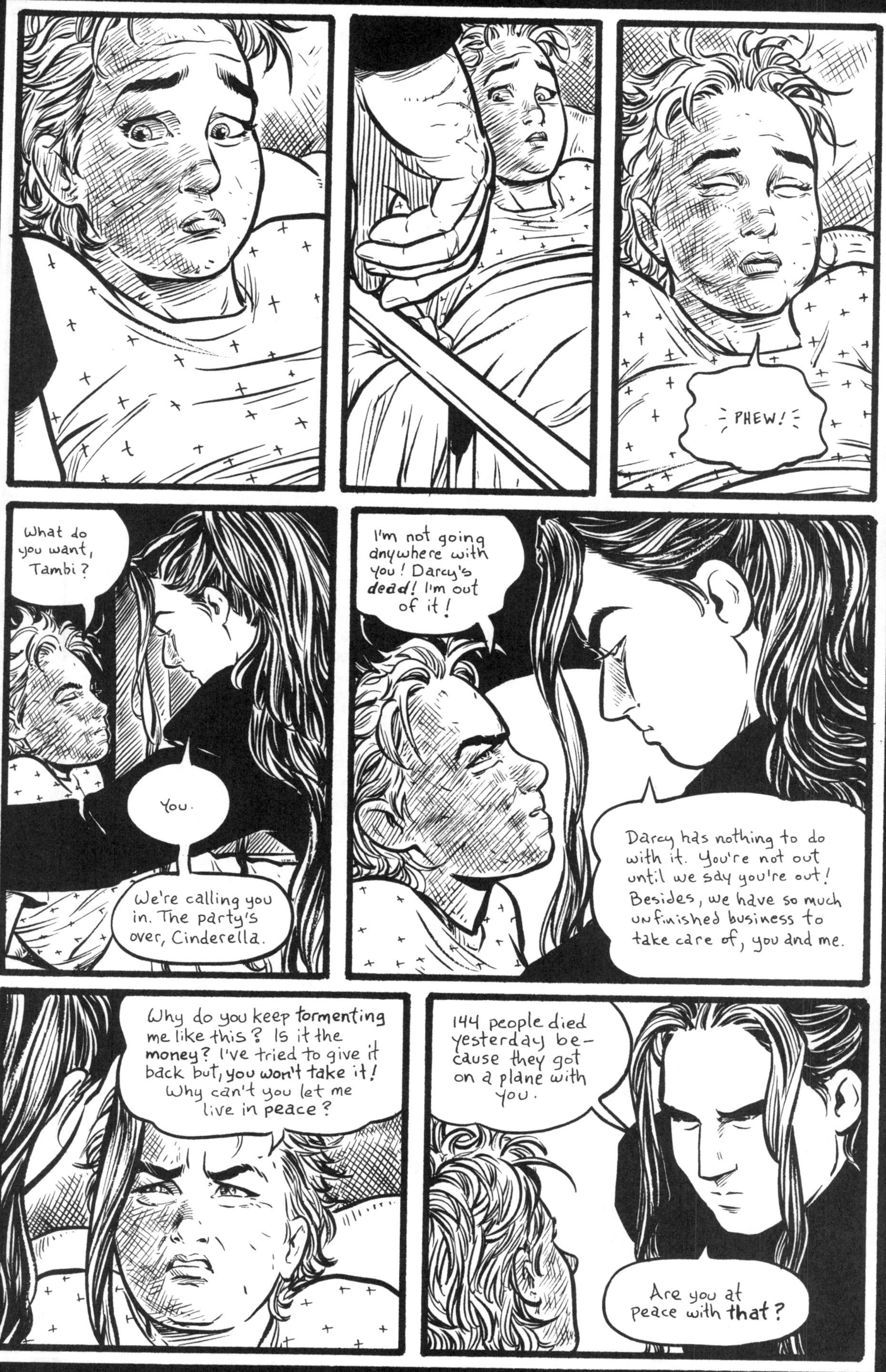
PHEW!
What do you want, Tambi?
You.
We're calling you in. The party's over, Cinderella.
I'm not going anywhere with you! Darcy's dead! I'm out of it!
Darcy has nothing to do with it. You're not out until we say you're out! Besides, we have so much unfinished business to take care of, you and me.
Why do you keep tormenting me like this? Is it the money? I've tried to give it back but, you won't take it! Why can't you let me live in peace?
144 people died yesterday because they got on a plane with you.
Are you at peace with that?

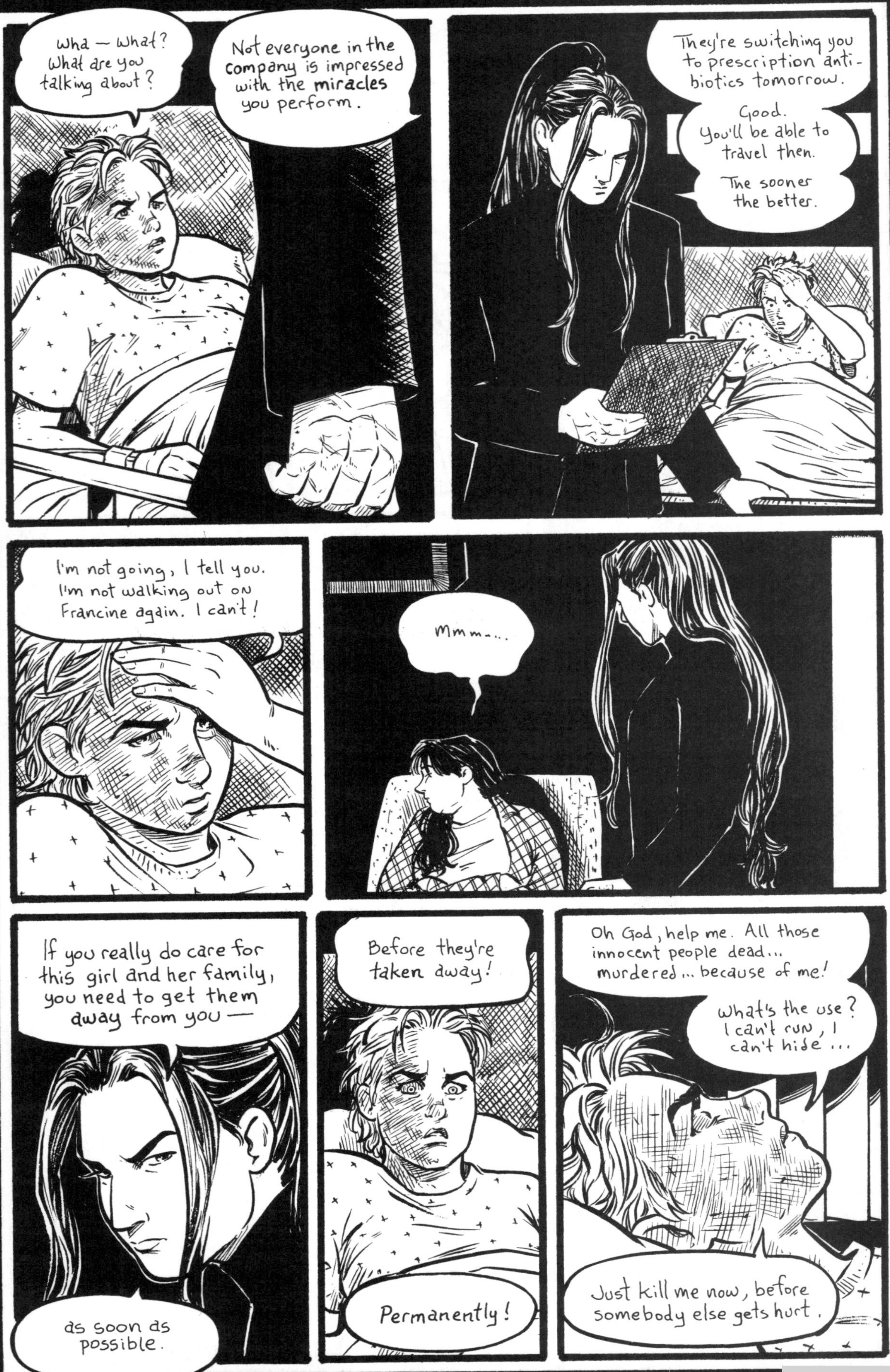
Wha — What? What are you talking about?
Not everyone in the company is impressed with the miracles you perform.
They're switching you to prescription anti-biotics tomorrow.
Good. You'll be able to travel then. The sooner the better.
I'm not going, I tell you. I'm not walking out on Francine again. I can't!
Mmm...
If you really do care for this girl and her family, you need to get them away from you —
as soon as possible.
Before they're taken away!
Permanently!
Oh God, help me. All those innocent people dead... murdered... because of me!
What's the use? I can't run, I can't hide...
Just kill me now, before somebody else gets hurt.

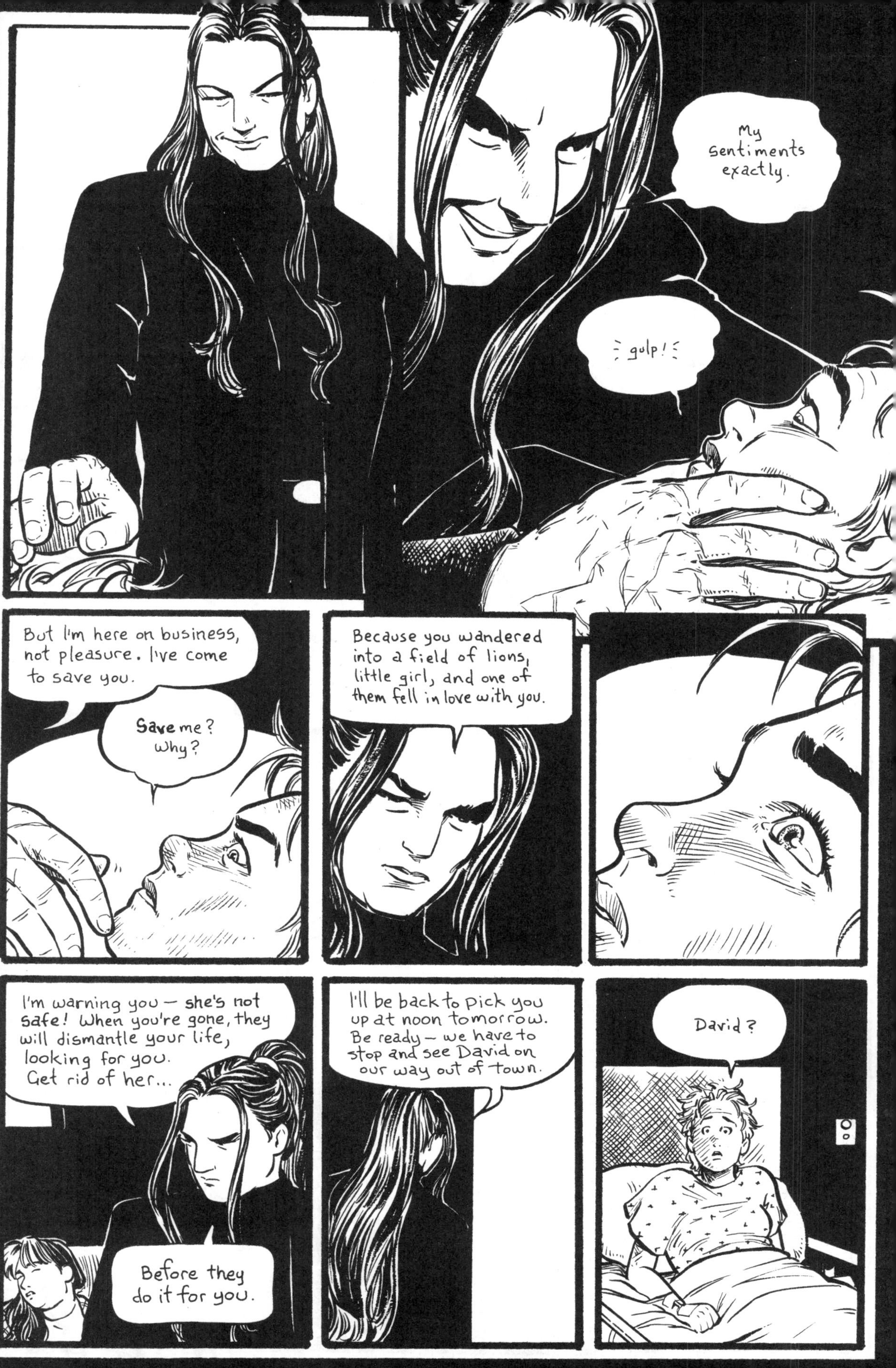
My sentiments exactly.
gulp!
But I'm here on business, not pleasure. I've come to save you.
Save me? Why?
Because you wandered into a field of lions, little girl, and one of them fell in love with you.
I'm warning you — she's not safe! When you're gone, they will dismantle your life, looking for you. Get rid of her...
Before they do it for you.
I'll be back to pick you up at noon tomorrow. Be ready — we have to stop and see David on our way out of town.
David?

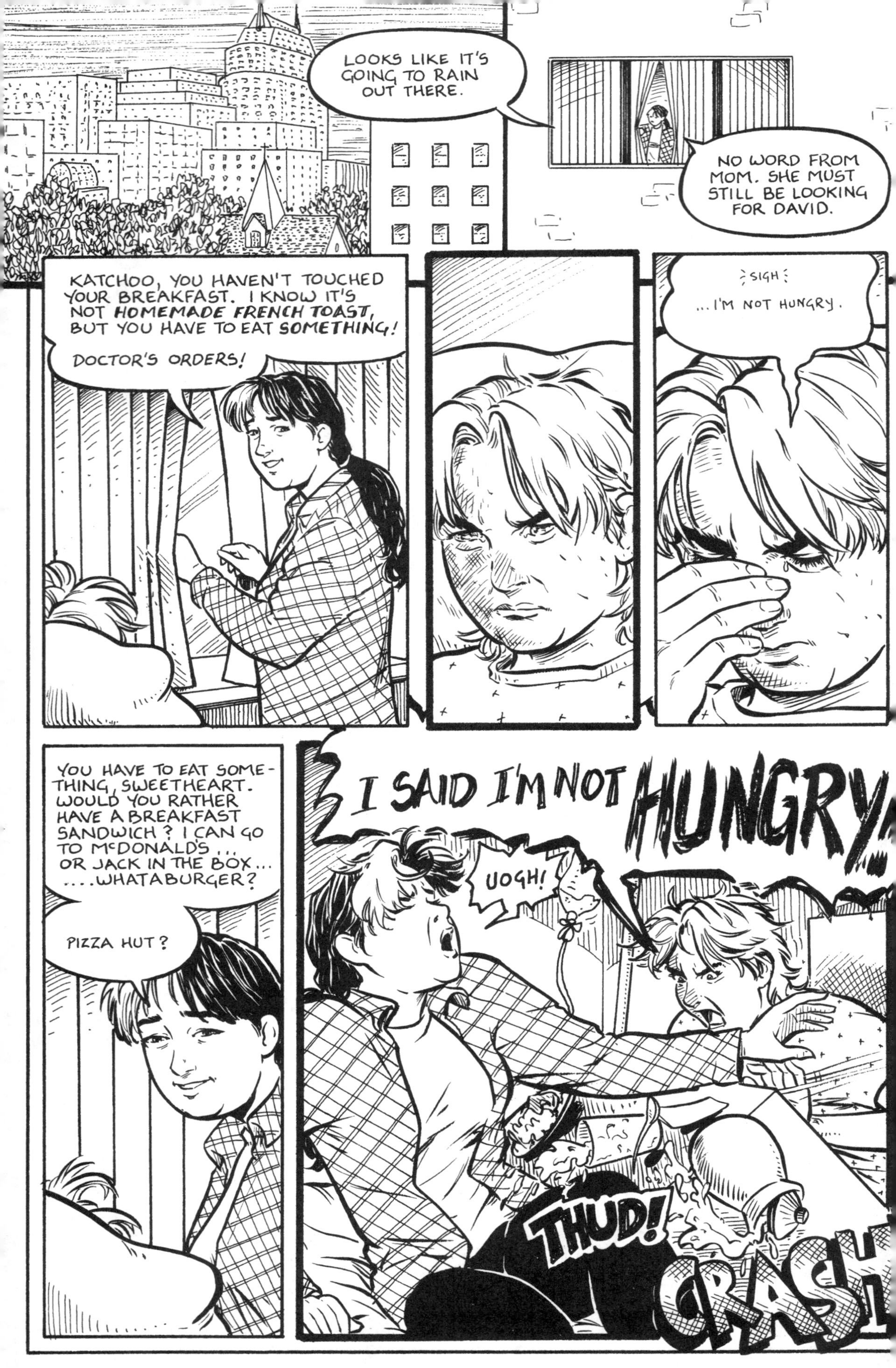

LOOKS LIKE IT'S GOING TO RAIN OUT THERE.
NO WORD FROM MOM. SHE MUST STILL BE LOOKING FOR DAVID.
KATCHOO, YOU HAVEN'T TOUCHED YOUR BREAKFAST. I KNOW IT'S NOT **HOMEMADE FRENCH TOAST**, BUT YOU HAVE TO EAT **SOMETHING**!
DOCTOR'S ORDERS!
SIGH
...I'M NOT HUNGRY.
YOU HAVE TO EAT SOME-THING, SWEETHEART. WOULD YOU RATHER HAVE A BREAKFAST SANDWICH? I CAN GO TO McDONALD'S... OR JACK IN THE BOX... ....WHATABURGER?
PIZZA HUT?
I SAID I'M NOT HUNGRY!
UOGH!
THUD!
CRASH

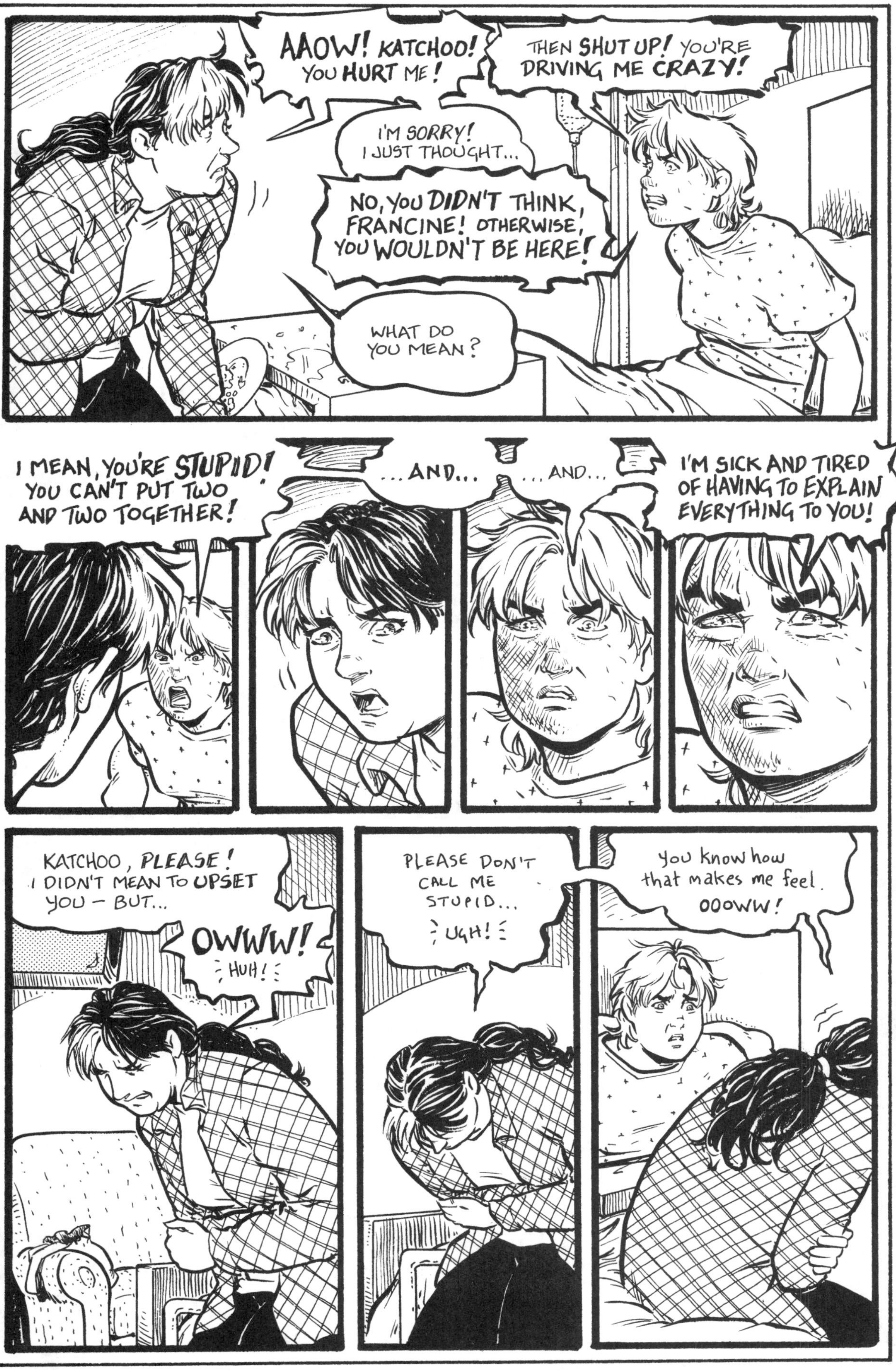

AAOW! KATCHOO! YOU HURT ME!
THEN SHUT UP! YOU'RE DRIVING ME CRAZY!
I'M SORRY! I JUST THOUGHT...
NO, YOU DIDN'T THINK, FRANCINE! OTHERWISE, YOU WOULDN'T BE HERE!
WHAT DO YOU MEAN?
I MEAN, YOU'RE STUPID! YOU CAN'T PUT TWO AND TWO TOGETHER!
...AND...
...AND...
I'M SICK AND TIRED OF HAVING TO EXPLAIN EVERYTHING TO YOU!
KATCHOO, PLEASE! I DIDN'T MEAN TO UPSET YOU — BUT...
OWWW!
HUH!
PLEASE DON'T CALL ME STUPID...
UGH!
You know how that makes me feel.
OOOWW!

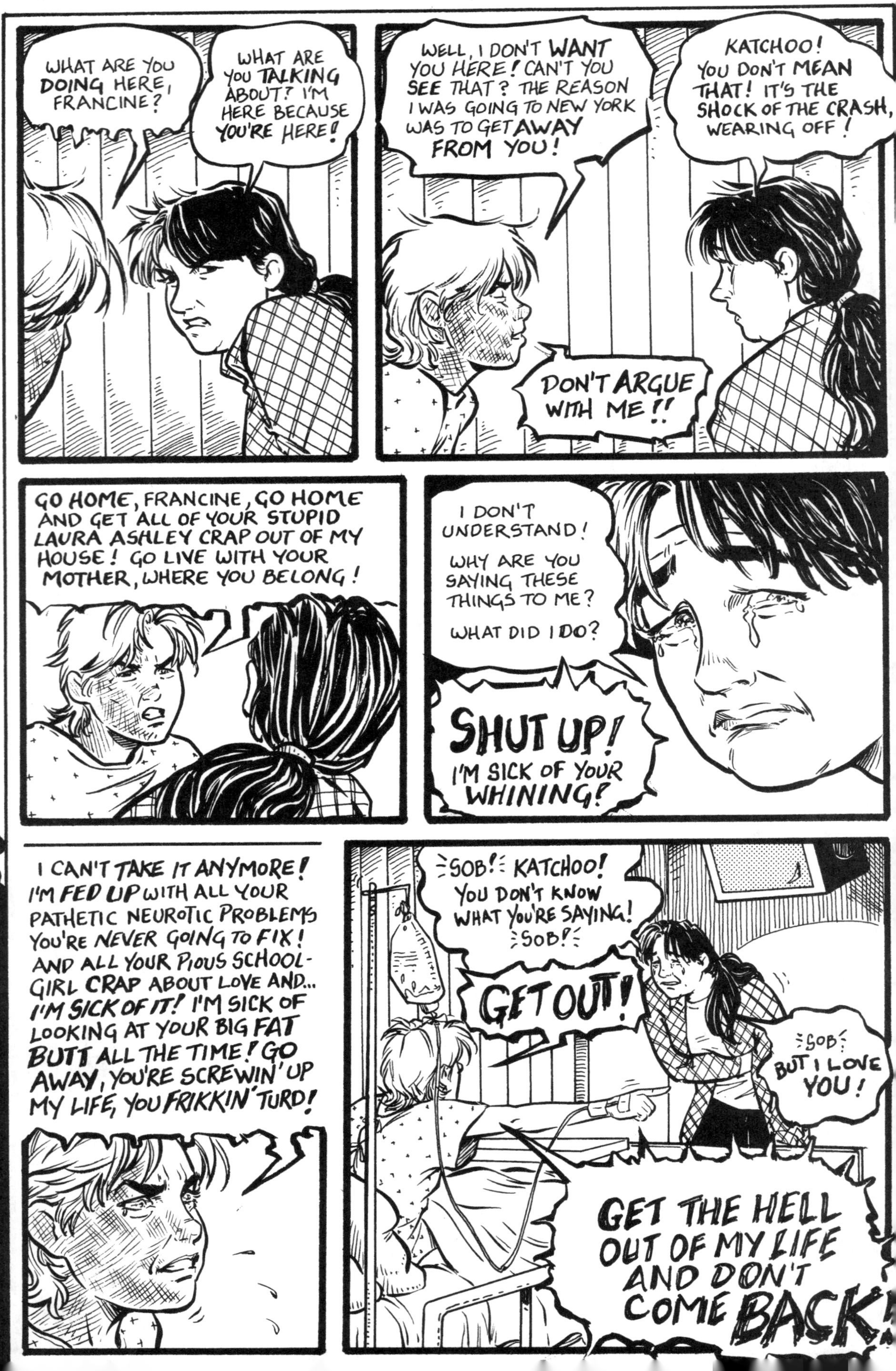
WHAT ARE YOU DOING HERE, FRANCINE?
WHAT ARE YOU TALKING ABOUT? I'M HERE BECAUSE YOU'RE HERE!
WELL, I DON'T WANT YOU HERE! CAN'T YOU SEE THAT? THE REASON I WAS GOING TO NEW YORK WAS TO GET AWAY FROM YOU!
KATCHOO! YOU DON'T MEAN THAT! IT'S THE SHOCK OF THE CRASH, WEARING OFF!
DON'T ARGUE WITH ME!!
GO HOME, FRANCINE, GO HOME AND GET ALL OF YOUR STUPID LAURA ASHLEY CRAP OUT OF MY HOUSE! GO LIVE WITH YOUR MOTHER, WHERE YOU BELONG!
I DON'T UNDERSTAND!
WHY ARE YOU SAYING THESE THINGS TO ME?
WHAT DID I DO?
SHUT UP! I'M SICK OF YOUR WHINING!
I CAN'T TAKE IT ANYMORE! I'M FED UP WITH ALL YOUR PATHETIC NEUROTIC PROBLEMS YOU'RE NEVER GOING TO FIX! AND ALL YOUR PIOUS SCHOOL-GIRL CRAP ABOUT LOVE AND... I'M SICK OF IT! I'M SICK OF LOOKING AT YOUR BIG FAT BUTT ALL THE TIME! GO AWAY, YOU'RE SCREWIN' UP MY LIFE, YOU FRIKKIN' TURD!
SOB! KATCHOO! YOU DON'T KNOW WHAT YOU'RE SAYING! SOB!
GET OUT!
SOB BUT I LOVE YOU!
GET THE HELL OUT OF MY LIFE AND DON'T COME BACK!

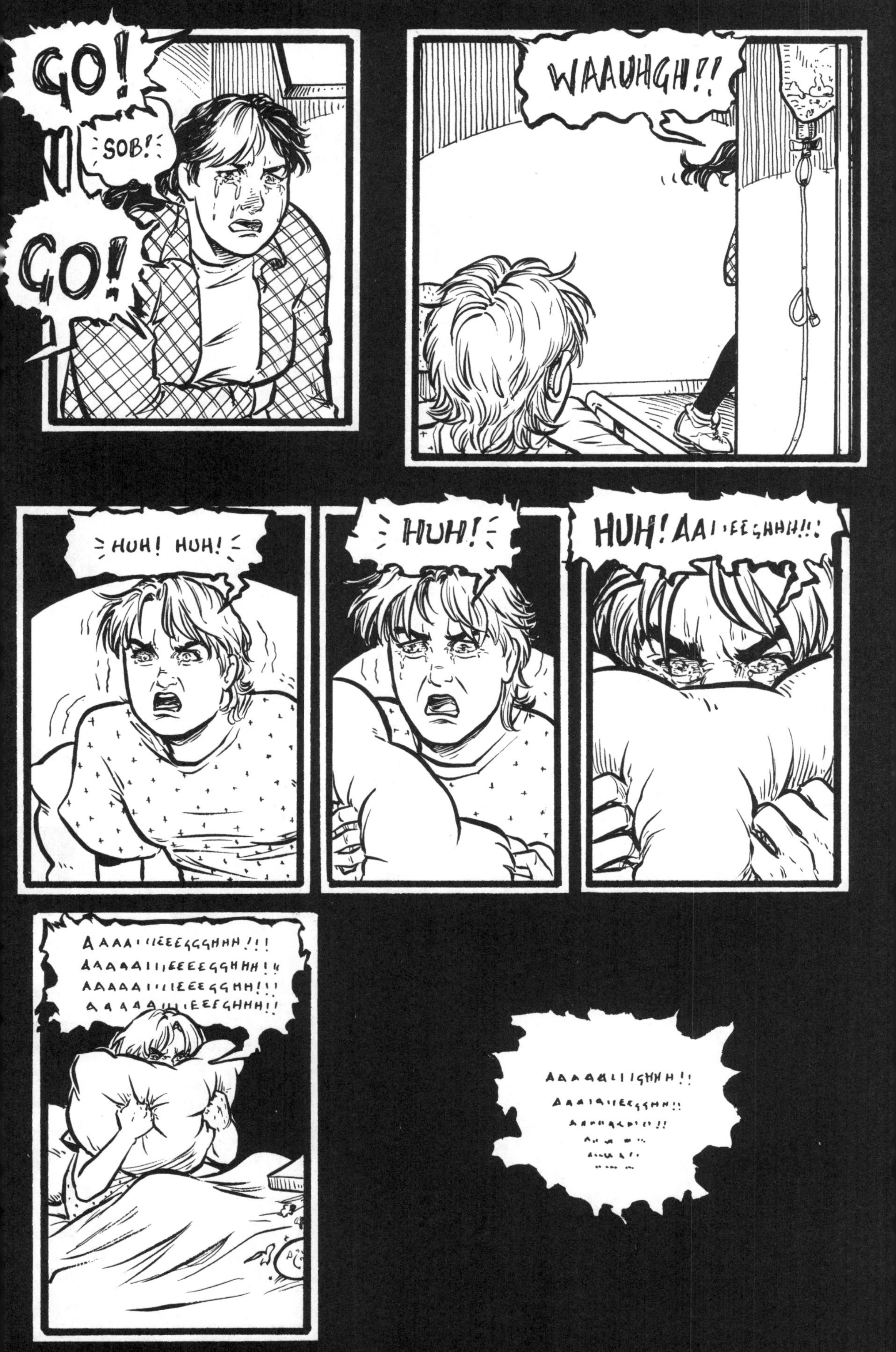

GO!
SOB!
GO!
WAAUHGH!!
HUH! HUH!
HUH!
HUH! AAIIEEGHHH!!!
AAAAIIIEEEGGGHHH!!!
AAAAAIIIEEEEEGGHHH!!!
AAAAAIIIIEEEGGHH!!!
AAAAAIIIIEEEGHHH!!
AAAAALIIGHHH!!
AAAIAIIEEEGGHH!!

ABSTRACT
STUDIO

**29**

2.75 U.S.
3.80 CAN

# STRANGERS IN PARADISE

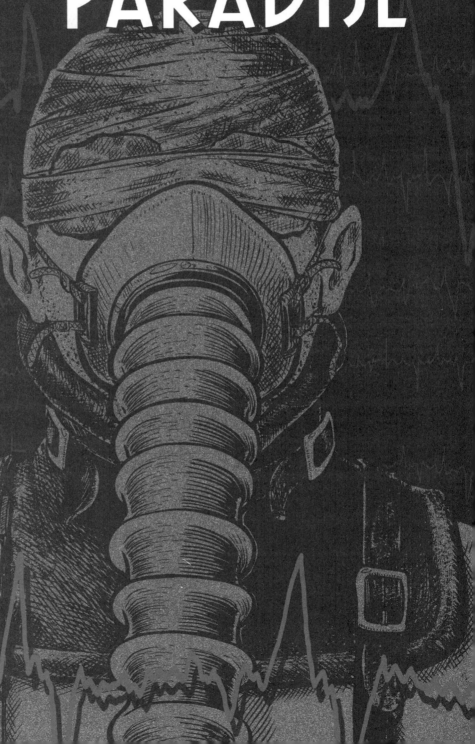

When I wake up at night
Remembering my other life,
I scream.
If I could find a way don't you believe
That I'd be there today?
But for my clever mind, to punish me,
I'm trapped inside this black design
My eyes are gallows and my heart's a nervous wreck
Trapped in confusion all around me I forget
My real name,
But they call me profane.

When I had angry eyes
To see beyond the veil of lies was nothing,
But now they're baby blue and don't see any answers,
I'm as blind as you.
If what they say is true then anything can happen
There are no border lines.
Tho' deep inside I hold the child I think I am,
My hands were midwife to the hell I'm living in.
Oh believe me,
I'm running out of time.

When I wake up at night
Remembering my other life,
I scream.
But every dawning day the faith in me
beyond my reach more distant fades.
My eyes are gallows and my heart's a nervous wreck;
My cries are fondled by the hangman's deadly kiss.
Oh believe me,
I'm running out of

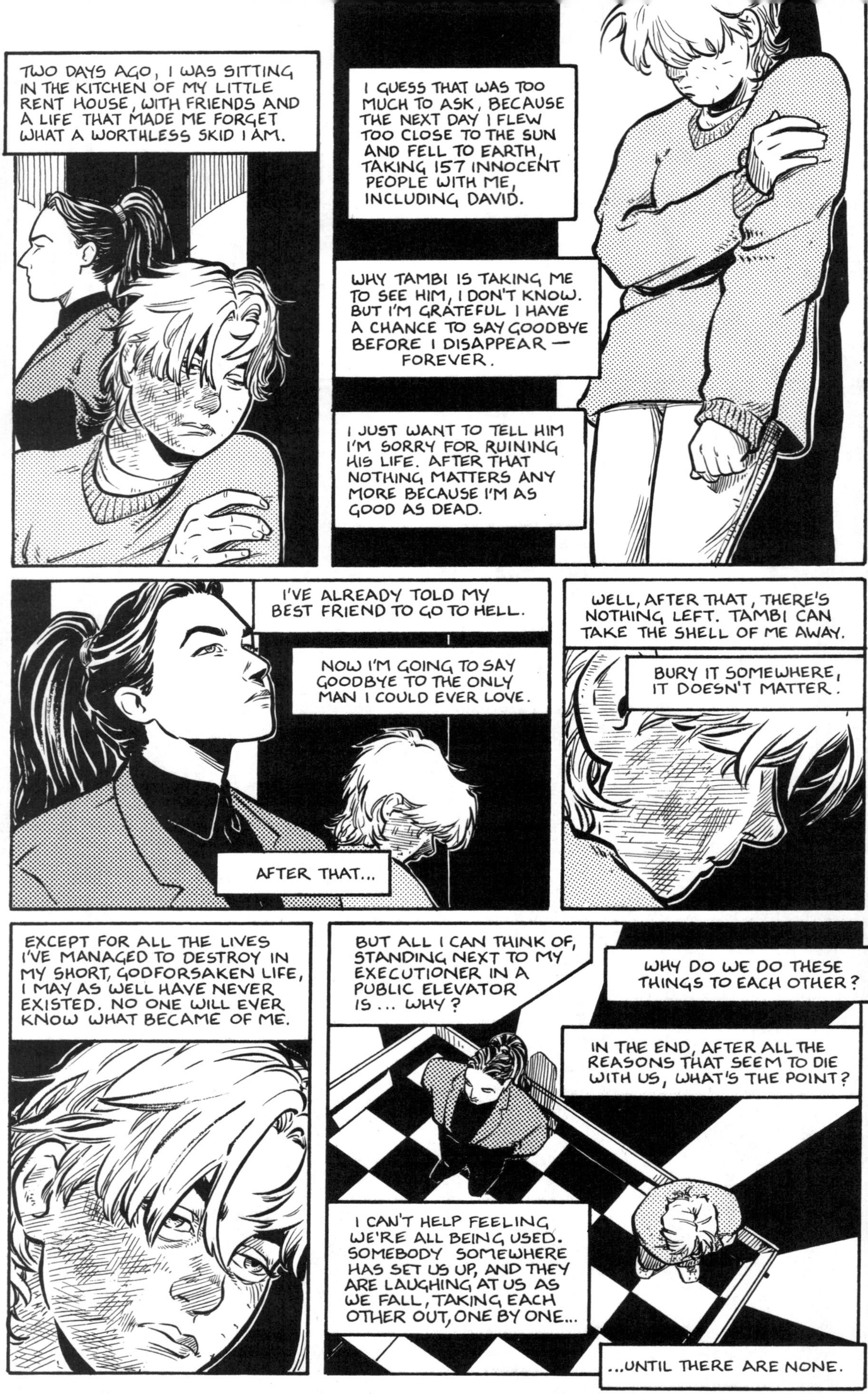
TWO DAYS AGO, I WAS SITTING IN THE KITCHEN OF MY LITTLE RENT HOUSE, WITH FRIENDS AND A LIFE THAT MADE ME FORGET WHAT A WORTHLESS SKID I AM.
I GUESS THAT WAS TOO MUCH TO ASK, BECAUSE THE NEXT DAY I FLEW TOO CLOSE TO THE SUN AND FELL TO EARTH, TAKING 157 INNOCENT PEOPLE WITH ME, INCLUDING DAVID.
WHY TAMBI IS TAKING ME TO SEE HIM, I DON'T KNOW. BUT I'M GRATEFUL I HAVE A CHANCE TO SAY GOODBYE BEFORE I DISAPPEAR — FOREVER.
I JUST WANT TO TELL HIM I'M SORRY FOR RUINING HIS LIFE. AFTER THAT NOTHING MATTERS ANY MORE BECAUSE I'M AS GOOD AS DEAD.
I'VE ALREADY TOLD MY BEST FRIEND TO GO TO HELL.
NOW I'M GOING TO SAY GOODBYE TO THE ONLY MAN I COULD EVER LOVE.
AFTER THAT...
WELL, AFTER THAT, THERE'S NOTHING LEFT. TAMBI CAN TAKE THE SHELL OF ME AWAY.
BURY IT SOMEWHERE, IT DOESN'T MATTER.
EXCEPT FOR ALL THE LIVES I'VE MANAGED TO DESTROY IN MY SHORT, GODFORSAKEN LIFE, I MAY AS WELL HAVE NEVER EXISTED. NO ONE WILL EVER KNOW WHAT BECAME OF ME.
BUT ALL I CAN THINK OF, STANDING NEXT TO MY EXECUTIONER IN A PUBLIC ELEVATOR IS ... WHY?
WHY DO WE DO THESE THINGS TO EACH OTHER?
IN THE END, AFTER ALL THE REASONS THAT SEEM TO DIE WITH US, WHAT'S THE POINT?
I CAN'T HELP FEELING WE'RE ALL BEING USED. SOMEBODY SOMEWHERE HAS SET US UP, AND THEY ARE LAUGHING AT US AS WE FALL, TAKING EACH OTHER OUT, ONE BY ONE...
...UNTIL THERE ARE NONE.

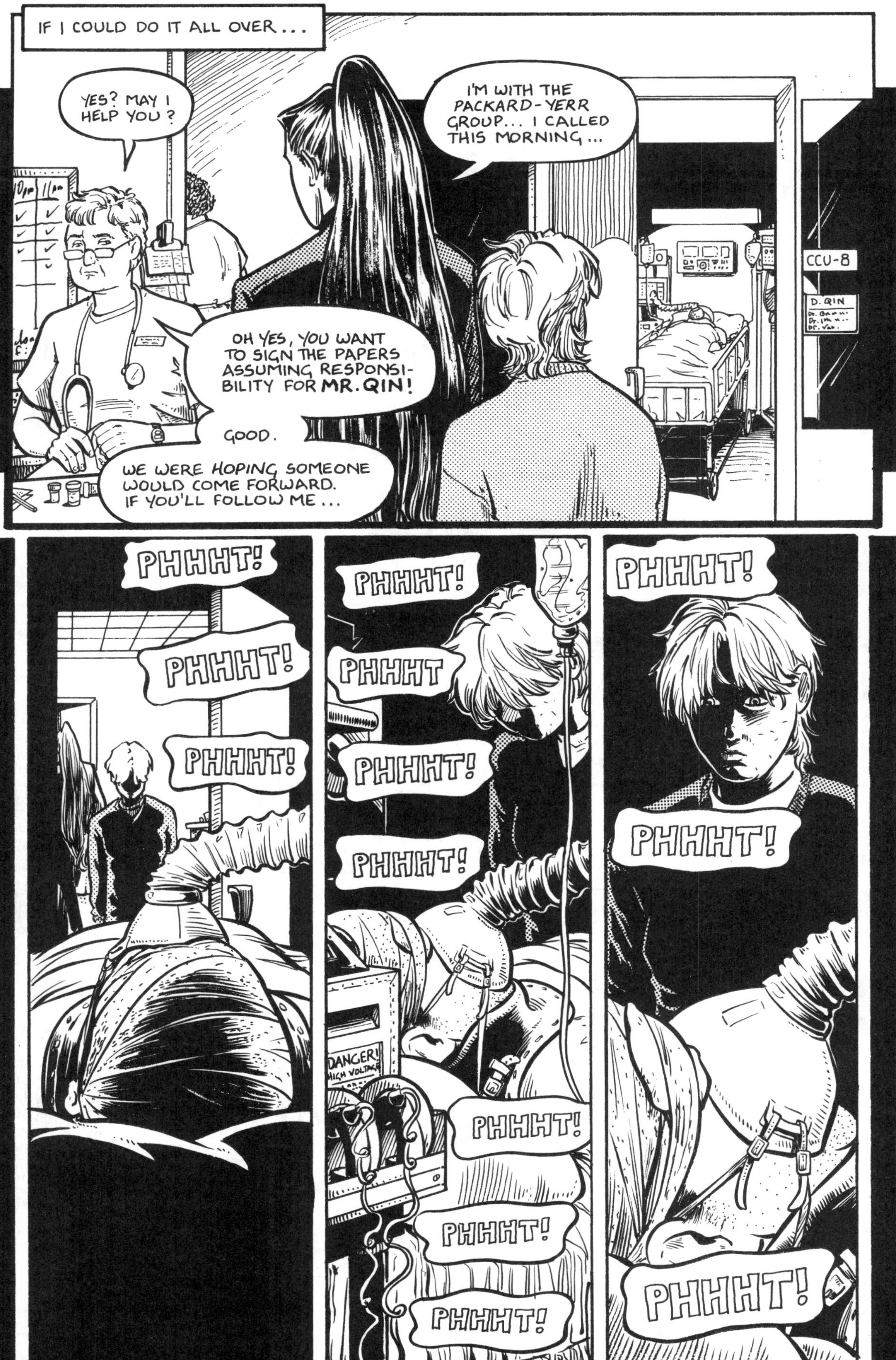
IF I COULD DO IT ALL OVER...
YES? MAY I HELP YOU?
I'M WITH THE PACKARD-YERR GROUP... I CALLED THIS MORNING...
CCU-8
D. QIN
OH YES, YOU WANT TO SIGN THE PAPERS ASSUMING RESPONSIBILITY FOR MR. QIN!
GOOD.
WE WERE HOPING SOMEONE WOULD COME FORWARD. IF YOU'LL FOLLOW ME...
PHHHT!
PHHHT!
PHHHT!
PHHHT!
PHHHT
PHHHT!
PHHHT!
DANGER! HIGH VOLTAGE
PHHHT!
PHHHT!
PHHHT!
PHHHT!
PHHHT!
PHHHT!

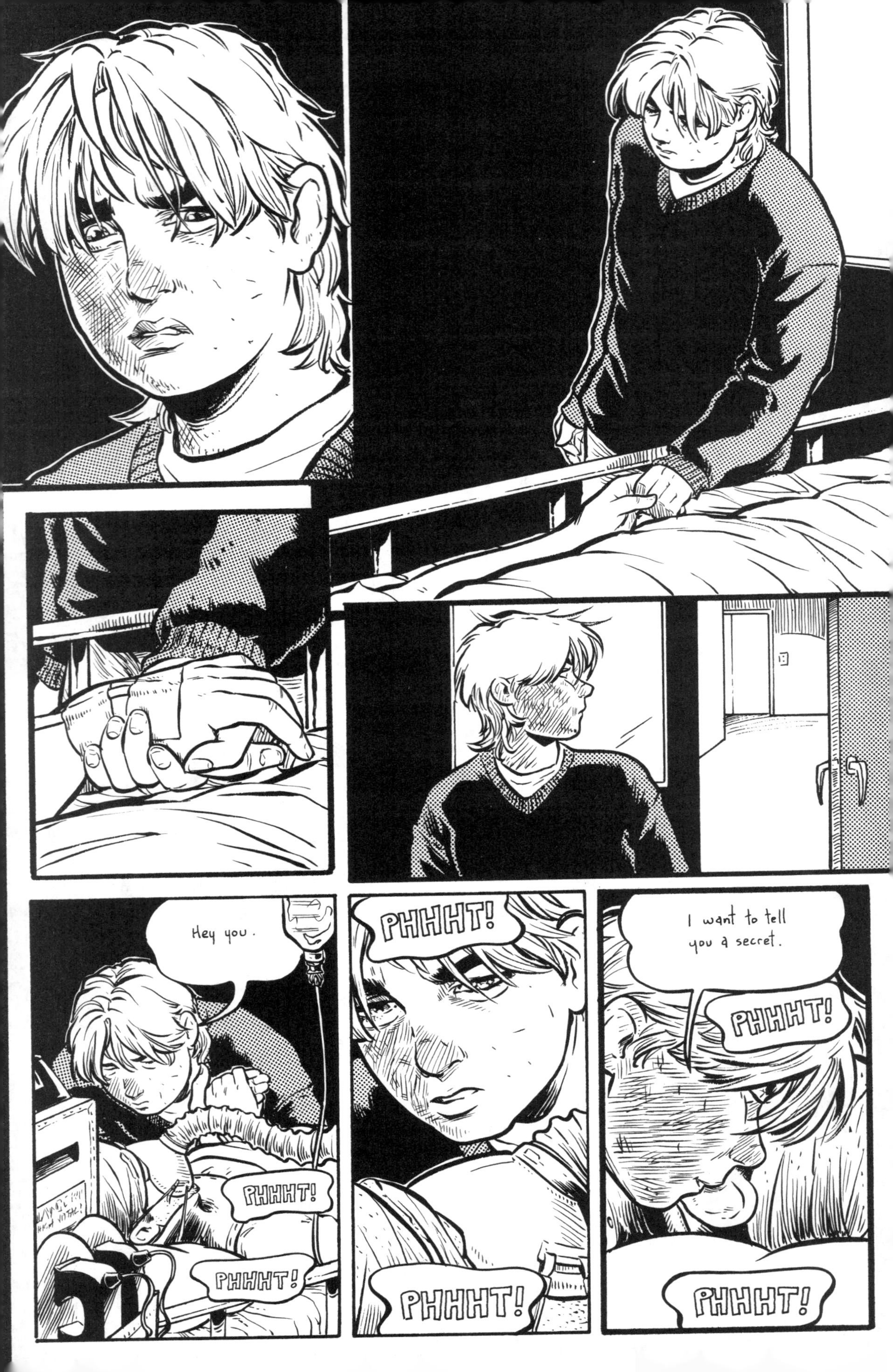
Hey you.
PHHHT!
PHHHT!
PHHHT!
PHHHT!
I want to tell you a secret.
PHHHT!
PHHHT!

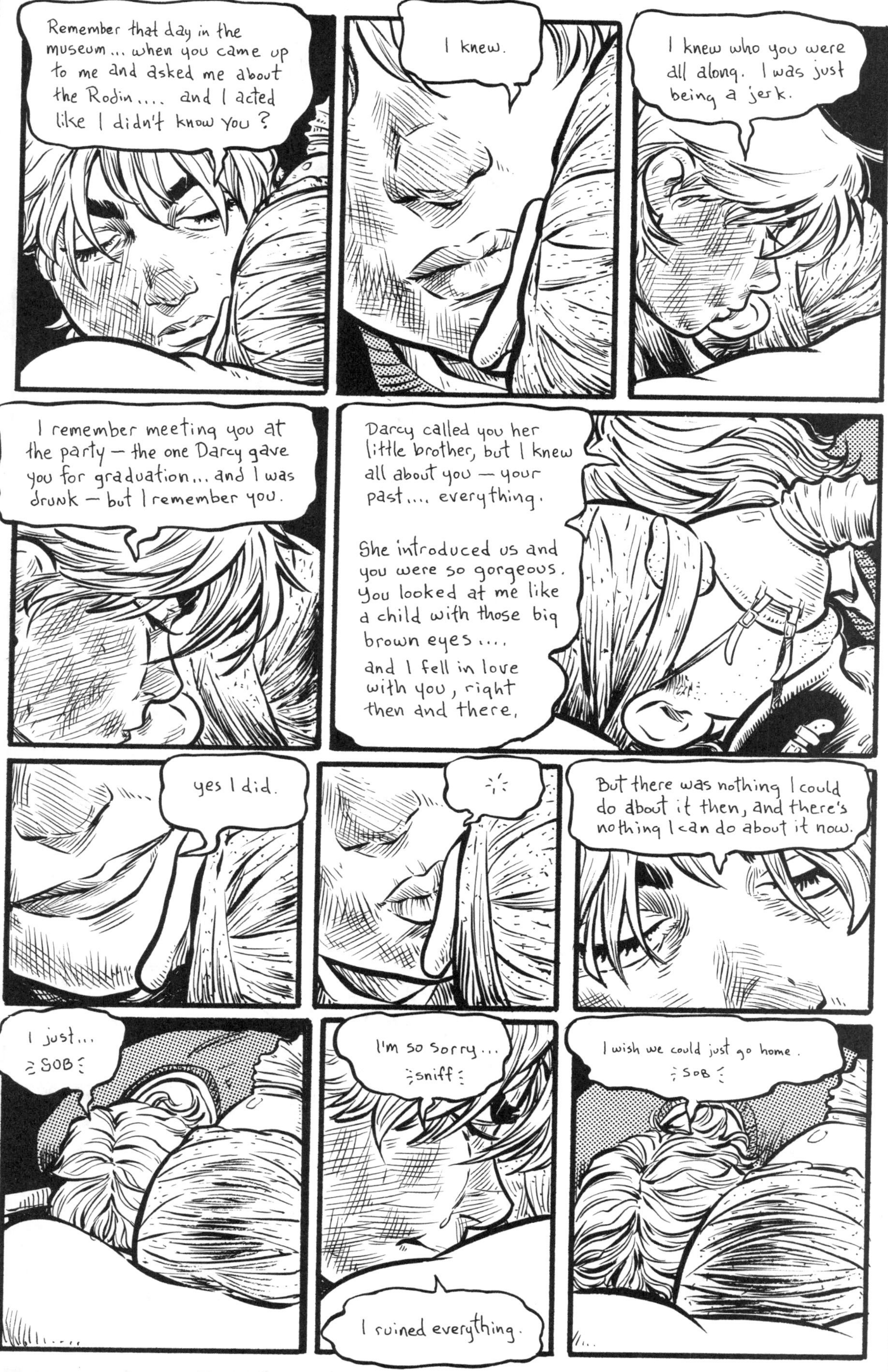

Remember that day in the museum... when you came up to me and asked me about the Rodin.... and I acted like I didn't know you?
I knew.
I knew who you were all along. I was just being a jerk.
I remember meeting you at the party — the one Darcy gave you for graduation... and I was drunk — but I remember you.
Darcy called you her little brother, but I knew all about you — your past.... everything.
She introduced us and you were so gorgeous. You looked at me like a child with those big brown eyes....
and I fell in love with you, right then and there,
...
yes I did.
But there was nothing I could do about it then, and there's nothing I can do about it now.
I just...
SOB
I'm so sorry...
sniff
I ruined everything.
I wish we could just go home.
SOB

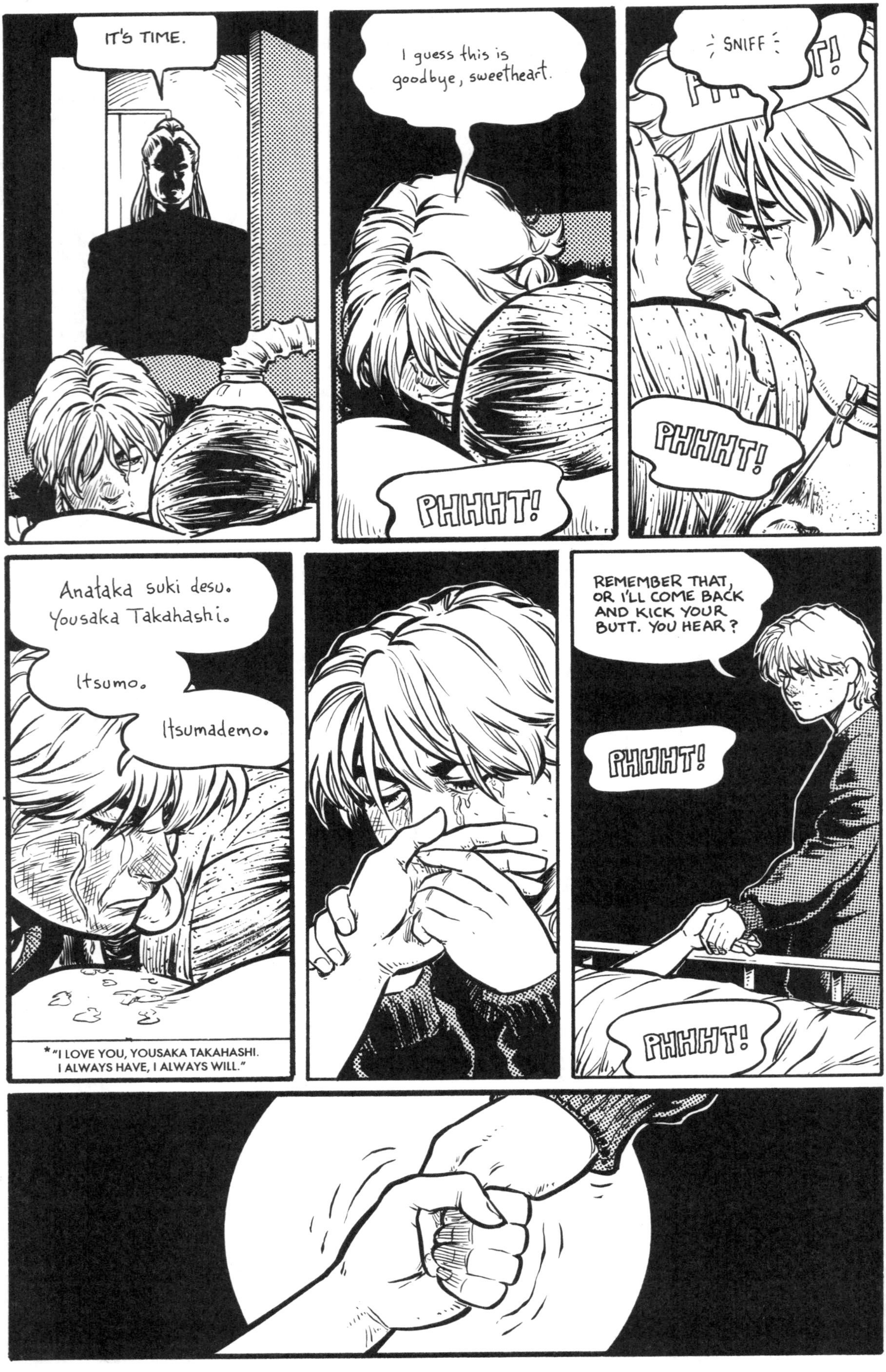
IT'S TIME.
I guess this is goodbye, sweetheart.
PHHHT!
SNIFF
PHHHT!
Anataka suki desu. Yousaka Takahashi.
Itsumo.
Itsumademo.
*"I LOVE YOU, YOUSAKA TAKAHASHI. I ALWAYS HAVE, I ALWAYS WILL."
REMEMBER THAT, OR I'LL COME BACK AND KICK YOUR BUTT. YOU HEAR?
PHHHT!
PHHHT!

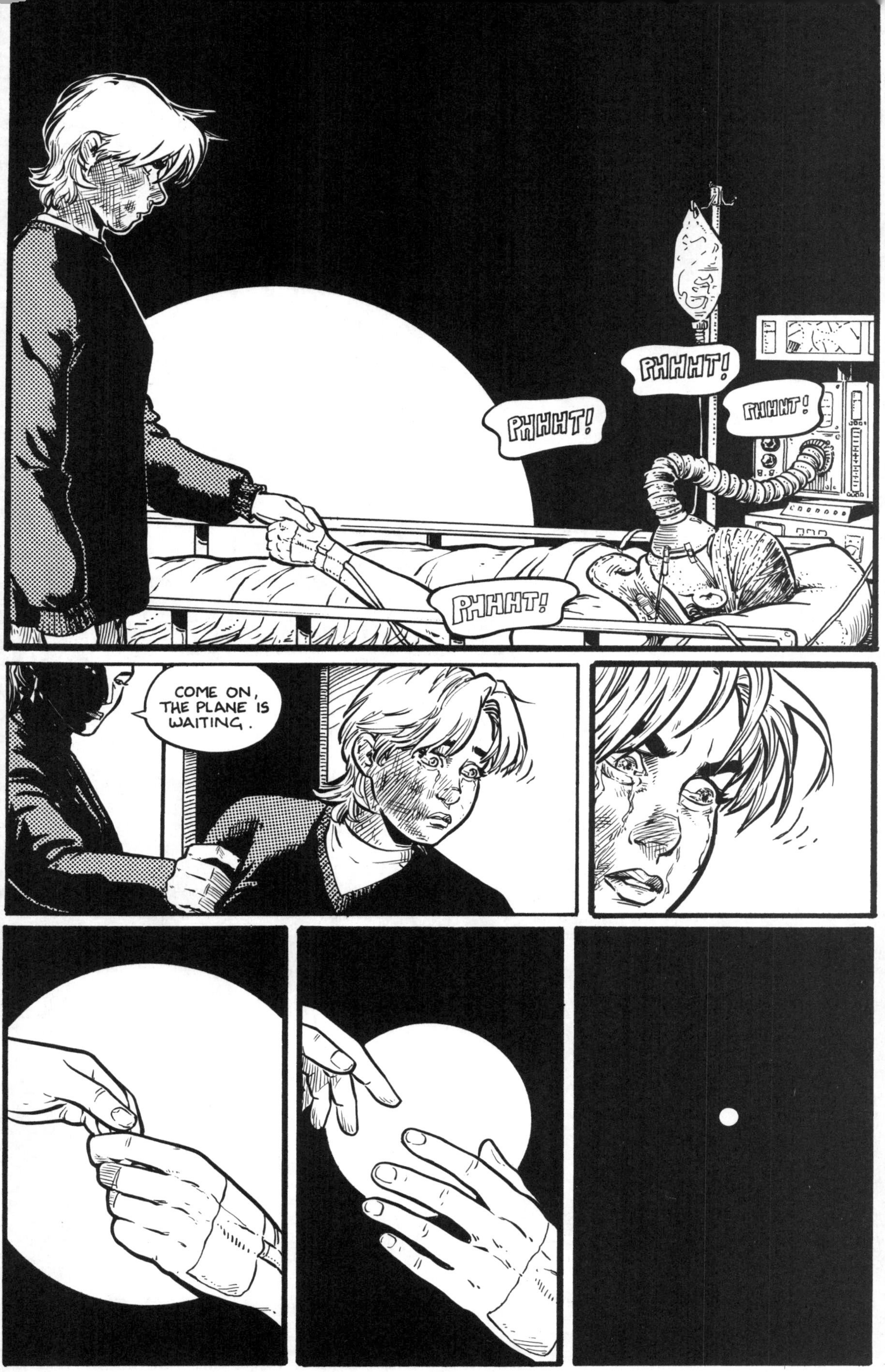
PHHHT!
PHHHT!
PHHHT!
PHHHT!
COME ON, THE PLANE IS WAITING.

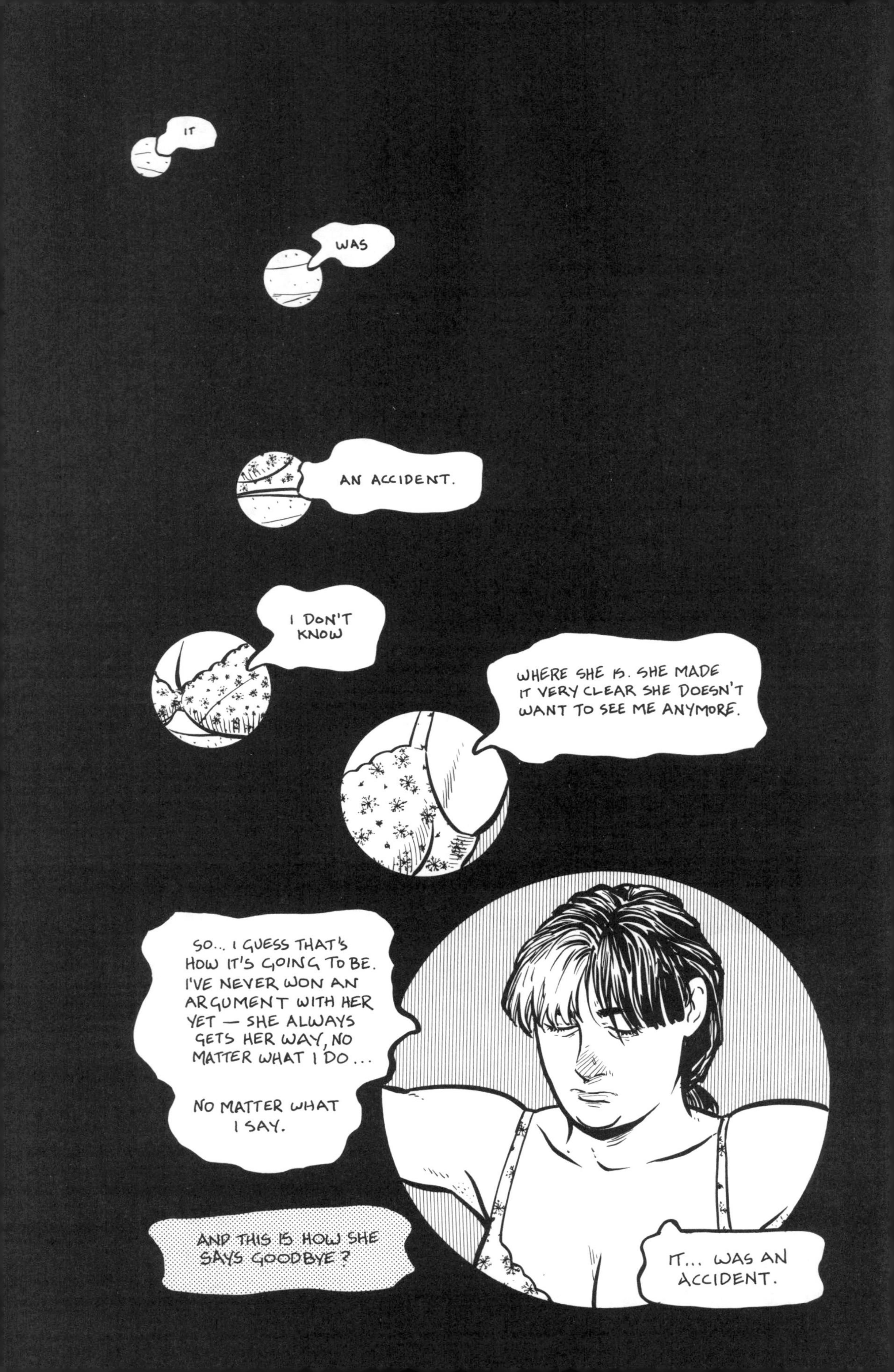
IT
WAS
AN ACCIDENT.
I DON'T KNOW
WHERE SHE IS. SHE MADE IT VERY CLEAR SHE DOESN'T WANT TO SEE ME ANYMORE.
SO... I GUESS THAT'S HOW IT'S GOING TO BE. I'VE NEVER WON AN ARGUMENT WITH HER YET — SHE ALWAYS GETS HER WAY, NO MATTER WHAT I DO...
NO MATTER WHAT I SAY.
AND THIS IS HOW SHE SAYS GOODBYE?
IT... WAS AN ACCIDENT.

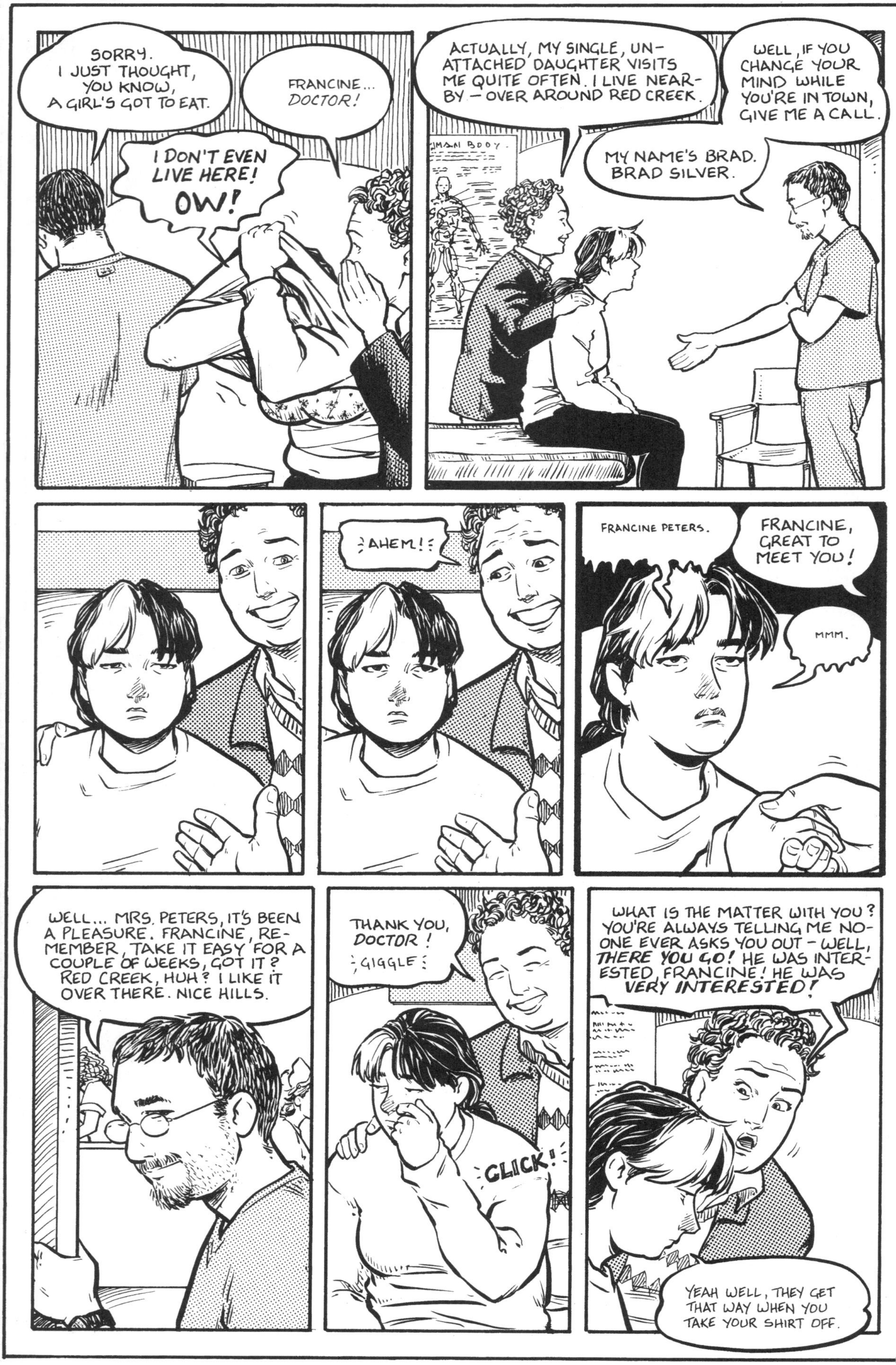
SORRY. I JUST THOUGHT, YOU KNOW, A GIRL'S GOT TO EAT.
FRANCINE... DOCTOR!
I DON'T EVEN LIVE HERE! OW!
ACTUALLY, MY SINGLE, UN-ATTACHED DAUGHTER VISITS ME QUITE OFTEN. I LIVE NEAR-BY — OVER AROUND RED CREEK.
WELL, IF YOU CHANGE YOUR MIND WHILE YOU'RE IN TOWN, GIVE ME A CALL.
MY NAME'S BRAD. BRAD SILVER.
AHEM!
FRANCINE PETERS.
FRANCINE, GREAT TO MEET YOU!
MMM.
WELL... MRS. PETERS, IT'S BEEN A PLEASURE. FRANCINE, RE-MEMBER, TAKE IT EASY FOR A COUPLE OF WEEKS, GOT IT? RED CREEK, HUH? I LIKE IT OVER THERE. NICE HILLS.
THANK YOU, DOCTOR! GIGGLE
CLICK!
WHAT IS THE MATTER WITH YOU? YOU'RE ALWAYS TELLING ME NO-ONE EVER ASKS YOU OUT — WELL, THERE YOU GO! HE WAS INTER-ESTED, FRANCINE! HE WAS VERY INTERESTED!
YEAH WELL, THEY GET THAT WAY WHEN YOU TAKE YOUR SHIRT OFF.

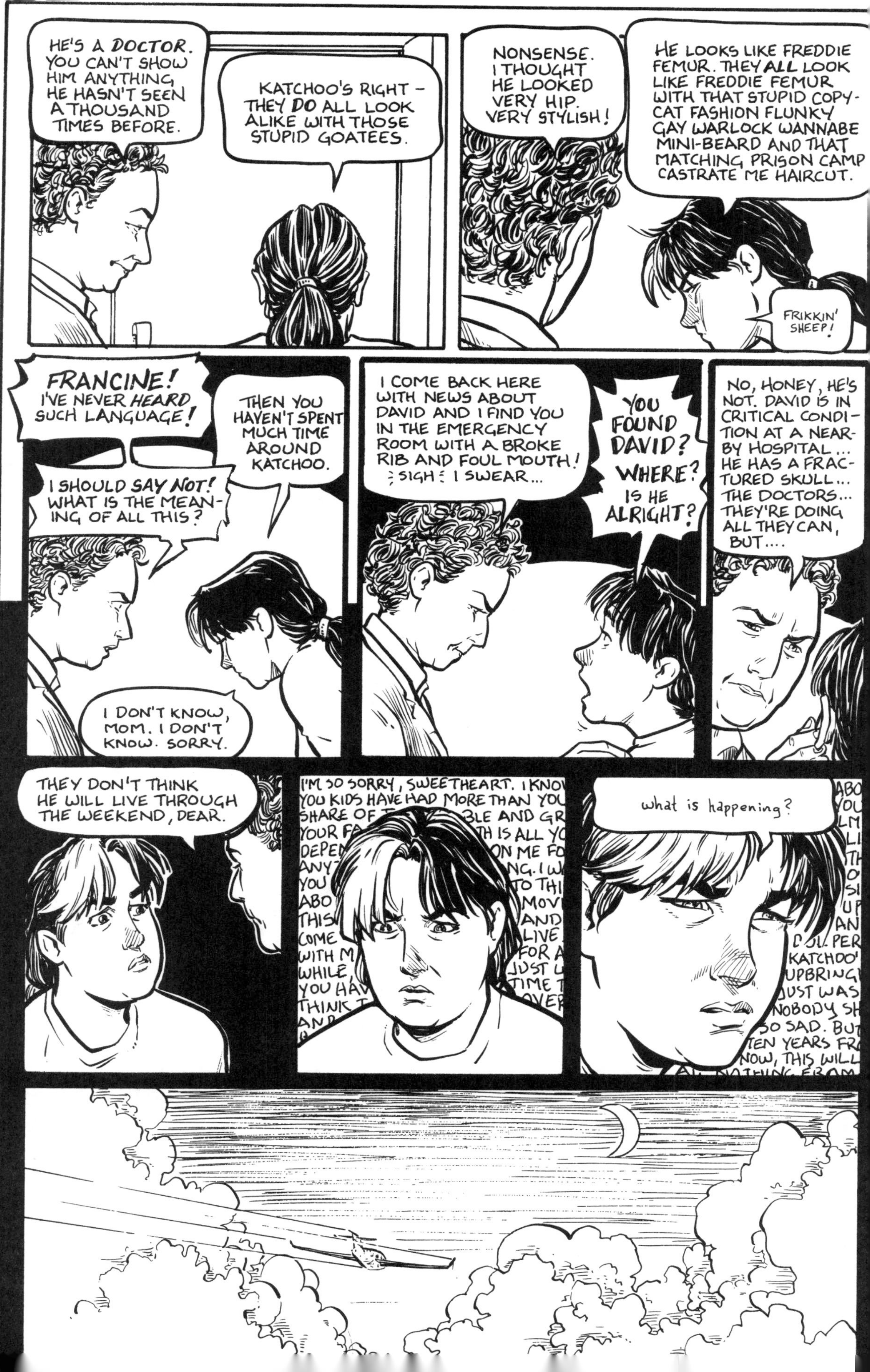
HE'S A DOCTOR. YOU CAN'T SHOW HIM ANYTHING HE HASN'T SEEN A THOUSAND TIMES BEFORE.
KATCHOO'S RIGHT - THEY DO ALL LOOK ALIKE WITH THOSE STUPID GOATEES.
NONSENSE. I THOUGHT HE LOOKED VERY HIP. VERY STYLISH!
HE LOOKS LIKE FREDDIE FEMUR. THEY ALL LOOK LIKE FREDDIE FEMUR WITH THAT STUPID COPY-CAT FASHION FLUNKY GAY WARLOCK WANNABE MINI-BEARD AND THAT MATCHING PRISON CAMP CASTRATE ME HAIRCUT.
FRIKKIN' SHEEP!
FRANCINE! I'VE NEVER HEARD SUCH LANGUAGE!
THEN YOU HAVEN'T SPENT MUCH TIME AROUND KATCHOO.
I SHOULD SAY NOT! WHAT IS THE MEANING OF ALL THIS?
I DON'T KNOW, MOM. I DON'T KNOW. SORRY.
I COME BACK HERE WITH NEWS ABOUT DAVID AND I FIND YOU IN THE EMERGENCY ROOM WITH A BROKE RIB AND FOUL MOUTH! ;SIGH; I SWEAR...
YOU FOUND DAVID? WHERE? IS HE ALRIGHT?
NO, HONEY, HE'S NOT. DAVID IS IN CRITICAL CONDITION AT A NEARBY HOSPITAL... HE HAS A FRACTURED SKULL... THE DOCTORS... THEY'RE DOING ALL THEY CAN, BUT....
THEY DON'T THINK HE WILL LIVE THROUGH THE WEEKEND, DEAR.
what is happening?

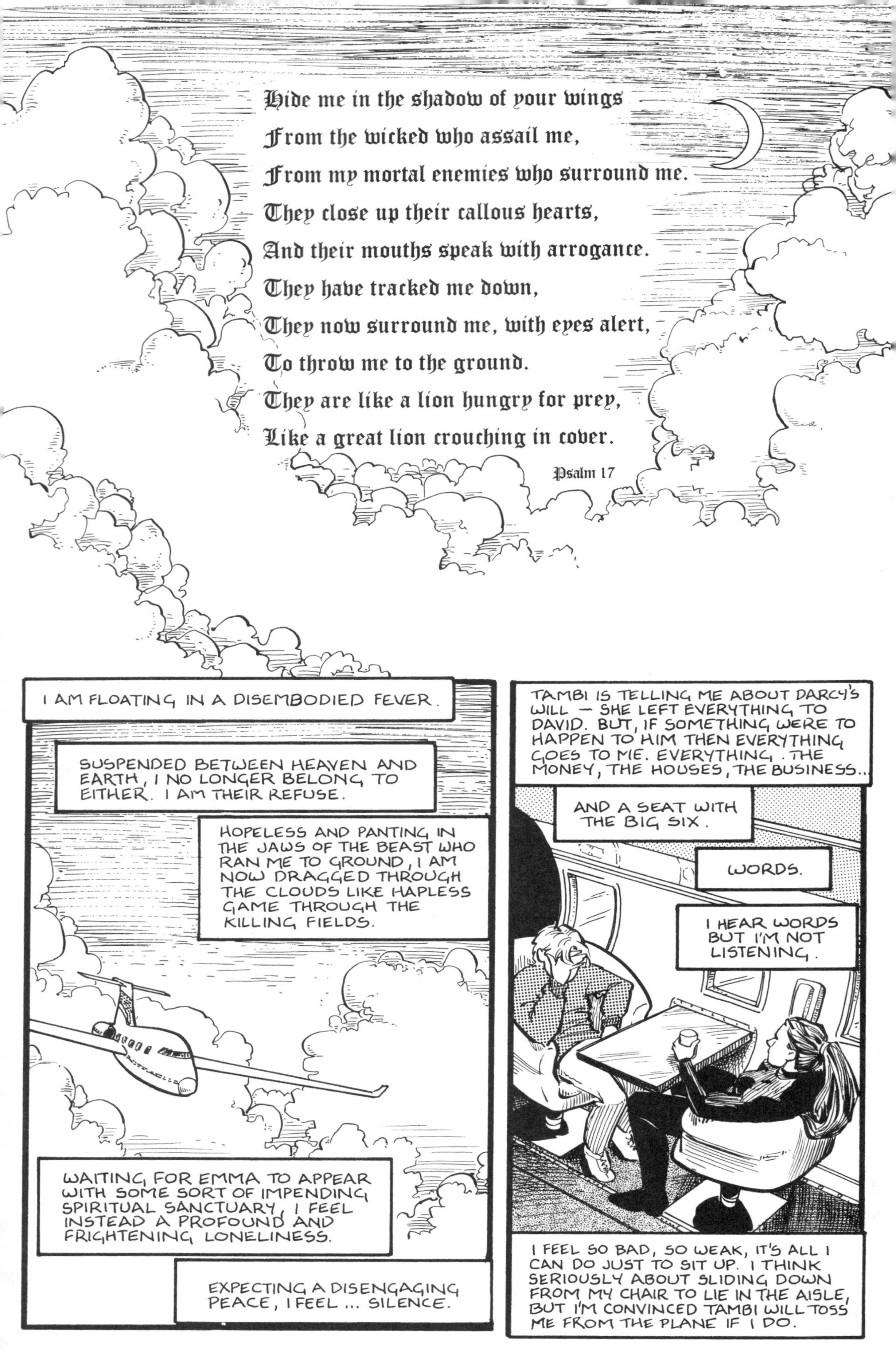
Hide me in the shadow of your wings
From the wicked who assail me,
From my mortal enemies who surround me.
They close up their callous hearts,
And their mouths speak with arrogance.
They have tracked me down,
They now surround me, with eyes alert,
To throw me to the ground.
They are like a lion hungry for prey,
Like a great lion crouching in cover.
Psalm 17
I AM FLOATING IN A DISEMBODIED FEVER.
SUSPENDED BETWEEN HEAVEN AND EARTH, I NO LONGER BELONG TO EITHER. I AM THEIR REFUSE.
HOPELESS AND PANTING IN THE JAWS OF THE BEAST WHO RAN ME TO GROUND, I AM NOW DRAGGED THROUGH THE CLOUDS LIKE HAPLESS GAME THROUGH THE KILLING FIELDS.
WAITING FOR EMMA TO APPEAR WITH SOME SORT OF IMPENDING SPIRITUAL SANCTUARY, I FEEL INSTEAD A PROFOUND AND FRIGHTENING LONELINESS.
EXPECTING A DISENGAGING PEACE, I FEEL ... SILENCE.
TAMBI IS TELLING ME ABOUT DARCY'S WILL — SHE LEFT EVERYTHING TO DAVID. BUT, IF SOMETHING WERE TO HAPPEN TO HIM THEN EVERYTHING GOES TO ME. EVERYTHING. THE MONEY, THE HOUSES, THE BUSINESS...
AND A SEAT WITH THE BIG SIX.
WORDS.
I HEAR WORDS BUT I'M NOT LISTENING.
I FEEL SO BAD, SO WEAK, IT'S ALL I CAN DO JUST TO SIT UP. I THINK SERIOUSLY ABOUT SLIDING DOWN FROM MY CHAIR TO LIE IN THE AISLE, BUT I'M CONVINCED TAMBI WILL TOSS ME FROM THE PLANE IF I DO.

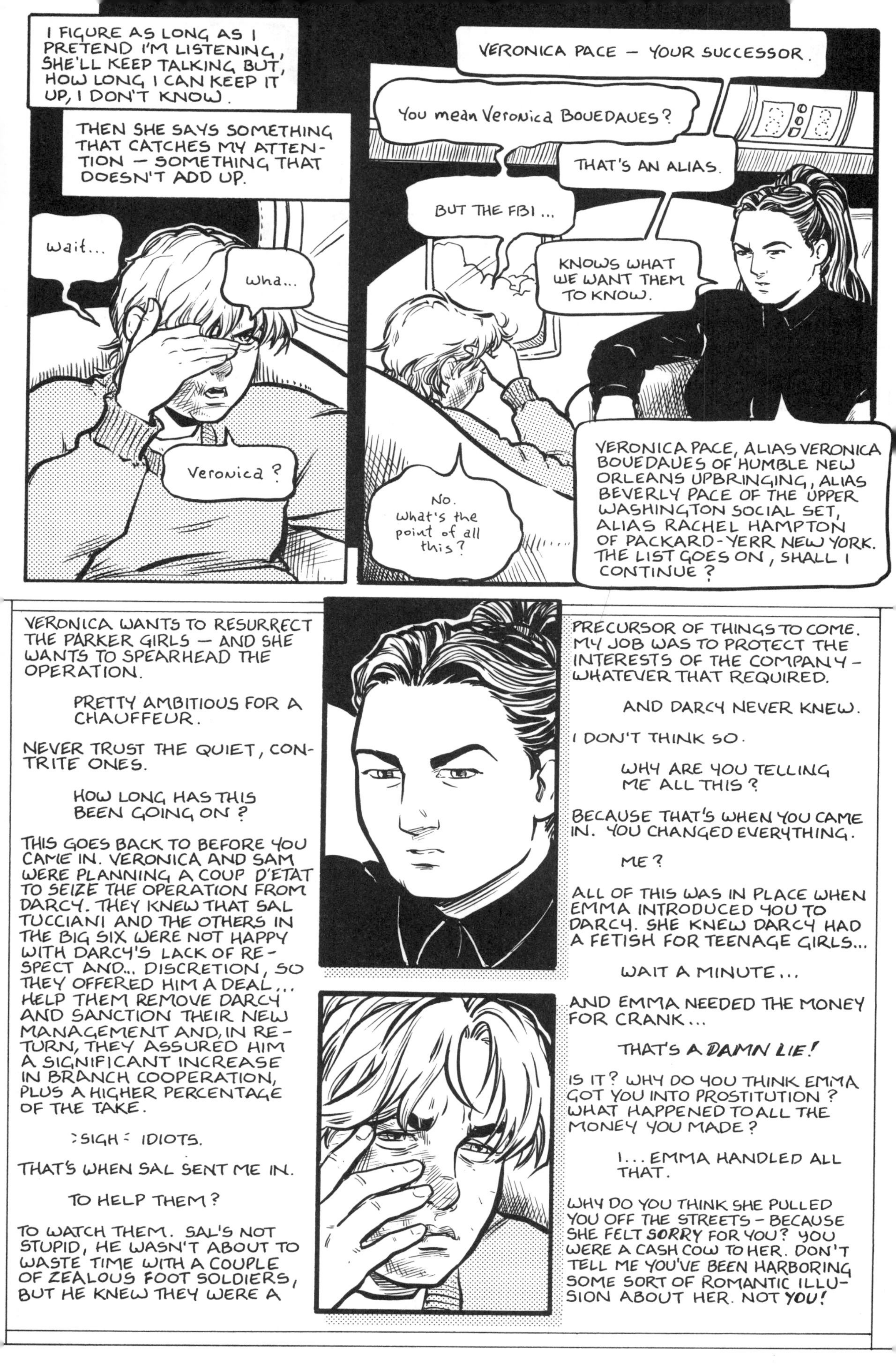
I FIGURE AS LONG AS I PRETEND I'M LISTENING, SHE'LL KEEP TALKING BUT, HOW LONG I CAN KEEP IT UP, I DON'T KNOW.
THEN SHE SAYS SOMETHING THAT CATCHES MY ATTENTION — SOMETHING THAT DOESN'T ADD UP.
wait...
whd...
Veronica?
VERONICA PACE — YOUR SUCCESSOR.
You mean Veronica BOUEDAUES?
THAT'S AN ALIAS.
BUT THE FBI...
KNOWS WHAT WE WANT THEM TO KNOW.
No. what's the point of all this?
VERONICA PACE, ALIAS VERONICA BOUEDAUES OF HUMBLE NEW ORLEANS UPBRINGING, ALIAS BEVERLY PACE OF THE UPPER WASHINGTON SOCIAL SET, ALIAS RACHEL HAMPTON OF PACKARD-YERR NEW YORK. THE LIST GOES ON, SHALL I CONTINUE?
VERONICA WANTS TO RESURRECT THE PARKER GIRLS — AND SHE WANTS TO SPEARHEAD THE OPERATION.
PRETTY AMBITIOUS FOR A CHAUFFEUR.
NEVER TRUST THE QUIET, CONTRITE ONES.
HOW LONG HAS THIS BEEN GOING ON?
THIS GOES BACK TO BEFORE YOU CAME IN. VERONICA AND SAM WERE PLANNING A COUP D'ETAT TO SEIZE THE OPERATION FROM DARCY. THEY KNEW THAT SAL TUCCIANI AND THE OTHERS IN THE BIG SIX WERE NOT HAPPY WITH DARCY'S LACK OF RESPECT AND... DISCRETION, SO THEY OFFERED HIM A DEAL... HELP THEM REMOVE DARCY AND SANCTION THEIR NEW MANAGEMENT AND, IN RETURN, THEY ASSURED HIM A SIGNIFICANT INCREASE IN BRANCH COOPERATION, PLUS A HIGHER PERCENTAGE OF THE TAKE.
:SIGH: IDIOTS.
THAT'S WHEN SAL SENT ME IN.
TO HELP THEM?
TO WATCH THEM. SAL'S NOT STUPID, HE WASN'T ABOUT TO WASTE TIME WITH A COUPLE OF ZEALOUS FOOT SOLDIERS, BUT HE KNEW THEY WERE A PRECURSOR OF THINGS TO COME. MY JOB WAS TO PROTECT THE INTERESTS OF THE COMPANY — WHATEVER THAT REQUIRED.
AND DARCY NEVER KNEW.
I DON'T THINK SO.
WHY ARE YOU TELLING ME ALL THIS?
BECAUSE THAT'S WHEN YOU CAME IN. YOU CHANGED EVERYTHING.
ME?
ALL OF THIS WAS IN PLACE WHEN EMMA INTRODUCED YOU TO DARCY. SHE KNEW DARCY HAD A FETISH FOR TEENAGE GIRLS...
WAIT A MINUTE...
AND EMMA NEEDED THE MONEY FOR CRANK...
THAT'S A DAMN LIE!
IS IT? WHY DO YOU THINK EMMA GOT YOU INTO PROSTITUTION? WHAT HAPPENED TO ALL THE MONEY YOU MADE?
I... EMMA HANDLED ALL THAT.
WHY DO YOU THINK SHE PULLED YOU OFF THE STREETS — BECAUSE SHE FELT SORRY FOR YOU? YOU WERE A CASH COW TO HER. DON'T TELL ME YOU'VE BEEN HARBORING SOME SORT OF ROMANTIC ILLUSION ABOUT HER. NOT YOU!

HMM.

I DIDN'T KNOW THAT.

LOOK, I'M NOT IN A HURRY TO DIE BUT, WHY ARE WE HAVING THIS CONVERSATION?

MY GOAL HERE IS TO TELL YOU THE TRUTH... ABOUT EVERYTHING.

WHY? WHAT DIFFERENCE DOES IT MAKE NOW?

DARCY FELL IN LOVE WITH YOU, SHE TRUSTED YOU, SHE EVEN CONFIDED IN YOU. YOU BEGAN TO OFFER YOUR OPINION AND YOUR OBSERVATIONS WERE ASTUTE. YOU DIRECTED HER THROUGH SEVERAL COMPLICATED SITUATIONS AND YOUR INFLUENCE EVENTUALLY MADE THE PARKER OPERATION MORE POWERFUL AND COMPLEX THAN ANYONE THOUGHT POSSIBLE. IN SHORT, TO EVERYONE'S SURPRISE, IT TURNS OUT YOU HAVE A GIFT FOR THIS LINE OF WORK. THAT'S WHY SAMANTHA AND VERONICA SET YOU UP.

THAT'S WHAT I'VE BEEN SAYING, AND YOU KNEW THIS ALL ALONG?

I TOLD YOU, MY JOB WAS TO PROTECT THE COMPANY, NOT FIX YOUR PROBLEMS. DARCY HAD A PARTY FOR DAVID AND INVITED SENATOR CHALMERS, WHO WAS BRINGING HER A PAYMENT FOR A BLACKMAIL DEAL SHE WAS WORKING ON HIM. SHE SENT YOU AND EMMA UPSTAIRS UNDER THE PRETEXT OF REWARDING HIS COOPERATION, BUT THE HIDDEN CAMERAS WOULD SERVE TO PERPETUATE HIS SERVITUDE. THE SENATOR HAD THE MONEY ON HIM. WHEN SAMANTHA WENT TO SWEEP THE ROOM OF LIABILITIES AFTER YOU AND EMMA FINISHED, SHE INTENDED TO TAKE THE MONEY AND HIDE IT. YOU AND EMMA WOULD BE ACCUSED OF THE CRIME AND, IF ALL WENT ACCORDING TO PLAN, THE TWO OF YOU WOULD NEVER SEE THE LIGHT OF DAY AGAIN. SIMPLE ENOUGH, RIGHT? WHAT COULD POSSIBLY GO WRONG?

BUT YOU BEAT THEM TO THE PUNCH – YOU DISAPPEARED WITH THE MONEY BEFORE THEY HAD A CHANCE TO NAIL YOU. I MUST SAY, I WAS IMPRESSED. YOUR TIMING HAS ALWAYS BEEN IMPECCABLE, MISS CHOOVANSKI.

I DIDN'T TAKE THE MONEY.

I KNOW. EMMA TOOK IT, DIDN'T SHE? YOU DIDN'T EVEN KNOW SHE HAD IT UNTIL SHE SHOWED YOU IN HAWAII, DID YOU? YOU JUST WANTED TO RUN AWAY – BUT SHE COMPLICATED MATTERS. HOW AM I DOING SO FAR?

IT'S PISSING ME OFF YOU KNEW ALL THIS AND DIDN'T SAY SOMETHING.

YOU FLEW TO ZURICH AND OPENED AN ACCOUNT IN SAMANTHA'S NAME – A BRILLIANT MOVE BY THE WAY, VERY FARSIGHTED – AND WHEN YOU REJOINED EMMA IN HAWAII, WE WERE WAITING FOR YOU. THE MONEY WAS NOWHERE TO BE FOUND. YOU ACTED LIKE YOU DIDN'T KNOW WHAT WE WERE TALKING ABOUT, EMMA OVERDOSES ON HER NEW CRANK AND NEARLY DROWNS, SAM AND VERONICA WANT TO CRUCIFY YOU AND DARCY WANTS THE PRODIGAL DAUGHTER TO COME HOME. WOULD YOU CARE FOR A DRINK?

NO.

DARCY WOULDN'T LET THEM KILL YOU, SO THEY LET YOU GO. YOU AND EMMA SPLIT UP TO FORK THE TRAIL – SHE GOES HOME TO TORONTO AND YOU TO HOUSTON. SAM'S PLAN WAS TO FOLLOW YOU, CONVINCED YOU'D LEAD THEM TO THE MONEY. THEN SHE COULD USE THE WHOLE MESS TO DISCREDIT DARCY AND GET WHAT SHE WANTED. BUT YOU DO NOTHING, YOU LAY LOW, AND SAM GROWS IMPATIENT. THE MONEY SHE'S SIPHONING OFF THE COMPANY ISN'T ENOUGH. SHE VILIFIES YOU TO PARKER – SO THEY SEND DAVID.

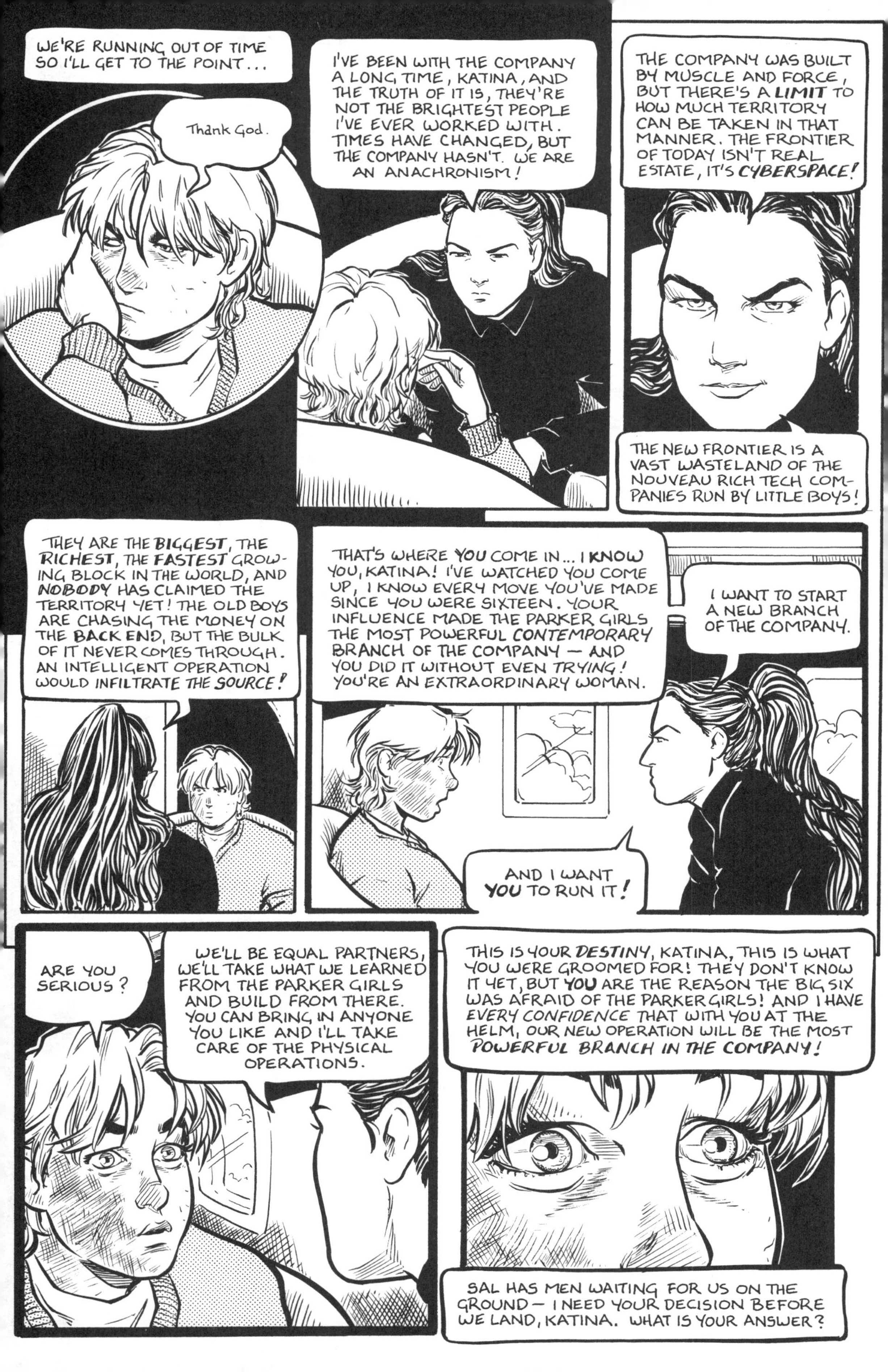
WE'RE RUNNING OUT OF TIME SO I'LL GET TO THE POINT...
Thank God.
I'VE BEEN WITH THE COMPANY A LONG TIME, KATINA, AND THE TRUTH OF IT IS, THEY'RE NOT THE BRIGHTEST PEOPLE I'VE EVER WORKED WITH. TIMES HAVE CHANGED, BUT THE COMPANY HASN'T. WE ARE AN ANACHRONISM!
THE COMPANY WAS BUILT BY MUSCLE AND FORCE, BUT THERE'S A LIMIT TO HOW MUCH TERRITORY CAN BE TAKEN IN THAT MANNER. THE FRONTIER OF TODAY ISN'T REAL ESTATE, IT'S CYBERSPACE!
THE NEW FRONTIER IS A VAST WASTELAND OF THE NOUVEAU RICH TECH COMPANIES RUN BY LITTLE BOYS!
THEY ARE THE BIGGEST, THE RICHEST, THE FASTEST GROWING BLOCK IN THE WORLD, AND NOBODY HAS CLAIMED THE TERRITORY YET! THE OLD BOYS ARE CHASING THE MONEY ON THE BACK END, BUT THE BULK OF IT NEVER COMES THROUGH. AN INTELLIGENT OPERATION WOULD INFILTRATE THE SOURCE!
THAT'S WHERE YOU COME IN... I KNOW YOU, KATINA! I'VE WATCHED YOU COME UP, I KNOW EVERY MOVE YOU'VE MADE SINCE YOU WERE SIXTEEN. YOUR INFLUENCE MADE THE PARKER GIRLS THE MOST POWERFUL CONTEMPORARY BRANCH OF THE COMPANY — AND YOU DID IT WITHOUT EVEN TRYING! YOU'RE AN EXTRAORDINARY WOMAN.
I WANT TO START A NEW BRANCH OF THE COMPANY.
AND I WANT YOU TO RUN IT!
ARE YOU SERIOUS?
WE'LL BE EQUAL PARTNERS, WE'LL TAKE WHAT WE LEARNED FROM THE PARKER GIRLS AND BUILD FROM THERE. YOU CAN BRING IN ANYONE YOU LIKE AND I'LL TAKE CARE OF THE PHYSICAL OPERATIONS.
THIS IS YOUR DESTINY, KATINA, THIS IS WHAT YOU WERE GROOMED FOR! THEY DON'T KNOW IT YET, BUT YOU ARE THE REASON THE BIG SIX WAS AFRAID OF THE PARKER GIRLS! AND I HAVE EVERY CONFIDENCE THAT WITH YOU AT THE HELM, OUR NEW OPERATION WILL BE THE MOST POWERFUL BRANCH IN THE COMPANY!
SAL HAS MEN WAITING FOR US ON THE GROUND — I NEED YOUR DECISION BEFORE WE LAND, KATINA. WHAT IS YOUR ANSWER?

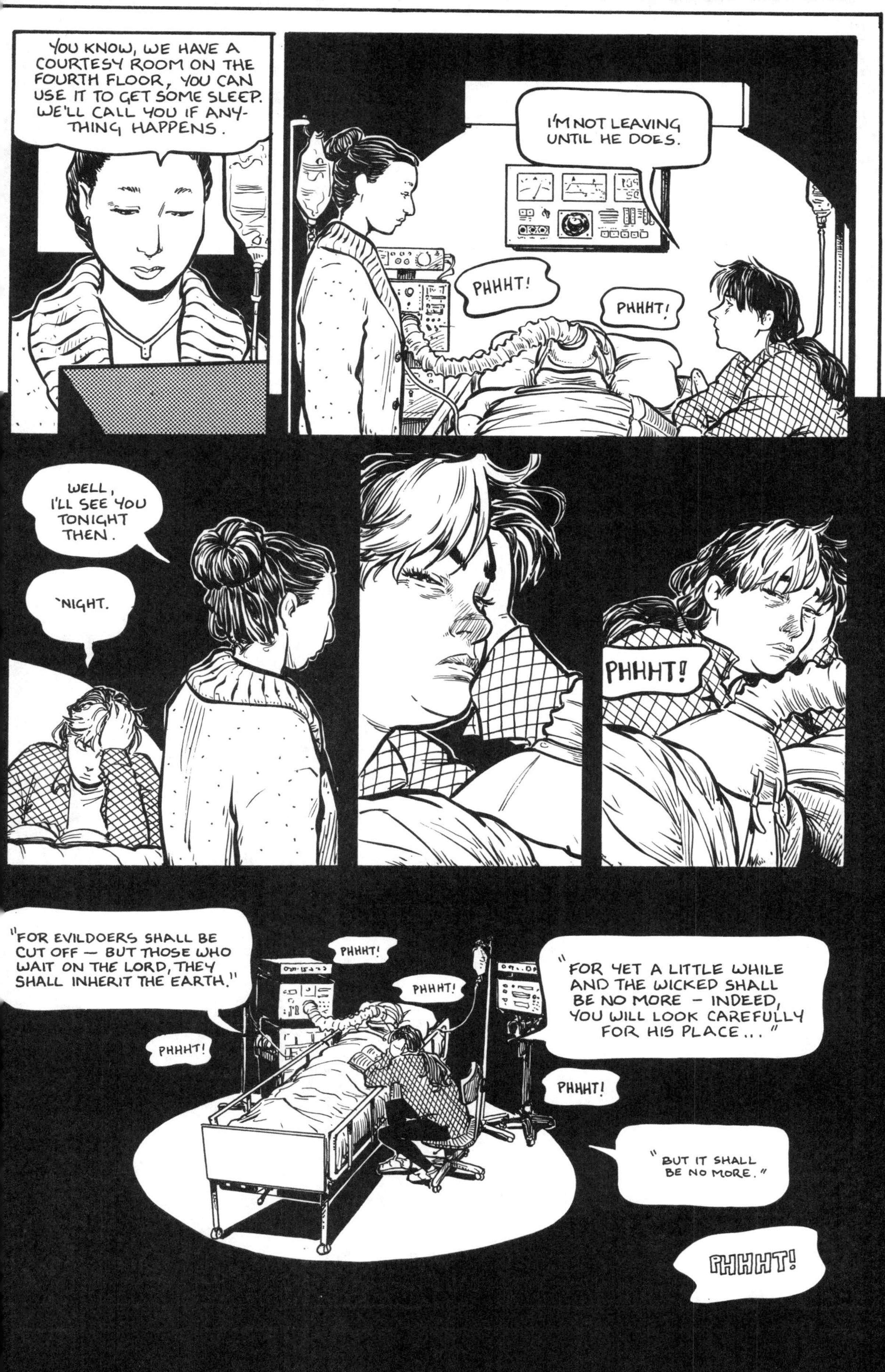
YOU KNOW, WE HAVE A COURTESY ROOM ON THE FOURTH FLOOR, YOU CAN USE IT TO GET SOME SLEEP. WE'LL CALL YOU IF ANY-THING HAPPENS.
I'M NOT LEAVING UNTIL HE DOES.
PHHHT!
PHHHT!
WELL, I'LL SEE YOU TONIGHT THEN.
`NIGHT.
PHHHT!
"FOR EVILDOERS SHALL BE CUT OFF — BUT THOSE WHO WAIT ON THE LORD, THEY SHALL INHERIT THE EARTH."
PHHHT!
PHHHT!
PHHHT!
"FOR YET A LITTLE WHILE AND THE WICKED SHALL BE NO MORE – INDEED, YOU WILL LOOK CAREFULLY FOR HIS PLACE..."
PHHHT!
"BUT IT SHALL BE NO MORE."
PHHHT!

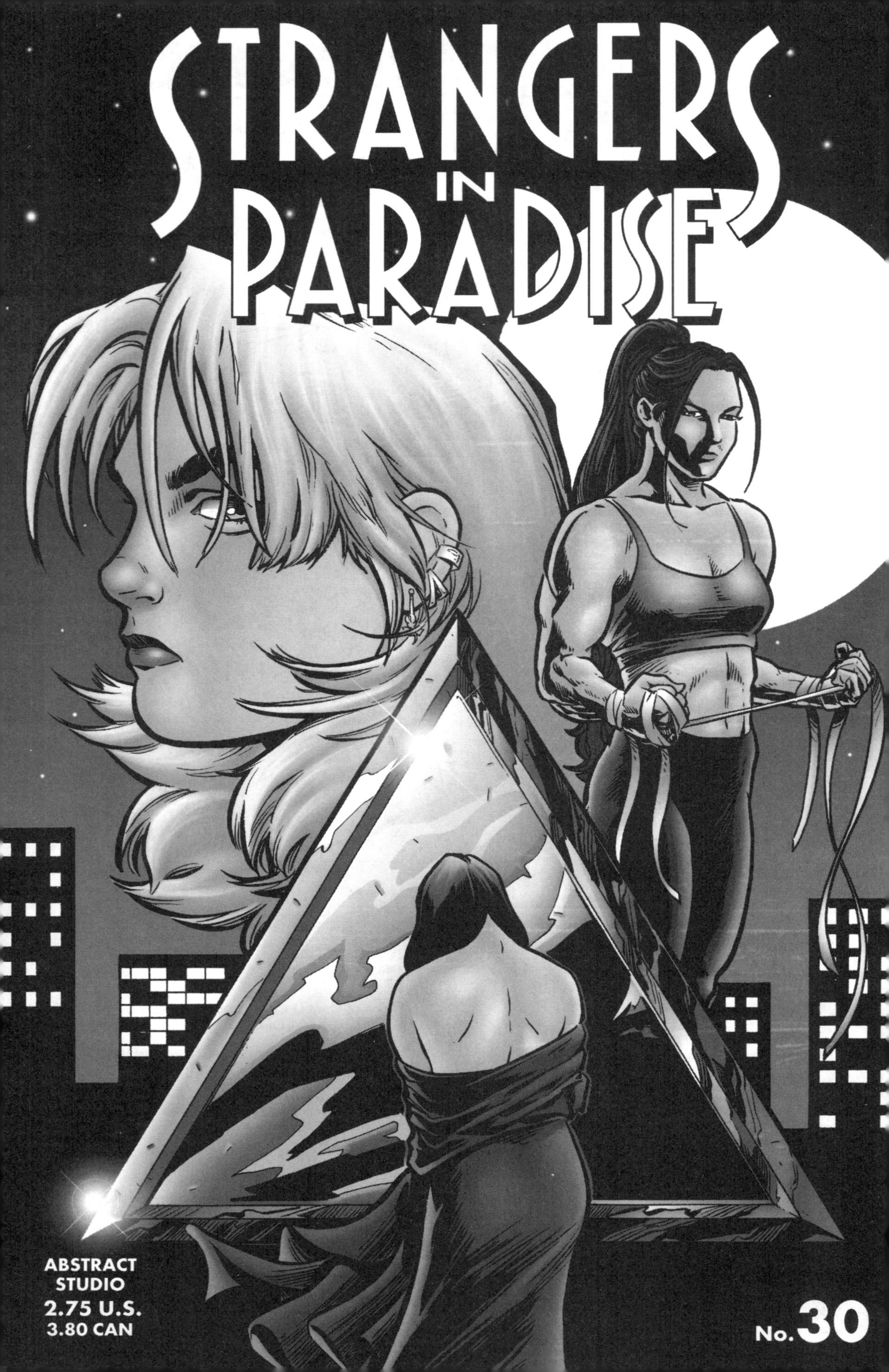
STRANGERS IN PARADISE
ABSTRACT STUDIO
2.75 U.S.
3.80 CAN
No. 30

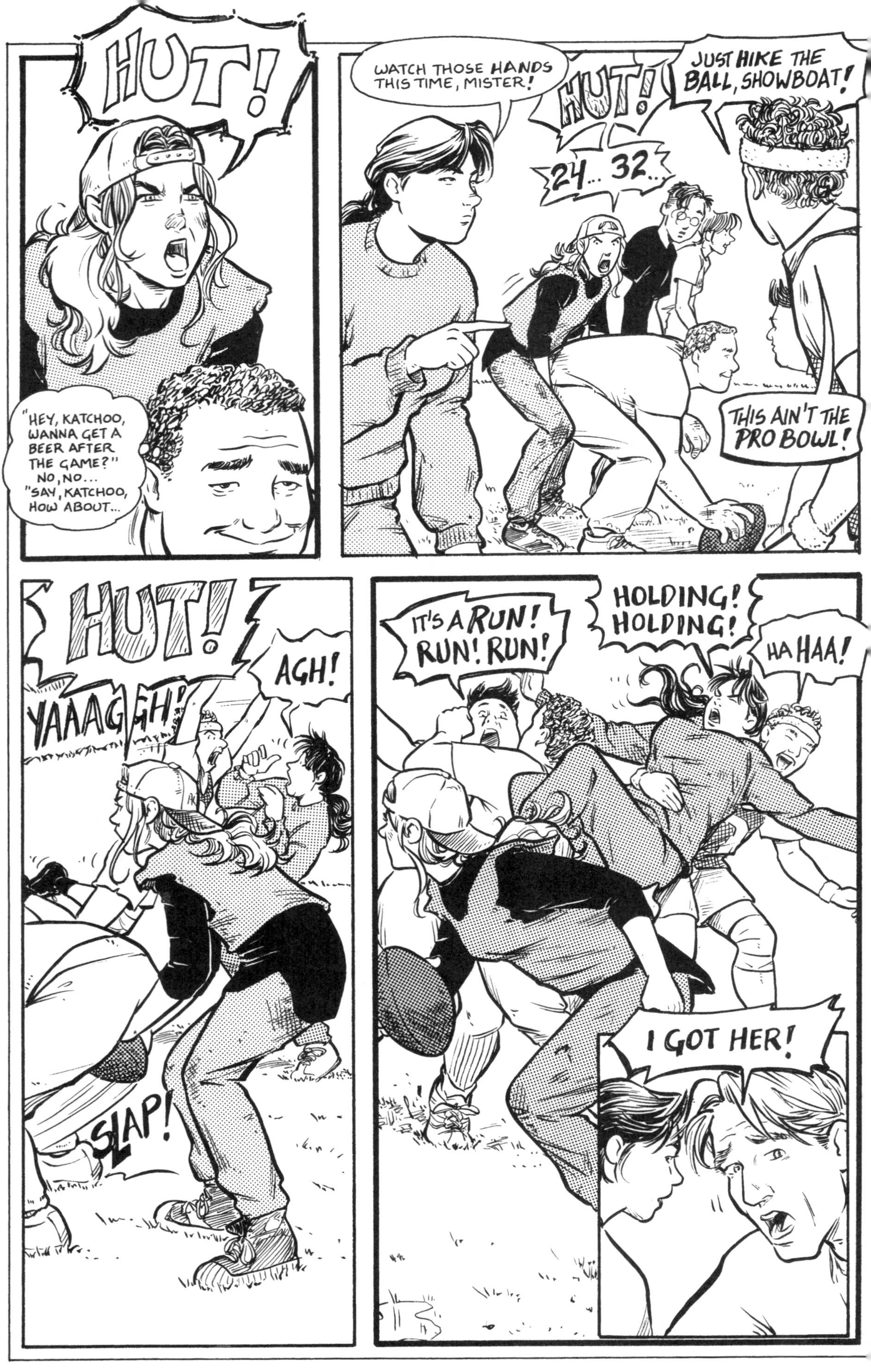
HUT!
"HEY, KATCHOO, WANNA GET A BEER AFTER THE GAME?" NO, NO... "SAY, KATCHOO, HOW ABOUT...
WATCH THOSE HANDS THIS TIME, MISTER!
HUT!
24... 32...
JUST HIKE THE BALL, SHOWBOAT!
THIS AIN'T THE PRO BOWL!
HUT!
YAAAGGH!
AGH!
SLAP!
IT'S A RUN! RUN! RUN!
HOLDING! HOLDING!
HA HAA!
I GOT HER!

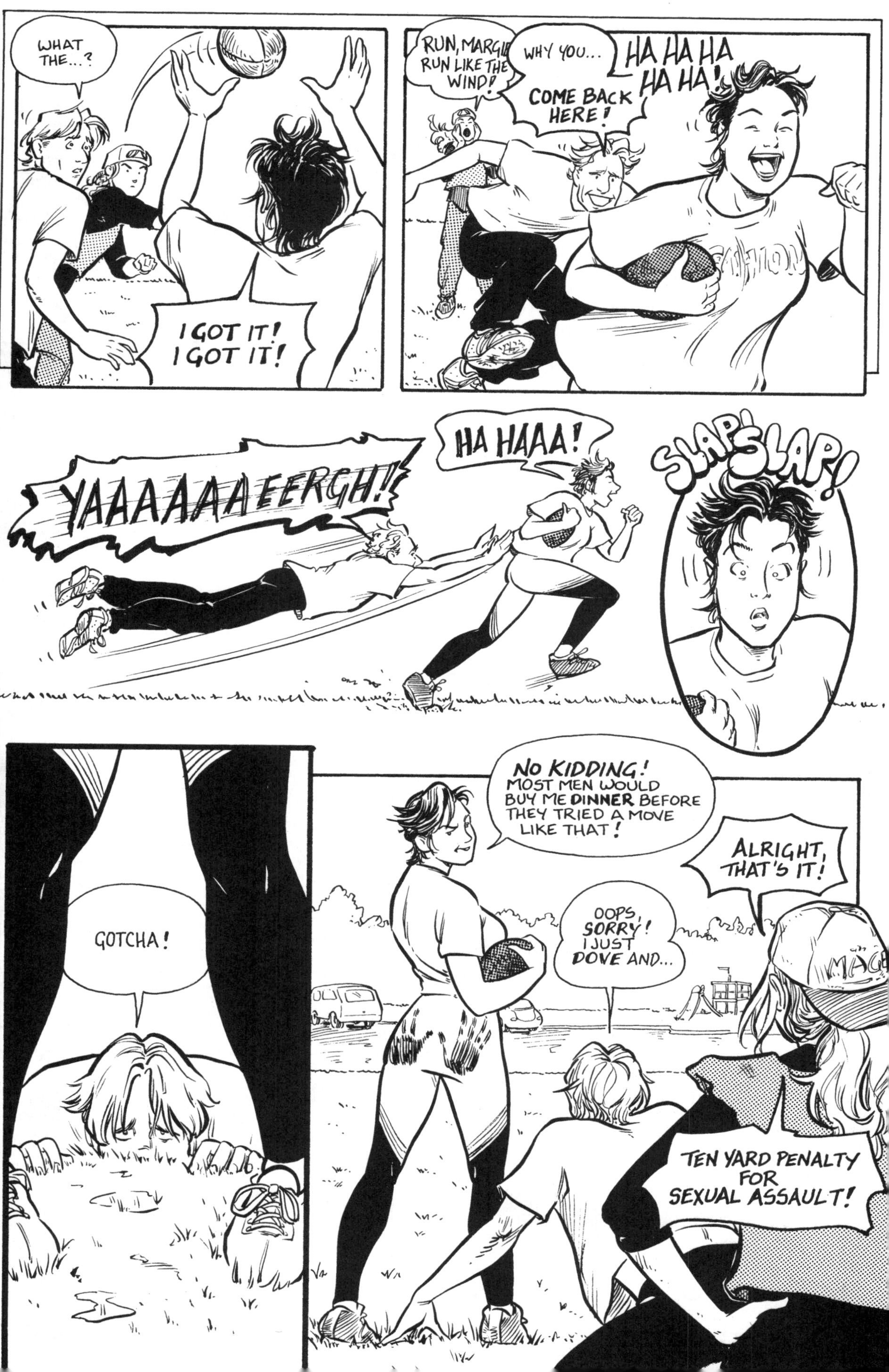
WHAT THE...?
I GOT IT! I GOT IT!
RUN, MARGIE RUN LIKE THE WIND!
WHY YOU...
COME BACK HERE!
HA HA HA HA HA!
YAAAAAAAEERGH!
HA HAAA!
SLAP! SLAP!
GOTCHA!
NO KIDDING! MOST MEN WOULD BUY ME DINNER BEFORE THEY TRIED A MOVE LIKE THAT!
ALRIGHT, THAT'S IT!
OOPS, SORRY! I JUST DOVE AND...
TEN YARD PENALTY FOR SEXUAL ASSAULT!

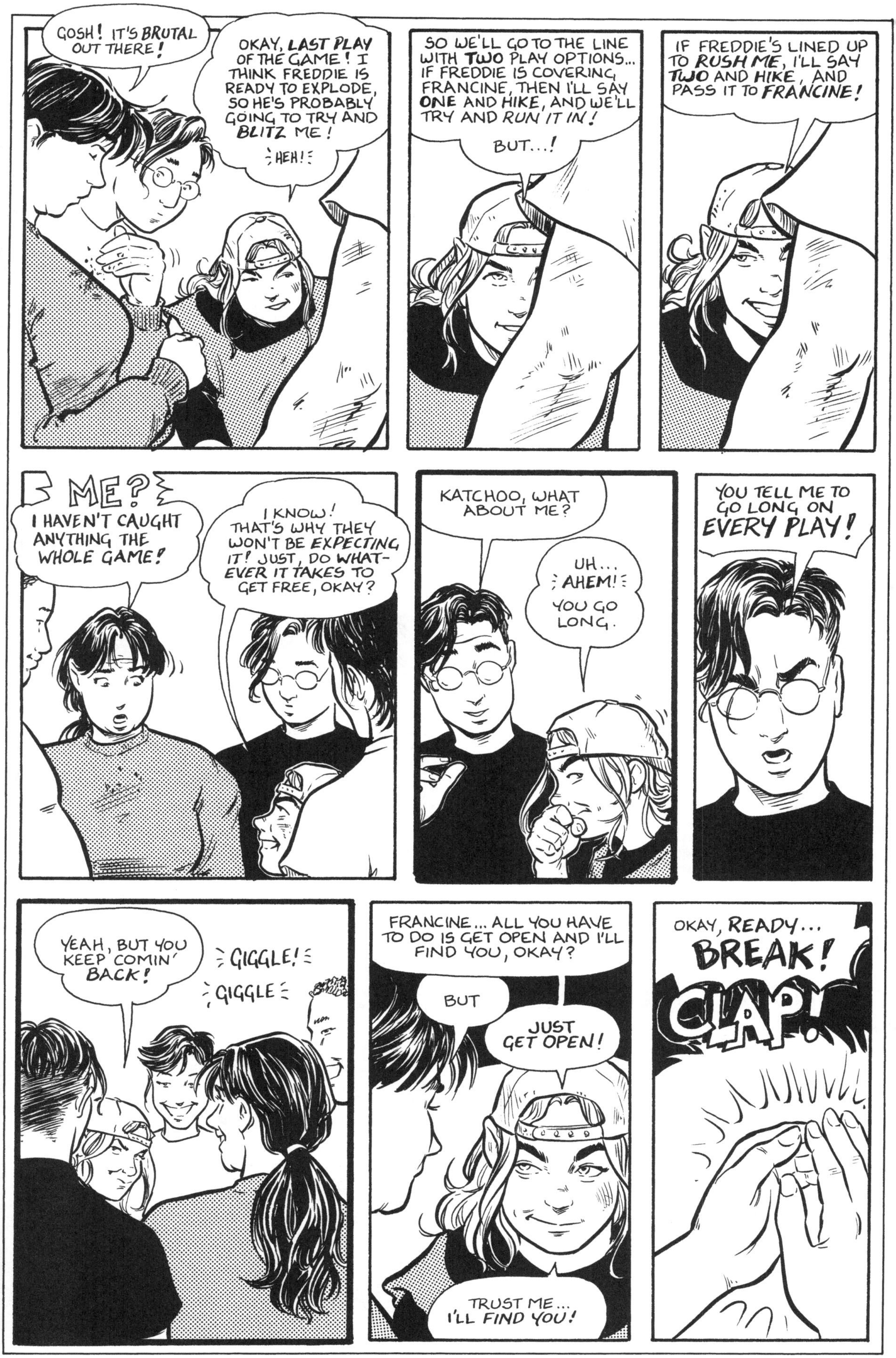
GOSH! IT'S BRUTAL OUT THERE!
OKAY, LAST PLAY OF THE GAME! I THINK FREDDIE IS READY TO EXPLODE, SO HE'S PROBABLY GOING TO TRY AND BLITZ ME!
HEH!
SO WE'LL GO TO THE LINE WITH TWO PLAY OPTIONS... IF FREDDIE IS COVERING FRANCINE, THEN I'LL SAY ONE AND HIKE, AND WE'LL TRY AND RUN IT IN!
BUT...!
IF FREDDIE'S LINED UP TO RUSH ME, I'LL SAY TWO AND HIKE, AND PASS IT TO FRANCINE!
ME?
I HAVEN'T CAUGHT ANYTHING THE WHOLE GAME!
I KNOW! THAT'S WHY THEY WON'T BE EXPECTING IT! JUST, DO WHATEVER IT TAKES TO GET FREE, OKAY?
KATCHOO, WHAT ABOUT ME?
UH... AHEM! YOU GO LONG.
YOU TELL ME TO GO LONG ON EVERY PLAY!
YEAH, BUT YOU KEEP COMIN' BACK!
GIGGLE!
GIGGLE
FRANCINE... ALL YOU HAVE TO DO IS GET OPEN AND I'LL FIND YOU, OKAY?
BUT
JUST GET OPEN!
TRUST ME... I'LL FIND YOU!
OKAY, READY... BREAK!
CLAP!

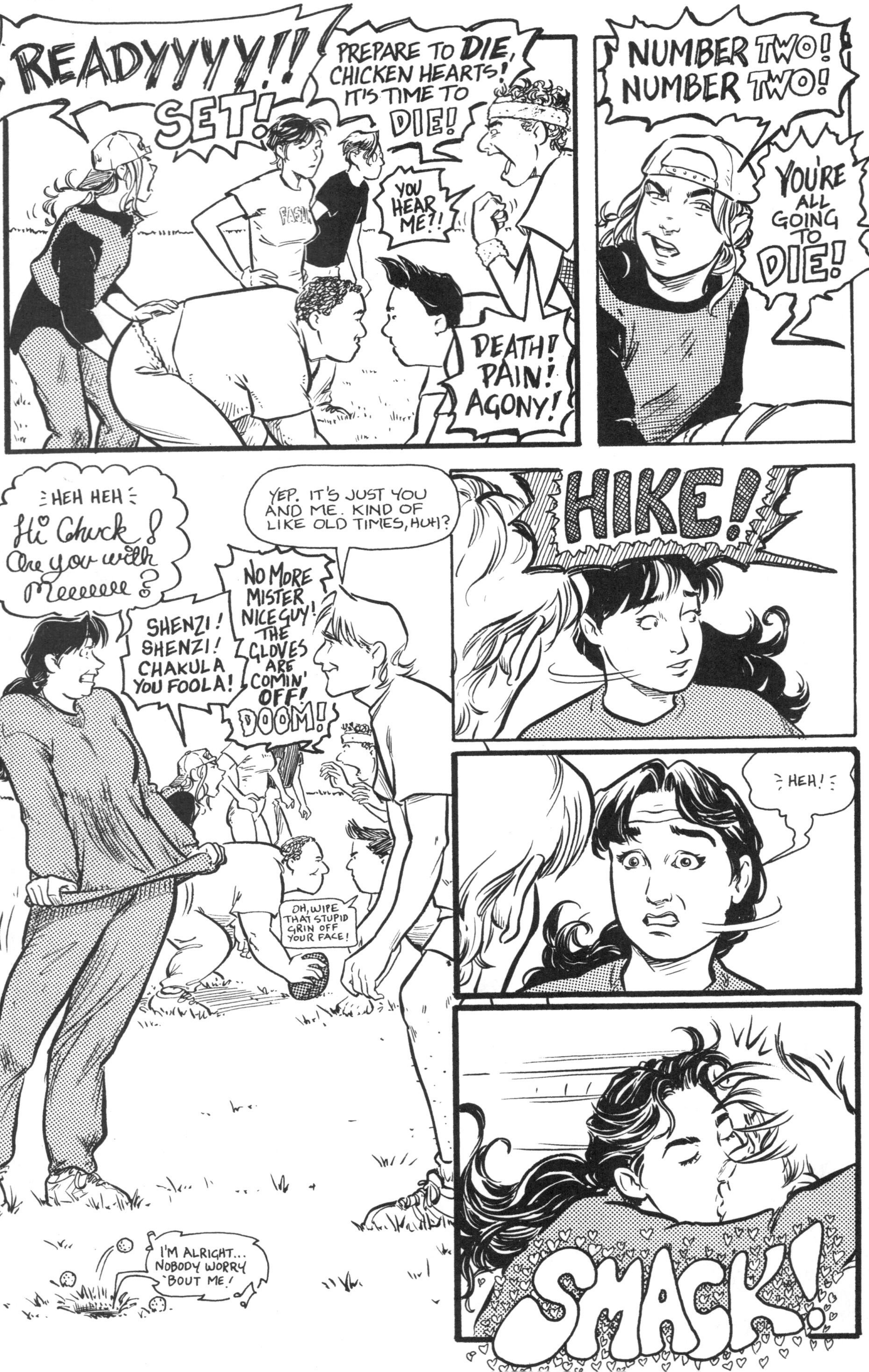
READYYYY!!
SET!
PREPARE TO DIE, CHICKEN HEARTS! IT'S TIME TO DIE!
YOU HEAR ME?!
DEATH! PAIN! AGONY!
NUMBER TWO! NUMBER TWO!
YOU'RE ALL GOING TO DIE!
HEH HEH Hi Chuck! Are you with Meeeeee?
YEP. IT'S JUST YOU AND ME. KIND OF LIKE OLD TIMES, HUH?
SHENZI! SHENZI! CHAKULA YOU FOOLA!
NO MORE MISTER NICE GUY! THE GLOVES ARE COMIN' OFF! DOOM!
OH, WIPE THAT STUPID GRIN OFF YOUR FACE!
I'M ALRIGHT... NOBODY WORRY 'BOUT ME!
HIKE!!
HEH!
SMACK!

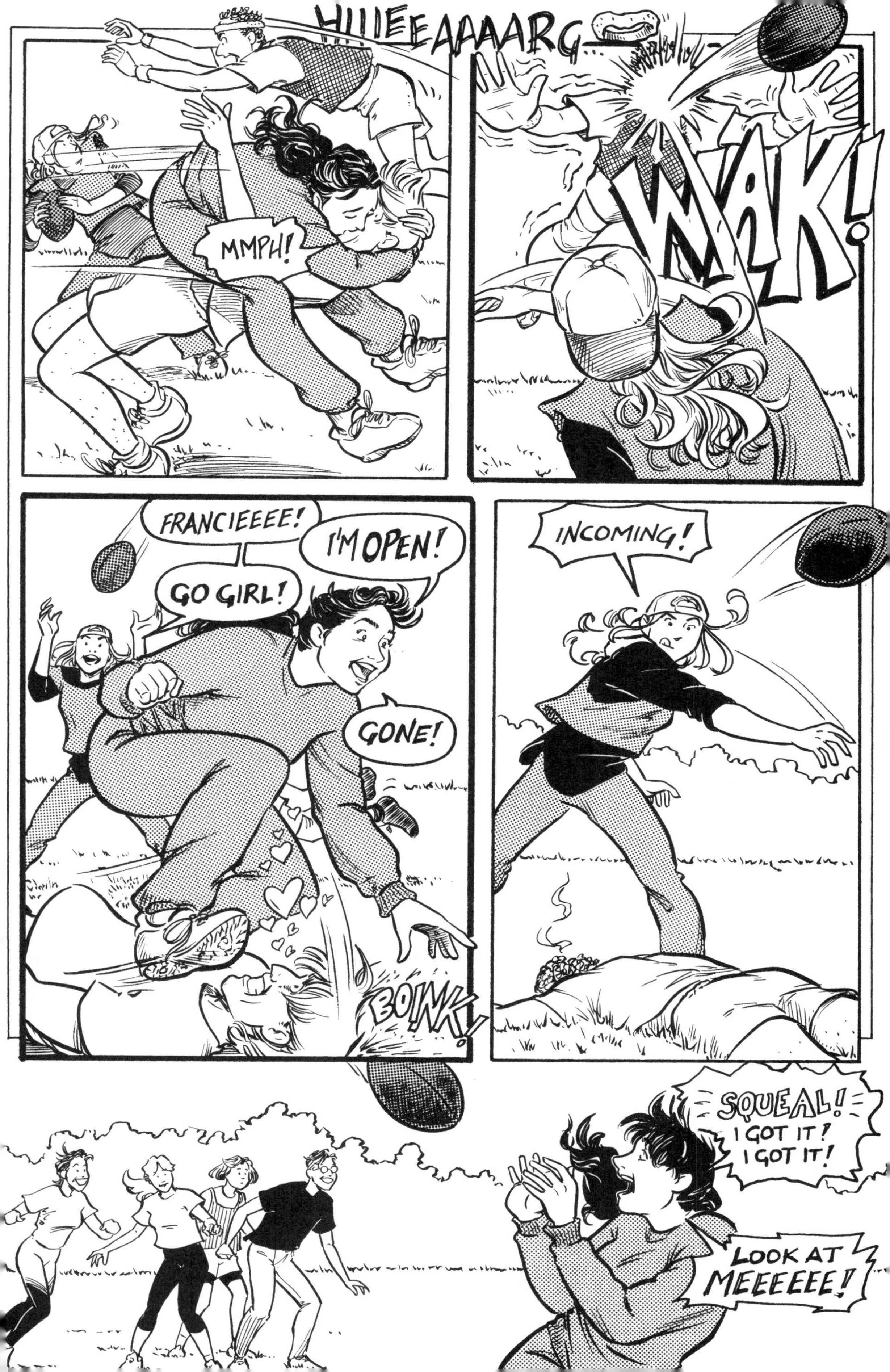
HIIIEEAAAAARG
MMPH!
WAK!
FRANCIEEEE!
GO GIRL!
I'M OPEN!
GONE!
BOINK!
INCOMING!
SQUEAL!
I GOT IT!
I GOT IT!
LOOK AT MEEEEEE!

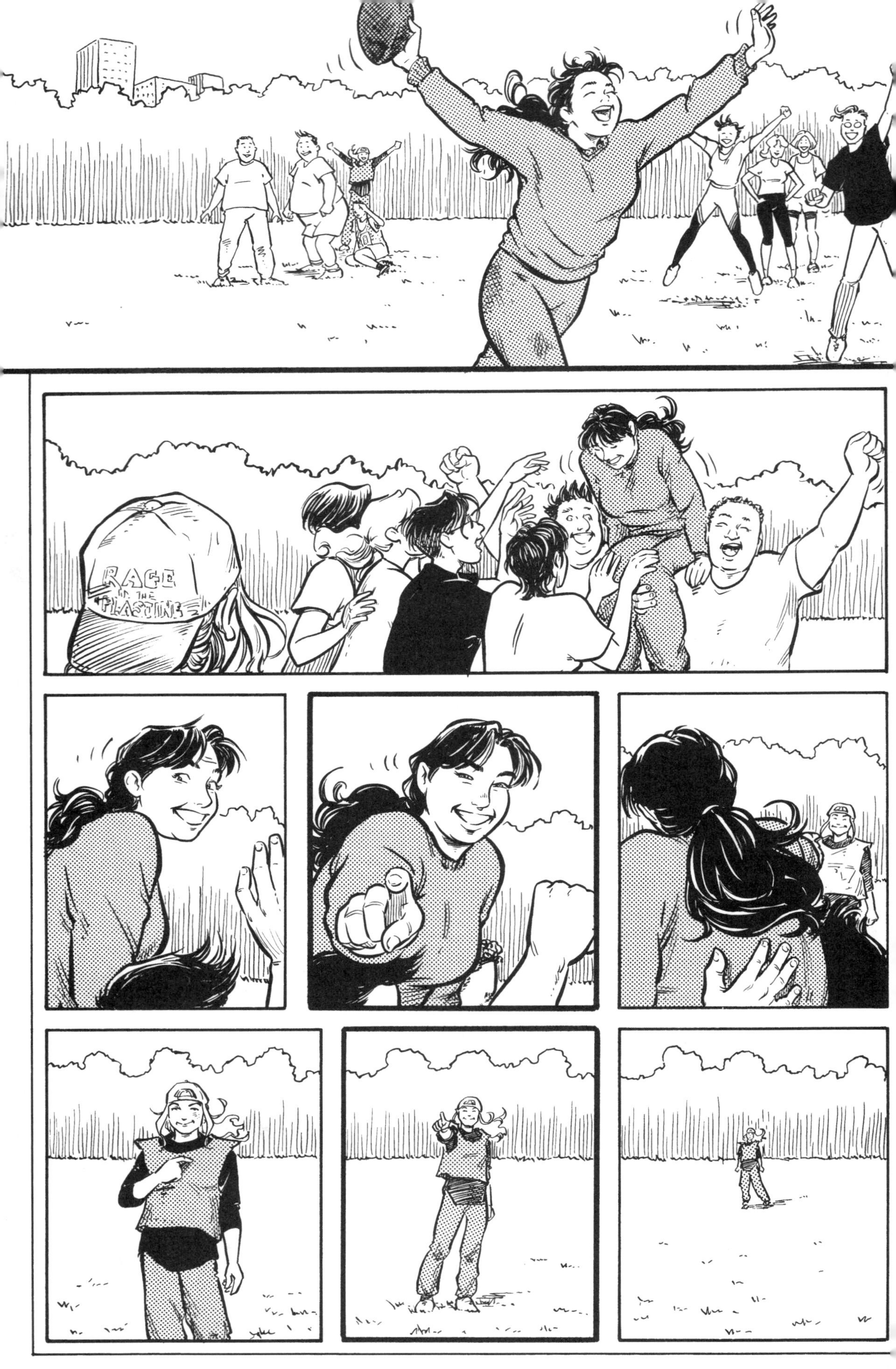
RAGE
THE
PLASTINE

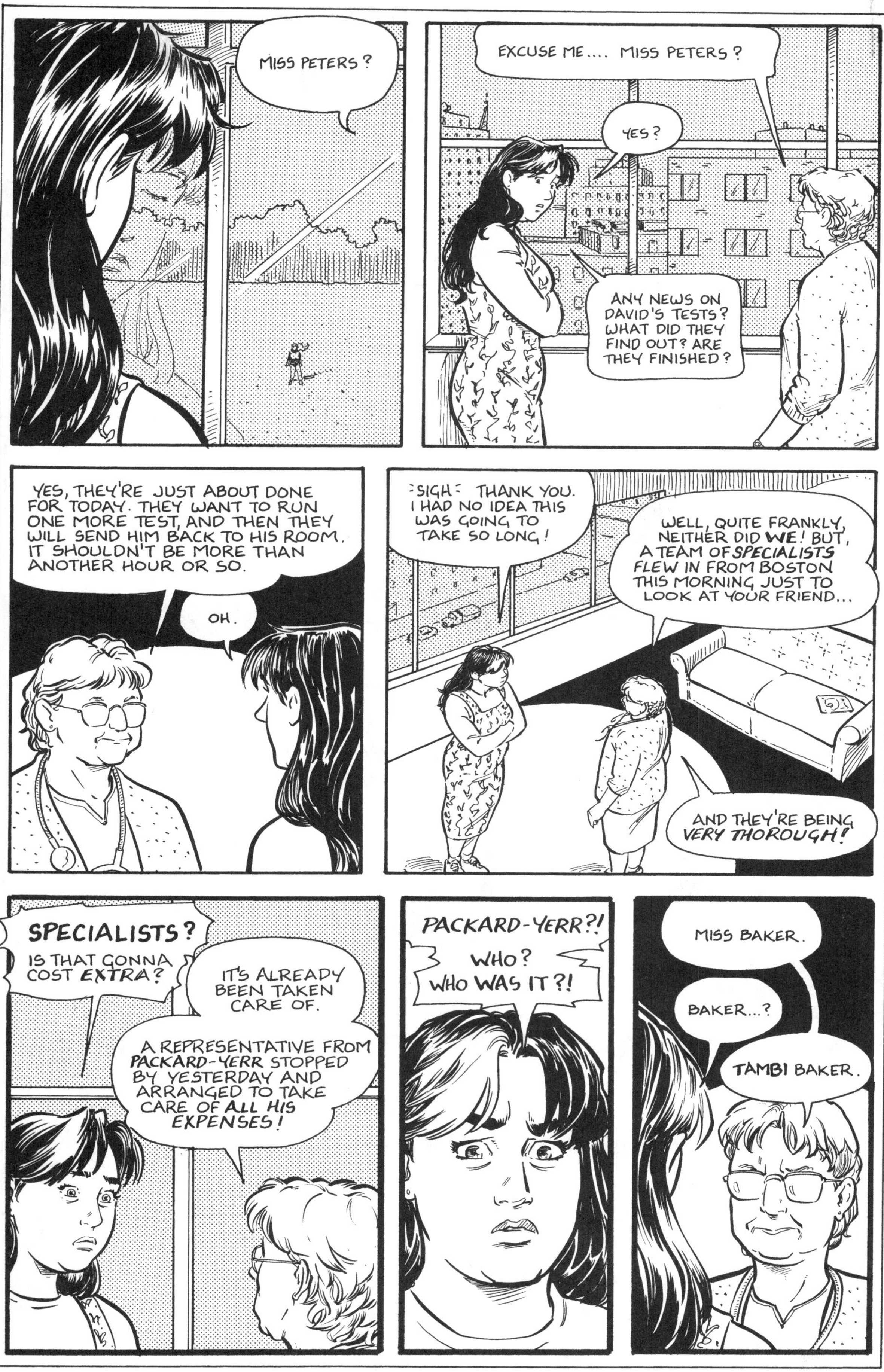

MISS PETERS?
EXCUSE ME.... MISS PETERS?
YES?
ANY NEWS ON DAVID'S TESTS? WHAT DID THEY FIND OUT? ARE THEY FINISHED?
YES, THEY'RE JUST ABOUT DONE FOR TODAY. THEY WANT TO RUN ONE MORE TEST, AND THEN THEY WILL SEND HIM BACK TO HIS ROOM. IT SHOULDN'T BE MORE THAN ANOTHER HOUR OR SO.
OH.
:SIGH: THANK YOU. I HAD NO IDEA THIS WAS GOING TO TAKE SO LONG!
WELL, QUITE FRANKLY, NEITHER DID WE! BUT, A TEAM OF SPECIALISTS FLEW IN FROM BOSTON THIS MORNING JUST TO LOOK AT YOUR FRIEND...
AND THEY'RE BEING VERY THOROUGH!
SPECIALISTS? IS THAT GONNA COST EXTRA?
IT'S ALREADY BEEN TAKEN CARE OF.
A REPRESENTATIVE FROM PACKARD-YERR STOPPED BY YESTERDAY AND ARRANGED TO TAKE CARE OF ALL HIS EXPENSES!
PACKARD-YERR?!
WHO? WHO WAS IT?!
MISS BAKER.
BAKER...?
TAMBI BAKER.

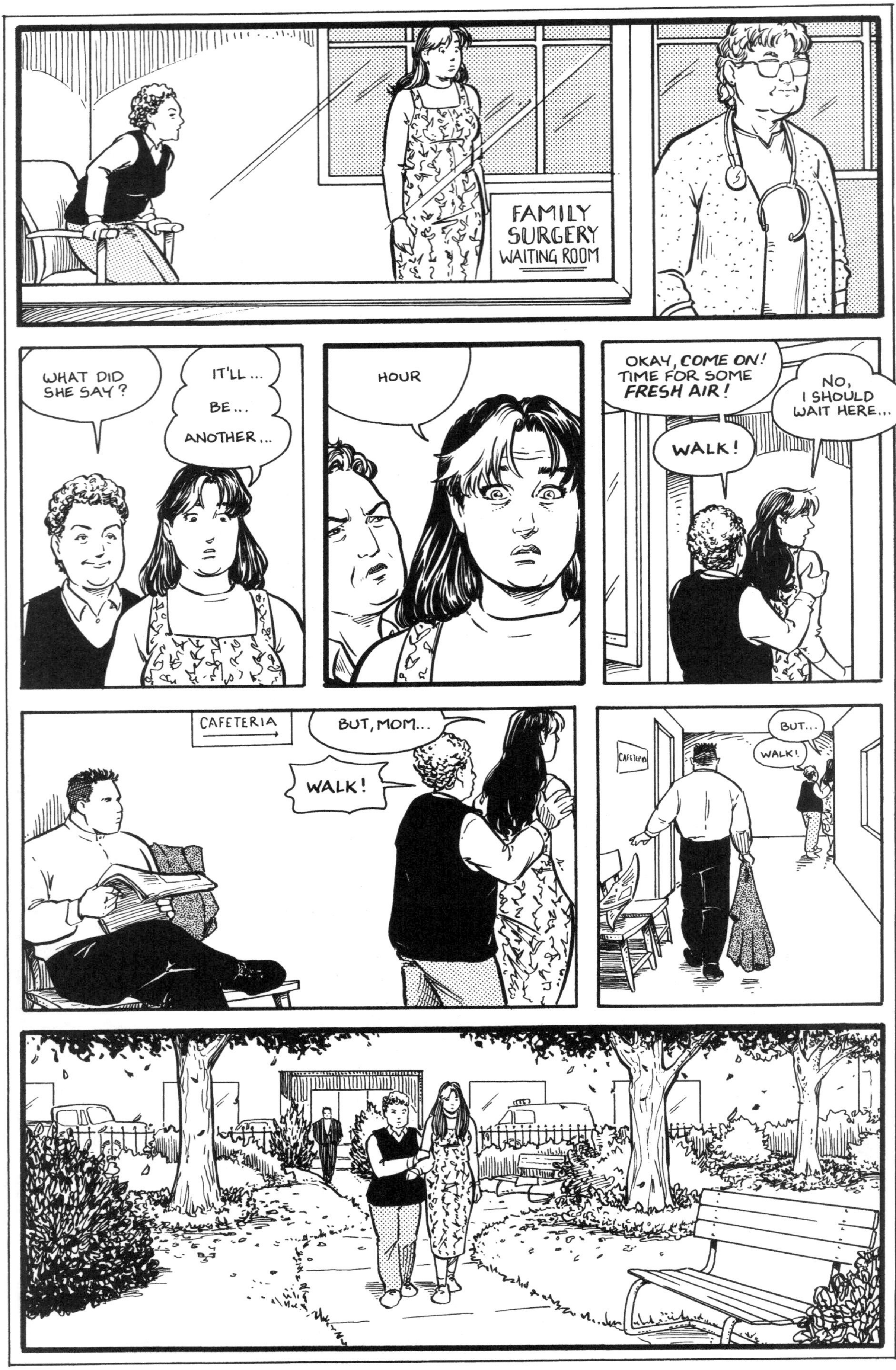
FAMILY
SURGERY
WAITING ROOM
WHAT DID SHE SAY?
IT'LL... BE... ANOTHER...
HOUR
OKAY, COME ON! TIME FOR SOME FRESH AIR!
NO, I SHOULD WAIT HERE...
WALK!
CAFETERIA
BUT, MOM...
WALK!
BUT...
WALK!

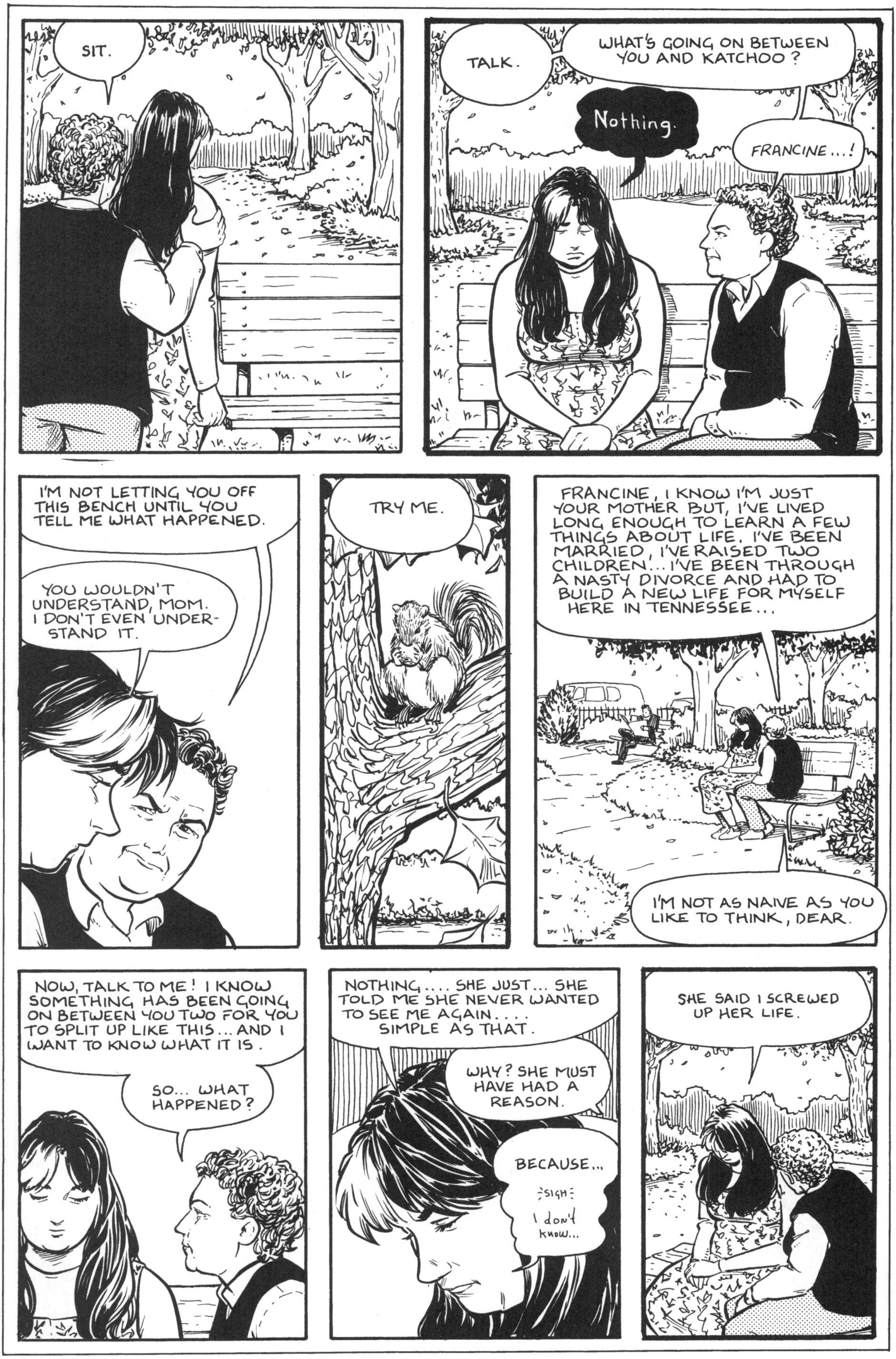
SIT.
TALK.
WHAT'S GOING ON BETWEEN YOU AND KATCHOO?
Nothing.
FRANCINE...!
I'M NOT LETTING YOU OFF THIS BENCH UNTIL YOU TELL ME WHAT HAPPENED.
YOU WOULDN'T UNDERSTAND, MOM. I DON'T EVEN UNDERSTAND IT.
TRY ME.
FRANCINE, I KNOW I'M JUST YOUR MOTHER BUT, I'VE LIVED LONG ENOUGH TO LEARN A FEW THINGS ABOUT LIFE. I'VE BEEN MARRIED, I'VE RAISED TWO CHILDREN... I'VE BEEN THROUGH A NASTY DIVORCE AND HAD TO BUILD A NEW LIFE FOR MYSELF HERE IN TENNESSEE...
I'M NOT AS NAIVE AS YOU LIKE TO THINK, DEAR.
NOW, TALK TO ME! I KNOW SOMETHING HAS BEEN GOING ON BETWEEN YOU TWO FOR YOU TO SPLIT UP LIKE THIS... AND I WANT TO KNOW WHAT IT IS.
SO... WHAT HAPPENED?
NOTHING.... SHE JUST... SHE TOLD ME SHE NEVER WANTED TO SEE ME AGAIN.... SIMPLE AS THAT.
WHY? SHE MUST HAVE HAD A REASON.
BECAUSE...
SIGH
I don't know...
SHE SAID I SCREWED UP HER LIFE.

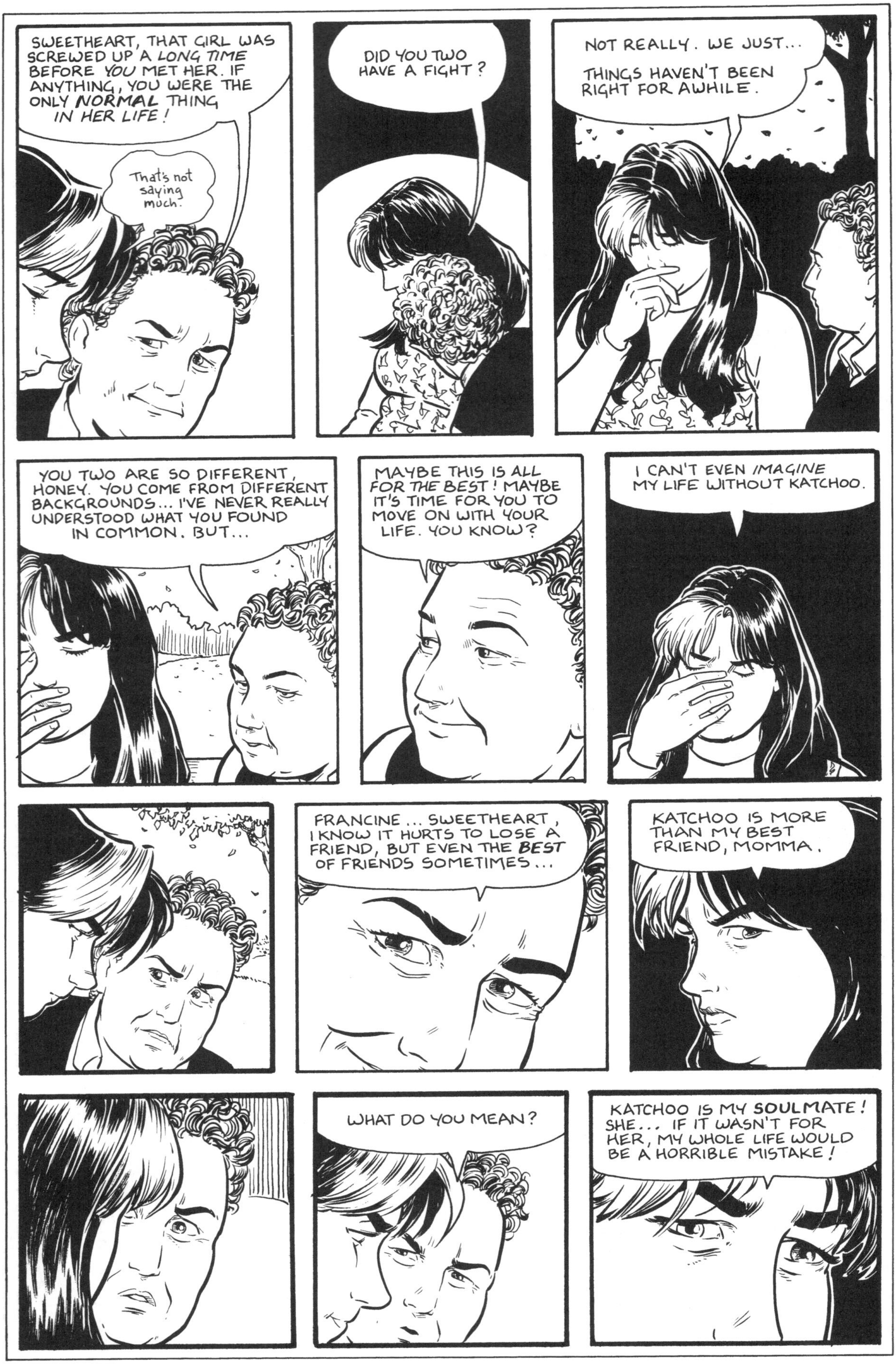

SWEETHEART, THAT GIRL WAS SCREWED UP A LONG TIME BEFORE YOU MET HER. IF ANYTHING, YOU WERE THE ONLY NORMAL THING IN HER LIFE!
That's not saying much.
DID YOU TWO HAVE A FIGHT?
NOT REALLY. WE JUST...
THINGS HAVEN'T BEEN RIGHT FOR AWHILE.
YOU TWO ARE SO DIFFERENT, HONEY. YOU COME FROM DIFFERENT BACKGROUNDS... I'VE NEVER REALLY UNDERSTOOD WHAT YOU FOUND IN COMMON. BUT...
MAYBE THIS IS ALL FOR THE BEST! MAYBE IT'S TIME FOR YOU TO MOVE ON WITH YOUR LIFE. YOU KNOW?
I CAN'T EVEN IMAGINE MY LIFE WITHOUT KATCHOO.
FRANCINE... SWEETHEART, I KNOW IT HURTS TO LOSE A FRIEND, BUT EVEN THE BEST OF FRIENDS SOMETIMES...
KATCHOO IS MORE THAN MY BEST FRIEND, MOMMA.
WHAT DO YOU MEAN?
KATCHOO IS MY SOULMATE! SHE... IF IT WASN'T FOR HER, MY WHOLE LIFE WOULD BE A HORRIBLE MISTAKE!

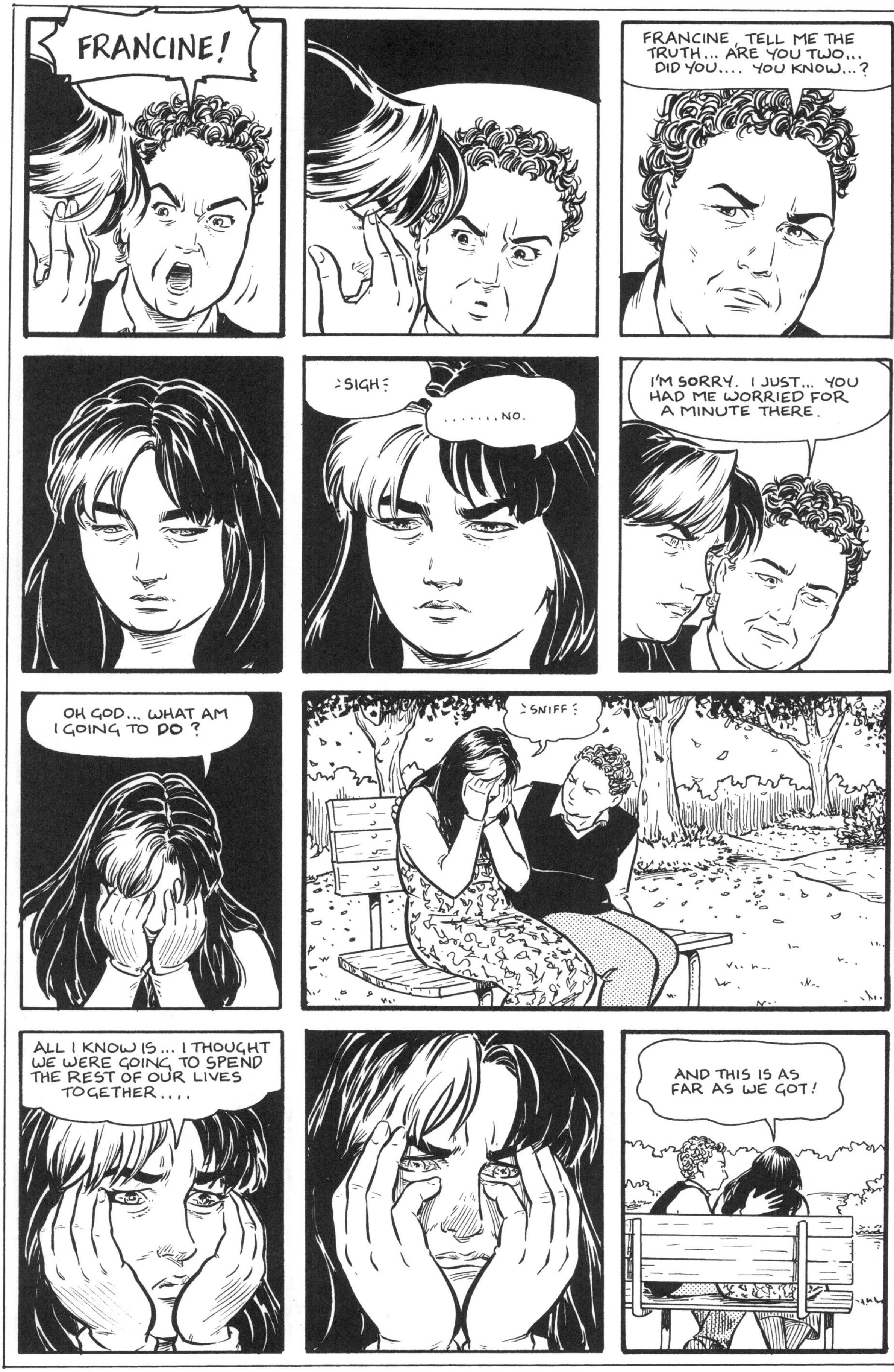
FRANCINE!
FRANCINE, TELL ME THE TRUTH... ARE YOU TWO... DID YOU.... YOU KNOW...?
SIGH
.......NO.
I'M SORRY. I JUST... YOU HAD ME WORRIED FOR A MINUTE THERE.
OH GOD... WHAT AM I GOING TO DO?
SNIFF
ALL I KNOW IS... I THOUGHT WE WERE GOING TO SPEND THE REST OF OUR LIVES TOGETHER....
AND THIS IS AS FAR AS WE GOT!

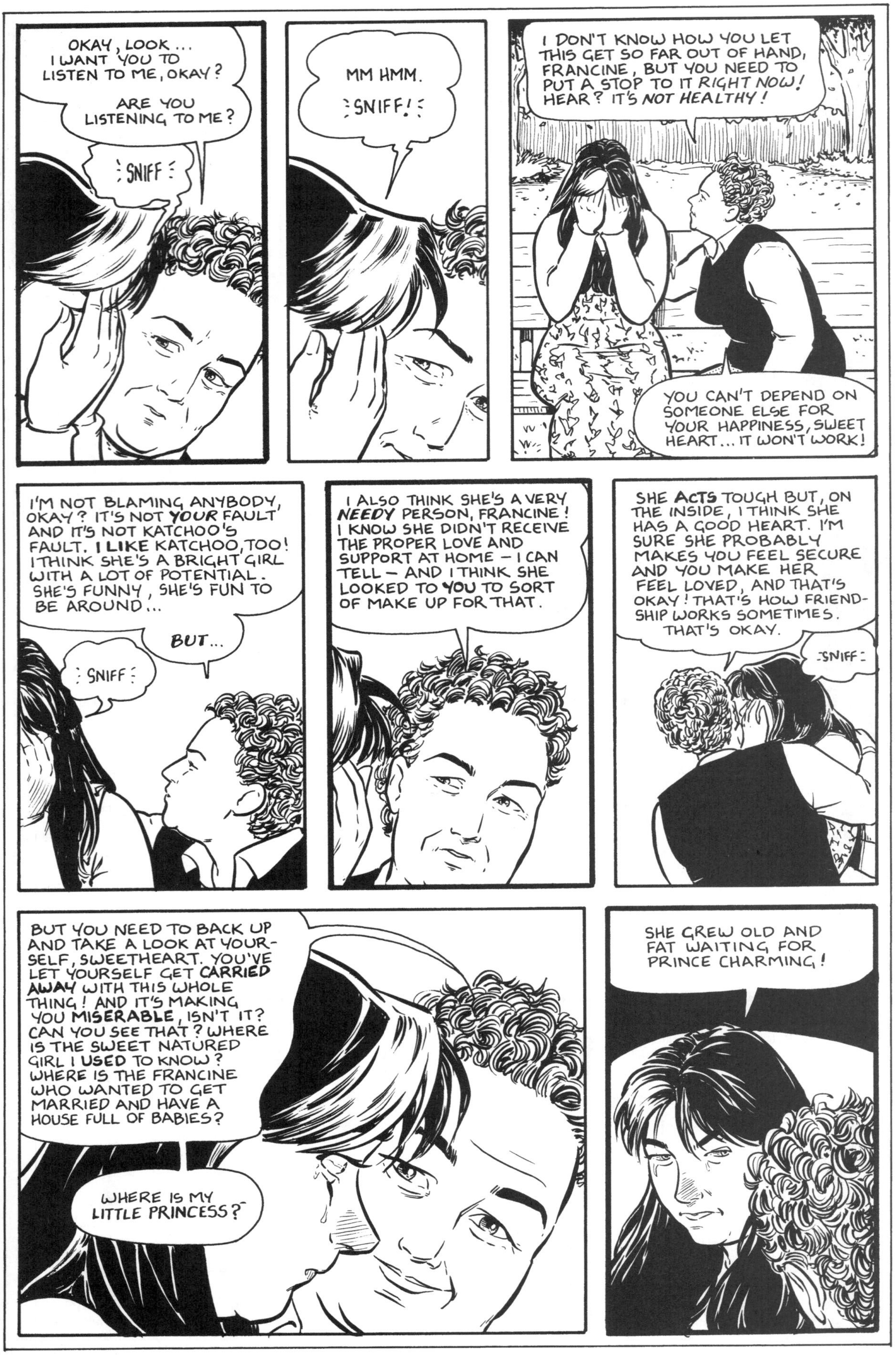
OKAY, LOOK... I WANT YOU TO LISTEN TO ME, OKAY?
ARE YOU LISTENING TO ME?
SNIFF
MM HMM.
SNIFF!
I DON'T KNOW HOW YOU LET THIS GET SO FAR OUT OF HAND, FRANCINE, BUT YOU NEED TO PUT A STOP TO IT RIGHT NOW! HEAR? IT'S NOT HEALTHY!
YOU CAN'T DEPEND ON SOMEONE ELSE FOR YOUR HAPPINESS, SWEET HEART... IT WON'T WORK!
I'M NOT BLAMING ANYBODY, OKAY? IT'S NOT YOUR FAULT AND IT'S NOT KATCHOO'S FAULT. I LIKE KATCHOO, TOO! I THINK SHE'S A BRIGHT GIRL WITH A LOT OF POTENTIAL. SHE'S FUNNY, SHE'S FUN TO BE AROUND...
BUT...
SNIFF
I ALSO THINK SHE'S A VERY NEEDY PERSON, FRANCINE! I KNOW SHE DIDN'T RECEIVE THE PROPER LOVE AND SUPPORT AT HOME – I CAN TELL – AND I THINK SHE LOOKED TO YOU TO SORT OF MAKE UP FOR THAT.
SHE ACTS TOUGH BUT, ON THE INSIDE, I THINK SHE HAS A GOOD HEART. I'M SURE SHE PROBABLY MAKES YOU FEEL SECURE AND YOU MAKE HER FEEL LOVED, AND THAT'S OKAY! THAT'S HOW FRIENDSHIP WORKS SOMETIMES. THAT'S OKAY.
SNIFF
BUT YOU NEED TO BACK UP AND TAKE A LOOK AT YOURSELF, SWEETHEART. YOU'VE LET YOURSELF GET CARRIED AWAY WITH THIS WHOLE THING! AND IT'S MAKING YOU MISERABLE, ISN'T IT? CAN YOU SEE THAT? WHERE IS THE SWEET NATURED GIRL I USED TO KNOW? WHERE IS THE FRANCINE WHO WANTED TO GET MARRIED AND HAVE A HOUSE FULL OF BABIES?
WHERE IS MY LITTLE PRINCESS?
SHE GREW OLD AND FAT WAITING FOR PRINCE CHARMING!

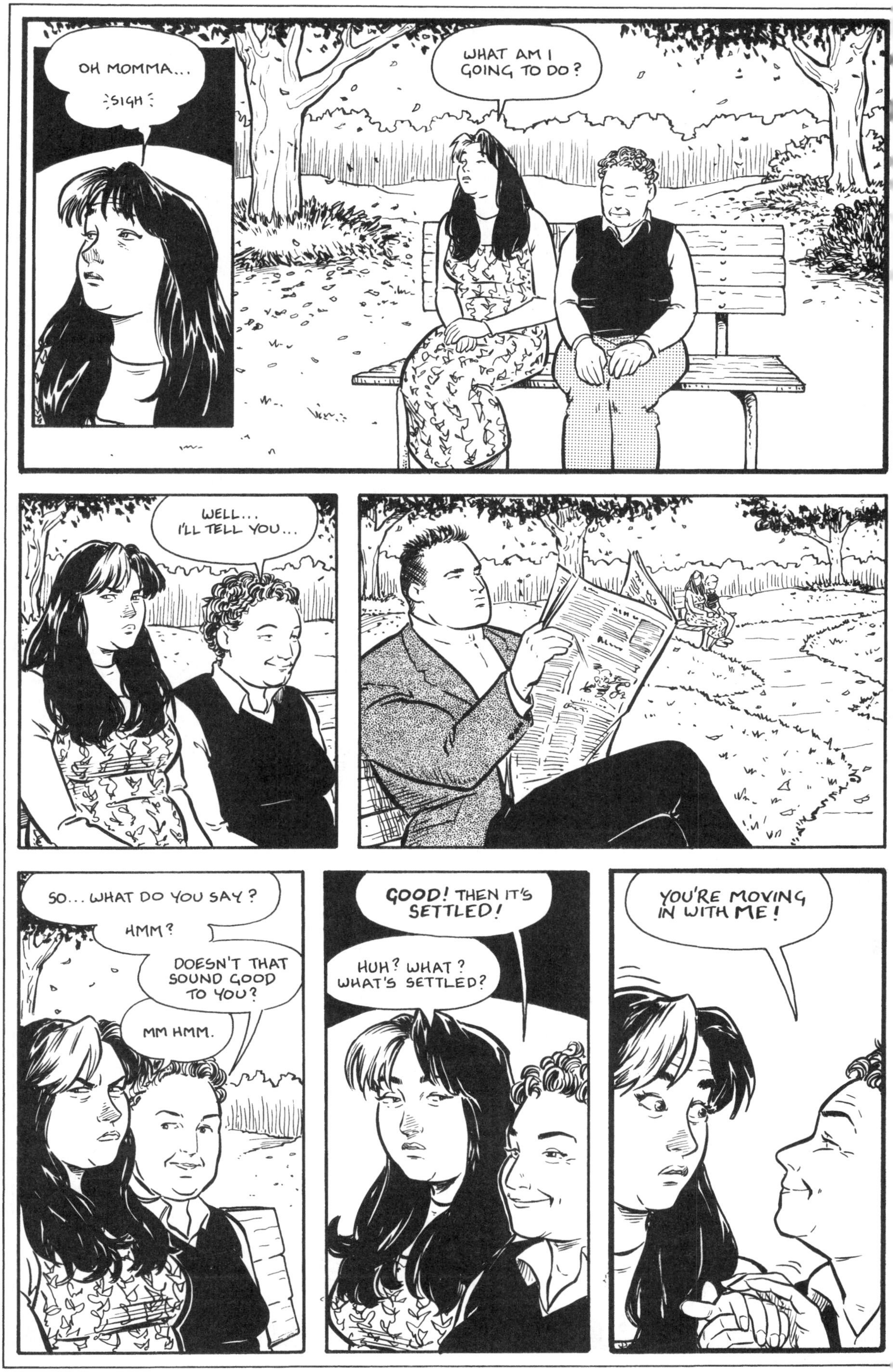
OH MOMMA...
SIGH
WHAT AM I GOING TO DO?
WELL... I'LL TELL YOU...
SO... WHAT DO YOU SAY?
HMM?
DOESN'T THAT SOUND GOOD TO YOU?
MM HMM.
GOOD! THEN IT'S SETTLED!
HUH? WHAT? WHAT'S SETTLED?
YOU'RE MOVING IN WITH ME!

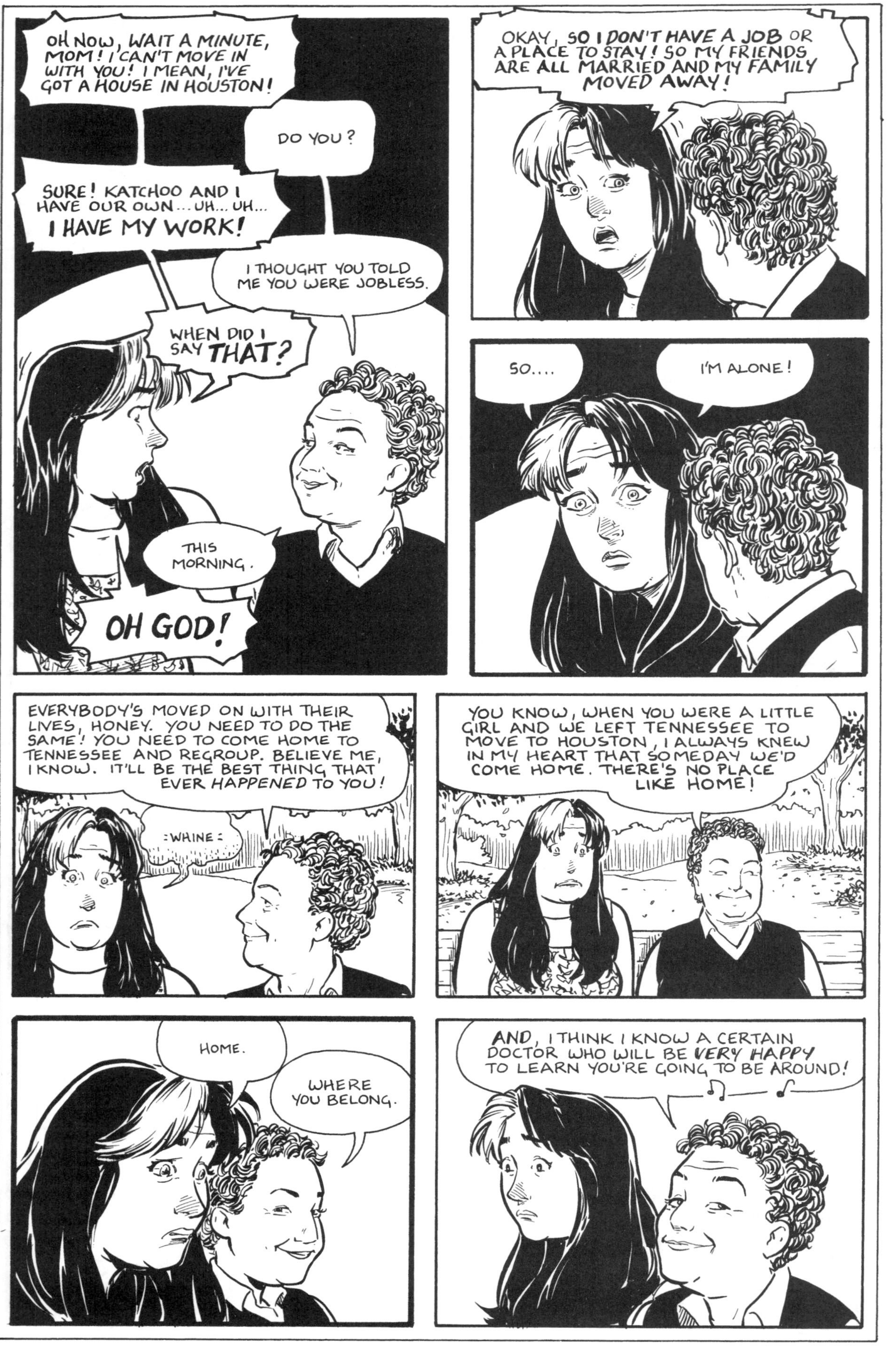
OH NOW, WAIT A MINUTE, MOM! I CAN'T MOVE IN WITH YOU! I MEAN, I'VE GOT A HOUSE IN HOUSTON!
DO YOU?
SURE! KATCHOO AND I HAVE OUR OWN... UH... UH... I HAVE MY WORK!
I THOUGHT YOU TOLD ME YOU WERE JOBLESS.
WHEN DID I SAY THAT?
THIS MORNING.
OH GOD!
OKAY, SO I DON'T HAVE A JOB OR A PLACE TO STAY! SO MY FRIENDS ARE ALL MARRIED AND MY FAMILY MOVED AWAY!
SO....
I'M ALONE!
EVERYBODY'S MOVED ON WITH THEIR LIVES, HONEY. YOU NEED TO DO THE SAME! YOU NEED TO COME HOME TO TENNESSEE AND REGROUP. BELIEVE ME, I KNOW. IT'LL BE THE BEST THING THAT EVER HAPPENED TO YOU!
:WHINE:
YOU KNOW, WHEN YOU WERE A LITTLE GIRL AND WE LEFT TENNESSEE TO MOVE TO HOUSTON, I ALWAYS KNEW IN MY HEART THAT SOMEDAY WE'D COME HOME. THERE'S NO PLACE LIKE HOME!
HOME.
WHERE YOU BELONG.
AND, I THINK I KNOW A CERTAIN DOCTOR WHO WILL BE VERY HAPPY TO LEARN YOU'RE GOING TO BE AROUND!

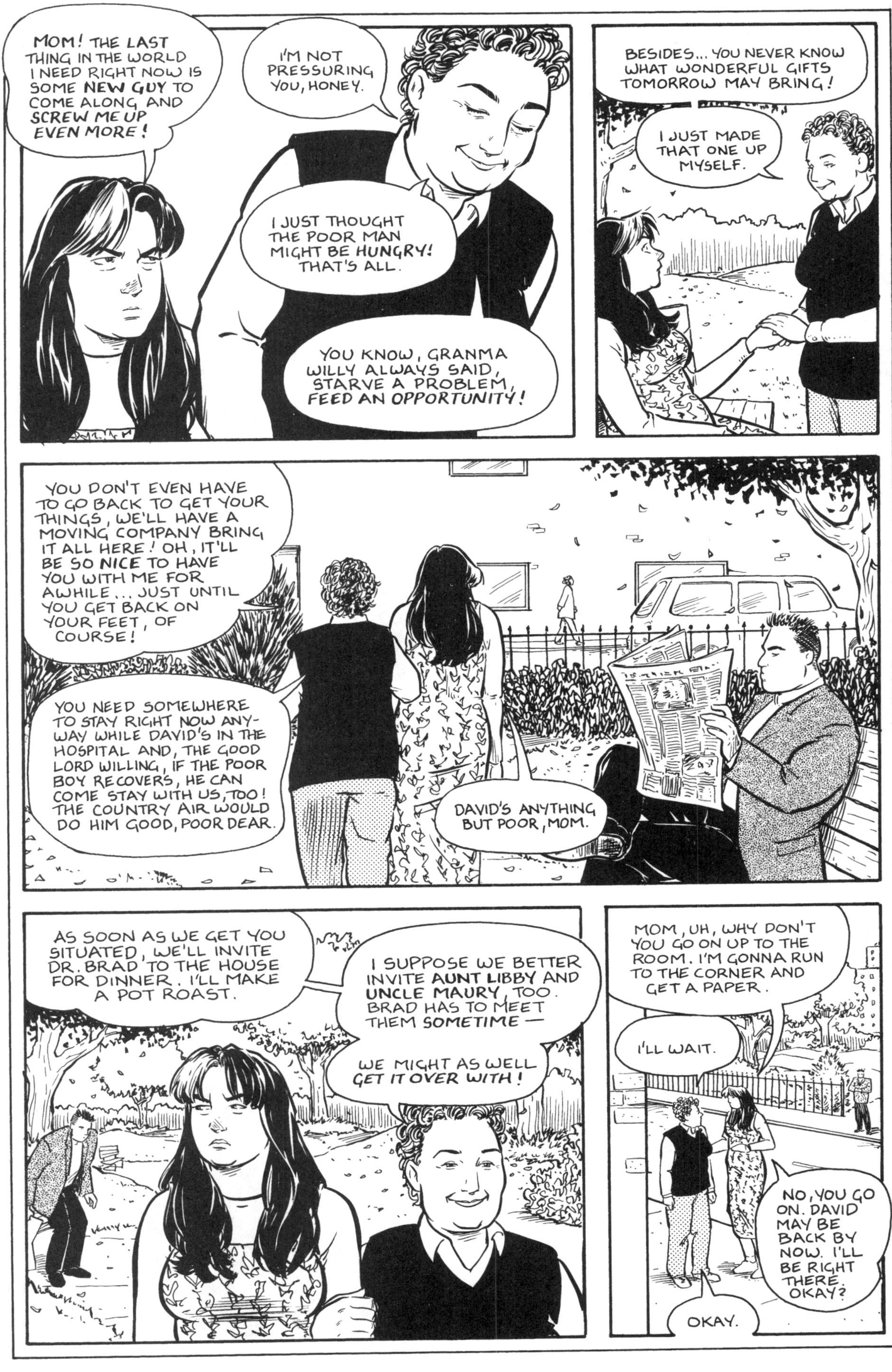
MOM! THE LAST THING IN THE WORLD I NEED RIGHT NOW IS SOME NEW GUY TO COME ALONG AND SCREW ME UP EVEN MORE!
I'M NOT PRESSURING YOU, HONEY.
I JUST THOUGHT THE POOR MAN MIGHT BE HUNGRY! THAT'S ALL.
YOU KNOW, GRANMA WILLY ALWAYS SAID, STARVE A PROBLEM, FEED AN OPPORTUNITY!
BESIDES... YOU NEVER KNOW WHAT WONDERFUL GIFTS TOMORROW MAY BRING!
I JUST MADE THAT ONE UP MYSELF.
YOU DON'T EVEN HAVE TO GO BACK TO GET YOUR THINGS, WE'LL HAVE A MOVING COMPANY BRING IT ALL HERE! OH, IT'LL BE SO NICE TO HAVE YOU WITH ME FOR AWHILE... JUST UNTIL YOU GET BACK ON YOUR FEET, OF COURSE!
YOU NEED SOMEWHERE TO STAY RIGHT NOW ANY-WAY WHILE DAVID'S IN THE HOSPITAL AND, THE GOOD LORD WILLING, IF THE POOR BOY RECOVERS, HE CAN COME STAY WITH US, TOO! THE COUNTRY AIR WOULD DO HIM GOOD, POOR DEAR.
DAVID'S ANYTHING BUT POOR, MOM.
AS SOON AS WE GET YOU SITUATED, WE'LL INVITE DR. BRAD TO THE HOUSE FOR DINNER. I'LL MAKE A POT ROAST.
I SUPPOSE WE BETTER INVITE AUNT LIBBY AND UNCLE MAURY, TOO. BRAD HAS TO MEET THEM SOMETIME —
WE MIGHT AS WELL GET IT OVER WITH!
MOM, UH, WHY DON'T YOU GO ON UP TO THE ROOM. I'M GONNA RUN TO THE CORNER AND GET A PAPER.
I'LL WAIT.
NO, YOU GO ON. DAVID MAY BE BACK BY NOW. I'LL BE RIGHT THERE. OKAY?
OKAY.

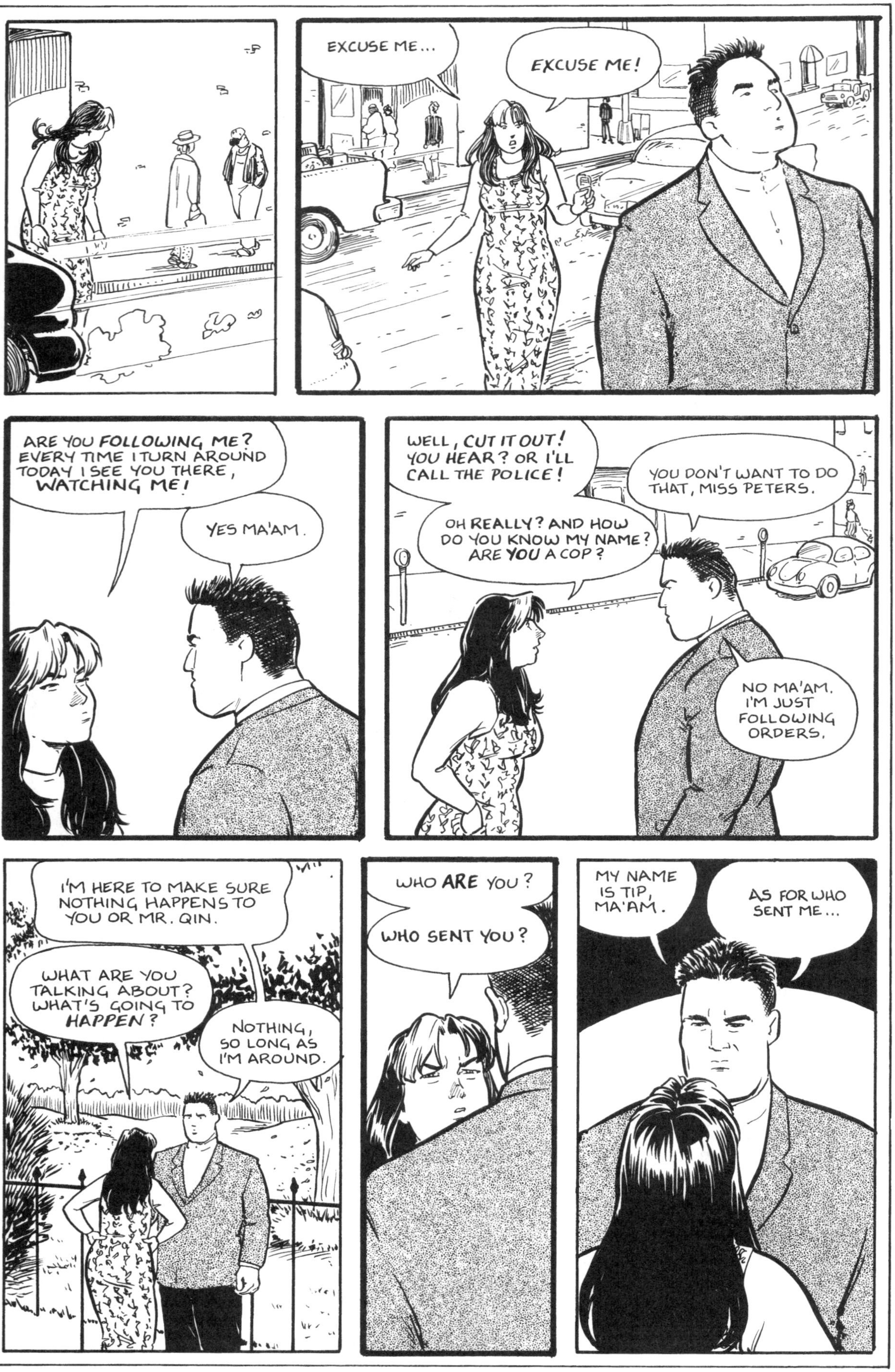
EXCUSE ME...
EXCUSE ME!
ARE YOU FOLLOWING ME? EVERY TIME I TURN AROUND TODAY I SEE YOU THERE, WATCHING ME!
YES MA'AM.
WELL, CUT IT OUT! YOU HEAR? OR I'LL CALL THE POLICE!
YOU DON'T WANT TO DO THAT, MISS PETERS.
OH REALLY? AND HOW DO YOU KNOW MY NAME? ARE YOU A COP?
NO MA'AM. I'M JUST FOLLOWING ORDERS.
I'M HERE TO MAKE SURE NOTHING HAPPENS TO YOU OR MR. QIN.
WHAT ARE YOU TALKING ABOUT? WHAT'S GOING TO HAPPEN?
NOTHING, SO LONG AS I'M AROUND.
WHO ARE YOU?
WHO SENT YOU?
MY NAME IS TIP, MA'AM.
AS FOR WHO SENT ME...

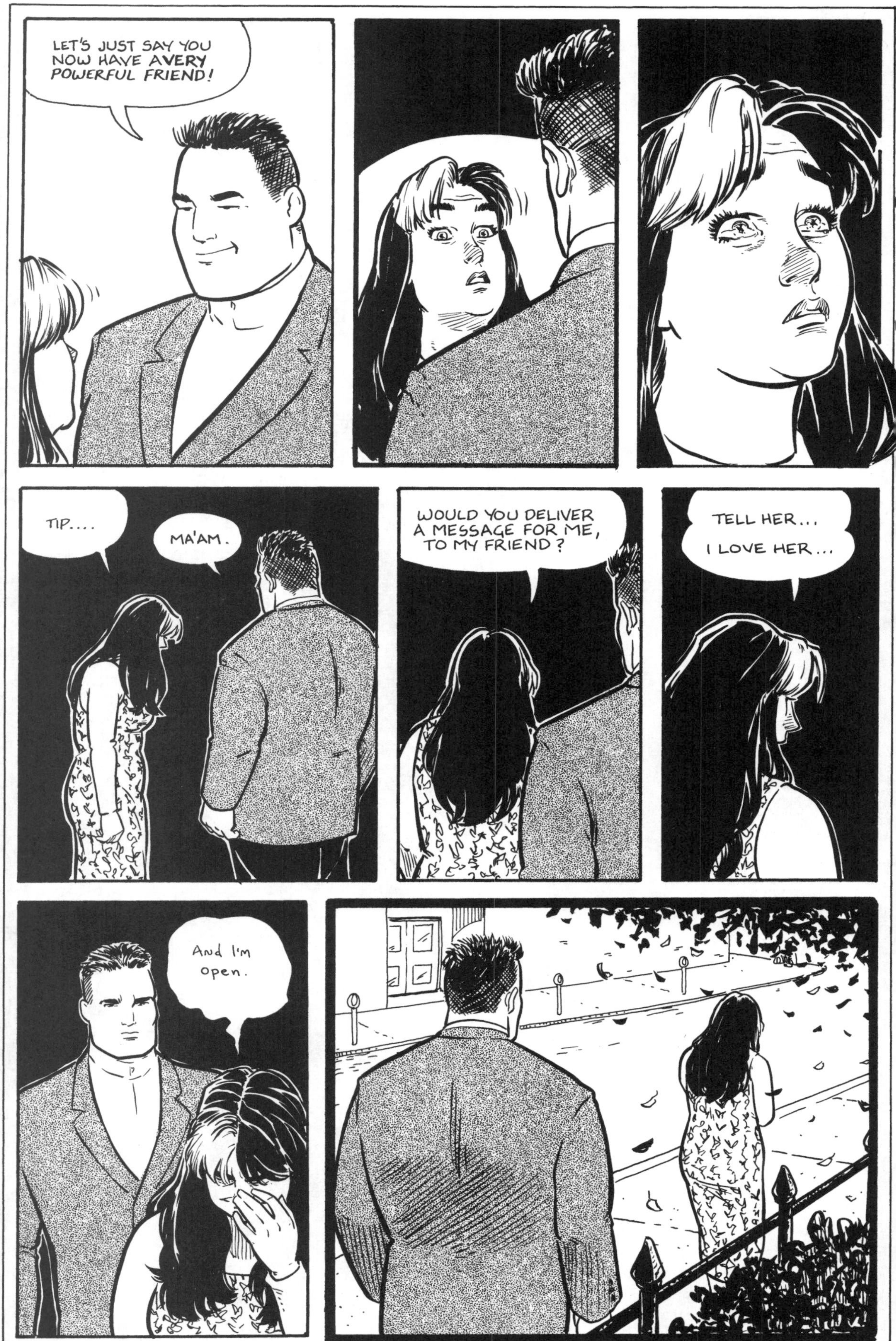

LET'S JUST SAY YOU NOW HAVE A VERY POWERFUL FRIEND!
TIP....
MA'AM.
WOULD YOU DELIVER A MESSAGE FOR ME, TO MY FRIEND?
TELL HER... I LOVE HER...
And I'm open.

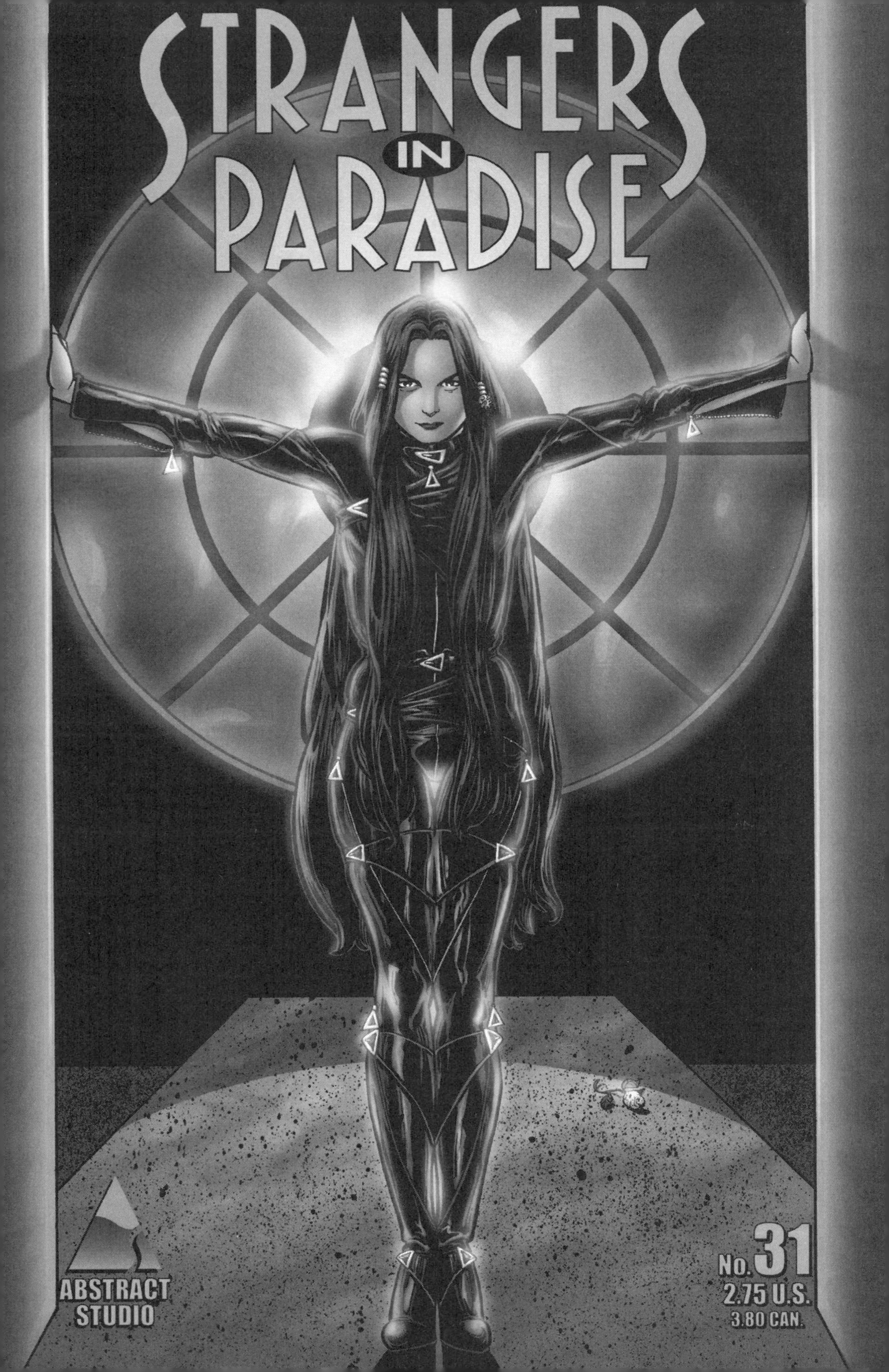
STRANGERS IN PARADISE
ABSTRACT STUDIO
No. 31
2.75 U.S.
3.80 CAN.

day by day we lose our civility when
night by night we play with hostility
seeding our hearts with constant desire
burning the proof in heavenly fire

hide me away in the black of your heart
hide me away and we'll make a new start
hide me away in the black of your heart
hide me away and pick me apart

hide me away in the black of your heart
hide me away in the black of your heart
hide me away in the black of your heart

in the black of your heart

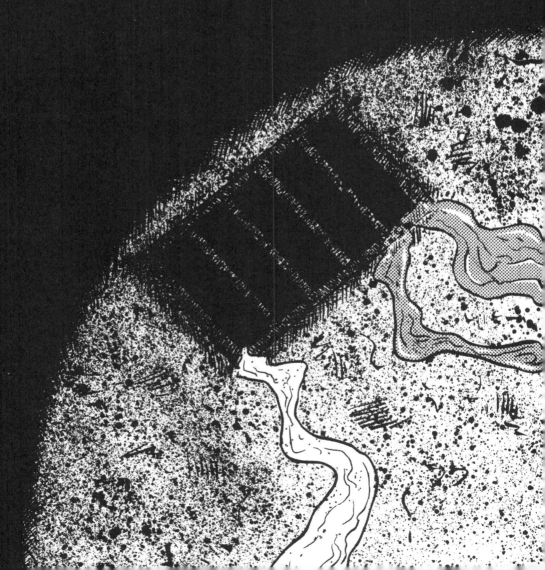

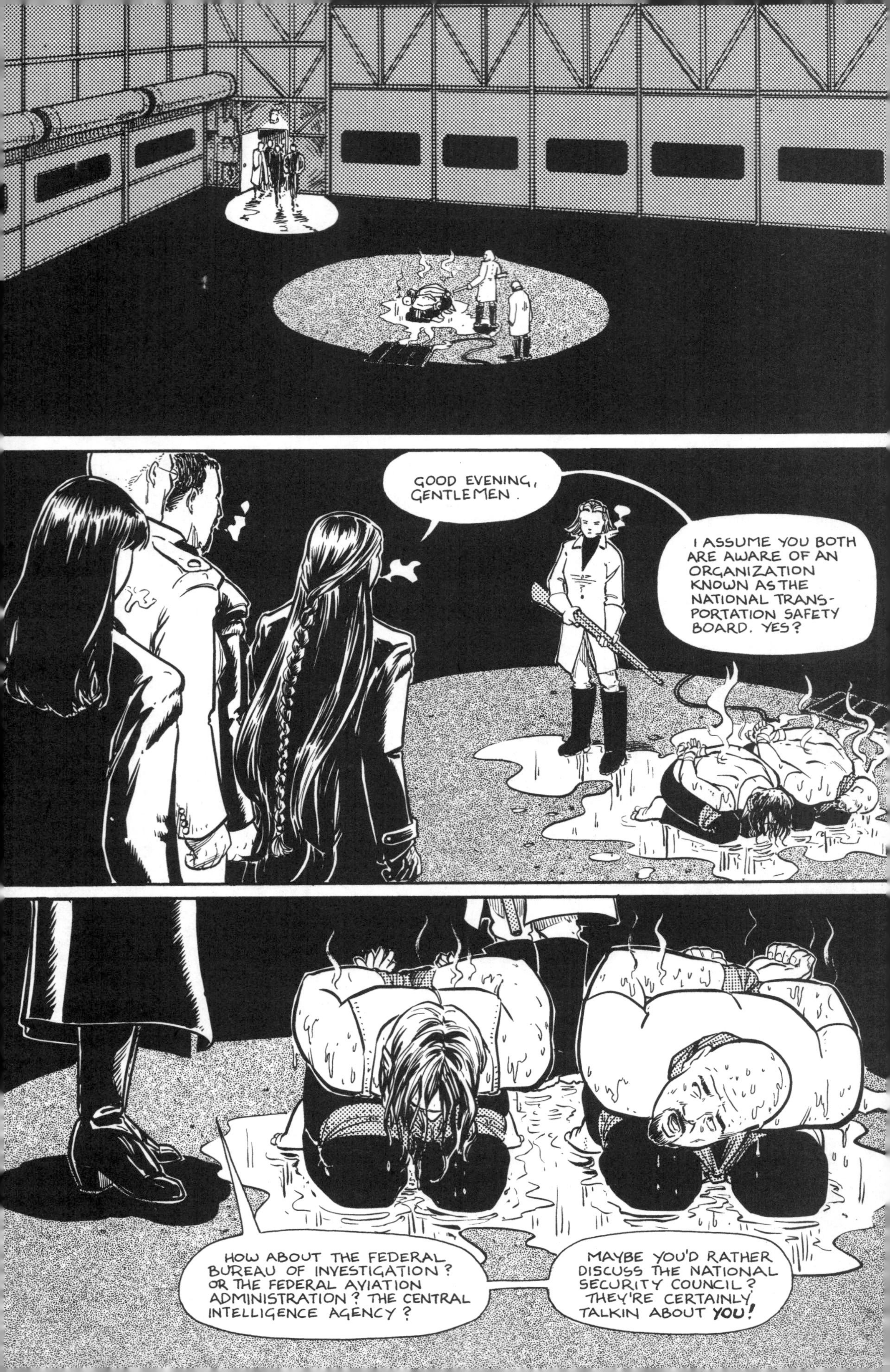
GOOD EVENING, GENTLEMEN.
I ASSUME YOU BOTH ARE AWARE OF AN ORGANIZATION KNOWN AS THE NATIONAL TRANSPORTATION SAFETY BOARD. YES?
HOW ABOUT THE FEDERAL BUREAU OF INVESTIGATION? OR THE FEDERAL AVIATION ADMINISTRATION? THE CENTRAL INTELLIGENCE AGENCY?
MAYBE YOU'D RATHER DISCUSS THE NATIONAL SECURITY COUNCIL? THEY'RE CERTAINLY TALKIN ABOUT **YOU**!

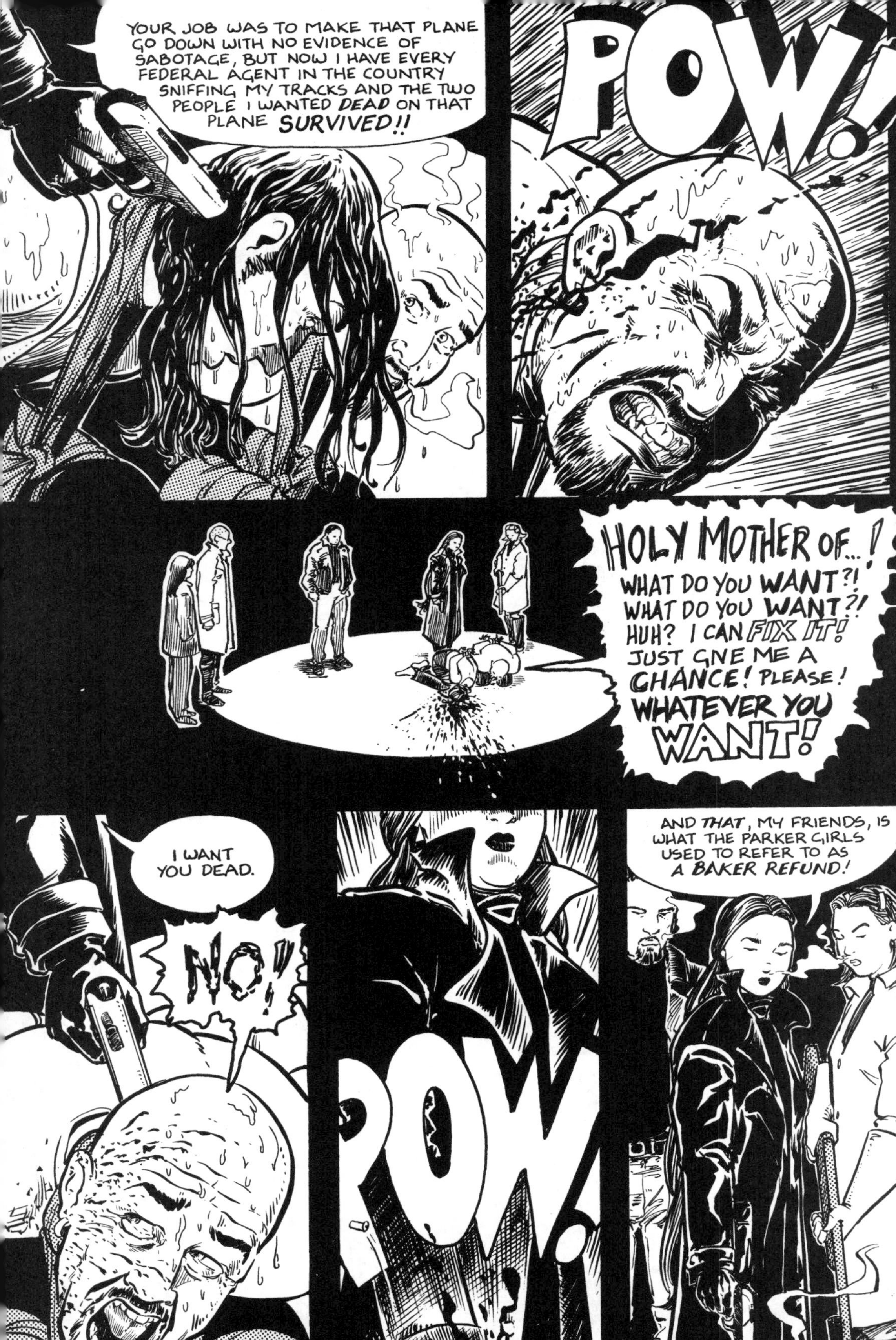
YOUR JOB WAS TO MAKE THAT PLANE GO DOWN WITH NO EVIDENCE OF SABOTAGE, BUT NOW I HAVE EVERY FEDERAL AGENT IN THE COUNTRY SNIFFING MY TRACKS AND THE TWO PEOPLE I WANTED DEAD ON THAT PLANE SURVIVED!!
POW!!
HOLY MOTHER OF...! WHAT DO YOU WANT?! WHAT DO YOU WANT?! HUH? I CAN FIX IT! JUST GIVE ME A CHANCE! PLEASE! WHATEVER YOU WANT!
I WANT YOU DEAD.
NO!!
POW!
AND THAT, MY FRIENDS, IS WHAT THE PARKER GIRLS USED TO REFER TO AS A BAKER REFUND!

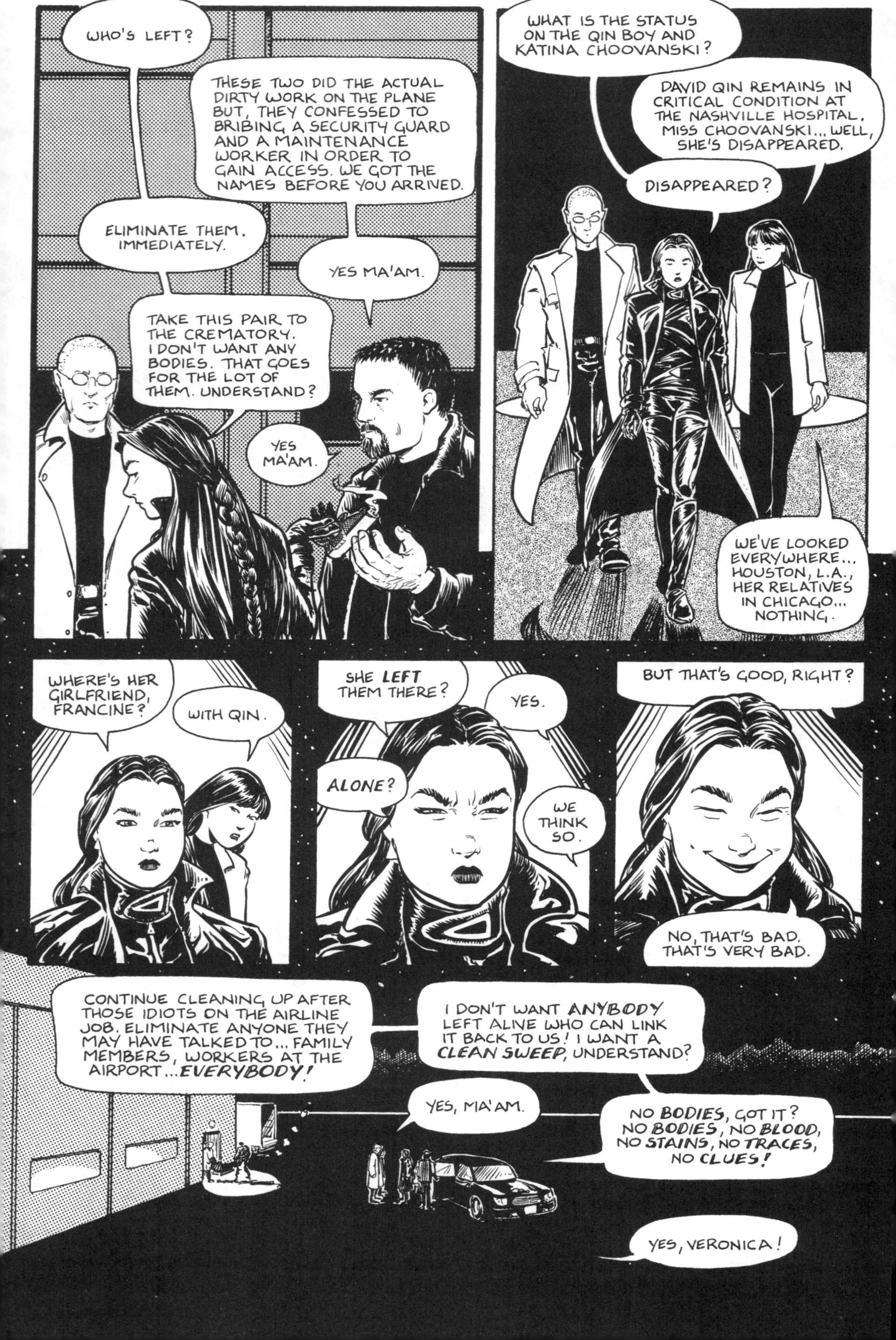
WHO'S LEFT?
THESE TWO DID THE ACTUAL DIRTY WORK ON THE PLANE BUT, THEY CONFESSED TO BRIBING A SECURITY GUARD AND A MAINTENANCE WORKER IN ORDER TO GAIN ACCESS. WE GOT THE NAMES BEFORE YOU ARRIVED.
ELIMINATE THEM. IMMEDIATELY.
YES MA'AM.
TAKE THIS PAIR TO THE CREMATORY. I DON'T WANT ANY BODIES. THAT GOES FOR THE LOT OF THEM. UNDERSTAND?
YES MA'AM.
WHAT IS THE STATUS ON THE QIN BOY AND KATINA CHOOVANSKI?
DAVID QIN REMAINS IN CRITICAL CONDITION AT THE NASHVILLE HOSPITAL. MISS CHOOVANSKI... WELL, SHE'S DISAPPEARED.
DISAPPEARED?
WE'VE LOOKED EVERYWHERE... HOUSTON, L.A., HER RELATIVES IN CHICAGO... NOTHING.
WHERE'S HER GIRLFRIEND, FRANCINE?
WITH QIN.
SHE **LEFT** THEM THERE?
YES.
**ALONE**?
WE THINK SO.
BUT THAT'S GOOD, RIGHT?
NO, THAT'S BAD. THAT'S VERY BAD.
CONTINUE CLEANING UP AFTER THOSE IDIOTS ON THE AIRLINE JOB. ELIMINATE ANYONE THEY MAY HAVE TALKED TO... FAMILY MEMBERS, WORKERS AT THE AIRPORT... **EVERYBODY!**
I DON'T WANT **ANYBODY** LEFT ALIVE WHO CAN LINK IT BACK TO US! I WANT A **CLEAN SWEEP**, UNDERSTAND?
YES, MA'AM.
NO **BODIES**, GOT IT? NO **BODIES**, NO **BLOOD**, NO **STAINS**, NO **TRACES**, NO **CLUES!**
YES, VERONICA!

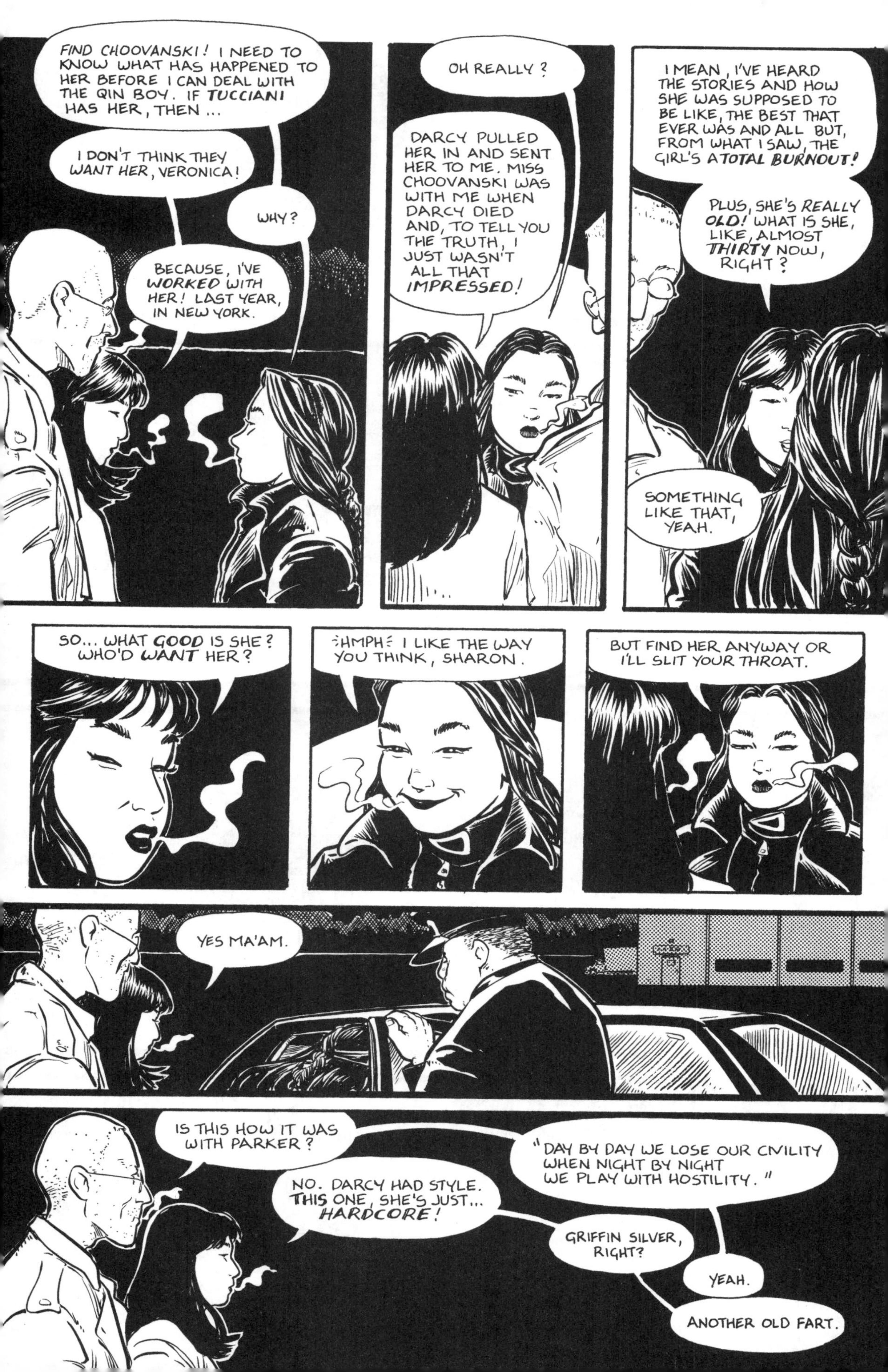

FIND CHOOVANSKI! I NEED TO KNOW WHAT HAS HAPPENED TO HER BEFORE I CAN DEAL WITH THE QIN BOY. IF TUCCIANI HAS HER, THEN ...
I DON'T THINK THEY WANT HER, VERONICA!
WHY?
BECAUSE, I'VE WORKED WITH HER! LAST YEAR, IN NEW YORK.
OH REALLY?
DARCY PULLED HER IN AND SENT HER TO ME. MISS CHOOVANSKI WAS WITH ME WHEN DARCY DIED AND, TO TELL YOU THE TRUTH, I JUST WASN'T ALL THAT IMPRESSED!
I MEAN, I'VE HEARD THE STORIES AND HOW SHE WAS SUPPOSED TO BE LIKE, THE BEST THAT EVER WAS AND ALL BUT, FROM WHAT I SAW, THE GIRL'S A TOTAL BURNOUT!
PLUS, SHE'S REALLY OLD! WHAT IS SHE, LIKE, ALMOST THIRTY NOW, RIGHT?
SOMETHING LIKE THAT, YEAH.
SO... WHAT GOOD IS SHE? WHO'D WANT HER?
HMPH I LIKE THE WAY YOU THINK, SHARON.
BUT FIND HER ANYWAY OR I'LL SLIT YOUR THROAT.
YES MA'AM.
IS THIS HOW IT WAS WITH PARKER?
NO. DARCY HAD STYLE. THIS ONE, SHE'S JUST... HARDCORE!
"DAY BY DAY WE LOSE OUR CIVILITY WHEN NIGHT BY NIGHT WE PLAY WITH HOSTILITY."
GRIFFIN SILVER, RIGHT?
YEAH.
ANOTHER OLD FART.

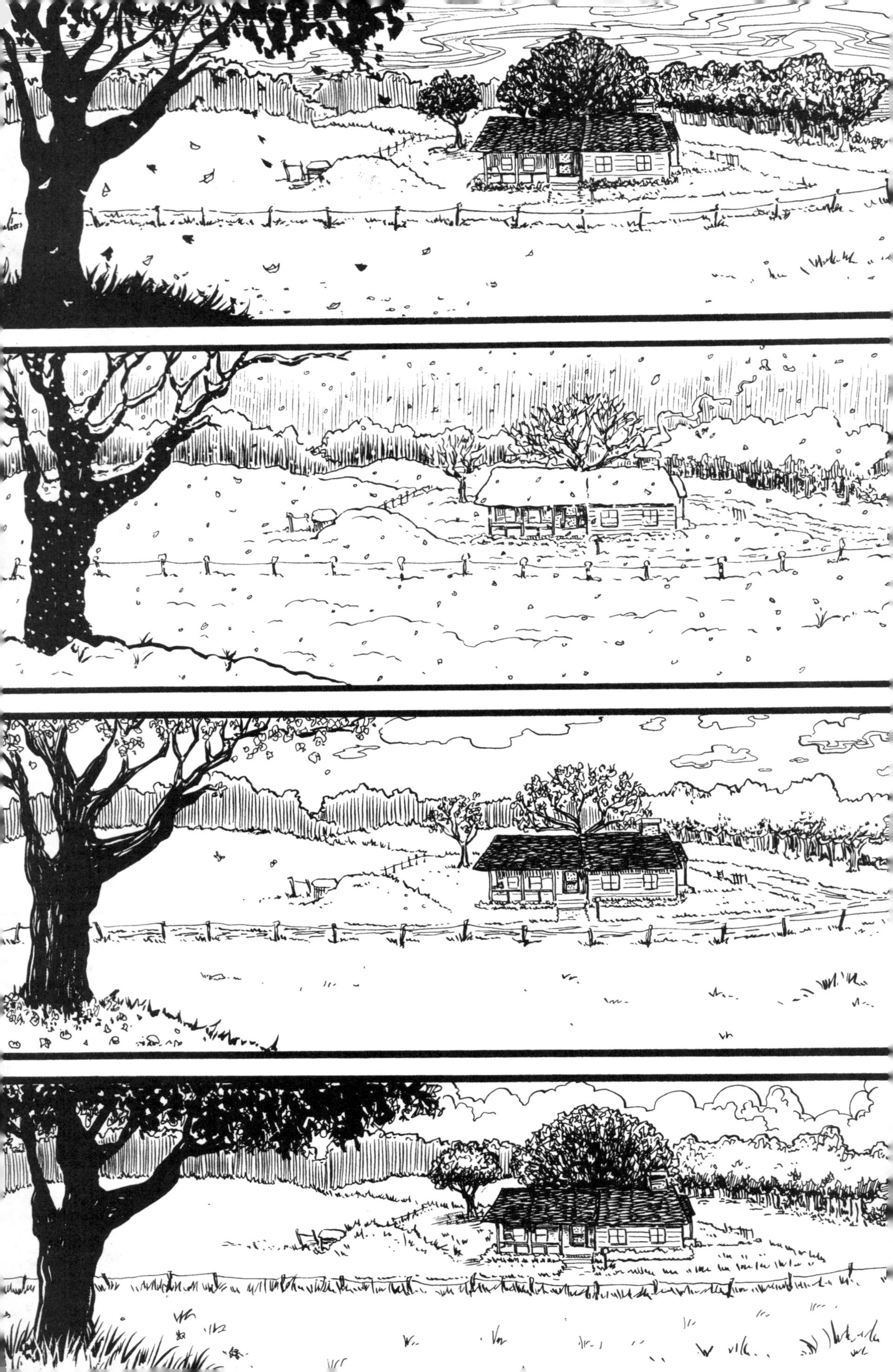

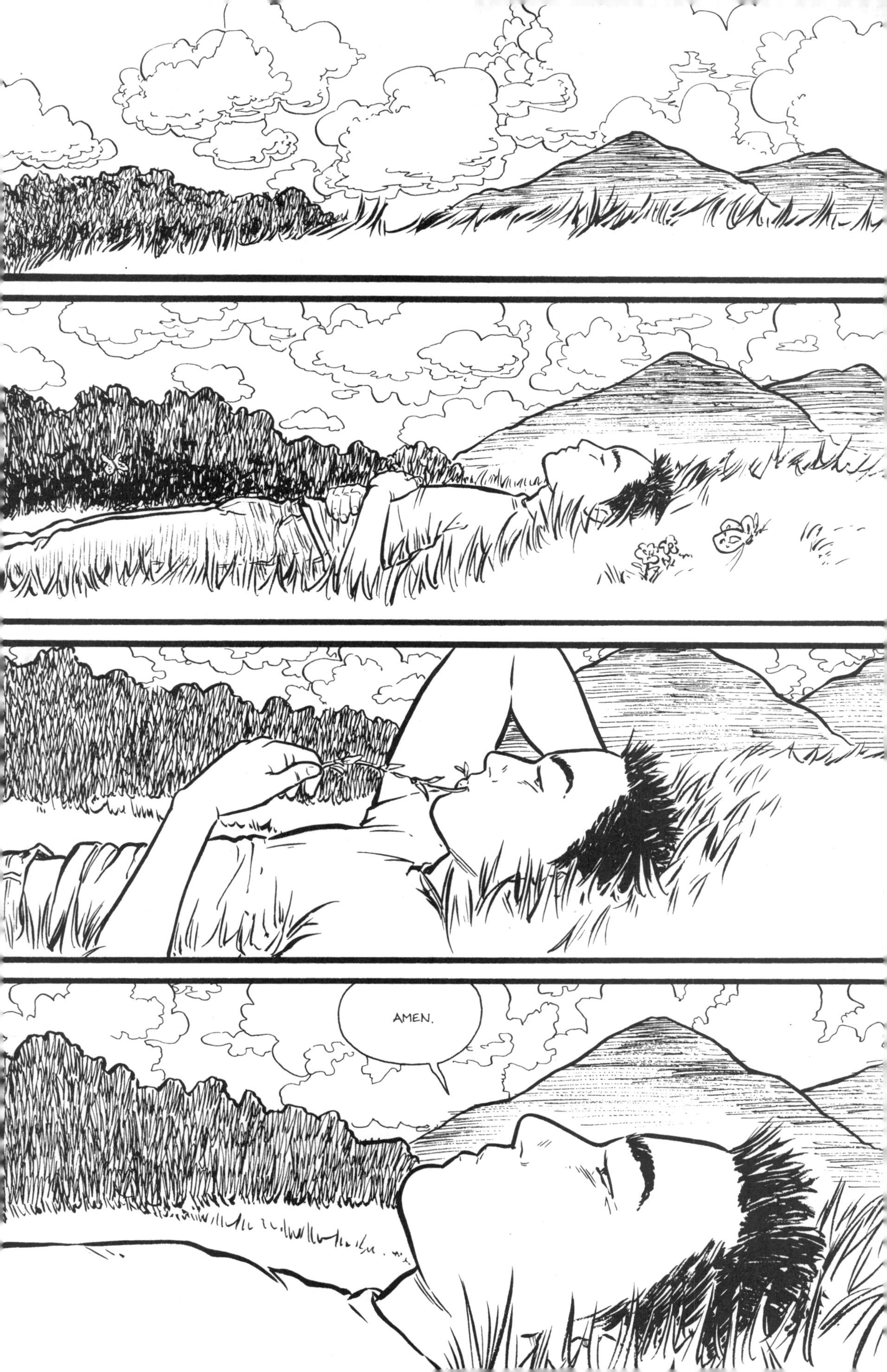
AMEN.

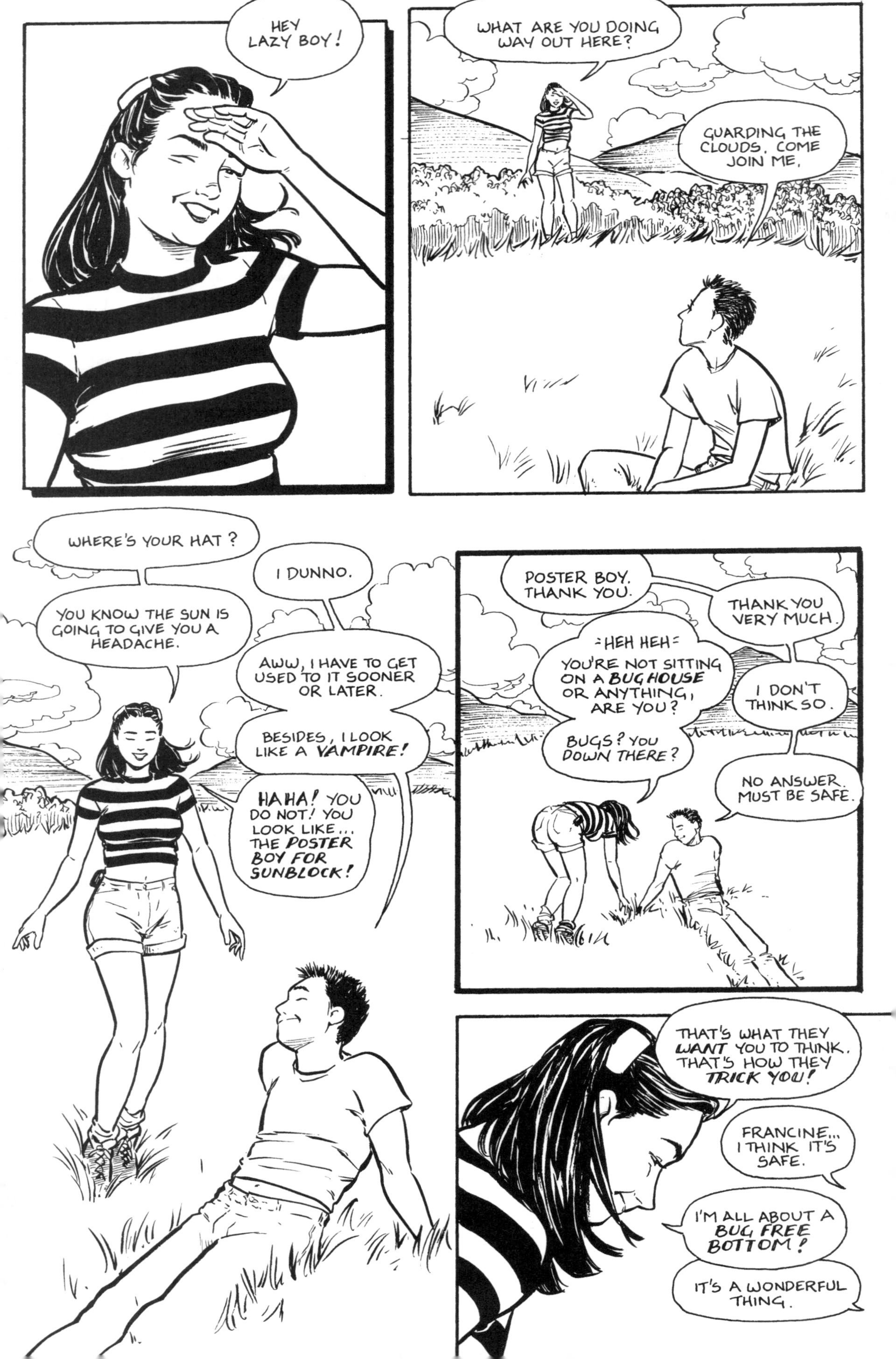
HEY LAZY BOY!
WHAT ARE YOU DOING WAY OUT HERE?
GUARDING THE CLOUDS. COME JOIN ME.
WHERE'S YOUR HAT?
YOU KNOW THE SUN IS GOING TO GIVE YOU A HEADACHE.
I DUNNO.
AWW, I HAVE TO GET USED TO IT SOONER OR LATER.
BESIDES, I LOOK LIKE A VAMPIRE!
HAHA! YOU DO NOT! YOU LOOK LIKE... THE POSTER BOY FOR SUNBLOCK!
POSTER BOY. THANK YOU.
THANK YOU VERY MUCH.
=HEH HEH=
YOU'RE NOT SITTING ON A BUG HOUSE OR ANYTHING, ARE YOU?
BUGS? YOU DOWN THERE?
I DON'T THINK SO.
NO ANSWER. MUST BE SAFE.
THAT'S WHAT THEY WANT YOU TO THINK. THAT'S HOW THEY TRICK YOU!
FRANCINE... I THINK IT'S SAFE.
I'M ALL ABOUT A BUG FREE BOTTOM!
IT'S A WONDERFUL THING.

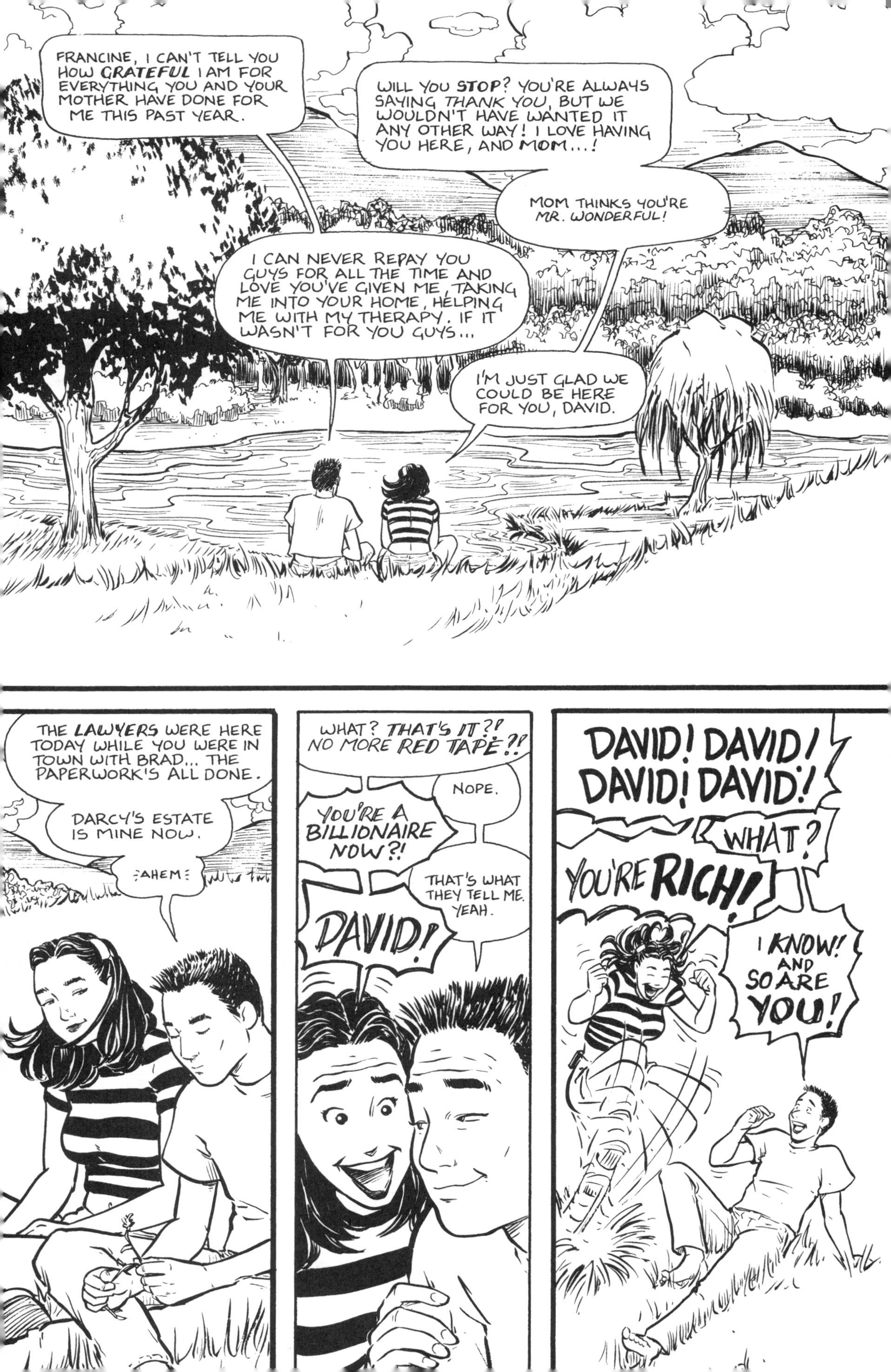
FRANCINE, I CAN'T TELL YOU HOW GRATEFUL I AM FOR EVERYTHING YOU AND YOUR MOTHER HAVE DONE FOR ME THIS PAST YEAR.
WILL YOU STOP? YOU'RE ALWAYS SAYING THANK YOU, BUT WE WOULDN'T HAVE WANTED IT ANY OTHER WAY! I LOVE HAVING YOU HERE, AND MOM...!
MOM THINKS YOU'RE MR. WONDERFUL!
I CAN NEVER REPAY YOU GUYS FOR ALL THE TIME AND LOVE YOU'VE GIVEN ME, TAKING ME INTO YOUR HOME, HELPING ME WITH MY THERAPY. IF IT WASN'T FOR YOU GUYS...
I'M JUST GLAD WE COULD BE HERE FOR YOU, DAVID.
THE LAWYERS WERE HERE TODAY WHILE YOU WERE IN TOWN WITH BRAD... THE PAPERWORK'S ALL DONE.
DARCY'S ESTATE IS MINE NOW.
AHEM
WHAT? THAT'S IT?! NO MORE RED TAPE?!
NOPE.
YOU'RE A BILLIONAIRE NOW?!
THAT'S WHAT THEY TELL ME. YEAH.
DAVID!
DAVID! DAVID! DAVID! DAVID!
WHAT?
YOU'RE RICH!
I KNOW! AND SO ARE YOU!

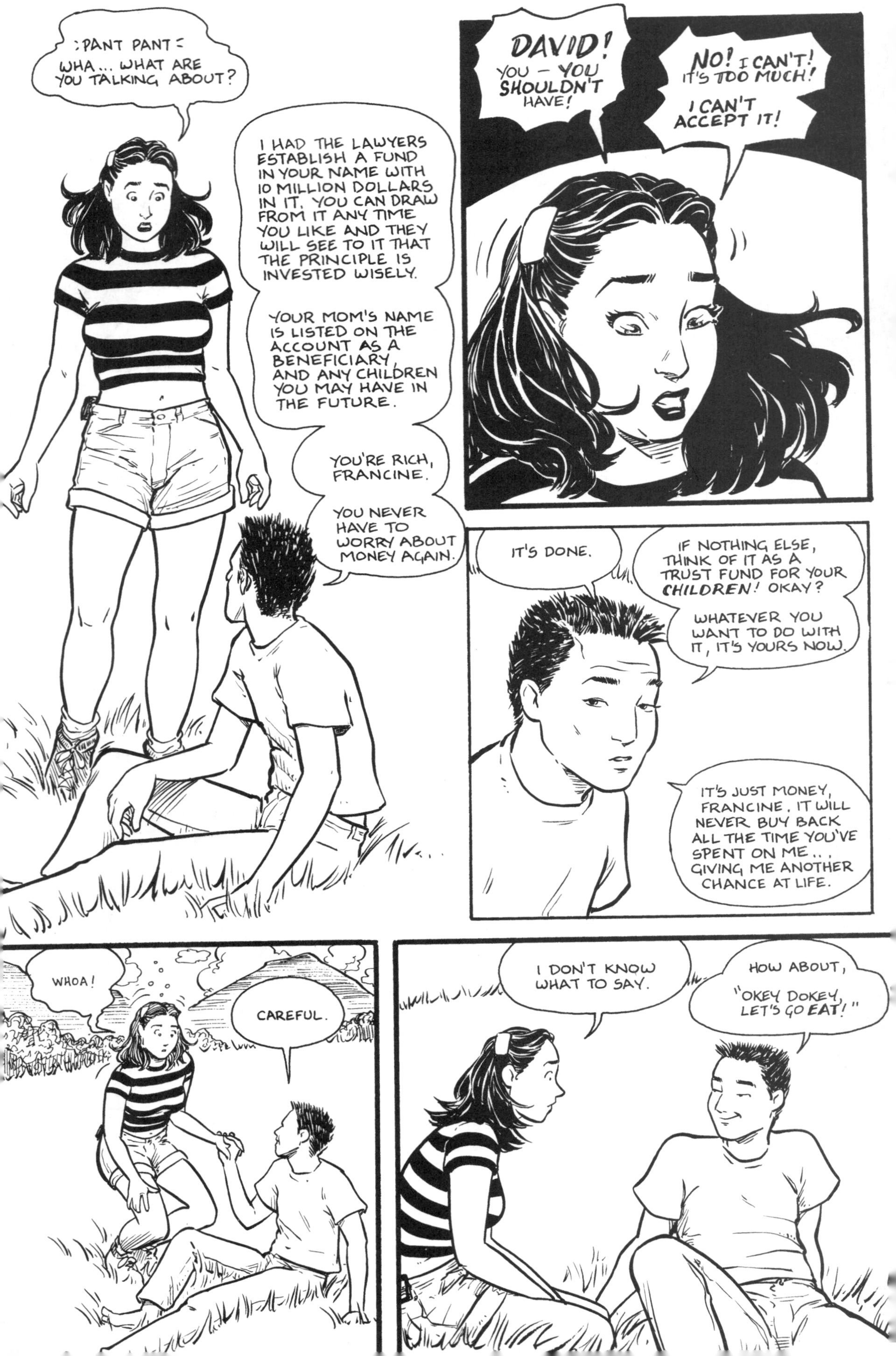
:PANT PANT:
WHA... WHAT ARE YOU TALKING ABOUT?
I HAD THE LAWYERS ESTABLISH A FUND IN YOUR NAME WITH 10 MILLION DOLLARS IN IT. YOU CAN DRAW FROM IT ANY TIME YOU LIKE AND THEY WILL SEE TO IT THAT THE PRINCIPLE IS INVESTED WISELY.
YOUR MOM'S NAME IS LISTED ON THE ACCOUNT AS A BENEFICIARY, AND ANY CHILDREN YOU MAY HAVE IN THE FUTURE.
YOU'RE RICH, FRANCINE.
YOU NEVER HAVE TO WORRY ABOUT MONEY AGAIN.
DAVID! YOU — YOU SHOULDN'T HAVE!
NO! I CAN'T! IT'S TOO MUCH!
I CAN'T ACCEPT IT!
IT'S DONE.
IF NOTHING ELSE, THINK OF IT AS A TRUST FUND FOR YOUR CHILDREN! OKAY?
WHATEVER YOU WANT TO DO WITH IT, IT'S YOURS NOW.
IT'S JUST MONEY, FRANCINE. IT WILL NEVER BUY BACK ALL THE TIME YOU'VE SPENT ON ME... GIVING ME ANOTHER CHANCE AT LIFE.
WHOA!
CAREFUL.
I DON'T KNOW WHAT TO SAY.
HOW ABOUT, "OKEY DOKEY, LET'S GO EAT!"

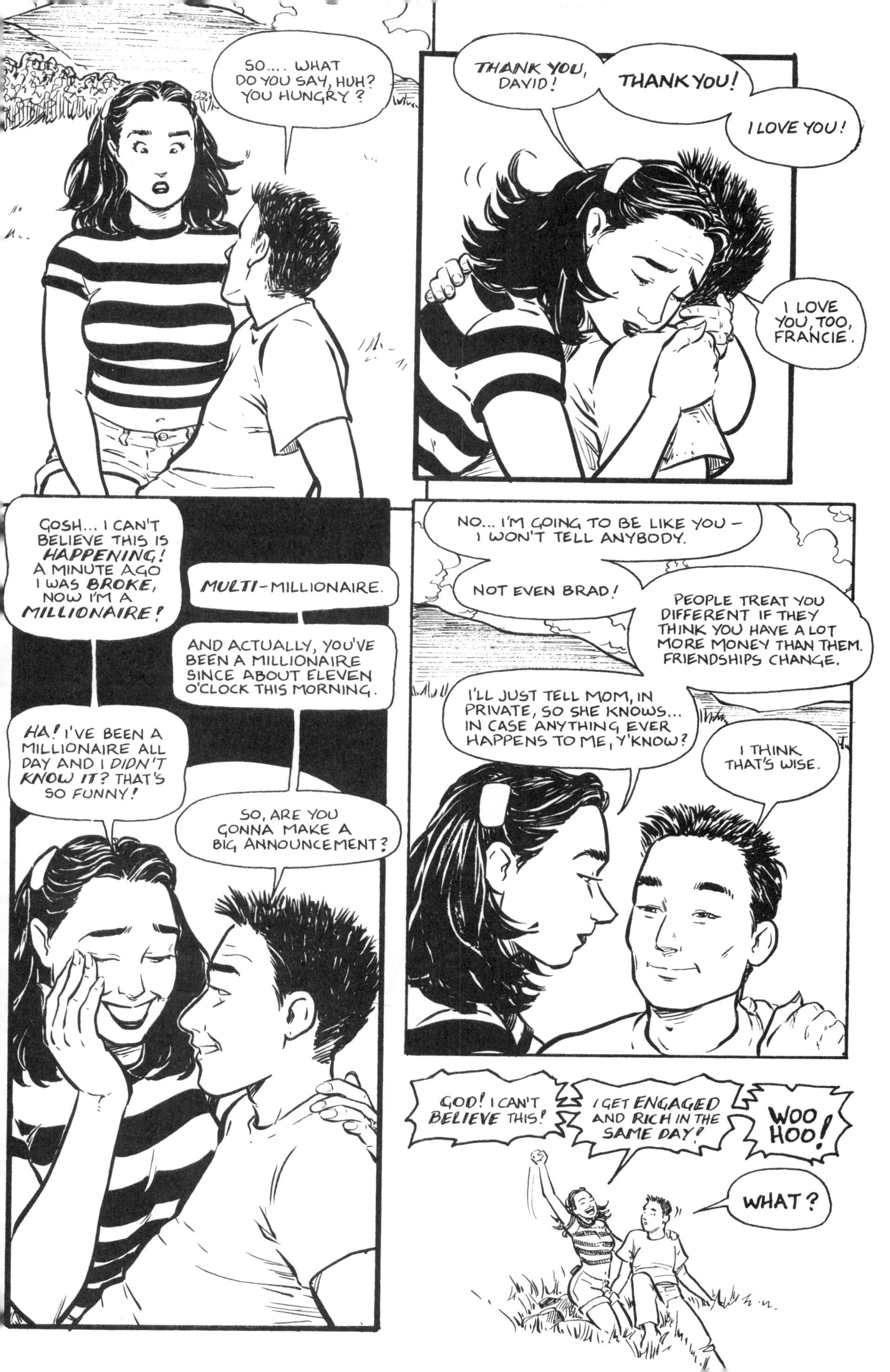
SO.... WHAT DO YOU SAY, HUH? YOU HUNGRY?
THANK YOU, DAVID!
THANK YOU!
I LOVE YOU!
I LOVE YOU, TOO, FRANCIE.
GOSH... I CAN'T BELIEVE THIS IS HAPPENING! A MINUTE AGO I WAS BROKE, NOW I'M A MILLIONAIRE!
MULTI-MILLIONAIRE.
AND ACTUALLY, YOU'VE BEEN A MILLIONAIRE SINCE ABOUT ELEVEN O'CLOCK THIS MORNING.
HA! I'VE BEEN A MILLIONAIRE ALL DAY AND I DIDN'T KNOW IT? THAT'S SO FUNNY!
SO, ARE YOU GONNA MAKE A BIG ANNOUNCEMENT?
NO... I'M GOING TO BE LIKE YOU – I WON'T TELL ANYBODY.
NOT EVEN BRAD!
PEOPLE TREAT YOU DIFFERENT IF THEY THINK YOU HAVE A LOT MORE MONEY THAN THEM. FRIENDSHIPS CHANGE.
I'LL JUST TELL MOM, IN PRIVATE, SO SHE KNOWS... IN CASE ANYTHING EVER HAPPENS TO ME, Y'KNOW?
I THINK THAT'S WISE.
GOD! I CAN'T BELIEVE THIS!
I GET ENGAGED AND RICH IN THE SAME DAY!
WOO HOO!
WHAT?

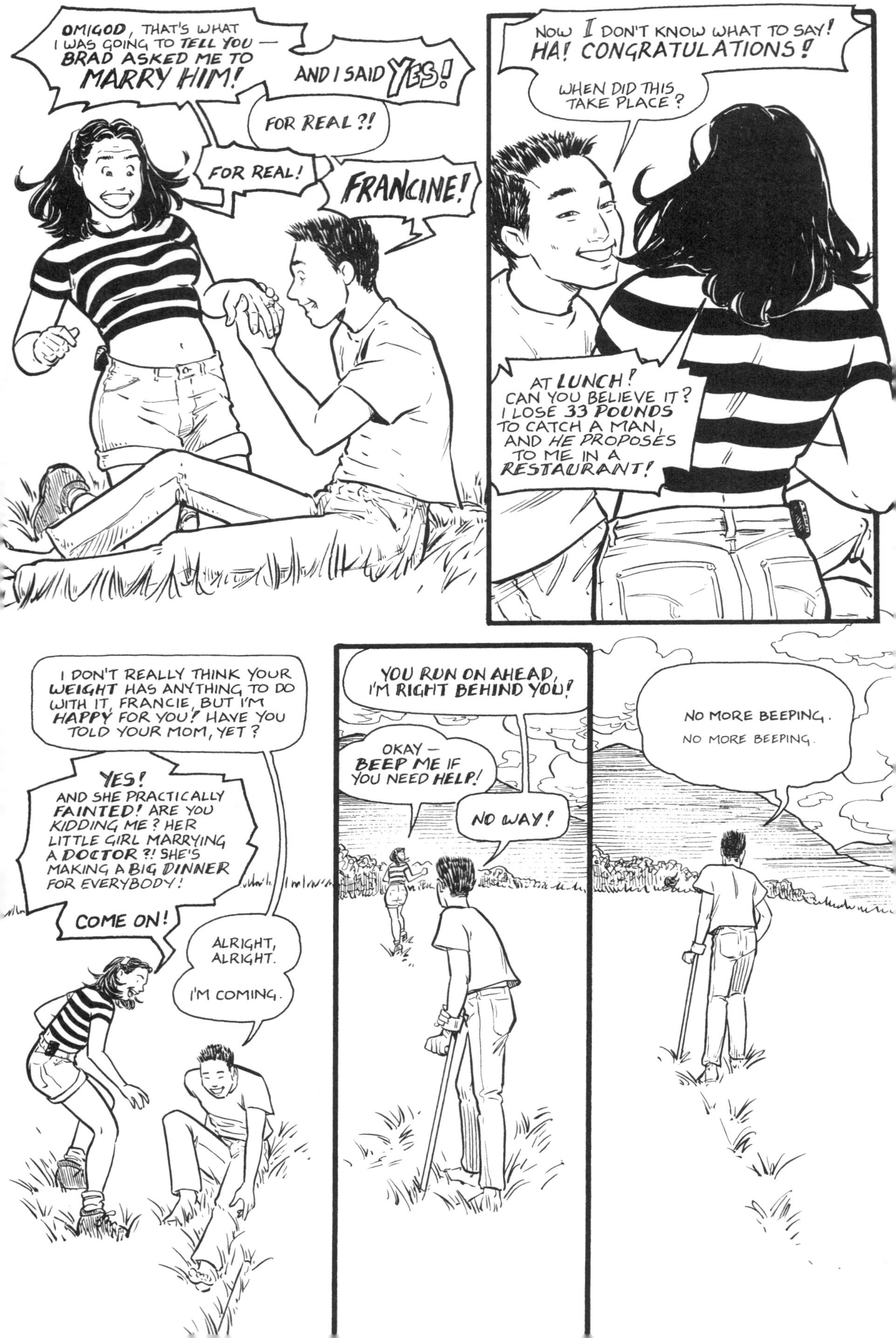

OMIGOD, THAT'S WHAT I WAS GOING TO TELL YOU — BRAD ASKED ME TO MARRY HIM!
AND I SAID YES!
FOR REAL?!
FOR REAL!
FRANCINE!
NOW I DON'T KNOW WHAT TO SAY! HA! CONGRATULATIONS!
WHEN DID THIS TAKE PLACE?
AT LUNCH! CAN YOU BELIEVE IT? I LOSE 33 POUNDS TO CATCH A MAN, AND HE PROPOSES TO ME IN A RESTAURANT!
I DON'T REALLY THINK YOUR WEIGHT HAS ANYTHING TO DO WITH IT, FRANCIE, BUT I'M HAPPY FOR YOU! HAVE YOU TOLD YOUR MOM, YET?
YES! AND SHE PRACTICALLY FAINTED! ARE YOU KIDDING ME? HER LITTLE GIRL MARRYING A DOCTOR?! SHE'S MAKING A BIG DINNER FOR EVERYBODY!
COME ON!
ALRIGHT, ALRIGHT.
I'M COMING.
YOU RUN ON AHEAD, I'M RIGHT BEHIND YOU!
OKAY — BEEP ME IF YOU NEED HELP!
NO WAY!
NO MORE BEEPING.
NO MORE BEEPING.

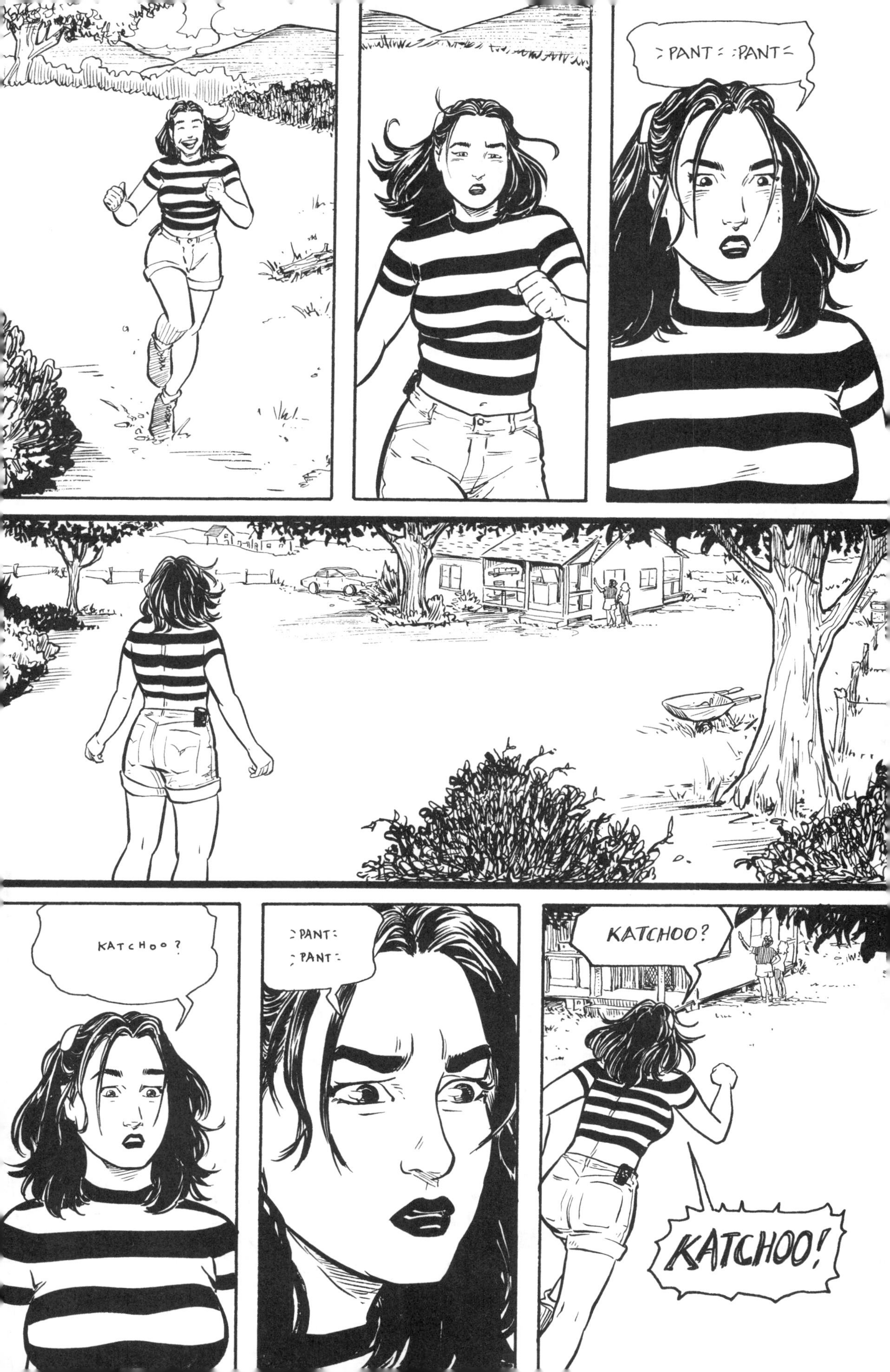

PANT PANT
KATCHOO?
PANT
PANT
KATCHOO?
KATCHOO!

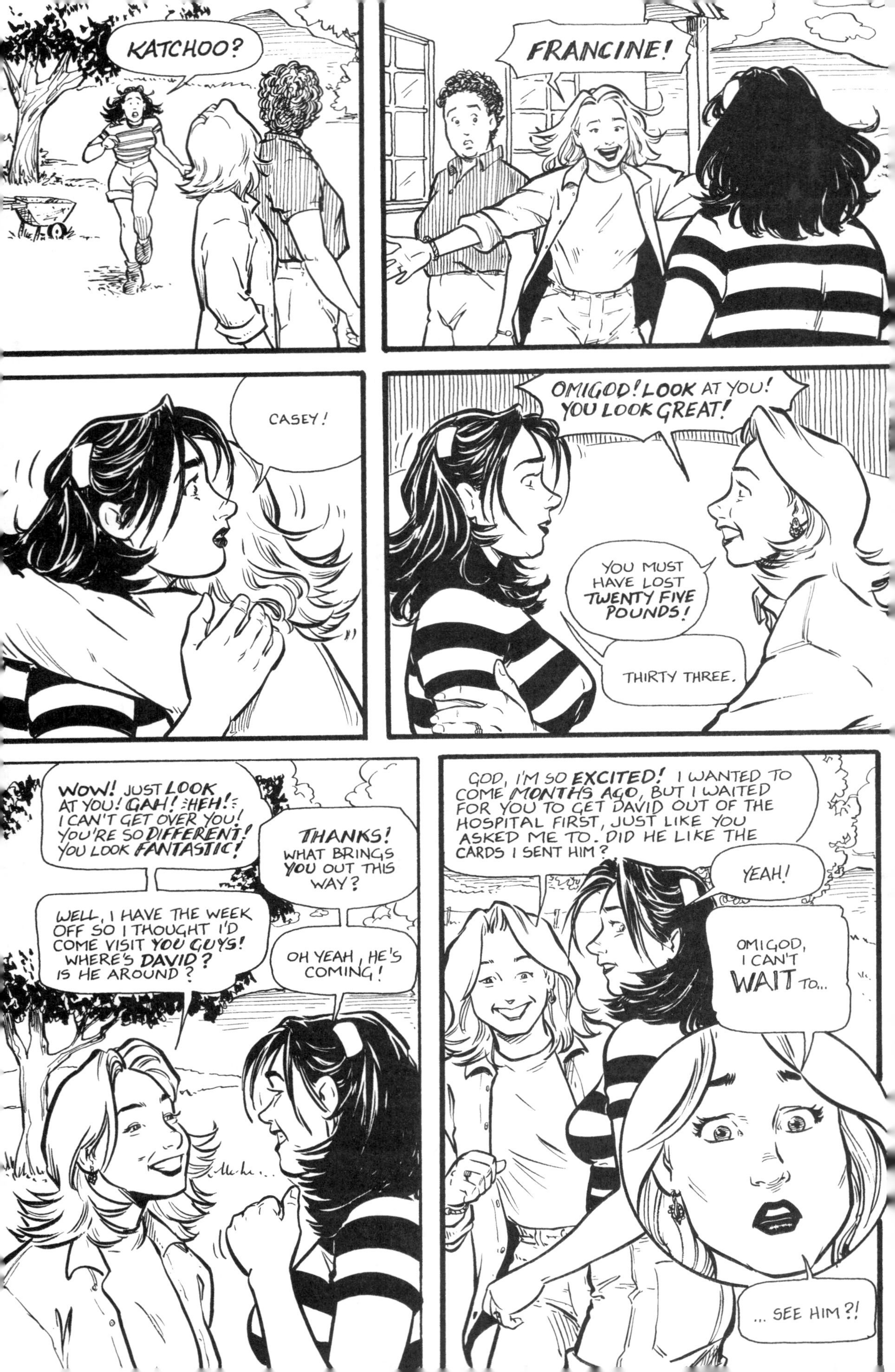
KATCHOO?
FRANCINE!
CASEY!
OMIGOD! LOOK AT YOU! YOU LOOK GREAT!
YOU MUST HAVE LOST TWENTY FIVE POUNDS!
THIRTY THREE.
WOW! JUST LOOK AT YOU! GAH! HEH! I CAN'T GET OVER YOU! YOU'RE SO DIFFERENT! YOU LOOK FANTASTIC!
THANKS! WHAT BRINGS YOU OUT THIS WAY?
WELL, I HAVE THE WEEK OFF SO I THOUGHT I'D COME VISIT YOU GUYS! WHERE'S DAVID? IS HE AROUND?
OH YEAH, HE'S COMING!
GOD, I'M SO EXCITED! I WANTED TO COME MONTHS AGO, BUT I WAITED FOR YOU TO GET DAVID OUT OF THE HOSPITAL FIRST, JUST LIKE YOU ASKED ME TO. DID HE LIKE THE CARDS I SENT HIM?
YEAH!
OMIGOD, I CAN'T WAIT TO...
... SEE HIM?!

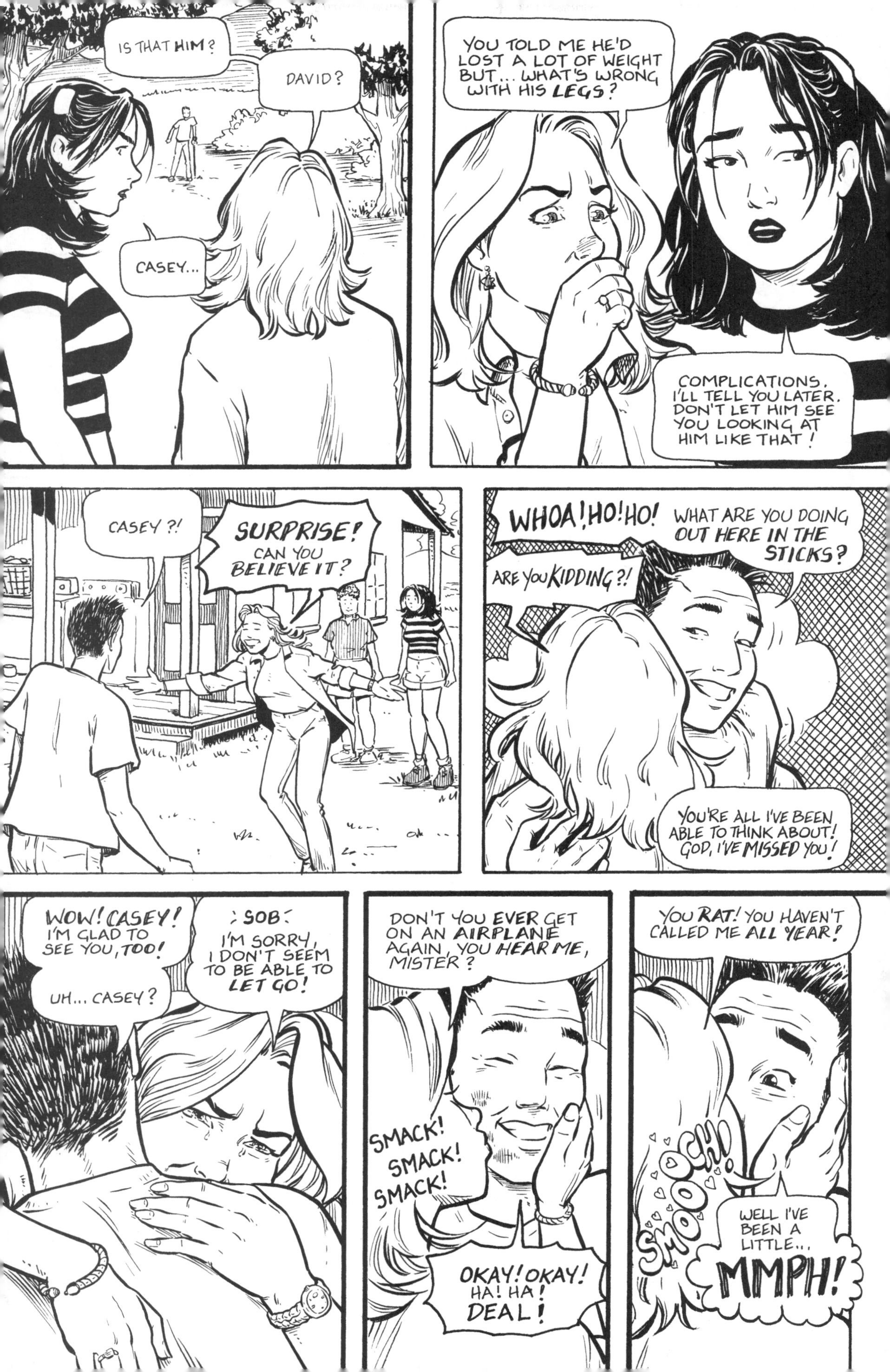
IS THAT HIM?
DAVID?
CASEY...
YOU TOLD ME HE'D LOST A LOT OF WEIGHT BUT... WHAT'S WRONG WITH HIS LEGS?
COMPLICATIONS. I'LL TELL YOU LATER. DON'T LET HIM SEE YOU LOOKING AT HIM LIKE THAT!
CASEY?!
SURPRISE! CAN YOU BELIEVE IT?
WHOA! HO! HO!
WHAT ARE YOU DOING OUT HERE IN THE STICKS?
ARE YOU KIDDING?!
YOU'RE ALL I'VE BEEN ABLE TO THINK ABOUT! GOD, I'VE MISSED YOU!
WOW! CASEY! I'M GLAD TO SEE YOU, TOO!
UH... CASEY?
SOB
I'M SORRY, I DON'T SEEM TO BE ABLE TO LET GO!
DON'T YOU EVER GET ON AN AIRPLANE AGAIN, YOU HEAR ME, MISTER?
SMACK! SMACK! SMACK!
OKAY! OKAY! HA! HA! DEAL!
YOU RAT! YOU HAVEN'T CALLED ME ALL YEAR!
SMOOOOCH!
WELL I'VE BEEN A LITTLE...
MMPH!

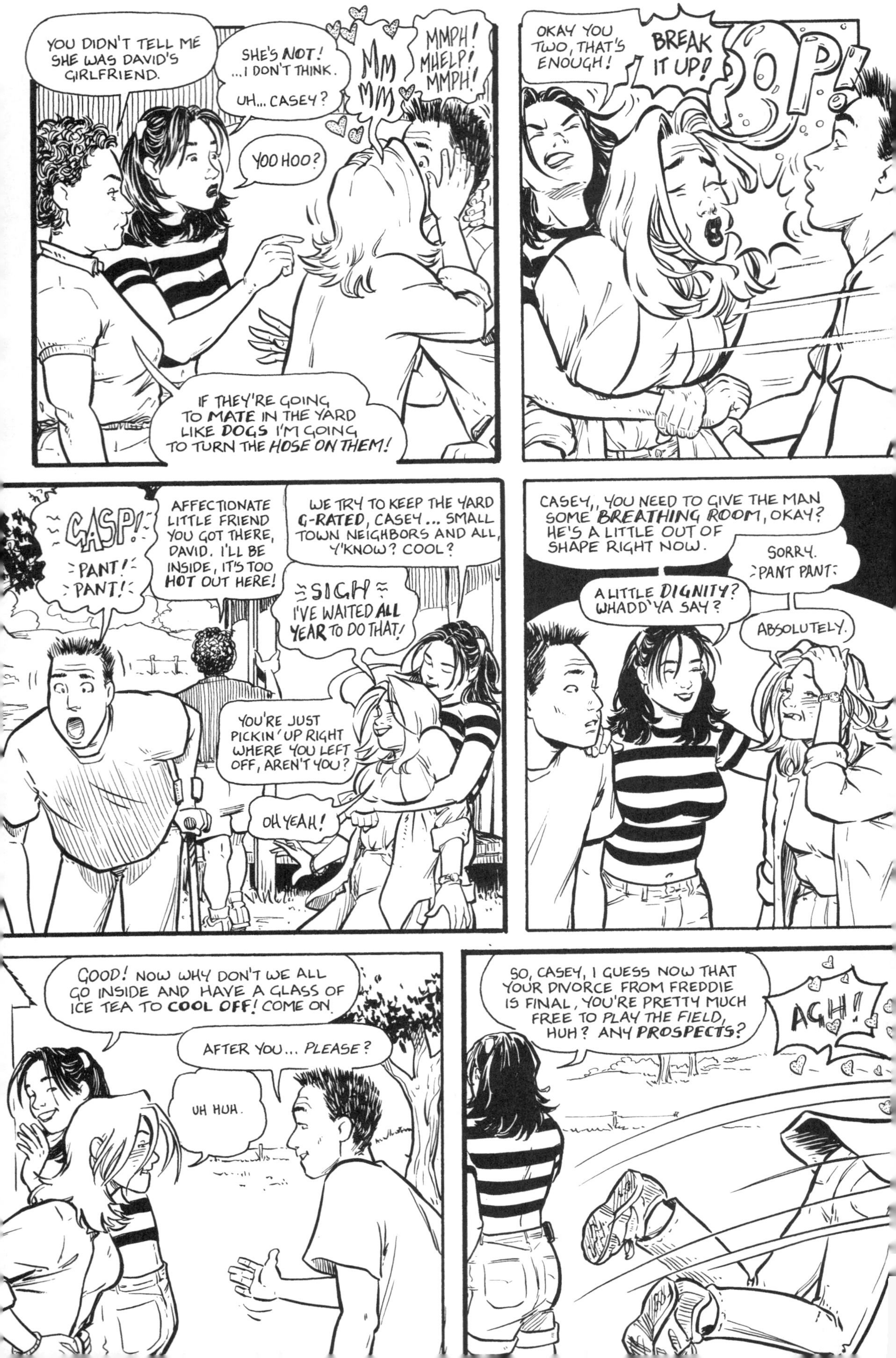

YOU DIDN'T TELL ME SHE WAS DAVID'S GIRLFRIEND.
SHE'S NOT! ...I DON'T THINK.
UH... CASEY?
YOO HOO?
MM MM
MMPH! MHELP! MMPH!
IF THEY'RE GOING TO MATE IN THE YARD LIKE DOGS I'M GOING TO TURN THE HOSE ON THEM!
OKAY YOU TWO, THAT'S ENOUGH!
BREAK IT UP!
POP!
GASP!
PANT! PANT!
AFFECTIONATE LITTLE FRIEND YOU GOT THERE, DAVID. I'LL BE INSIDE, IT'S TOO HOT OUT HERE!
WE TRY TO KEEP THE YARD G-RATED, CASEY... SMALL TOWN NEIGHBORS AND ALL, Y'KNOW? COOL?
SIGH
I'VE WAITED ALL YEAR TO DO THAT!
YOU'RE JUST PICKIN' UP RIGHT WHERE YOU LEFT OFF, AREN'T YOU?
OH YEAH!
CASEY,, YOU NEED TO GIVE THE MAN SOME BREATHING ROOM, OKAY? HE'S A LITTLE OUT OF SHAPE RIGHT NOW.
SORRY. PANT PANT
A LITTLE DIGNITY? WHADD'YA SAY?
ABSOLUTELY.
GOOD! NOW WHY DON'T WE ALL GO INSIDE AND HAVE A GLASS OF ICE TEA TO COOL OFF! COME ON.
AFTER YOU... PLEASE?
UH HUH.
SO, CASEY, I GUESS NOW THAT YOUR DIVORCE FROM FREDDIE IS FINAL, YOU'RE PRETTY MUCH FREE TO PLAY THE FIELD, HUH? ANY PROSPECTS?
AGH!!

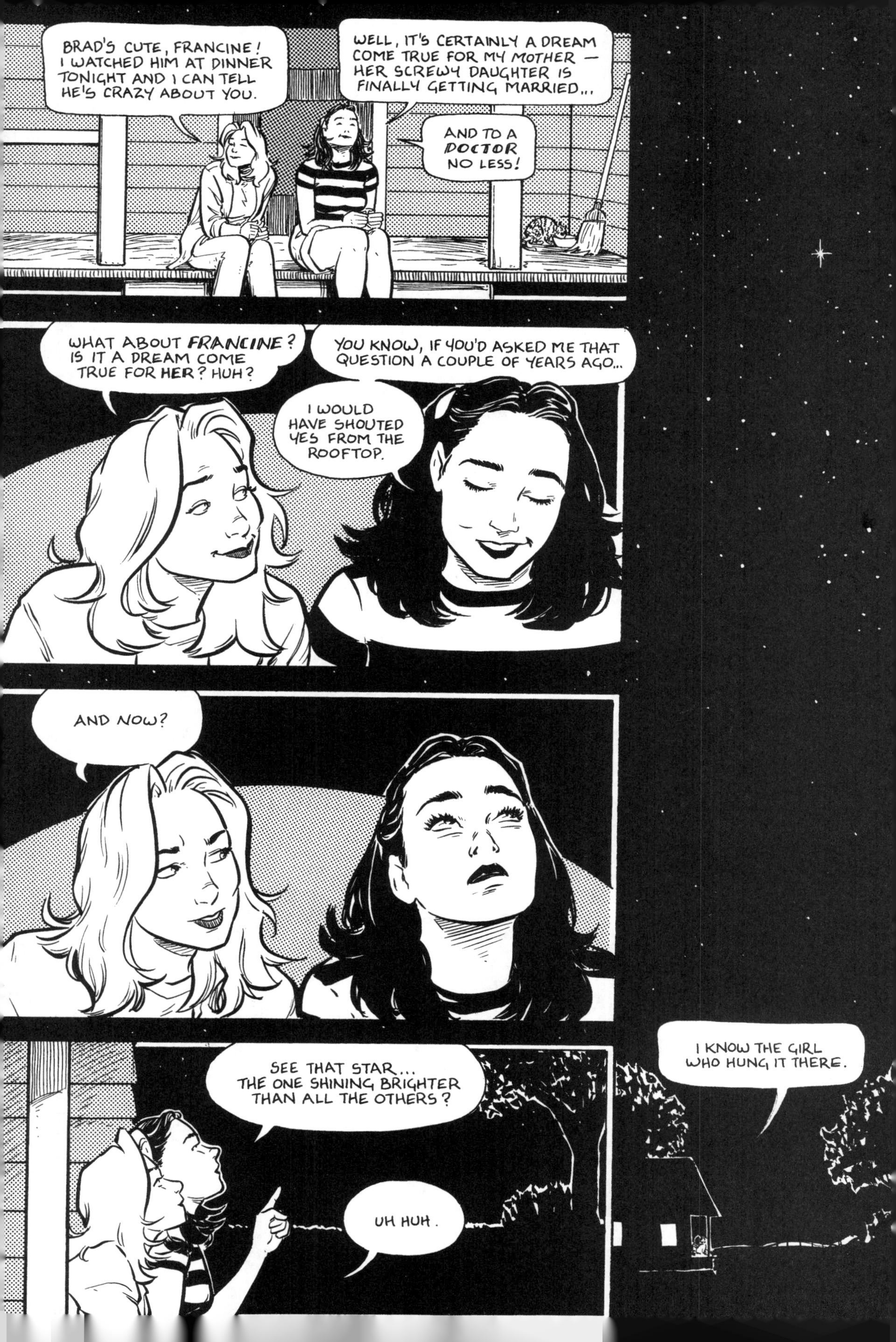

BRAD'S CUTE, FRANCINE! I WATCHED HIM AT DINNER TONIGHT AND I CAN TELL HE'S CRAZY ABOUT YOU.
WELL, IT'S CERTAINLY A DREAM COME TRUE FOR MY MOTHER — HER SCREWY DAUGHTER IS FINALLY GETTING MARRIED...
AND TO A DOCTOR NO LESS!
WHAT ABOUT FRANCINE? IS IT A DREAM COME TRUE FOR HER? HUH?
YOU KNOW, IF YOU'D ASKED ME THAT QUESTION A COUPLE OF YEARS AGO...
I WOULD HAVE SHOUTED YES FROM THE ROOFTOP.
AND NOW?
SEE THAT STAR... THE ONE SHINING BRIGHTER THAN ALL THE OTHERS?
UH HUH.
I KNOW THE GIRL WHO HUNG IT THERE.

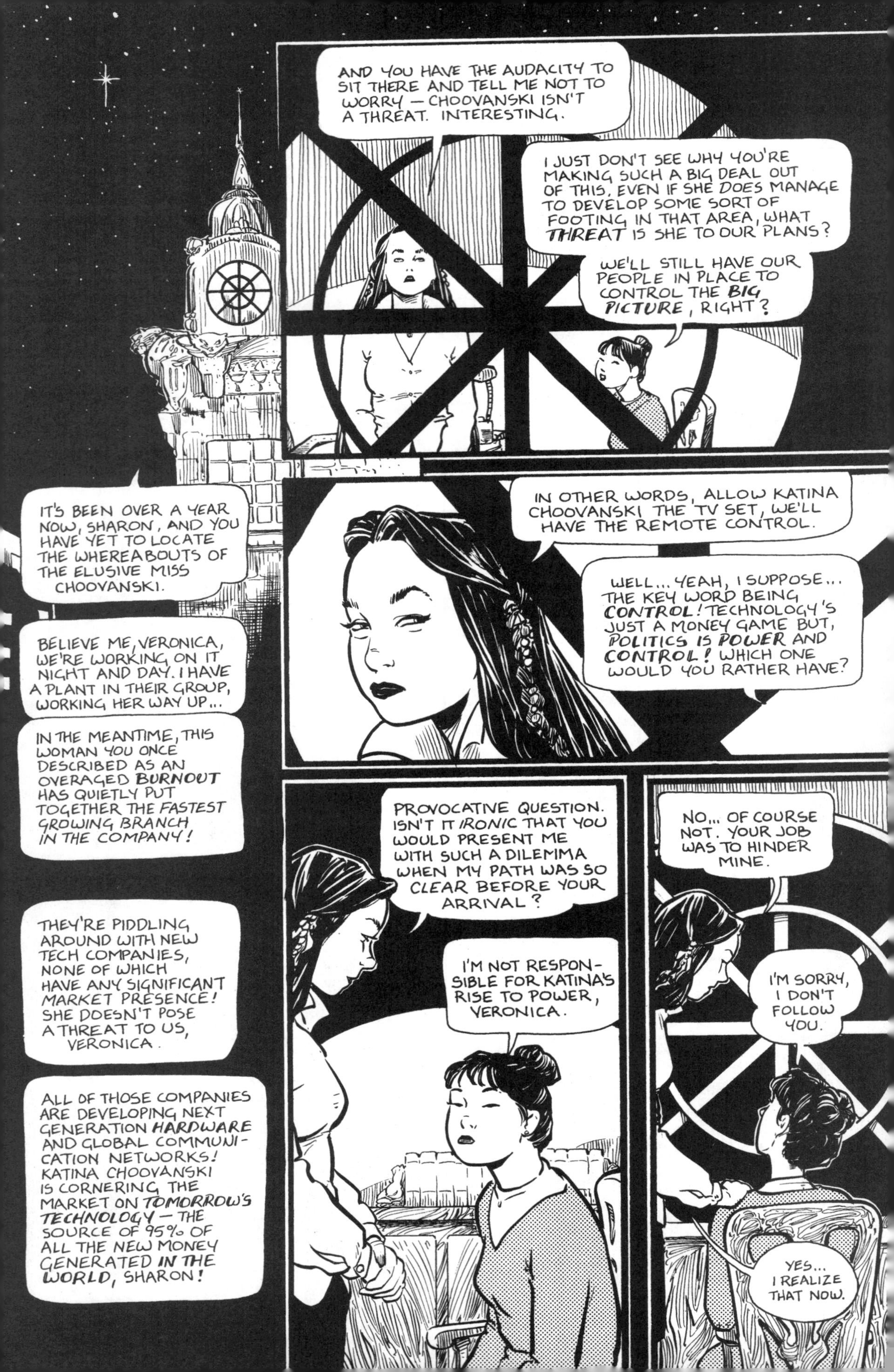
IT'S BEEN OVER A YEAR NOW, SHARON, AND YOU HAVE YET TO LOCATE THE WHEREABOUTS OF THE ELUSIVE MISS CHOOVANSKI.
BELIEVE ME, VERONICA, WE'RE WORKING ON IT NIGHT AND DAY. I HAVE A PLANT IN THEIR GROUP, WORKING HER WAY UP...
IN THE MEANTIME, THIS WOMAN *YOU* ONCE DESCRIBED AS AN OVERAGED **BURNOUT** HAS QUIETLY PUT TOGETHER THE *FASTEST GROWING BRANCH IN THE COMPANY!*
THEY'RE PIDDLING AROUND WITH NEW TECH COMPANIES, NONE OF WHICH HAVE ANY SIGNIFICANT *MARKET PRESENCE!* SHE DOESN'T POSE A THREAT TO US, VERONICA.
ALL OF THOSE COMPANIES ARE DEVELOPING NEXT GENERATION **HARDWARE** AND GLOBAL COMMUNICATION NETWORKS! KATINA CHOOVANSKI IS CORNERING THE MARKET ON ***TOMORROW'S TECHNOLOGY*** — THE SOURCE OF 95% OF ALL THE NEW MONEY GENERATED **IN THE WORLD**, SHARON!
AND YOU HAVE THE AUDACITY TO SIT THERE AND TELL ME NOT TO WORRY — CHOOVANSKI ISN'T A THREAT. INTERESTING.
I JUST DON'T SEE WHY YOU'RE MAKING SUCH A BIG DEAL OUT OF THIS. EVEN IF SHE *DOES* MANAGE TO DEVELOP SOME SORT OF FOOTING IN THAT AREA, WHAT **THREAT** IS SHE TO OUR PLANS?
WE'LL STILL HAVE OUR PEOPLE IN PLACE TO CONTROL THE ***BIG PICTURE***, RIGHT?
IN OTHER WORDS, ALLOW KATINA CHOOVANSKI THE TV SET, WE'LL HAVE THE REMOTE CONTROL.
WELL... YEAH, I SUPPOSE... THE KEY WORD BEING **CONTROL!** TECHNOLOGY'S JUST A MONEY GAME BUT, ***POLITICS IS POWER*** AND **CONTROL!** WHICH ONE WOULD YOU RATHER HAVE?
PROVOCATIVE QUESTION. ISN'T IT *IRONIC* THAT YOU WOULD PRESENT ME WITH SUCH A DILEMMA WHEN MY PATH WAS SO *CLEAR* BEFORE YOUR ARRIVAL?
I'M NOT RESPONSIBLE FOR KATINA'S RISE TO POWER, VERONICA.
NO... OF COURSE NOT. YOUR JOB WAS TO HINDER MINE.
I'M SORRY, I DON'T FOLLOW YOU.
YES... I REALIZE THAT NOW.

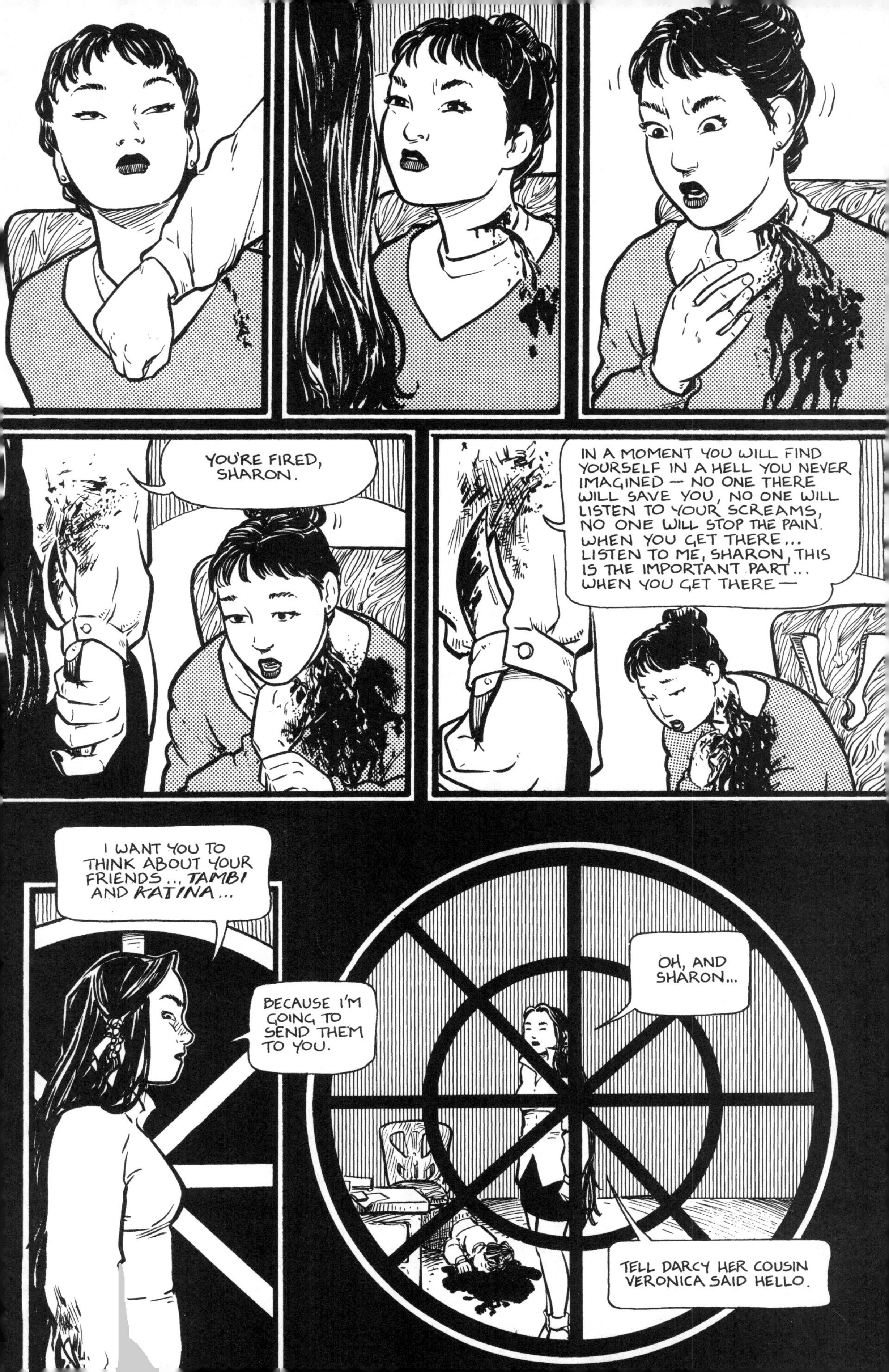
YOU'RE FIRED, SHARON.
IN A MOMENT YOU WILL FIND YOURSELF IN A HELL YOU NEVER IMAGINED — NO ONE THERE WILL SAVE YOU, NO ONE WILL LISTEN TO YOUR SCREAMS, NO ONE WILL STOP THE PAIN. WHEN YOU GET THERE... LISTEN TO ME, SHARON, THIS IS THE IMPORTANT PART... WHEN YOU GET THERE—
I WANT YOU TO THINK ABOUT YOUR FRIENDS... *TAMBI* AND *KATINA*...
BECAUSE I'M GOING TO SEND THEM TO YOU.
OH, AND SHARON...
TELL DARCY HER COUSIN VERONICA SAID HELLO.

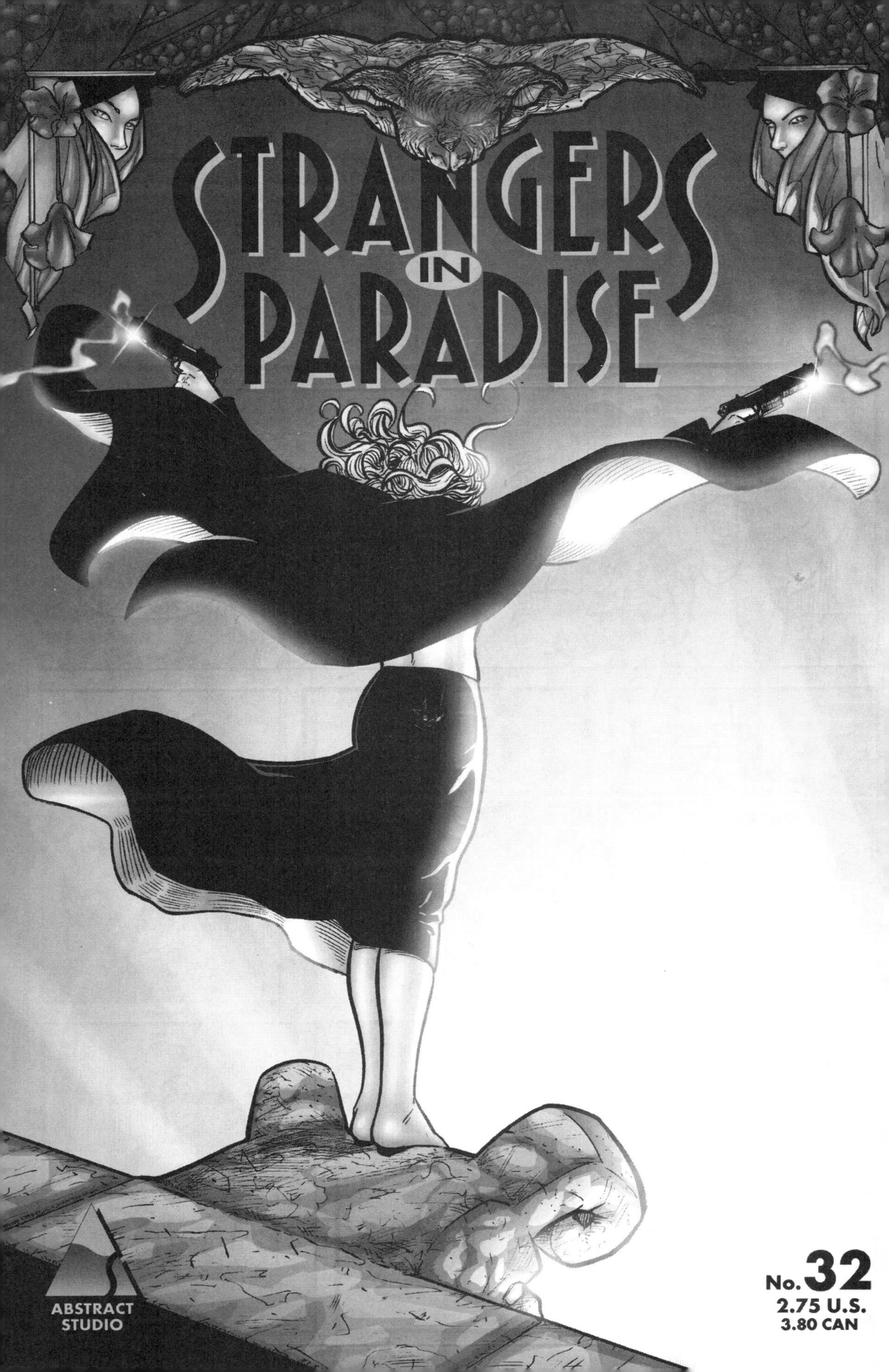
STRANGERS IN PARADISE
ABSTRACT STUDIO
No. 32
2.75 U.S.
3.80 CAN

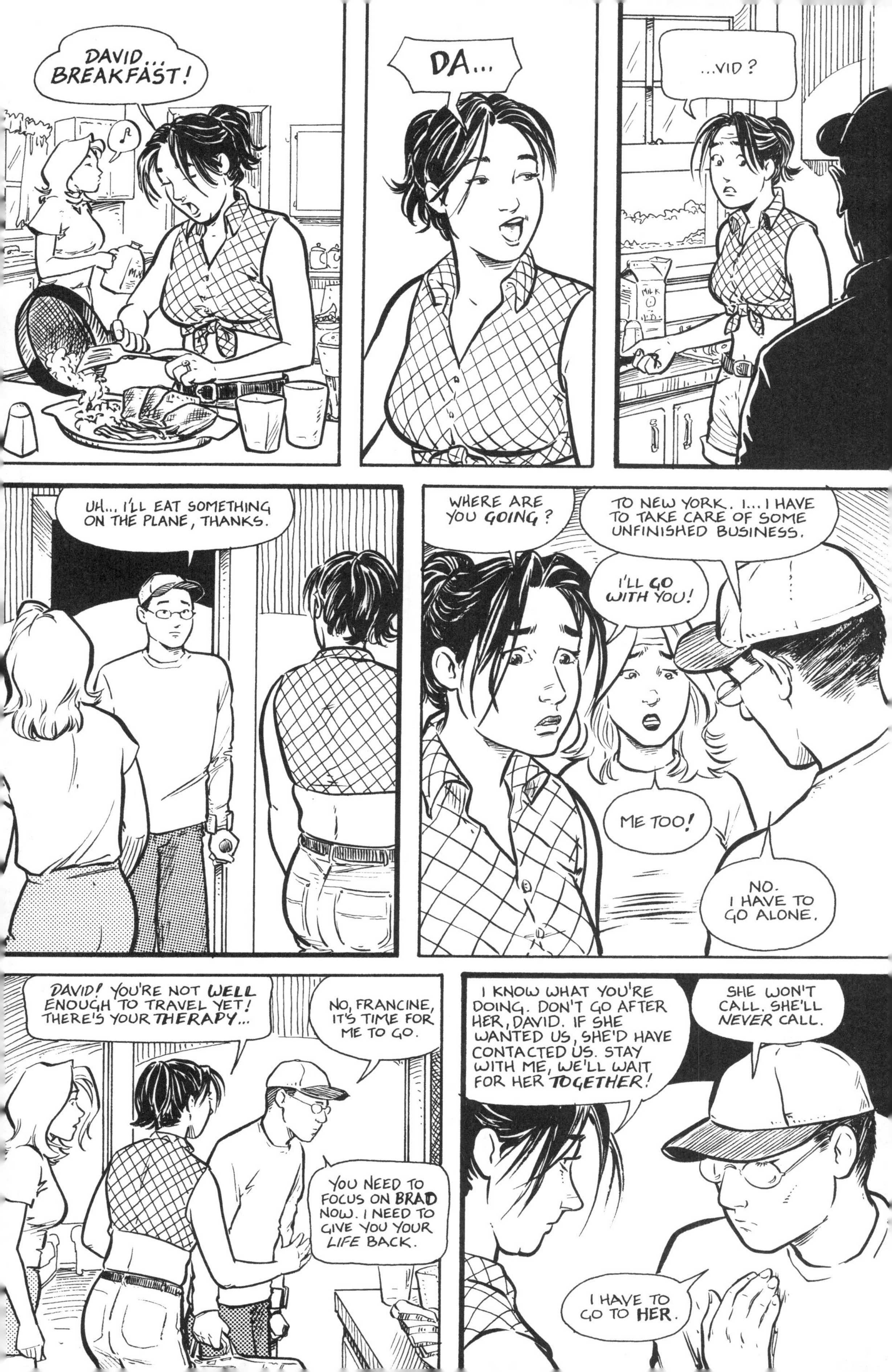

DAVID... BREAKFAST!
DA...
...VID?
UH... I'LL EAT SOMETHING ON THE PLANE, THANKS.
WHERE ARE YOU GOING?
TO NEW YORK. I... I HAVE TO TAKE CARE OF SOME UNFINISHED BUSINESS.
I'LL GO WITH YOU!
ME TOO!
NO. I HAVE TO GO ALONE.
DAVID! YOU'RE NOT WELL ENOUGH TO TRAVEL YET! THERE'S YOUR THERAPY...
NO, FRANCINE, IT'S TIME FOR ME TO GO.
YOU NEED TO FOCUS ON BRAD NOW. I NEED TO GIVE YOU YOUR LIFE BACK.
I KNOW WHAT YOU'RE DOING. DON'T GO AFTER HER, DAVID. IF SHE WANTED US, SHE'D HAVE CONTACTED US. STAY WITH ME, WE'LL WAIT FOR HER TOGETHER!
SHE WON'T CALL. SHE'LL NEVER CALL.
I HAVE TO GO TO HER.

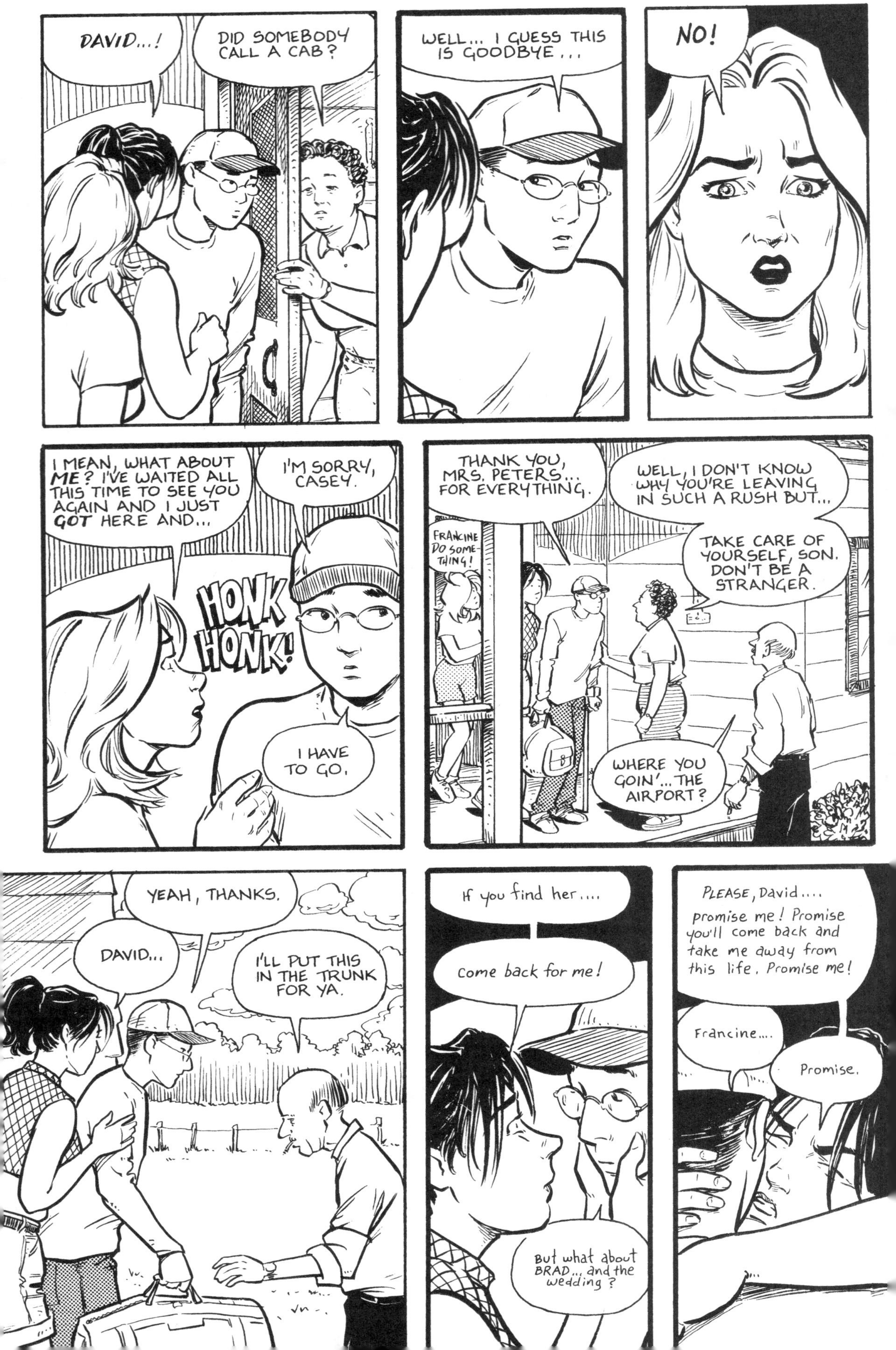
DAVID...!
DID SOMEBODY CALL A CAB?
WELL... I GUESS THIS IS GOODBYE...
NO!
I MEAN, WHAT ABOUT ME? I'VE WAITED ALL THIS TIME TO SEE YOU AGAIN AND I JUST GOT HERE AND...
I'M SORRY, CASEY.
HONK HONK!
I HAVE TO GO.
THANK YOU, MRS. PETERS... FOR EVERYTHING.
FRANCINE DO SOMETHING!
WELL, I DON'T KNOW WHY YOU'RE LEAVING IN SUCH A RUSH BUT...
TAKE CARE OF YOURSELF, SON. DON'T BE A STRANGER.
WHERE YOU GOIN'... THE AIRPORT?
YEAH, THANKS.
DAVID...
I'LL PUT THIS IN THE TRUNK FOR YA.
If you find her....
Come back for me!
But what about BRAD... and the wedding?
PLEASE, David.... promise me! Promise you'll come back and take me away from this life. Promise me!
Francine....
Promise.

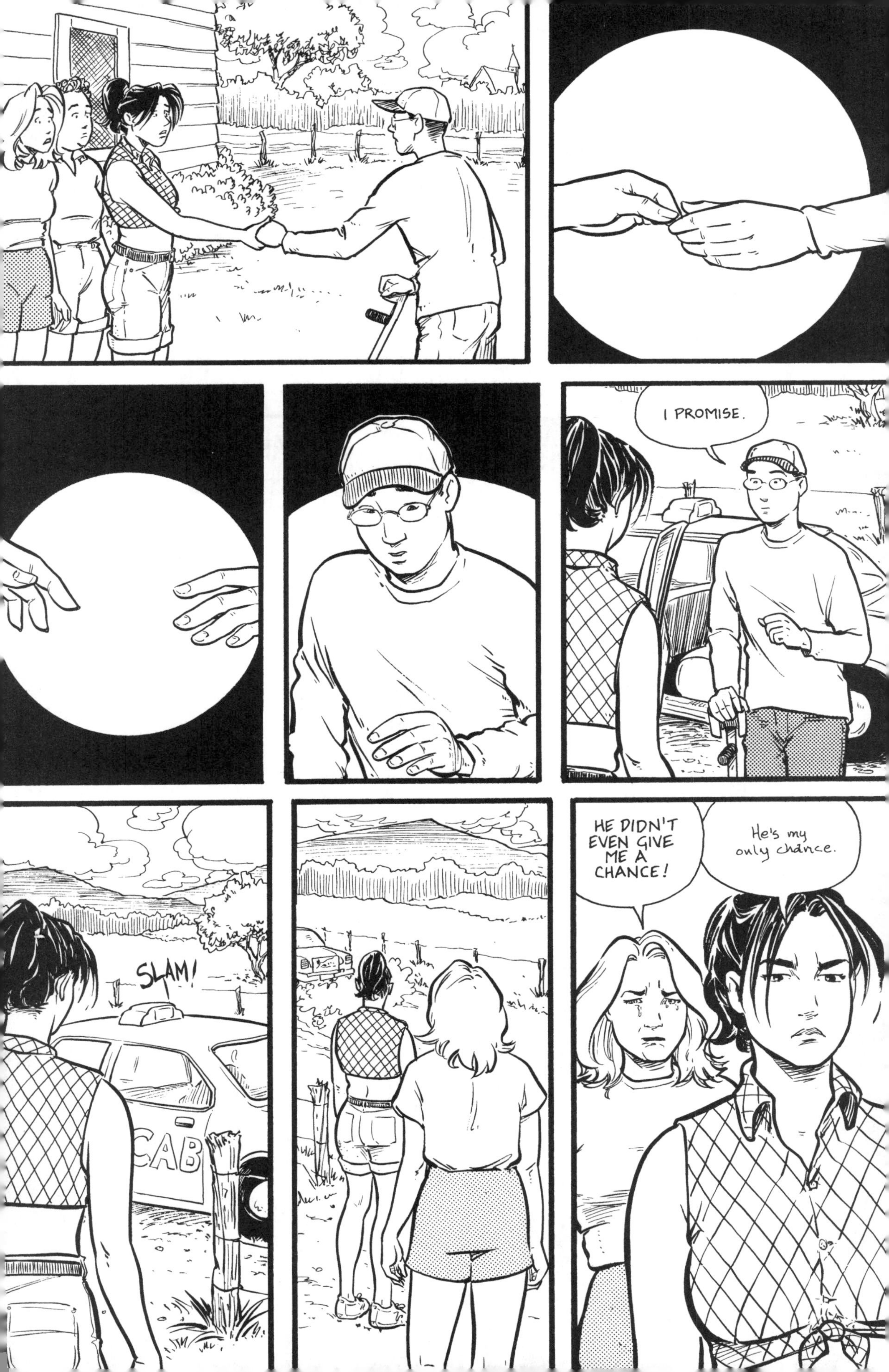
I PROMISE.
SLAM!
CAB
HE DIDN'T EVEN GIVE ME A CHANCE!
He's my only chance.

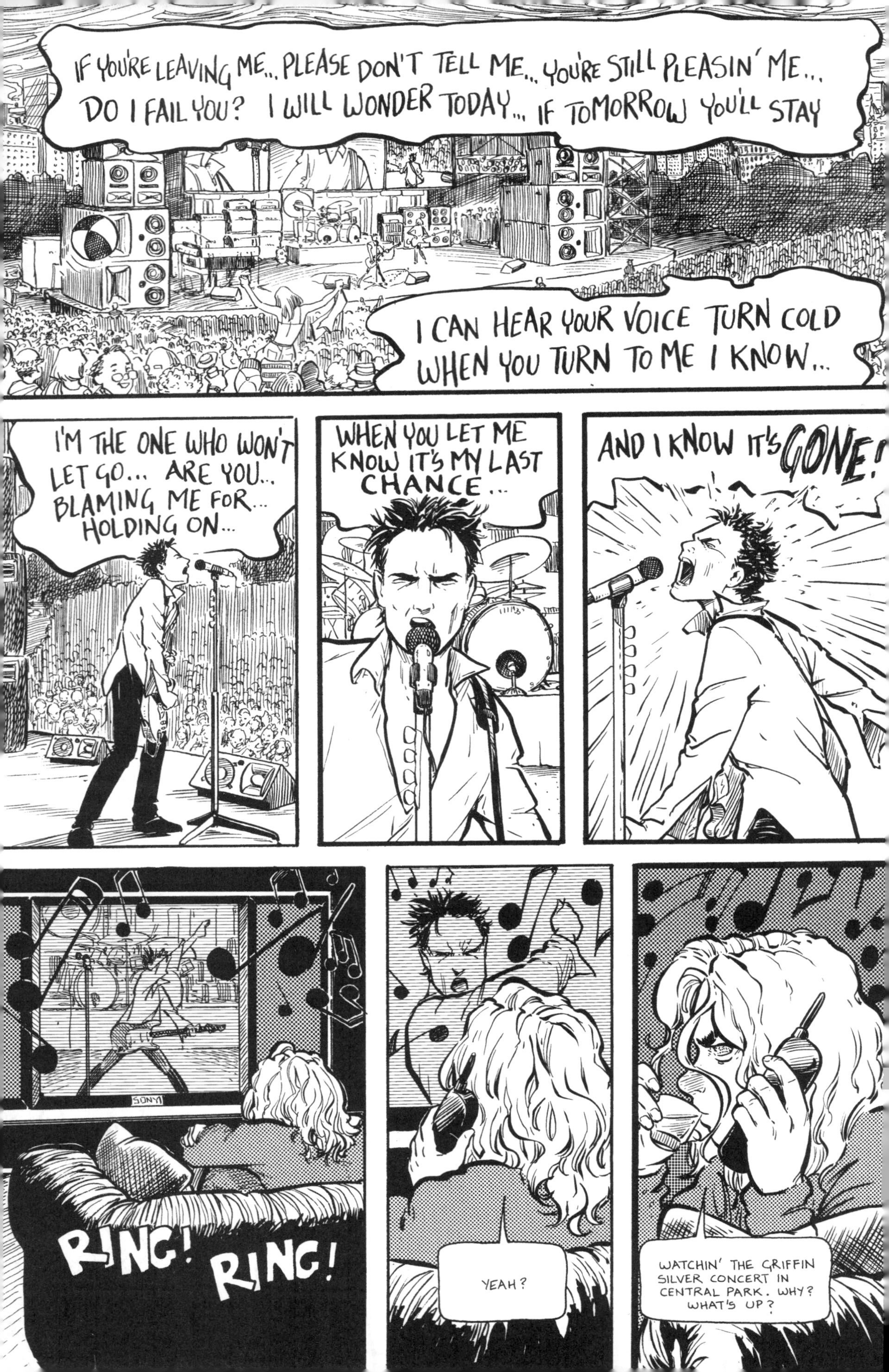

IF YOU'RE LEAVING ME... PLEASE DON'T TELL ME... YOU'RE STILL PLEASIN' ME... DO I FAIL YOU? I WILL WONDER TODAY... IF TOMORROW YOU'LL STAY
I CAN HEAR YOUR VOICE TURN COLD WHEN YOU TURN TO ME I KNOW...
I'M THE ONE WHO WON'T LET GO... ARE YOU... BLAMING ME FOR... HOLDING ON...
WHEN YOU LET ME KNOW IT'S MY LAST CHANCE...
AND I KNOW IT'S GONE!
SONY
RING! RING!
YEAH?
WATCHIN' THE GRIFFIN SILVER CONCERT IN CENTRAL PARK. WHY? WHAT'S UP?

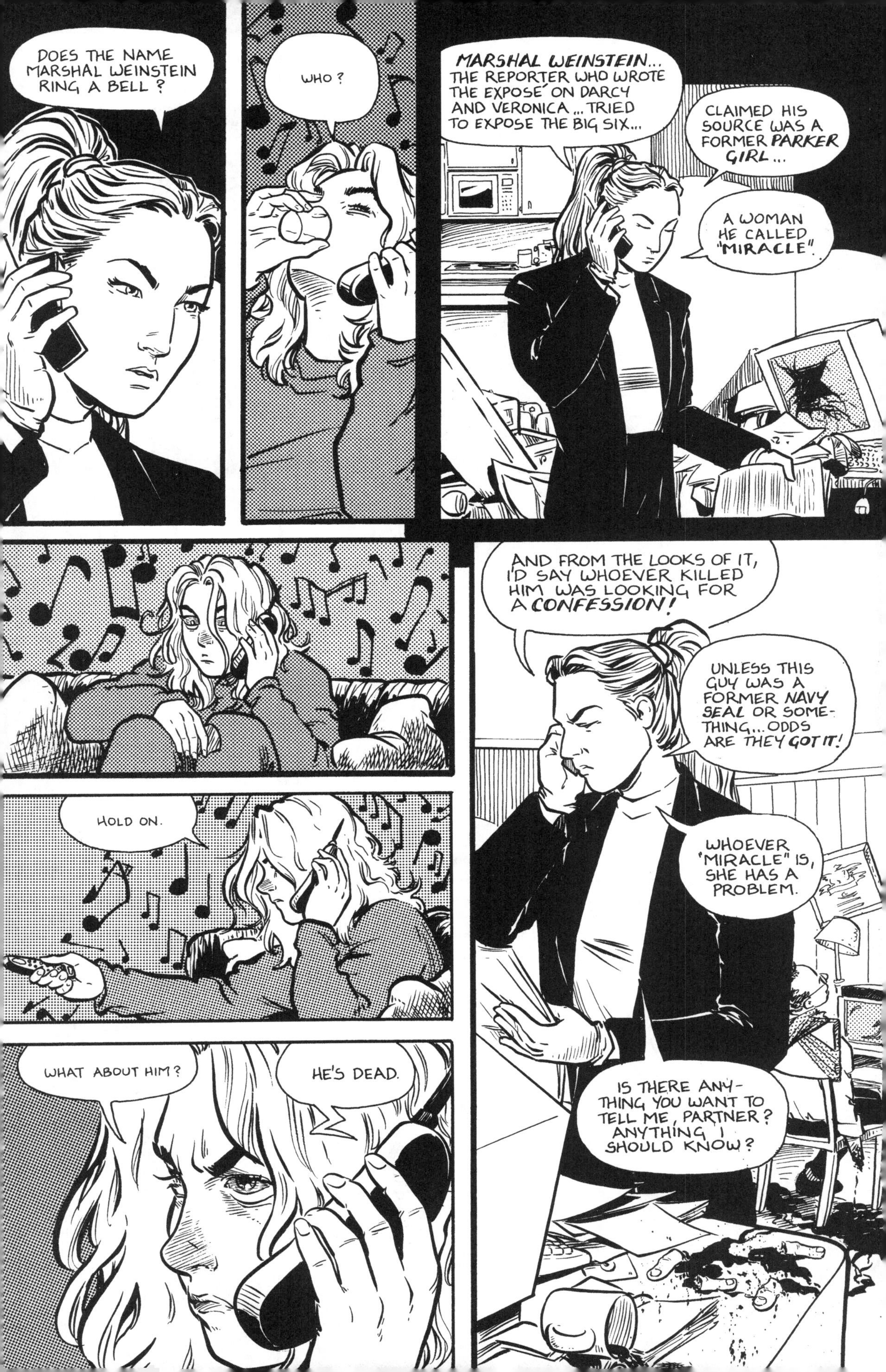
DOES THE NAME MARSHAL WEINSTEIN RING A BELL ?
WHO ?
MARSHAL WEINSTEIN... THE REPORTER WHO WROTE THE EXPOSÉ ON DARCY AND VERONICA... TRIED TO EXPOSE THE BIG SIX...
CLAIMED HIS SOURCE WAS A FORMER PARKER GIRL...
A WOMAN HE CALLED "MIRACLE".
HOLD ON.
WHAT ABOUT HIM ?
HE'S DEAD.
AND FROM THE LOOKS OF IT, I'D SAY WHOEVER KILLED HIM WAS LOOKING FOR A CONFESSION!
UNLESS THIS GUY WAS A FORMER NAVY SEAL OR SOME-THING... ODDS ARE THEY GOT IT!
WHOEVER "MIRACLE" IS, SHE HAS A PROBLEM.
IS THERE ANY-THING YOU WANT TO TELL ME, PARTNER ? ANYTHING I SHOULD KNOW ?

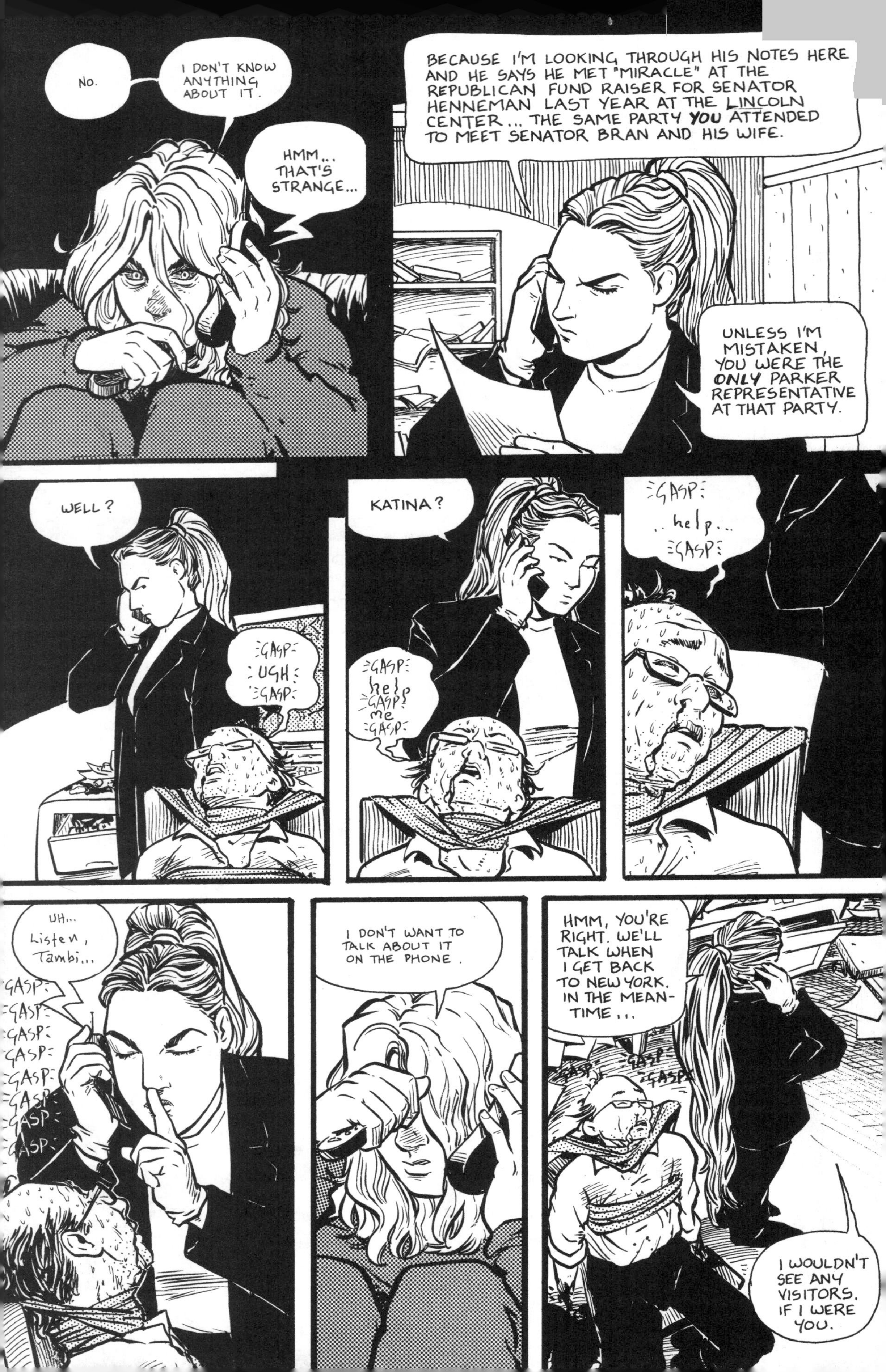
NO.
I DON'T KNOW ANYTHING ABOUT IT.
HMM... THAT'S STRANGE...
BECAUSE I'M LOOKING THROUGH HIS NOTES HERE AND HE SAYS HE MET "MIRACLE" AT THE REPUBLICAN FUND RAISER FOR SENATOR HENNEMAN LAST YEAR AT THE LINCOLN CENTER... THE SAME PARTY YOU ATTENDED TO MEET SENATOR BRAN AND HIS WIFE.
UNLESS I'M MISTAKEN, YOU WERE THE ONLY PARKER REPRESENTATIVE AT THAT PARTY.
WELL?
GASP UGH GASP
KATINA?
GASP help GASP me GASP
GASP ..help.. GASP
UH... Listen, Tambi...
GASP GASP GASP GASP GASP GASP GASP GASP
I DON'T WANT TO TALK ABOUT IT ON THE PHONE.
HMM, YOU'RE RIGHT. WE'LL TALK WHEN I GET BACK TO NEW YORK. IN THE MEANTIME...
GASP GASP GASP
I WOULDN'T SEE ANY VISITORS. IF I WERE YOU.

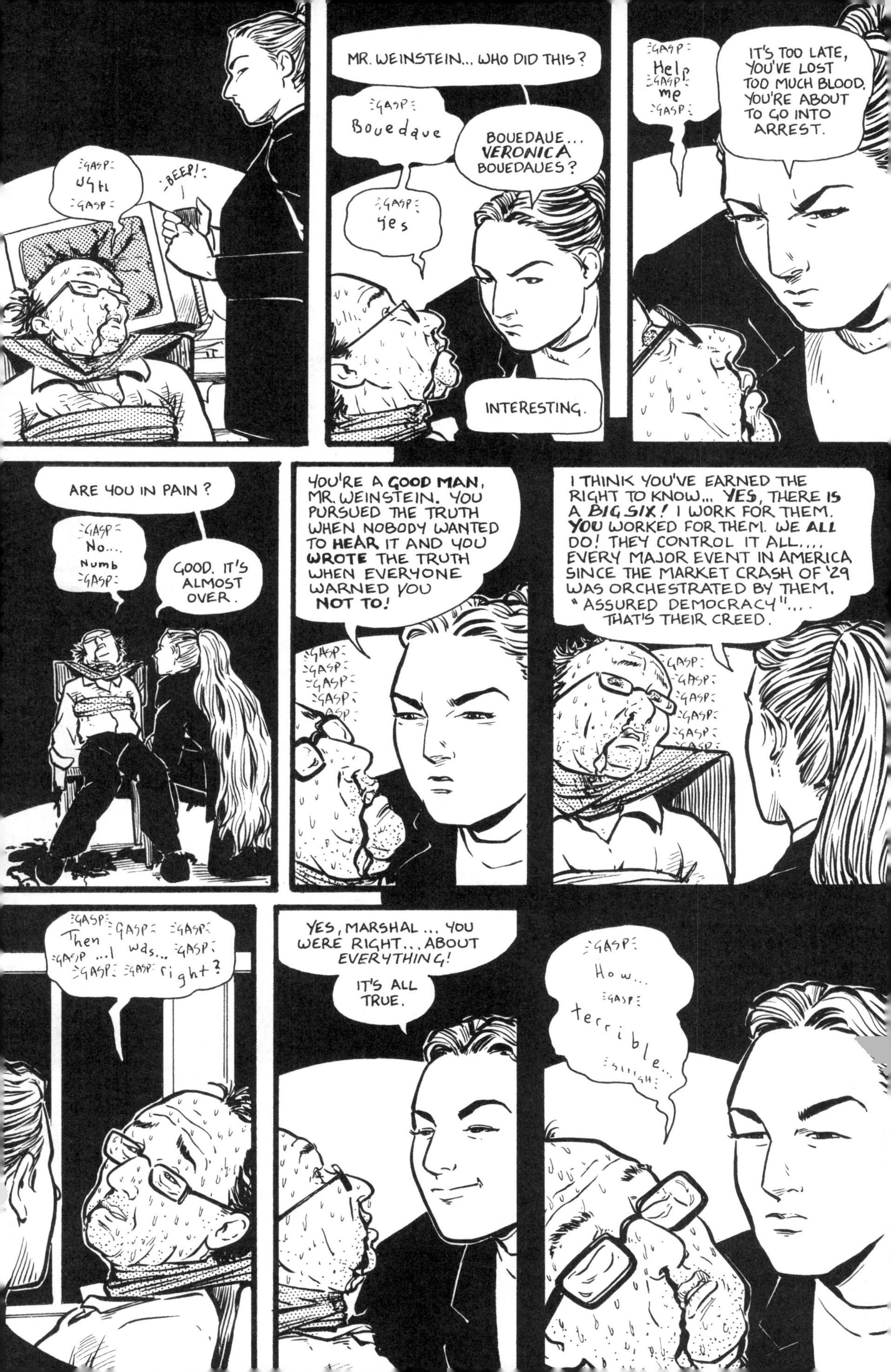
GASP Ugh GASP
BEEP!
MR. WEINSTEIN... WHO DID THIS?
GASP Bouedaue
BOUEDAUE... VERONICA BOUEDAUES?
GASP yes
INTERESTING.
GASP Help GASP me GASP
IT'S TOO LATE, YOU'VE LOST TOO MUCH BLOOD. YOU'RE ABOUT TO GO INTO ARREST.
ARE YOU IN PAIN?
GASP No.... Numb GASP
GOOD. IT'S ALMOST OVER.
YOU'RE A GOOD MAN, MR. WEINSTEIN. YOU PURSUED THE TRUTH WHEN NOBODY WANTED TO HEAR IT AND YOU WROTE THE TRUTH WHEN EVERYONE WARNED YOU NOT TO!
GASP GASP GASP GASP
I THINK YOU'VE EARNED THE RIGHT TO KNOW... YES, THERE IS A BIG SIX! I WORK FOR THEM. YOU WORKED FOR THEM. WE ALL DO! THEY CONTROL IT ALL.... EVERY MAJOR EVENT IN AMERICA SINCE THE MARKET CRASH OF '29 WAS ORCHESTRATED BY THEM. "ASSURED DEMOCRACY"... THAT'S THEIR CREED.
GASP GASP GASP GASP GASP
GASP Then GASP ...I GASP was... GASP GASP GASP GASP right?
YES, MARSHAL... YOU WERE RIGHT... ABOUT EVERYTHING!
IT'S ALL TRUE.
GASP How... GASP terrible...

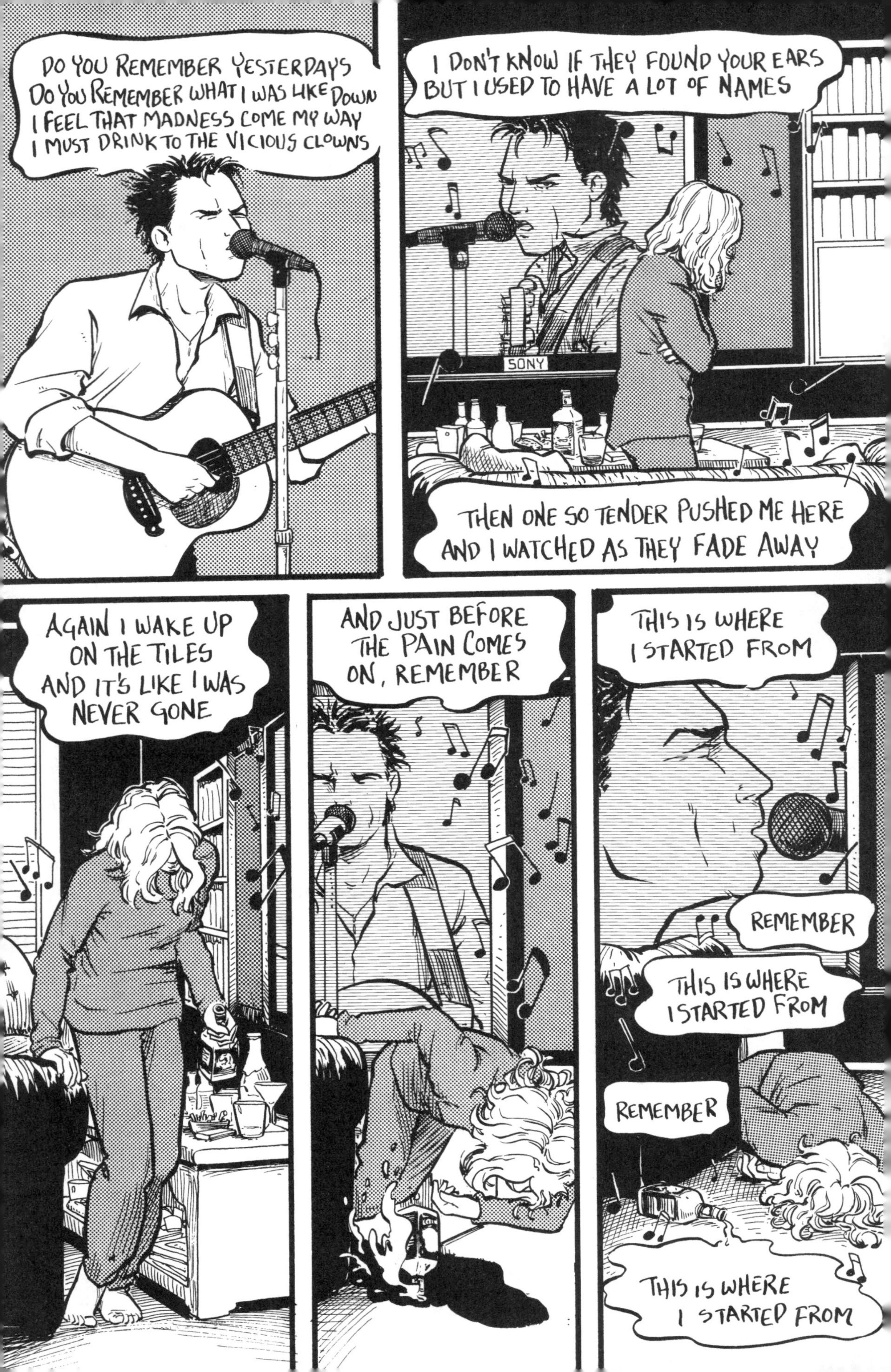
DO YOU REMEMBER YESTERDAYS
DO YOU REMEMBER WHAT I WAS LIKE DOWN
I FEEL THAT MADNESS COME MY WAY
I MUST DRINK TO THE VICIOUS CLOWNS
I DON'T KNOW IF THEY FOUND YOUR EARS
BUT I USED TO HAVE A LOT OF NAMES
SONY
THEN ONE SO TENDER PUSHED ME HERE
AND I WATCHED AS THEY FADE AWAY
AGAIN I WAKE UP ON THE TILES AND IT'S LIKE I WAS NEVER GONE
AND JUST BEFORE THE PAIN COMES ON, REMEMBER
THIS IS WHERE I STARTED FROM
REMEMBER
THIS IS WHERE I STARTED FROM
REMEMBER
THIS IS WHERE I STARTED FROM

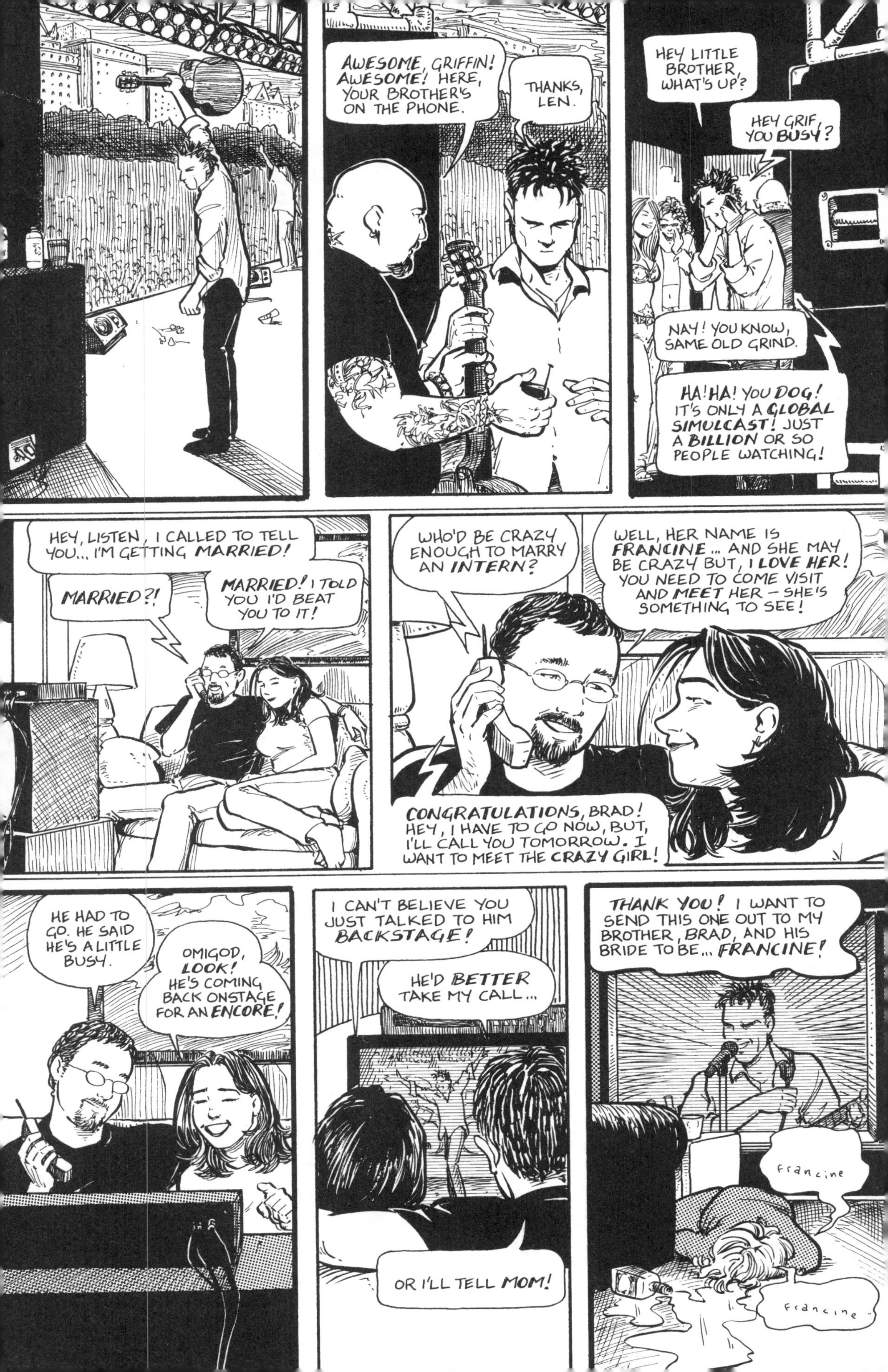
AWESOME, GRIFFIN! AWESOME! HERE, YOUR BROTHER'S ON THE PHONE.
THANKS, LEN.
HEY LITTLE BROTHER WHAT'S UP?
HEY GRIF, YOU BUSY?
NAY! YOU KNOW, SAME OLD GRIND.
HA! HA! YOU DOG! IT'S ONLY A GLOBAL SIMULCAST! JUST A BILLION OR SO PEOPLE WATCHING!
HEY, LISTEN, I CALLED TO TELL YOU... I'M GETTING MARRIED!
MARRIED?!
MARRIED! I TOLD YOU I'D BEAT YOU TO IT!
WHO'D BE CRAZY ENOUGH TO MARRY AN INTERN?
WELL, HER NAME IS FRANCINE... AND SHE MAY BE CRAZY BUT, I LOVE HER! YOU NEED TO COME VISIT AND MEET HER - SHE'S SOMETHING TO SEE!
CONGRATULATIONS, BRAD! HEY, I HAVE TO GO NOW, BUT, I'LL CALL YOU TOMORROW. I WANT TO MEET THE CRAZY GIRL!
HE HAD TO GO. HE SAID HE'S A LITTLE BUSY.
OMIGOD, LOOK! HE'S COMING BACK ONSTAGE FOR AN ENCORE!
I CAN'T BELIEVE YOU JUST TALKED TO HIM BACKSTAGE!
HE'D BETTER TAKE MY CALL...
OR I'LL TELL MOM!
THANK YOU! I WANT TO SEND THIS ONE OUT TO MY BROTHER, BRAD, AND HIS BRIDE TO BE... FRANCINE!
Francine
Francine..

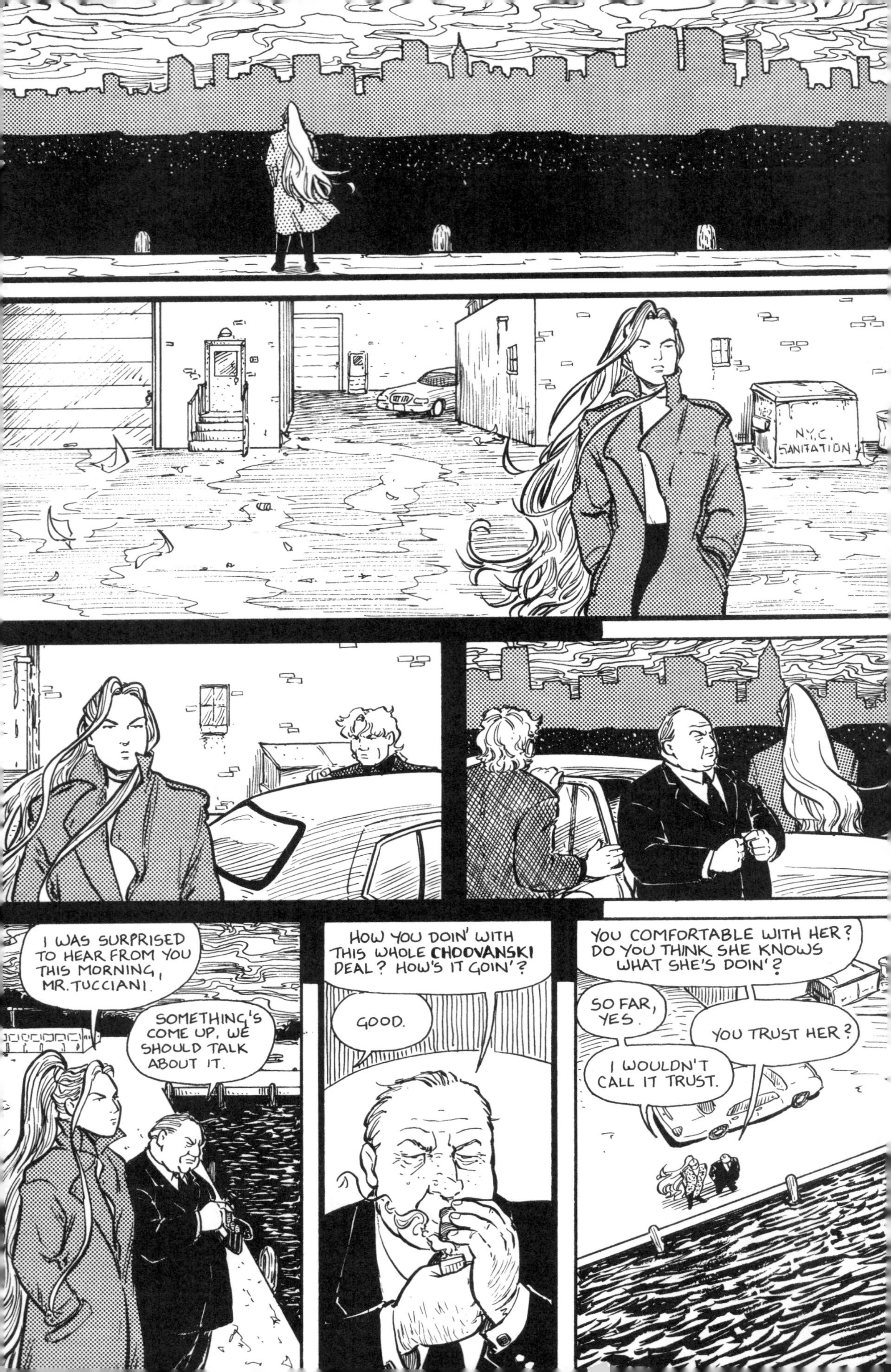
N.Y.C. SANITATION
I WAS SURPRISED TO HEAR FROM YOU THIS MORNING, MR. TUCCIANI.
SOMETHING'S COME UP, WE SHOULD TALK ABOUT IT.
HOW YOU DOIN' WITH THIS WHOLE **CHOOVANSKI** DEAL? HOW'S IT GOIN'?
GOOD.
YOU COMFORTABLE WITH HER? DO YOU THINK SHE KNOWS WHAT SHE'S DOIN'?
SO FAR, YES.
YOU TRUST HER?
I WOULDN'T CALL IT TRUST.

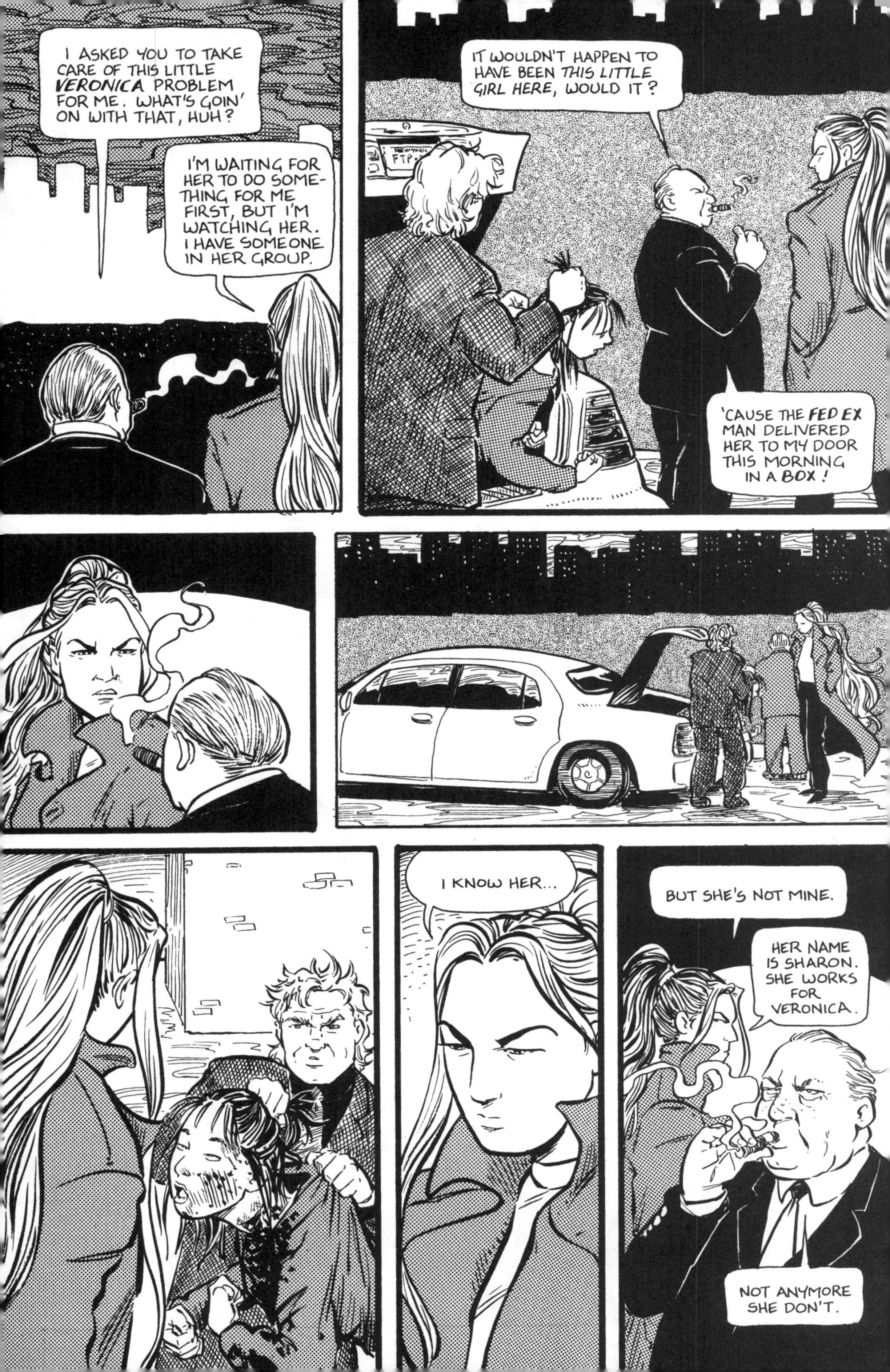
I ASKED YOU TO TAKE CARE OF THIS LITTLE VERONICA PROBLEM FOR ME. WHAT'S GOIN' ON WITH THAT, HUH?
I'M WAITING FOR HER TO DO SOMETHING FOR ME FIRST, BUT I'M WATCHING HER. I HAVE SOMEONE IN HER GROUP.
IT WOULDN'T HAPPEN TO HAVE BEEN THIS LITTLE GIRL HERE, WOULD IT?
'CAUSE THE FED EX MAN DELIVERED HER TO MY DOOR THIS MORNING IN A BOX!
I KNOW HER...
BUT SHE'S NOT MINE.
HER NAME IS SHARON. SHE WORKS FOR VERONICA.
NOT ANYMORE SHE DON'T.

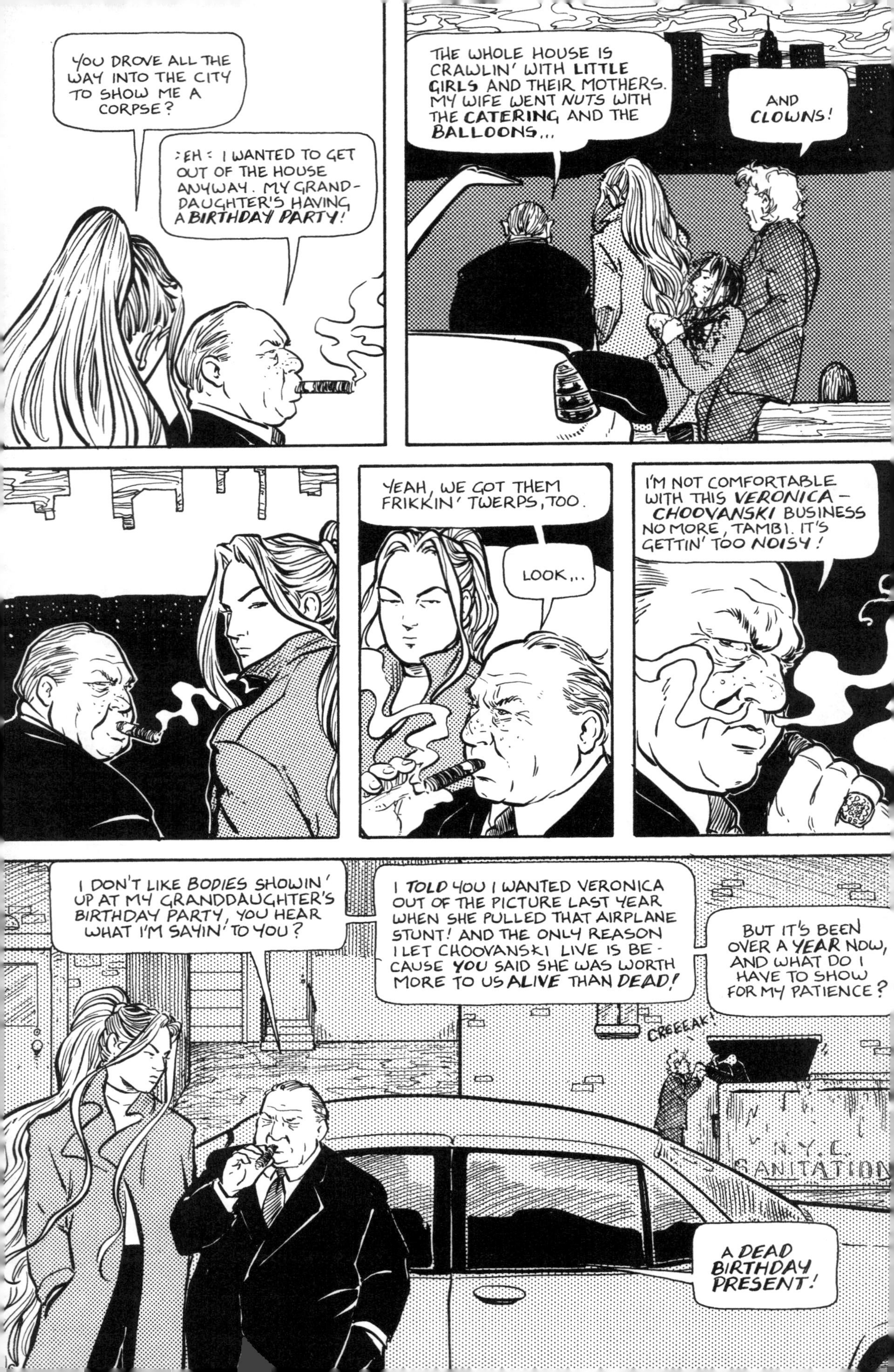

YOU DROVE ALL THE WAY INTO THE CITY TO SHOW ME A CORPSE?
:EH: I WANTED TO GET OUT OF THE HOUSE ANYWAY. MY GRAND-DAUGHTER'S HAVING A BIRTHDAY PARTY!
THE WHOLE HOUSE IS CRAWLIN' WITH LITTLE GIRLS AND THEIR MOTHERS. MY WIFE WENT NUTS WITH THE CATERING AND THE BALLOONS...
AND CLOWNS!
YEAH, WE GOT THEM FRIKKIN' TWERPS, TOO.
LOOK,..
I'M NOT COMFORTABLE WITH THIS VERONICA-CHOOVANSKI BUSINESS NO MORE, TAMBI. IT'S GETTIN' TOO NOISY!
I DON'T LIKE BODIES SHOWIN' UP AT MY GRANDDAUGHTER'S BIRTHDAY PARTY, YOU HEAR WHAT I'M SAYIN' TO YOU?
I TOLD YOU I WANTED VERONICA OUT OF THE PICTURE LAST YEAR WHEN SHE PULLED THAT AIRPLANE STUNT! AND THE ONLY REASON I LET CHOOVANSKI LIVE IS BE-CAUSE YOU SAID SHE WAS WORTH MORE TO US ALIVE THAN DEAD!
BUT IT'S BEEN OVER A YEAR NOW, AND WHAT DO I HAVE TO SHOW FOR MY PATIENCE?
CREEEAK!
N.Y.C. SANITATION
A DEAD BIRTHDAY PRESENT!

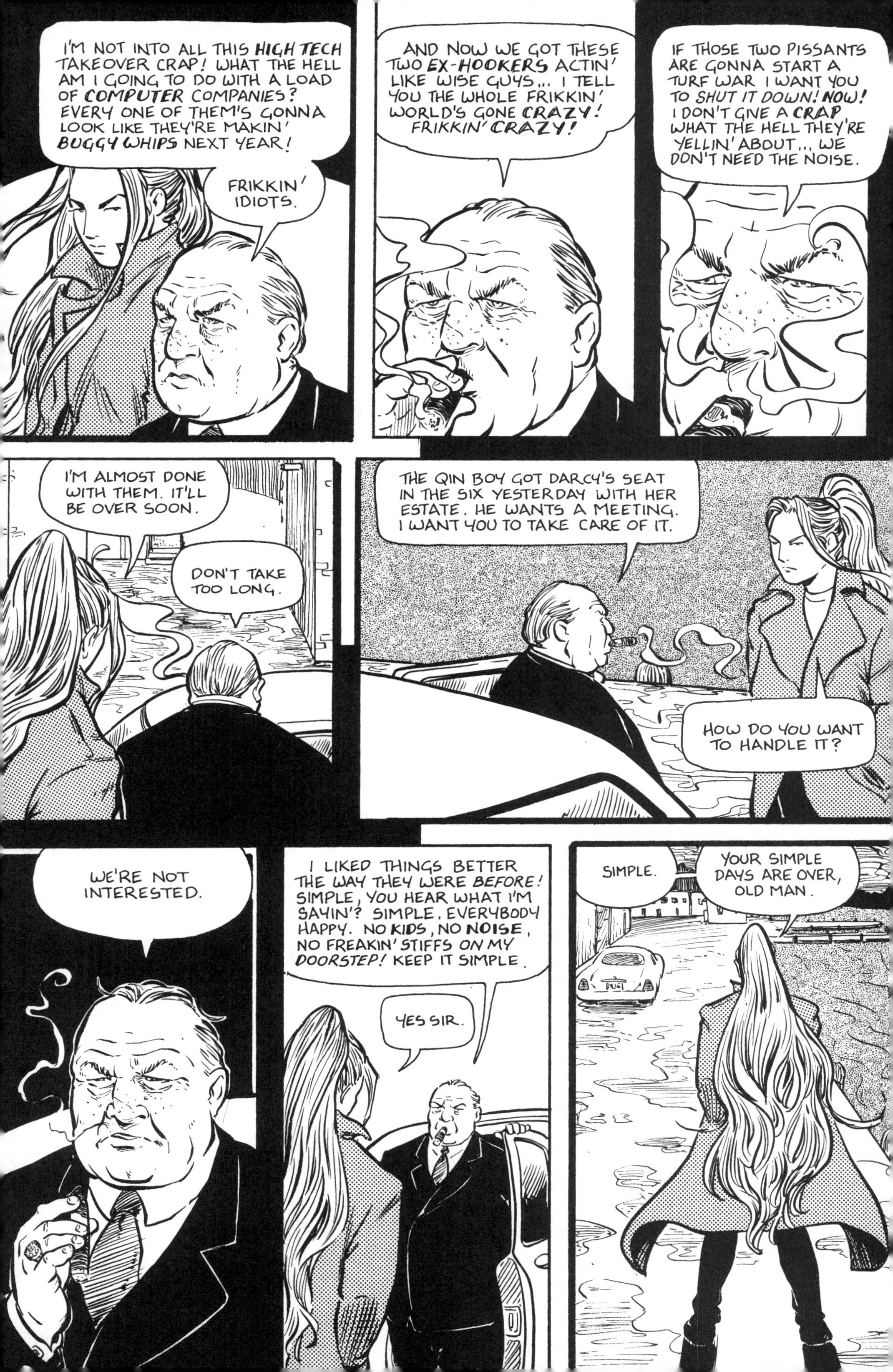
I'M NOT INTO ALL THIS HIGH TECH TAKEOVER CRAP! WHAT THE HELL AM I GOING TO DO WITH A LOAD OF COMPUTER COMPANIES? EVERY ONE OF THEM'S GONNA LOOK LIKE THEY'RE MAKIN' BUGGY WHIPS NEXT YEAR!
FRIKKIN' IDIOTS.
AND NOW WE GOT THESE TWO EX-HOOKERS ACTIN' LIKE WISE GUYS... I TELL YOU THE WHOLE FRIKKIN' WORLD'S GONE CRAZY! FRIKKIN' CRAZY!
IF THOSE TWO PISSANTS ARE GONNA START A TURF WAR I WANT YOU TO SHUT IT DOWN! NOW! I DON'T GIVE A CRAP WHAT THE HELL THEY'RE YELLIN' ABOUT... WE DON'T NEED THE NOISE.
I'M ALMOST DONE WITH THEM. IT'LL BE OVER SOON.
DON'T TAKE TOO LONG.
THE QIN BOY GOT DARCY'S SEAT IN THE SIX YESTERDAY WITH HER ESTATE. HE WANTS A MEETING. I WANT YOU TO TAKE CARE OF IT.
HOW DO YOU WANT TO HANDLE IT?
WE'RE NOT INTERESTED.
I LIKED THINGS BETTER THE WAY THEY WERE BEFORE! SIMPLE, YOU HEAR WHAT I'M SAYIN'? SIMPLE. EVERYBODY HAPPY. NO KIDS, NO NOISE, NO FREAKIN' STIFFS ON MY DOORSTEP! KEEP IT SIMPLE.
YES SIR.
SIMPLE.
YOUR SIMPLE DAYS ARE OVER, OLD MAN.

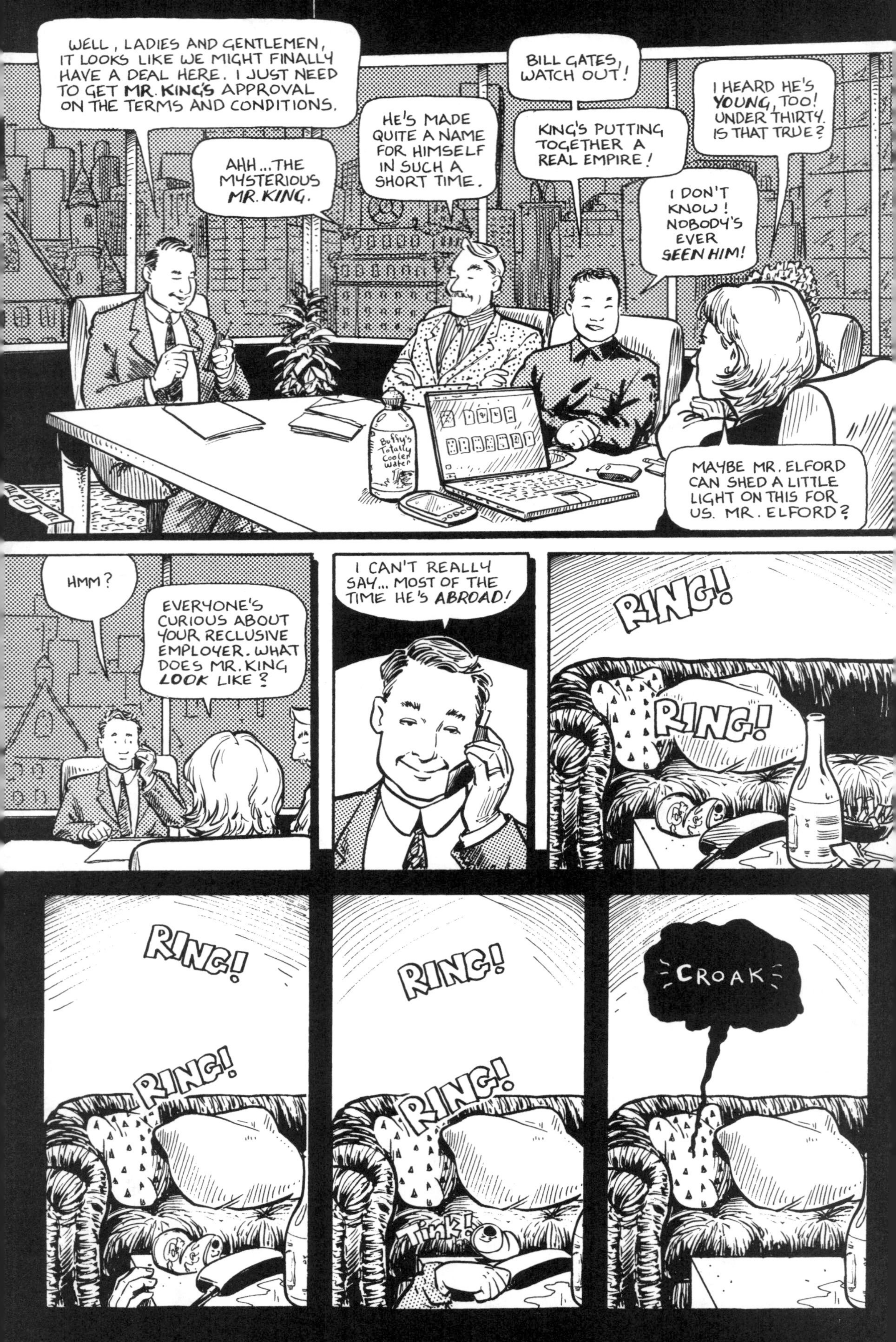

WELL, LADIES AND GENTLEMEN, IT LOOKS LIKE WE MIGHT FINALLY HAVE A DEAL HERE. I JUST NEED TO GET MR. KING'S APPROVAL ON THE TERMS AND CONDITIONS.
AHH... THE MYSTERIOUS MR. KING.
HE'S MADE QUITE A NAME FOR HIMSELF IN SUCH A SHORT TIME.
BILL GATES, WATCH OUT!
KING'S PUTTING TOGETHER A REAL EMPIRE!
I HEARD HE'S YOUNG, TOO! UNDER THIRTY. IS THAT TRUE?
I DON'T KNOW! NOBODY'S EVER SEEN HIM!
Buffy's Totally Cooler water
MAYBE MR. ELFORD CAN SHED A LITTLE LIGHT ON THIS FOR US. MR. ELFORD?
HMM?
EVERYONE'S CURIOUS ABOUT YOUR RECLUSIVE EMPLOYER. WHAT DOES MR. KING LOOK LIKE?
I CAN'T REALLY SAY... MOST OF THE TIME HE'S ABROAD!
RING!
RING!
RING!
RING!
RING!
RING!
TINK!
CROAK

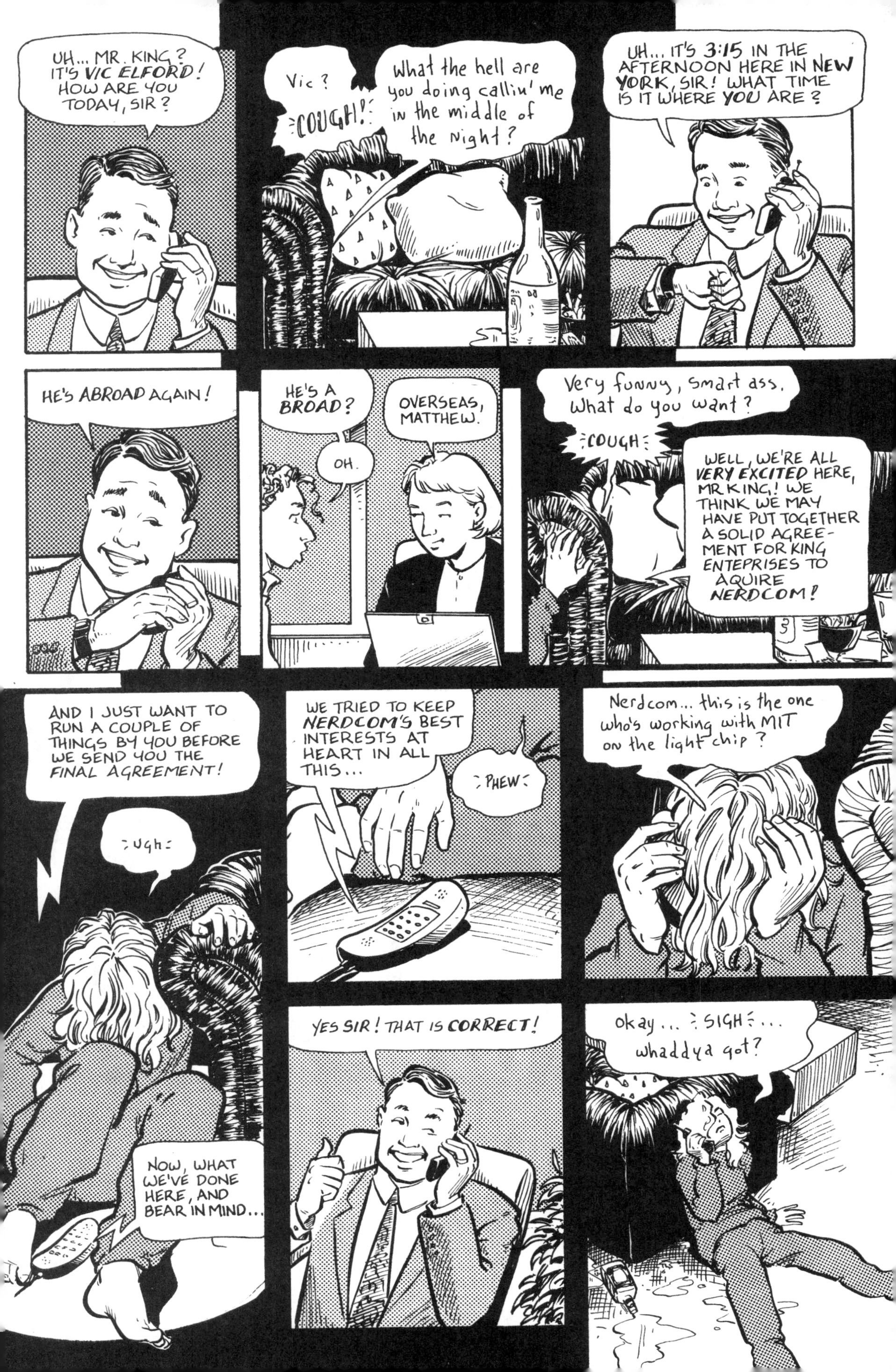
UH... MR. KING? IT'S VIC ELFORD! HOW ARE YOU TODAY, SIR?
Vic?
COUGH!
What the hell are you doing callin' me in the middle of the night?
UH... IT'S 3:15 IN THE AFTERNOON HERE IN NEW YORK, SIR! WHAT TIME IS IT WHERE YOU ARE?
HE'S ABROAD AGAIN!
HE'S A BROAD?
OVERSEAS, MATTHEW.
OH.
Very funny, smart ass. What do you want?
COUGH
WELL, WE'RE ALL VERY EXCITED HERE, MR KING! WE THINK WE MAY HAVE PUT TOGETHER A SOLID AGREEMENT FOR KING ENTEPRISES TO AQUIRE NERDCOM!
AND I JUST WANT TO RUN A COUPLE OF THINGS BY YOU BEFORE WE SEND YOU THE FINAL AGREEMENT!
Ugh
NOW, WHAT WE'VE DONE HERE, AND BEAR IN MIND...
WE TRIED TO KEEP NERDCOM'S BEST INTERESTS AT HEART IN ALL THIS...
PHEW
Nerdcom... this is the one who's working with MIT on the light chip?
YES SIR! THAT IS CORRECT!
Okay... SIGH... whaddya got?

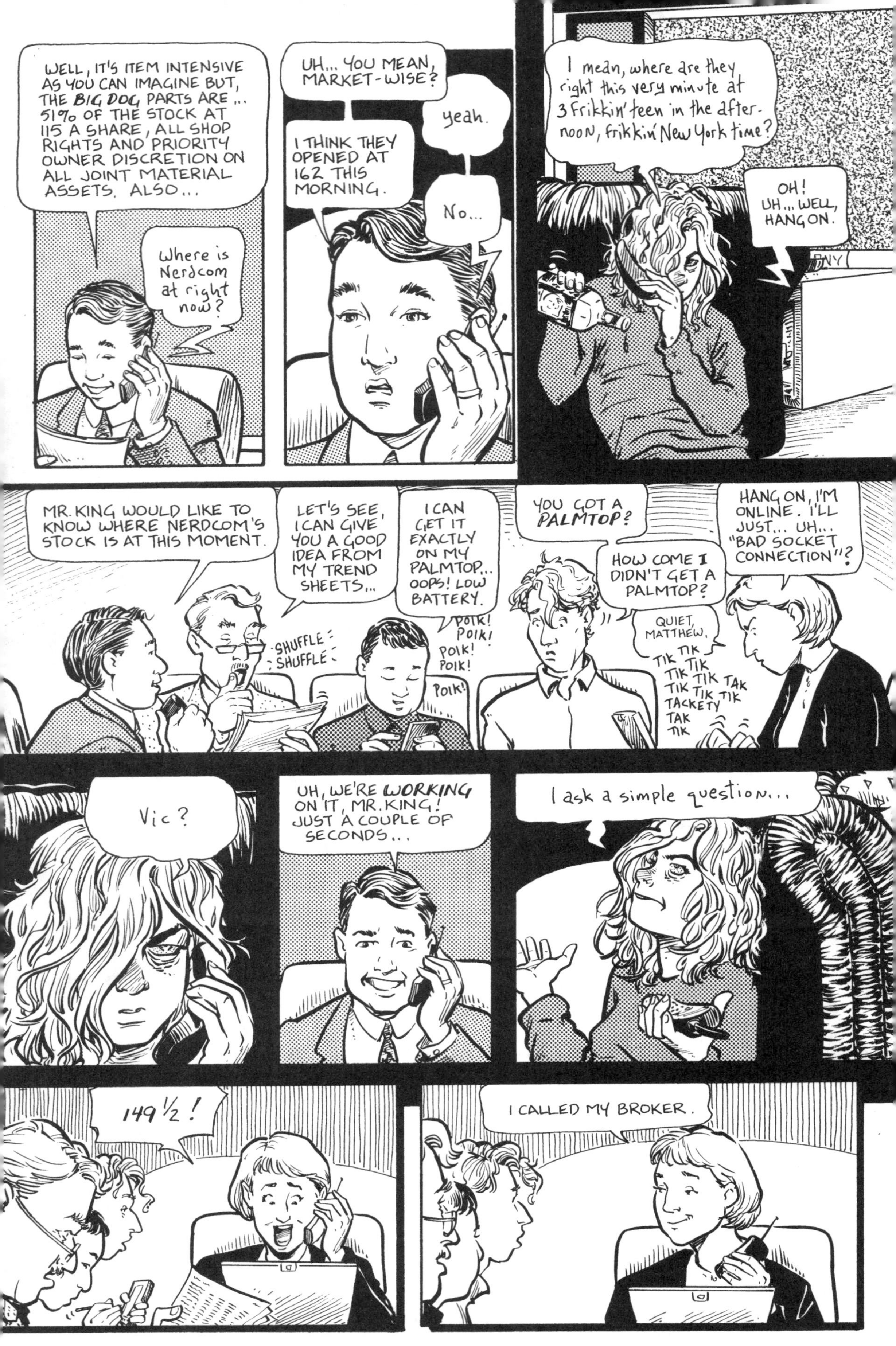

WELL, IT'S ITEM INTENSIVE AS YOU CAN IMAGINE BUT, THE BIG DOG PARTS ARE... 51% OF THE STOCK AT 115 A SHARE, ALL SHOP RIGHTS AND PRIORITY OWNER DISCRETION ON ALL JOINT MATERIAL ASSETS. ALSO...
Where is Nerdcom at right now?
UH... YOU MEAN, MARKET-WISE?
yeah.
I THINK THEY OPENED AT 162 THIS MORNING.
No...
I mean, where are they right this very minute at 3 frikkin' teen in the after-noon, frikkin' New York time?
OH! UH... WELL, HANG ON.
MR. KING WOULD LIKE TO KNOW WHERE NERDCOM'S STOCK IS AT THIS MOMENT.
LET'S SEE, I CAN GIVE YOU A GOOD IDEA FROM MY TREND SHEETS...
SHUFFLE SHUFFLE
I CAN GET IT EXACTLY ON MY PALMTOP... OOPS! LOW BATTERY.
POIK! POIK! POIK! POIK! POIK!
YOU GOT A PALMTOP?
HOW COME I DIDN'T GET A PALMTOP?
QUIET, MATTHEW.
HANG ON, I'M ONLINE. I'LL JUST... UH... "BAD SOCKET CONNECTION"?
TIK TIK TIK TIK TIK TIK TAK TIK TIK TIK TACKETY TAK TIK
Vic?
UH, WE'RE WORKING ON IT, MR. KING! JUST A COUPLE OF SECONDS...
I ask a simple question...
149 1/2!
I CALLED MY BROKER.

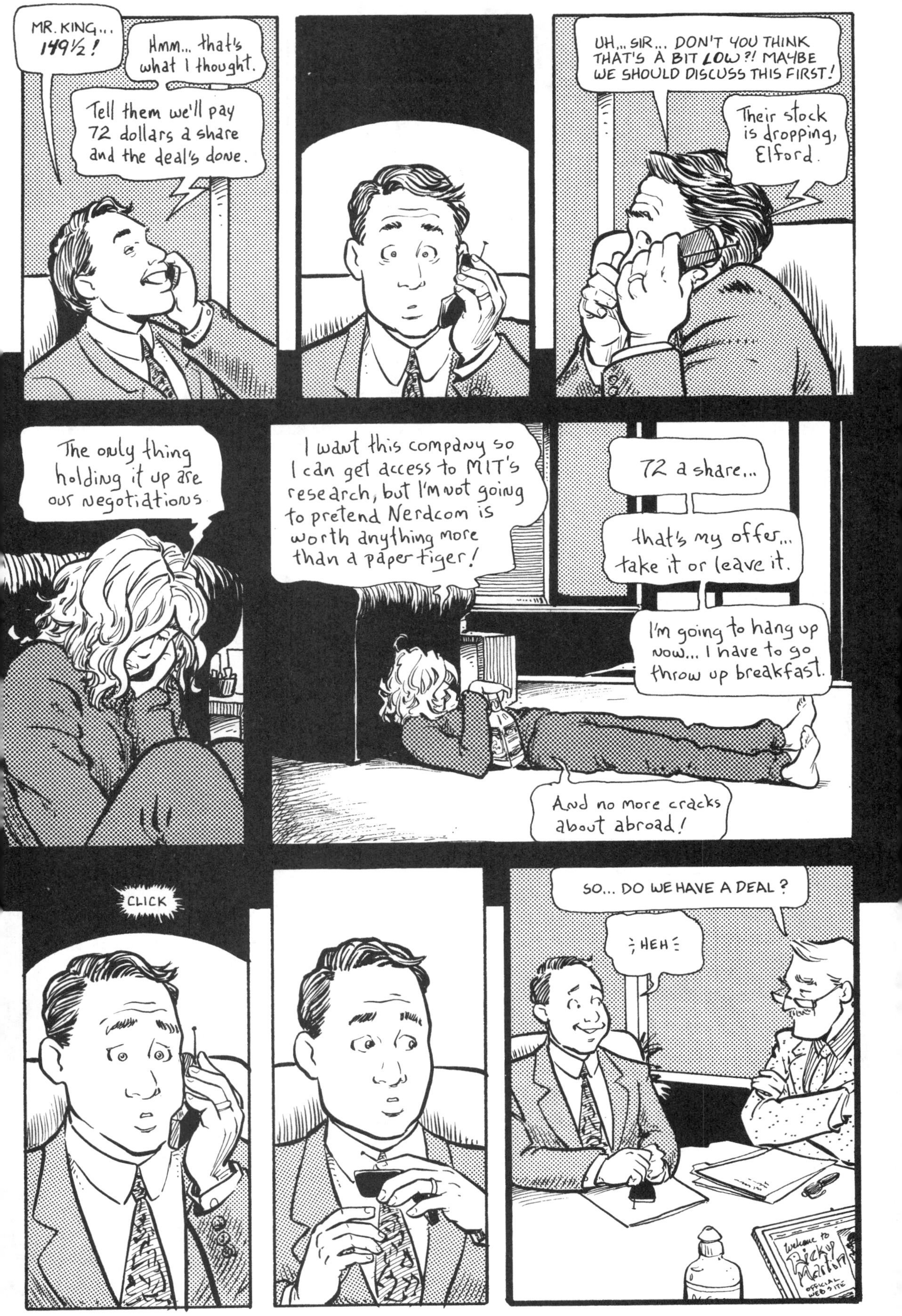

MR. KING... 149½!
Hmm... that's what I thought.
Tell them we'll pay 72 dollars a share and the deal's done.
UH,... SIR... DON'T YOU THINK THAT'S A BIT LOW?! MAYBE WE SHOULD DISCUSS THIS FIRST!
Their stock is dropping, Elford.
The only thing holding it up are our negotiations
I want this company so I can get access to MIT's research, but I'm not going to pretend Nerdcom is worth anything more than a paper tiger!
72 a share...
that's my offer... take it or leave it.
I'm going to hang up now... I have to go throw up breakfast.
And no more cracks about abroad!
CLICK
SO... DO WE HAVE A DEAL?
HEH
Welcome to Pickup Martin Official Web Site

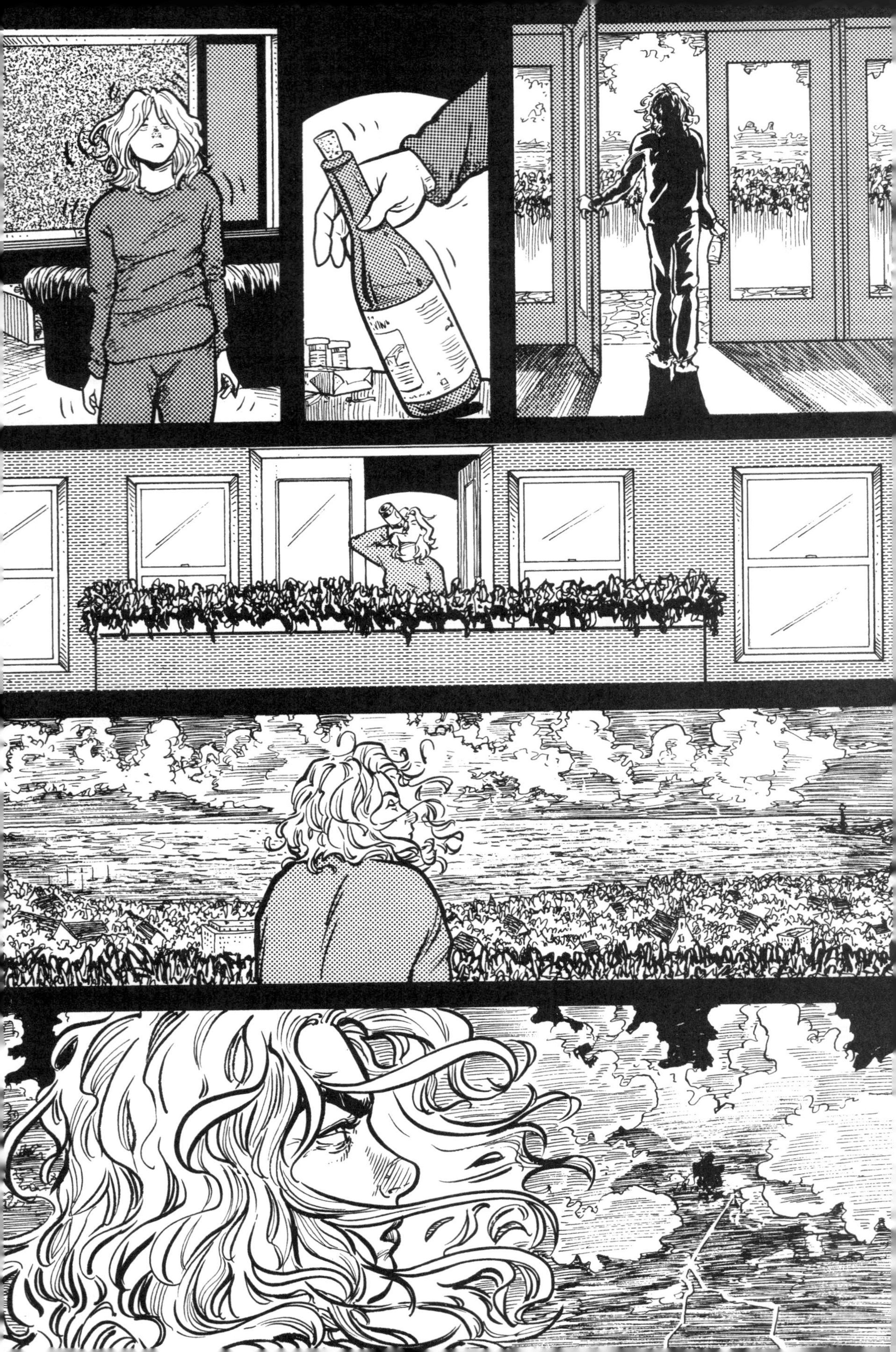

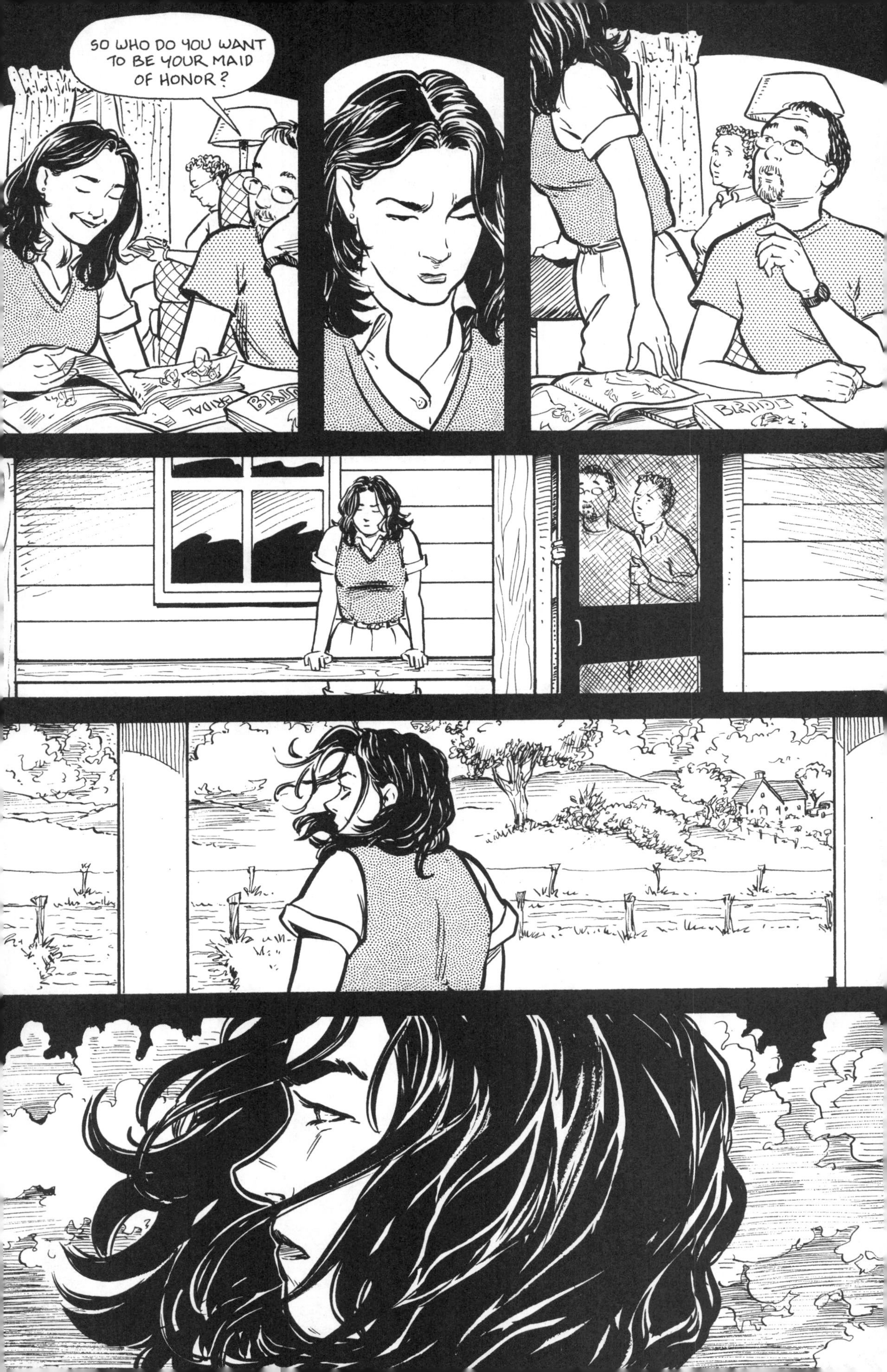
SO WHO DO YOU WANT TO BE YOUR MAID OF HONOR?
BRIDAL

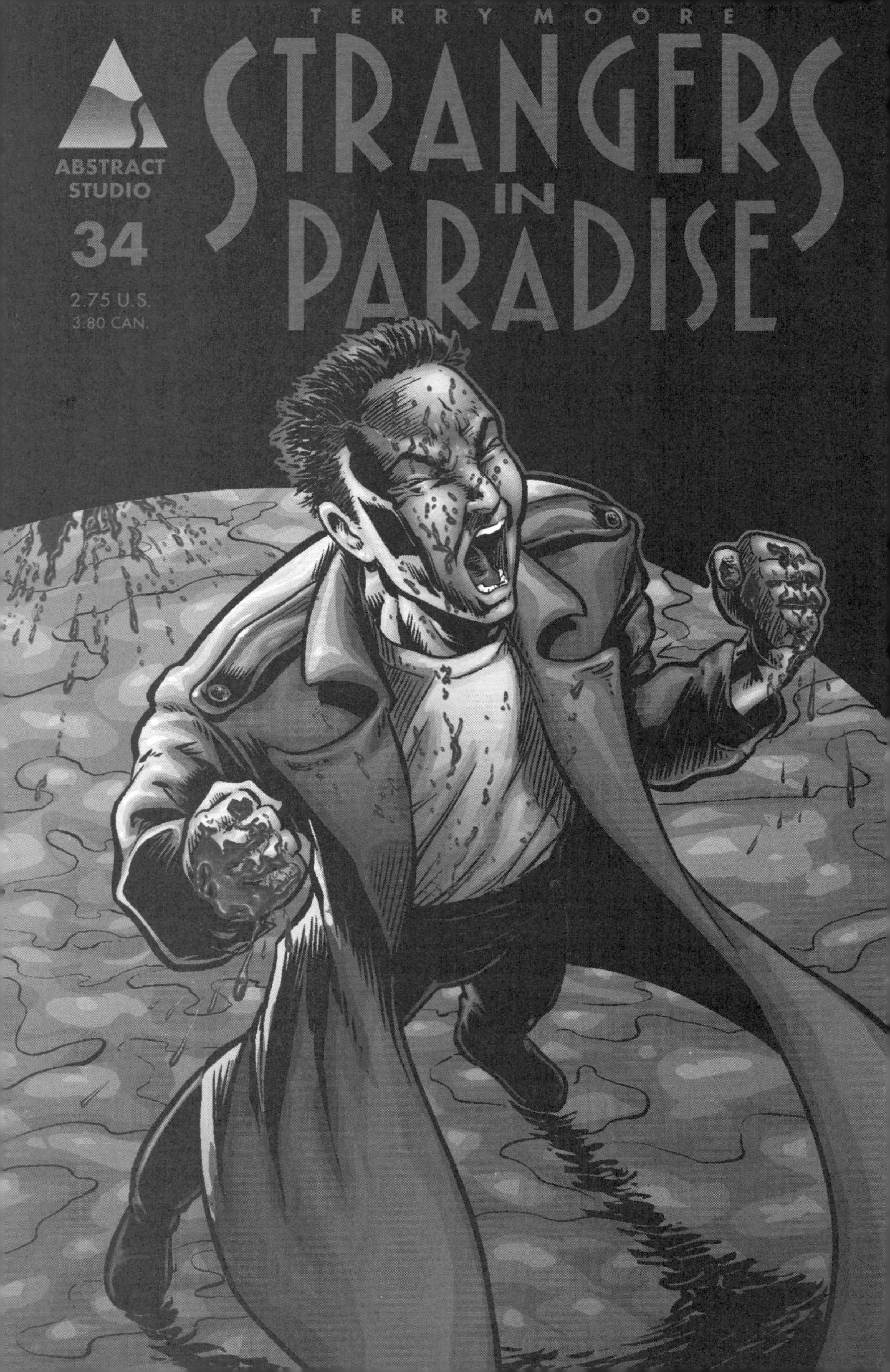
TERRY MOORE
STRANGERS IN PARADISE
ABSTRACT STUDIO
34
2.75 U.S.
3.80 CAN.

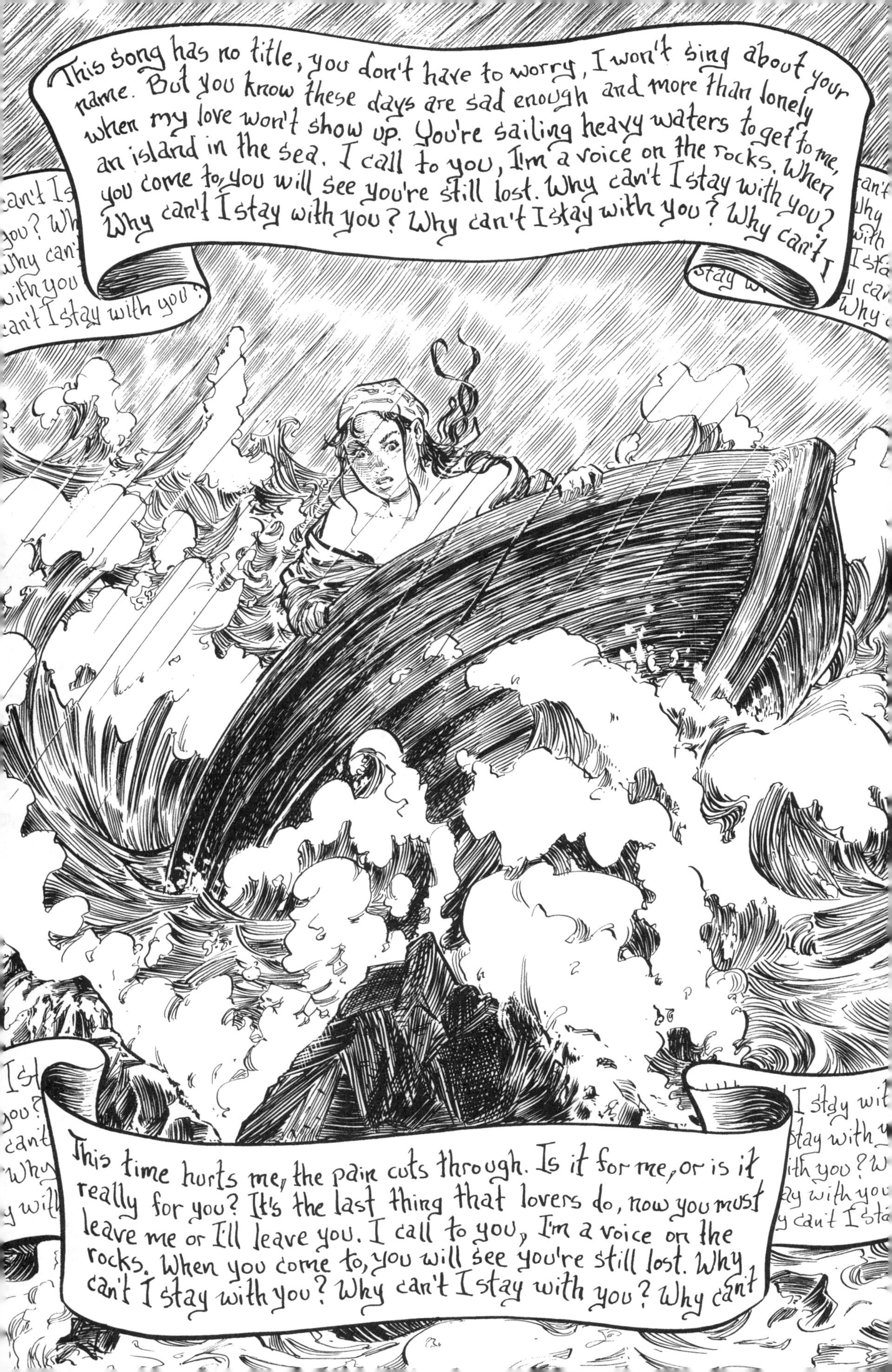

This song has no title, you don't have to worry, I won't sing about your name. But you know these days are sad enough and more than lonely when my love won't show up. You're sailing heavy waters to get to me, an island in the sea. I call to you, I'm a voice on the rocks. When you come to, you will see you're still lost. Why can't I stay with you? Why can't I stay with you? Why can't I stay with you? Why can't I
This time hurts me, the pain cuts through. Is it for me, or is it really for you? It's the last thing that lovers do, now you must leave me or I'll leave you. I call to you, I'm a voice on the rocks. When you come to, you will see you're still lost. Why can't I stay with you? Why can't I stay with you? Why can't

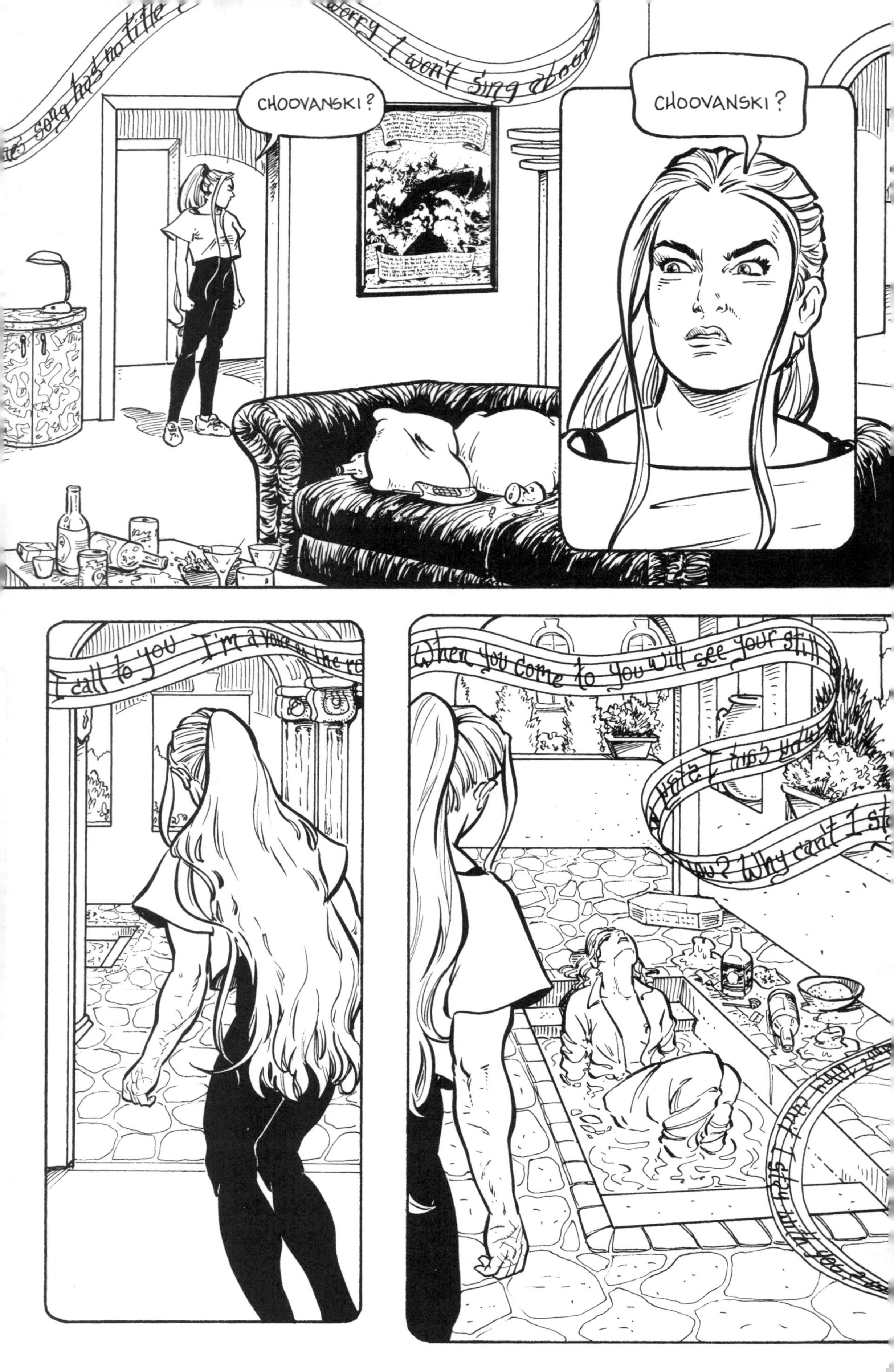
song has no title
worry I won't sing about
CHOOVANSKI?
CHOOVANSKI?
I call to you I'm a voice
When you come to you will see your
Why can't I

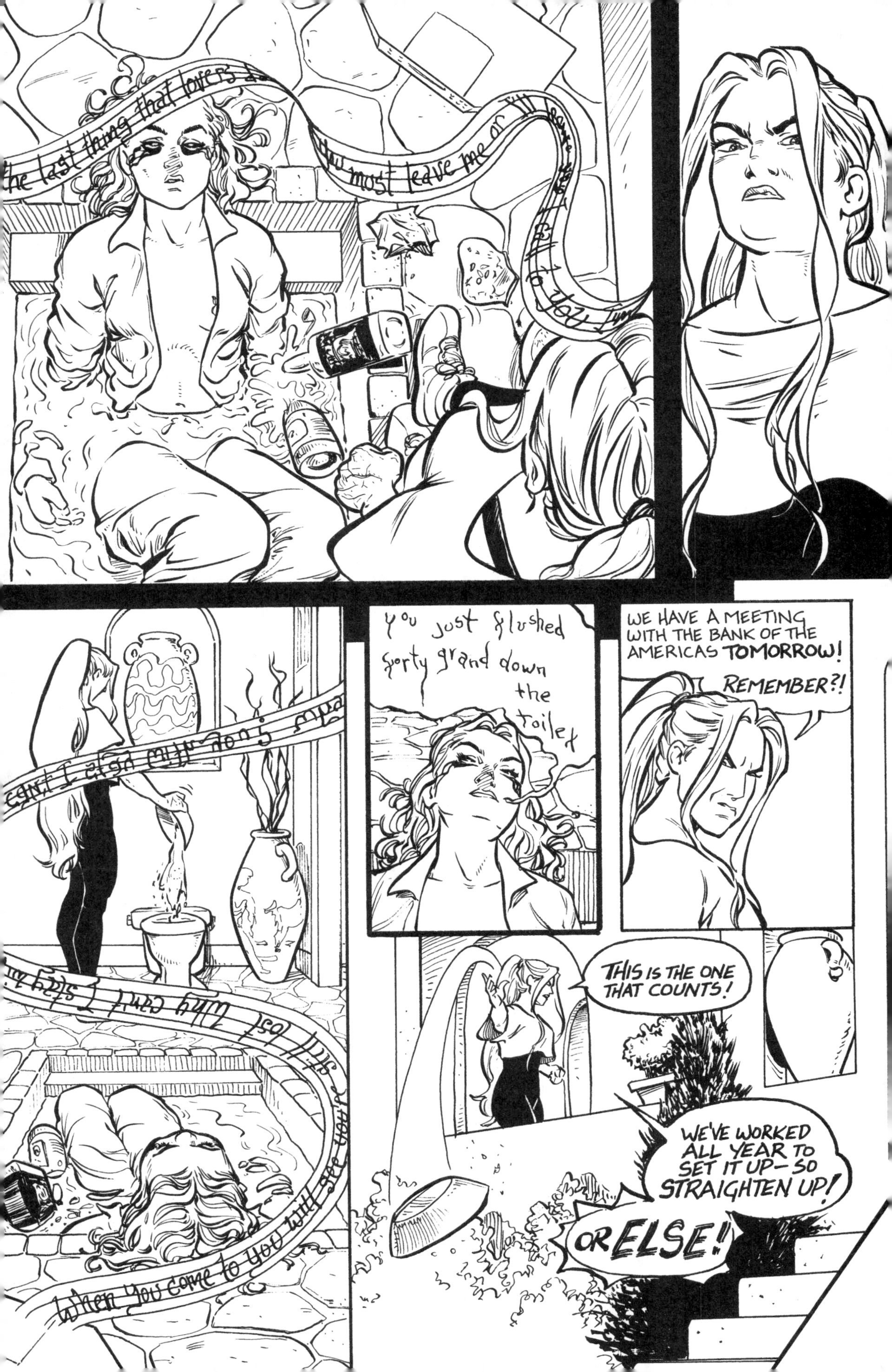

the last thing that lovers
you most leave me or
you just flushed forty grand down the toilet
WE HAVE A MEETING WITH THE BANK OF THE AMERICAS TOMORROW!
REMEMBER?!
THIS IS THE ONE THAT COUNTS!
When you come to you will see
WE'VE WORKED ALL YEAR TO SET IT UP— SO STRAIGHTEN UP!
OR ELSE!

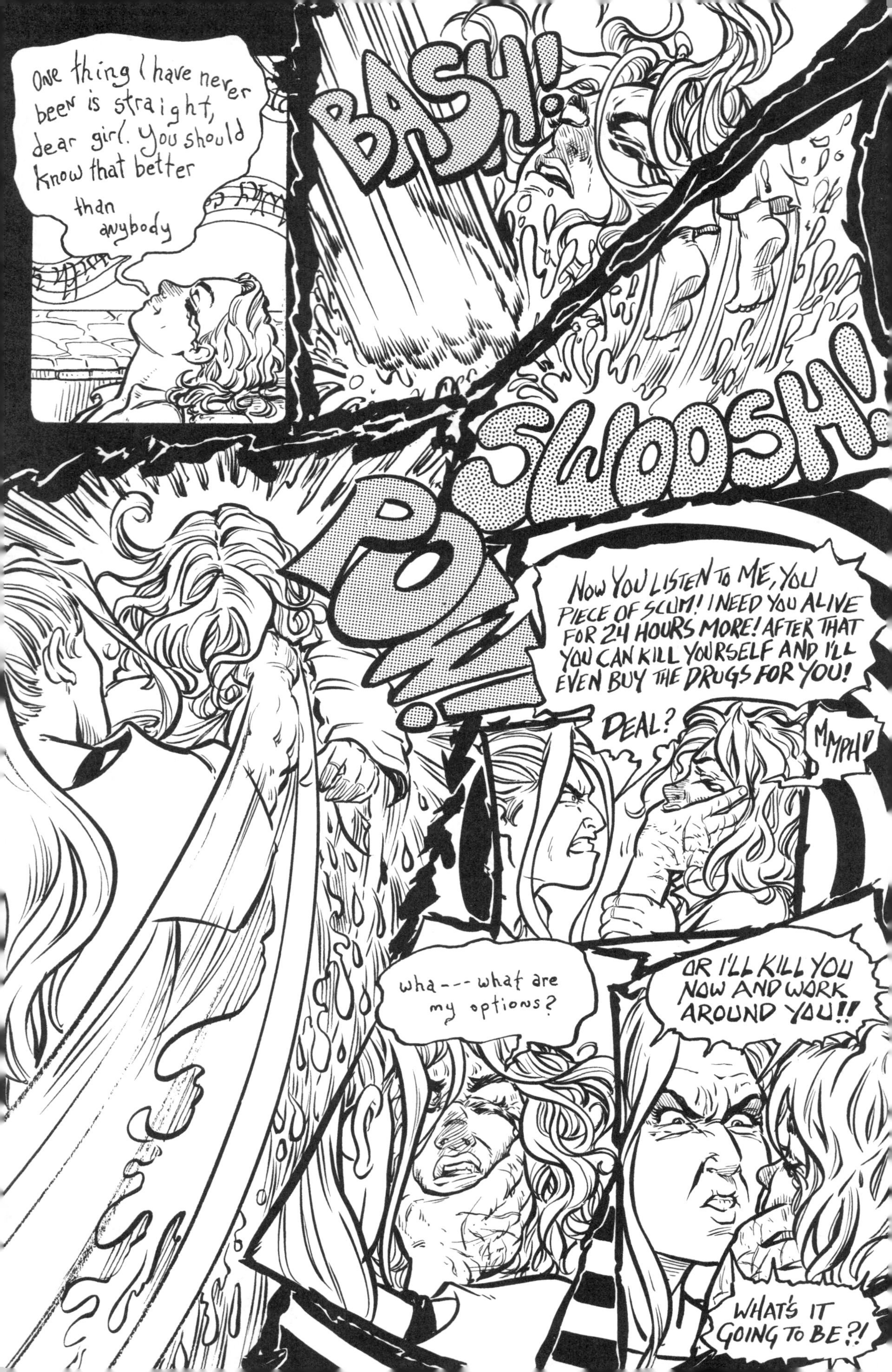
One thing I have never been is straight, dear girl. You should know that better than anybody
BASH!
SWOOSH!
POW
NOW YOU LISTEN TO ME, YOU PIECE OF SCUM! I NEED YOU ALIVE FOR 24 HOURS MORE! AFTER THAT YOU CAN KILL YOURSELF AND I'LL EVEN BUY THE DRUGS FOR YOU!
DEAL?
MMPH
wha--- what are my options?
OR I'LL KILL YOU NOW AND WORK AROUND YOU!!
WHAT'S IT GOING TO BE?!

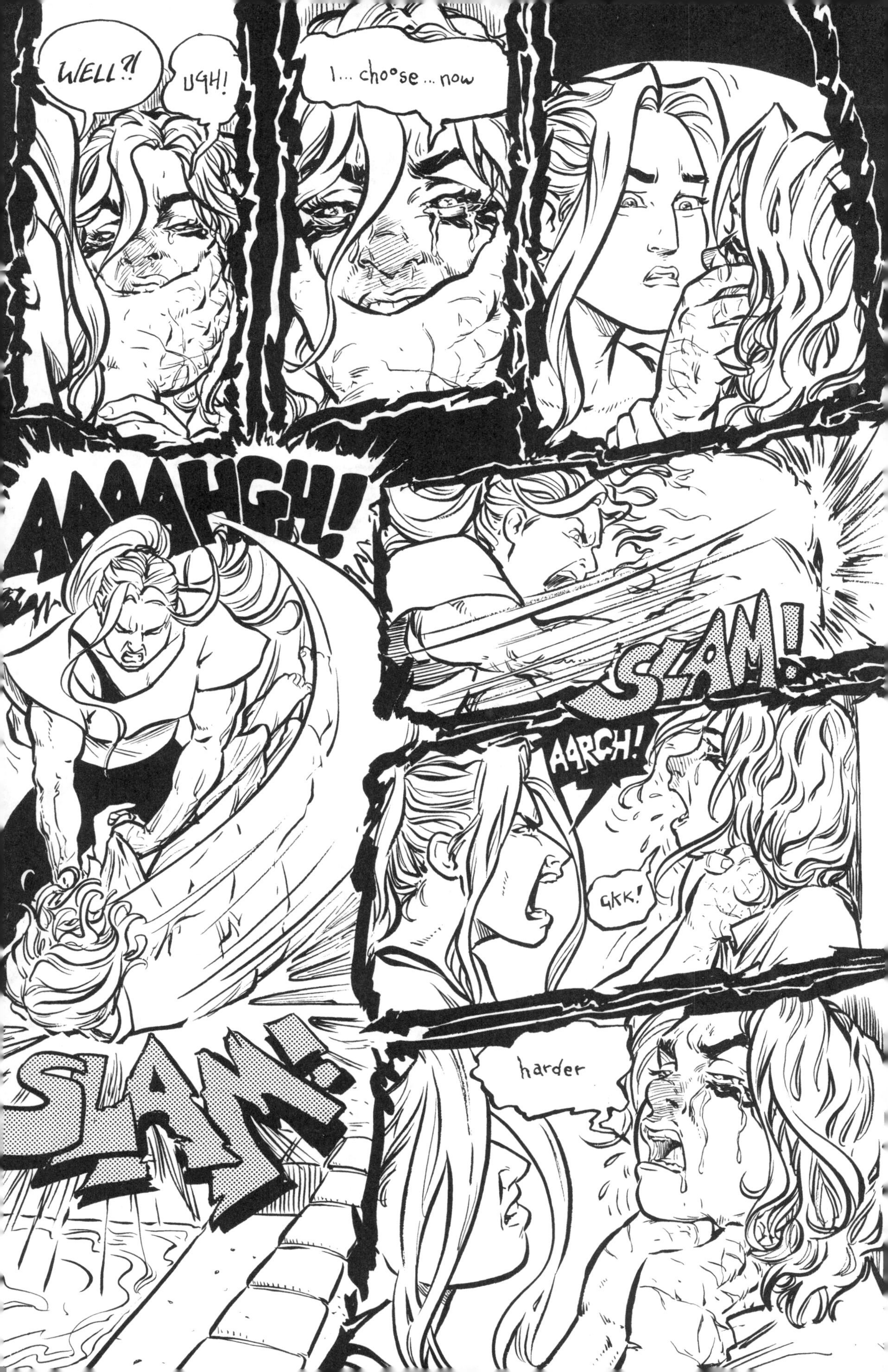

WELL?!
UGH!
I... choose... now
AAAAHGH!
SLAM!
AARCH!
GKK!
SLAM!
harder

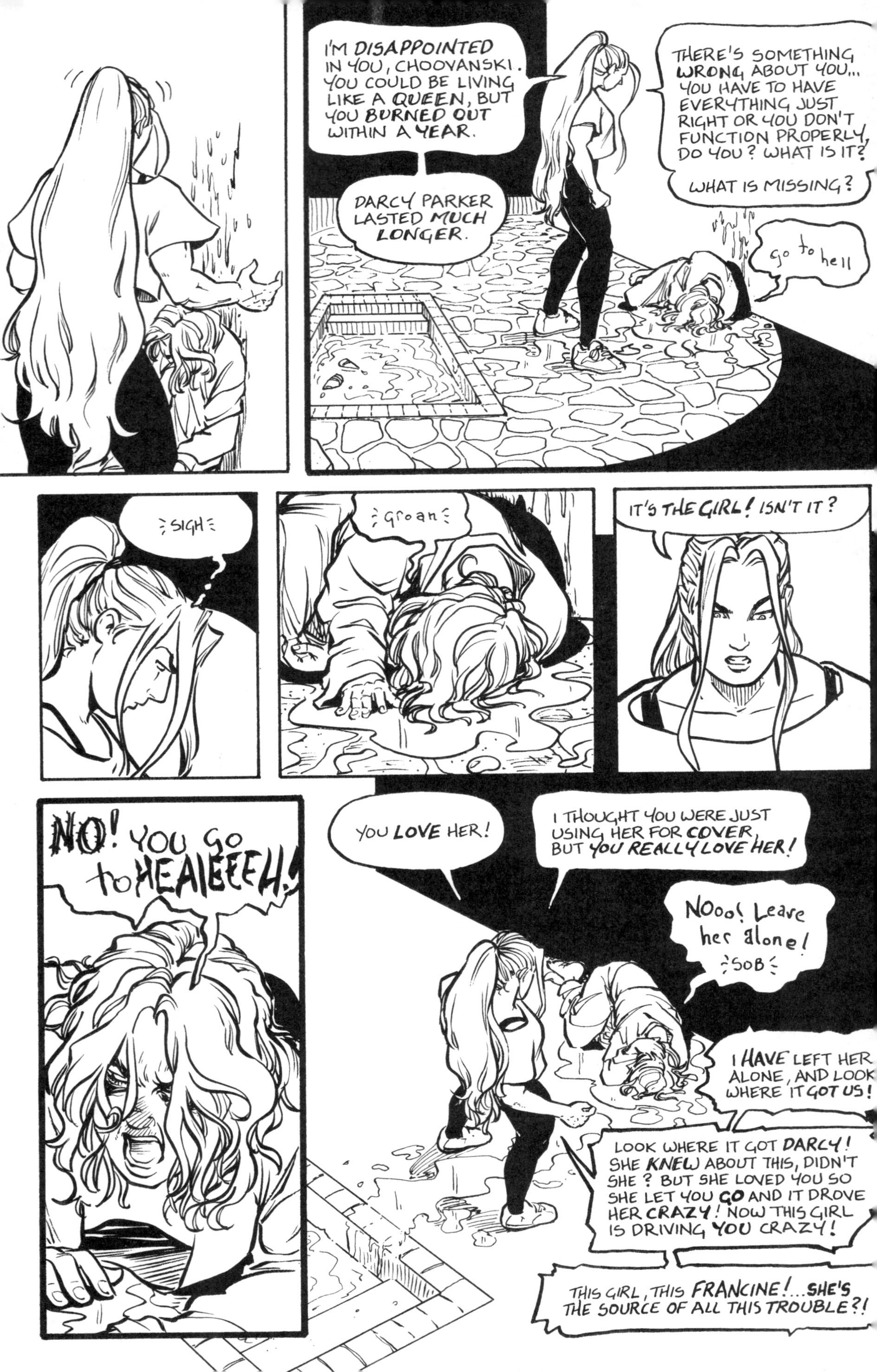
I'M DISAPPOINTED IN YOU, CHOOVANSKI. YOU COULD BE LIVING LIKE A QUEEN, BUT YOU BURNED OUT WITHIN A YEAR.
DARCY PARKER LASTED MUCH LONGER.
THERE'S SOMETHING WRONG ABOUT YOU... YOU HAVE TO HAVE EVERYTHING JUST RIGHT OR YOU DON'T FUNCTION PROPERLY, DO YOU? WHAT IS IT?
WHAT IS MISSING?
go to hell
SIGH
groan
IT'S THE GIRL! ISN'T IT?
NO! YOU GO to HEAIEEEH!
YOU LOVE HER!
I THOUGHT YOU WERE JUST USING HER FOR COVER, BUT YOU REALLY LOVE HER!
NOoo! Leave her alone!
SOB
I HAVE LEFT HER ALONE, AND LOOK WHERE IT GOT US!
LOOK WHERE IT GOT DARCY! SHE KNEW ABOUT THIS, DIDN'T SHE? BUT SHE LOVED YOU SO SHE LET YOU GO AND IT DROVE HER CRAZY! NOW THIS GIRL IS DRIVING YOU CRAZY!
THIS GIRL, THIS FRANCINE!...SHE'S THE SOURCE OF ALL THIS TROUBLE?!

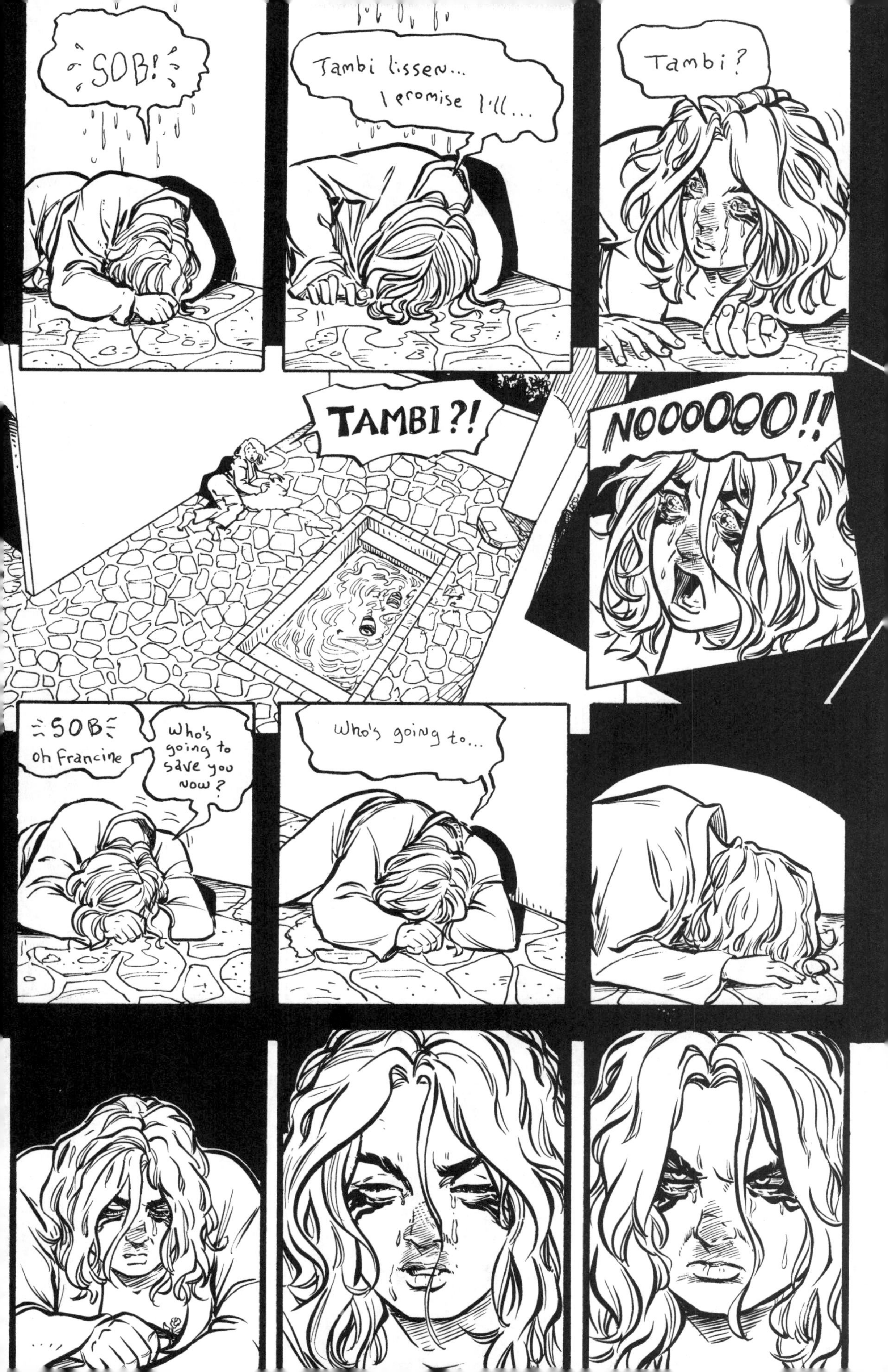

SOB!
Tambi lissen... I promise I'll...
Tambi?
TAMBI?!
NOOOOOO!!
SOB
oh Francine
Who's going to save you now?
Who's going to...

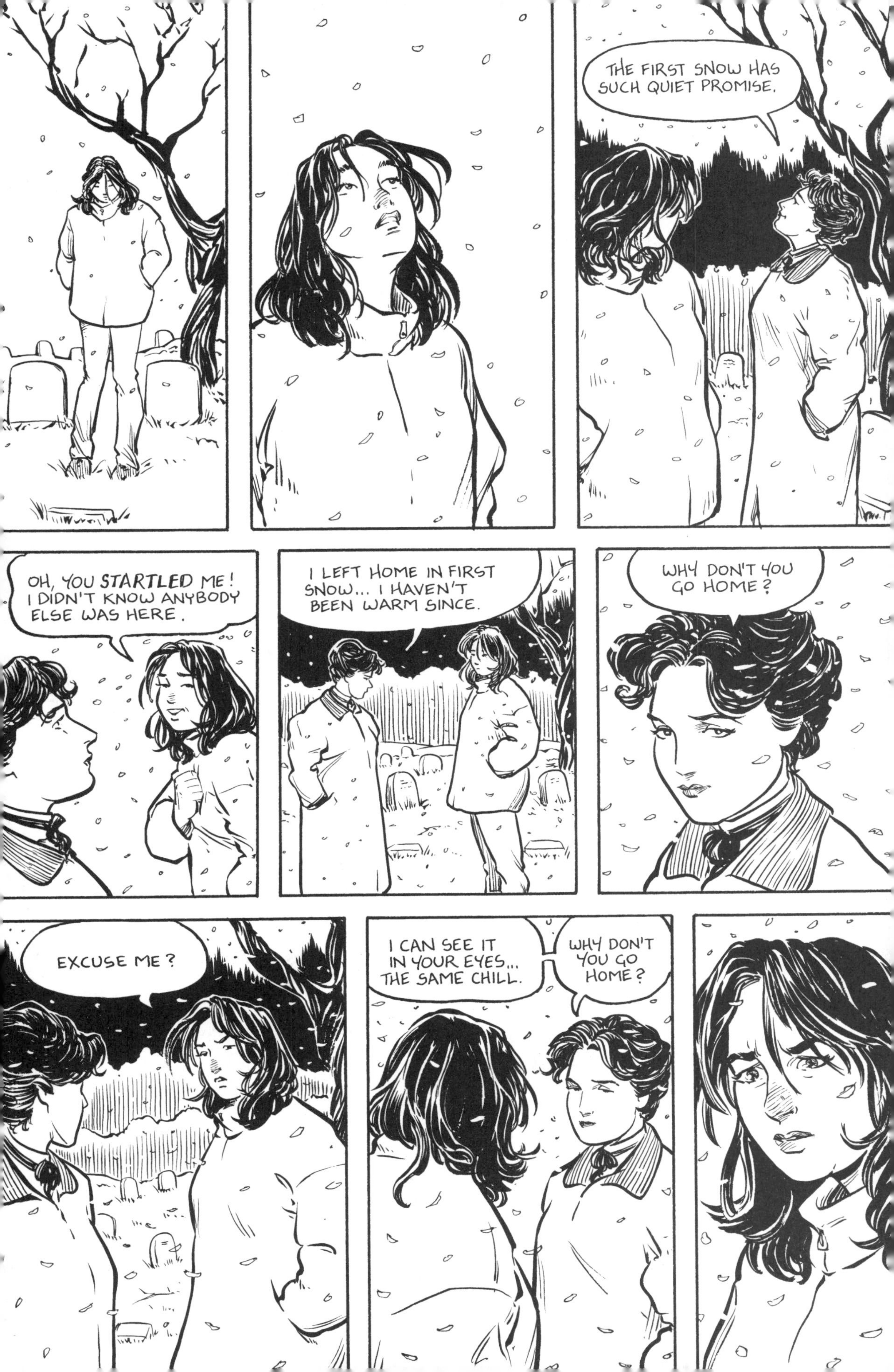
THE FIRST SNOW HAS SUCH QUIET PROMISE.
OH, YOU STARTLED ME! I DIDN'T KNOW ANYBODY ELSE WAS HERE.
I LEFT HOME IN FIRST SNOW... I HAVEN'T BEEN WARM SINCE.
WHY DON'T YOU GO HOME?
EXCUSE ME?
I CAN SEE IT IN YOUR EYES... THE SAME CHILL.
WHY DON'T YOU GO HOME?

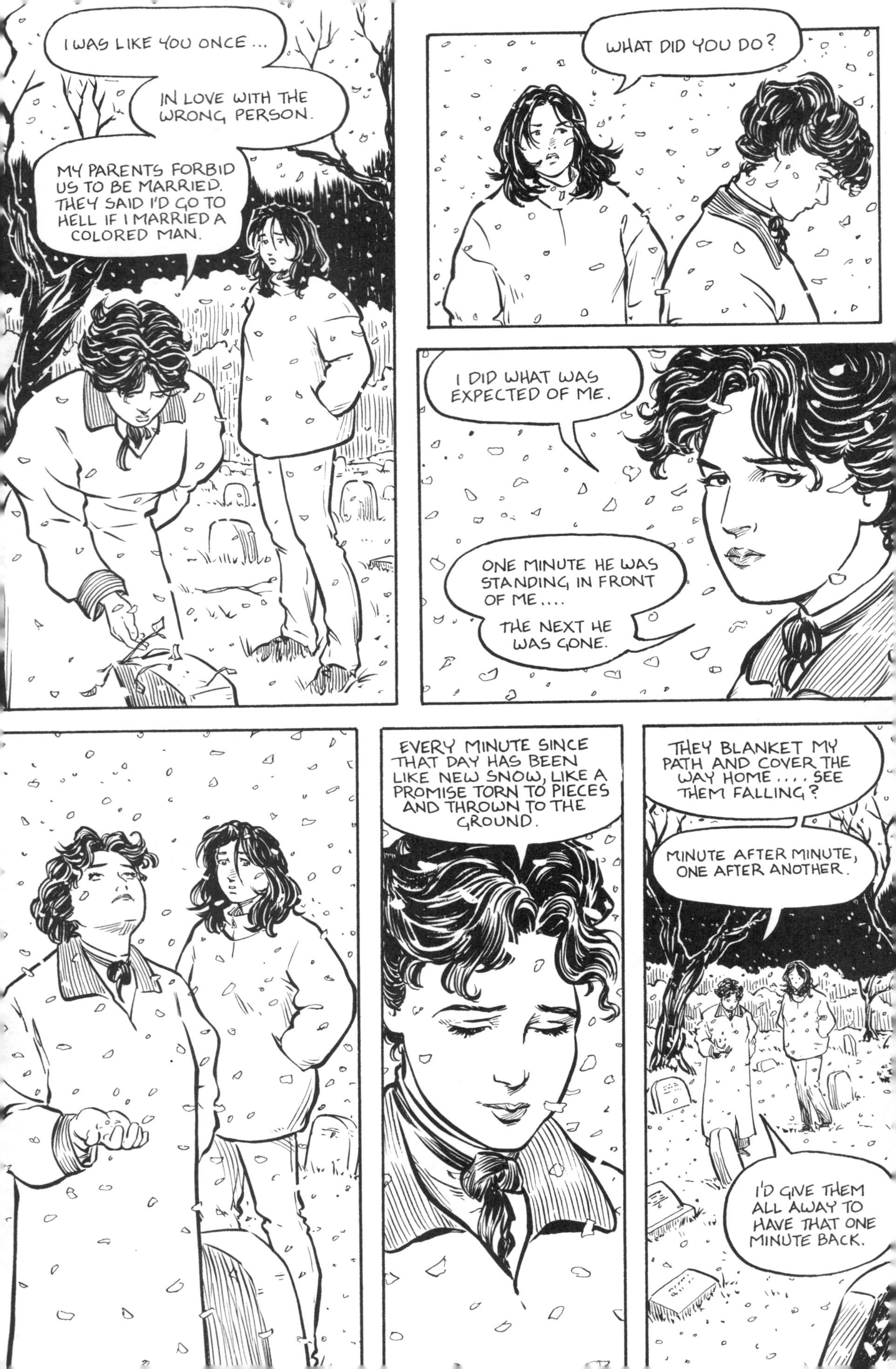

I WAS LIKE YOU ONCE...
IN LOVE WITH THE WRONG PERSON.
MY PARENTS FORBID US TO BE MARRIED. THEY SAID I'D GO TO HELL IF I MARRIED A COLORED MAN.
WHAT DID YOU DO?
I DID WHAT WAS EXPECTED OF ME.
ONE MINUTE HE WAS STANDING IN FRONT OF ME....
THE NEXT HE WAS GONE.
EVERY MINUTE SINCE THAT DAY HAS BEEN LIKE NEW SNOW, LIKE A PROMISE TORN TO PIECES AND THROWN TO THE GROUND.
THEY BLANKET MY PATH AND COVER THE WAY HOME.... SEE THEM FALLING?
MINUTE AFTER MINUTE, ONE AFTER ANOTHER.
I'D GIVE THEM ALL AWAY TO HAVE THAT ONE MINUTE BACK.

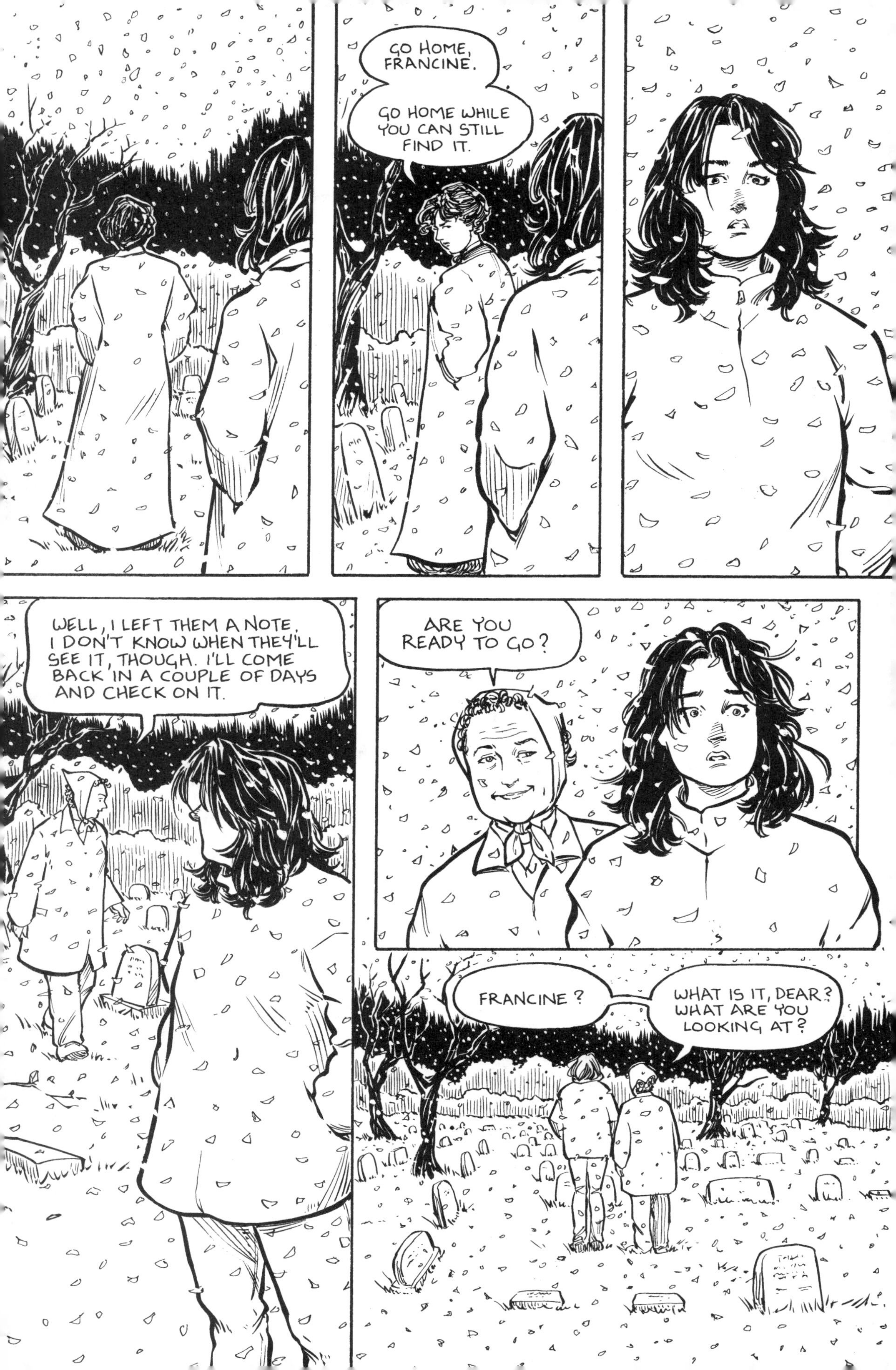
GO HOME, FRANCINE.
GO HOME WHILE YOU CAN STILL FIND IT.
WELL, I LEFT THEM A NOTE. I DON'T KNOW WHEN THEY'LL SEE IT, THOUGH. I'LL COME BACK IN A COUPLE OF DAYS AND CHECK ON IT.
ARE YOU READY TO GO?
FRANCINE?
WHAT IS IT, DEAR? WHAT ARE YOU LOOKING AT?

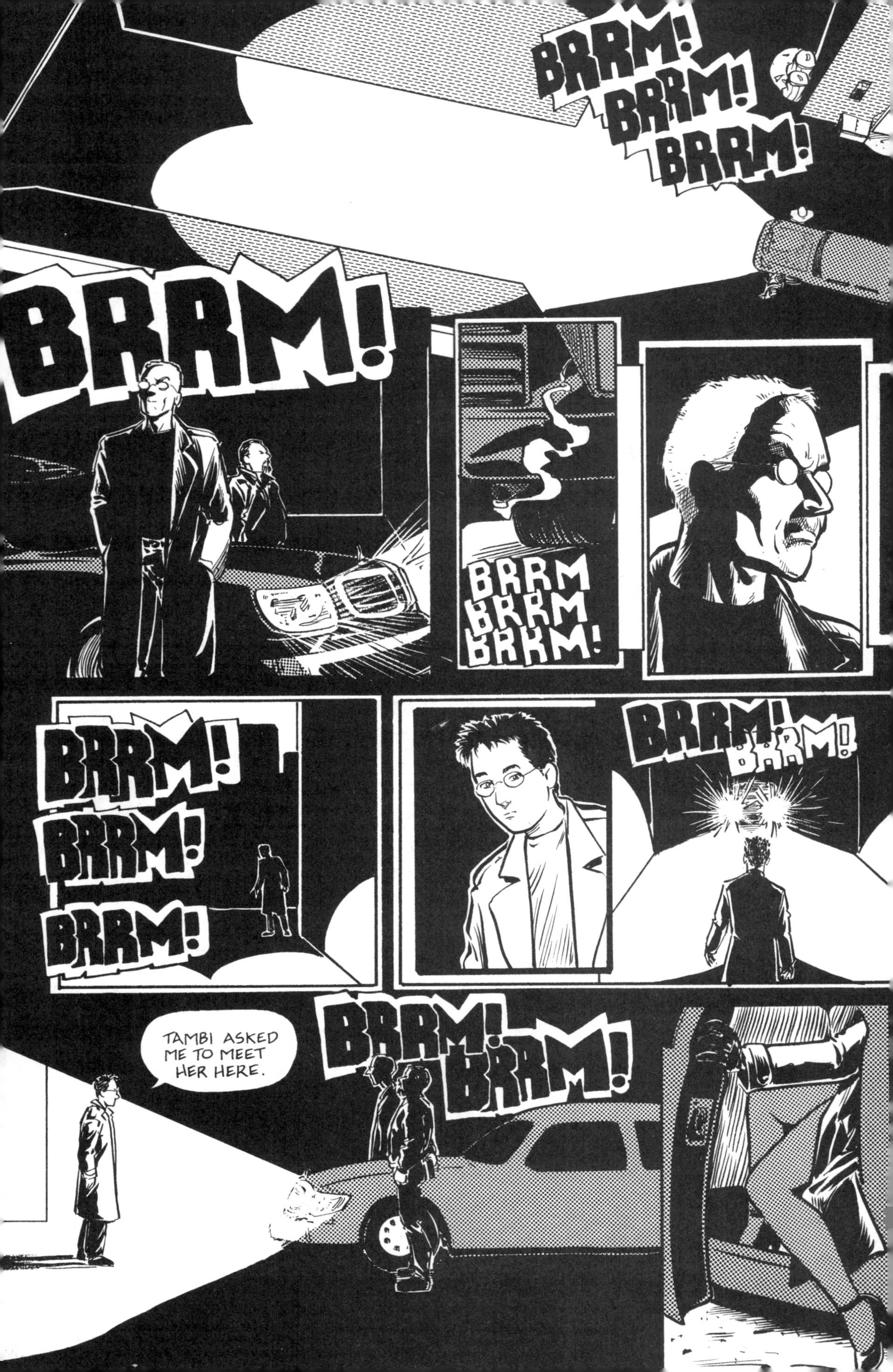
BRRM! BRRM! BRRM!
BRRM!
BRRM
BRRM
BRRM!
BRRM!
BRRM!
BRRM!
BRRM! BRRM!
TAMBI ASKED ME TO MEET HER HERE.
BRRM! BRRM!

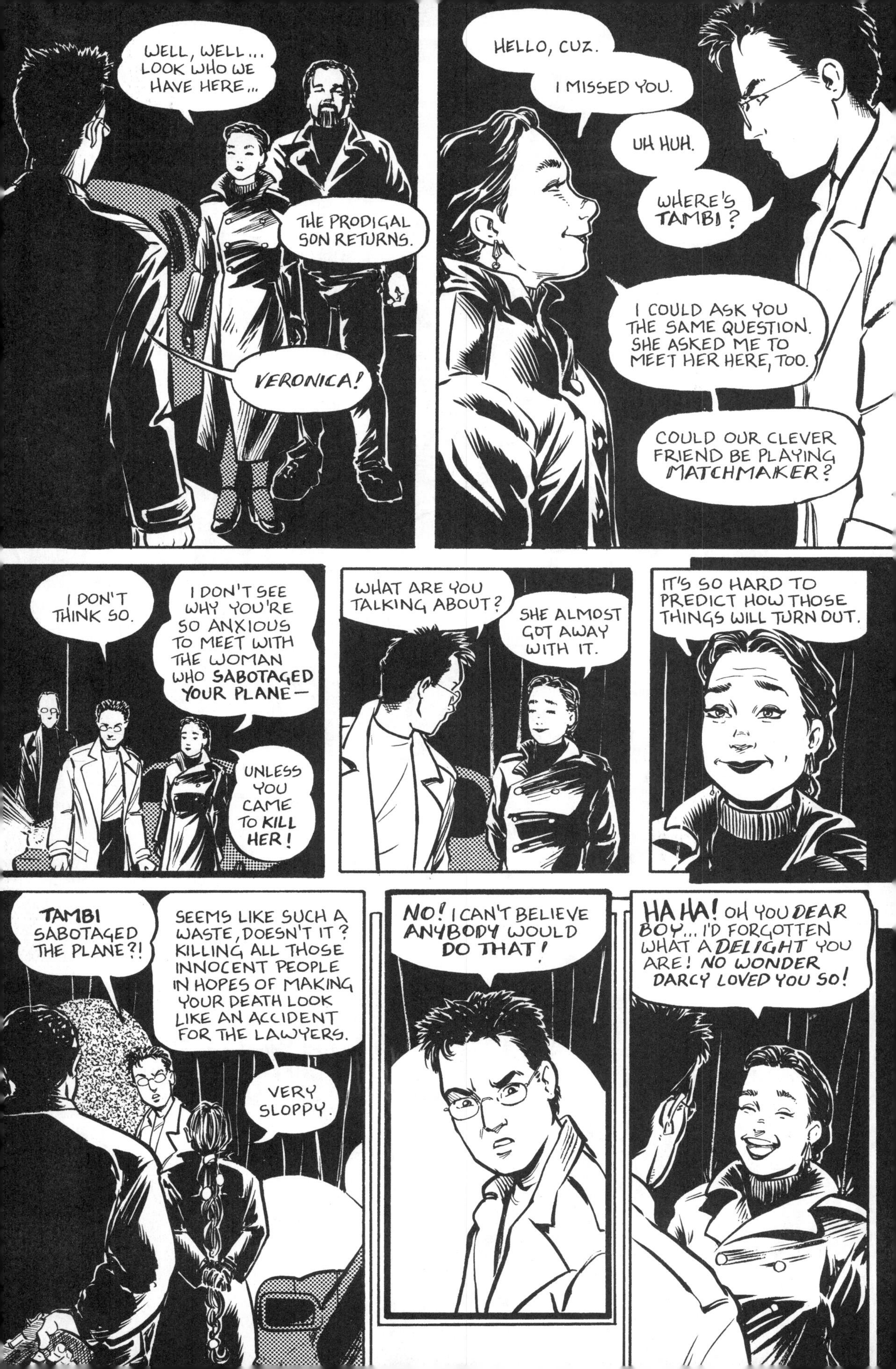

WELL, WELL... LOOK WHO WE HAVE HERE...
THE PRODIGAL SON RETURNS.
VERONICA!
HELLO, CUZ.
I MISSED YOU.
UH HUH.
WHERE'S TAMBI?
I COULD ASK YOU THE SAME QUESTION. SHE ASKED ME TO MEET HER HERE, TOO.
COULD OUR CLEVER FRIEND BE PLAYING MATCHMAKER?
I DON'T THINK SO.
I DON'T SEE WHY YOU'RE SO ANXIOUS TO MEET WITH THE WOMAN WHO SABOTAGED YOUR PLANE—
UNLESS YOU CAME TO KILL HER!
WHAT ARE YOU TALKING ABOUT?
SHE ALMOST GOT AWAY WITH IT.
IT'S SO HARD TO PREDICT HOW THOSE THINGS WILL TURN OUT.
TAMBI SABOTAGED THE PLANE?!
SEEMS LIKE SUCH A WASTE, DOESN'T IT? KILLING ALL THOSE INNOCENT PEOPLE IN HOPES OF MAKING YOUR DEATH LOOK LIKE AN ACCIDENT FOR THE LAWYERS.
VERY SLOPPY.
NO! I CAN'T BELIEVE ANYBODY WOULD DO THAT!
HA HA! OH YOU DEAR BOY... I'D FORGOTTEN WHAT A DELIGHT YOU ARE! NO WONDER DARCY LOVED YOU SO!

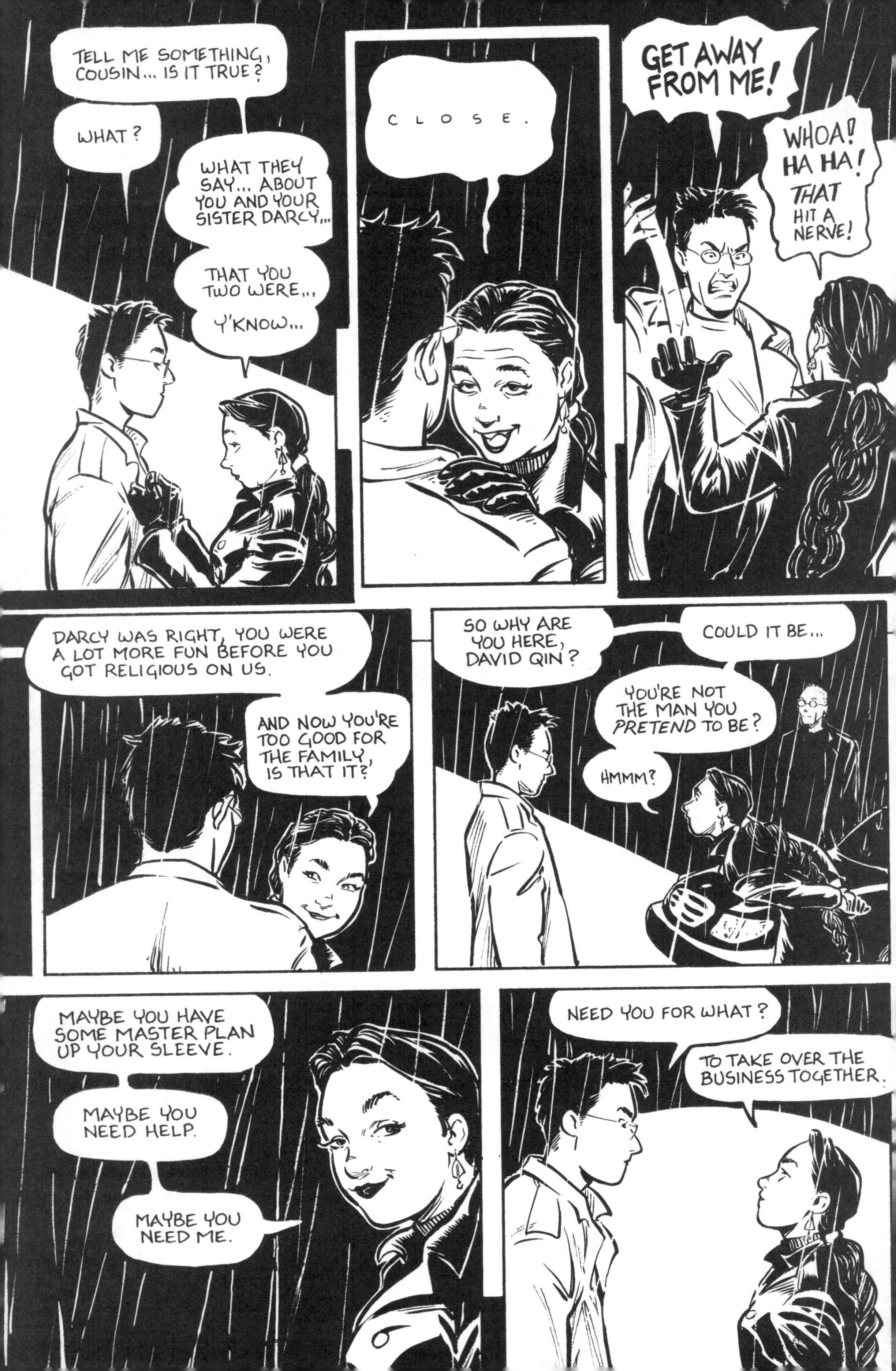
TELL ME SOMETHING, COUSIN... IS IT TRUE?
WHAT?
WHAT THEY SAY... ABOUT YOU AND YOUR SISTER DARCY...
THAT YOU TWO WERE...
Y'KNOW...
C L O S E.
GET AWAY FROM ME!
WHOA! HA HA! THAT HIT A NERVE!
DARCY WAS RIGHT, YOU WERE A LOT MORE FUN BEFORE YOU GOT RELIGIOUS ON US.
AND NOW YOU'RE TOO GOOD FOR THE FAMILY, IS THAT IT?
SO WHY ARE YOU HERE, DAVID QIN?
COULD IT BE...
YOU'RE NOT THE MAN YOU PRETEND TO BE?
HMMM?
MAYBE YOU HAVE SOME MASTER PLAN UP YOUR SLEEVE.
MAYBE YOU NEED HELP.
MAYBE YOU NEED ME.
NEED YOU FOR WHAT?
TO TAKE OVER THE BUSINESS TOGETHER.

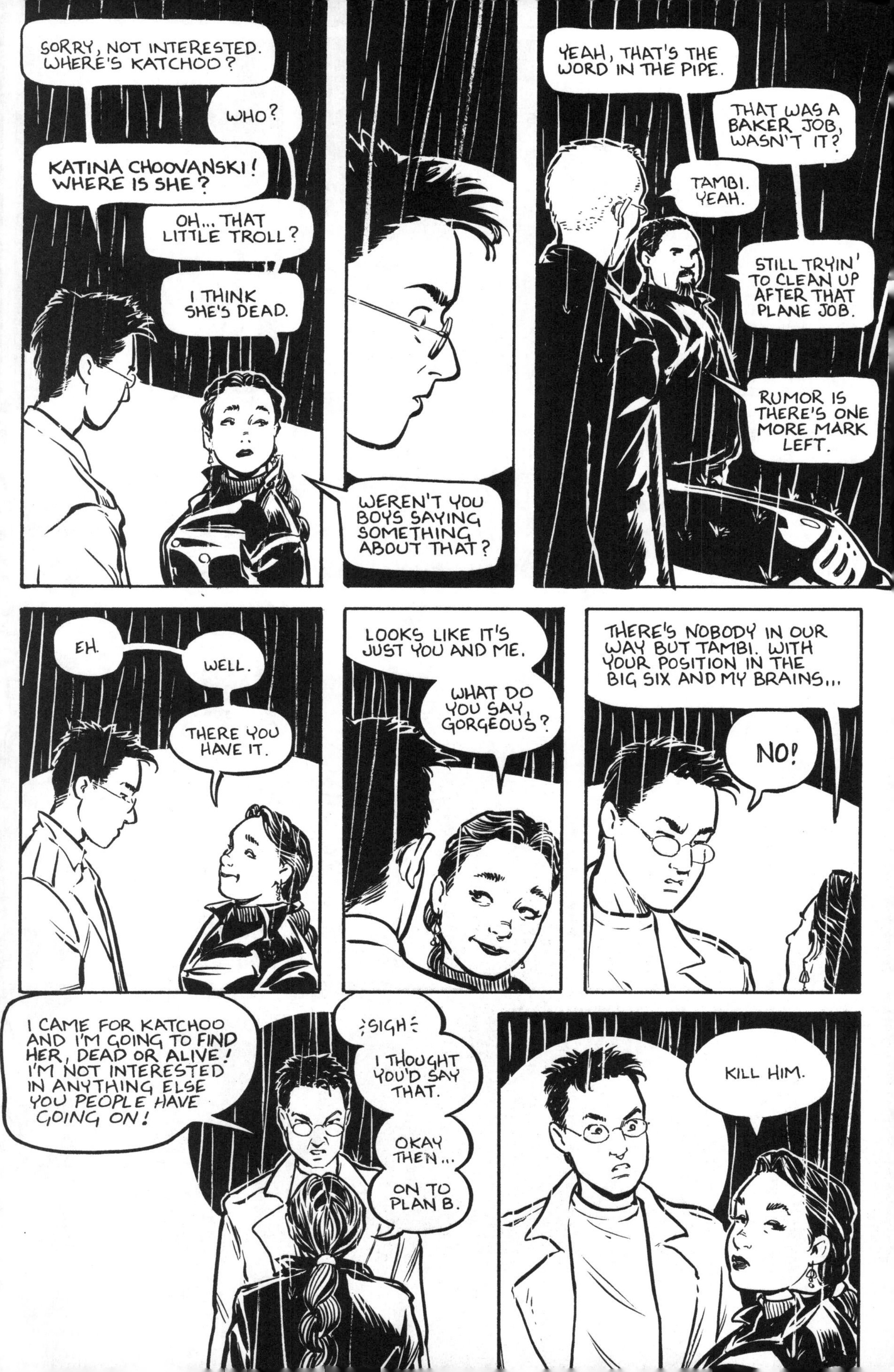
SORRY, NOT INTERESTED. WHERE'S KATCHOO?
WHO?
KATINA CHOOVANSKI! WHERE IS SHE?
OH... THAT LITTLE TROLL?
I THINK SHE'S DEAD.
WEREN'T YOU BOYS SAYING SOMETHING ABOUT THAT?
YEAH, THAT'S THE WORD IN THE PIPE.
THAT WAS A BAKER JOB, WASN'T IT?
TAMBI. YEAH.
STILL TRYIN' TO CLEAN UP AFTER THAT PLANE JOB.
RUMOR IS THERE'S ONE MORE MARK LEFT.
EH.
WELL.
THERE YOU HAVE IT.
LOOKS LIKE IT'S JUST YOU AND ME.
WHAT DO YOU SAY, GORGEOUS?
THERE'S NOBODY IN OUR WAY BUT TAMBI. WITH YOUR POSITION IN THE BIG SIX AND MY BRAINS...
NO!
I CAME FOR KATCHOO AND I'M GOING TO FIND HER, DEAD OR ALIVE! I'M NOT INTERESTED IN ANYTHING ELSE YOU PEOPLE HAVE GOING ON!
SIGH
I THOUGHT YOU'D SAY THAT.
OKAY THEN...
ON TO PLAN B.
KILL HIM.

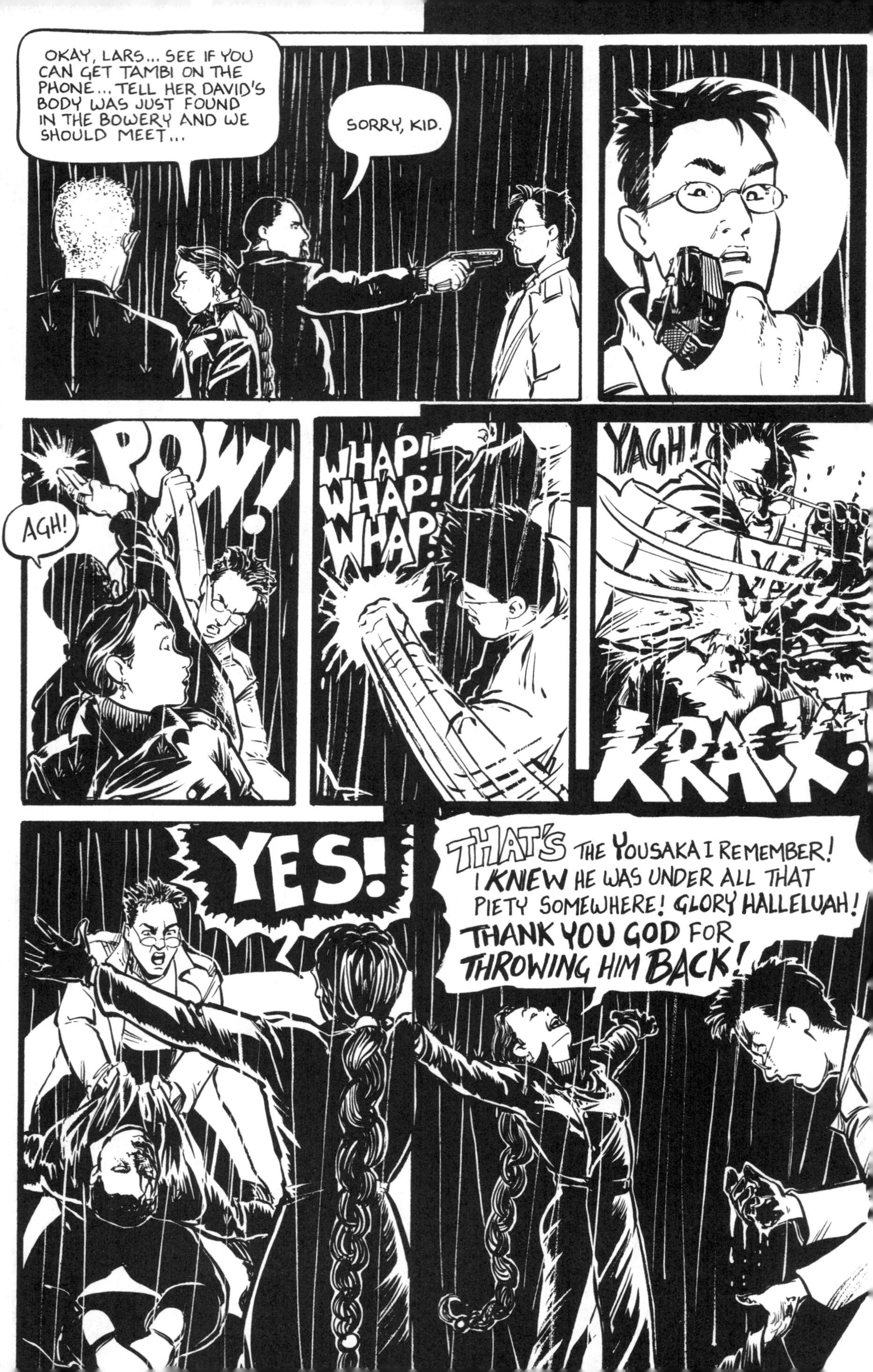

OKAY, LARS... SEE IF YOU CAN GET TAMBI ON THE PHONE... TELL HER DAVID'S BODY WAS JUST FOUND IN THE BOWERY AND WE SHOULD MEET...
SORRY, KID.
POW!
AGH!
WHAP! WHAP! WHAP!
YAGH!
KRACK!
YES!
THAT'S THE YOUSAKA I REMEMBER! I KNEW HE WAS UNDER ALL THAT PIETY SOMEWHERE! GLORY HALLELUAH! THANK YOU GOD FOR THROWING HIM BACK!

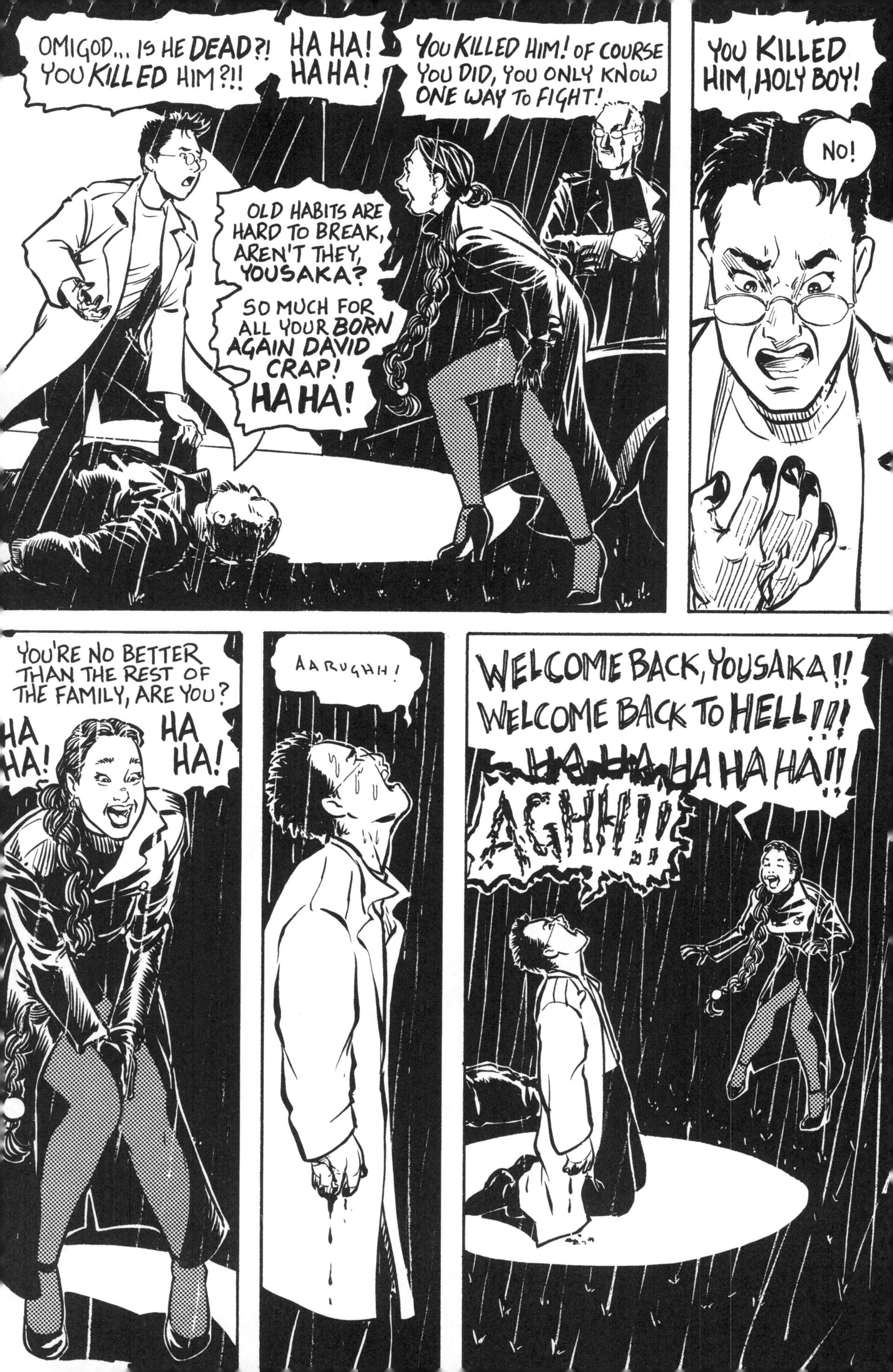

OMIGOD... IS HE DEAD?! YOU KILLED HIM?!!
HA HA! HA HA!
YOU KILLED HIM! OF COURSE YOU DID, YOU ONLY KNOW ONE WAY TO FIGHT!
OLD HABITS ARE HARD TO BREAK, AREN'T THEY, YOUSAKA?
SO MUCH FOR ALL YOUR BORN AGAIN DAVID CRAP! HA HA!
YOU KILLED HIM, HOLY BOY!
NO!
YOU'RE NO BETTER THAN THE REST OF THE FAMILY, ARE YOU?
HA HA!
HA HA!
AARUGHH!
WELCOME BACK, YOUSAKA!! WELCOME BACK TO HELL!!!
HA HA HA HA HA!!
AGHH!!

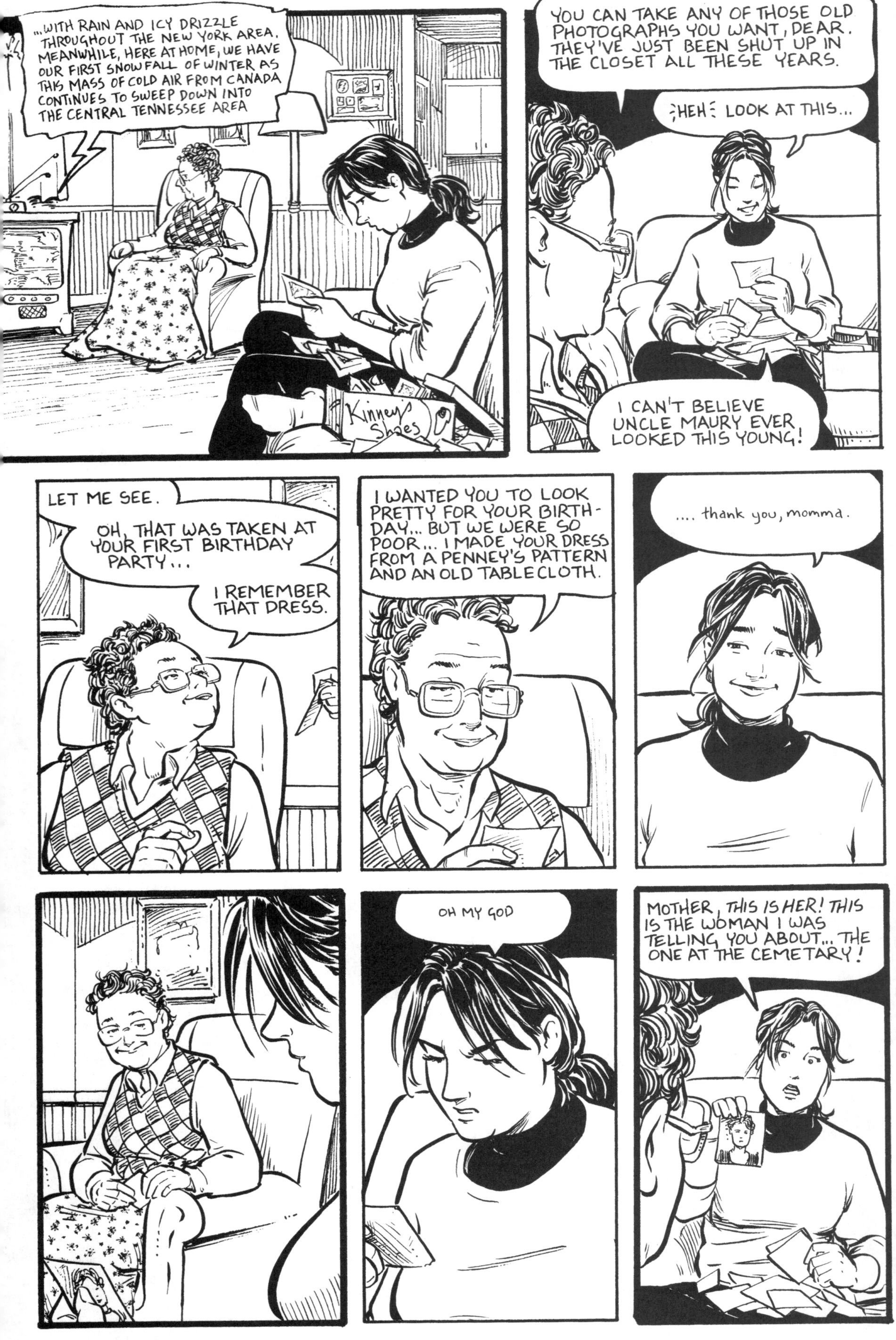
...WITH RAIN AND ICY DRIZZLE THROUGHOUT THE NEW YORK AREA. MEANWHILE, HERE AT HOME, WE HAVE OUR FIRST SNOWFALL OF WINTER AS THIS MASS OF COLD AIR FROM CANADA CONTINUES TO SWEEP DOWN INTO THE CENTRAL TENNESSEE AREA
Kinney's Shoes
YOU CAN TAKE ANY OF THOSE OLD PHOTOGRAPHS YOU WANT, DEAR. THEY'VE JUST BEEN SHUT UP IN THE CLOSET ALL THESE YEARS.
HEH LOOK AT THIS...
I CAN'T BELIEVE UNCLE MAURY EVER LOOKED THIS YOUNG!
LET ME SEE.
OH, THAT WAS TAKEN AT YOUR FIRST BIRTHDAY PARTY...
I REMEMBER THAT DRESS.
I WANTED YOU TO LOOK PRETTY FOR YOUR BIRTHDAY... BUT WE WERE SO POOR... I MADE YOUR DRESS FROM A PENNEY'S PATTERN AND AN OLD TABLECLOTH.
.... thank you, momma.
OH MY GOD
MOTHER, THIS IS HER! THIS IS THE WOMAN I WAS TELLING YOU ABOUT... THE ONE AT THE CEMETARY!

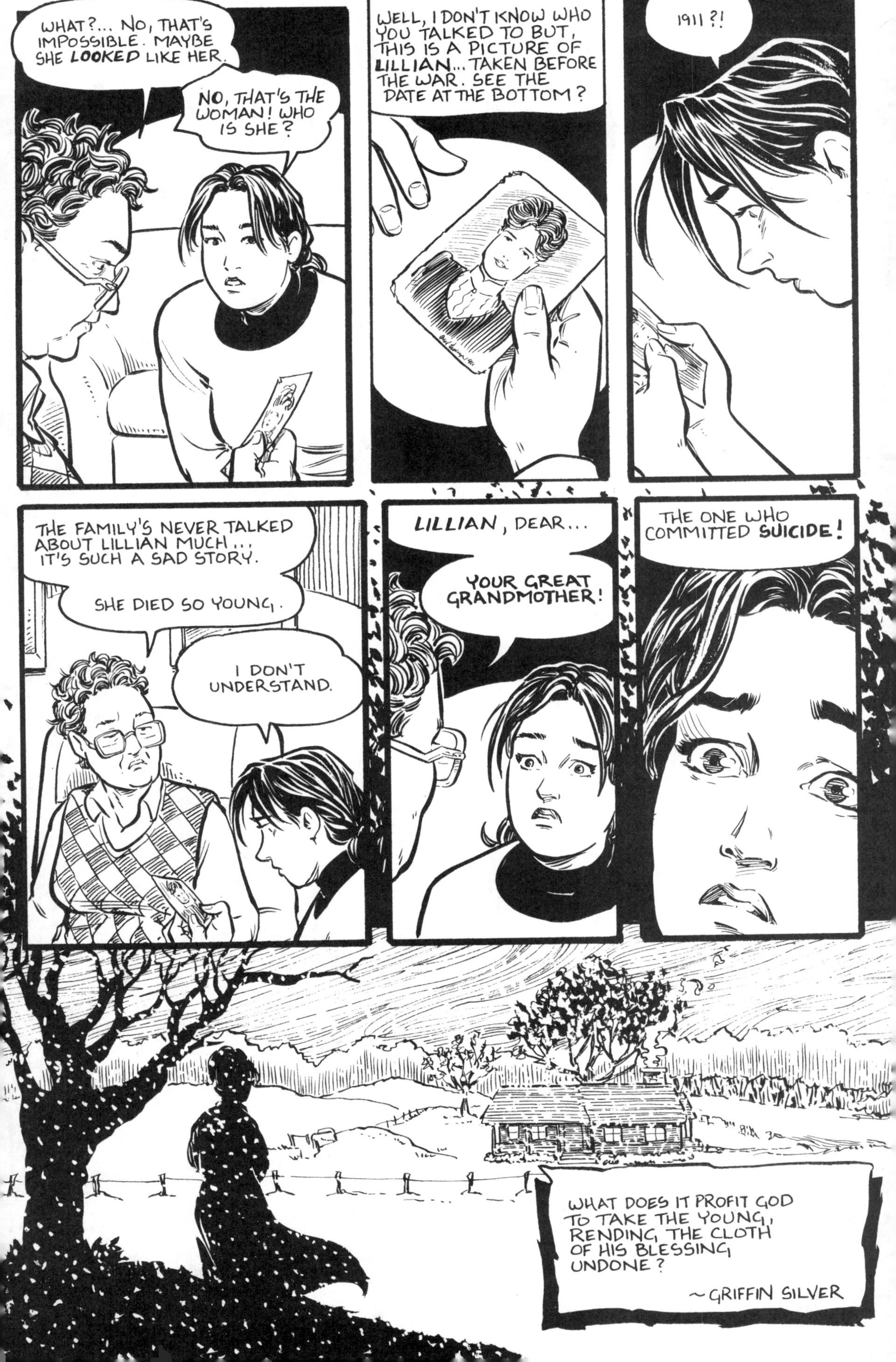

WHAT?... NO, THAT'S IMPOSSIBLE. MAYBE SHE LOOKED LIKE HER.
NO, THAT'S THE WOMAN! WHO IS SHE?
WELL, I DON'T KNOW WHO YOU TALKED TO BUT, THIS IS A PICTURE OF LILLIAN... TAKEN BEFORE THE WAR. SEE THE DATE AT THE BOTTOM?
1911?!
THE FAMILY'S NEVER TALKED ABOUT LILLIAN MUCH... IT'S SUCH A SAD STORY.
SHE DIED SO YOUNG.
I DON'T UNDERSTAND.
LILLIAN, DEAR...
YOUR GREAT GRANDMOTHER!
THE ONE WHO COMMITTED SUICIDE!
WHAT DOES IT PROFIT GOD TO TAKE THE YOUNG, RENDING THE CLOTH OF HIS BLESSING UNDONE?
~GRIFFIN SILVER

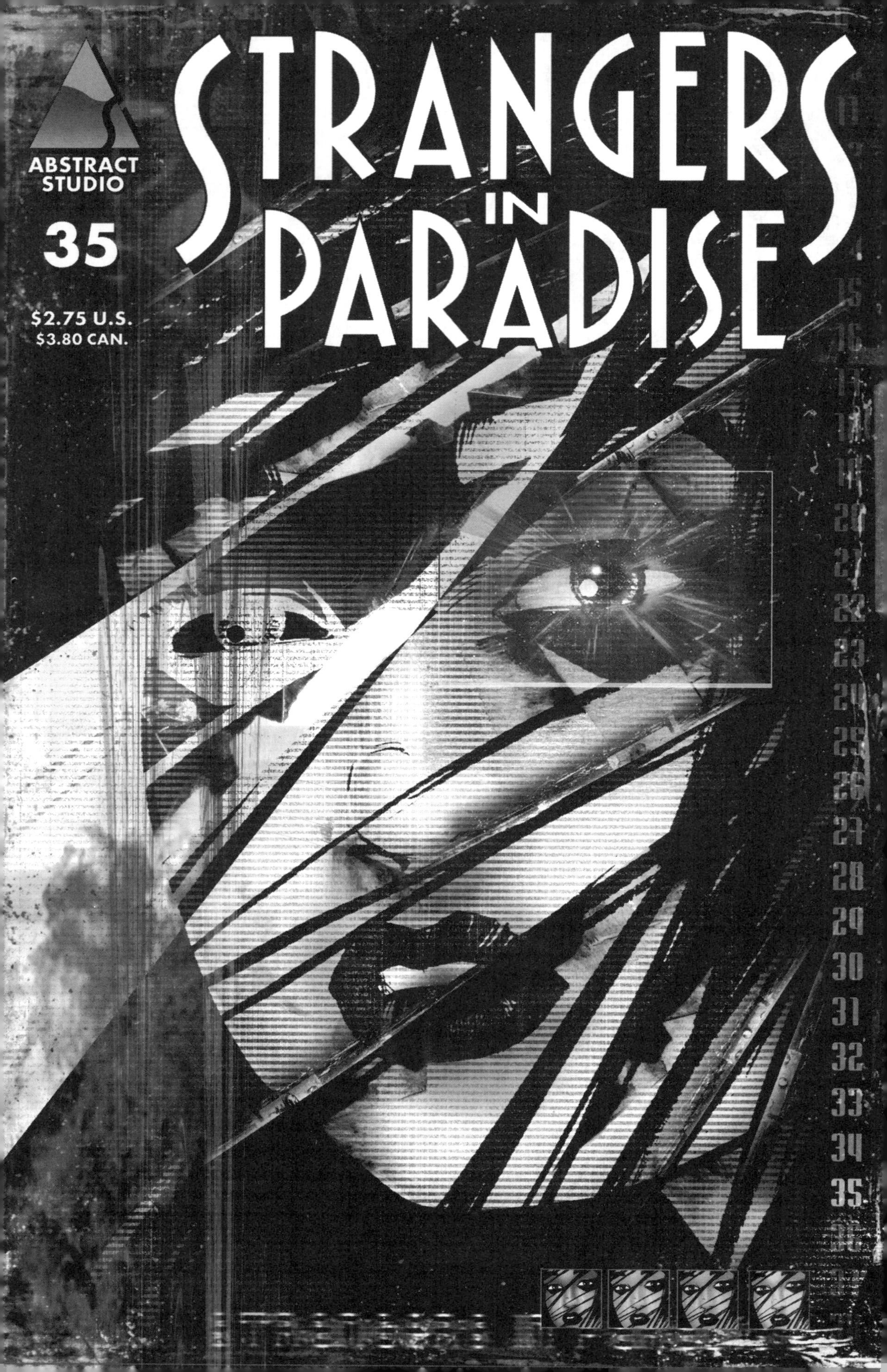
ABSTRACT STUDIO
35
$2.75 U.S.
$3.80 CAN.
STRANGERS IN PARADISE

## Pretty Maids All In A Row

Hi there, how are ya?
It's been a long time
Seems like we've come a long way
My, but we learn so slow
And heroes they come and they go
And leave us behind
As if we're supposed to know why
Why do we give up our hearts to the past?
And why must we grow up so fast?

And all you wishing well fools with your fortunes
Someone should send you a rose
With love from a friend
It's nice to hear from you again
And the storybook comes to a close
Gone are the ribbons and bows
Things to remember
Places to go
Pretty maids all in a row

art by Alphonse Mucha

Pretty Maids All In A Row by Joe Walsh & Joe Vitale

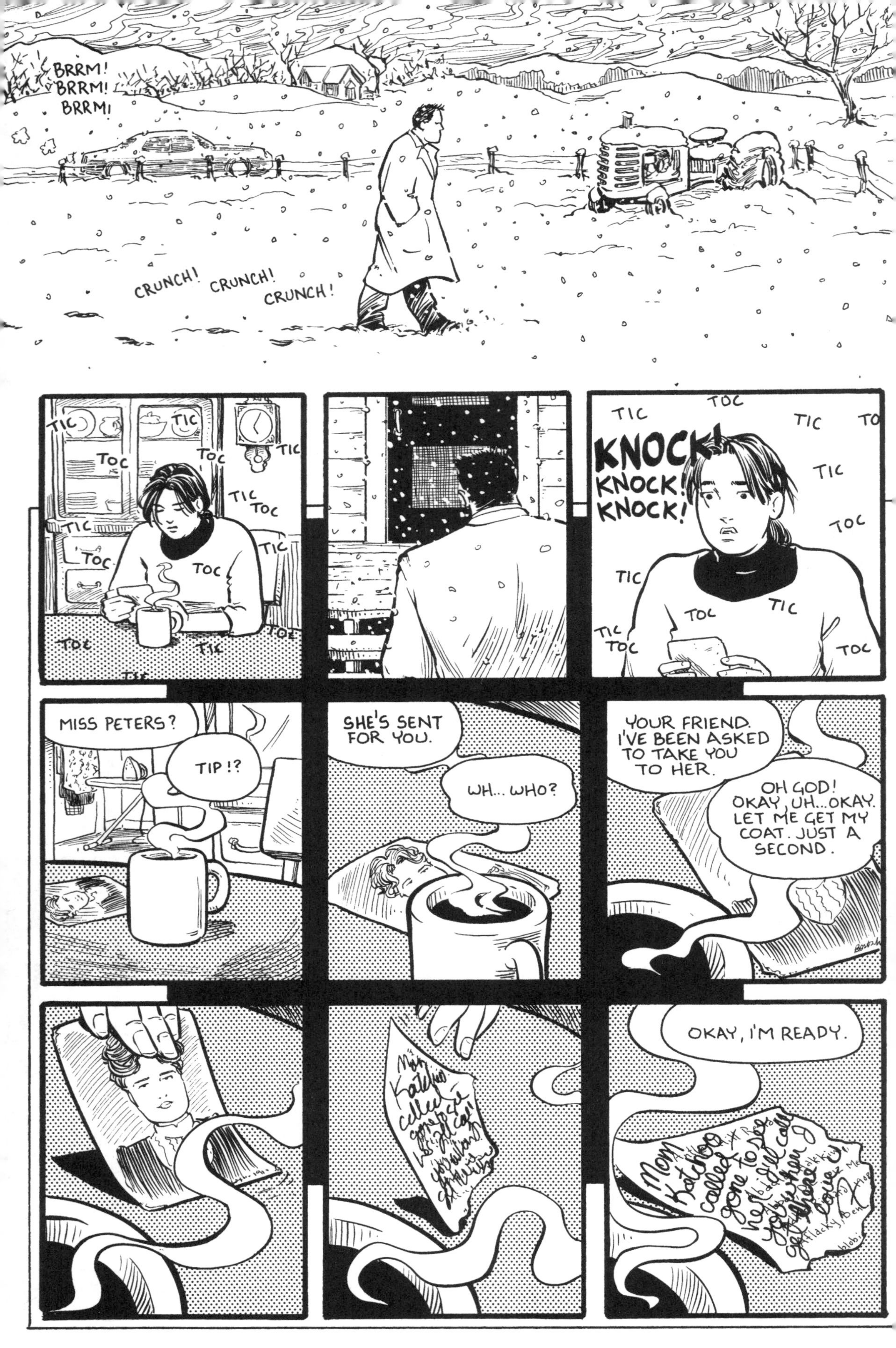
BRRM! BRRM! BRRM!
CRUNCH! CRUNCH! CRUNCH!
TIC TIC TOC TOC TIC TIC TOC TIC TOC TIC TOC TOC TIC
TIC TOC TIC TO
KNOCK! KNOCK! KNOCK!
TIC TOC TIC TIC TOC TIC TOC TOC
MISS PETERS?
TIP!?
SHE'S SENT FOR YOU.
WH... WHO?
YOUR FRIEND. I'VE BEEN ASKED TO TAKE YOU TO HER.
OH GOD! OKAY, UH... OKAY. LET ME GET MY COAT. JUST A SECOND.
OKAY, I'M READY.

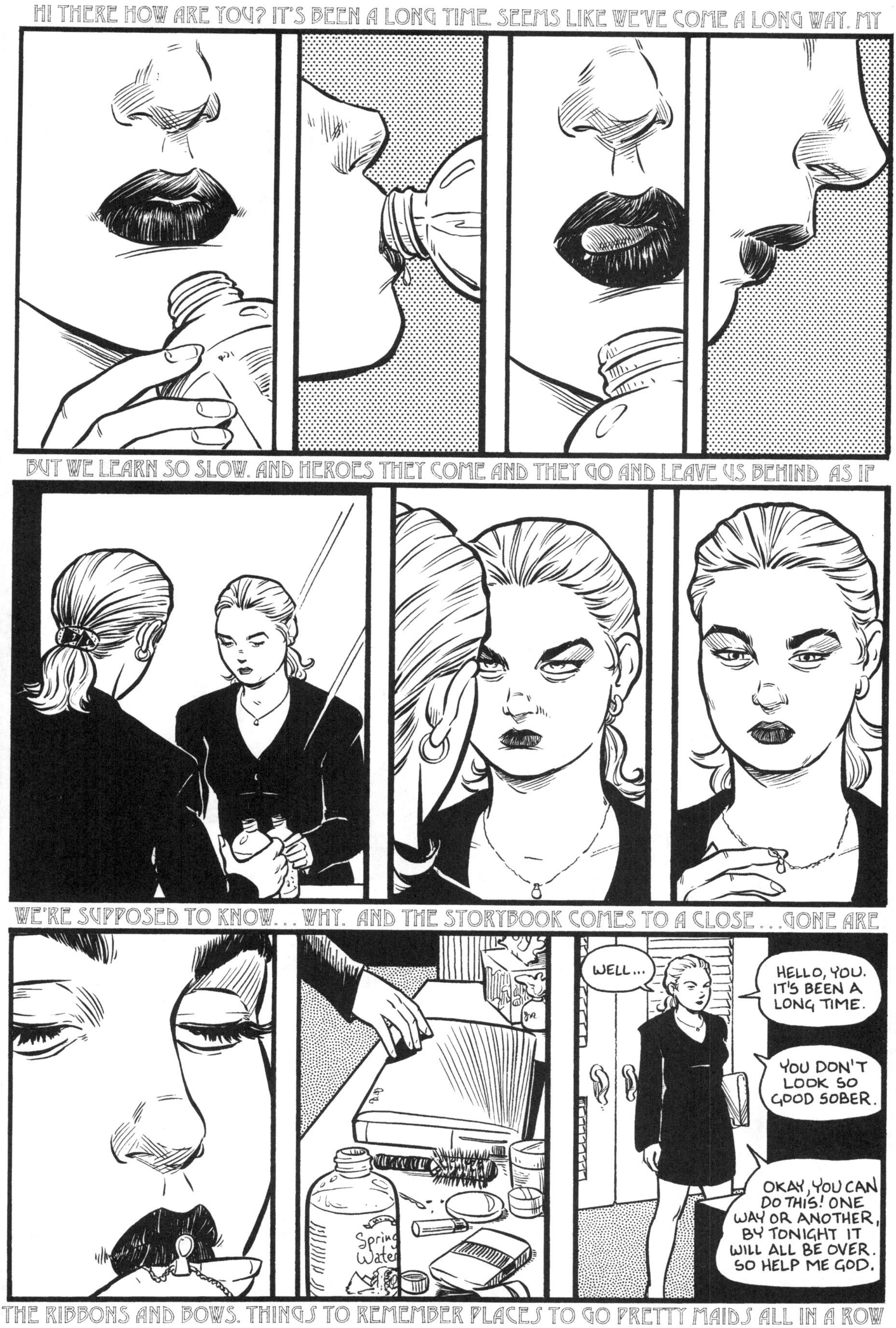
HI THERE HOW ARE YOU? IT'S BEEN A LONG TIME. SEEMS LIKE WE'VE COME A LONG WAY. MY
BUT WE LEARN SO SLOW. AND HEROES THEY COME AND THEY GO AND LEAVE US BEHIND AS IF
WE'RE SUPPOSED TO KNOW... WHY. AND THE STORYBOOK COMES TO A CLOSE... GONE ARE
WELL...
HELLO, YOU. IT'S BEEN A LONG TIME.
YOU DON'T LOOK SO GOOD SOBER.
OKAY, YOU CAN DO THIS! ONE WAY OR ANOTHER, BY TONIGHT IT WILL ALL BE OVER. SO HELP ME GOD.
Spring Water
THE RIBBONS AND BOWS. THINGS TO REMEMBER PLACES TO GO PRETTY MAIDS ALL IN A ROW

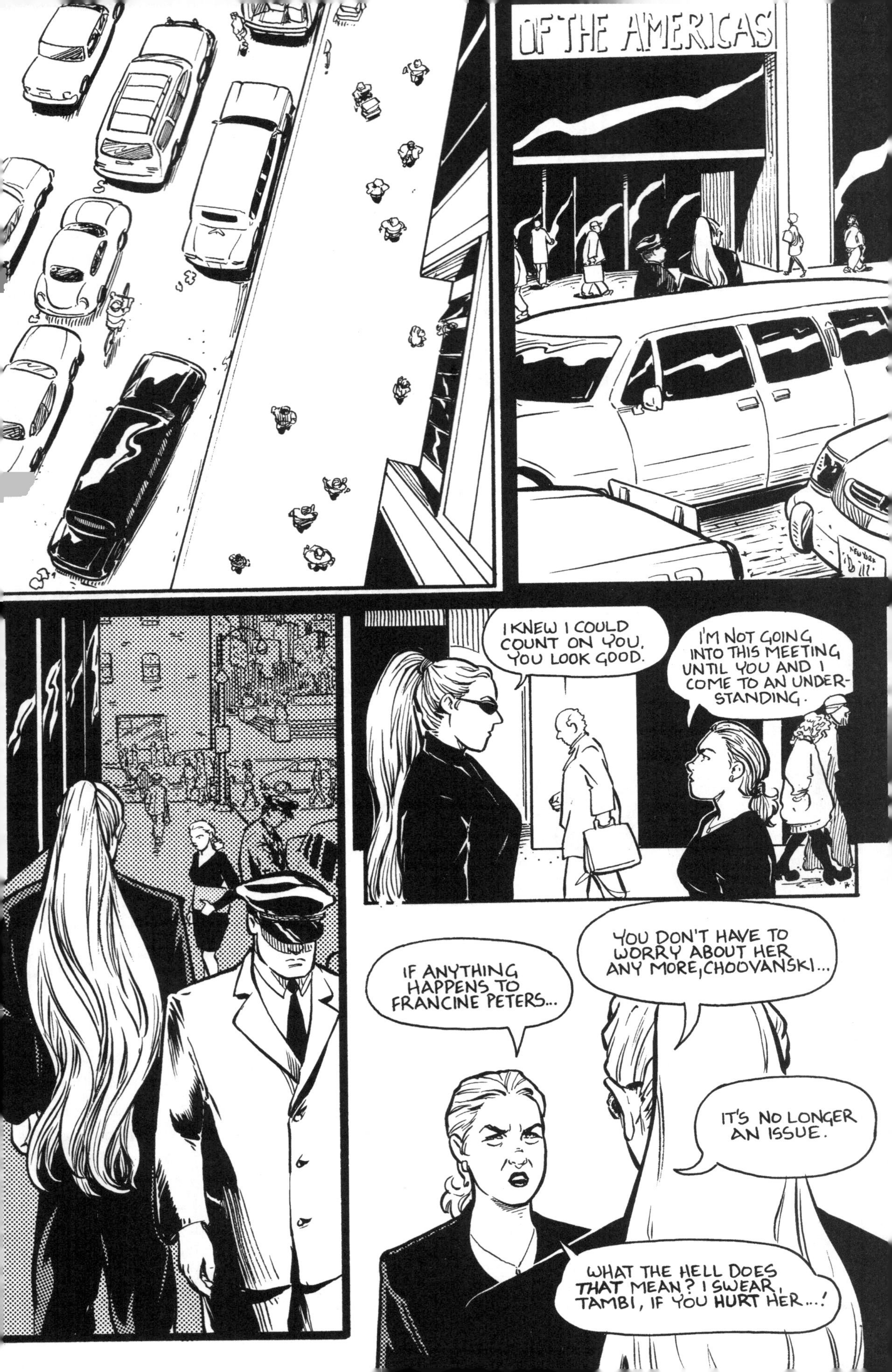
OF THE AMERICAS
I KNEW I COULD COUNT ON YOU. YOU LOOK GOOD.
I'M NOT GOING INTO THIS MEETING UNTIL YOU AND I COME TO AN UNDER-STANDING.
IF ANYTHING HAPPENS TO FRANCINE PETERS...
YOU DON'T HAVE TO WORRY ABOUT HER ANY MORE, CHOOVANSKI...
IT'S NO LONGER AN ISSUE.
WHAT THE HELL DOES *THAT* MEAN? I SWEAR, TAMBI, IF YOU **HURT** HER...!

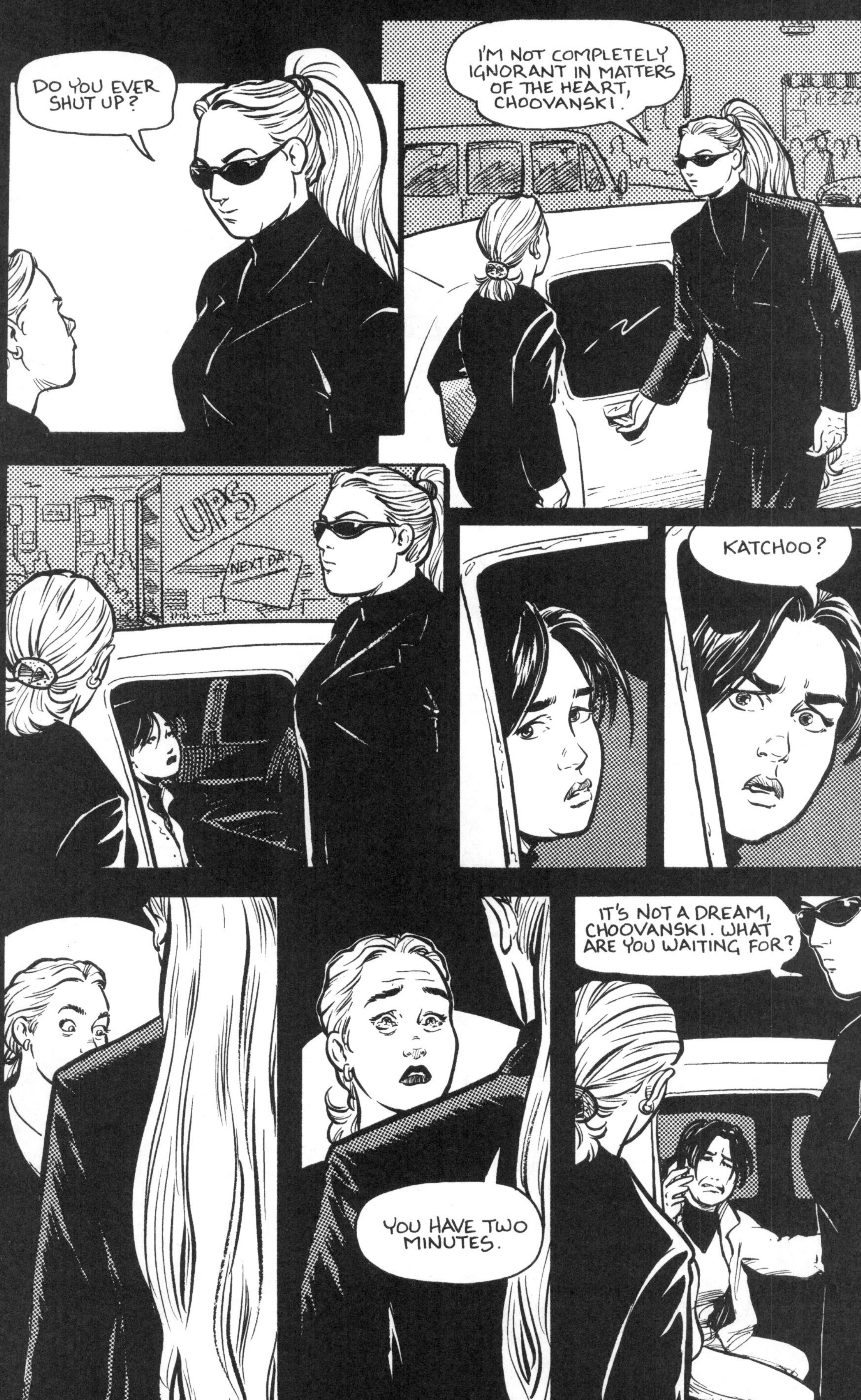
DO YOU EVER SHUT UP?
I'M NOT COMPLETELY IGNORANT IN MATTERS OF THE HEART, CHOOVANSKI.
PIZZA
UPS
NEXT DAY
KATCHOO?
YOU HAVE TWO MINUTES.
IT'S NOT A DREAM, CHOOVANSKI. WHAT ARE YOU WAITING FOR?

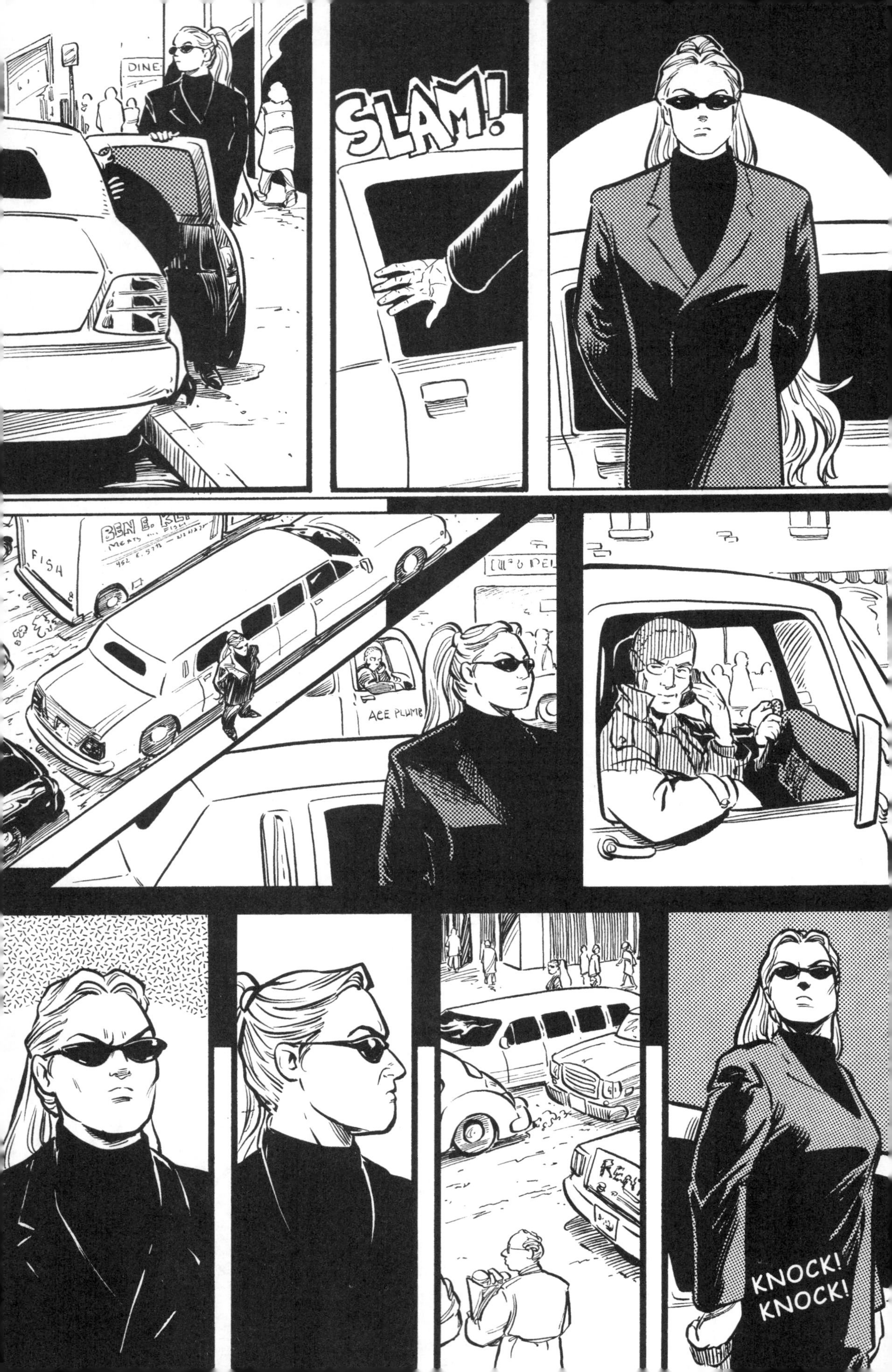

SLAM!
ACE PLUMB
KNOCK! KNOCK!

The long white limousine pulled slowly to the curb in front of the Bank Of The Americas building in Manhattan's lower east side at precisely two minutes before noon. The driver put the car into park and left the engine idling, waiting for a signal from the rear that his passengers were ready to get out, but no signal came. Five minutes passed. Ten. He would wait until hell froze over if that's what she wanted. Fifteen.

Francine watched her own reflection in the sunglasses of the amazon blonde who sat across from her in the back of the limo. With the exception of a curt introduction at the airport, Tambi had not spoken to her since her arrival this morning in the private jet that brought her from Nashville.

Introductions had not been necessary, Francine recognized her grim host on sight – Tambi Baker, the woman who worked for Darcy Parker's Packard-Yerr corporation. The woman who had arranged to pay for all of David's medical expenses after the plane crash. The woman Katchoo once called a killer. This was her, right? The same woman who had taken her and David by force to Darcy Parker's hotel room that awful night two years ago, then shot Katchoo?

"Aren't you supposed to be in jail?" Francine asked, as they walked to the waiting limousine.

Tambi looked at her, the face stoic behind the sunglasses.

"I mean, kidnapping me and David, shooting Katchoo... I thought you were in jail."

"You're thinking of someone else."

"Huh. She sure looked like you."

Francine thought she saw a slight twitch at the corner of the mouth but the face remained expressionless. Tambi held the door for her and Francine got in. Something was different about this woman, but too much time had passed since that night to be sure. Still, how many long haired, bleached-blonde, body builder killer babes could there be in the world?

Conversation had been useless after that. Francine's questions were met with stony silence. She resolved to be patient and go with it, suppressing the urge to roll down the window and scream for help because salvation might keep her from Katchoo.

"Wait here," Tambi said suddenly. In one quick move she was out of the car, closing the door firmly behind her. Francine turned around to see another limousine had pulled up to the curb behind them. It was difficult to see clearly through the dark tinted glass but Francine watched as a small, slender woman emerged and approached the waiting Tambi. They spoke a moment before Tambi reached over and opened the car door. Francine looked up at Tambi to see if this was her cue to get out, but Tambi seemed to be waiting on the other woman.

Turning her attention, Francine saw an elegant woman in an expensive dress and matching shoes. Her thick blonde hair was pulled back tight, her mouth striking in dark, rose colored lipstick that highlighted the delicate pale of her skin. Makeup failed to hide dark circles and heavy bags that seemed to anchor sad green eyes.

Francine's first thought was, Darcy Parker. Or at least, how she remembered Mrs. Parker. But, she was dead. Suicide. David's inheritance. And brunette. This blonde... who recognized her...

Francine's heart stopped. "Katchoo?" she said in disbelief.

Katchoo's face turned white, her mouth open in disbelief.

"You have two minutes," said Tambi.

Francine choked back tears and impulsively held her arms out to the soul mate she had not seen in over a year.

"It's not a dream, Choovanski. What are you waiting for?" Tambi said.

Katchoo blinked in disbelief. Stepping into the dream, Katchoo leaned over and fell into waiting arms that held her tight and wouldn't let go. The car door shut behind them, sealing them off from the outside world.

Francine sobbed uncontrollably into Katchoo's shoulder. "I thought I'd never see you again," she said.

Only then, when she heard the familiar southern drawl, and felt the soft crush of her friend's embrace, did Katchoo realize the dream was real. She tried to speak, to offer the apology she'd been waiting a year to deliver, but no words came. She could only close her eyes and hold on for dear life. The faint aroma of baby powder tickled her nose, making Katchoo smile. "I'm home" she whispered hoarsely.

No more words were spoken until a sharp knock came on the window.

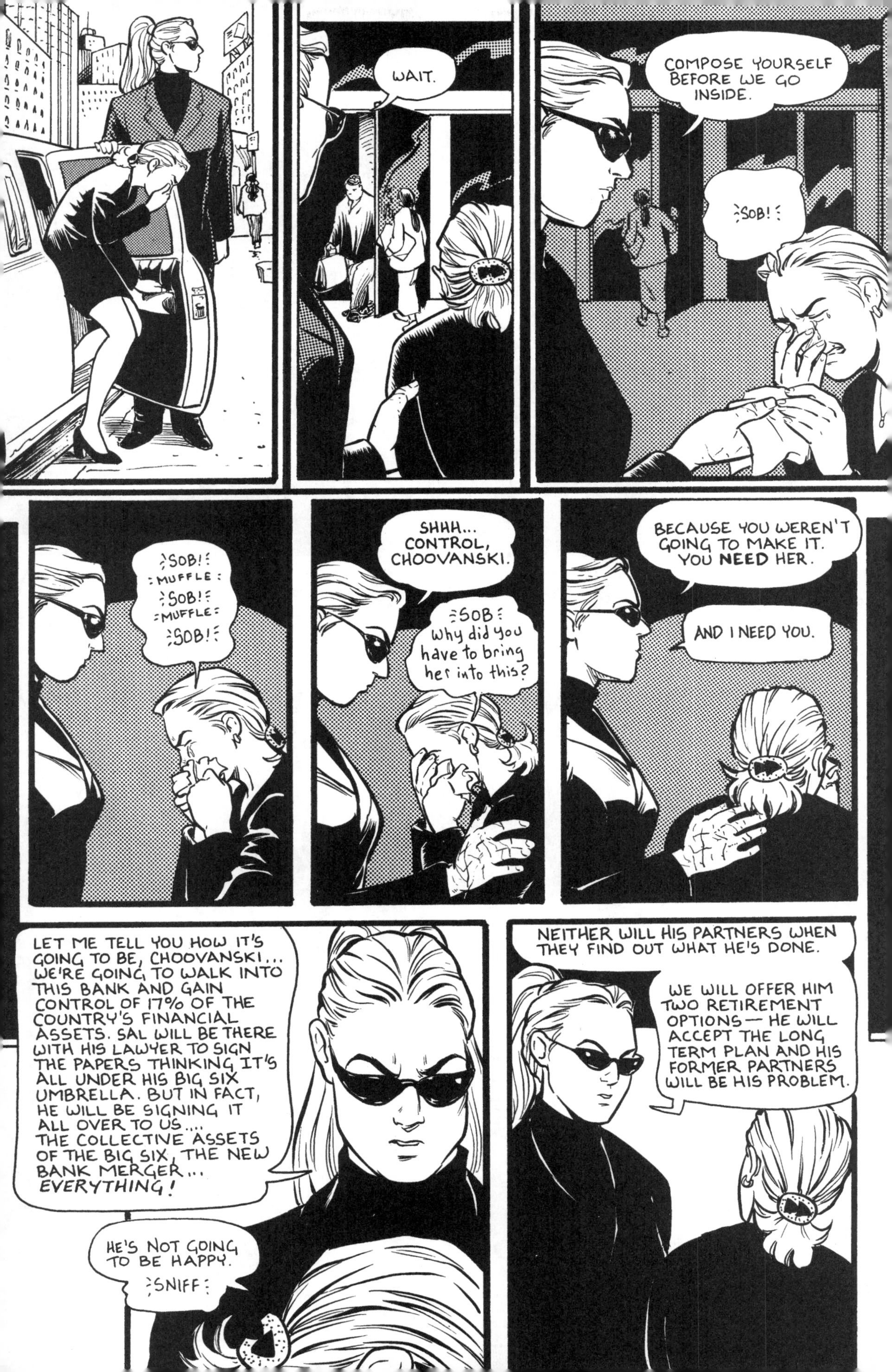
WAIT.
COMPOSE YOURSELF BEFORE WE GO INSIDE.
SOB!
SOB! MUFFLE SOB! MUFFLE SOB!
SHHH... CONTROL, CHOOVANSKI.
SOB why did you have to bring her into this?
BECAUSE YOU WEREN'T GOING TO MAKE IT. YOU NEED HER.
AND I NEED YOU.
LET ME TELL YOU HOW IT'S GOING TO BE, CHOOVANSKI... WE'RE GOING TO WALK INTO THIS BANK AND GAIN CONTROL OF 17% OF THE COUNTRY'S FINANCIAL ASSETS. SAL WILL BE THERE WITH HIS LAWYER TO SIGN THE PAPERS THINKING IT'S ALL UNDER HIS BIG SIX UMBRELLA. BUT IN FACT, HE WILL BE SIGNING IT ALL OVER TO US.... THE COLLECTIVE ASSETS OF THE BIG SIX, THE NEW BANK MERGER... EVERYTHING!
HE'S NOT GOING TO BE HAPPY.
SNIFF
NEITHER WILL HIS PARTNERS WHEN THEY FIND OUT WHAT HE'S DONE.
WE WILL OFFER HIM TWO RETIREMENT OPTIONS— HE WILL ACCEPT THE LONG TERM PLAN AND HIS FORMER PARTNERS WILL BE HIS PROBLEM.

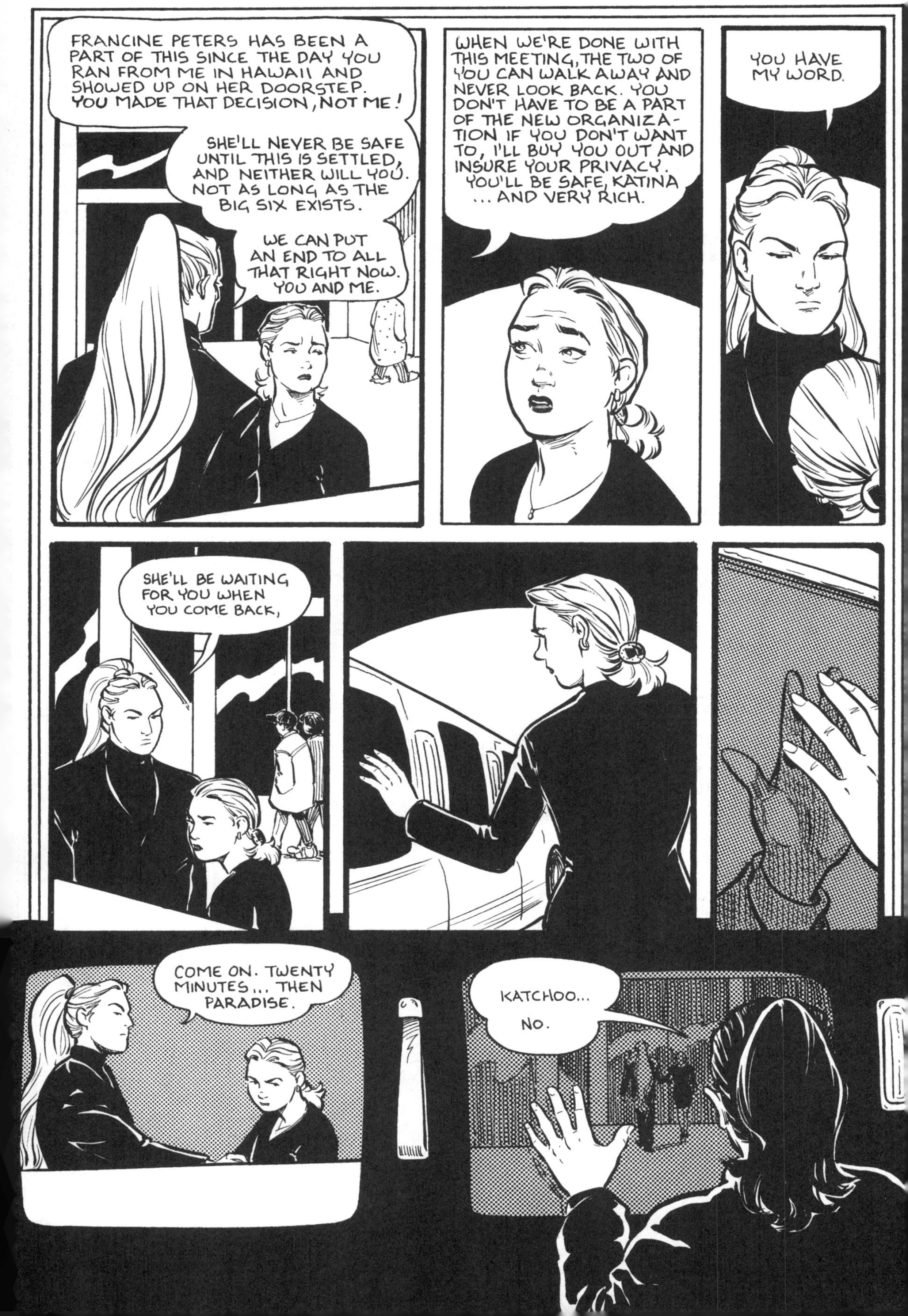
FRANCINE PETERS HAS BEEN A PART OF THIS SINCE THE DAY YOU RAN FROM ME IN HAWAII AND SHOWED UP ON HER DOORSTEP. YOU MADE THAT DECISION, NOT ME!
SHE'LL NEVER BE SAFE UNTIL THIS IS SETTLED, AND NEITHER WILL YOU. NOT AS LONG AS THE BIG SIX EXISTS.
WE CAN PUT AN END TO ALL THAT RIGHT NOW. YOU AND ME.
WHEN WE'RE DONE WITH THIS MEETING, THE TWO OF YOU CAN WALK AWAY AND NEVER LOOK BACK. YOU DON'T HAVE TO BE A PART OF THE NEW ORGANIZATION IF YOU DON'T WANT TO, I'LL BUY YOU OUT AND INSURE YOUR PRIVACY. YOU'LL BE SAFE, KATINA ... AND VERY RICH.
YOU HAVE MY WORD.
SHE'LL BE WAITING FOR YOU WHEN YOU COME BACK,
COME ON. TWENTY MINUTES... THEN PARADISE.
KATCHOO...
NO.

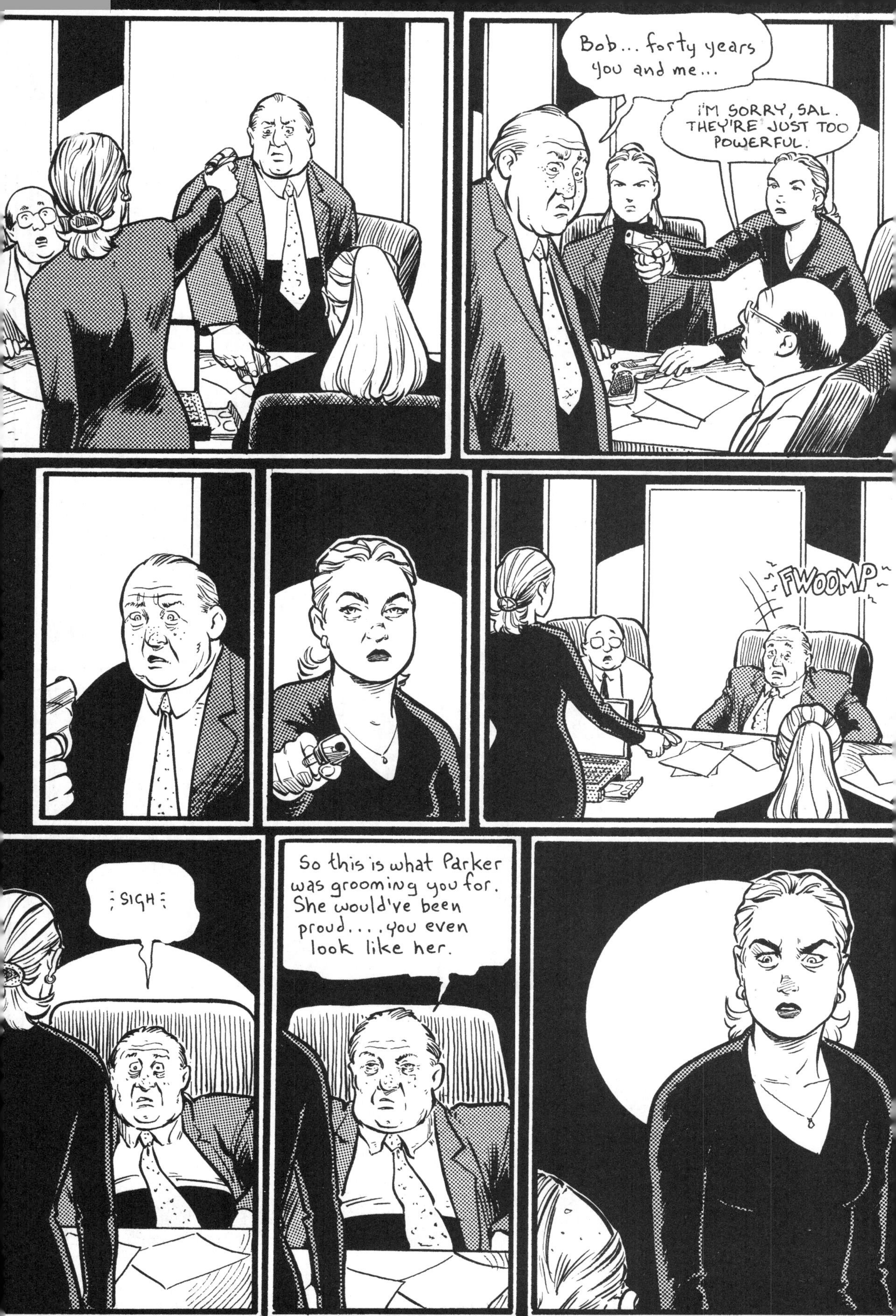
Bob... forty years you and me...
I'M SORRY, SAL. THEY'RE JUST TOO POWERFUL.
FWOOMP
SIGH
So this is what Parker was grooming you for. She would've been proud....you even look like her.

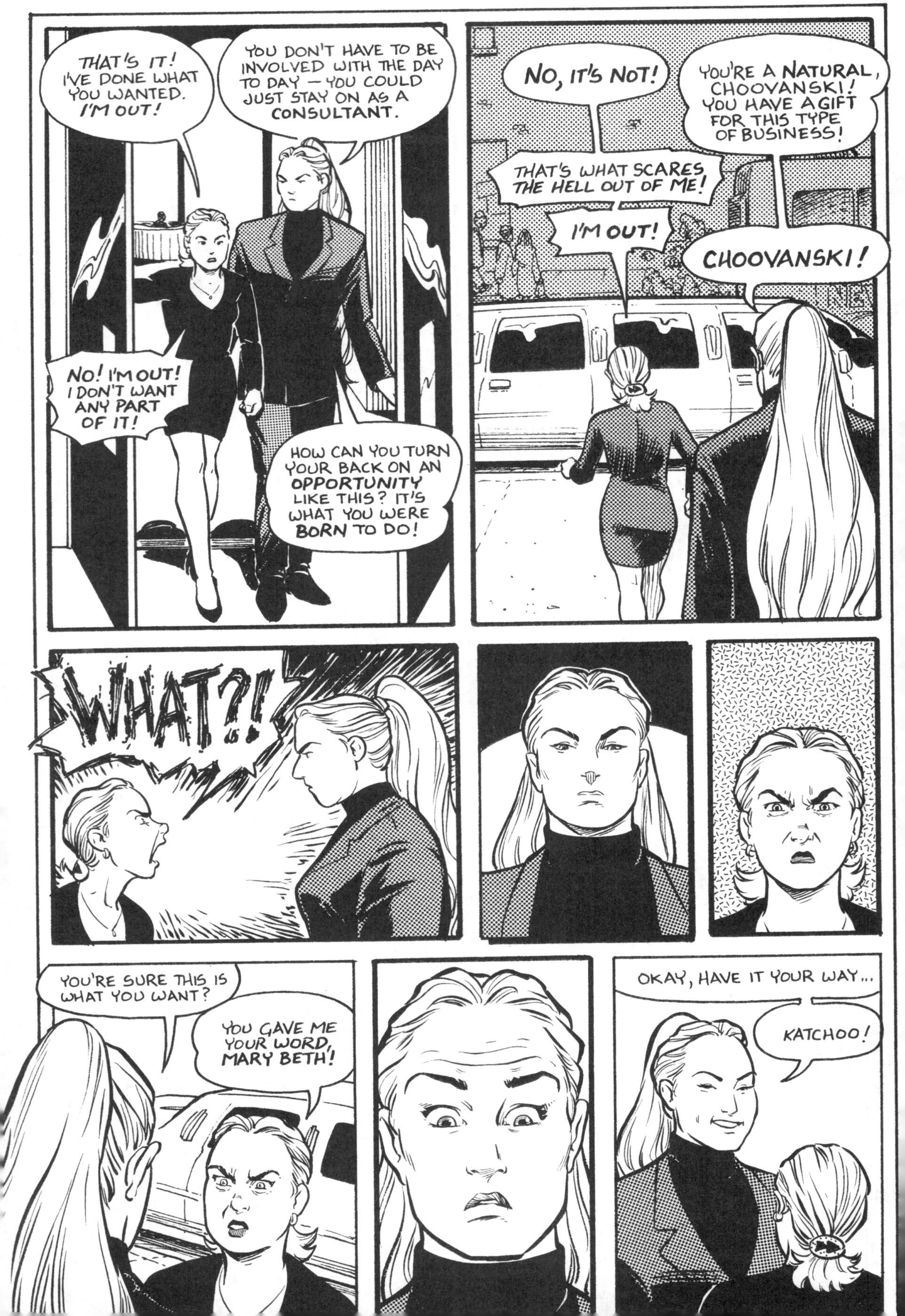
THAT'S IT! I'VE DONE WHAT YOU WANTED. I'M OUT!
YOU DON'T HAVE TO BE INVOLVED WITH THE DAY TO DAY — YOU COULD JUST STAY ON AS A CONSULTANT.
NO! I'M OUT! I DON'T WANT ANY PART OF IT!
HOW CAN YOU TURN YOUR BACK ON AN OPPORTUNITY LIKE THIS? IT'S WHAT YOU WERE BORN TO DO!
YOU'RE A NATURAL, CHOOVANSKI! YOU HAVE A GIFT FOR THIS TYPE OF BUSINESS!
NO, IT'S NOT!
THAT'S WHAT SCARES THE HELL OUT OF ME!
I'M OUT!
CHOOVANSKI!
WHAT?!
YOU'RE SURE THIS IS WHAT YOU WANT?
YOU GAVE ME YOUR WORD, MARY BETH!
OKAY, HAVE IT YOUR WAY...
KATCHOO!

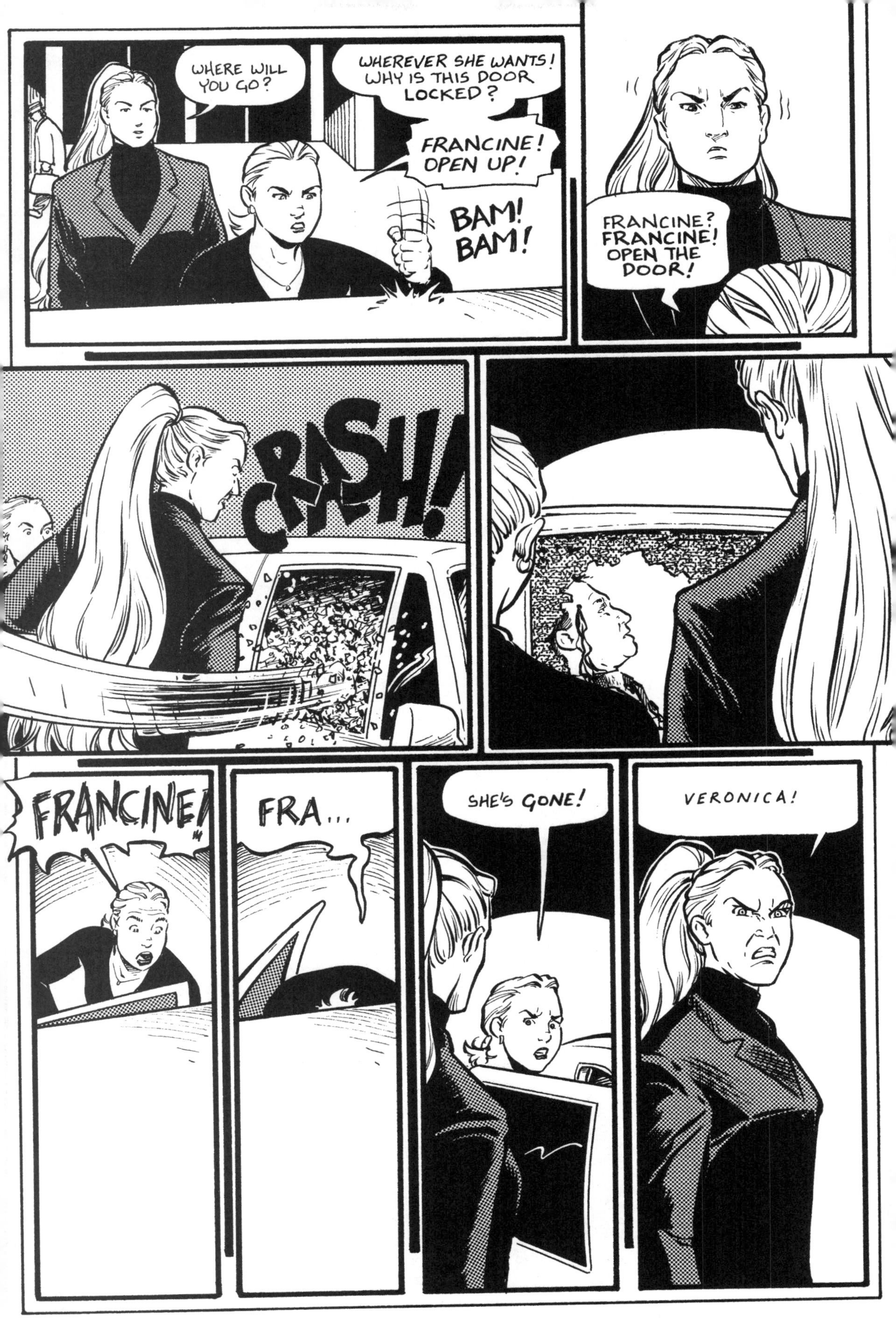
WHERE WILL YOU GO?
WHEREVER SHE WANTS! WHY IS THIS DOOR LOCKED?
FRANCINE! OPEN UP!
BAM! BAM!
FRANCINE? FRANCINE! OPEN THE DOOR!
CRASH!
FRANCINE!
FRA...
SHE'S GONE!
VERONICA!

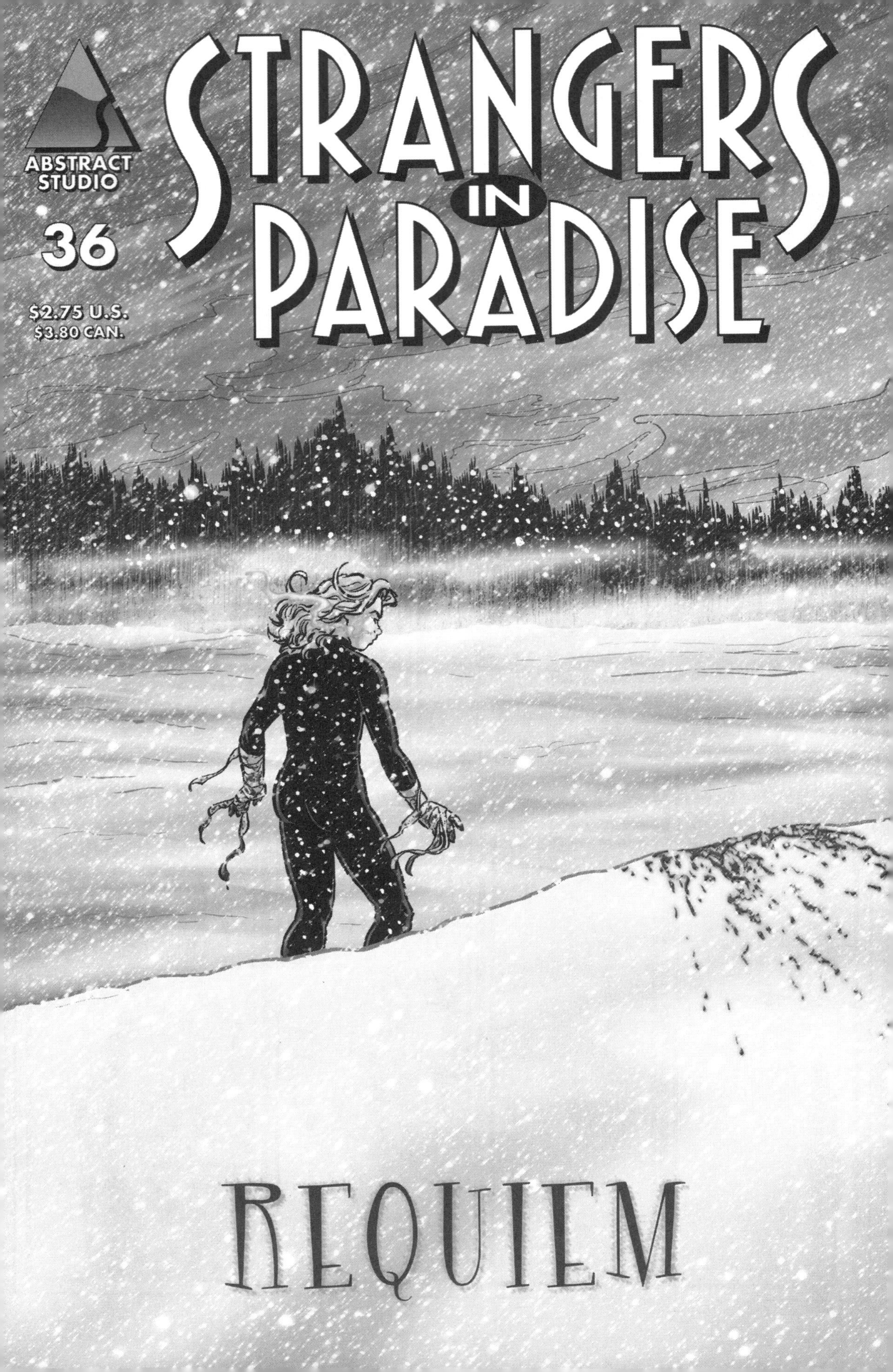
ABSTRACT STUDIO
STRANGERS IN PARADISE
36
$2.75 U.S.
$3.80 CAN.
REQUIEM

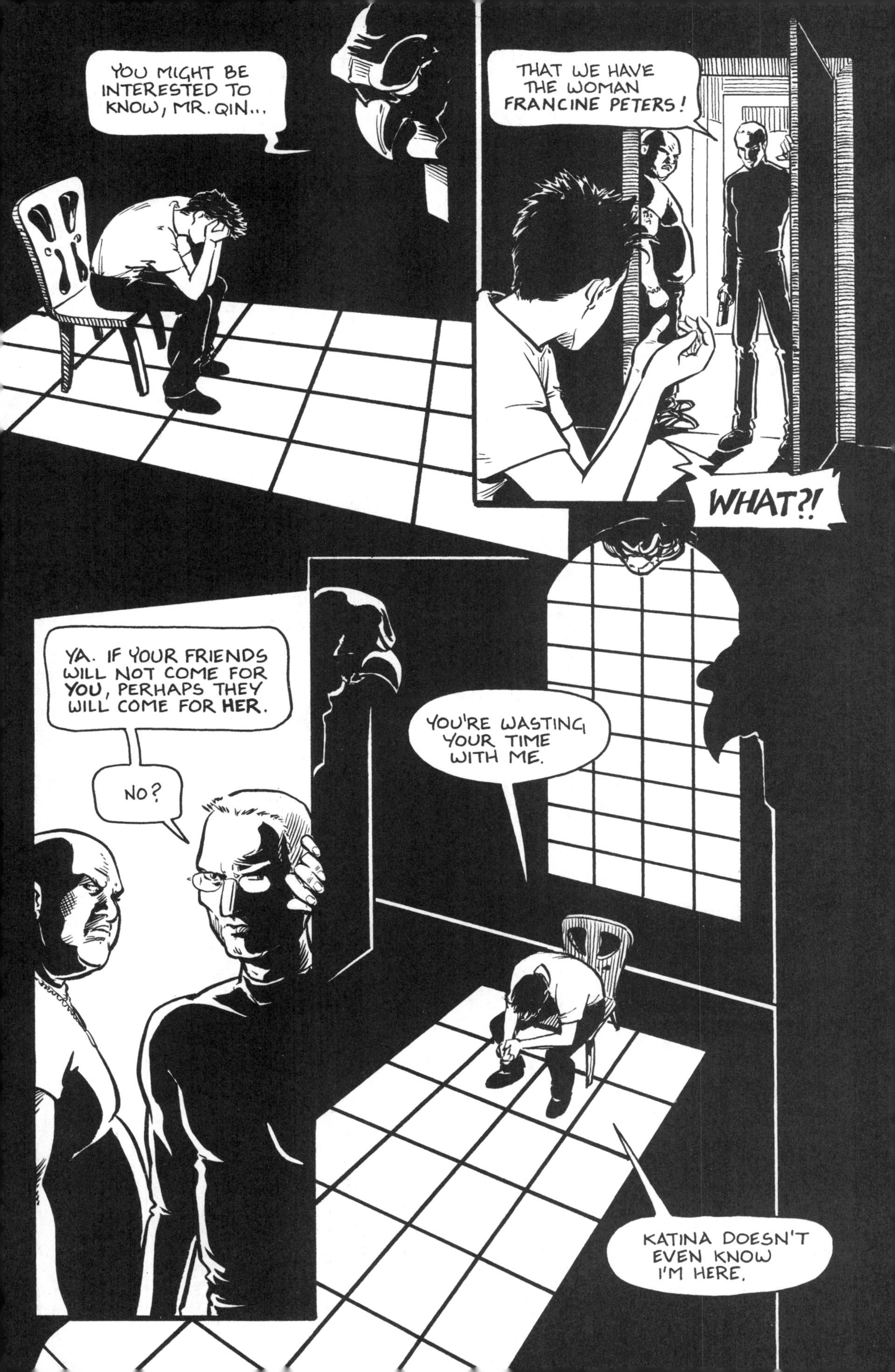
YOU MIGHT BE INTERESTED TO KNOW, MR. QIN...
THAT WE HAVE THE WOMAN FRANCINE PETERS!
WHAT?!
YA. IF YOUR FRIENDS WILL NOT COME FOR YOU, PERHAPS THEY WILL COME FOR HER.
NO?
YOU'RE WASTING YOUR TIME WITH ME.
KATINA DOESN'T EVEN KNOW I'M HERE.

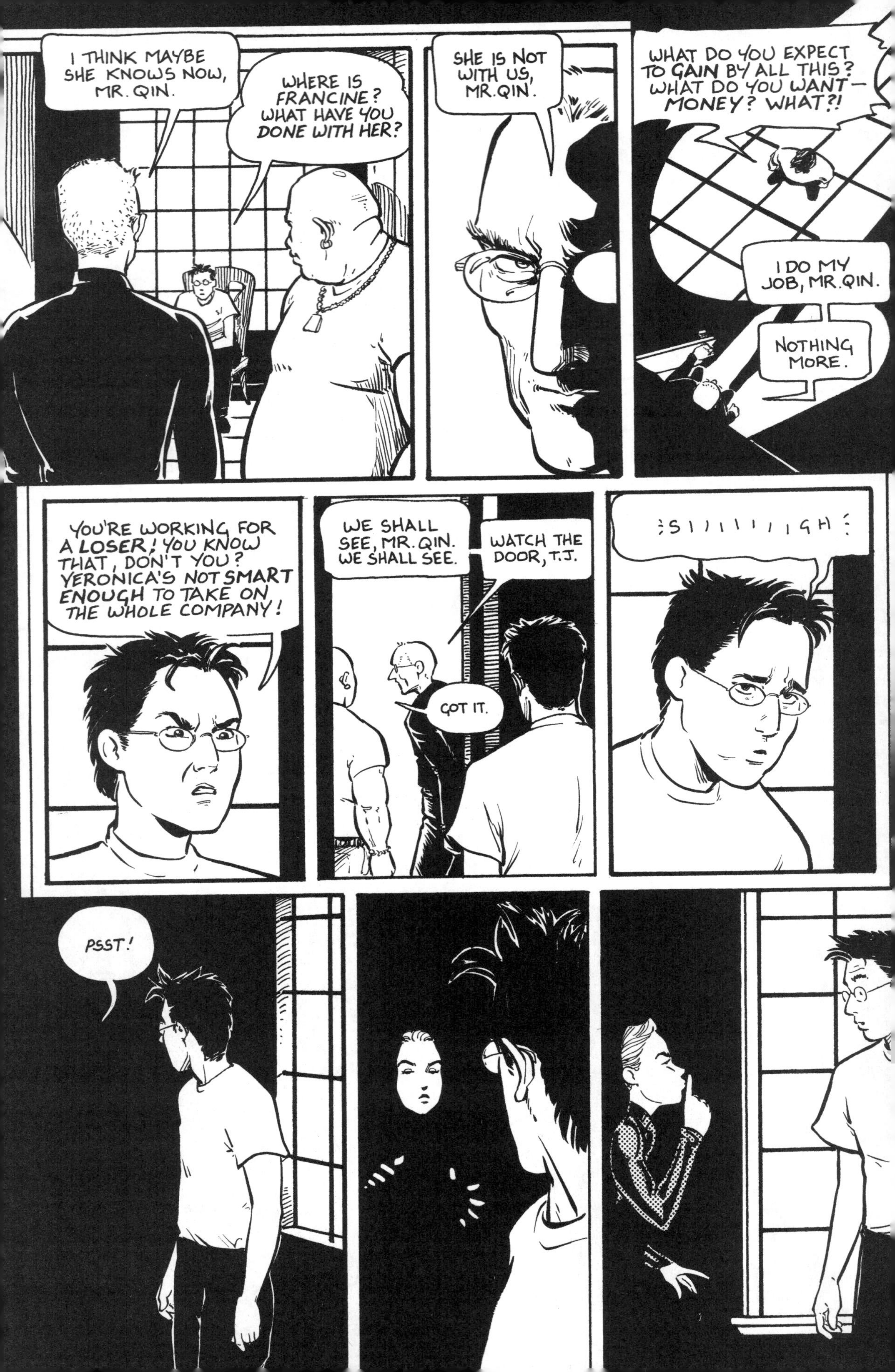
I THINK MAYBE SHE KNOWS NOW, MR. QIN.
WHERE IS FRANCINE? WHAT HAVE YOU DONE WITH HER?
SHE IS NOT WITH US, MR. QIN.
WHAT DO YOU EXPECT TO GAIN BY ALL THIS? WHAT DO YOU WANT— MONEY? WHAT?!
I DO MY JOB, MR. QIN.
NOTHING MORE.
YOU'RE WORKING FOR A LOSER! YOU KNOW THAT, DON'T YOU? VERONICA'S NOT SMART ENOUGH TO TAKE ON THE WHOLE COMPANY!
WE SHALL SEE, MR. QIN. WE SHALL SEE.
WATCH THE DOOR, T.J.
GOT IT.
SIIIIIIIGH
PSST!

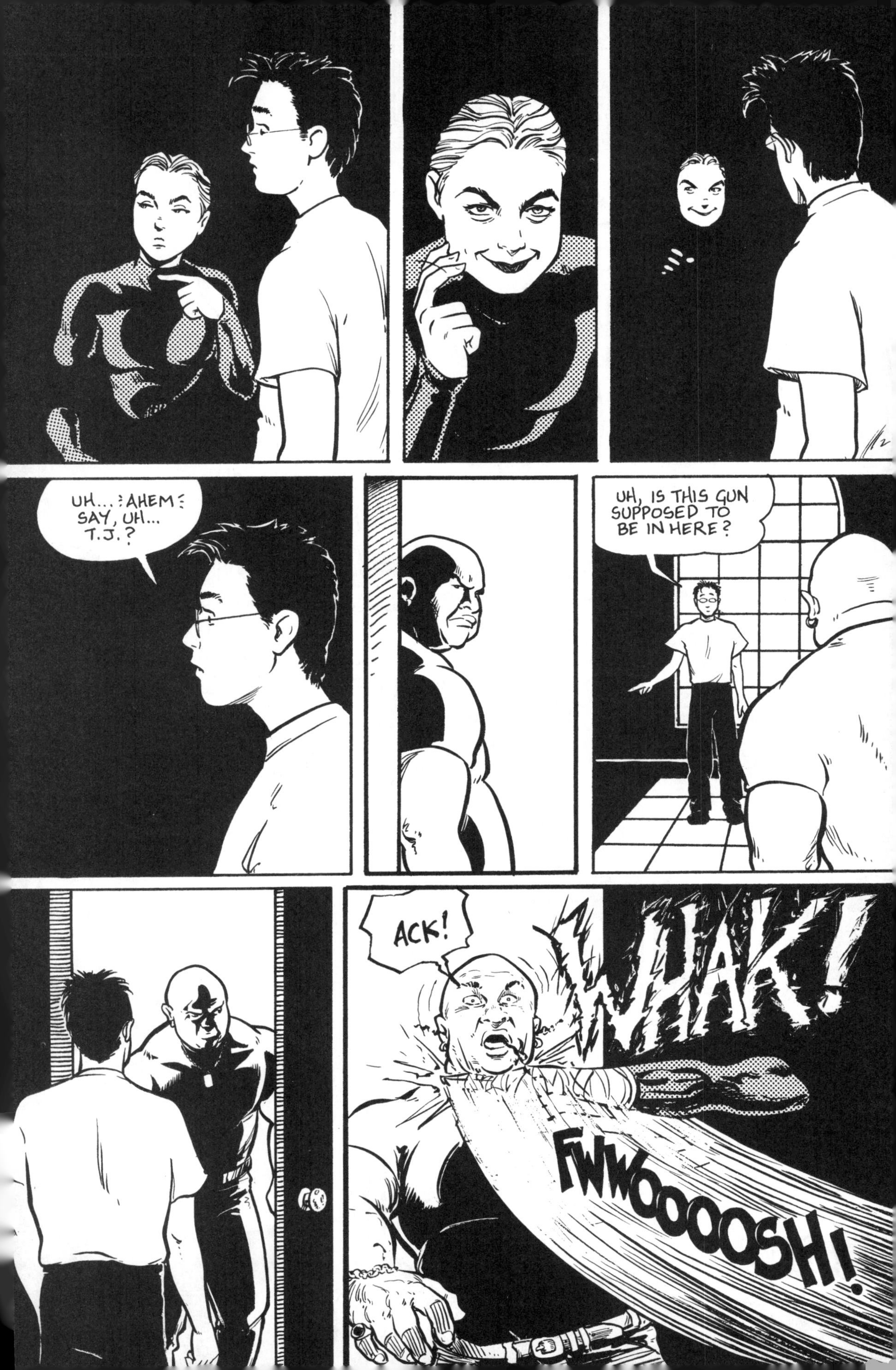

UH... :AHEM: SAY, UH... T.J.?
UH, IS THIS GUN SUPPOSED TO BE IN HERE?
ACK!
WHAK!
FWWOOOOOSH!

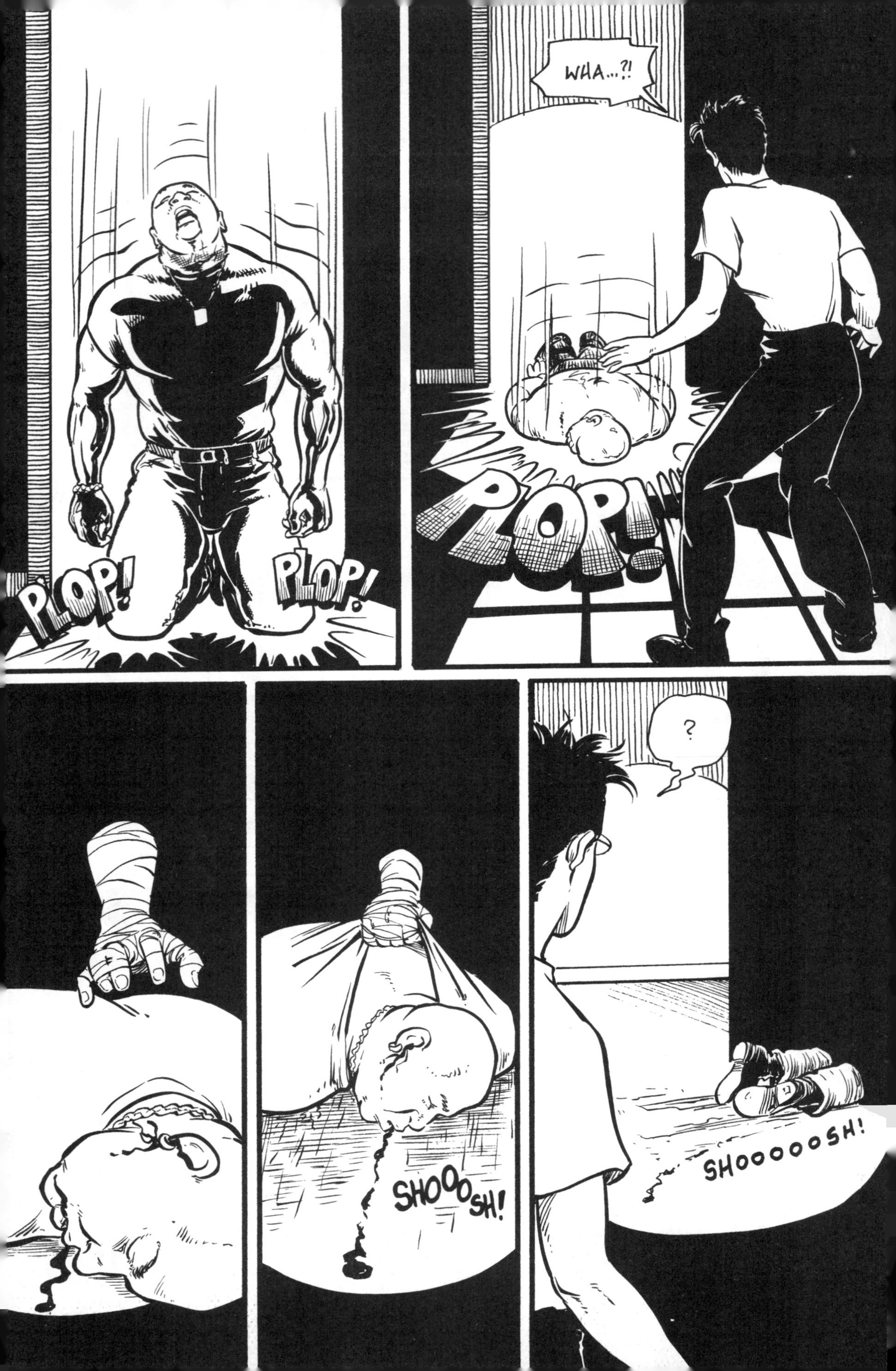
PLOP!
PLOP!
WHA...?!
PLOP!
SHOOOSH!
?
SHOOOOOSH!

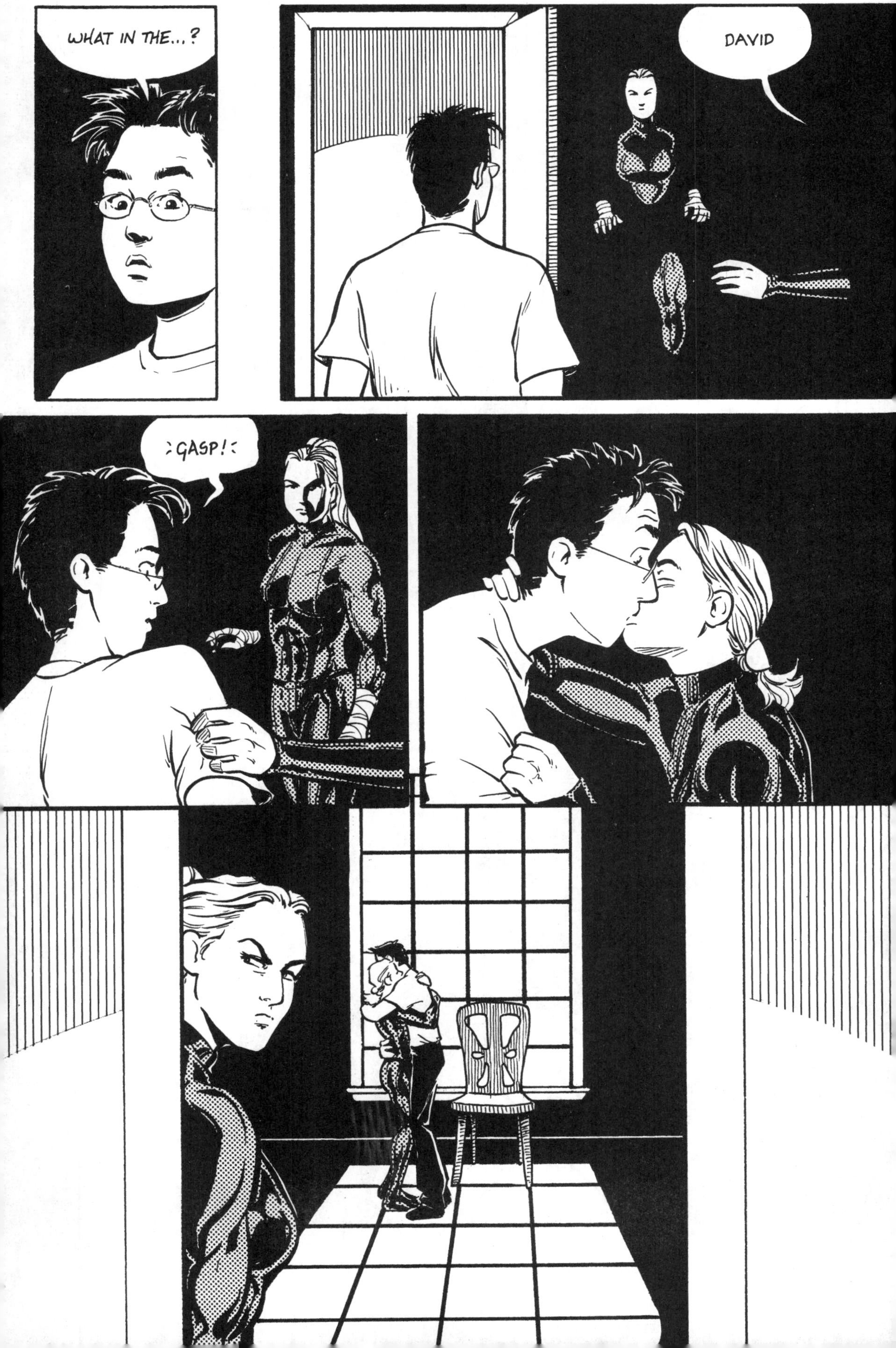
WHAT IN THE...?
DAVID
:GASP!:

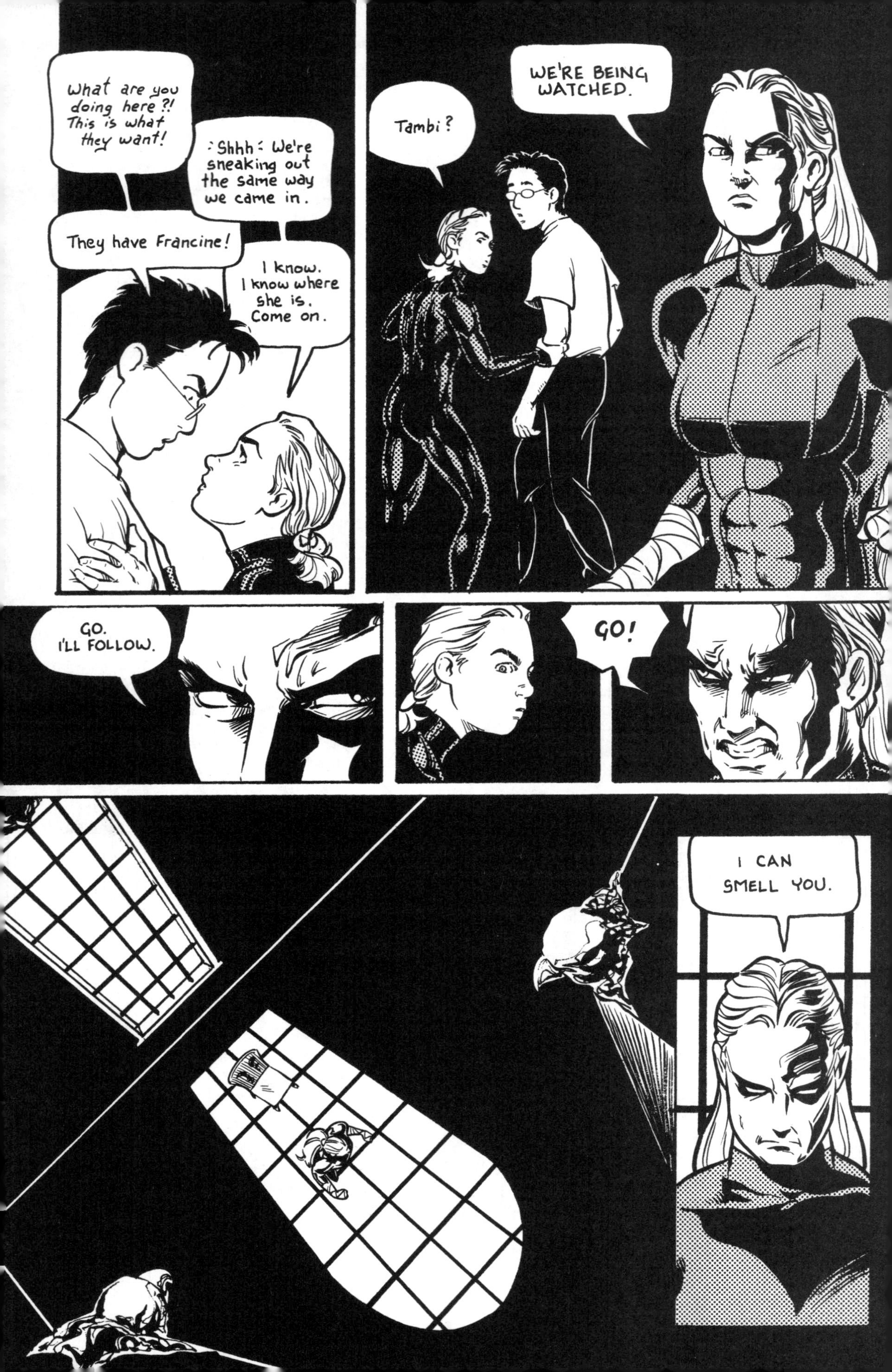
What are you doing here?! This is what they want!
:Shhh: We're sneaking out the same way we came in.
They have Francine!
I know. I know where she is. Come on.
Tambi?
WE'RE BEING WATCHED.
GO. I'LL FOLLOW.
GO!
I CAN SMELL YOU.

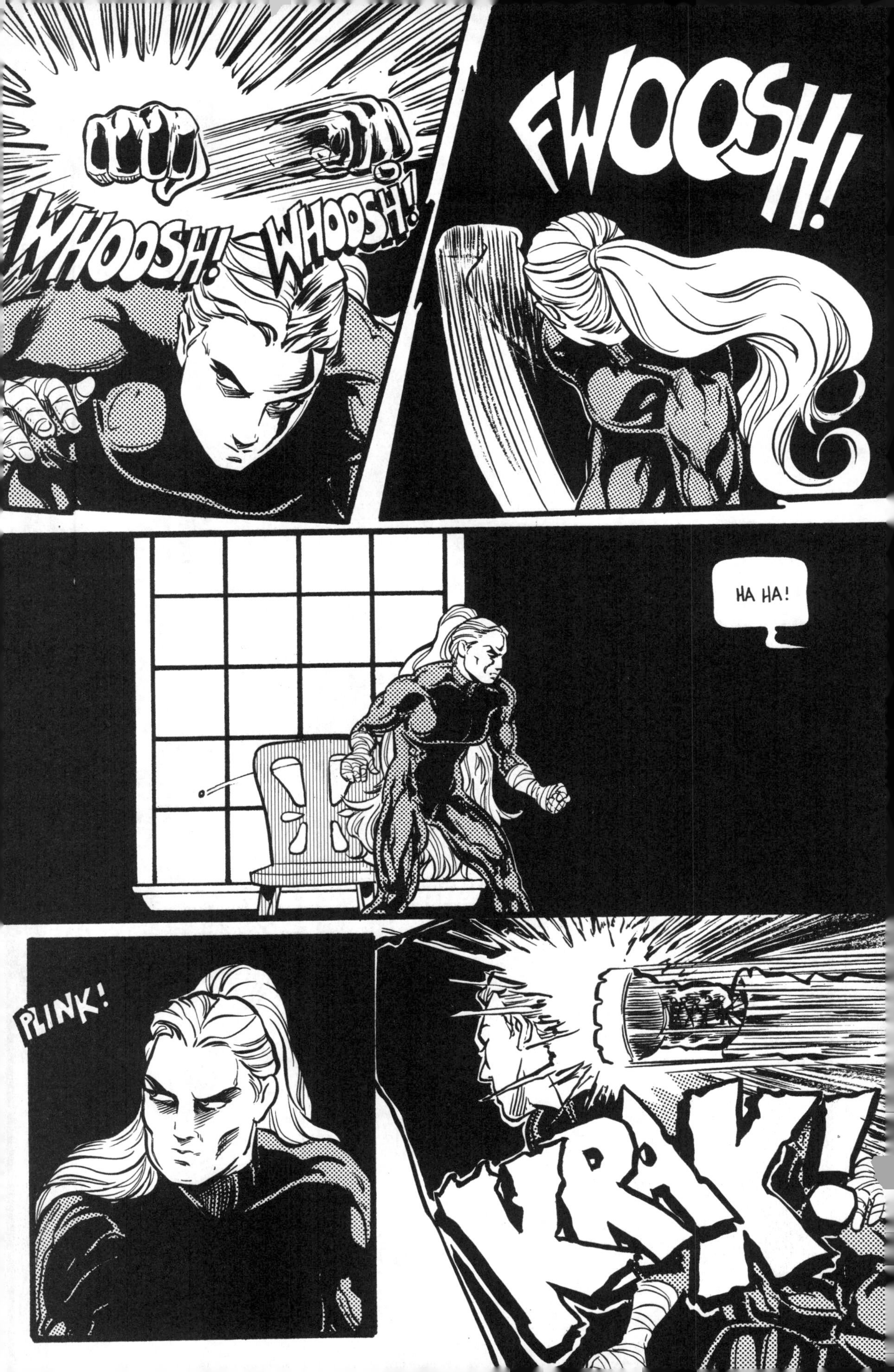
WHOOSH!
WHOOSH!
FWOOSH!
HA HA!
PLINK!
KRAK!

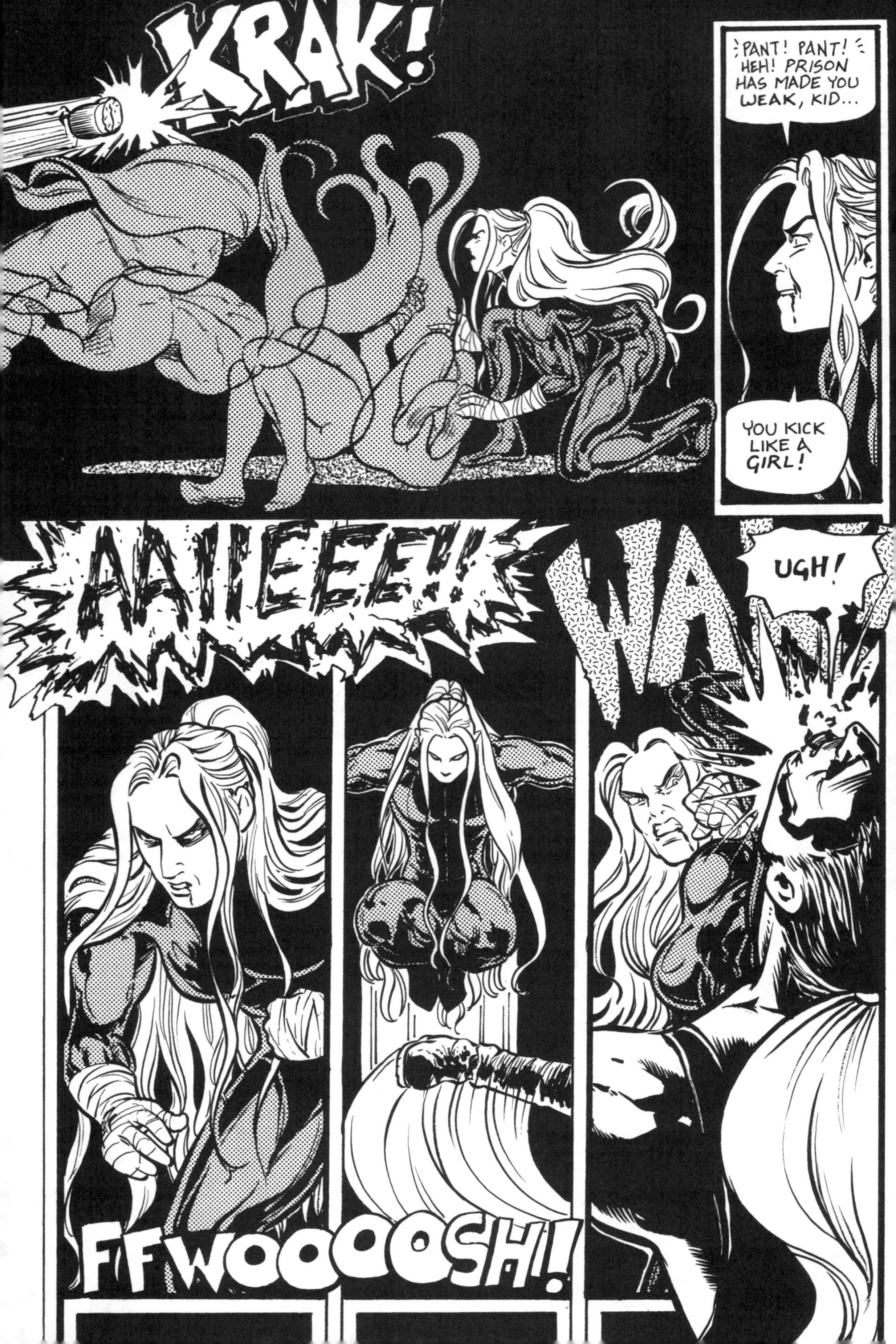
KRAK!
PANT! PANT! HEH! PRISON HAS MADE YOU WEAK, KID...
YOU KICK LIKE A GIRL!
AAIIEEE!!
UGH!
FFWOOOOOSH!

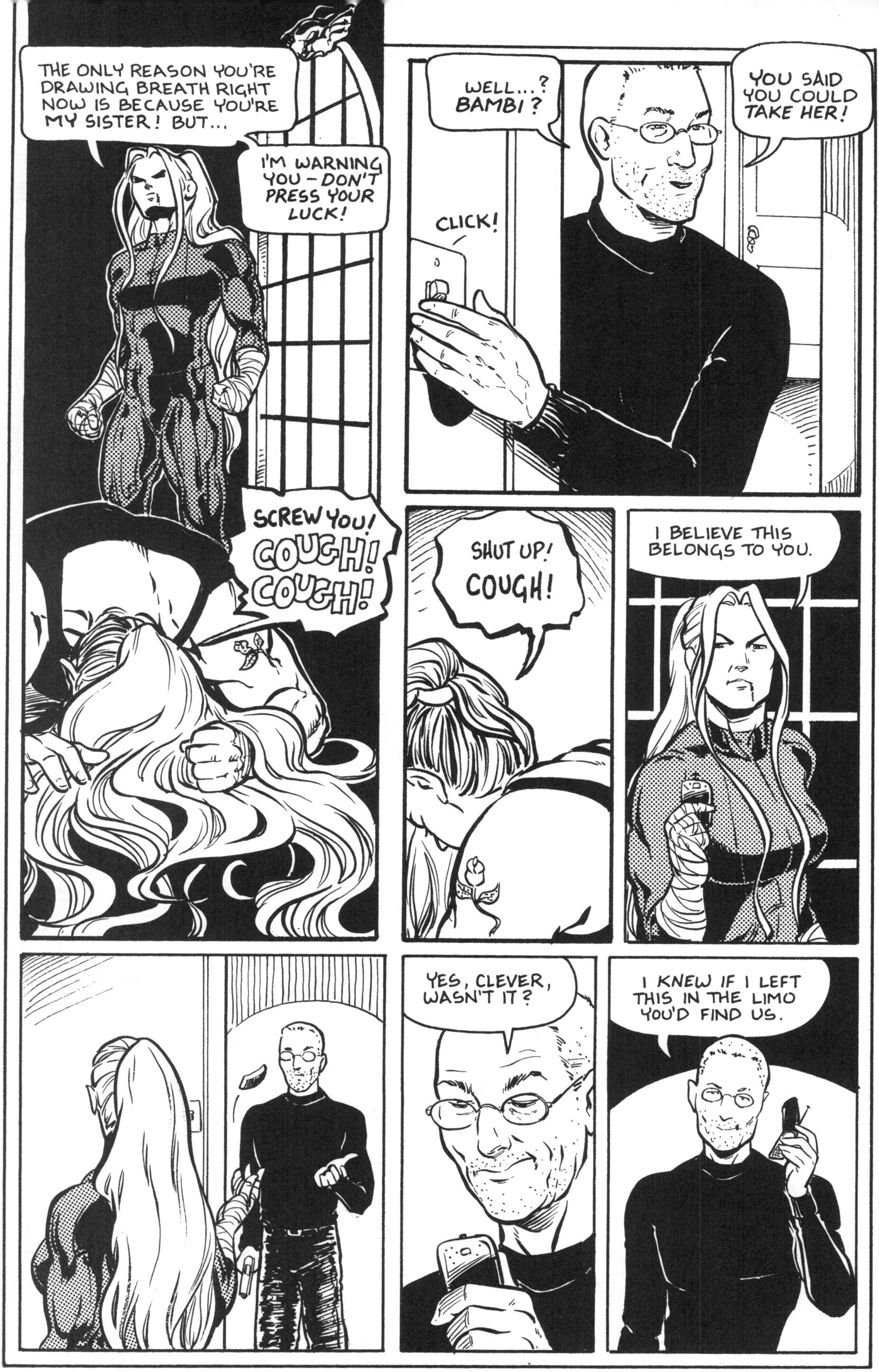
THE ONLY REASON YOU'RE DRAWING BREATH RIGHT NOW IS BECAUSE YOU'RE MY SISTER! BUT...
I'M WARNING YOU – DON'T PRESS YOUR LUCK!
WELL...? BAMBI?
YOU SAID YOU COULD TAKE HER!
CLICK!
SCREW YOU! COUGH! COUGH!
SHUT UP! COUGH!
I BELIEVE THIS BELONGS TO YOU.
YES, CLEVER, WASN'T IT?
I KNEW IF I LEFT THIS IN THE LIMO YOU'D FIND US.

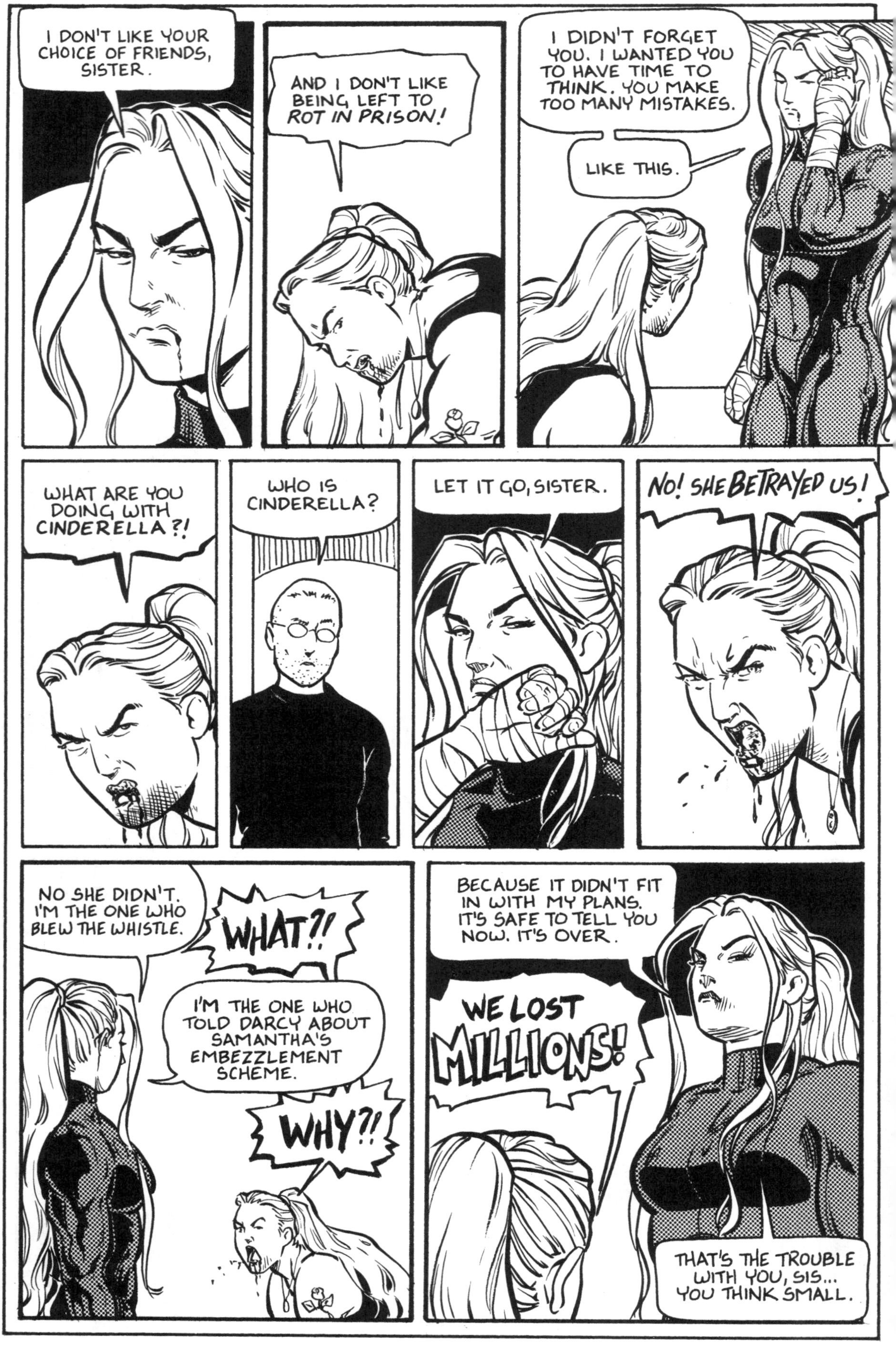

I DON'T LIKE YOUR CHOICE OF FRIENDS, SISTER.
AND I DON'T LIKE BEING LEFT TO ROT IN PRISON!
I DIDN'T FORGET YOU. I WANTED YOU TO HAVE TIME TO THINK. YOU MAKE TOO MANY MISTAKES.
LIKE THIS.
WHAT ARE YOU DOING WITH CINDERELLA?!
WHO IS CINDERELLA?
LET IT GO, SISTER.
NO! SHE BETRAYED US!
NO SHE DIDN'T. I'M THE ONE WHO BLEW THE WHISTLE.
WHAT?!
I'M THE ONE WHO TOLD DARCY ABOUT SAMANTHA'S EMBEZZLEMENT SCHEME.
WHY?!
BECAUSE IT DIDN'T FIT IN WITH MY PLANS. IT'S SAFE TO TELL YOU NOW. IT'S OVER.
WE LOST MILLIONS!
THAT'S THE TROUBLE WITH YOU, SIS... YOU THINK SMALL.

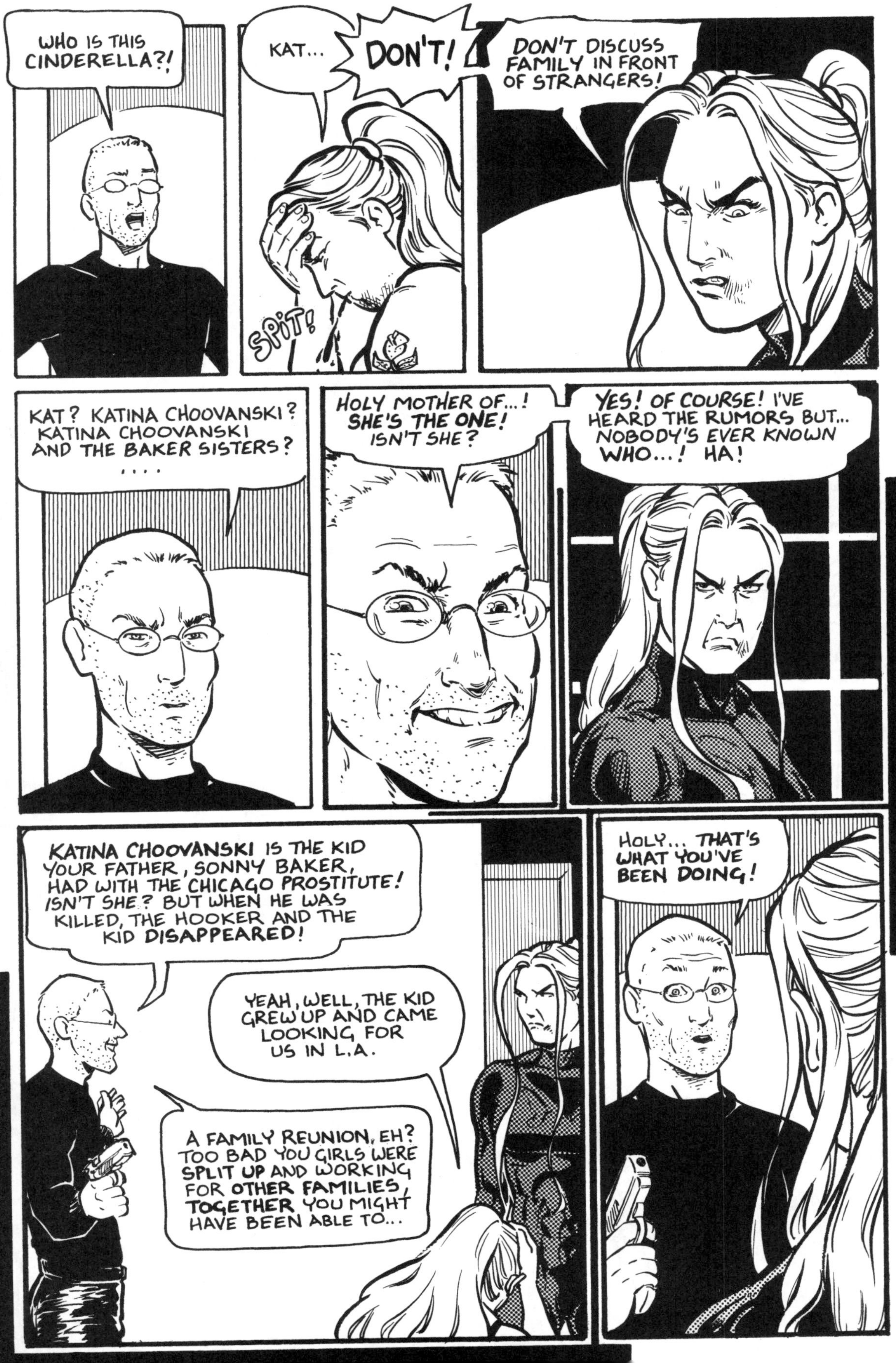
WHO IS THIS CINDERELLA?!
KAT...
DON'T!
SPIT!
DON'T DISCUSS FAMILY IN FRONT OF STRANGERS!
KAT? KATINA CHOOVANSKI? KATINA CHOOVANSKI AND THE BAKER SISTERS? ....
HOLY MOTHER OF...! SHE'S THE ONE! ISN'T SHE?
YES! OF COURSE! I'VE HEARD THE RUMORS BUT... NOBODY'S EVER KNOWN WHO...! HA!
KATINA CHOOVANSKI IS THE KID YOUR FATHER, SONNY BAKER, HAD WITH THE CHICAGO PROSTITUTE! ISN'T SHE? BUT WHEN HE WAS KILLED, THE HOOKER AND THE KID DISAPPEARED!
YEAH, WELL, THE KID GREW UP AND CAME LOOKING FOR US IN L.A.
A FAMILY REUNION, EH? TOO BAD YOU GIRLS WERE SPLIT UP AND WORKING FOR OTHER FAMILIES, TOGETHER YOU MIGHT HAVE BEEN ABLE TO...
HOLY... THAT'S WHAT YOU'VE BEEN DOING!

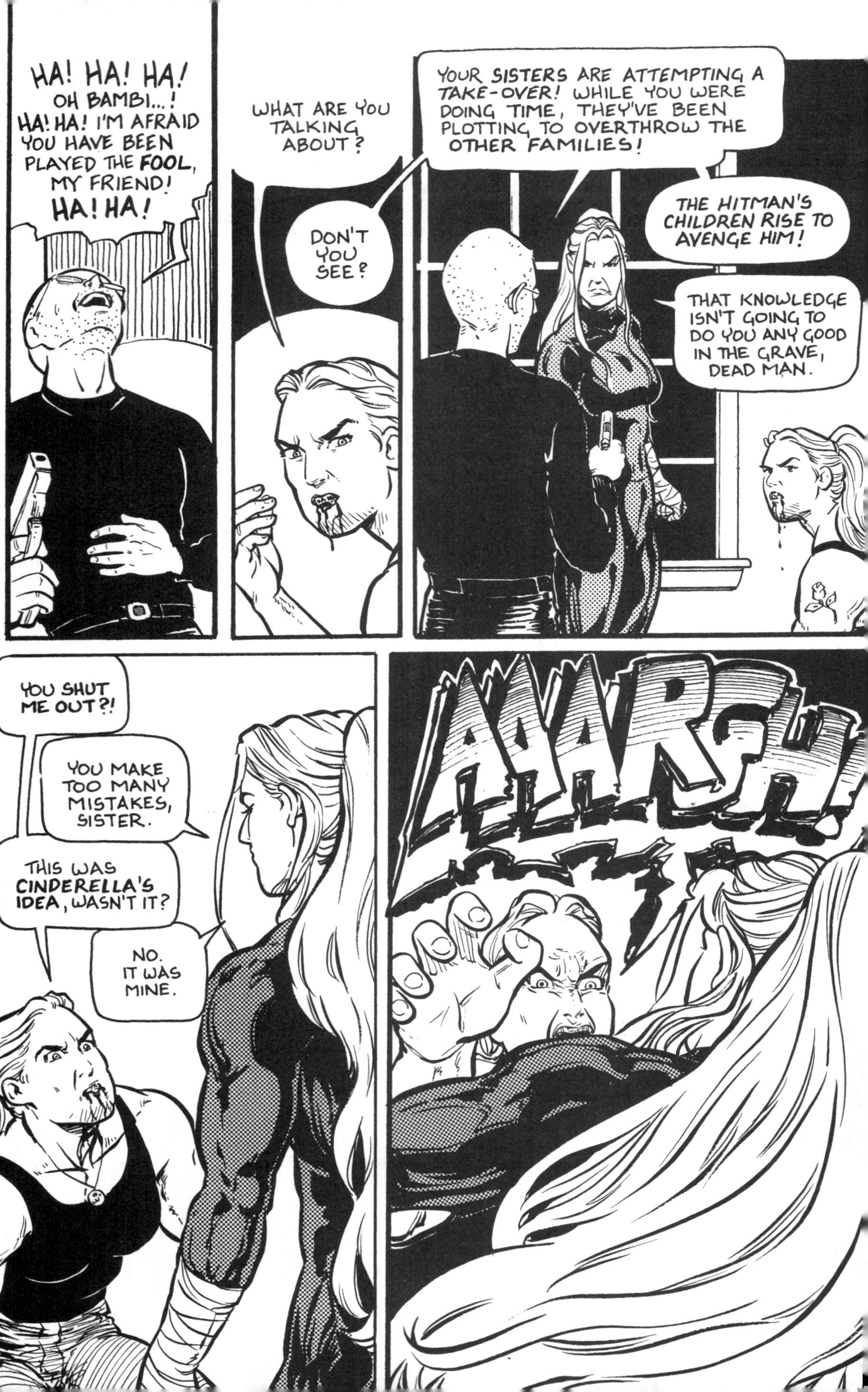
HA! HA! HA! OH BAMBI...! HA! HA! I'M AFRAID YOU HAVE BEEN PLAYED THE FOOL, MY FRIEND! HA! HA!
WHAT ARE YOU TALKING ABOUT?
DON'T YOU SEE?
YOUR SISTERS ARE ATTEMPTING A TAKE-OVER! WHILE YOU WERE DOING TIME, THEY'VE BEEN PLOTTING TO OVERTHROW THE OTHER FAMILIES!
THE HITMAN'S CHILDREN RISE TO AVENGE HIM!
THAT KNOWLEDGE ISN'T GOING TO DO YOU ANY GOOD IN THE GRAVE, DEAD MAN.
YOU SHUT ME OUT?!
YOU MAKE TOO MANY MISTAKES, SISTER.
THIS WAS CINDERELLA'S IDEA, WASN'T IT?
NO. IT WAS MINE.
AAARGH!

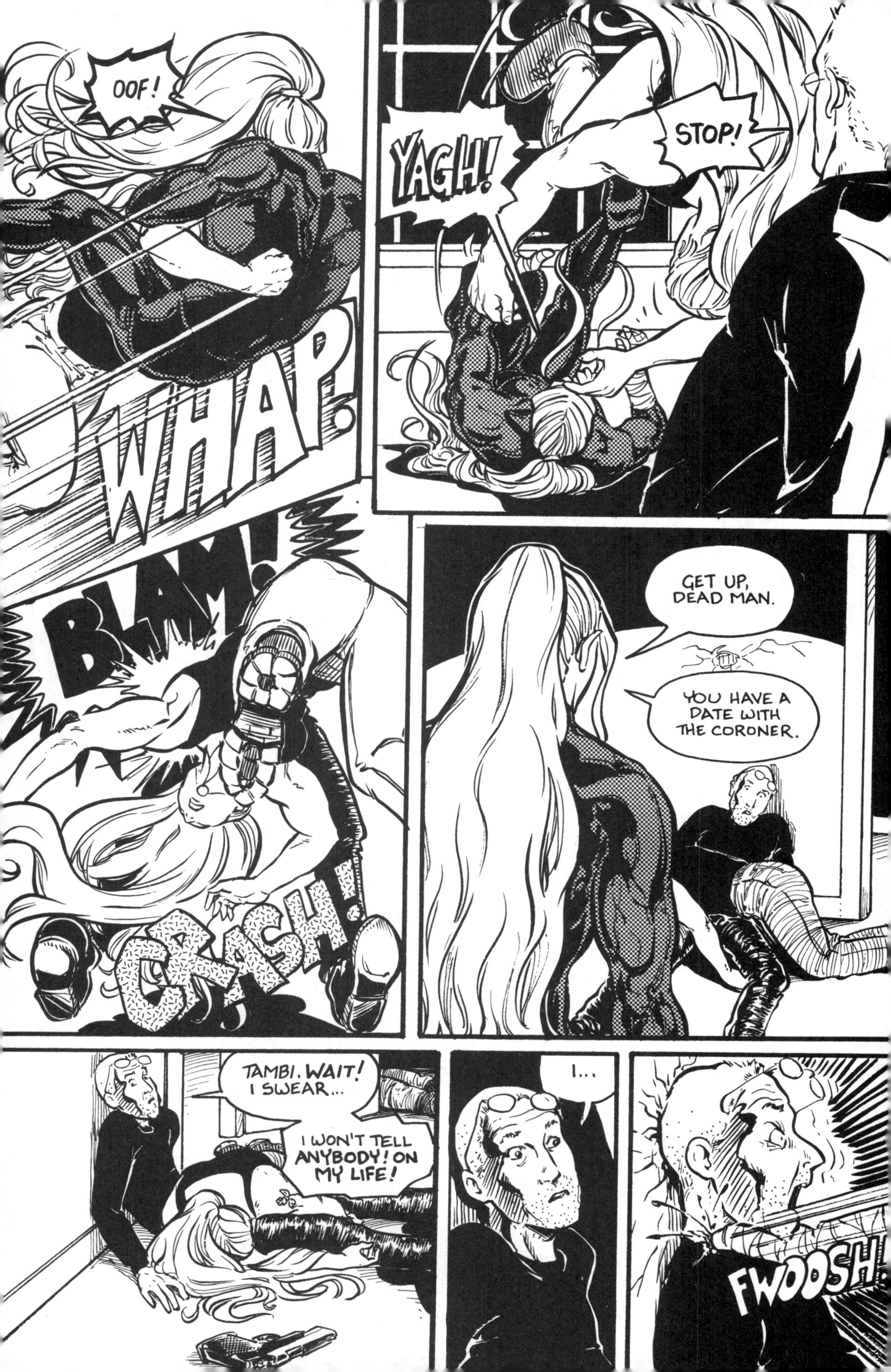
OOF!
WHAP!
YAGH!
STOP!
BLAM!
CRASH!
GET UP, DEAD MAN.
YOU HAVE A DATE WITH THE CORONER.
TAMBI. WAIT! I SWEAR...
I WON'T TELL ANYBODY! ON MY LIFE!
I...
FWOOSH!

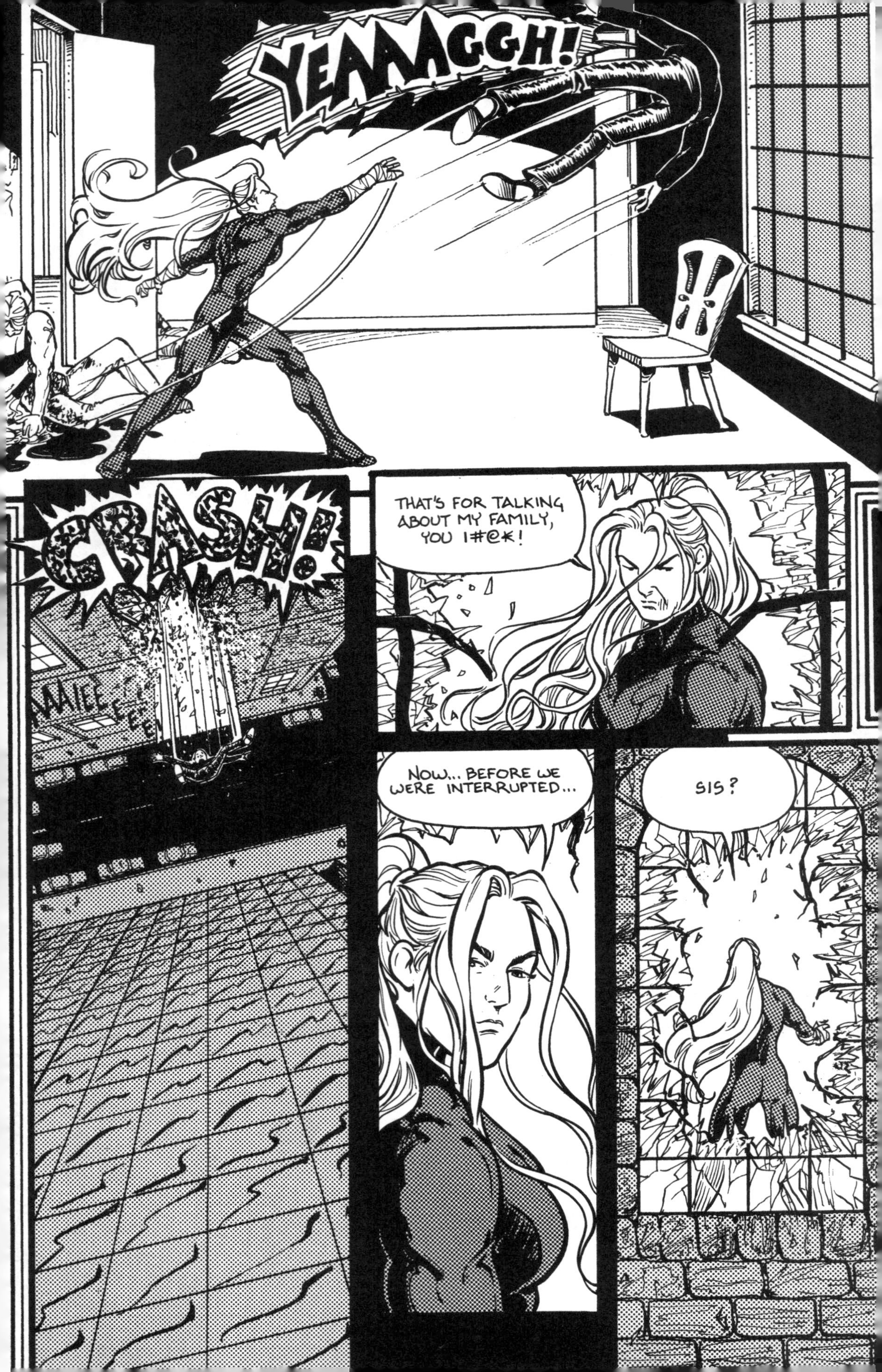

YEAAAGGH!
CRASH!
THAT'S FOR TALKING ABOUT MY FAMILY, YOU !#@*!
NOW... BEFORE WE WERE INTERRUPTED...
SIS?

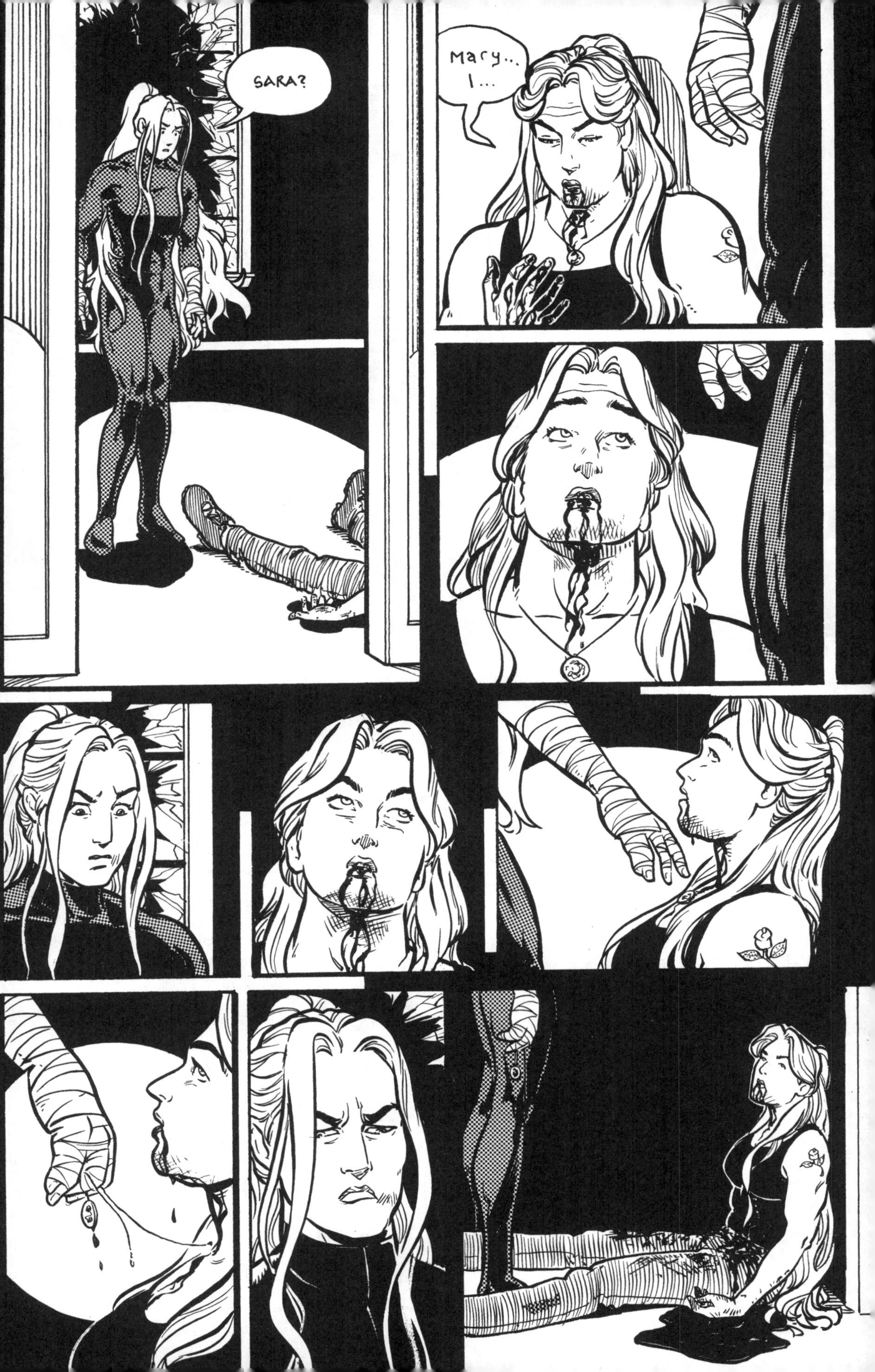
SARA?
Mary... I...

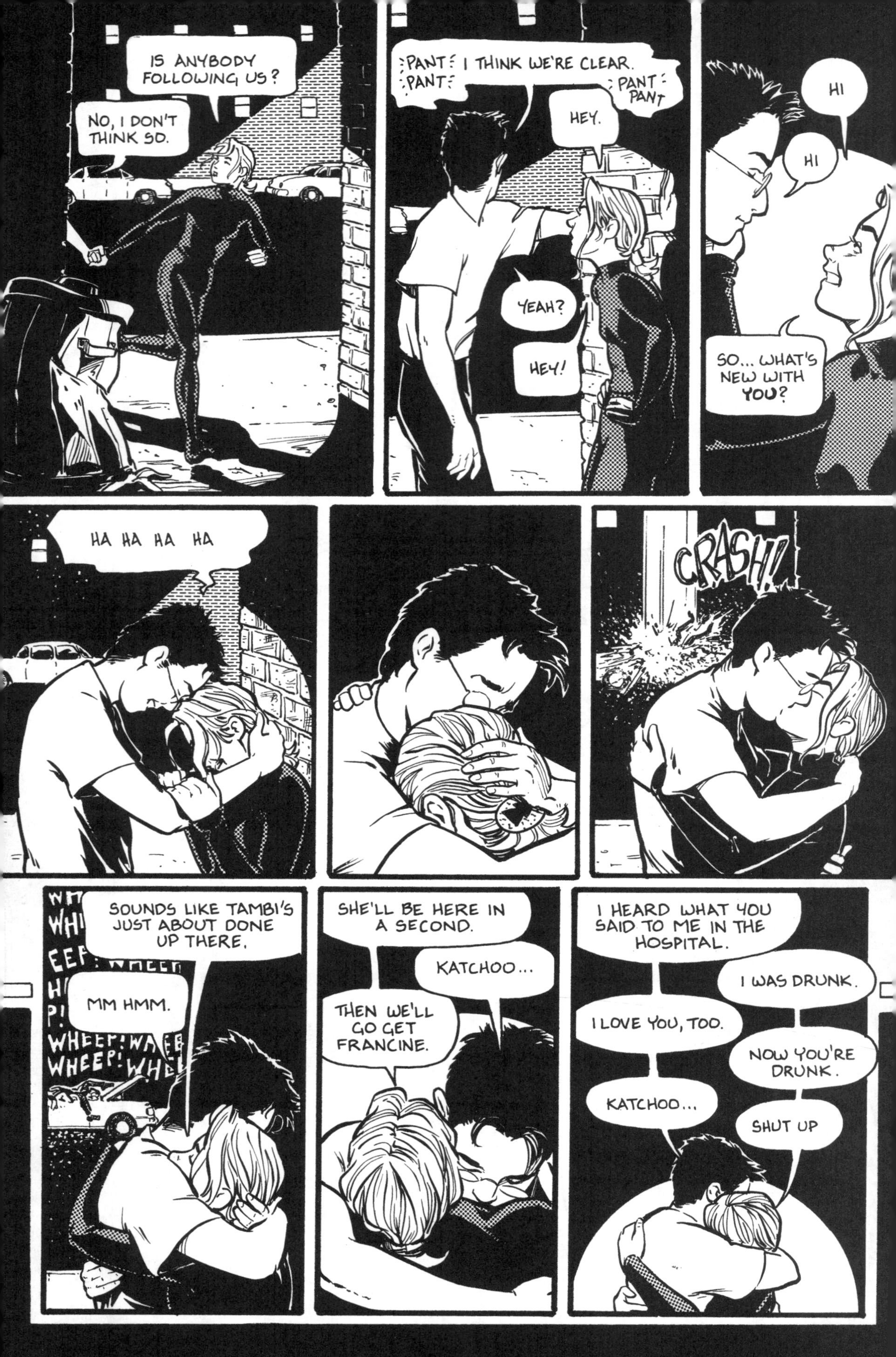
IS ANYBODY FOLLOWING US?
NO, I DON'T THINK SO.
PANT PANT
I THINK WE'RE CLEAR.
PANT PANT
HEY.
YEAH?
HEY!
HI
HI
SO... WHAT'S NEW WITH YOU?
HA HA HA HA
CRASH!
SOUNDS LIKE TAMBI'S JUST ABOUT DONE UP THERE.
MM HMM.
WHEEP! WHEEP!
SHE'LL BE HERE IN A SECOND.
KATCHOO...
THEN WE'LL GO GET FRANCINE.
I HEARD WHAT YOU SAID TO ME IN THE HOSPITAL.
I WAS DRUNK.
I LOVE YOU, TOO.
NOW YOU'RE DRUNK.
KATCHOO...
SHUT UP

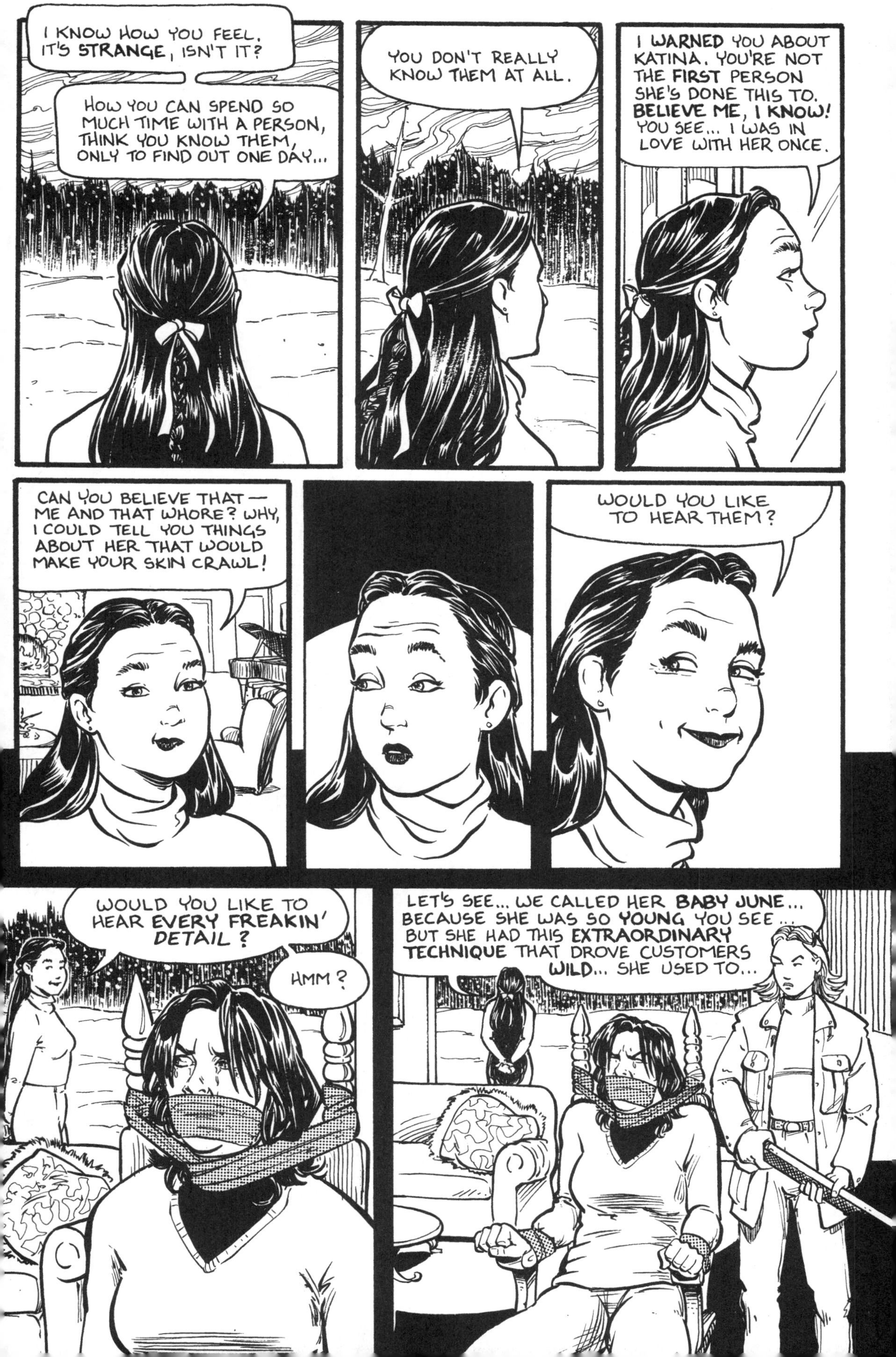
I KNOW HOW YOU FEEL. IT'S STRANGE, ISN'T IT?
HOW YOU CAN SPEND SO MUCH TIME WITH A PERSON, THINK YOU KNOW THEM, ONLY TO FIND OUT ONE DAY...
YOU DON'T REALLY KNOW THEM AT ALL.
I WARNED YOU ABOUT KATINA. YOU'RE NOT THE FIRST PERSON SHE'S DONE THIS TO. BELIEVE ME, I KNOW! YOU SEE... I WAS IN LOVE WITH HER ONCE.
CAN YOU BELIEVE THAT — ME AND THAT WHORE? WHY, I COULD TELL YOU THINGS ABOUT HER THAT WOULD MAKE YOUR SKIN CRAWL!
WOULD YOU LIKE TO HEAR THEM?
WOULD YOU LIKE TO HEAR EVERY FREAKIN' DETAIL?
HMM?
LET'S SEE... WE CALLED HER BABY JUNE... BECAUSE SHE WAS SO YOUNG YOU SEE... BUT SHE HAD THIS EXTRAORDINARY TECHNIQUE THAT DROVE CUSTOMERS WILD... SHE USED TO...

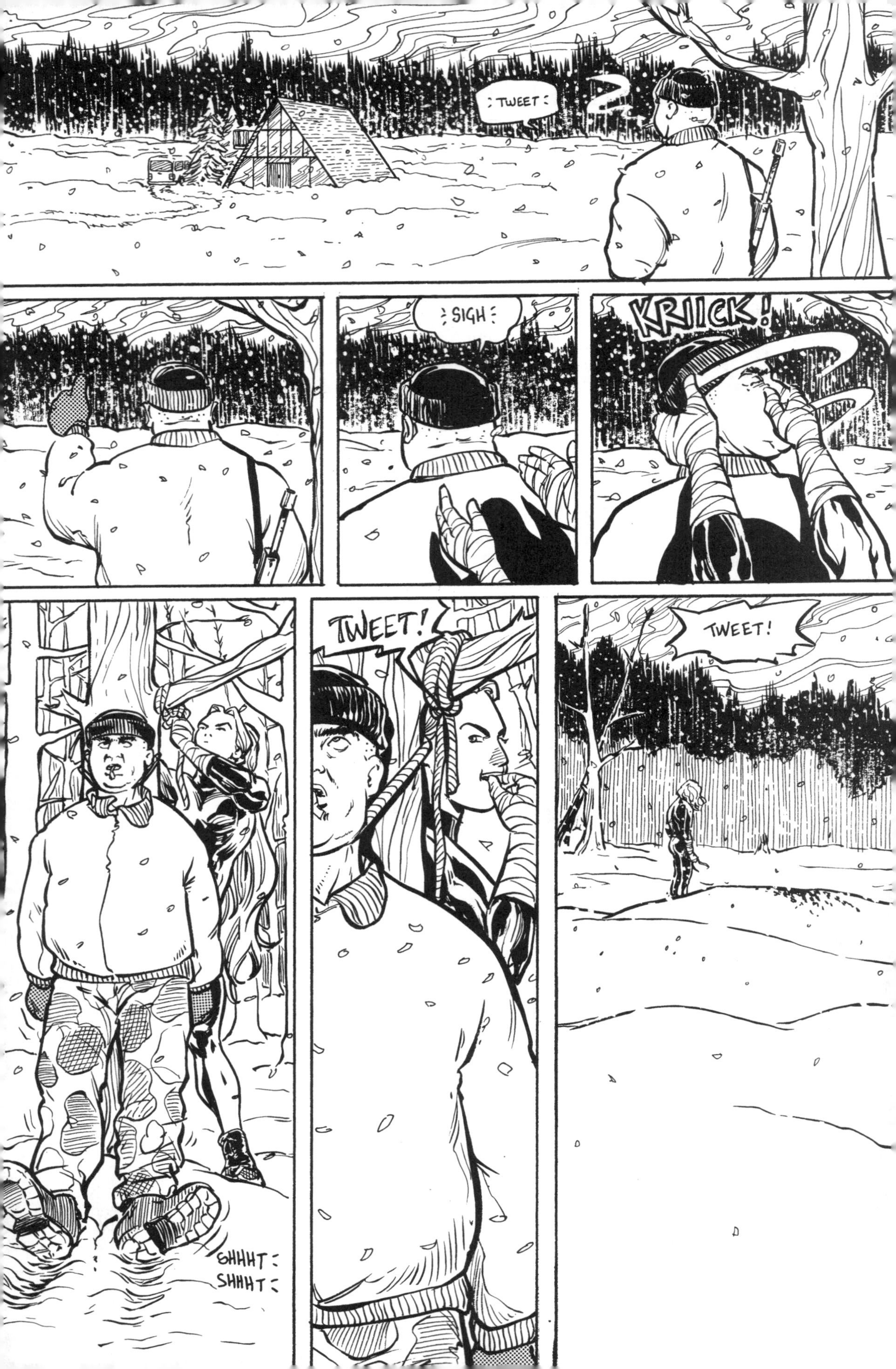
TWEET
SIGH
KRIICK!
SHHHT
SHHHT
TWEET!
TWEET!

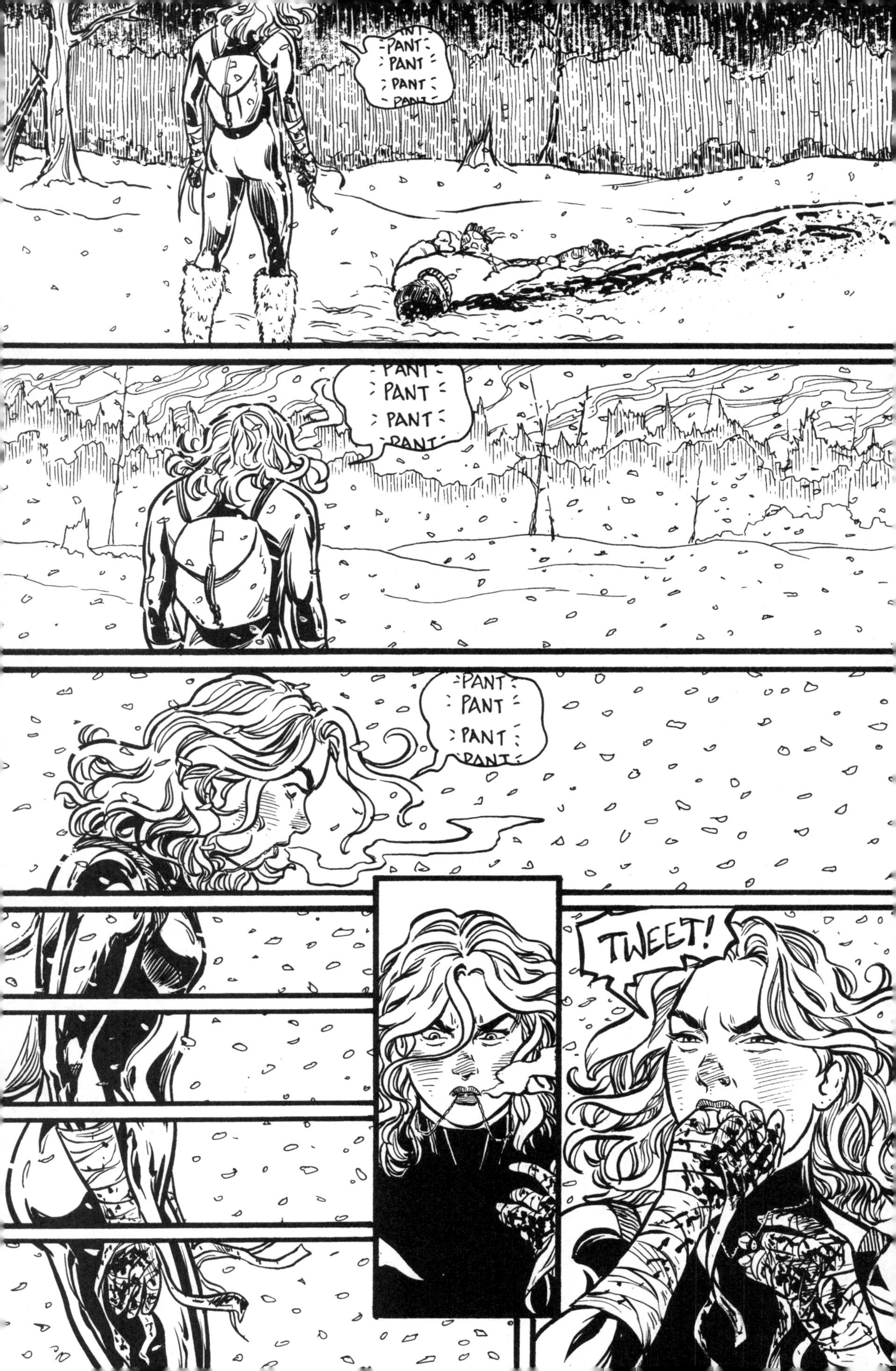
PANT PANT PANT
PANT PANT PANT
PANT PANT PANT
TWEET!

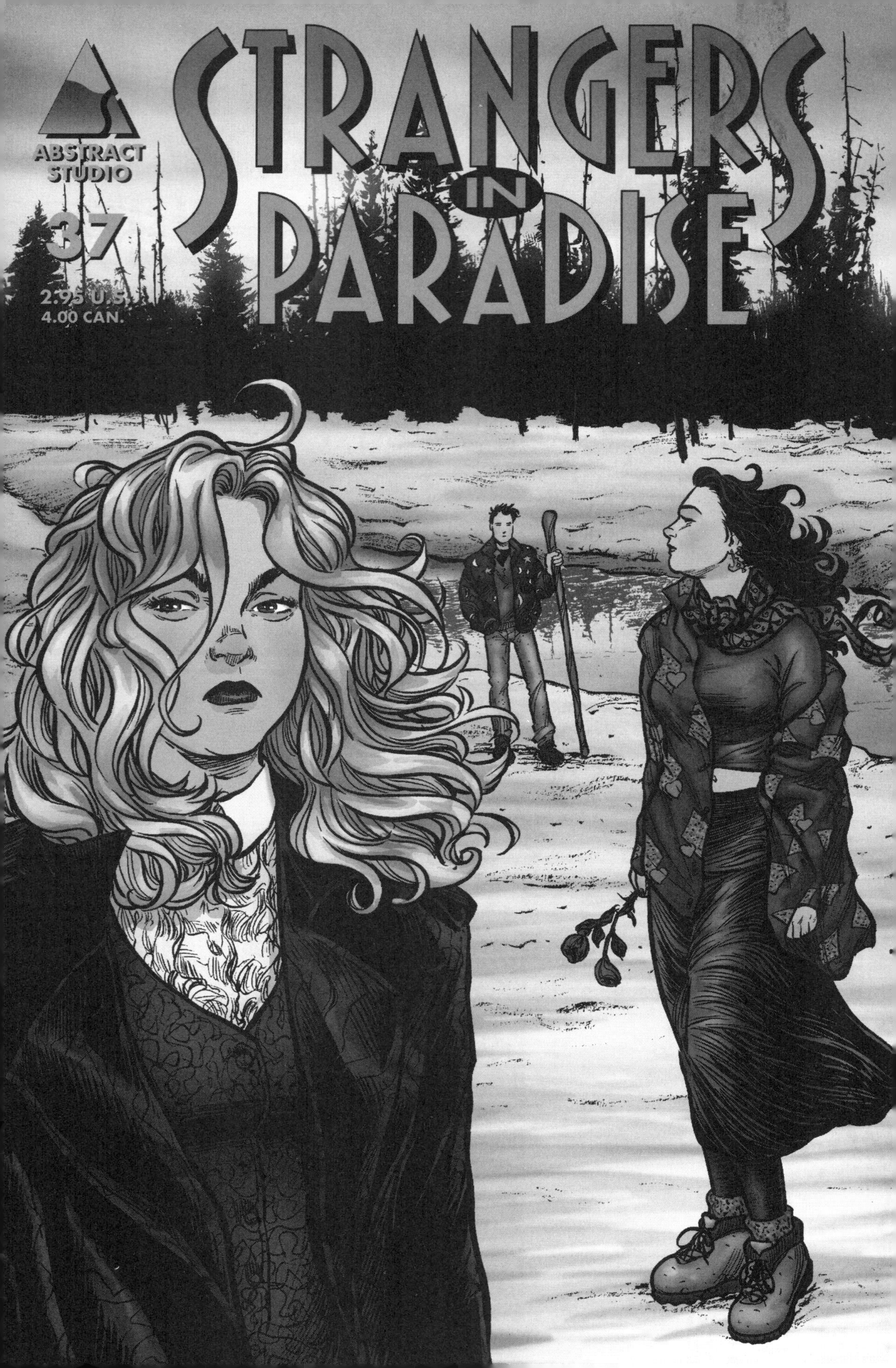
ABSTRACT STUDIO
37
2.95 U.S.
4.00 CAN.
STRANGERS IN PARADISE

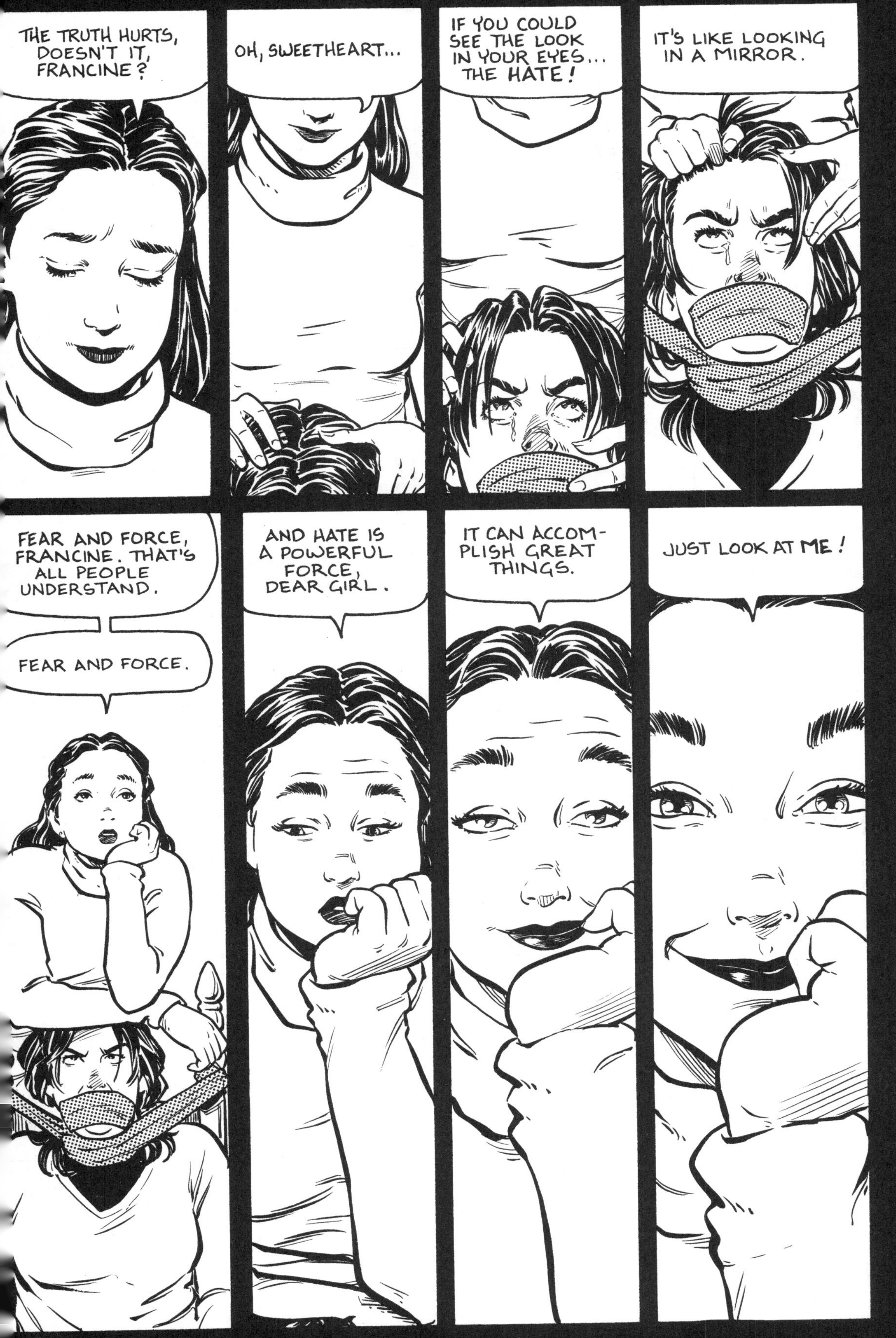
THE TRUTH HURTS, DOESN'T IT, FRANCINE?
OH, SWEETHEART...
IF YOU COULD SEE THE LOOK IN YOUR EYES... THE HATE!
IT'S LIKE LOOKING IN A MIRROR.
FEAR AND FORCE, FRANCINE. THAT'S ALL PEOPLE UNDERSTAND.
FEAR AND FORCE.
AND HATE IS A POWERFUL FORCE, DEAR GIRL.
IT CAN ACCOMPLISH GREAT THINGS.
JUST LOOK AT ME!

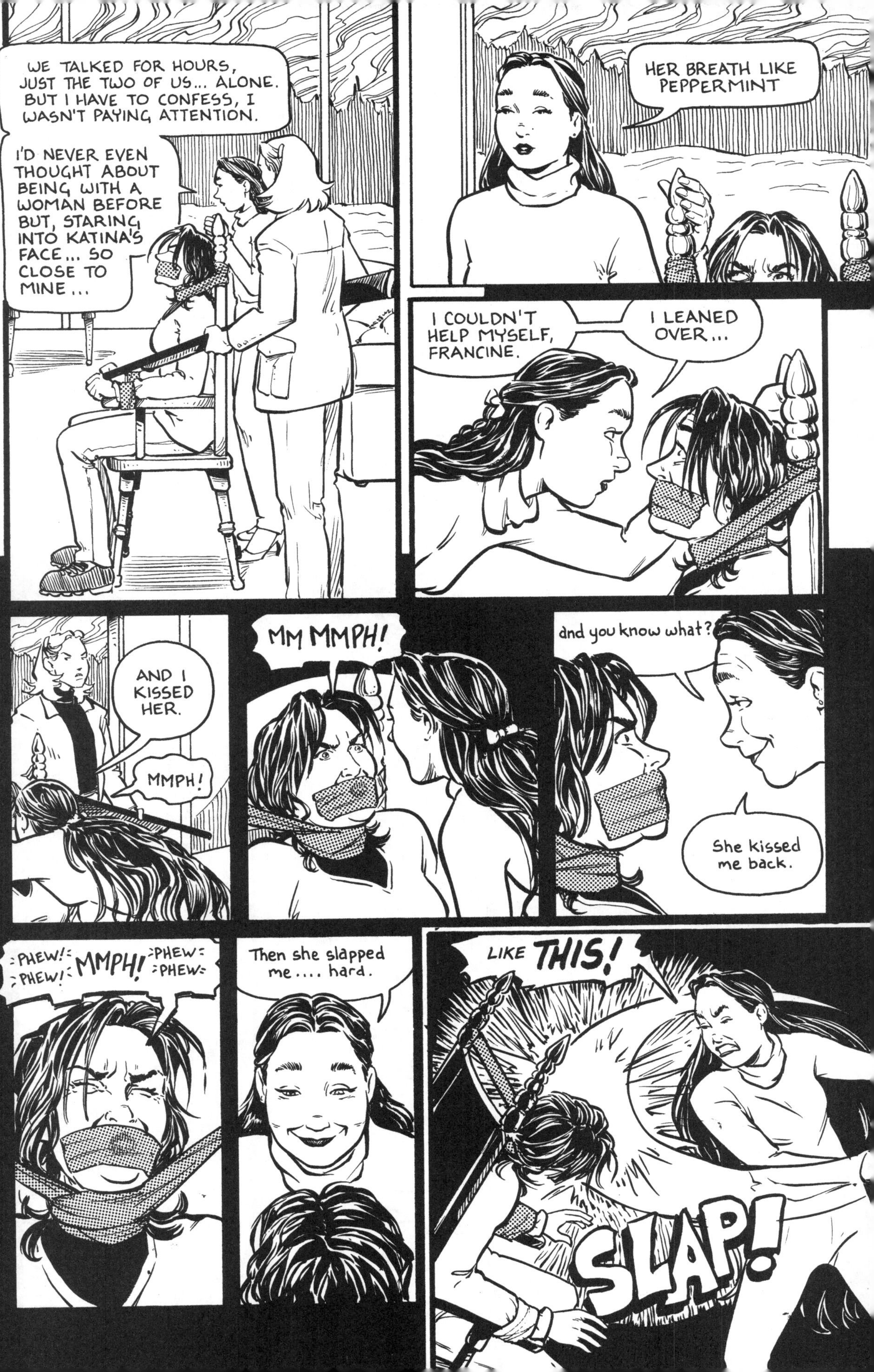
WE TALKED FOR HOURS, JUST THE TWO OF US... ALONE. BUT I HAVE TO CONFESS, I WASN'T PAYING ATTENTION.
I'D NEVER EVEN THOUGHT ABOUT BEING WITH A WOMAN BEFORE BUT, STARING INTO KATINA'S FACE... SO CLOSE TO MINE...
HER BREATH LIKE PEPPERMINT
I COULDN'T HELP MYSELF, FRANCINE.
I LEANED OVER...
AND I KISSED HER.
MMPH!
MM MMPH!
and you know what?
She kissed me back.
PHEW! PHEW! MMPH! PHEW PHEW
Then she slapped me.... hard.
LIKE THIS!
SLAP!

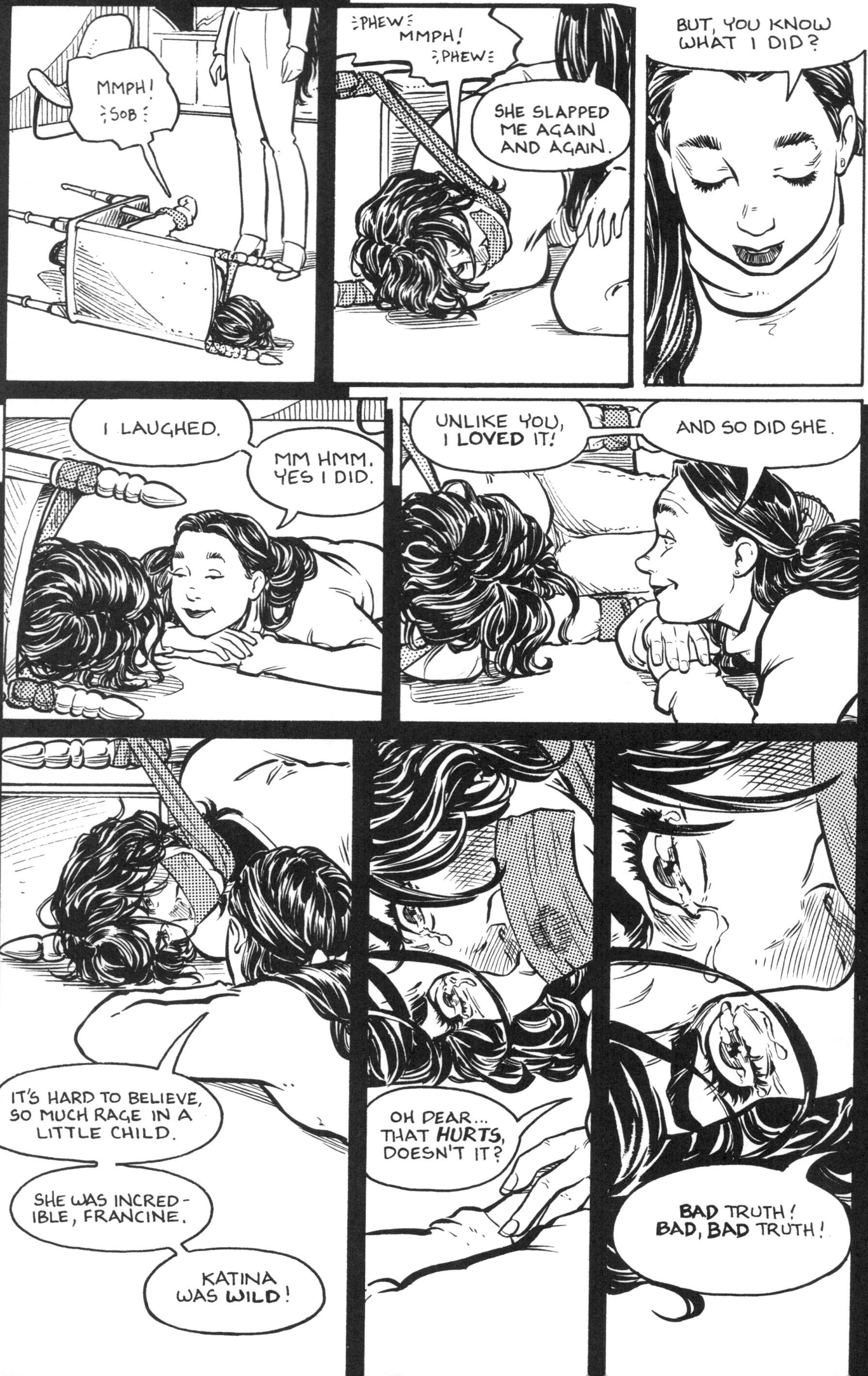
MMPH!
SOB
PHEW
MMPH!
PHEW
SHE SLAPPED ME AGAIN AND AGAIN.
BUT, YOU KNOW WHAT I DID?
I LAUGHED.
MM HMM. YES I DID.
UNLIKE YOU, I **LOVED** IT!
AND SO DID SHE.
IT'S HARD TO BELIEVE, SO MUCH RAGE IN A LITTLE CHILD.
SHE WAS INCRED-IBLE, FRANCINE.
KATINA WAS **WILD**!
OH DEAR... THAT **HURTS**, DOESN'T IT?
**BAD** TRUTH! **BAD, BAD** TRUTH!

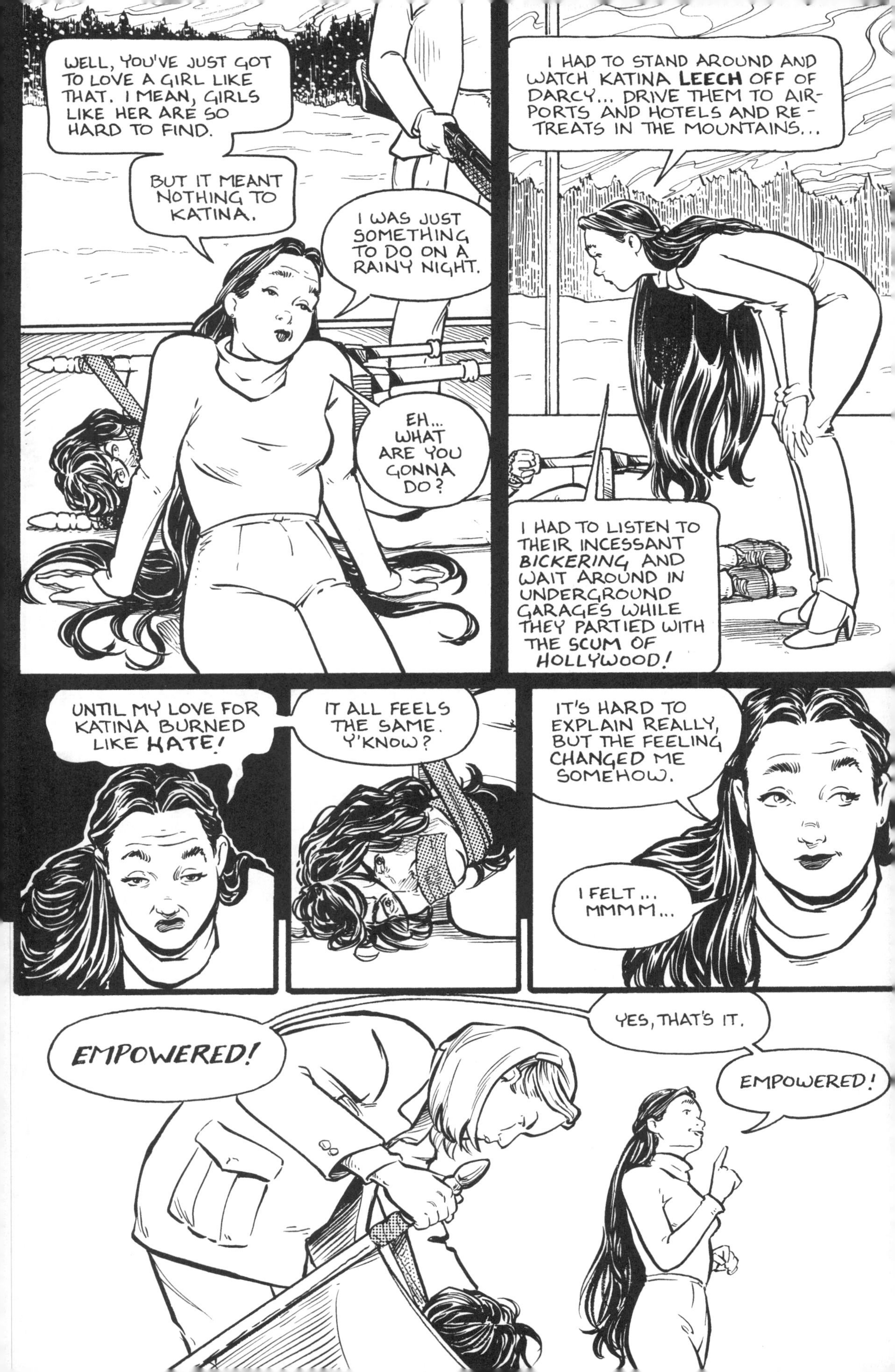
WELL, YOU'VE JUST GOT TO LOVE A GIRL LIKE THAT. I MEAN, GIRLS LIKE HER ARE SO HARD TO FIND.
BUT IT MEANT NOTHING TO KATINA.
I WAS JUST SOMETHING TO DO ON A RAINY NIGHT.
EH... WHAT ARE YOU GONNA DO?
I HAD TO STAND AROUND AND WATCH KATINA **LEECH** OFF OF DARCY... DRIVE THEM TO AIR-PORTS AND HOTELS AND RE-TREATS IN THE MOUNTAINS...
I HAD TO LISTEN TO THEIR INCESSANT *BICKERING* AND WAIT AROUND IN UNDERGROUND GARAGES WHILE THEY PARTIED WITH THE **SCUM** OF **HOLLYWOOD**!
UNTIL MY LOVE FOR KATINA BURNED LIKE **HATE**!
IT ALL FEELS THE SAME. Y'KNOW?
IT'S HARD TO EXPLAIN REALLY, BUT THE FEELING **CHANGED** ME SOMEHOW.
I FELT... MMMM...
YES, THAT'S IT.
EMPOWERED!
*EMPOWERED!*

EVERYBODY AND EVERY-THING LOOKED DIFFERENT TO ME AFTER KATINA... NOBODY HAD ANY POWER OVER ME THAT I DIDN'T GIVE THEM.

AND THE DAY I REALIZED THAT WAS THE DAY I STOPPED GIVING IT AWAY.

YOU SEE, THAT'S THE DIFFERENCE BETWEEN US, FRANCINE... THAT'S WHY I'M ON TOP OF THE WORLD AND YOU'RE TIED TO A CHAIR.

IT'S VERY SYMBOLIC, DON'T YOU THINK?

IN MANY WAYS...

YOU REMIND ME...

OF EMMA.

THE LAST TIME I SAW EMMA SHE WAS IN A CHAIR, JUST LIKE YOU ARE NOW. IT WAS PATHETIC.

SHE LOVED KATINA, TOO.

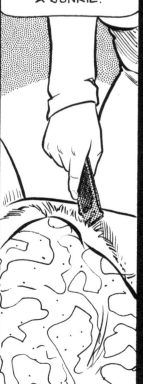

BUT SHE WAS A JUNKIE.

SO I FILLED HER FULL OF HEROIN WITH AN INFECTED NEEDLE AND SENT HER ON HER WAY.

FLIK

IT TOOK SIX YEARS FOR HER TO DIE... AND I LOVED EVERY MINUTE OF IT.

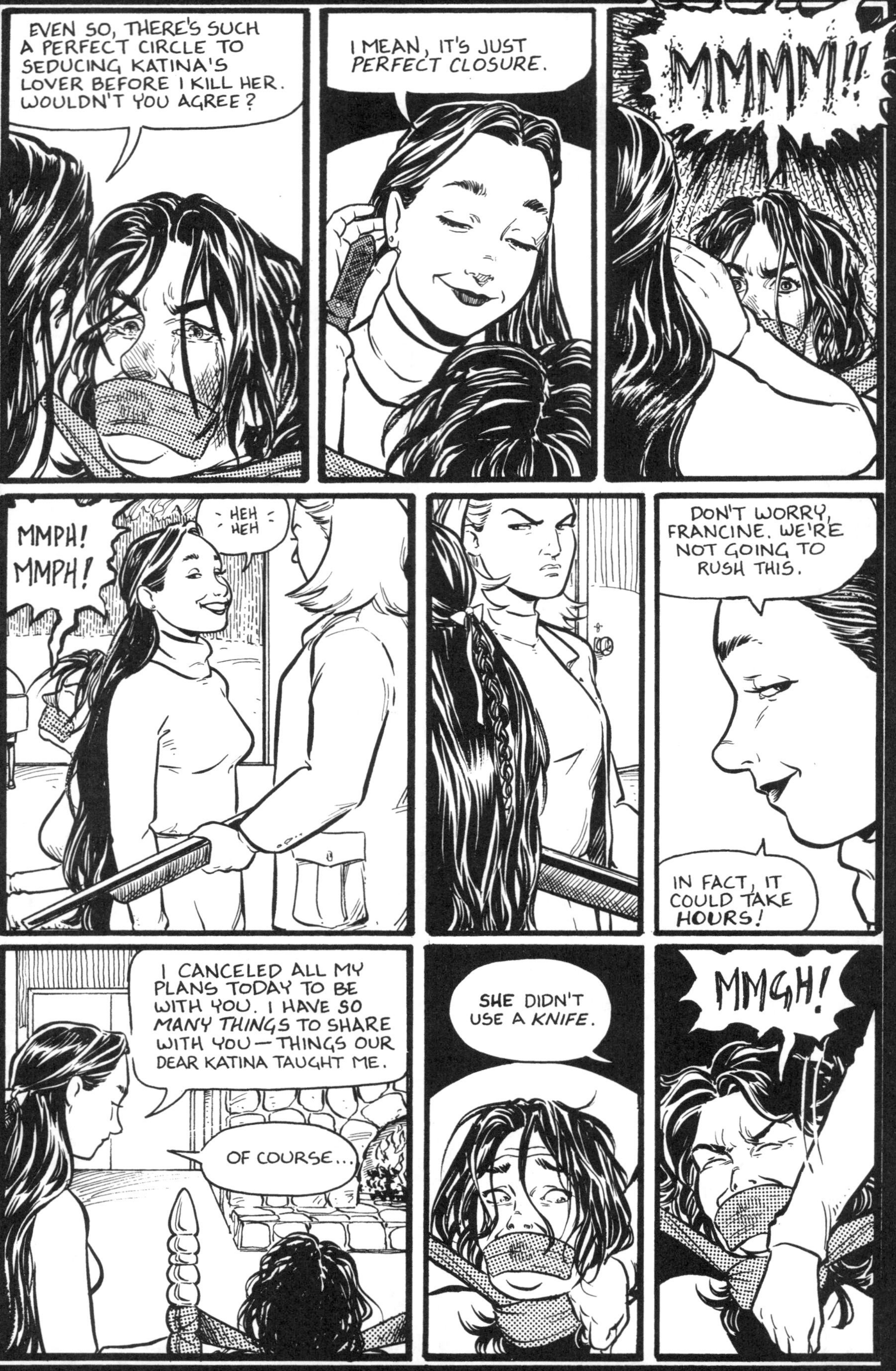
EVEN SO, THERE'S SUCH A PERFECT CIRCLE TO SEDUCING KATINA'S LOVER BEFORE I KILL HER. WOULDN'T YOU AGREE?
I MEAN, IT'S JUST PERFECT CLOSURE.
MMMM!!
MMPH! MMPH!
HEH HEH
DON'T WORRY, FRANCINE. WE'RE NOT GOING TO RUSH THIS.
IN FACT, IT COULD TAKE HOURS!
I CANCELED ALL MY PLANS TODAY TO BE WITH YOU. I HAVE SO MANY THINGS TO SHARE WITH YOU—THINGS OUR DEAR KATINA TAUGHT ME.
OF COURSE...
SHE DIDN'T USE A KNIFE.
MMGH!

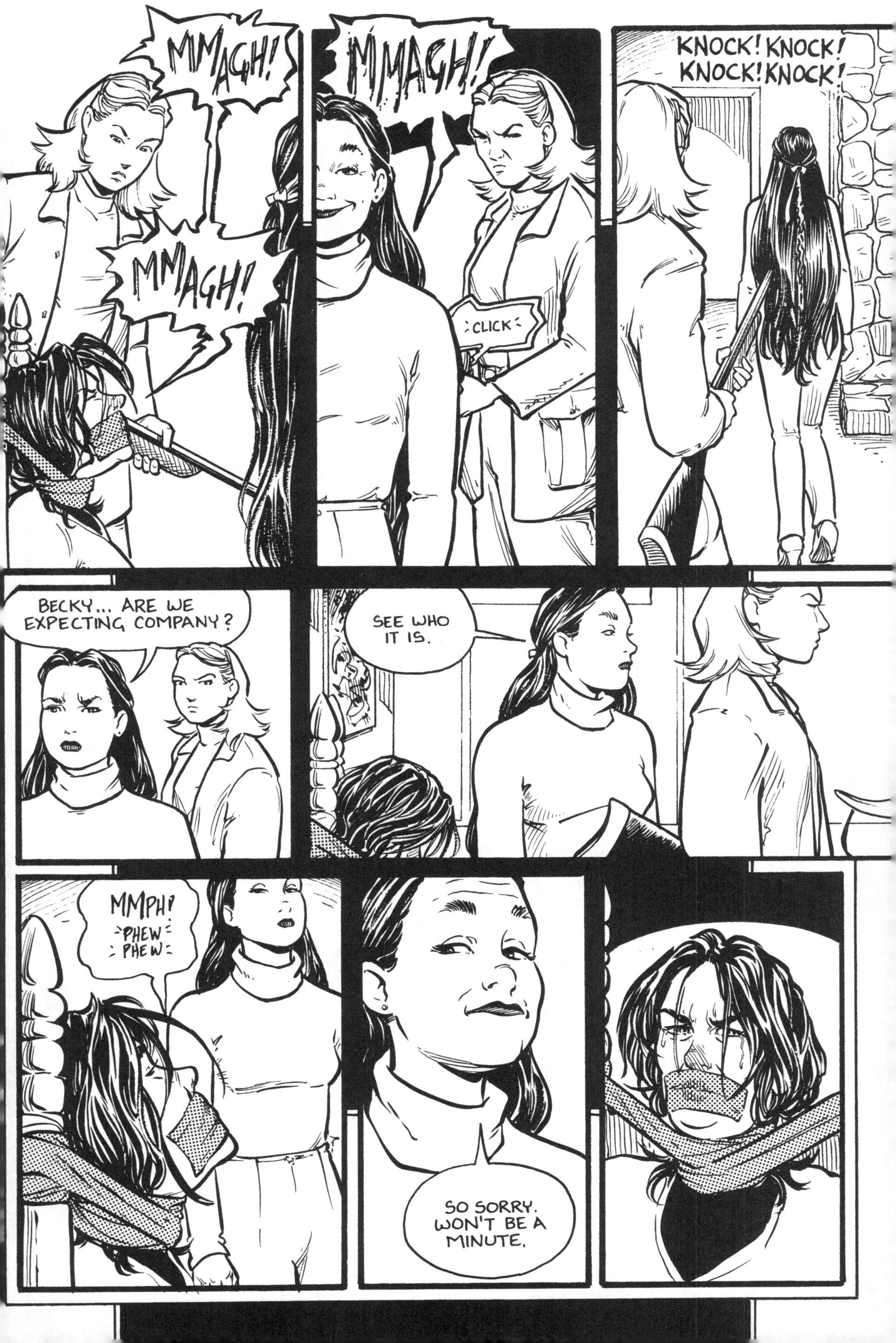
MMAGH!
MMAGH!
MMAGH!
CLICK
KNOCK! KNOCK! KNOCK! KNOCK!
BECKY... ARE WE EXPECTING COMPANY?
SEE WHO IT IS.
MMPH! PHEW PHEW
SO SORRY. WON'T BE A MINUTE.

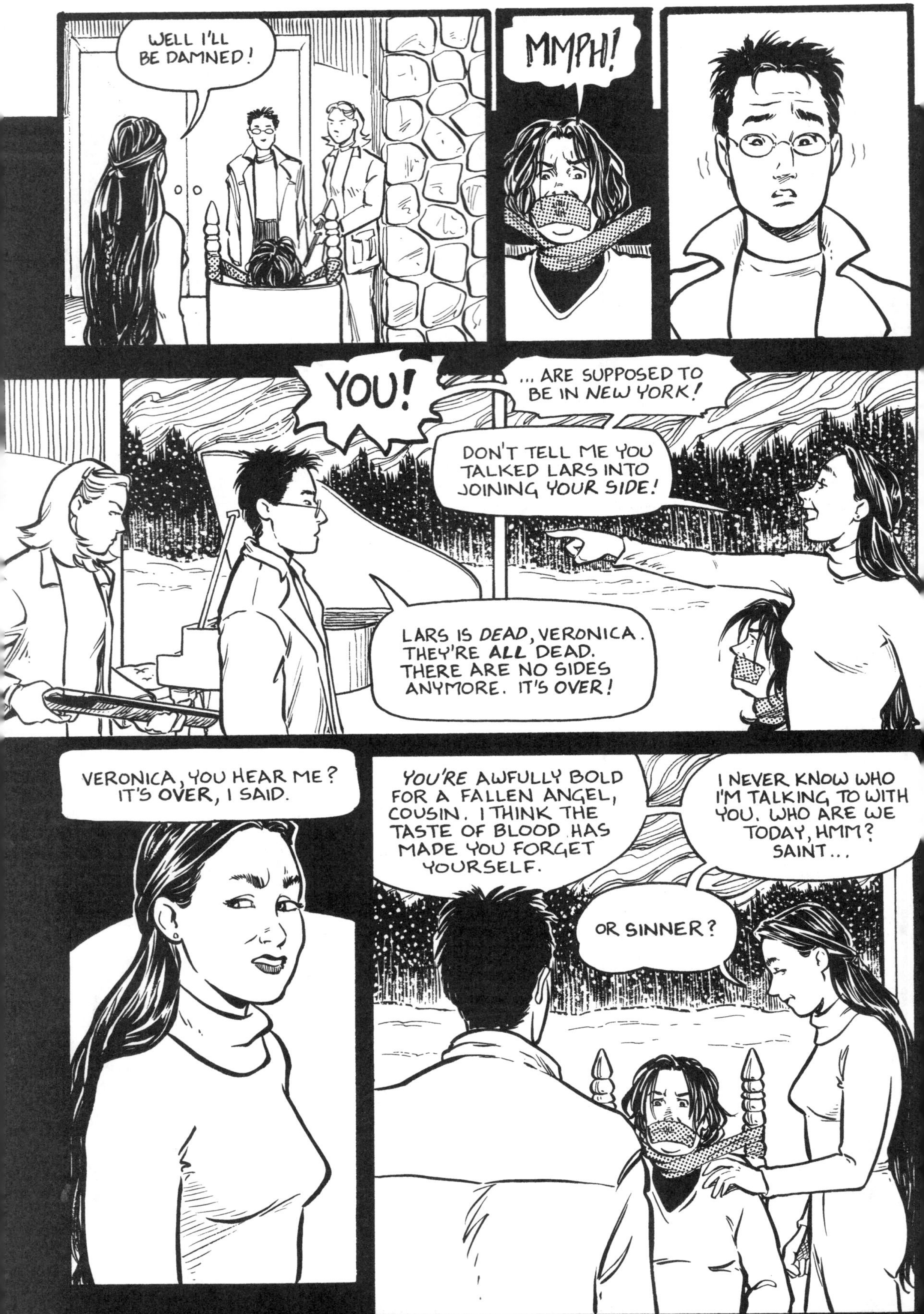

WELL I'LL BE DAMNED!
MMPH!
YOU!
... ARE SUPPOSED TO BE IN NEW YORK!
DON'T TELL ME YOU TALKED LARS INTO JOINING YOUR SIDE!
LARS IS DEAD, VERONICA. THEY'RE ALL DEAD. THERE ARE NO SIDES ANYMORE. IT'S OVER!
VERONICA, YOU HEAR ME? IT'S OVER, I SAID.
YOU'RE AWFULLY BOLD FOR A FALLEN ANGEL, COUSIN. I THINK THE TASTE OF BLOOD HAS MADE YOU FORGET YOURSELF.
I NEVER KNOW WHO I'M TALKING TO WITH YOU. WHO ARE WE TODAY, HMM? SAINT...
OR SINNER?

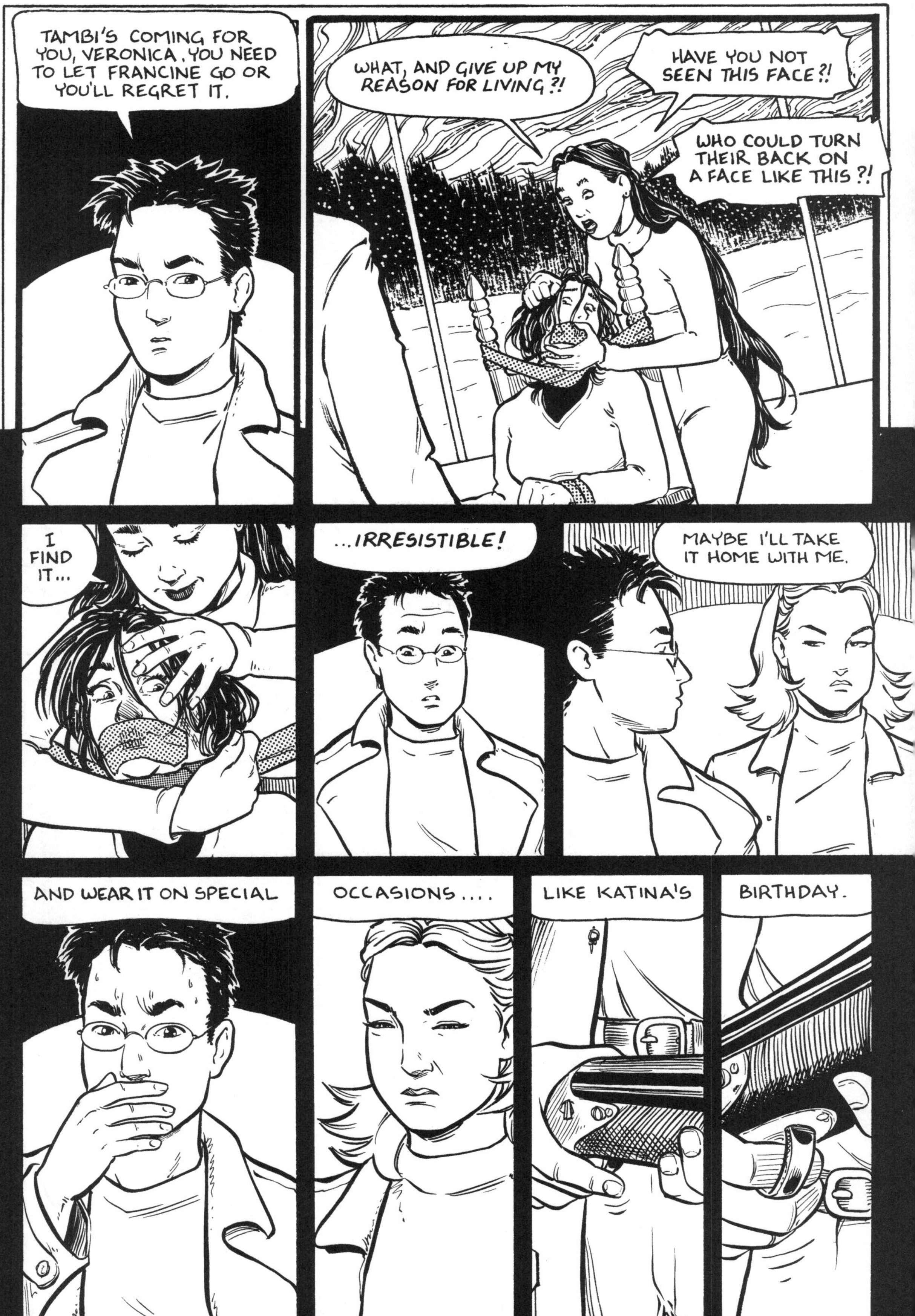
TAMBI'S COMING FOR YOU, VERONICA. YOU NEED TO LET FRANCINE GO OR YOU'LL REGRET IT.
WHAT, AND GIVE UP MY REASON FOR LIVING?!
HAVE YOU NOT SEEN THIS FACE?!
WHO COULD TURN THEIR BACK ON A FACE LIKE THIS?!
I FIND IT...
...IRRESISTIBLE!
MAYBE I'LL TAKE IT HOME WITH ME.
AND WEAR IT ON SPECIAL
OCCASIONS....
LIKE KATINA'S
BIRTHDAY.

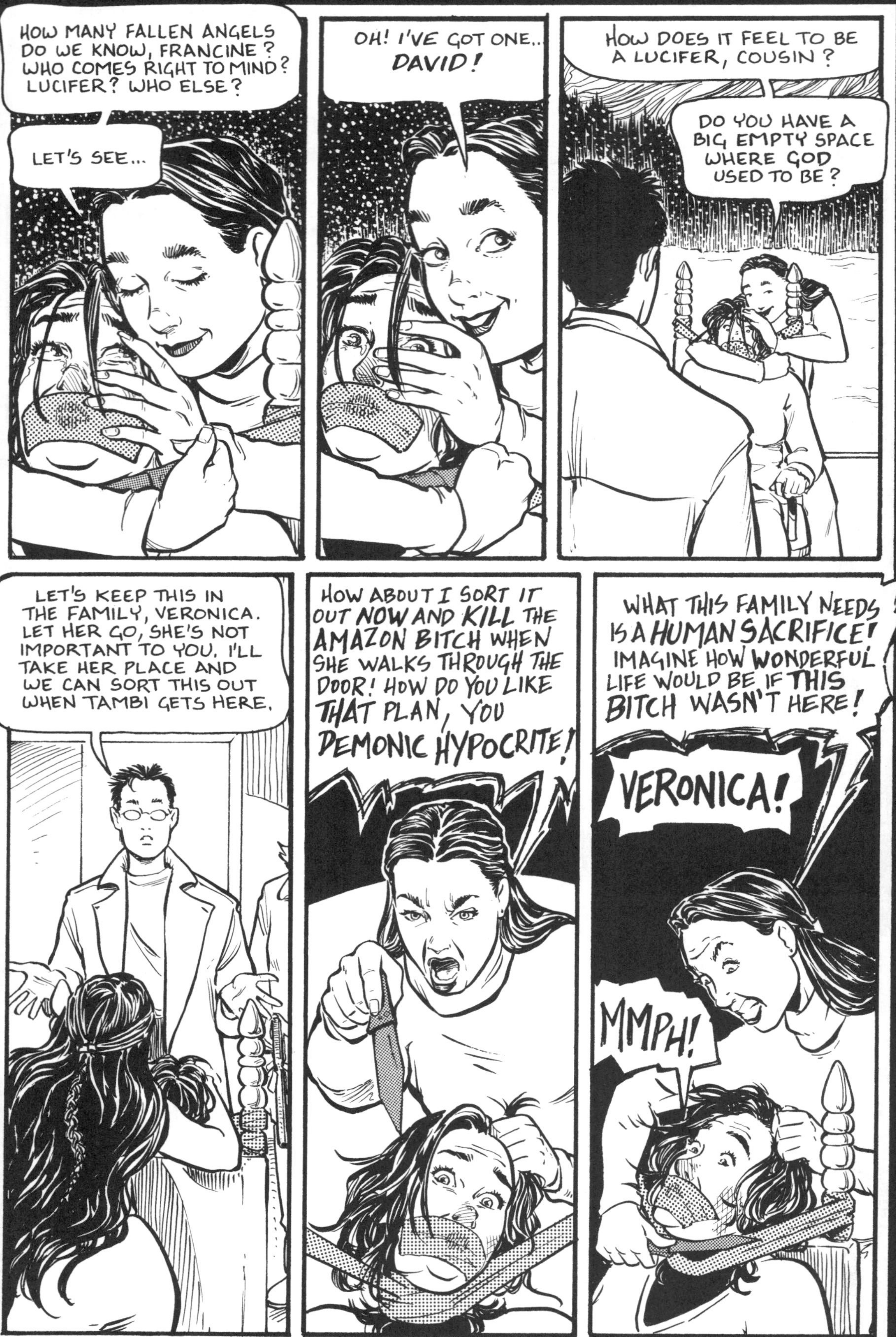
HOW MANY FALLEN ANGELS DO WE KNOW, FRANCINE? WHO COMES RIGHT TO MIND? LUCIFER? WHO ELSE?
LET'S SEE...
OH! I'VE GOT ONE.. DAVID!
HOW DOES IT FEEL TO BE A LUCIFER, COUSIN?
DO YOU HAVE A BIG EMPTY SPACE WHERE GOD USED TO BE?
LET'S KEEP THIS IN THE FAMILY, VERONICA. LET HER GO, SHE'S NOT IMPORTANT TO YOU. I'LL TAKE HER PLACE AND WE CAN SORT THIS OUT WHEN TAMBI GETS HERE.
HOW ABOUT I SORT IT OUT NOW AND KILL THE AMAZON BITCH WHEN SHE WALKS THROUGH THE DOOR! HOW DO YOU LIKE THAT PLAN, YOU DEMONIC HYPOCRITE!
WHAT THIS FAMILY NEEDS IS A HUMAN SACRIFICE! IMAGINE HOW WONDERFUL LIFE WOULD BE IF THIS BITCH WASN'T HERE!
VERONICA!
MMPH!

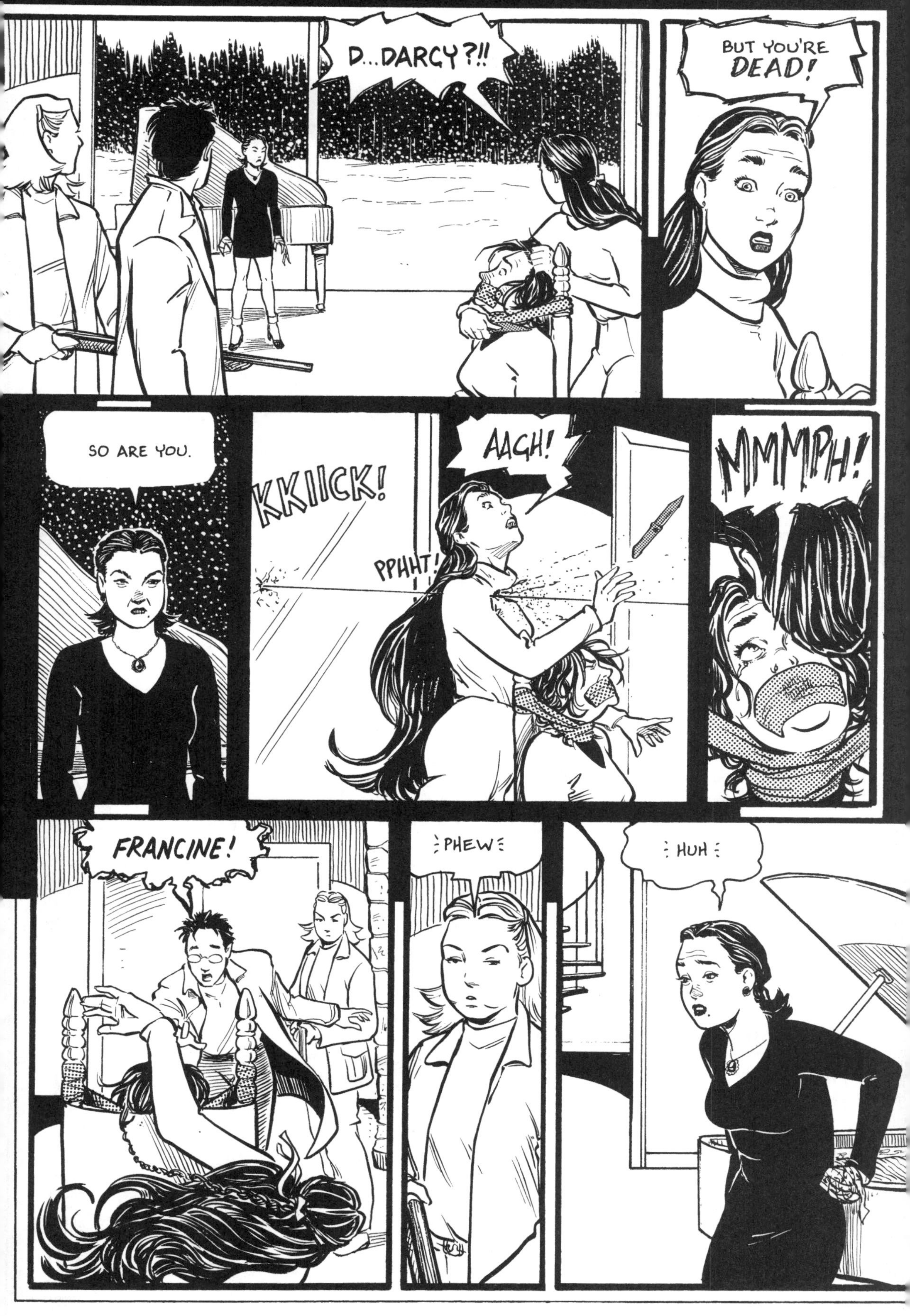
D...DARCY?!!
BUT YOU'RE DEAD!
SO ARE YOU.
KKIICK!
AAGH!
PPHHT!
MMMPH!
FRANCINE!
PHEW
HUH

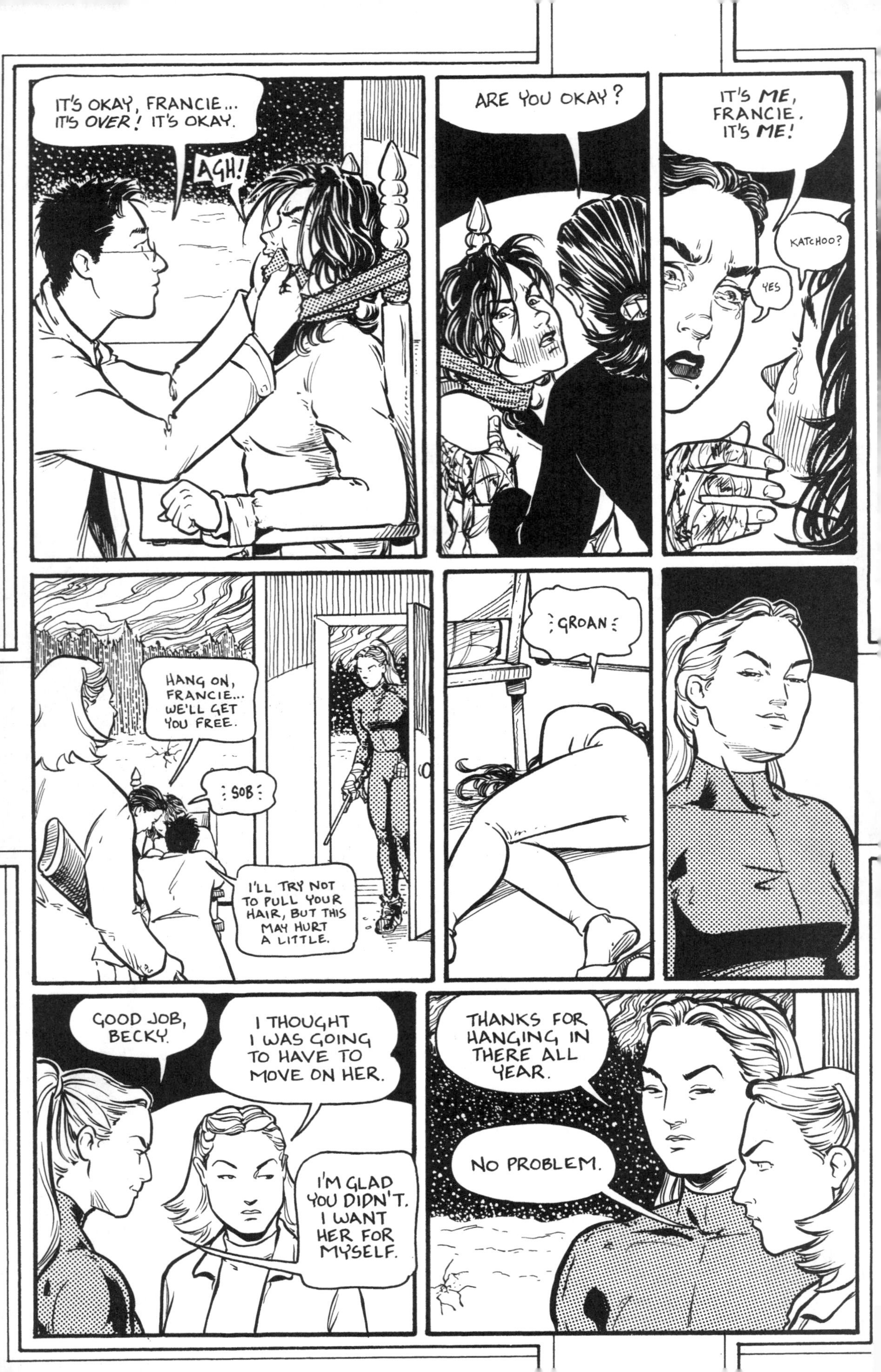
IT'S OKAY, FRANCIE... IT'S OVER! IT'S OKAY.
AGH!
ARE YOU OKAY?
IT'S ME, FRANCIE. IT'S ME!
KATCHOO?
YES
HANG ON, FRANCIE... WE'LL GET YOU FREE.
SOB
I'LL TRY NOT TO PULL YOUR HAIR, BUT THIS MAY HURT A LITTLE.
GROAN
GOOD JOB, BECKY.
I THOUGHT I WAS GOING TO HAVE TO MOVE ON HER.
I'M GLAD YOU DIDN'T. I WANT HER FOR MYSELF.
THANKS FOR HANGING IN THERE ALL YEAR.
NO PROBLEM.

TAMBI, I NEED TO GET HER OUT OF HERE. NOW.

GO AHEAD. TAKE THE ROVER OUTSIDE. BECKY WILL DRIVE YOU TO THE AIRPORT.

I'LL CALL THE PLANE. THEY'LL BE READY FOR YOU WHEN YOU GET THERE TO TAKE YOU ANYWHERE YOU WANT.

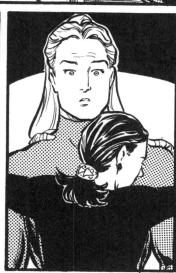

Thank you, Mary.

You're welcome.... sis.

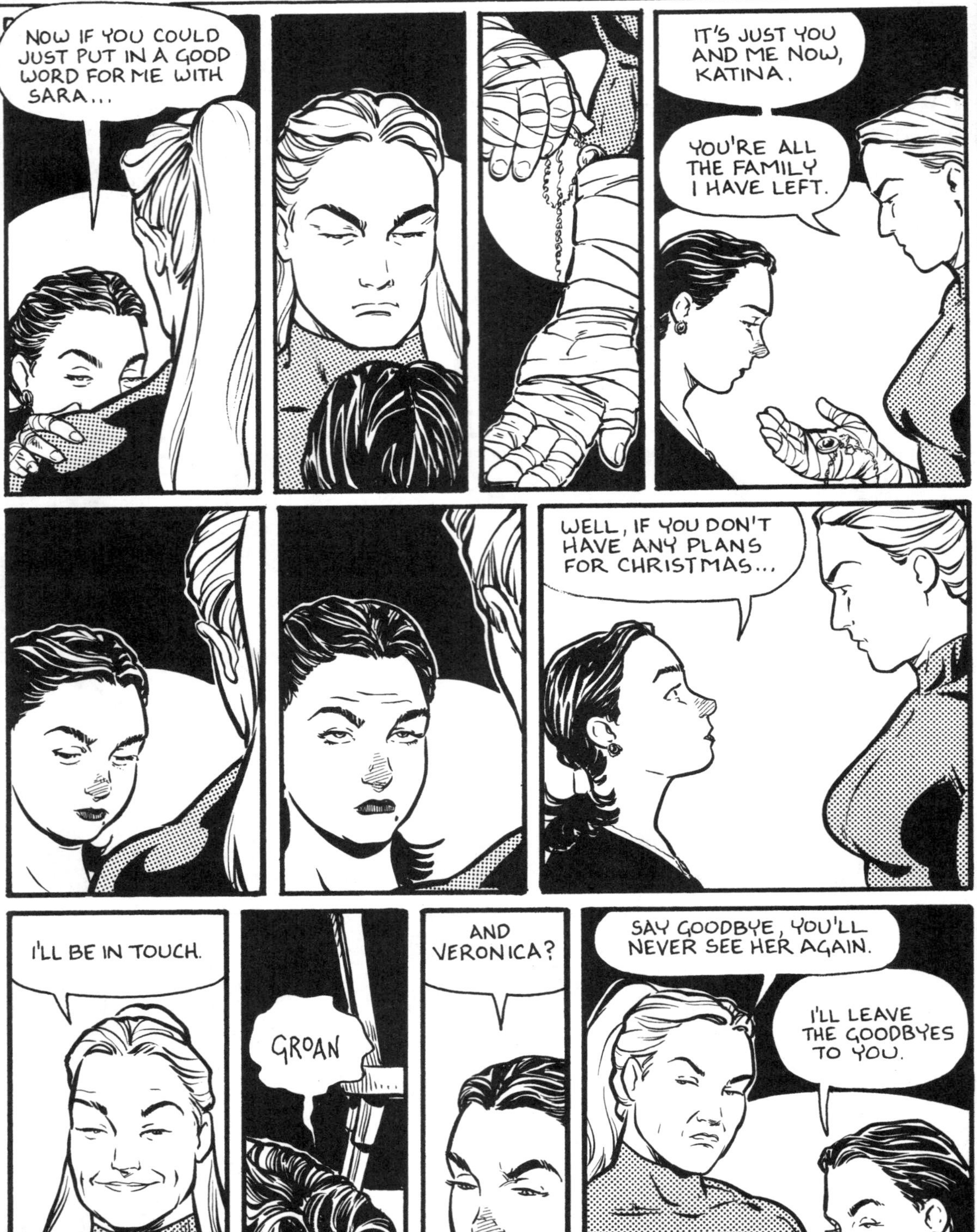
NOW IF YOU COULD JUST PUT IN A GOOD WORD FOR ME WITH SARA...
IT'S JUST YOU AND ME NOW, KATINA.
YOU'RE ALL THE FAMILY I HAVE LEFT.
WELL, IF YOU DON'T HAVE ANY PLANS FOR CHRISTMAS...
I'LL BE IN TOUCH.
GROAN
AND VERONICA?
SAY GOODBYE, YOU'LL NEVER SEE HER AGAIN.
I'LL LEAVE THE GOODBYES TO YOU.

GROAN

I WANT **YOU**....!

AAIGH!

IN THE CHAIR!

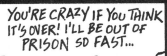

YOU'RE CRAZY IF YOU THINK IT'S OVER! I'LL BE OUT OF PRISON SO FAST...

YOU'RE NOT GOING TO PRISON, VERONICA. I DON'T WORK THAT WAY.

FRIIIP!

GO **AHEAD!** CALL THE POLICE! TELL THEM TO SEND AN AMBULANCE**!!**

FRIIIP!

DO YOU BELIEVE IN KARMA, VERONICA?

WHAT?!

REMEMBER MARSHAL WEINSTEIN?

DID YOU EVER WONDER WHAT IT MUST HAVE BEEN LIKE FOR HIM TO DIE LIKE THAT, VERONICA?

ONE FINGER AT A TIME ... ONE LIMB AT A TIME ....

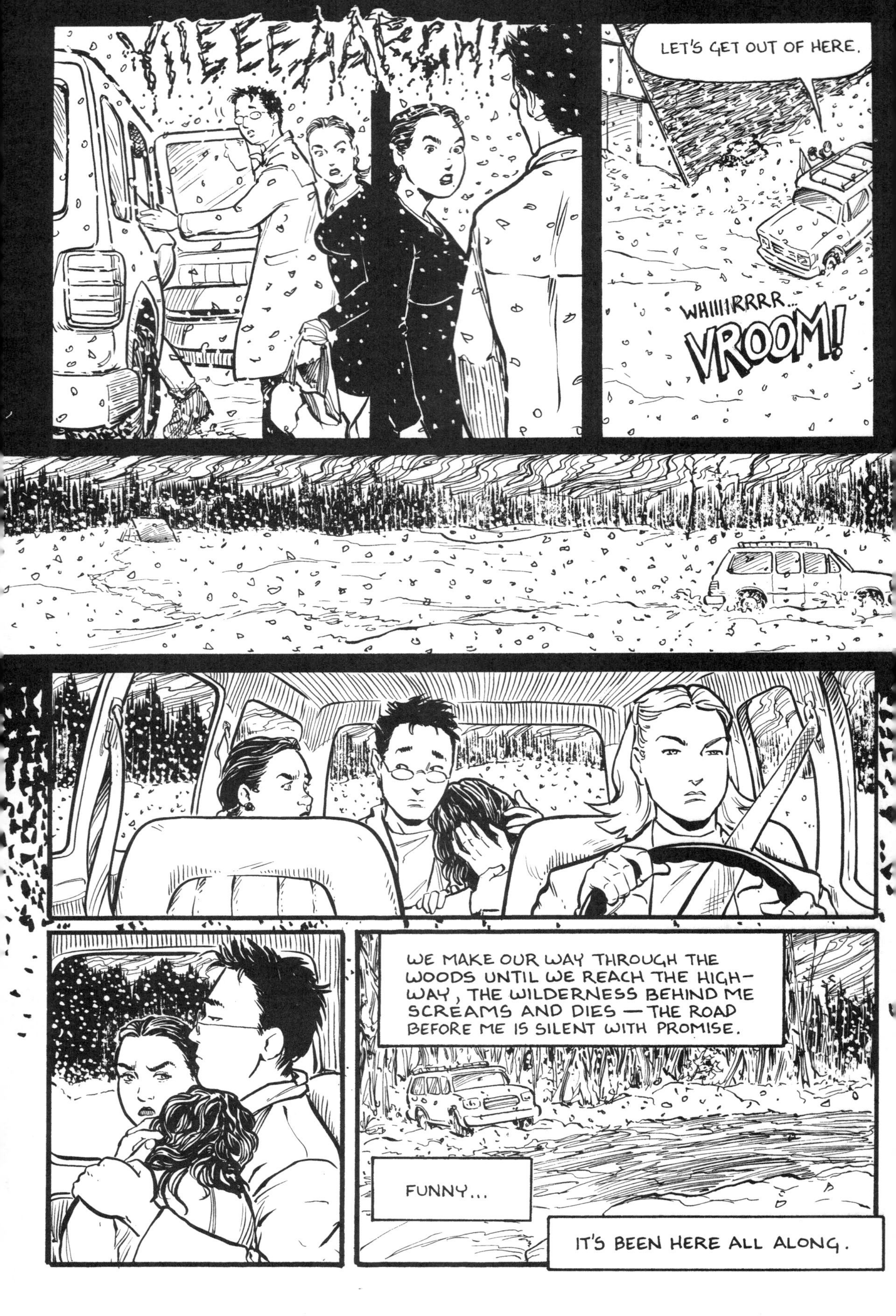

YIEEEAARGH!
LET'S GET OUT OF HERE.
WHIIIIRRRR...
VROOM!
WE MAKE OUR WAY THROUGH THE WOODS UNTIL WE REACH THE HIGH-WAY, THE WILDERNESS BEHIND ME SCREAMS AND DIES — THE ROAD BEFORE ME IS SILENT WITH PROMISE.
FUNNY...
IT'S BEEN HERE ALL ALONG.

ABSTRACT
STUDIO

**38**

2.95 US
4.00 CAN

TERRY MOORE

# STRANGERS IN PARADISE

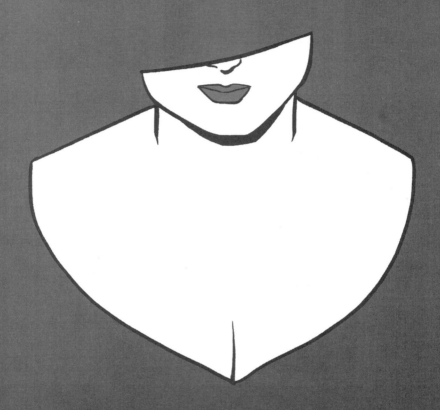

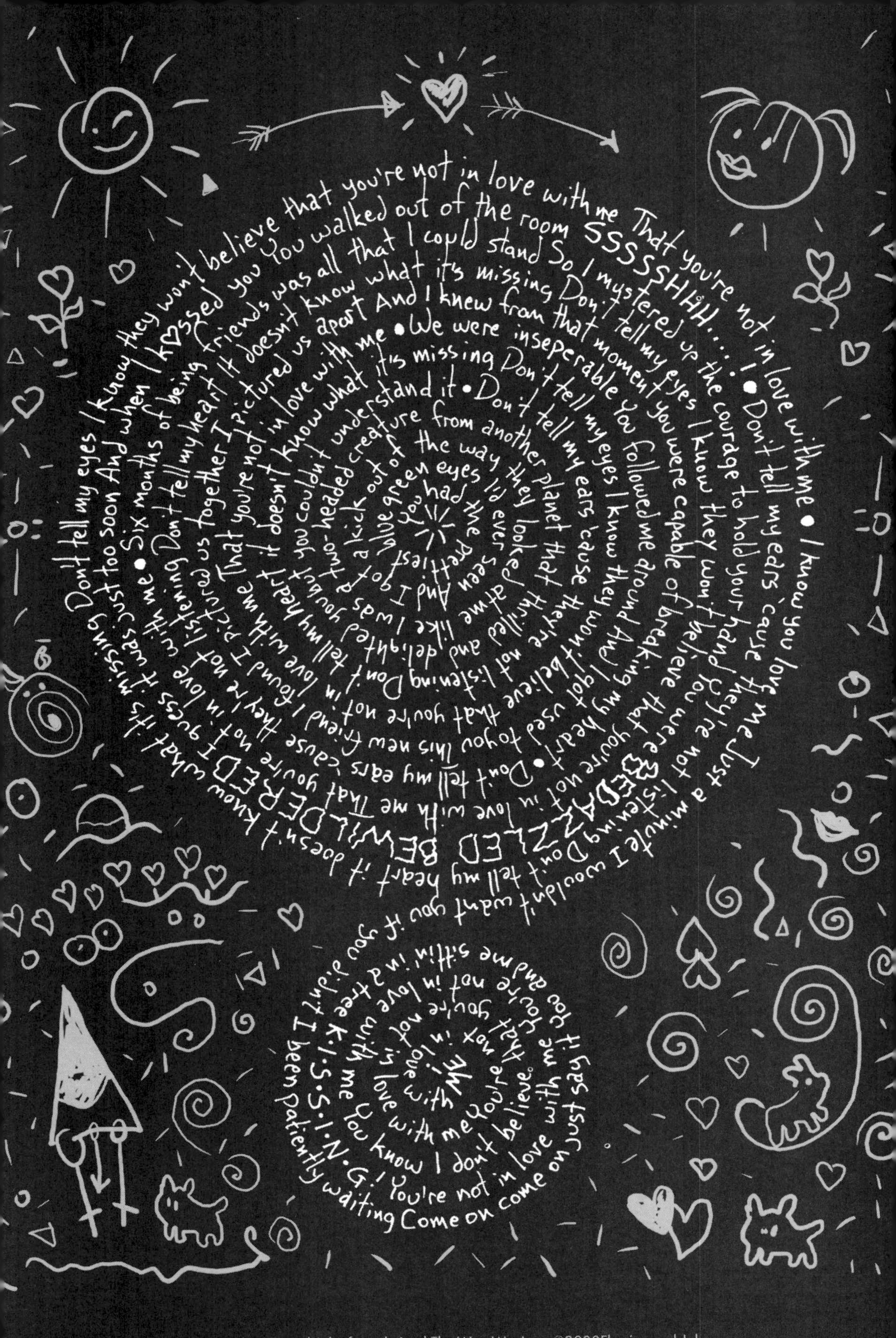
You had the prettiest blue green eyes I've ever seen And I got a kick out of the way they looked at me like I was a two-headed creature from another planet that thrilled and delighted you but you couldn't understand it •
Don't tell my eyes I know they won't believe that you're not in love with me Don't tell my ears 'cause they're not listening Don't tell my heart it doesn't know what it's missing •
We were inseperable You followed me around And I got used to you This new friend I found I pictured us together I pictured us apart And I knew from that moment you were capable of breaking my heart •
Don't tell my eyes I know they won't believe that you're not in love with me That you're not in love with me Don't tell my ears 'cause they're not listening Don't tell my heart it doesn't know what it's missing •
Six months of being friends was all that I could stand So I mustered up the courage to hold your hand You were BEDAZZLED BEWILDERED I guess it was just too soon And when I kissed you You walked out of the room SSSSHHH....! •
Don't tell my eyes I know they won't believe that you're not in love with me That you're not in love with me • I know you love me Just a minute I wouldn't want you if you didn't I been patiently waiting Come on come on just say it too you and me sittin' in a tree K.I.S.S.I.N.G.! You're not in love with me You know I don't believe that you're not in love with me You're not in love with me!

Sssh! by Fleming and John from their cd The Way We Are ©2000Fleming and John

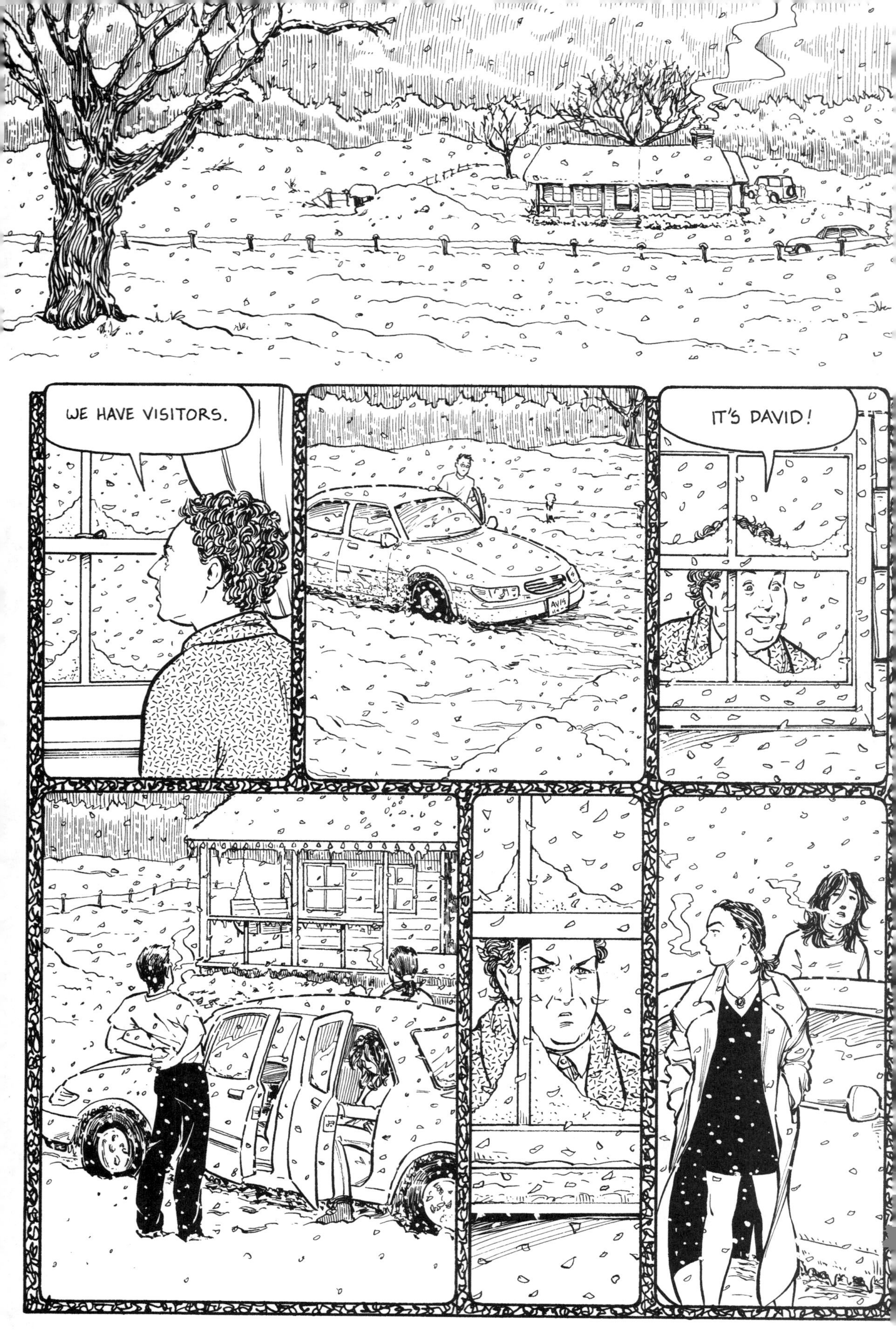
WE HAVE VISITORS.
IT'S DAVID!

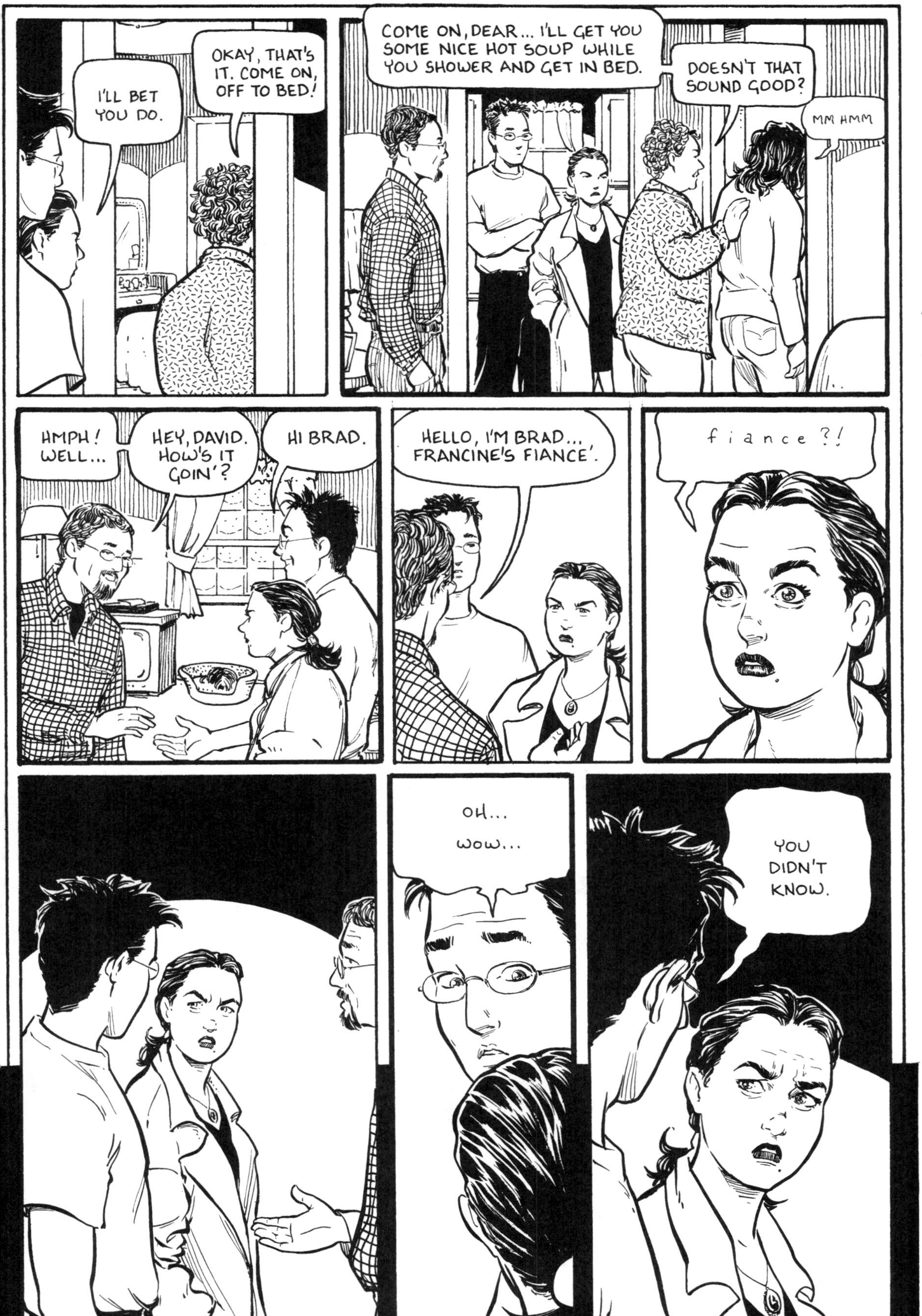
I'LL BET YOU DO.
OKAY, THAT'S IT. COME ON, OFF TO BED!
COME ON, DEAR... I'LL GET YOU SOME NICE HOT SOUP WHILE YOU SHOWER AND GET IN BED.
DOESN'T THAT SOUND GOOD?
MM HMM
HMPH! WELL...
HEY, DAVID. HOW'S IT GOIN'?
HI BRAD.
HELLO, I'M BRAD... FRANCINE'S FIANCE'.
fiance?!
OH...
WOW...
YOU DIDN'T KNOW.

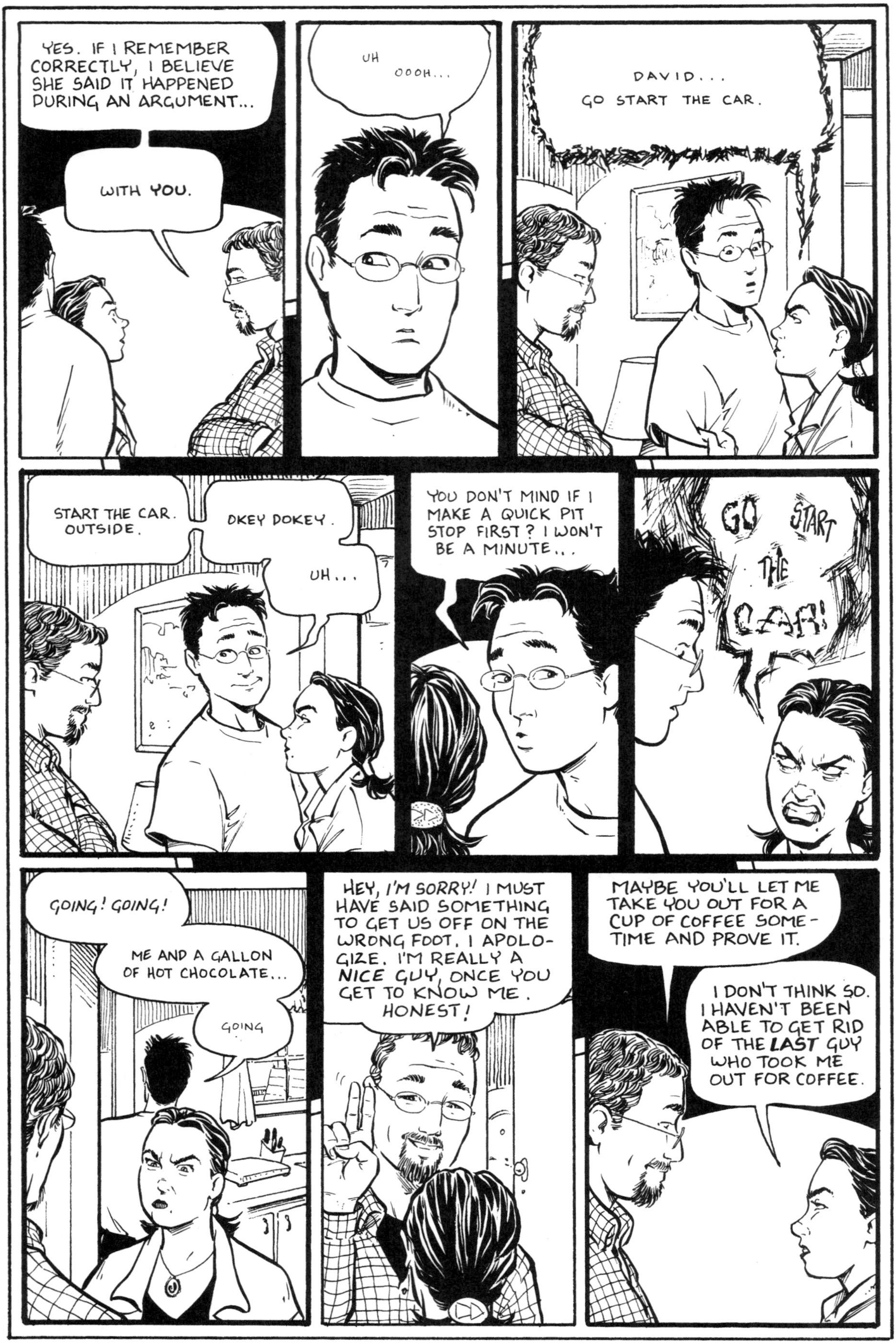
YES. IF I REMEMBER CORRECTLY, I BELIEVE SHE SAID IT HAPPENED DURING AN ARGUMENT...
WITH **YOU**.
UH OOOH...
DAVID... GO START THE CAR.
START THE CAR. OUTSIDE.
OKEY DOKEY.
UH...
YOU DON'T MIND IF I MAKE A QUICK PIT STOP FIRST? I WON'T BE A MINUTE...
GO START THE CAR!
GOING! GOING!
ME AND A GALLON OF HOT CHOCOLATE...
GOING
HEY, *I'M SORRY!* I MUST HAVE SAID SOMETHING TO GET US OFF ON THE WRONG FOOT. I APOLOGIZE. I'M REALLY A **NICE GUY**, ONCE YOU GET TO KNOW ME. HONEST!
MAYBE YOU'LL LET ME TAKE YOU OUT FOR A CUP OF COFFEE SOMETIME AND PROVE IT.
I DON'T THINK SO. I HAVEN'T BEEN ABLE TO GET RID OF THE ***LAST*** GUY WHO TOOK ME OUT FOR COFFEE.

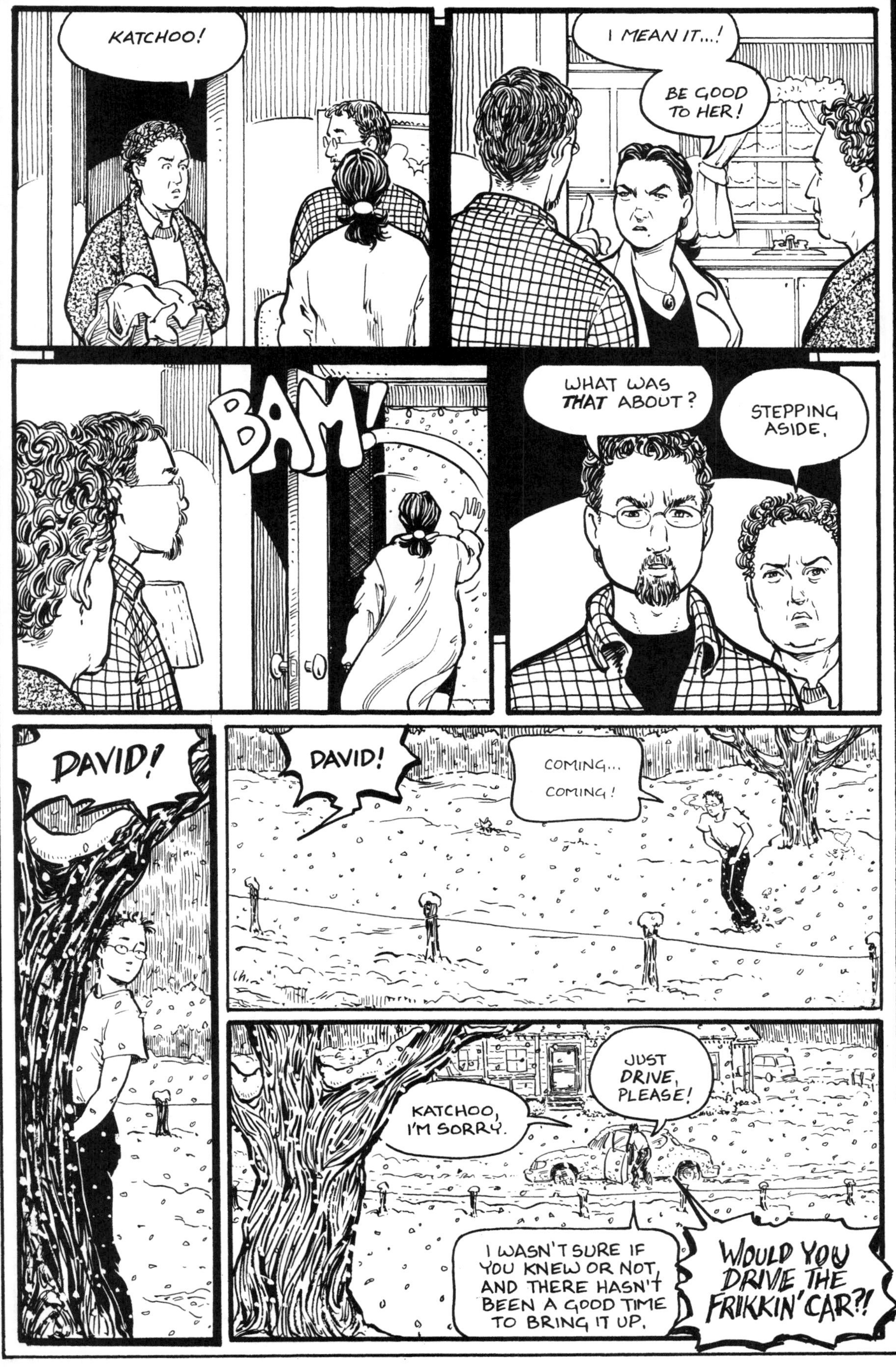

KATCHOO!
I MEAN IT...!
BE GOOD TO HER!
BAM!
WHAT WAS THAT ABOUT?
STEPPING ASIDE.
DAVID!
DAVID!
COMING... COMING!
KATCHOO, I'M SORRY.
JUST DRIVE, PLEASE!
I WASN'T SURE IF YOU KNEW OR NOT, AND THERE HASN'T BEEN A GOOD TIME TO BRING IT UP.
WOULD YOU DRIVE THE FRIKKIN' CAR?!

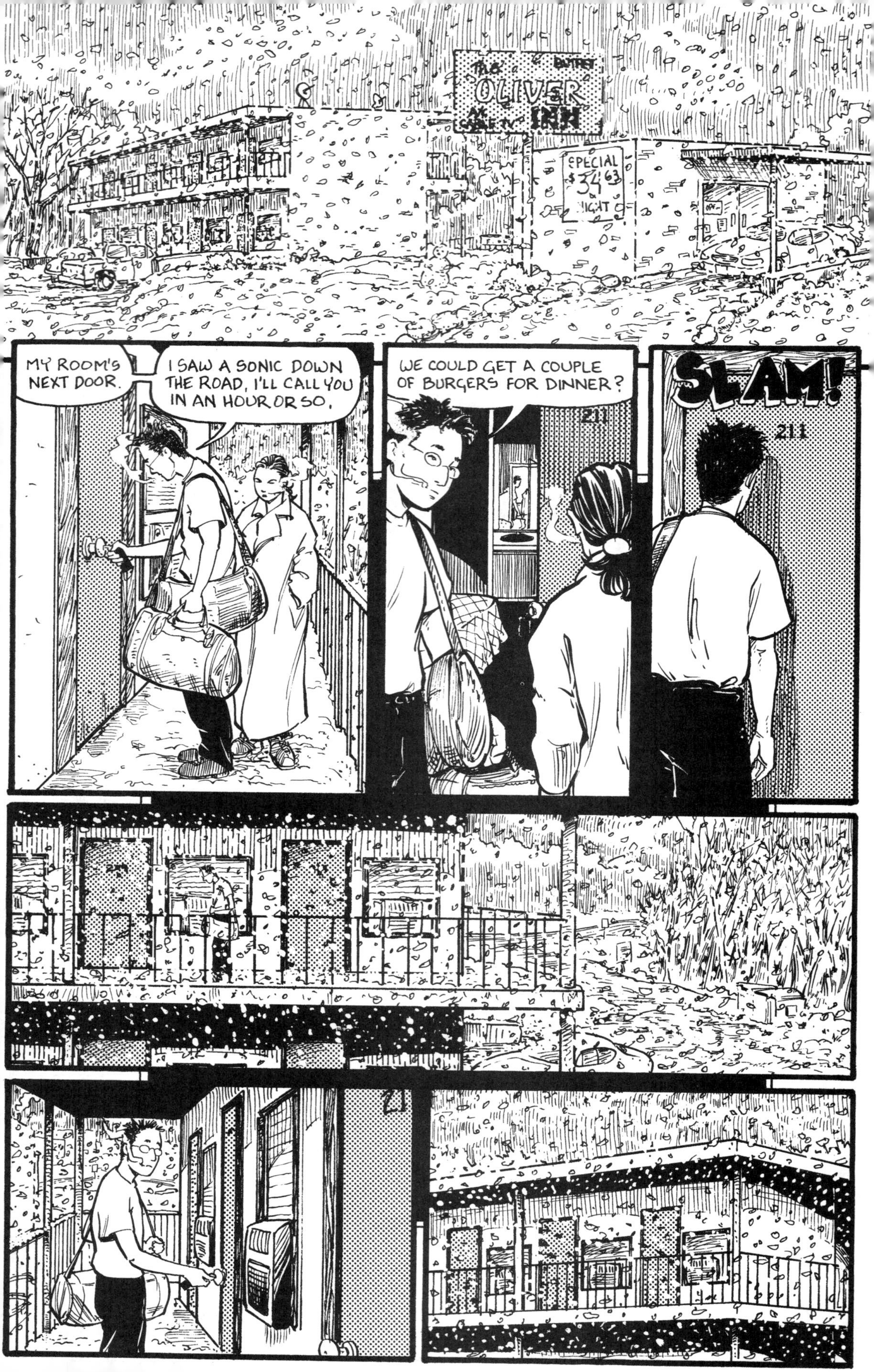
OLIVER
INN
SPECIAL
MY ROOM'S NEXT DOOR.
I SAW A SONIC DOWN THE ROAD, I'LL CALL YOU IN AN HOUR OR SO.
WE COULD GET A COUPLE OF BURGERS FOR DINNER?
211
SLAM!
211

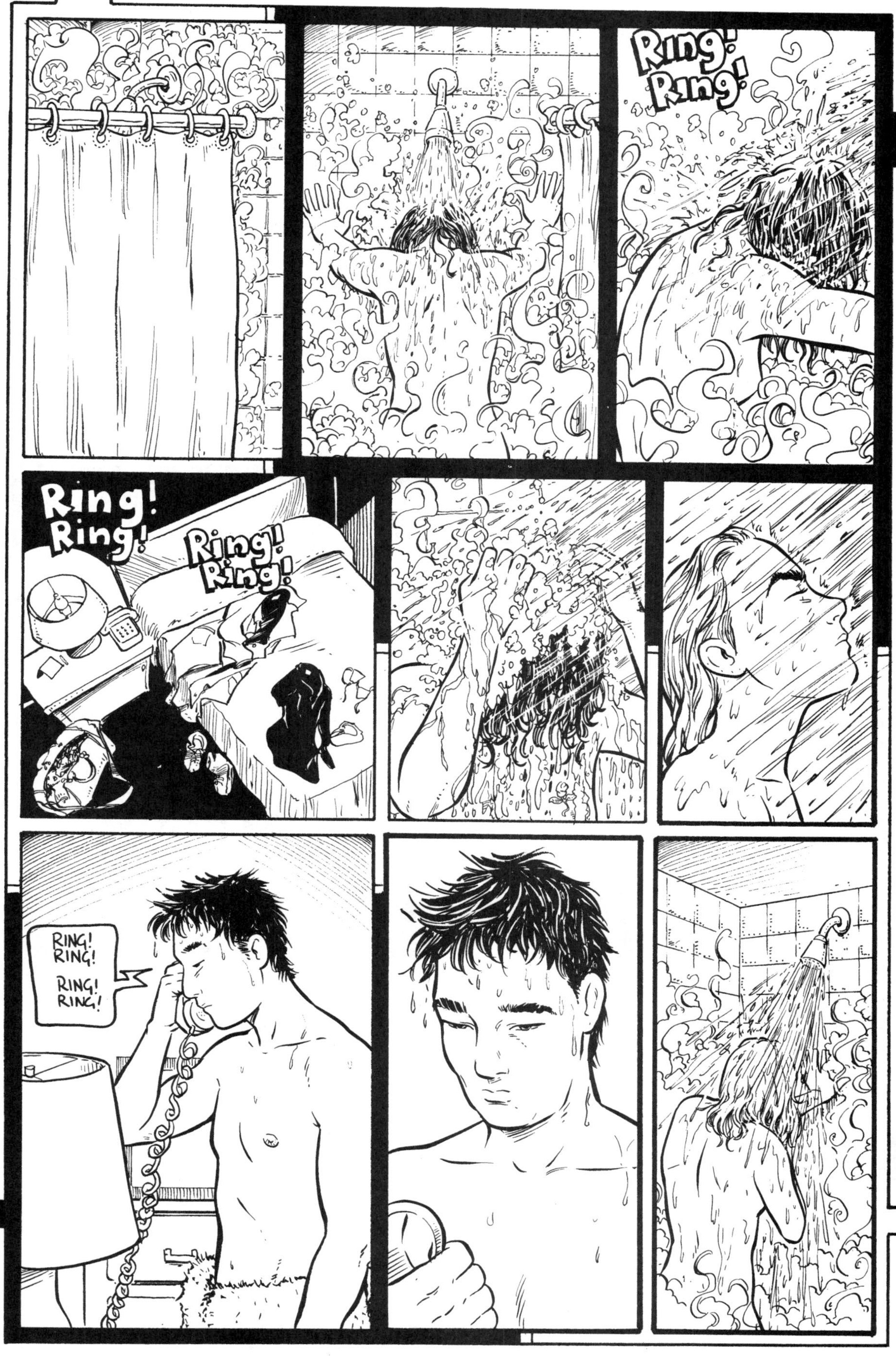
Ring! Ring!
Ring! Ring!
Ring! Ring!
RING! RING! RING! RING!

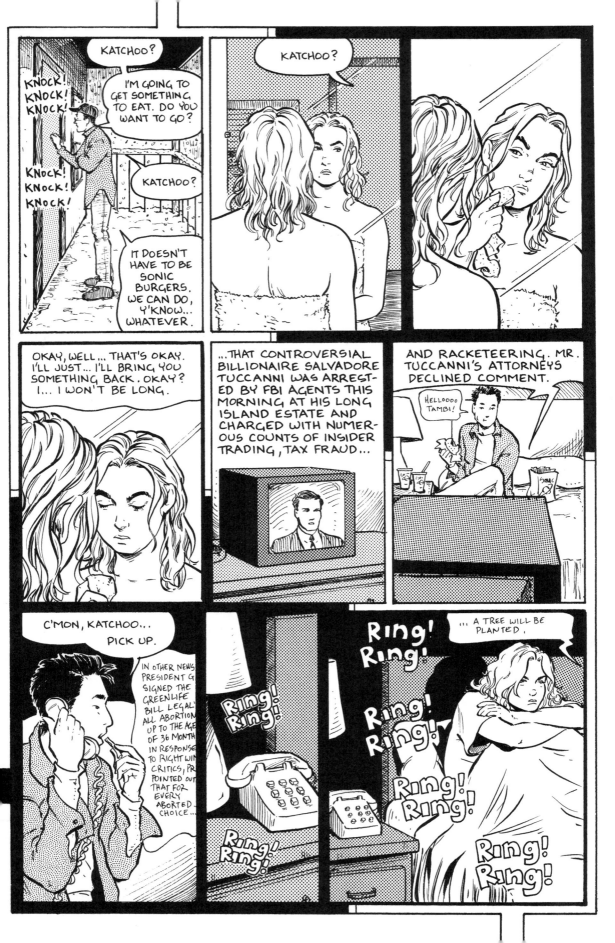

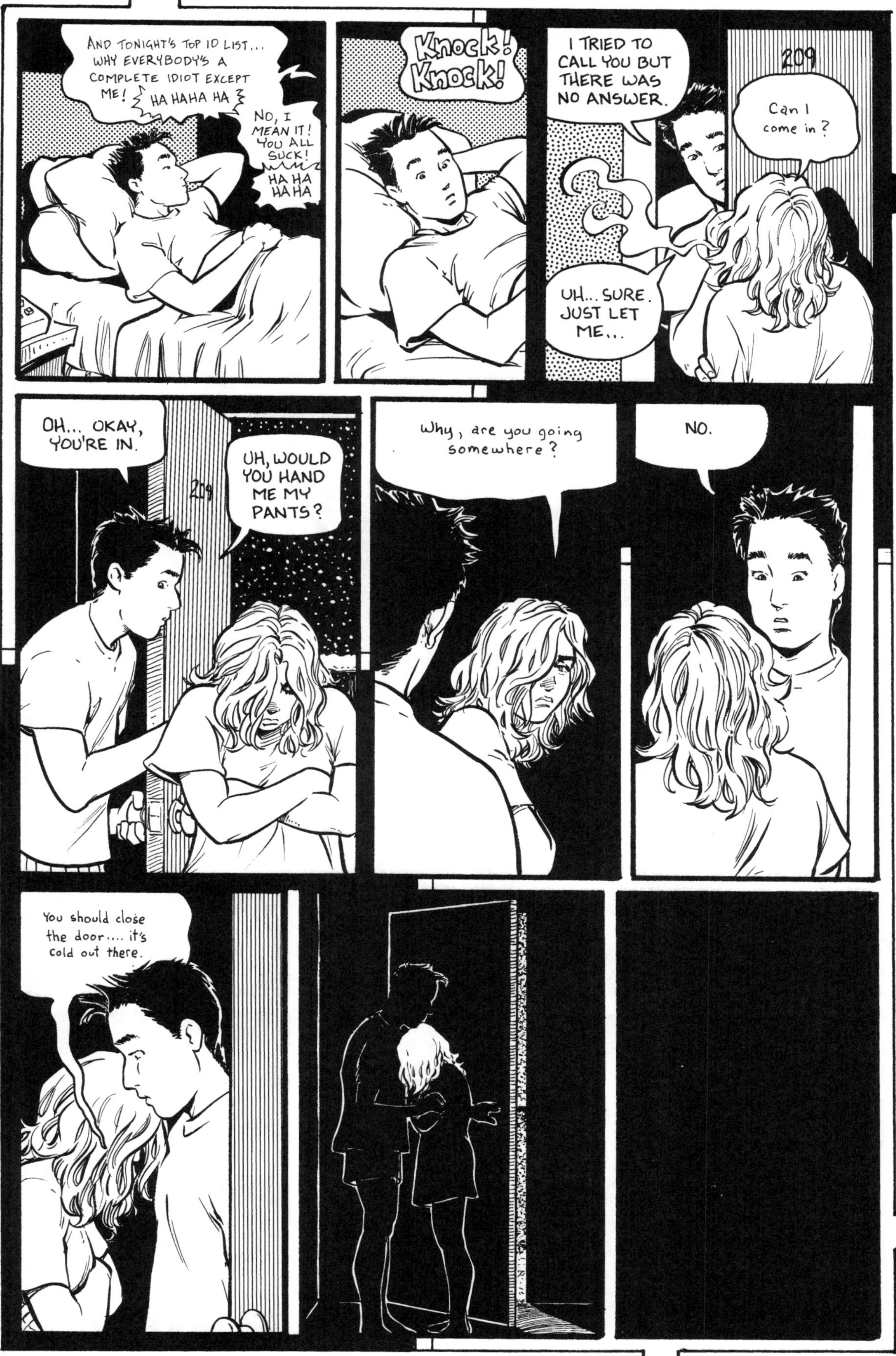
AND TONIGHT'S TOP 10 LIST... WHY EVERYBODY'S A COMPLETE IDIOT EXCEPT ME!
HA HAHA HA
NO, I MEAN IT! YOU ALL SUCK!
HA HA HA HA
Knock! Knock!
I TRIED TO CALL YOU BUT THERE WAS NO ANSWER.
209
Can I come in?
UH... SURE. JUST LET ME...
OH... OKAY, YOU'RE IN.
209
UH, WOULD YOU HAND ME MY PANTS?
Why, are you going somewhere?
NO.
You should close the door.... it's cold out there.

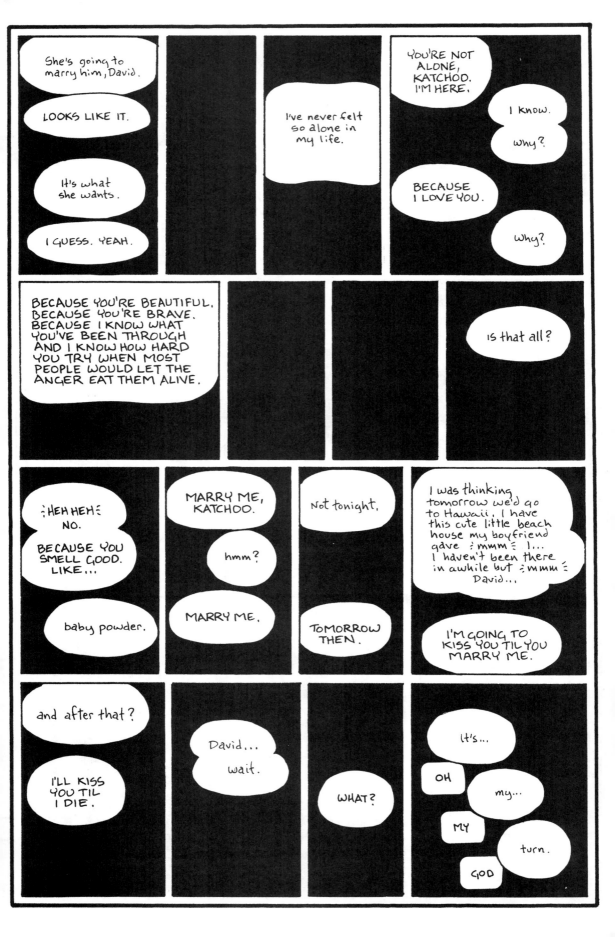

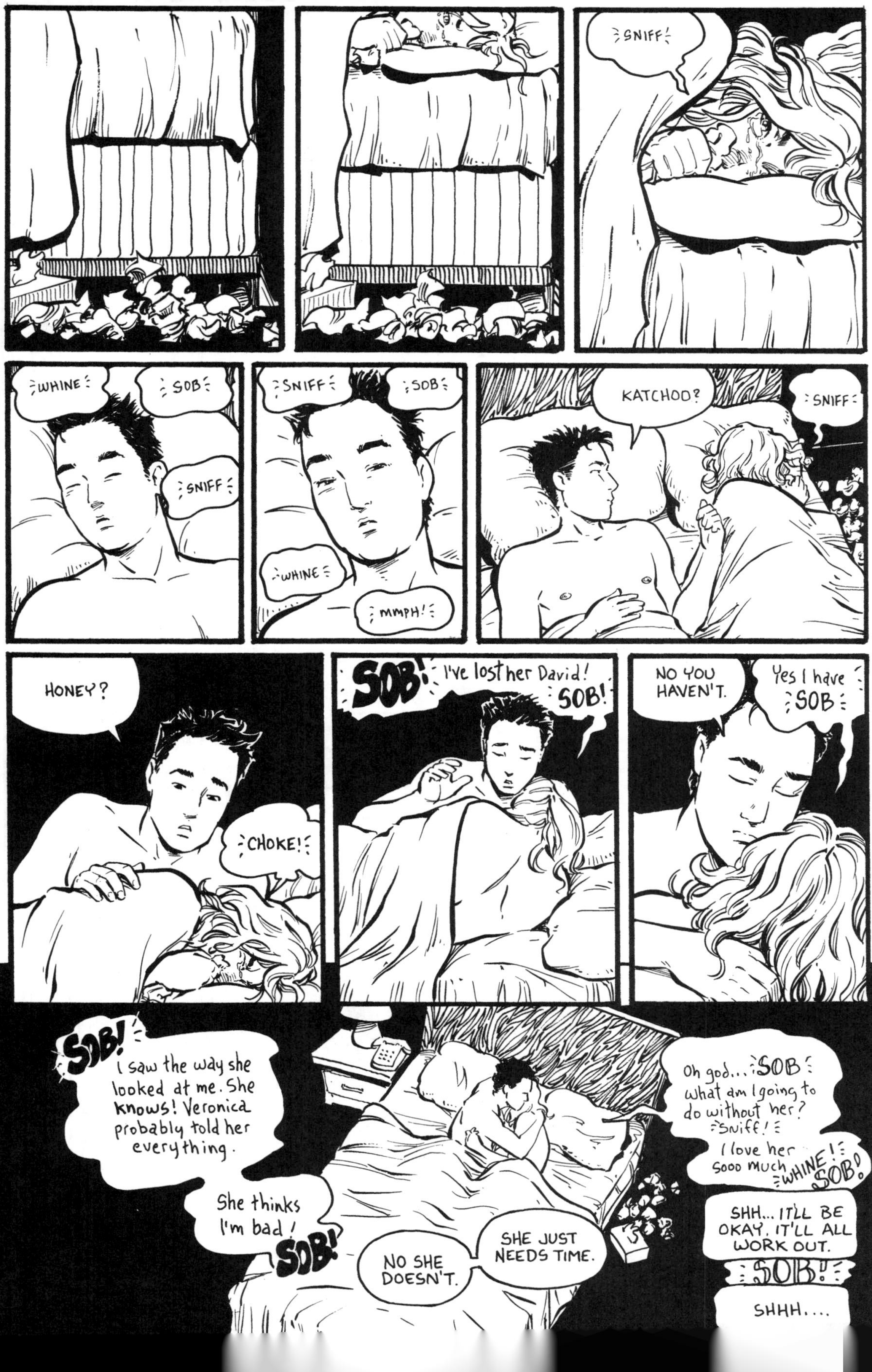
SNIFF!
WHINE
SOB
SNIFF
SNIFF
SOB
WHINE
MMPH!
KATCHOO?
SNIFF
HONEY?
CHOKE!
SOB! I've lost her David! SOB!
NO YOU HAVEN'T.
Yes I have SOB
SOB! I saw the way she looked at me. She knows! Veronica probably told her everything.
She thinks I'm bad! SOB!
Oh god... SOB what am I going to do without her? Sniff! I love her sooo much WHINE! SOB!
NO SHE DOESN'T.
SHE JUST NEEDS TIME.
SHH... IT'LL BE OKAY. IT'LL ALL WORK OUT.
SOB!
SHHH....

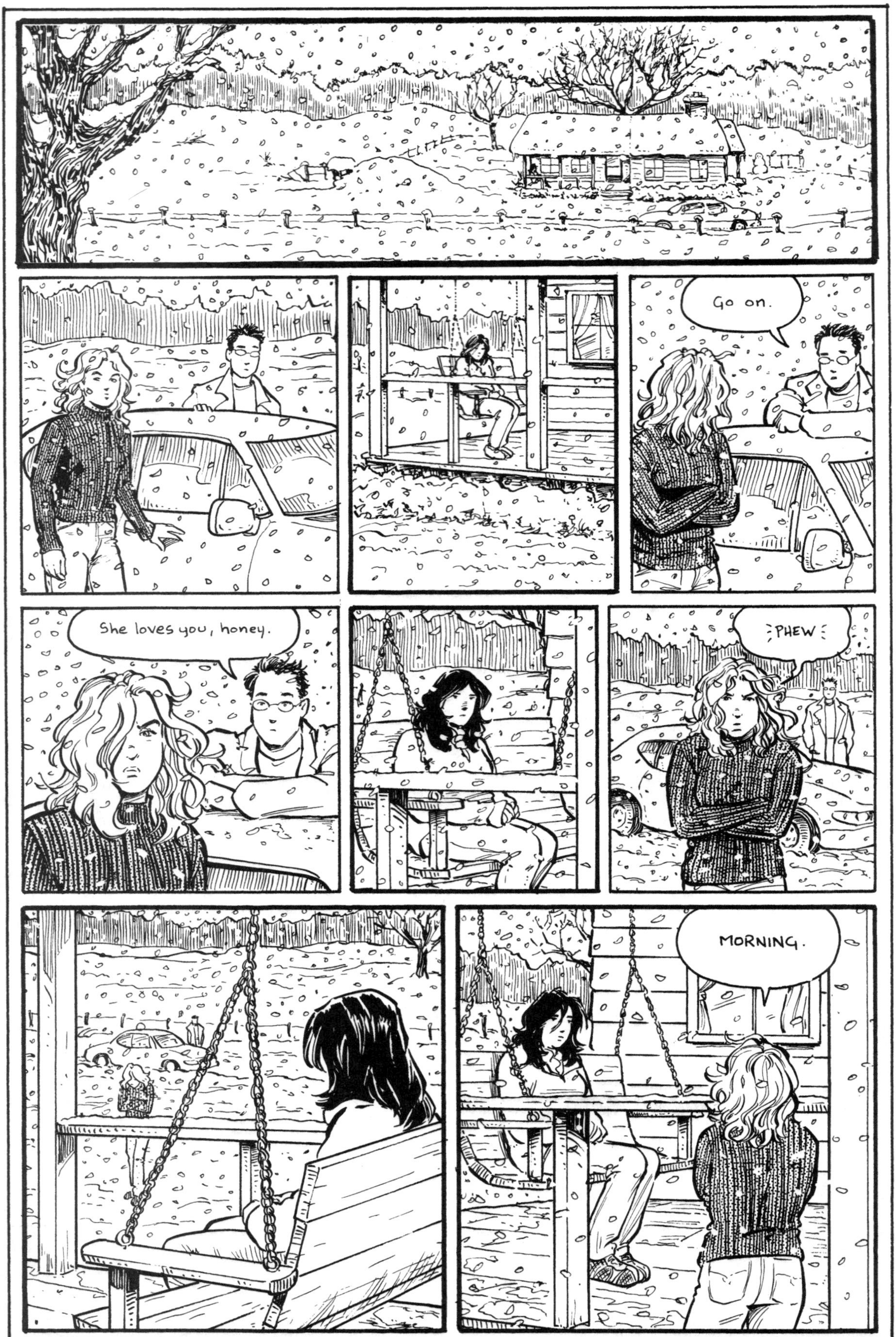
Go on.
She loves you, honey.
PHEW
MORNING.

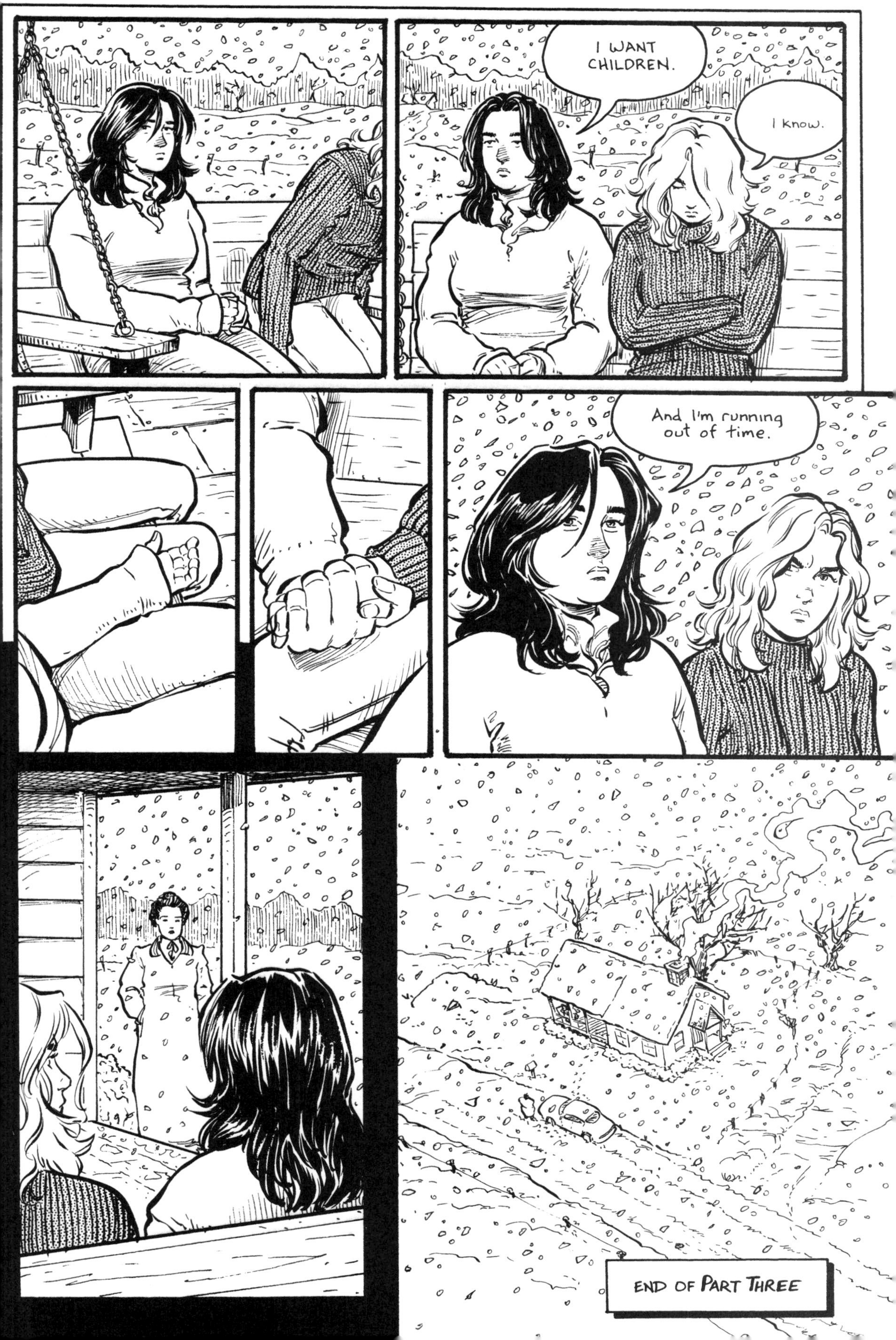
I WANT CHILDREN.
I know.
And I'm running out of time.
END OF PART THREE

What if a very bad man had delusions of power and wanted to take over the world? What if he rented an Atomic Laser Blaster and actually attempted to launch his master plan for world domination while wearing a cape? Sound familiar? No, it's not the latest issue of your favorite superhero comic. It's...

Be brave, dear hearts, your eyes do not deceive you, for this is a side of Strangers In Paradise wise men dare not discuss! This is a no holds barred, all out, freeform toxic phenomenon! A terrifying tale of what might happen when...

ABSTRACT
STUDIO

# STRANGERS IN PARADISE

**33**

$2.75 U.S.
$3.80 CAN

WHEN WORLDS COLLIDE!

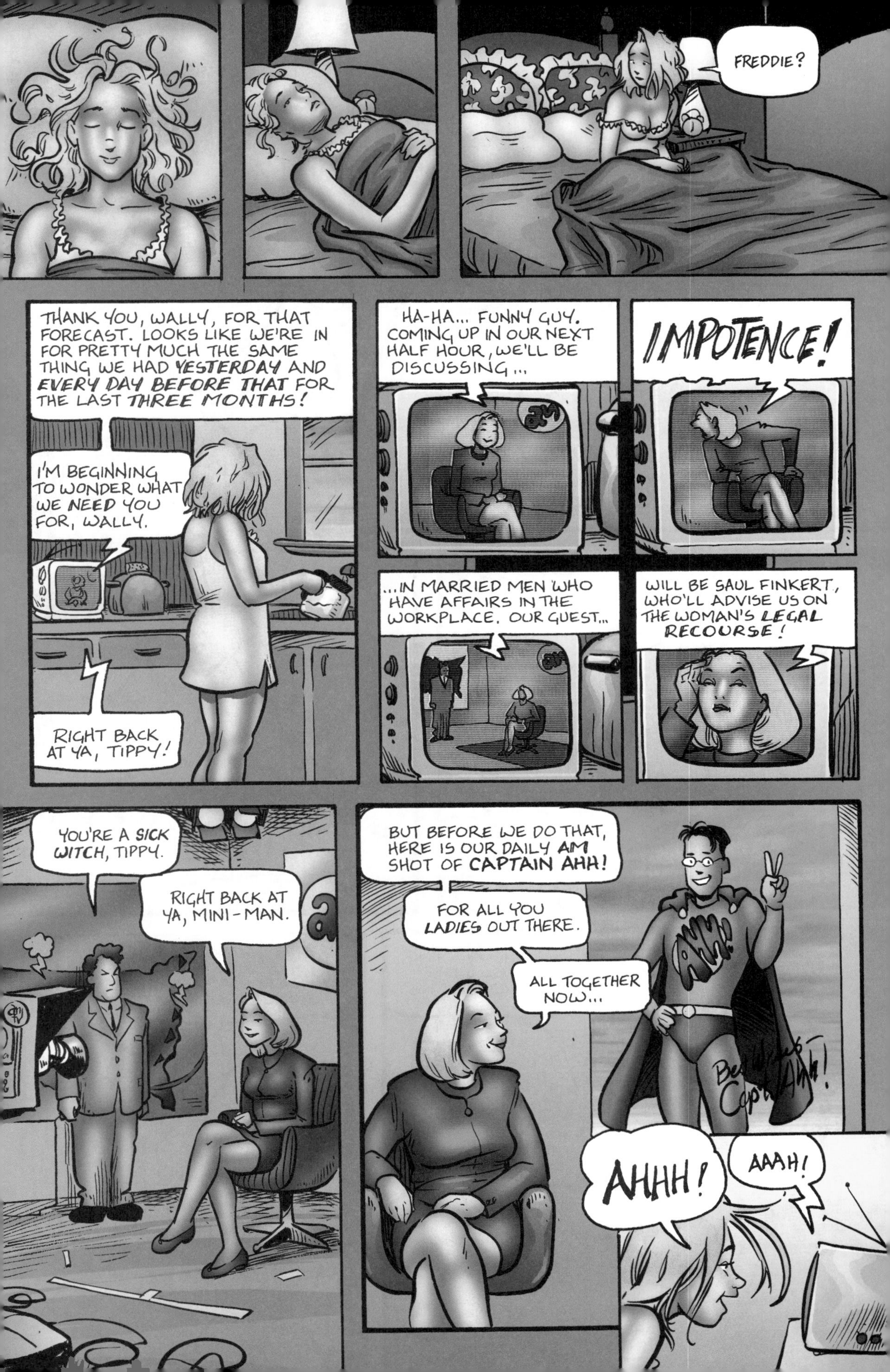

FREDDIE?
THANK YOU, WALLY, FOR THAT FORECAST. LOOKS LIKE WE'RE IN FOR PRETTY MUCH THE SAME THING WE HAD YESTERDAY AND EVERY DAY BEFORE THAT FOR THE LAST THREE MONTHS!
I'M BEGINNING TO WONDER WHAT WE NEED YOU FOR, WALLY.
RIGHT BACK AT YA, TIPPY!
HA-HA... FUNNY GUY. COMING UP IN OUR NEXT HALF HOUR, WE'LL BE DISCUSSING...
IMPOTENCE!
...IN MARRIED MEN WHO HAVE AFFAIRS IN THE WORKPLACE. OUR GUEST...
WILL BE SAUL FINKERT, WHO'LL ADVISE US ON THE WOMAN'S LEGAL RECOURSE!
YOU'RE A SICK WITCH, TIPPY.
RIGHT BACK AT YA, MINI-MAN.
BUT BEFORE WE DO THAT, HERE IS OUR DAILY AM SHOT OF CAPTAIN AHH!
FOR ALL YOU LADIES OUT THERE.
ALL TOGETHER NOW...
AHHH!
AAAH!

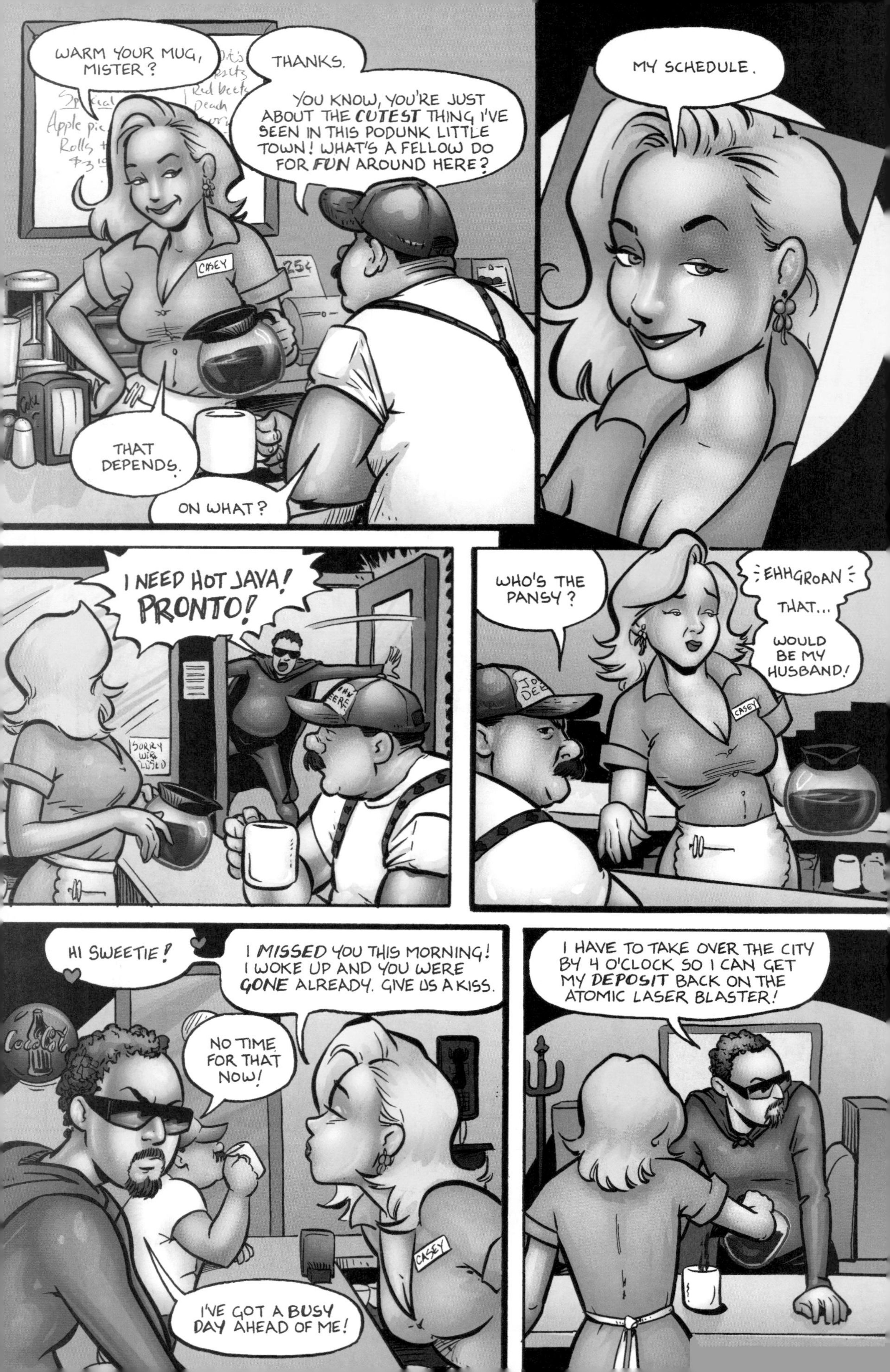

WARM YOUR MUG, MISTER?
THANKS.
YOU KNOW, YOU'RE JUST ABOUT THE CUTEST THING I'VE SEEN IN THIS PODUNK LITTLE TOWN! WHAT'S A FELLOW DO FOR FUN AROUND HERE?
THAT DEPENDS.
ON WHAT?
MY SCHEDULE.
I NEED HOT JAVA! PRONTO!
SORRY WE'RE CLOSED
WHO'S THE PANSY?
EHHGROAN
THAT...
WOULD BE MY HUSBAND!
CASEY
HI SWEETIE!
I MISSED YOU THIS MORNING! I WOKE UP AND YOU WERE GONE ALREADY. GIVE US A KISS.
NO TIME FOR THAT NOW!
I'VE GOT A BUSY DAY AHEAD OF ME!
I HAVE TO TAKE OVER THE CITY BY 4 O'CLOCK SO I CAN GET MY DEPOSIT BACK ON THE ATOMIC LASER BLASTER!

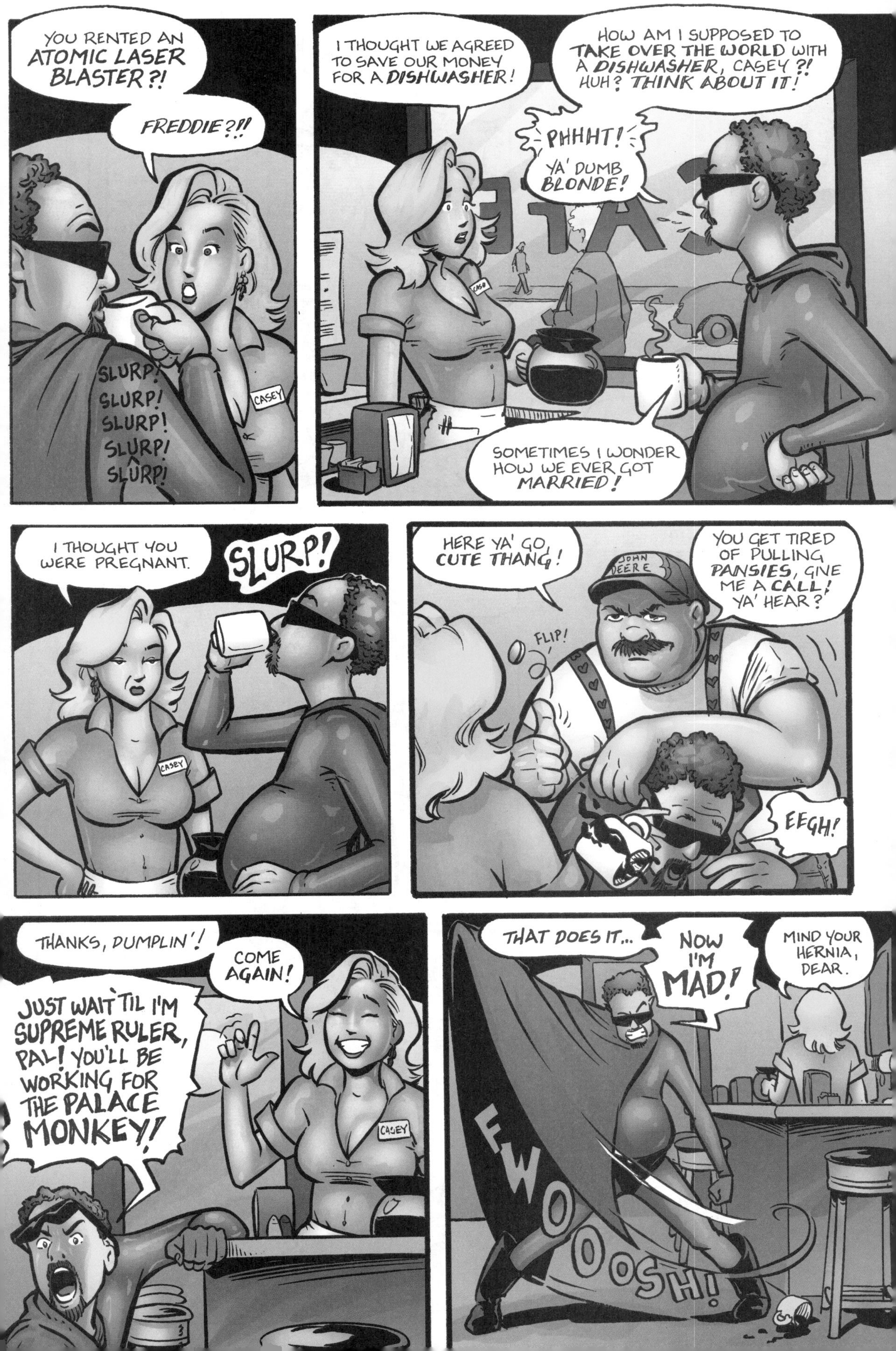

YOU RENTED AN ATOMIC LASER BLASTER ?!
FREDDIE ?!!
SLURP! SLURP! SLURP! SLURP! SLURP!
CASEY
I THOUGHT WE AGREED TO SAVE OUR MONEY FOR A DISHWASHER!
HOW AM I SUPPOSED TO TAKE OVER THE WORLD WITH A DISHWASHER, CASEY ?! HUH? THINK ABOUT IT!
PHHHT!
YA' DUMB BLONDE!
SOMETIMES I WONDER HOW WE EVER GOT MARRIED!
I THOUGHT YOU WERE PREGNANT.
SLURP!
CASEY
HERE YA' GO, CUTE THANG!
YOU GET TIRED OF PULLING PANSIES, GIVE ME A CALL! YA' HEAR?
JOHN DEERE
FLIP!
EEGH!
THANKS, DUMPLIN'!
COME AGAIN!
JUST WAIT 'TIL I'M SUPREME RULER, PAL! YOU'LL BE WORKING FOR THE PALACE MONKEY!
CASEY
THAT DOES IT...
NOW I'M MAD!
MIND YOUR HERNIA, DEAR.
FWOOOOSH!

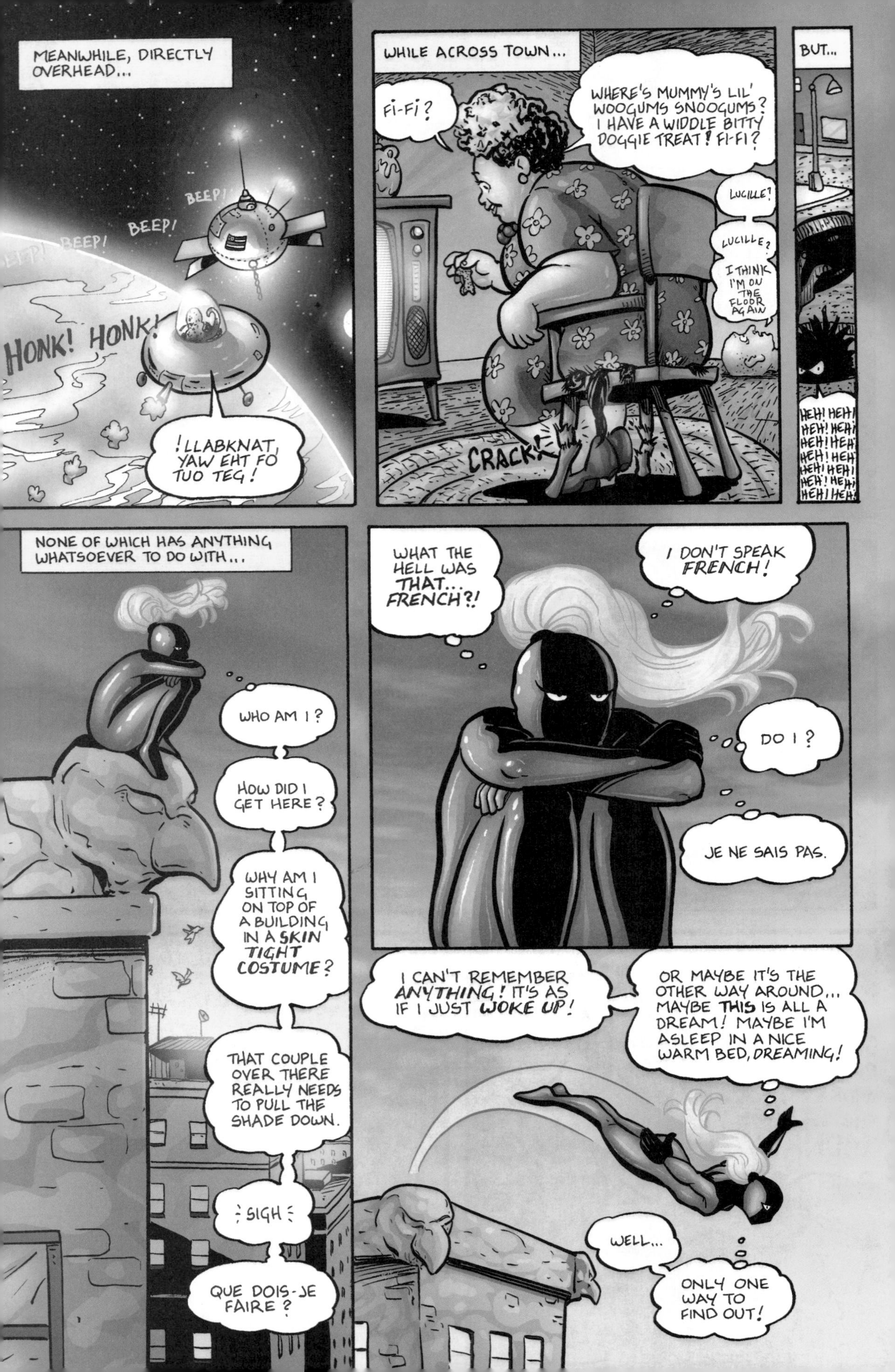

MEANWHILE, DIRECTLY OVERHEAD...
BEEP!
BEEP!
BEEP!
HONK! HONK!
!LLABKNAT, YAW EHT FO TUO TEG!
WHILE ACROSS TOWN...
FI-FI?
WHERE'S MUMMY'S LIL' WOOGUMS SNOOGUMS? I HAVE A WIDDLE BITTY DOGGIE TREAT! FI-FI?
LUCILLE?
LUCILLE?
I THINK I'M ON THE FLOOR AGAIN
CRACK!
BUT...
HEH! HEH! HEH! HEH! HEH! HEH! HEH! HEH! HEH! HEH! HEH! HEH! HEH! HEH!
NONE OF WHICH HAS ANYTHING WHATSOEVER TO DO WITH...
WHO AM I?
HOW DID I GET HERE?
WHY AM I SITTING ON TOP OF A BUILDING IN A SKIN TIGHT COSTUME?
THAT COUPLE OVER THERE REALLY NEEDS TO PULL THE SHADE DOWN.
SIGH
QUE DOIS-JE FAIRE?
WHAT THE HELL WAS THAT... FRENCH?!
I DON'T SPEAK FRENCH!
DO I?
JE NE SAIS PAS.
I CAN'T REMEMBER ANYTHING! IT'S AS IF I JUST WOKE UP!
OR MAYBE IT'S THE OTHER WAY AROUND... MAYBE THIS IS ALL A DREAM! MAYBE I'M ASLEEP IN A NICE WARM BED, DREAMING!
WELL...
ONLY ONE WAY TO FIND OUT!

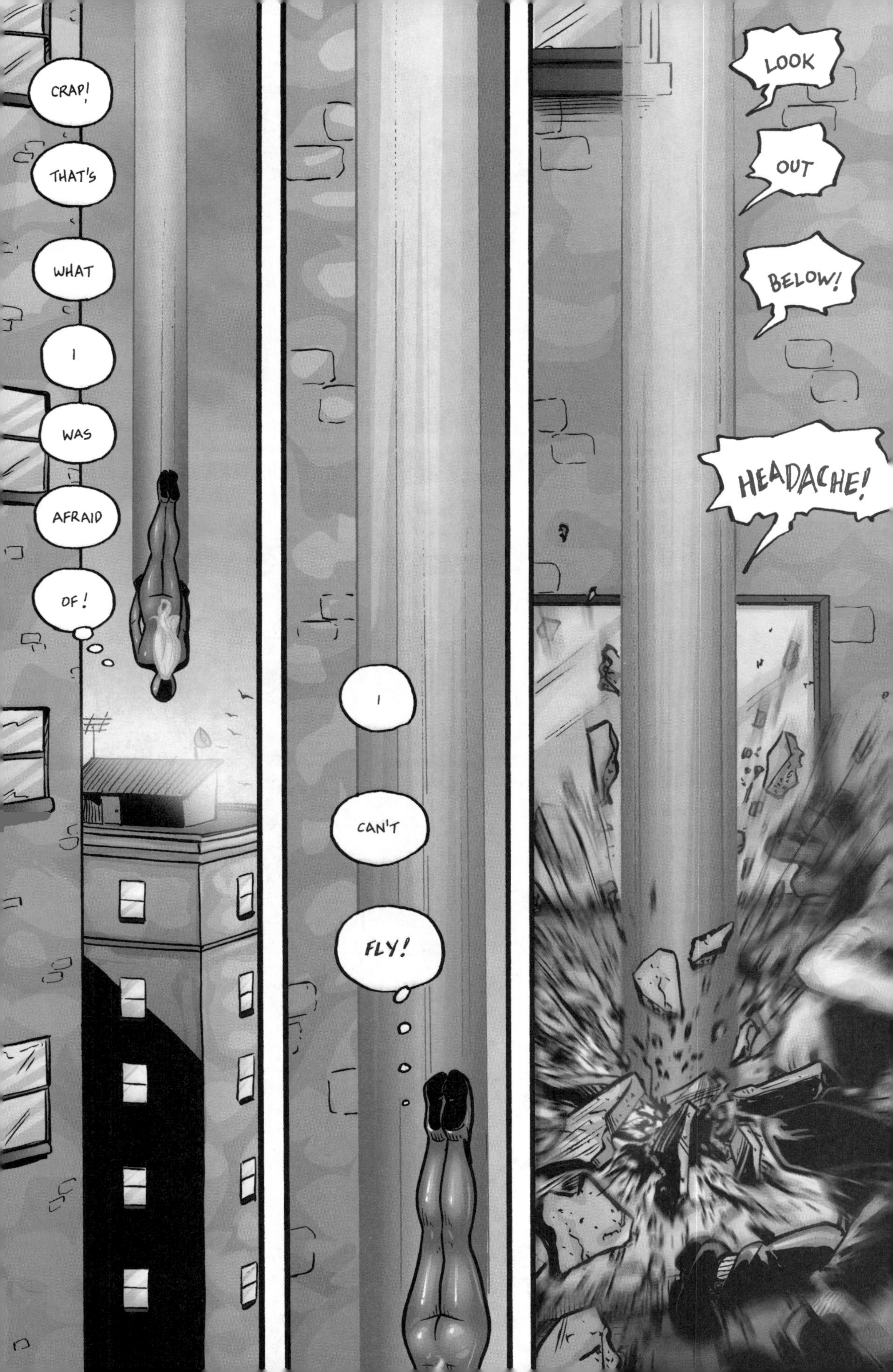

CRAP!
THAT'S
WHAT
I
WAS
AFRAID
OF!
I
CAN'T
FLY!
LOOK
OUT
BELOW!
HEADACHE!

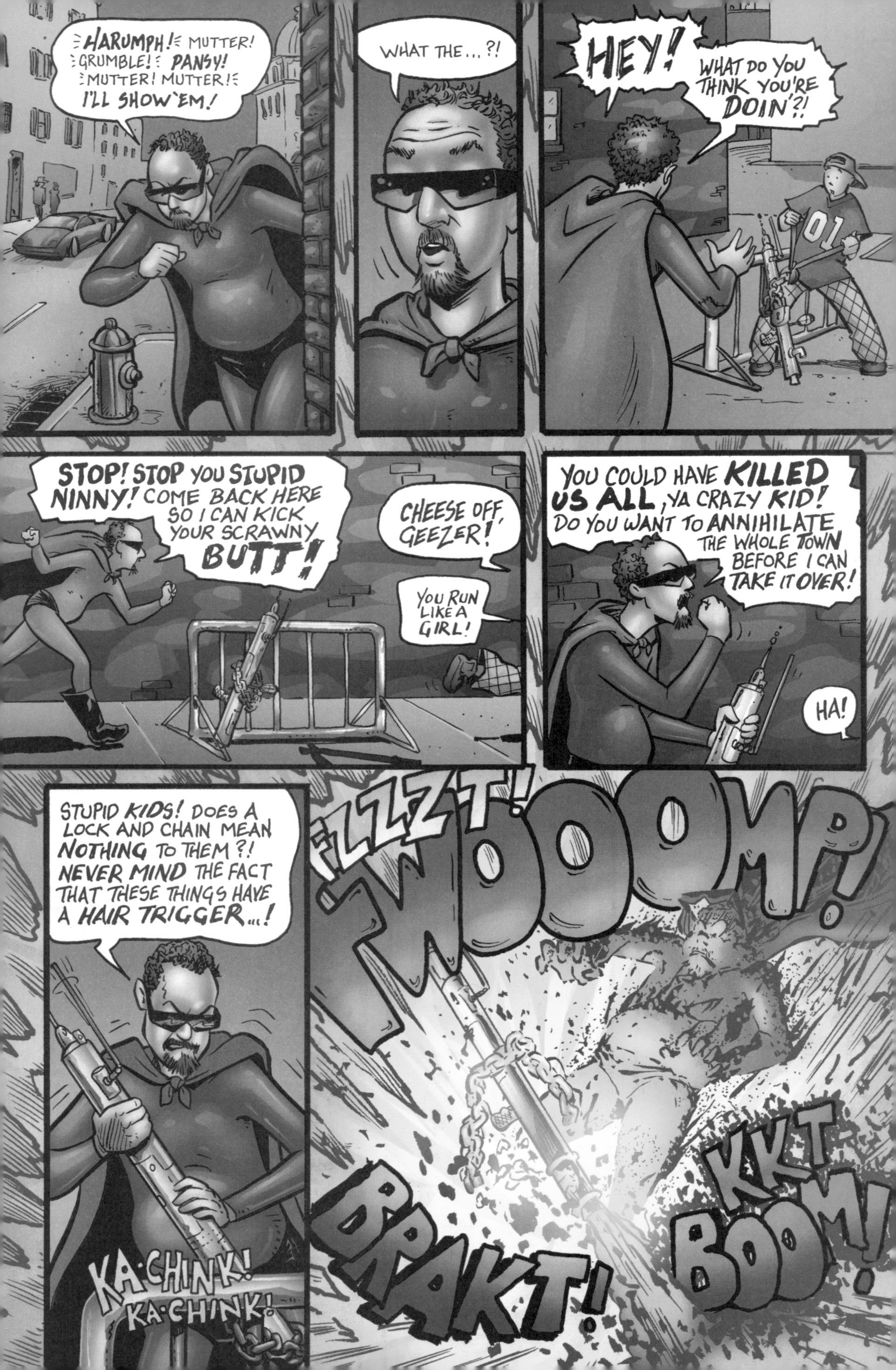
HARUMPH! MUTTER! GRUMBLE! PANSY! MUTTER! MUTTER! I'LL SHOW 'EM!
WHAT THE...?!
HEY!
WHAT DO YOU THINK YOU'RE DOIN'?!
STOP! STOP YOU STUPID NINNY! COME BACK HERE SO I CAN KICK YOUR SCRAWNY BUTT!
CHEESE OFF, GEEZER!
YOU RUN LIKE A GIRL!
YOU COULD HAVE KILLED US ALL, YA CRAZY KID! DO YOU WANT TO ANNIHILATE THE WHOLE TOWN BEFORE I CAN TAKE IT OVER!
HA!
STUPID KIDS! DOES A LOCK AND CHAIN MEAN NOTHING TO THEM?! NEVER MIND THE FACT THAT THESE THINGS HAVE A HAIR TRIGGER...!
KA-CHINK! KA-CHINK!
FZZZT!
WOOOMP!
BRAKT!
KKT BOOM!

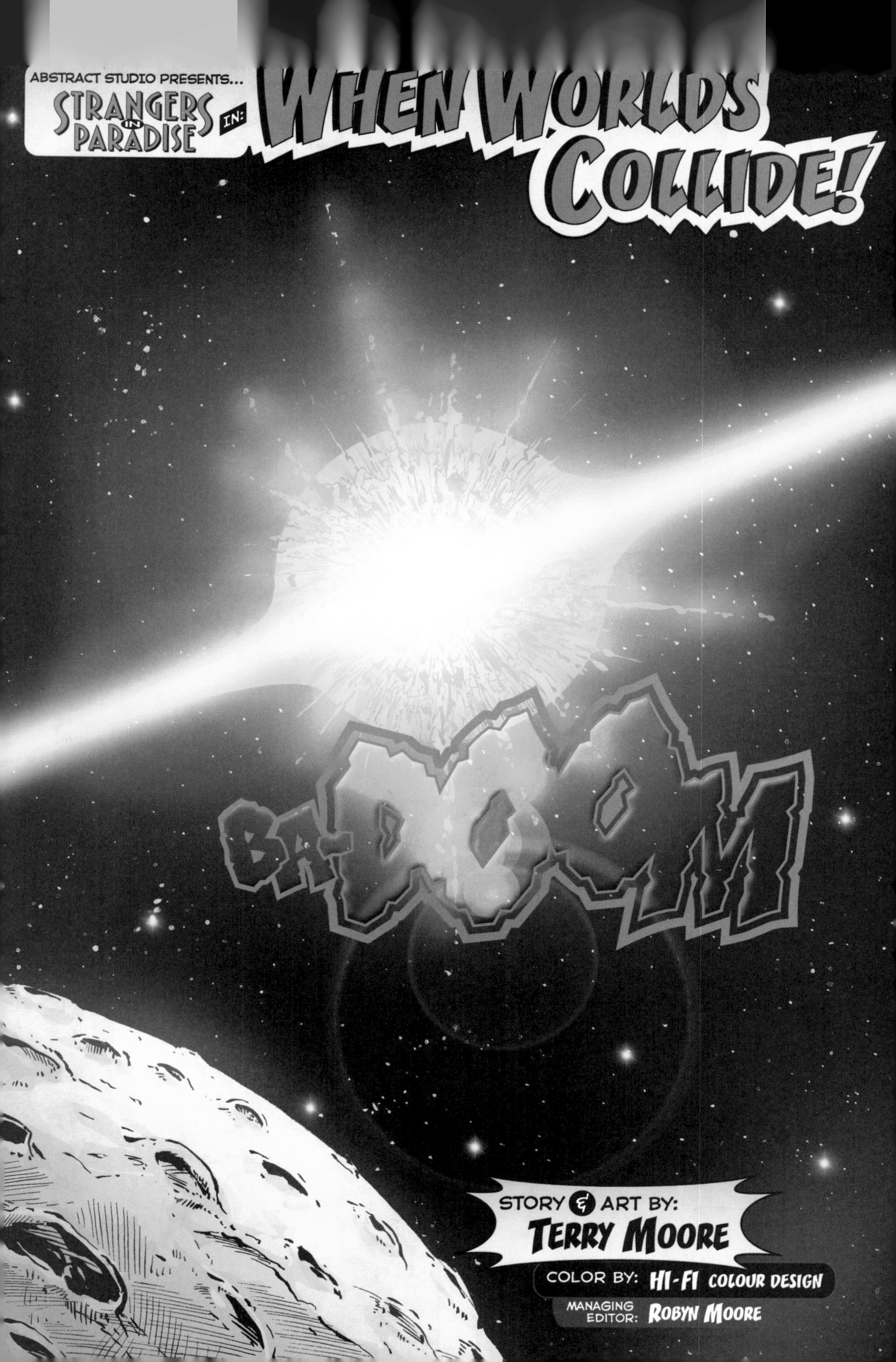

ABSTRACT STUDIO PRESENTS...
STRANGERS IN PARADISE IN: WHEN WORLDS COLLIDE!
BA-DOOM
STORY & ART BY: TERRY MOORE
COLOR BY: HI-FI COLOUR DESIGN
MANAGING EDITOR: ROBYN MOORE

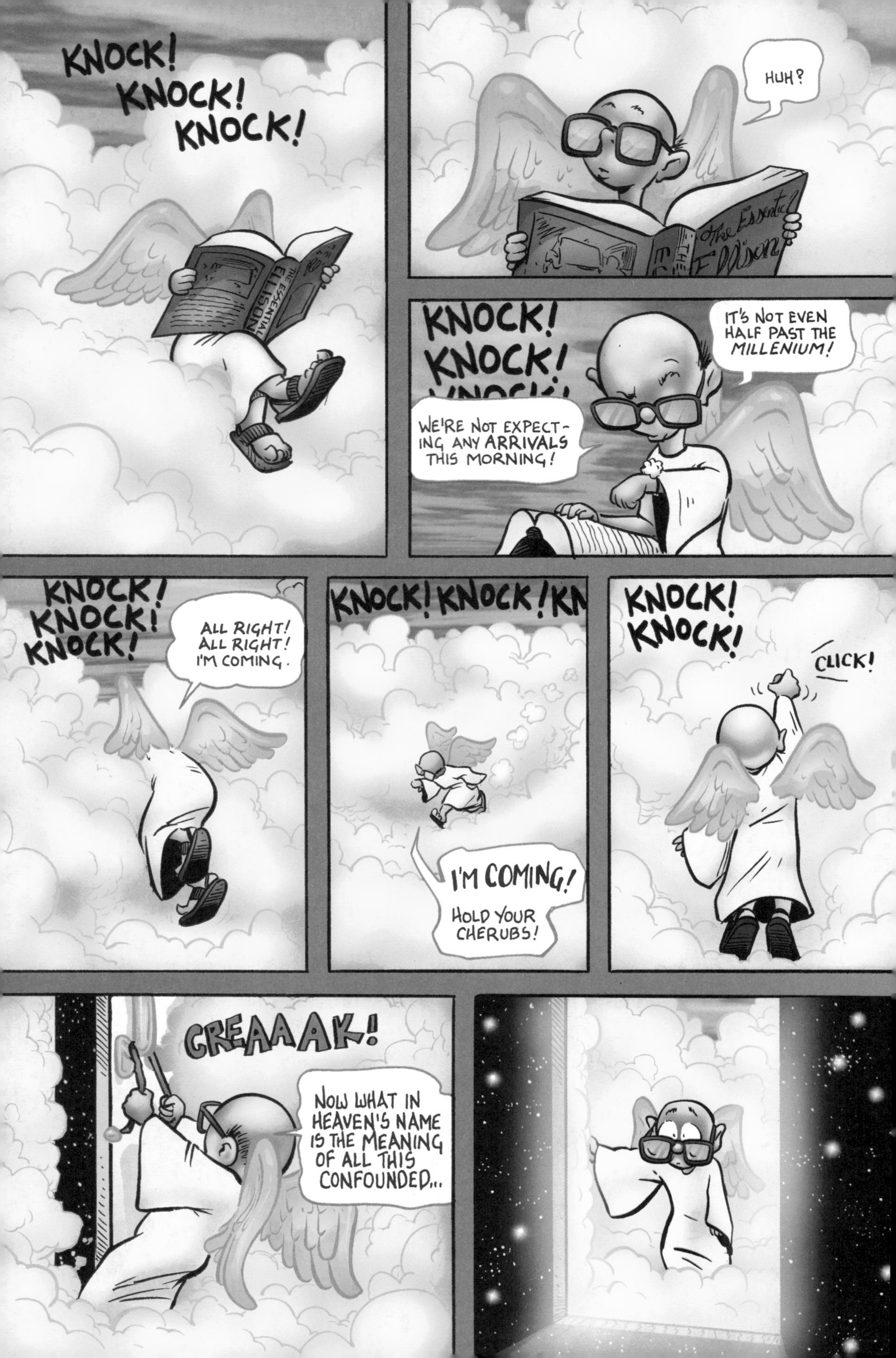
KNOCK! KNOCK! KNOCK!
THE ESSENTIAL ELLISON
HUH?
The Essential Ellison
KNOCK! KNOCK!
IT'S NOT EVEN HALF PAST THE MILLENIUM!
WE'RE NOT EXPECTING ANY ARRIVALS THIS MORNING!
KNOCK! KNOCK! KNOCK!
ALL RIGHT! ALL RIGHT! I'M COMING.
KNOCK! KNOCK! KN
I'M COMING!
HOLD YOUR CHERUBS!
KNOCK! KNOCK!
CLICK!
CREAAAK!
NOW WHAT IN HEAVEN'S NAME IS THE MEANING OF ALL THIS CONFOUNDED...

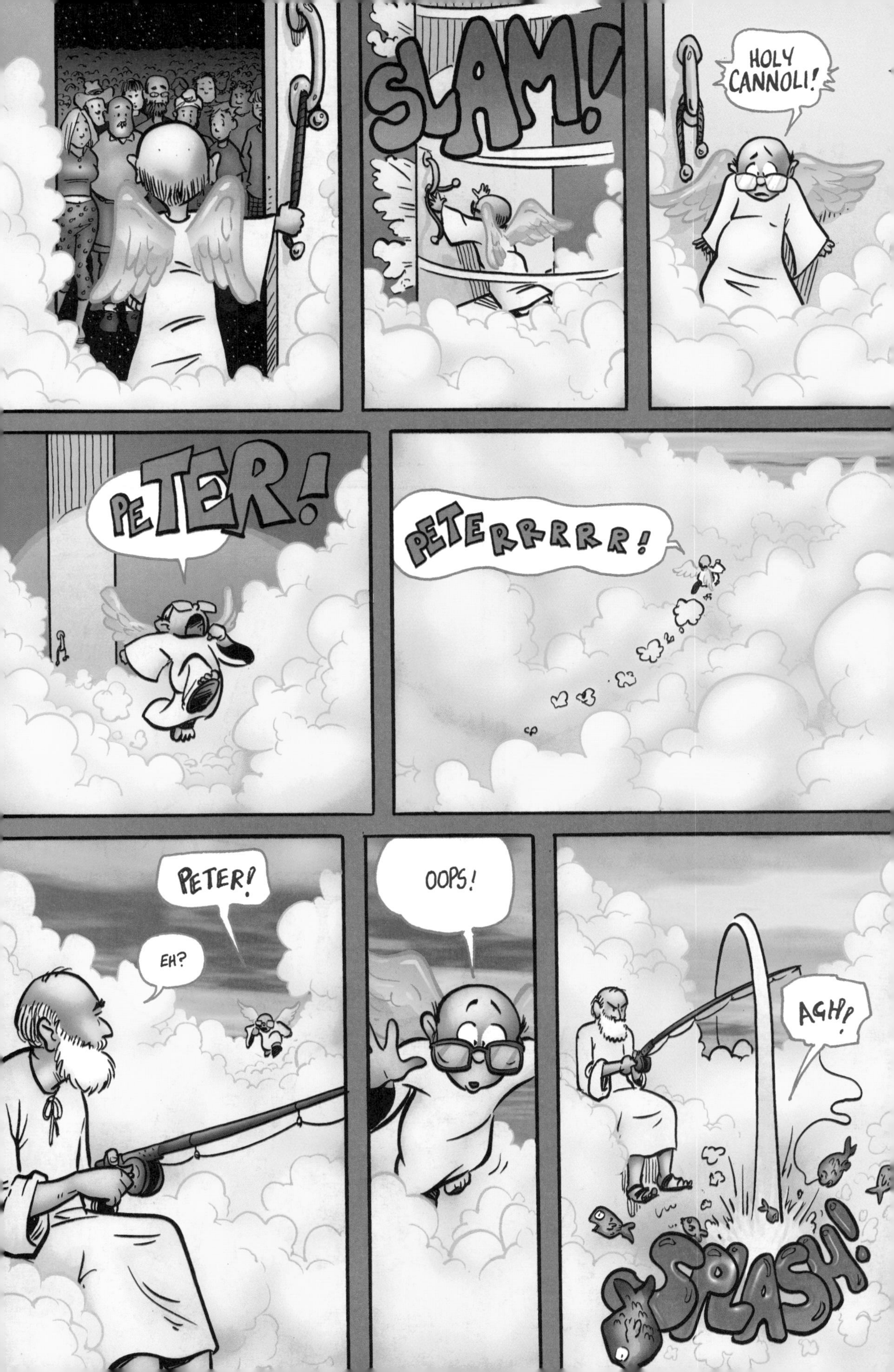
SLAM!
HOLY CANNOLI!
PETER!
PETERRRRRR!
PETER!
EH?
OOPS!
AGH!
SPLASH!

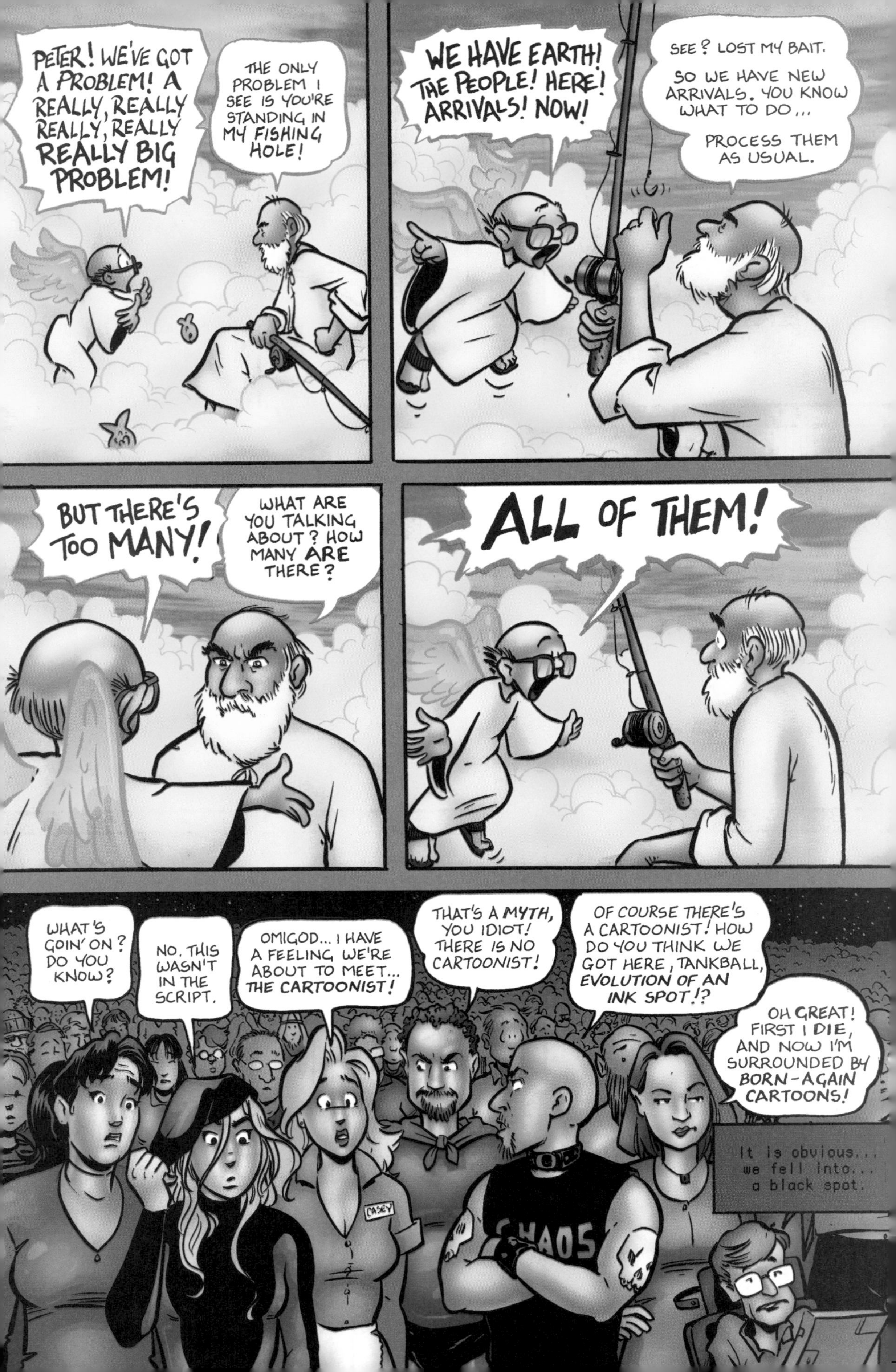

PETER! WE'VE GOT A PROBLEM! A REALLY, REALLY REALLY, REALLY REALLY BIG PROBLEM!
THE ONLY PROBLEM I SEE IS YOU'RE STANDING IN MY FISHING HOLE!
WE HAVE EARTH! THE PEOPLE! HERE! ARRIVALS! NOW!
SEE? LOST MY BAIT.
SO WE HAVE NEW ARRIVALS. YOU KNOW WHAT TO DO...
PROCESS THEM AS USUAL.
BUT THERE'S TOO MANY!
WHAT ARE YOU TALKING ABOUT? HOW MANY ARE THERE?
ALL OF THEM!
WHAT'S GOIN' ON? DO YOU KNOW?
NO. THIS WASN'T IN THE SCRIPT.
OMIGOD... I HAVE A FEELING WE'RE ABOUT TO MEET... THE CARTOONIST!
THAT'S A MYTH, YOU IDIOT! THERE IS NO CARTOONIST!
OF COURSE THERE'S A CARTOONIST! HOW DO YOU THINK WE GOT HERE, TANKBALL, EVOLUTION OF AN INK SPOT!?
OH GREAT! FIRST I DIE, AND NOW I'M SURROUNDED BY BORN-AGAIN CARTOONS!
It is obvious... we fell into... a black spot.
CASEY
CHAOS

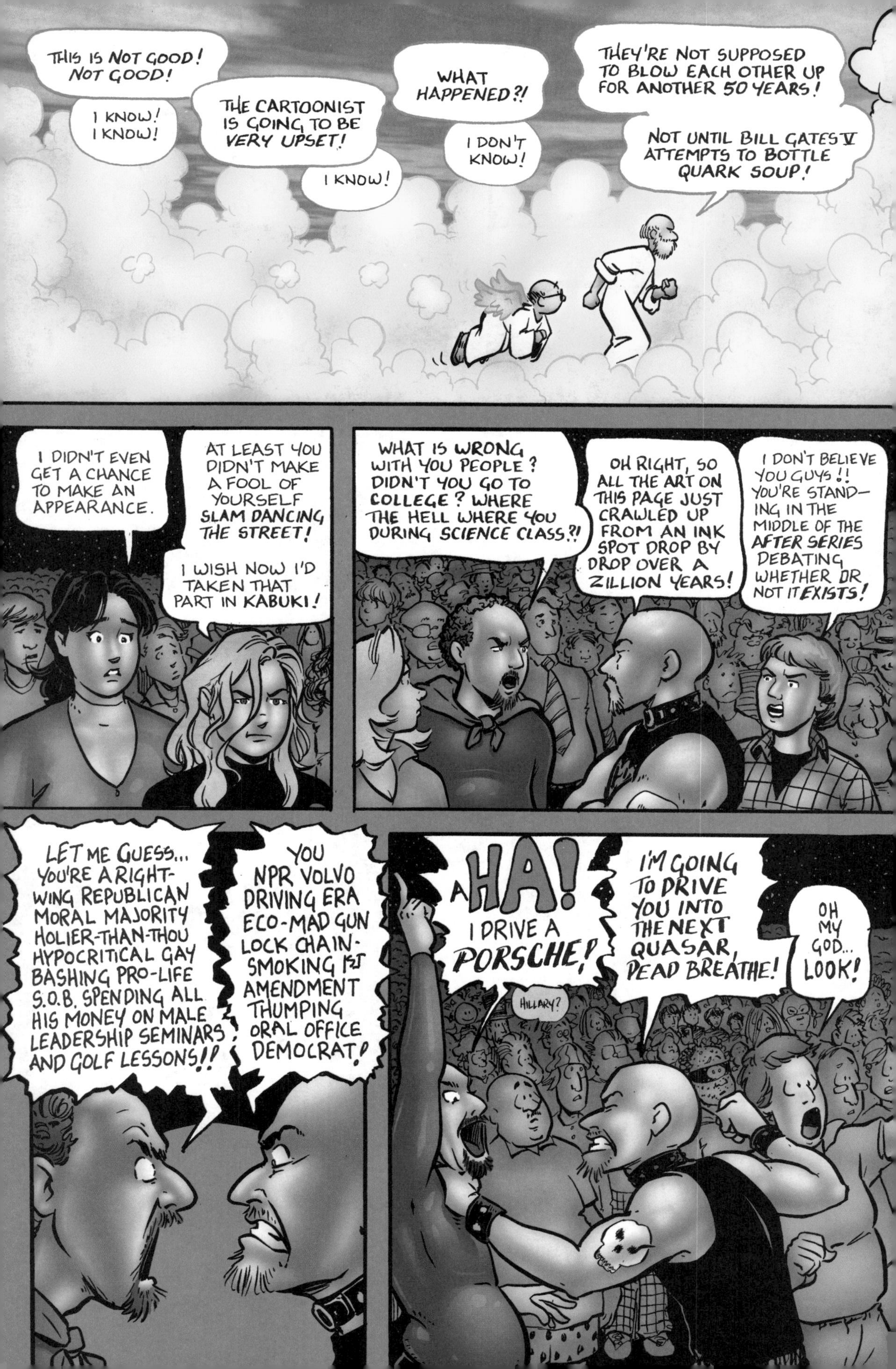

THIS IS NOT GOOD! NOT GOOD!
I KNOW! I KNOW!
THE CARTOONIST IS GOING TO BE VERY UPSET!
I KNOW!
WHAT HAPPENED?!
I DON'T KNOW!
THEY'RE NOT SUPPOSED TO BLOW EACH OTHER UP FOR ANOTHER 50 YEARS!
NOT UNTIL BILL GATES V ATTEMPTS TO BOTTLE QUARK SOUP!
I DIDN'T EVEN GET A CHANCE TO MAKE AN APPEARANCE.
AT LEAST YOU DIDN'T MAKE A FOOL OF YOURSELF SLAM DANCING THE STREET!
I WISH NOW I'D TAKEN THAT PART IN KABUKI!
WHAT IS WRONG WITH YOU PEOPLE? DIDN'T YOU GO TO COLLEGE? WHERE THE HELL WHERE YOU DURING SCIENCE CLASS?!
OH RIGHT, SO ALL THE ART ON THIS PAGE JUST CRAWLED UP FROM AN INK SPOT DROP BY DROP OVER A ZILLION YEARS!
I DON'T BELIEVE YOU GUYS!! YOU'RE STANDING IN THE MIDDLE OF THE AFTER SERIES DEBATING WHETHER OR NOT IT EXISTS!
LET ME GUESS... YOU'RE A RIGHT-WING REPUBLICAN MORAL MAJORITY HOLIER-THAN-THOU HYPOCRITICAL GAY BASHING PRO-LIFE S.O.B. SPENDING ALL HIS MONEY ON MALE LEADERSHIP SEMINARS AND GOLF LESSONS!!
YOU NPR VOLVO DRIVING ERA ECO-MAD GUN LOCK CHAIN-SMOKING 1ST AMENDMENT THUMPING ORAL OFFICE DEMOCRAT!
A HA! I DRIVE A PORSCHE!
HILLARY?
I'M GOING TO DRIVE YOU INTO THE NEXT QUASAR, DEAD BREATHE!
OH MY GOD... LOOK!

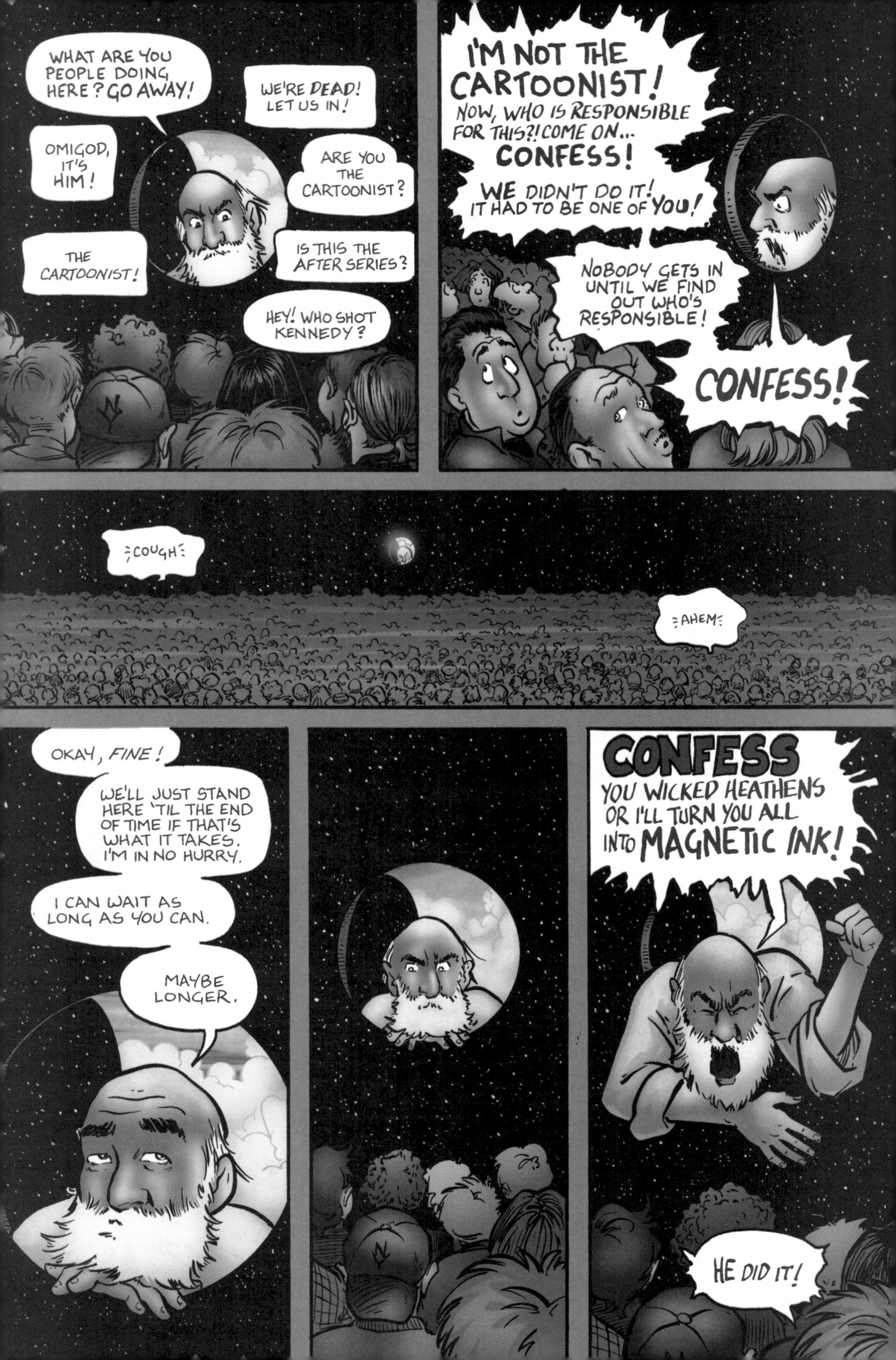
WHAT ARE YOU PEOPLE DOING HERE? GO AWAY!
WE'RE DEAD! LET US IN!
OMIGOD, IT'S HIM!
ARE YOU THE CARTOONIST?
THE CARTOONIST!
IS THIS THE AFTER SERIES?
HEY! WHO SHOT KENNEDY?
I'M NOT THE CARTOONIST! NOW, WHO IS RESPONSIBLE FOR THIS?! COME ON... CONFESS!
WE DIDN'T DO IT! IT HAD TO BE ONE OF YOU!
NOBODY GETS IN UNTIL WE FIND OUT WHO'S RESPONSIBLE!
CONFESS!
COUGH
AHEM
OKAY, FINE!
WE'LL JUST STAND HERE 'TIL THE END OF TIME IF THAT'S WHAT IT TAKES. I'M IN NO HURRY.
I CAN WAIT AS LONG AS YOU CAN.
MAYBE LONGER.
CONFESS YOU WICKED HEATHENS OR I'LL TURN YOU ALL INTO MAGNETIC INK!
HE DID IT!

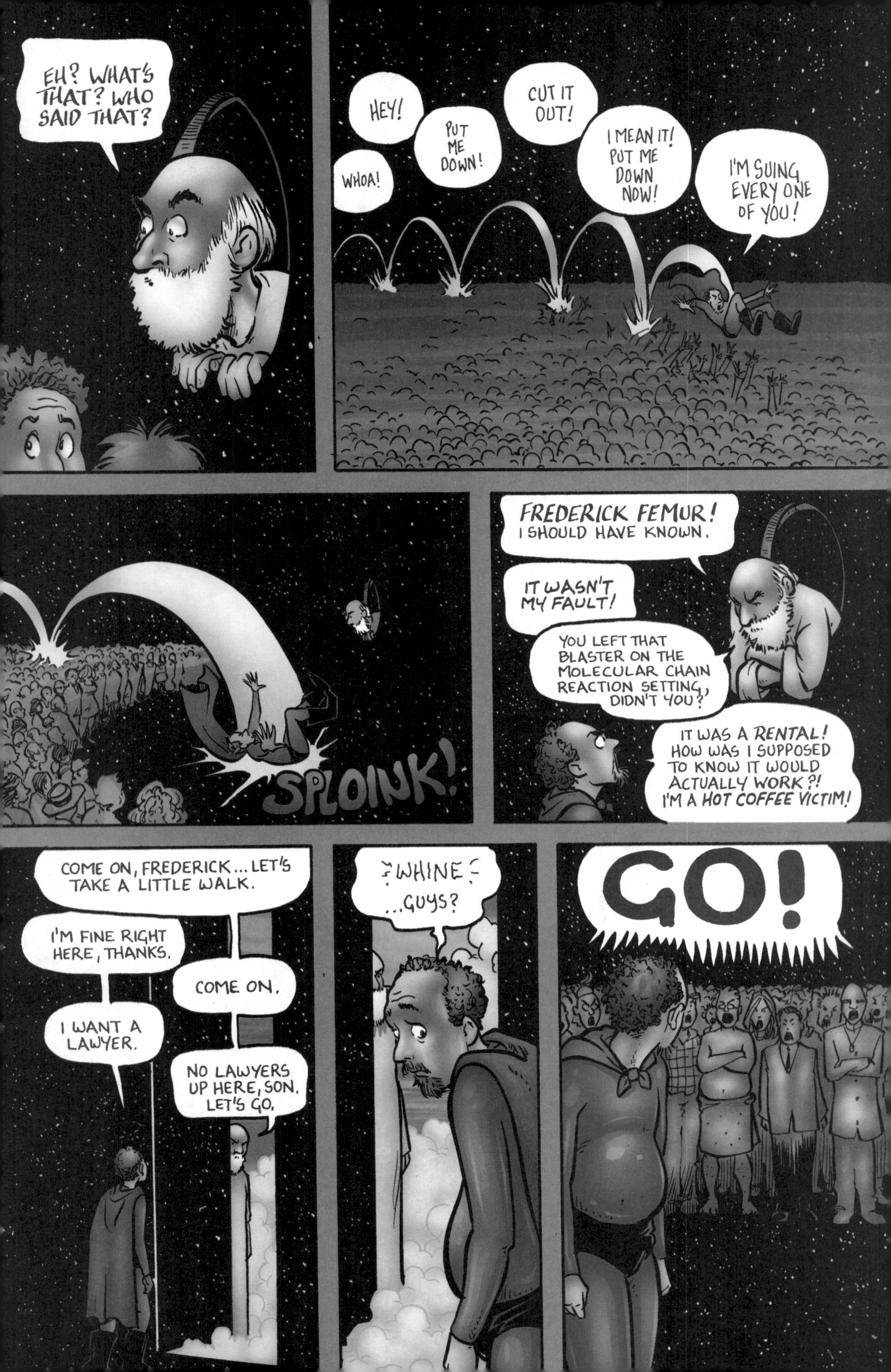
EH? WHAT'S THAT? WHO SAID THAT?
WHOA!
HEY!
PUT ME DOWN!
CUT IT OUT!
I MEAN IT! PUT ME DOWN NOW!
I'M SUING EVERY ONE OF YOU!
SPLOINK!
FREDERICK FEMUR! I SHOULD HAVE KNOWN.
IT WASN'T MY FAULT!
YOU LEFT THAT BLASTER ON THE MOLECULAR CHAIN REACTION SETTING, DIDN'T YOU?
IT WAS A RENTAL! HOW WAS I SUPPOSED TO KNOW IT WOULD ACTUALLY WORK?! I'M A HOT COFFEE VICTIM!
COME ON, FREDERICK... LET'S TAKE A LITTLE WALK.
I'M FINE RIGHT HERE, THANKS.
COME ON.
I WANT A LAWYER.
NO LAWYERS UP HERE, SON. LET'S GO.
WHINE
...GUYS?
GO!

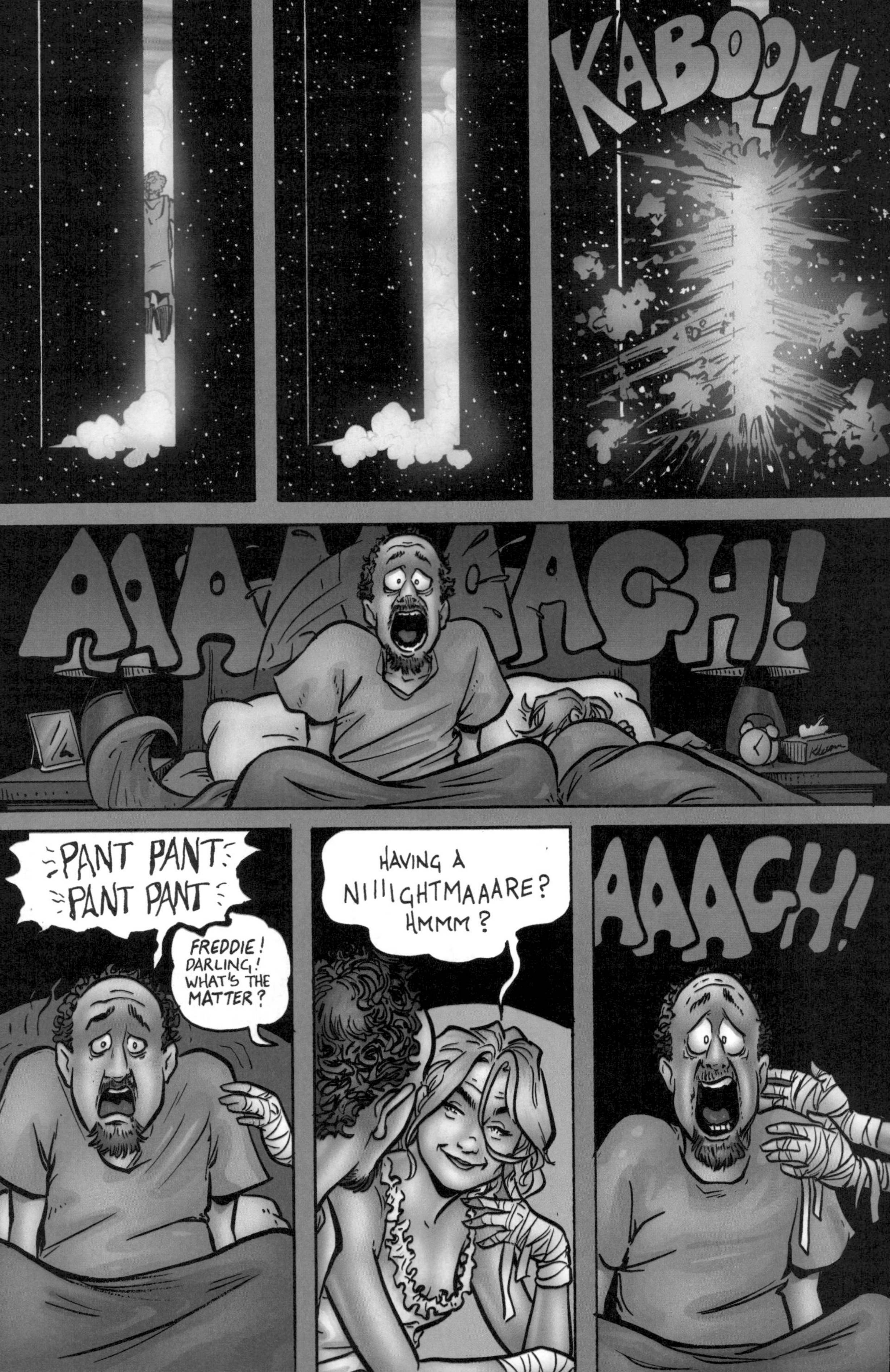
KABOOM!
AAAAAAGH!
PANT PANT
PANT PANT
FREDDIE! DARLING! WHAT'S THE MATTER?
HAVING A NIIIIGHTMAAARE? HMMM?
AAAGH!

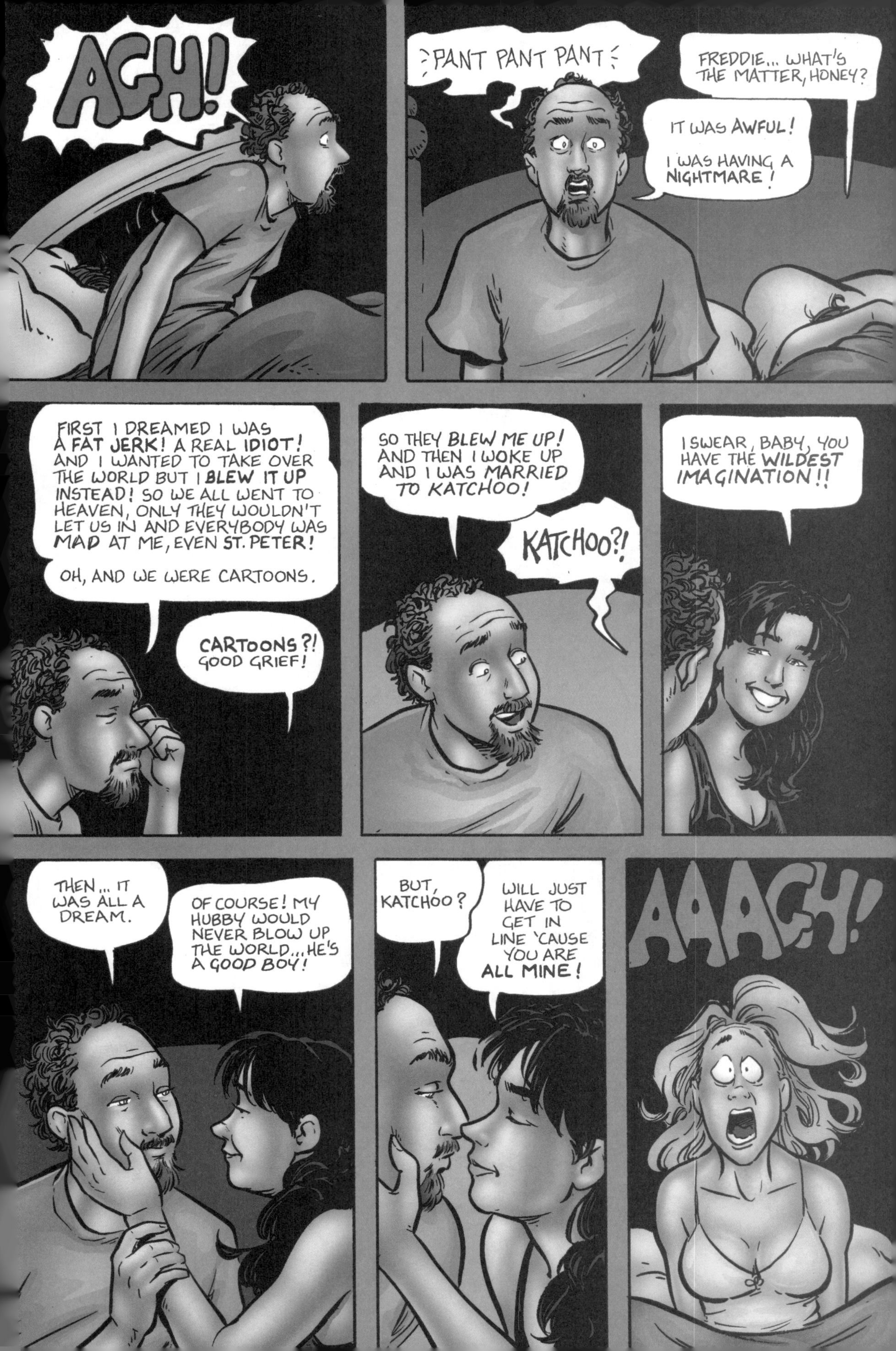
AGH!
PANT PANT PANT
FREDDIE... WHAT'S THE MATTER, HONEY?
IT WAS AWFUL!
I WAS HAVING A NIGHTMARE!
FIRST I DREAMED I WAS A FAT JERK! A REAL IDIOT! AND I WANTED TO TAKE OVER THE WORLD BUT I BLEW IT UP INSTEAD! SO WE ALL WENT TO HEAVEN, ONLY THEY WOULDN'T LET US IN AND EVERYBODY WAS MAD AT ME, EVEN ST. PETER!
OH, AND WE WERE CARTOONS.
CARTOONS?! GOOD GRIEF!
SO THEY BLEW ME UP! AND THEN I WOKE UP AND I WAS MARRIED TO KATCHOO!
KATCHOO?!
I SWEAR, BABY, YOU HAVE THE WILDEST IMAGINATION!!
THEN... IT WAS ALL A DREAM.
OF COURSE! MY HUBBY WOULD NEVER BLOW UP THE WORLD... HE'S A GOOD BOY!
BUT, KATCHOO?
WILL JUST HAVE TO GET IN LINE 'CAUSE YOU ARE ALL MINE!
AAACH!

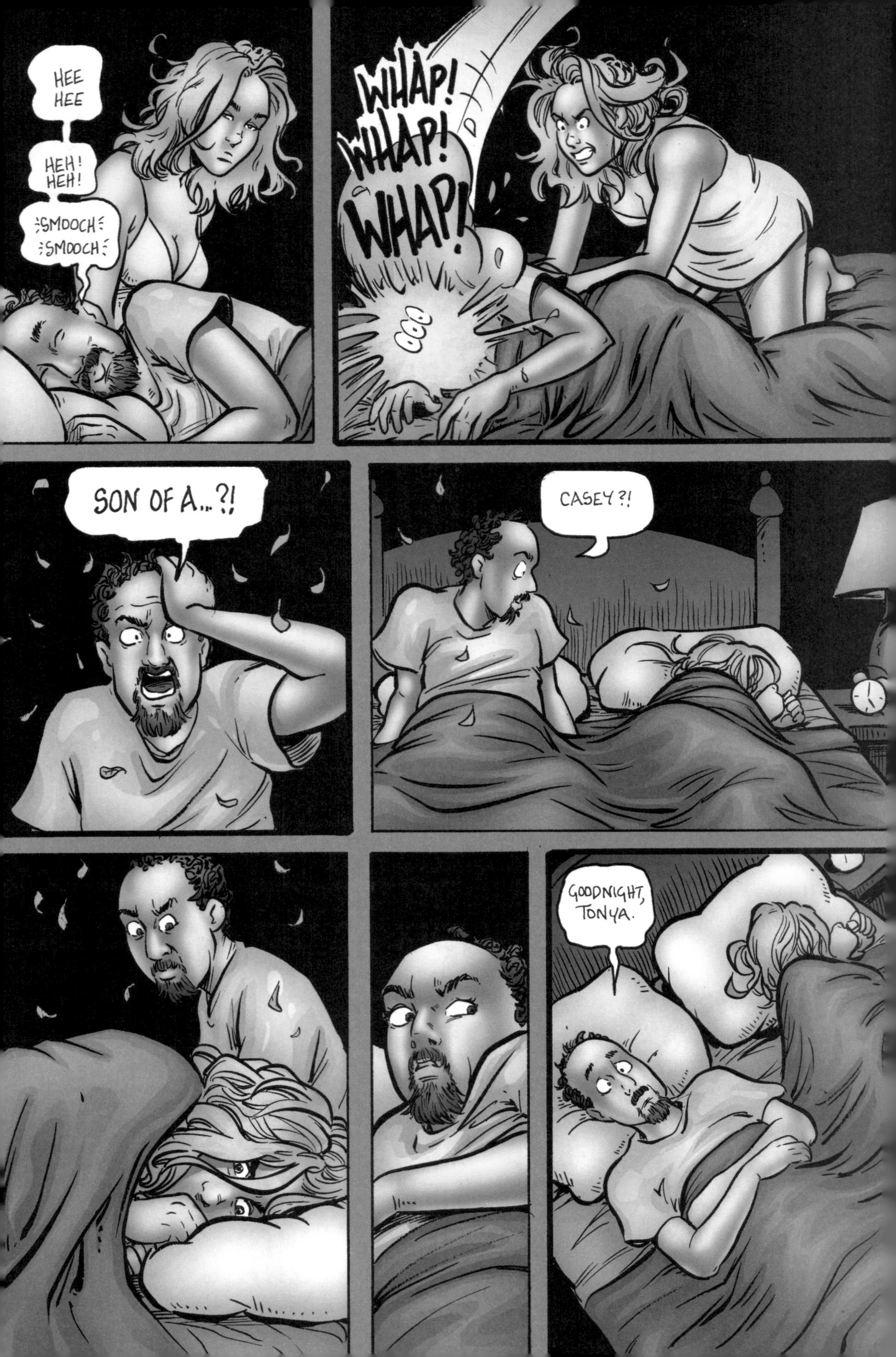
HEE HEE
HEH! HEH!
SMOOCH SMOOCH
WHAP! WHAP! WHAP!
SON OF A...?!
CASEY?!
GOODNIGHT, TONYA.

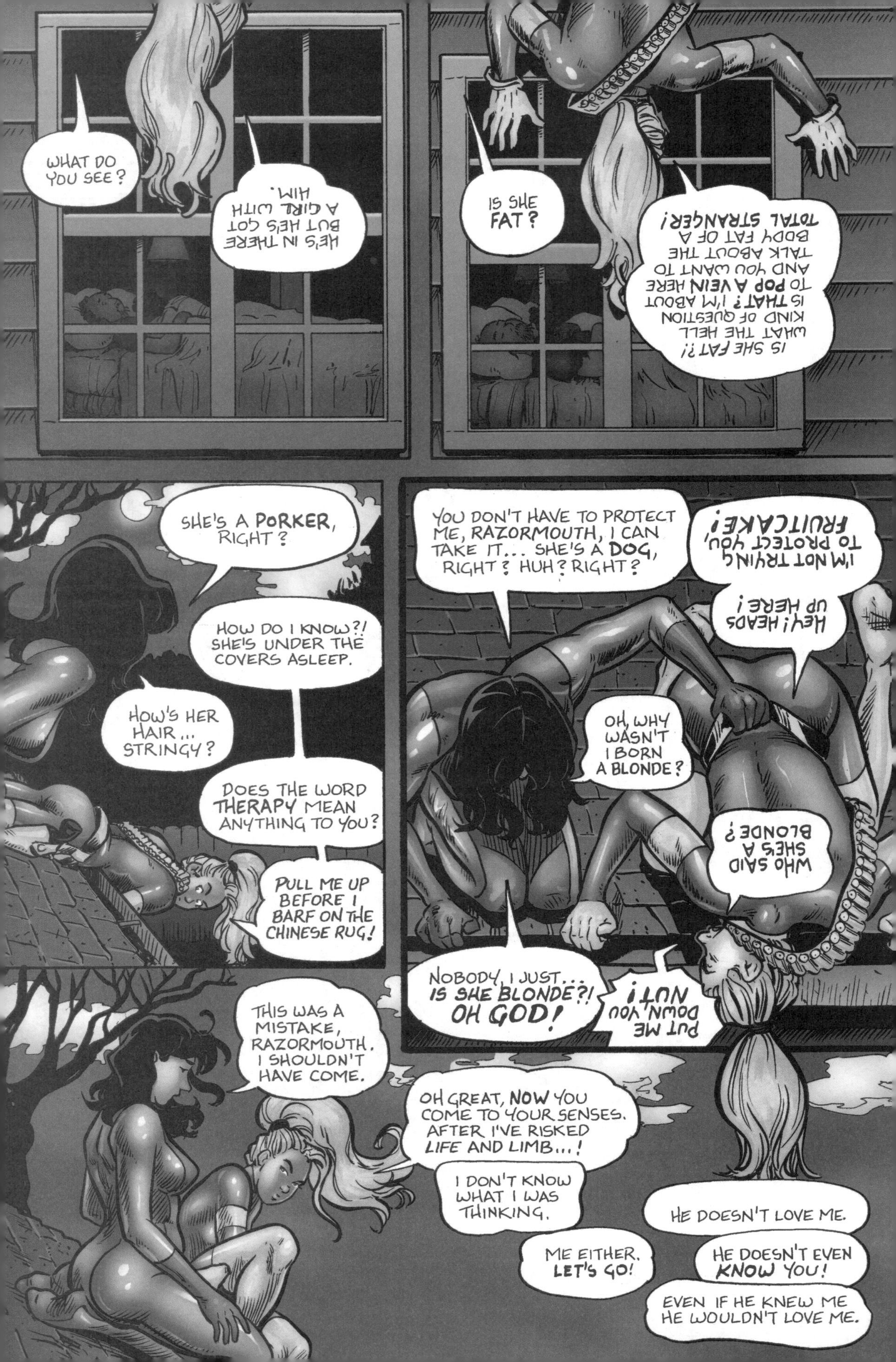

WHAT DO YOU SEE?
HE'S IN THERE BUT HE'S GOT A GIRL WITH HIM.
IS SHE FAT?
IS SHE FAT?! WHAT THE HELL KIND OF QUESTION IS THAT? I'M ABOUT TO POP A VEIN HERE AND YOU WANT TO TALK ABOUT THE BODY FAT OF A TOTAL STRANGER!
SHE'S A PORKER, RIGHT?
HOW DO I KNOW?! SHE'S UNDER THE COVERS ASLEEP.
HOW'S HER HAIR... STRINGY?
DOES THE WORD THERAPY MEAN ANYTHING TO YOU?
PULL ME UP BEFORE I BARF ON THE CHINESE RUG!
YOU DON'T HAVE TO PROTECT ME, RAZORMOUTH, I CAN TAKE IT... SHE'S A DOG, RIGHT? HUH? RIGHT?
I'M NOT TRYING TO PROTECT YOU, FRUITCAKE!
HEY! HEADS UP HERE!
OH, WHY WASN'T I BORN A BLONDE?
WHO SAID SHE'S A BLONDE?
NOBODY, I JUST... IS SHE BLONDE?! OH GOD!
PUT ME DOWN, YOU NUT!
THIS WAS A MISTAKE, RAZORMOUTH. I SHOULDN'T HAVE COME.
OH GREAT, NOW YOU COME TO YOUR SENSES. AFTER I'VE RISKED LIFE AND LIMB...!
I DON'T KNOW WHAT I WAS THINKING.
ME EITHER. LET'S GO!
HE DOESN'T LOVE ME.
HE DOESN'T EVEN KNOW YOU!
EVEN IF HE KNEW ME HE WOULDN'T LOVE ME.

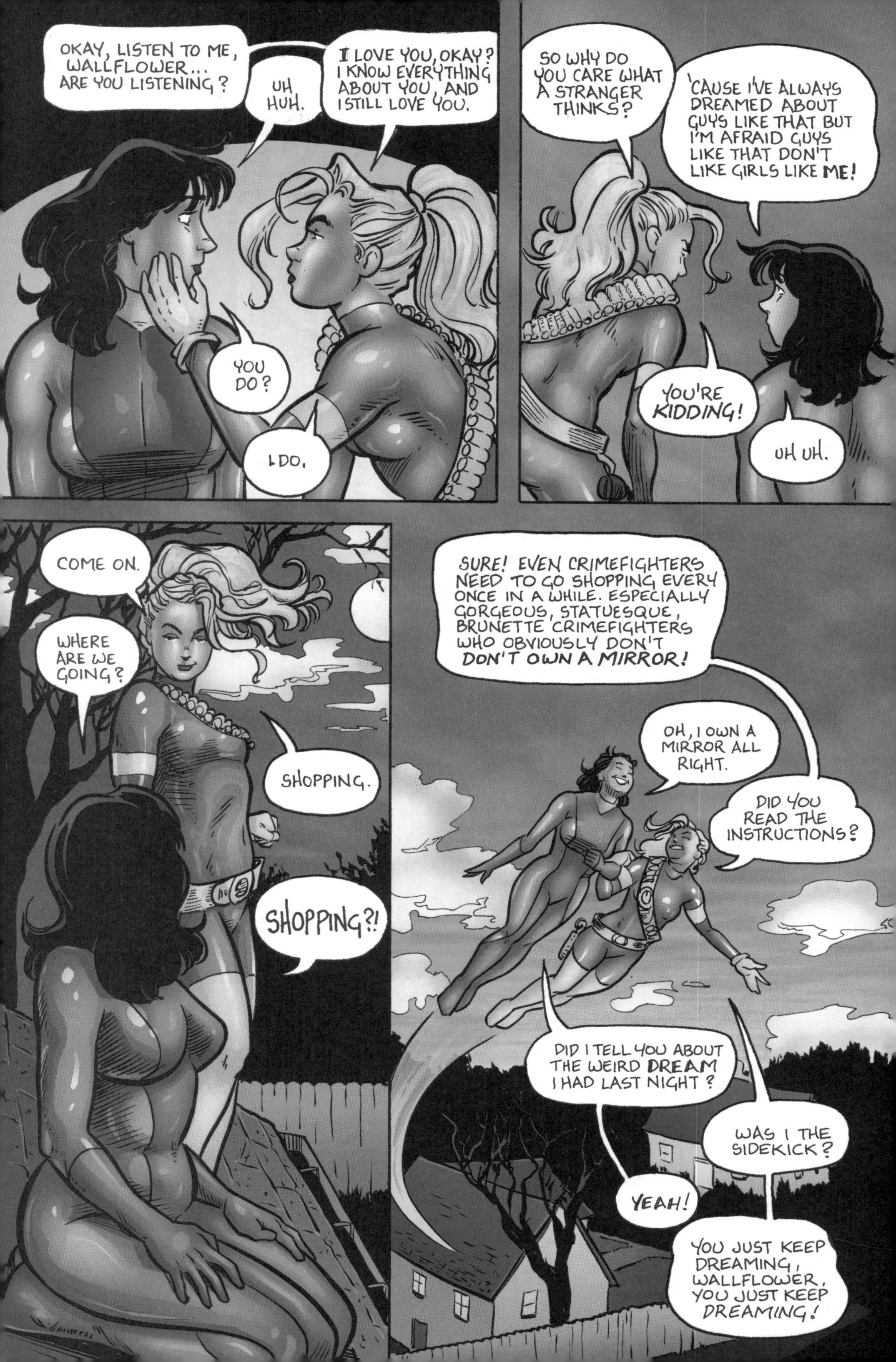

OKAY, LISTEN TO ME, WALLFLOWER... ARE YOU LISTENING?
UH HUH.
I LOVE YOU, OKAY? I KNOW EVERYTHING ABOUT YOU, AND I STILL LOVE YOU.
YOU DO?
I DO.
SO WHY DO YOU CARE WHAT A STRANGER THINKS?
'CAUSE I'VE ALWAYS DREAMED ABOUT GUYS LIKE THAT BUT I'M AFRAID GUYS LIKE THAT DON'T LIKE GIRLS LIKE ME!
YOU'RE KIDDING!
UH UH.
COME ON.
WHERE ARE WE GOING?
SHOPPING.
SHOPPING?!
SURE! EVEN CRIMEFIGHTERS NEED TO GO SHOPPING EVERY ONCE IN A WHILE. ESPECIALLY GORGEOUS, STATUESQUE, BRUNETTE CRIMEFIGHTERS WHO OBVIOUSLY DON'T DON'T OWN A MIRROR!
OH, I OWN A MIRROR ALL RIGHT.
DID YOU READ THE INSTRUCTIONS?
DID I TELL YOU ABOUT THE WEIRD DREAM I HAD LAST NIGHT?
WAS I THE SIDEKICK?
YEAH!
YOU JUST KEEP DREAMING, WALLFLOWER, YOU JUST KEEP DREAMING!

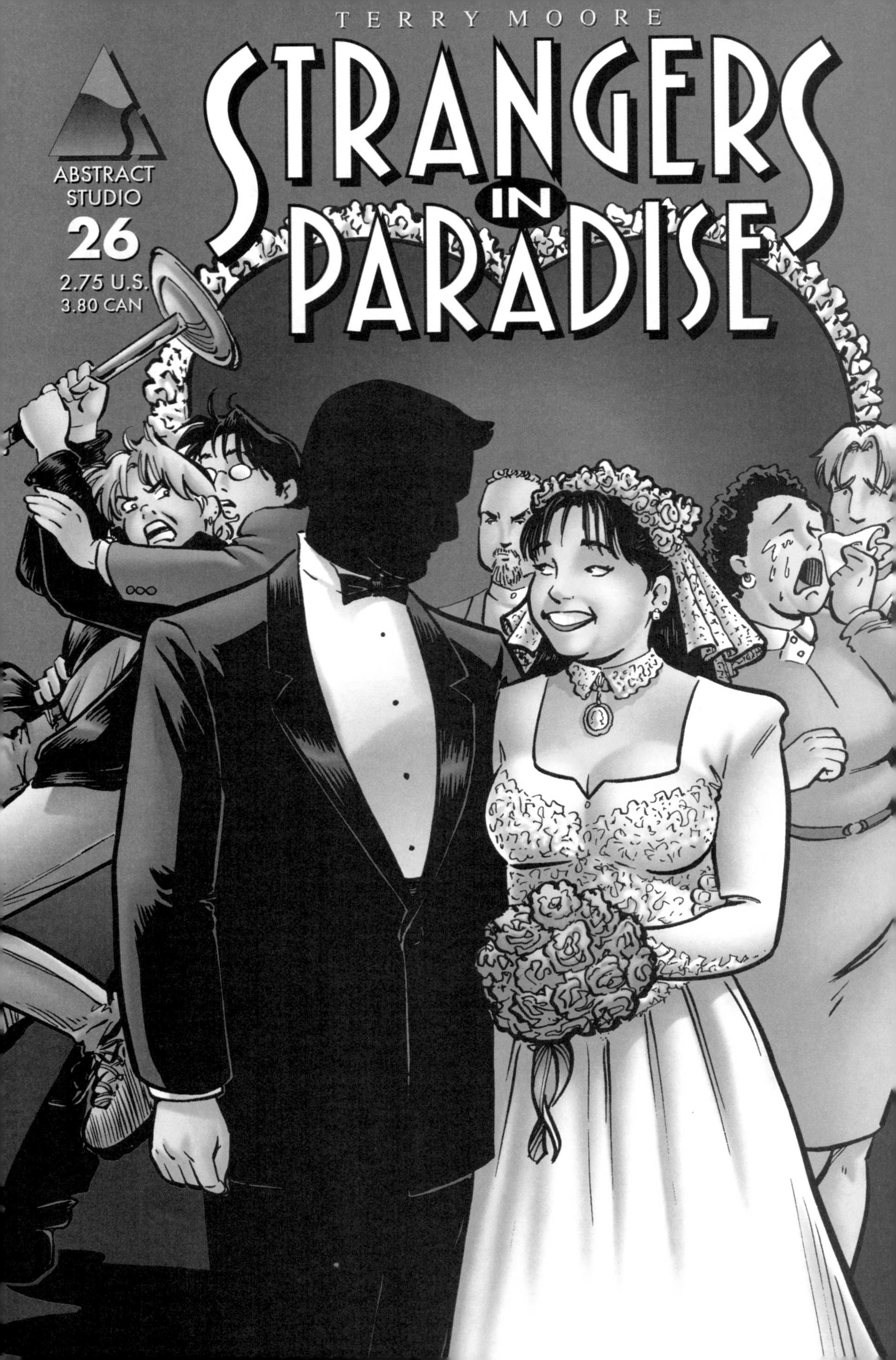

TERRY MOORE
STRANGERS IN PARADISE
ABSTRACT STUDIO
26
2.75 U.S.
3.80 CAN

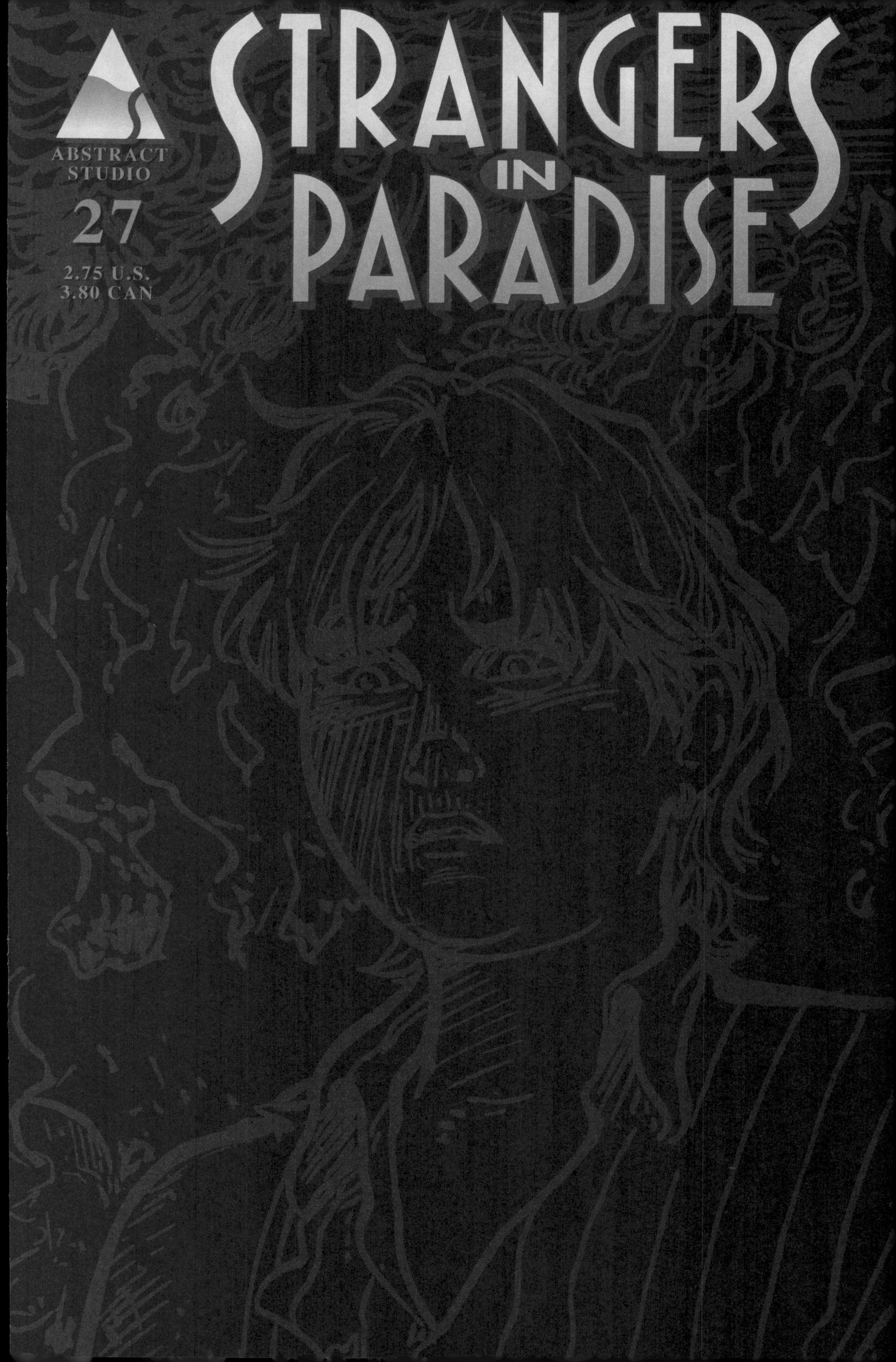
ABSTRACT
STUDIO
27
2.75 U.S.
3.80 CAN
STRANGERS
IN
PARADISE

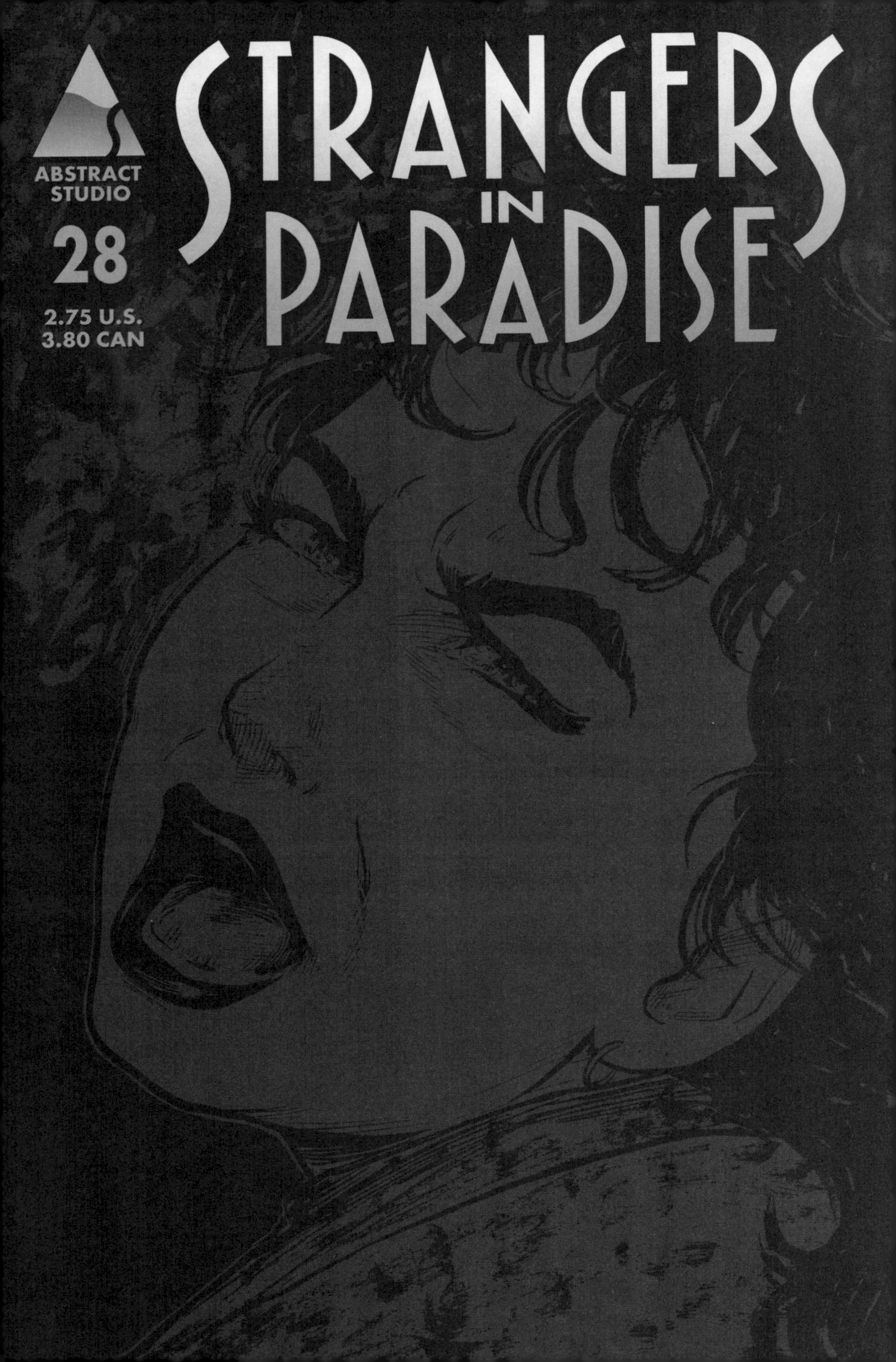
ABSTRACT
STUDIO
28
2.75 U.S.
3.80 CAN
STRANGERS
IN
PARADISE

ABSTRACT
STUDIO

**29**

2.75 U.S.
3.80 CAN

# STRANGERS IN PARADISE

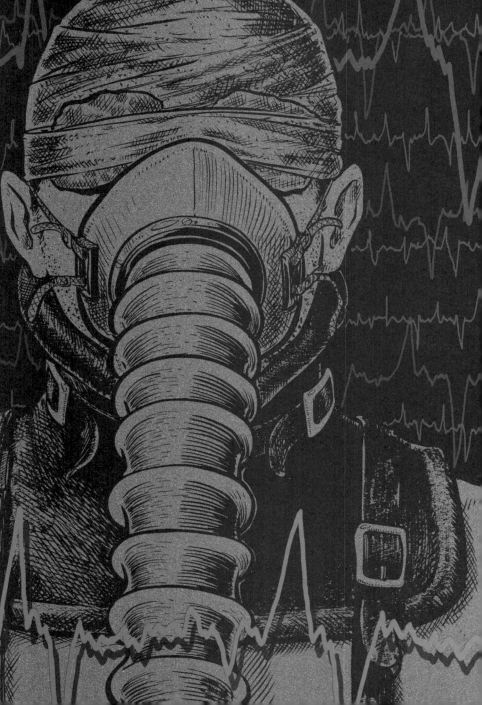

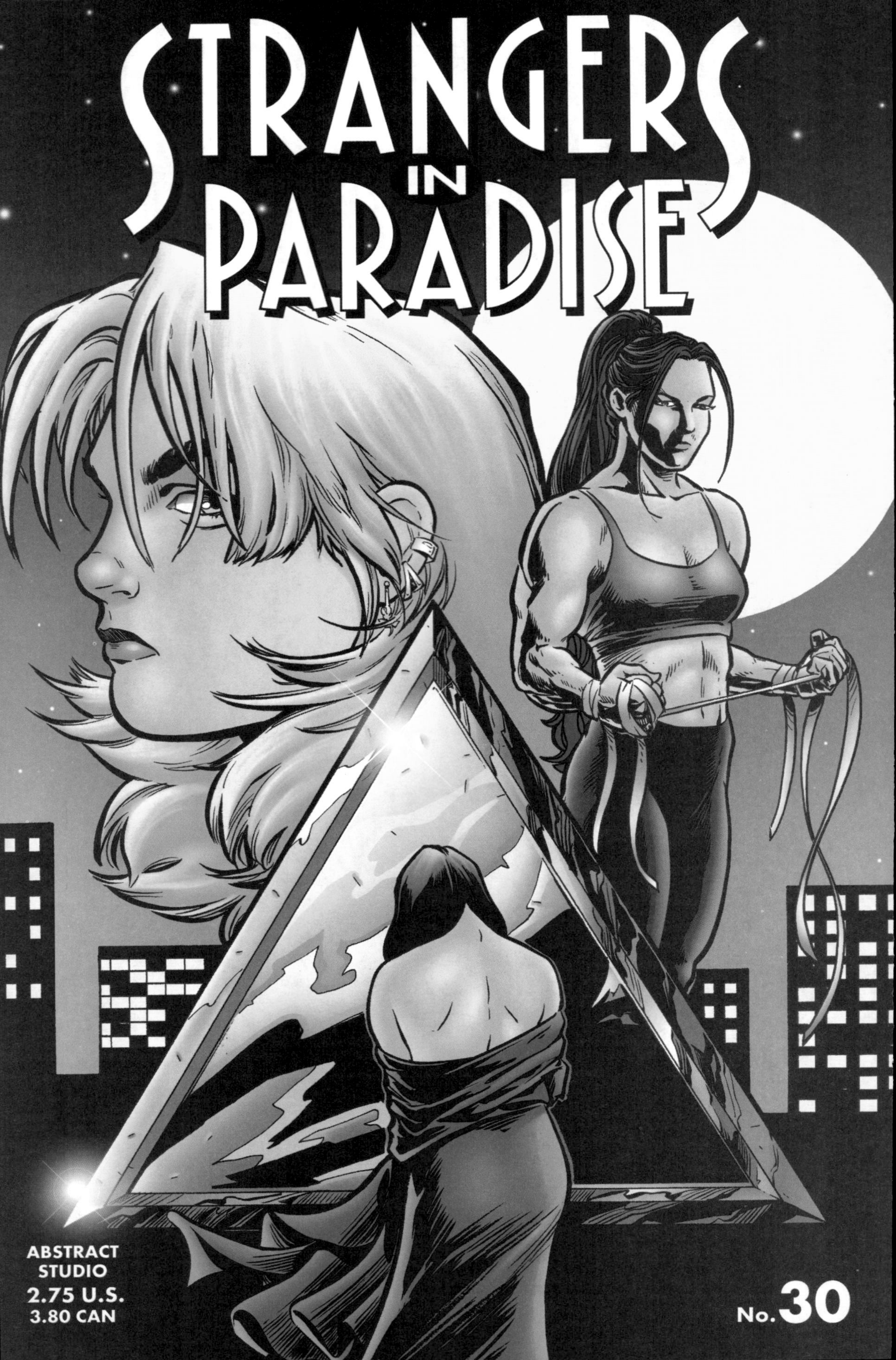
STRANGERS IN PARADISE
ABSTRACT STUDIO
2.75 U.S.
3.80 CAN
No. 30

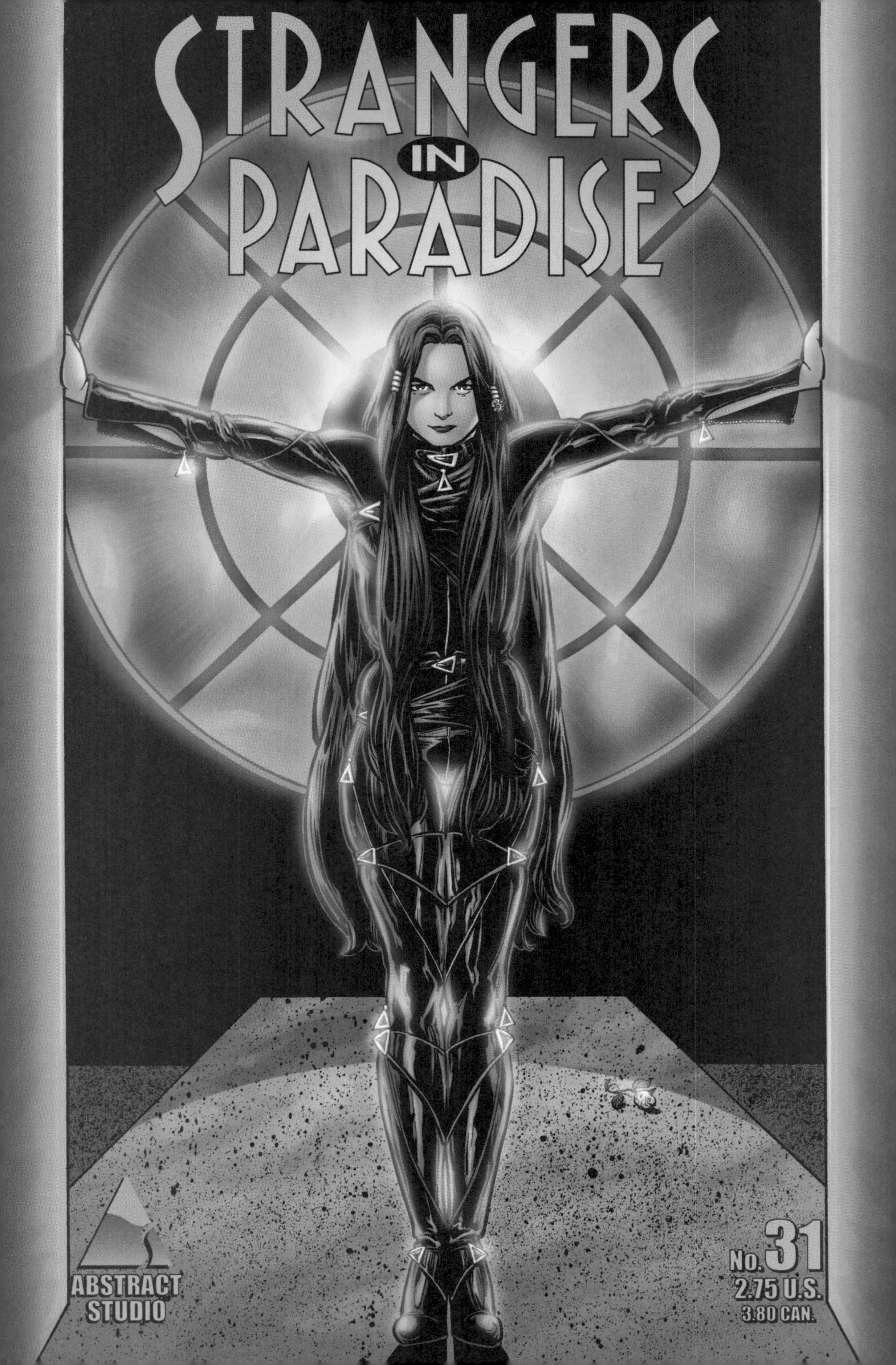

STRANGERS IN PARADISE
ABSTRACT STUDIO
No. 31
2.75 U.S.
3.80 CAN.

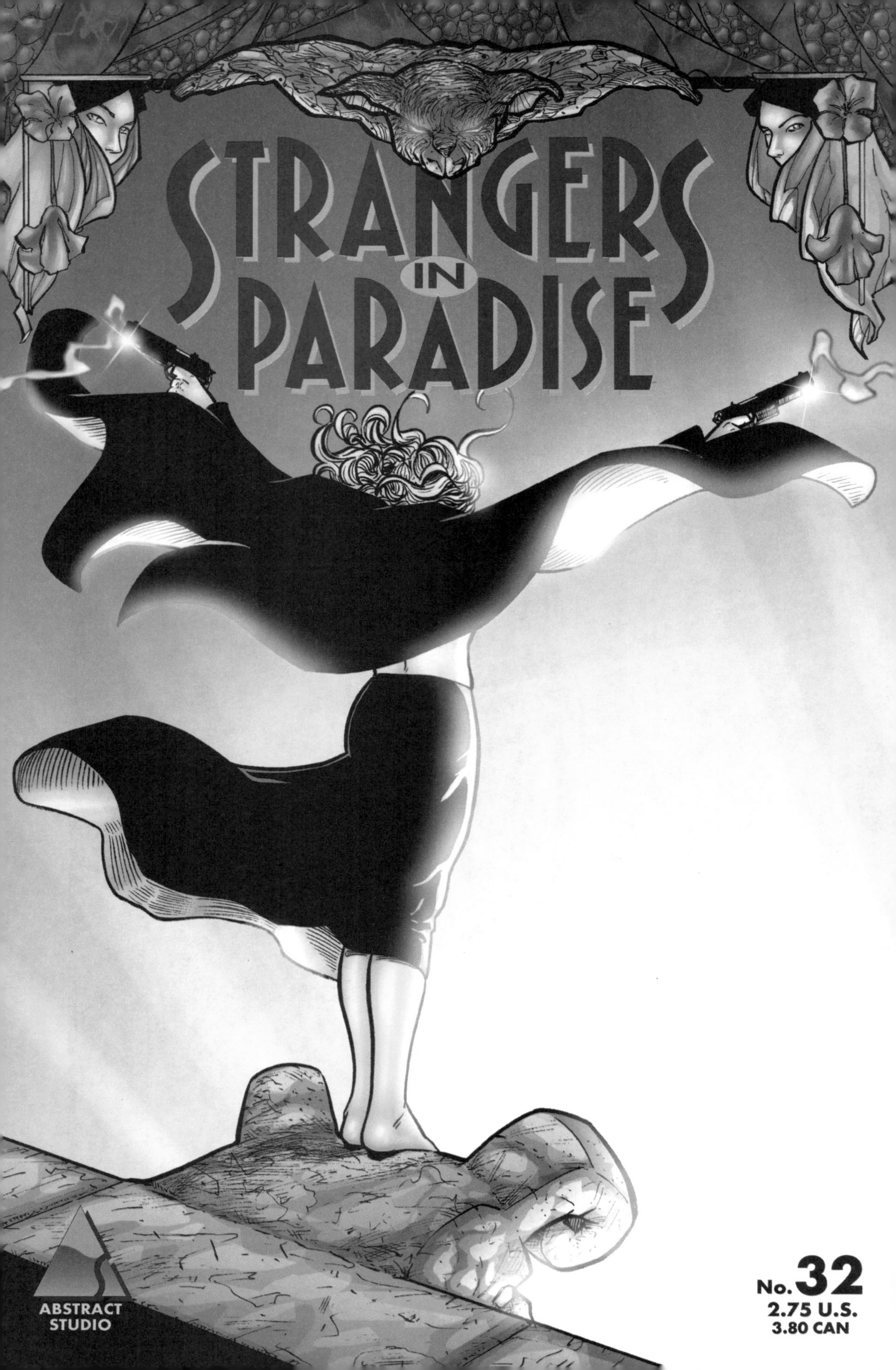

STRANGERS
IN
PARADISE
ABSTRACT STUDIO
No. 32
2.75 U.S.
3.80 CAN

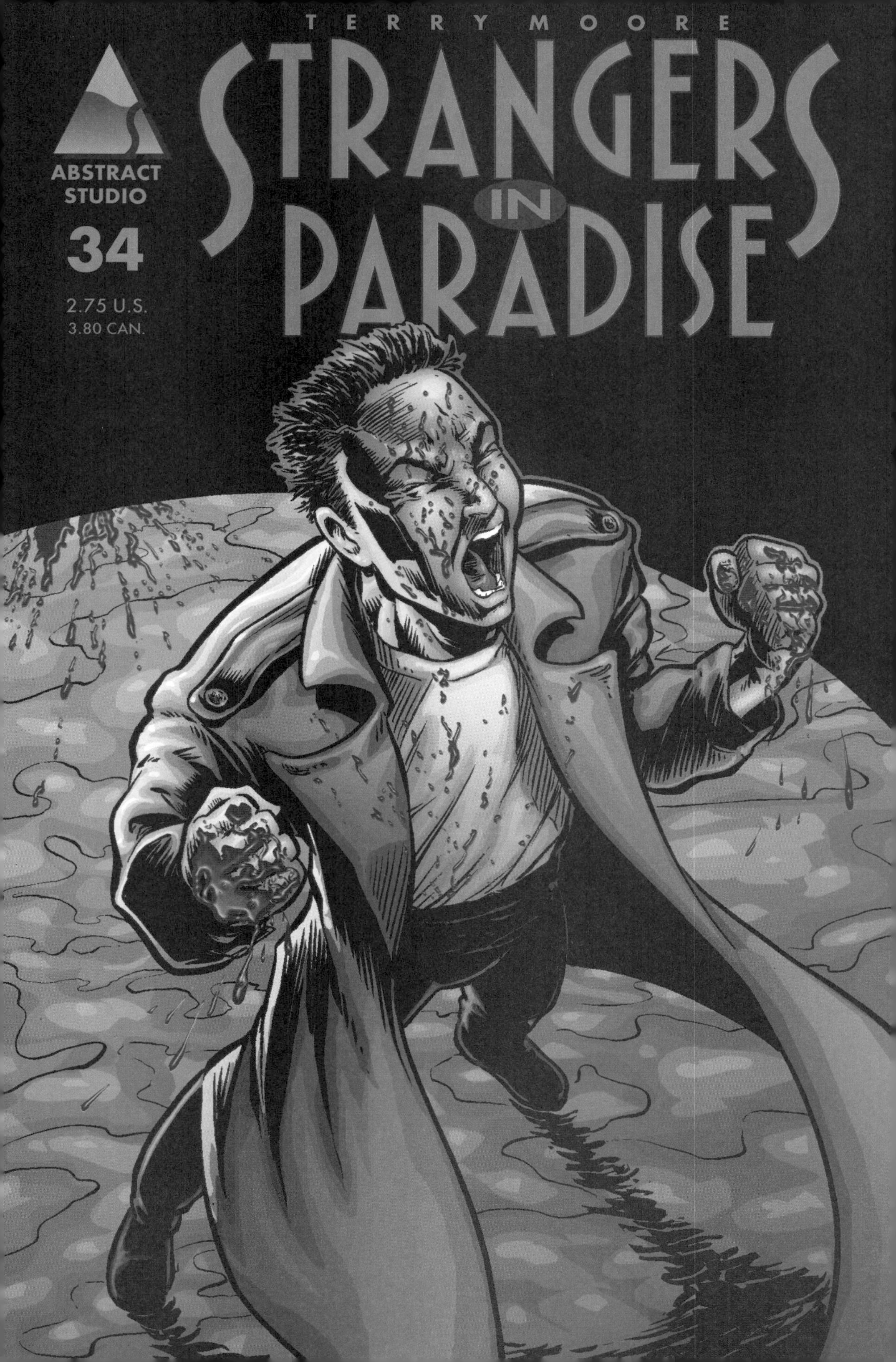
TERRY MOORE
STRANGERS IN PARADISE
ABSTRACT STUDIO
34
2.75 U.S.
3.80 CAN.

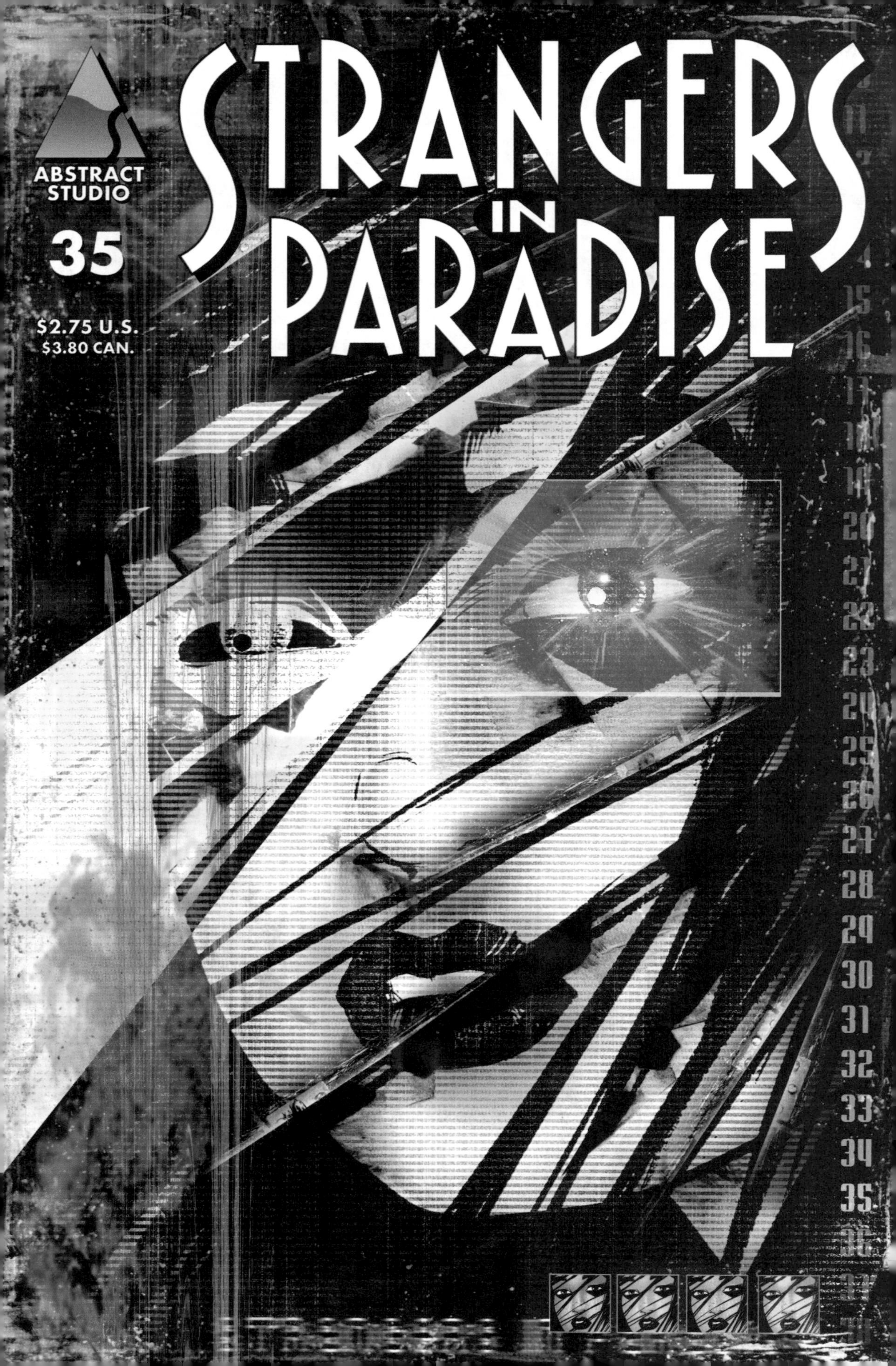

ABSTRACT STUDIO
STRANGERS IN PARADISE
35
$2.75 U.S.
$3.80 CAN.

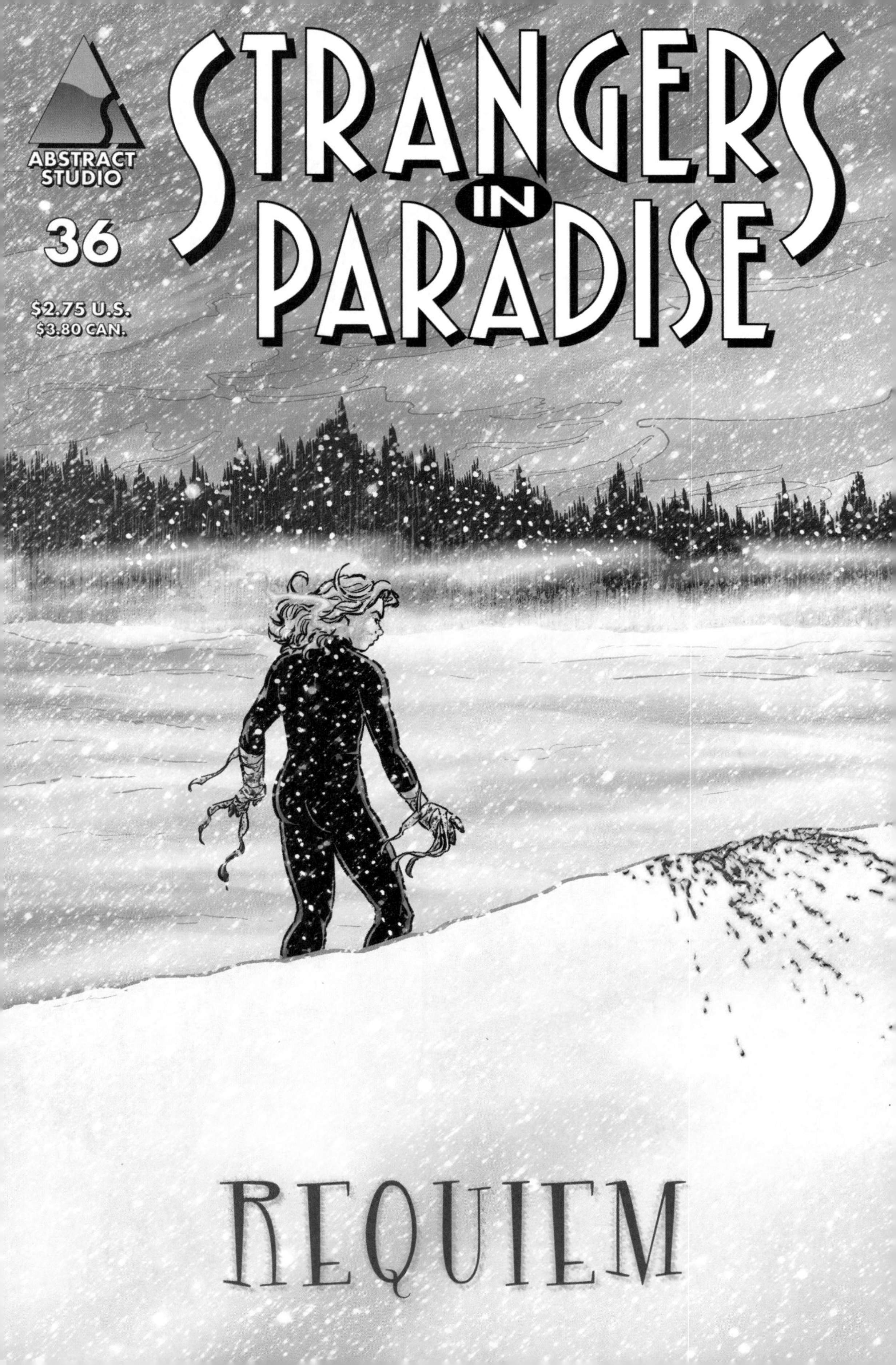
ABSTRACT STUDIO
36
$2.75 U.S.
$3.80 CAN.
STRANGERS IN PARADISE
REQUIEM

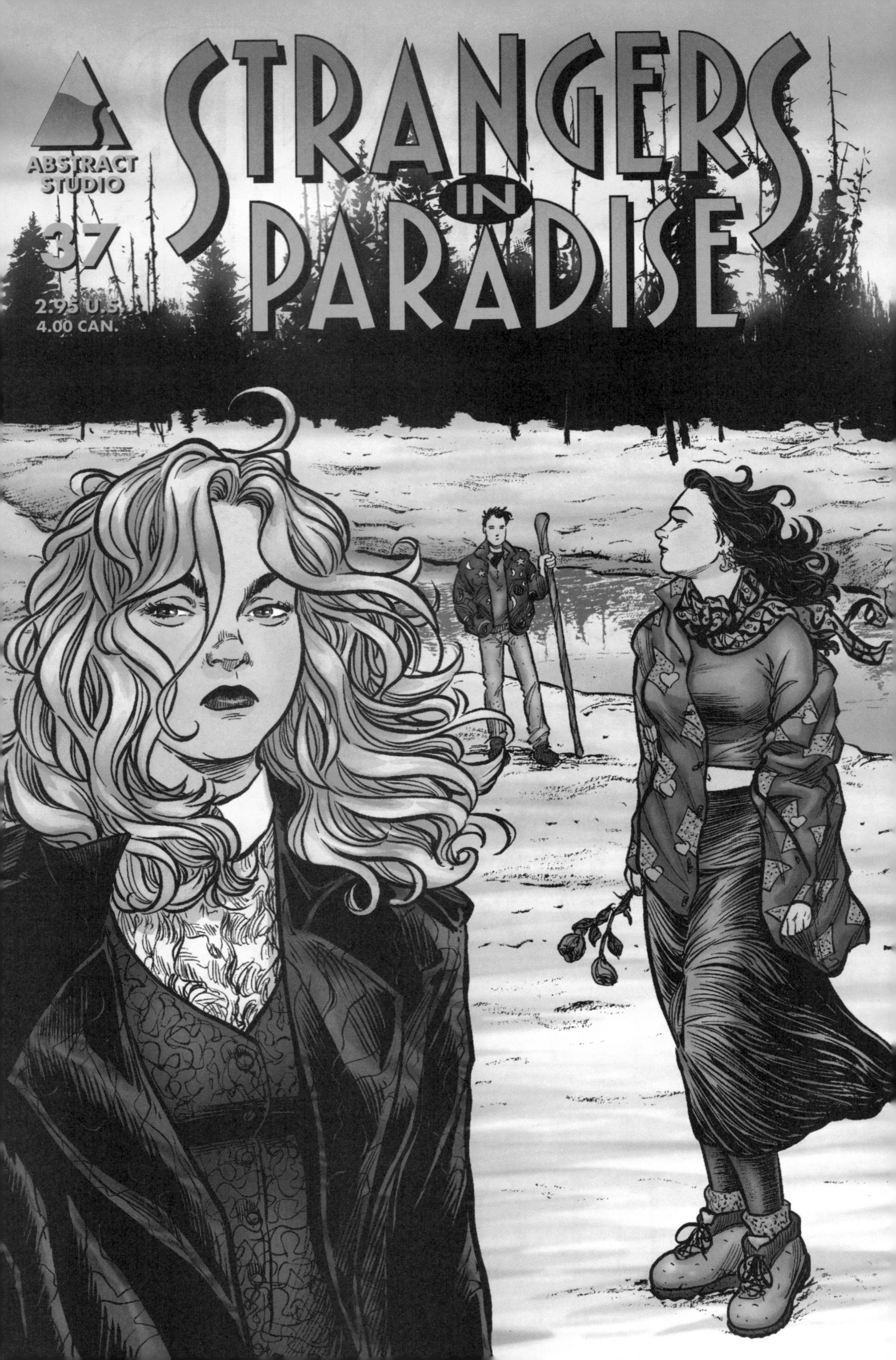

ABSTRACT STUDIO
STRANGERS IN PARADISE
37
2.95 U.S.
4.00 CAN.

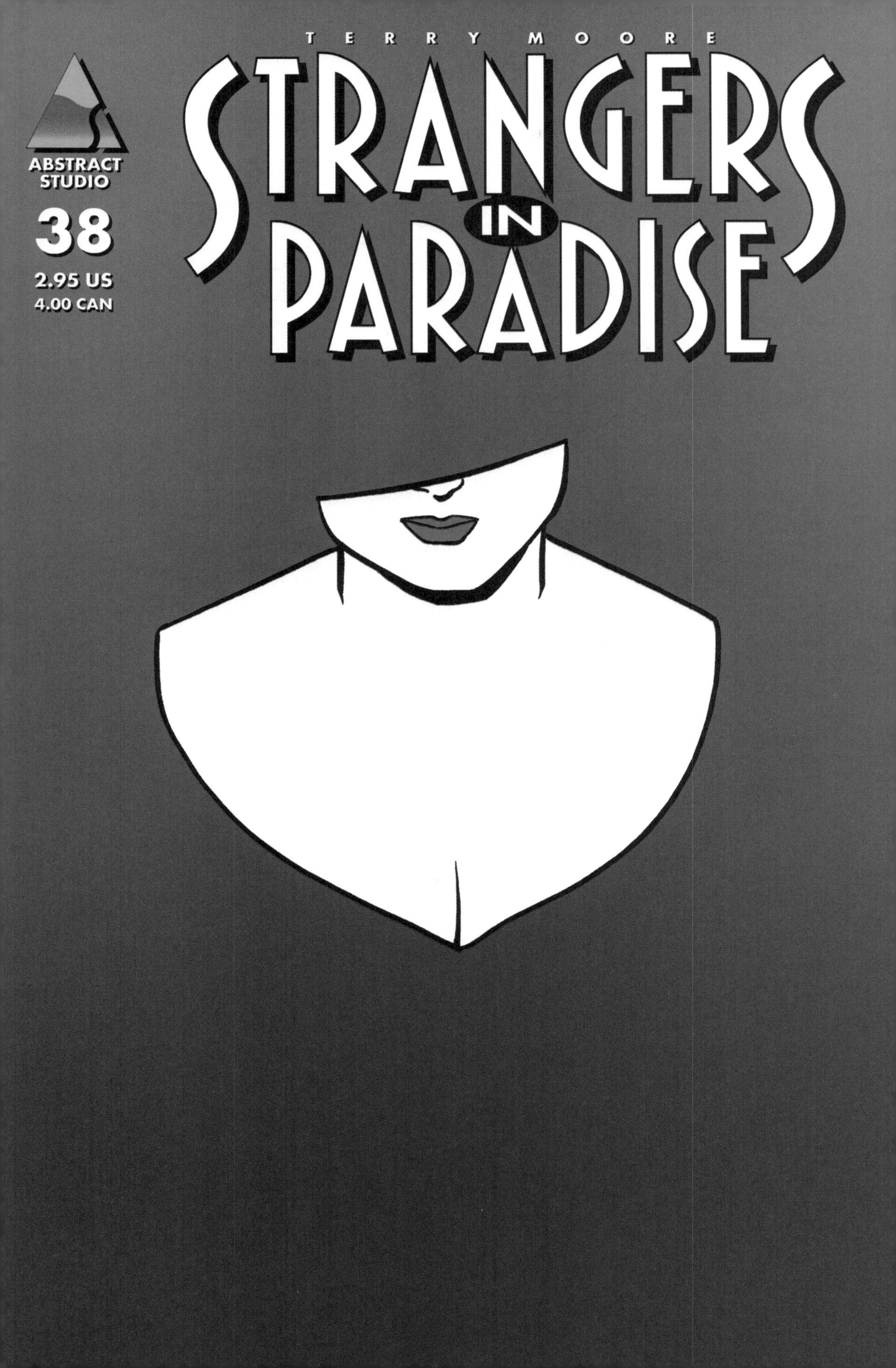
TERRY MOORE
STRANGERS IN PARADISE
ABSTRACT STUDIO
38
2.95 US
4.00 CAN

S k e t c h b o o k

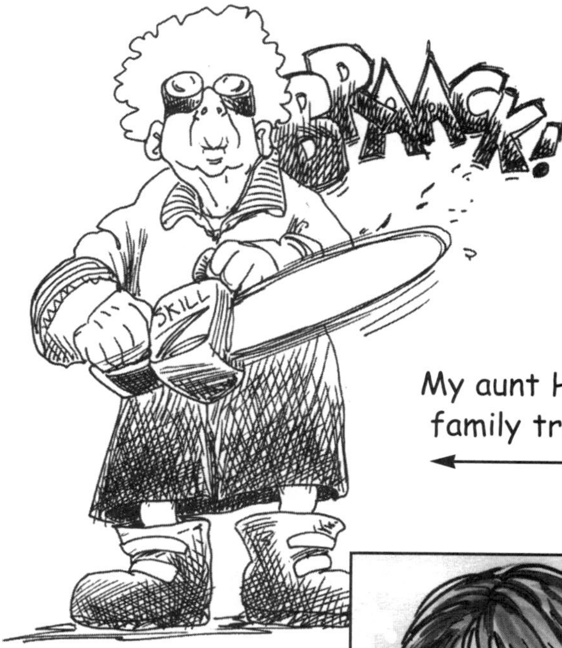
SKILL

My aunt Hildie. A family treasure.

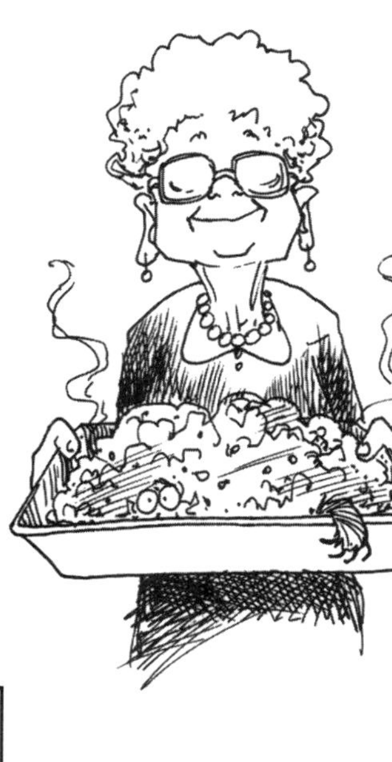

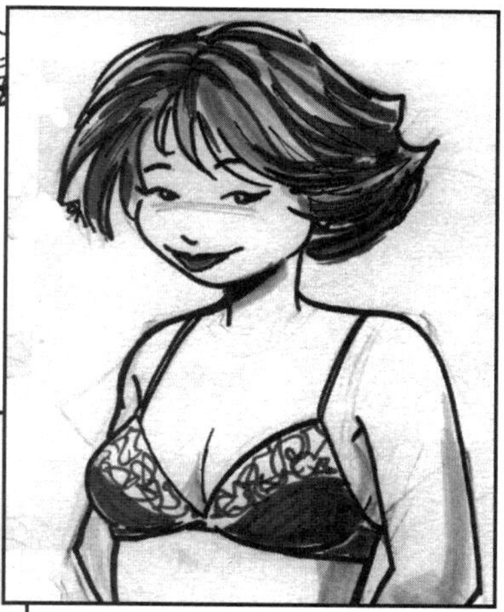

I don't expect the aging of the Gen-Xer's to be a pretty sight, what with millions of tattooed old ladies and pierced old men.

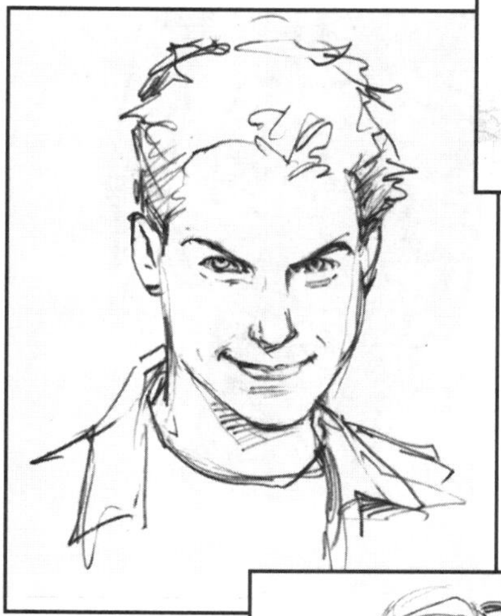

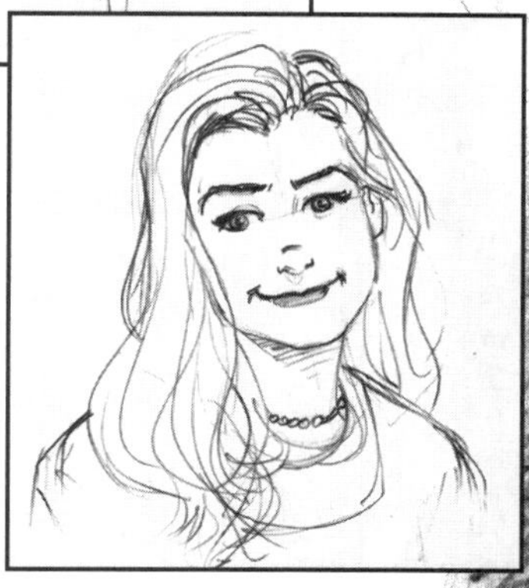

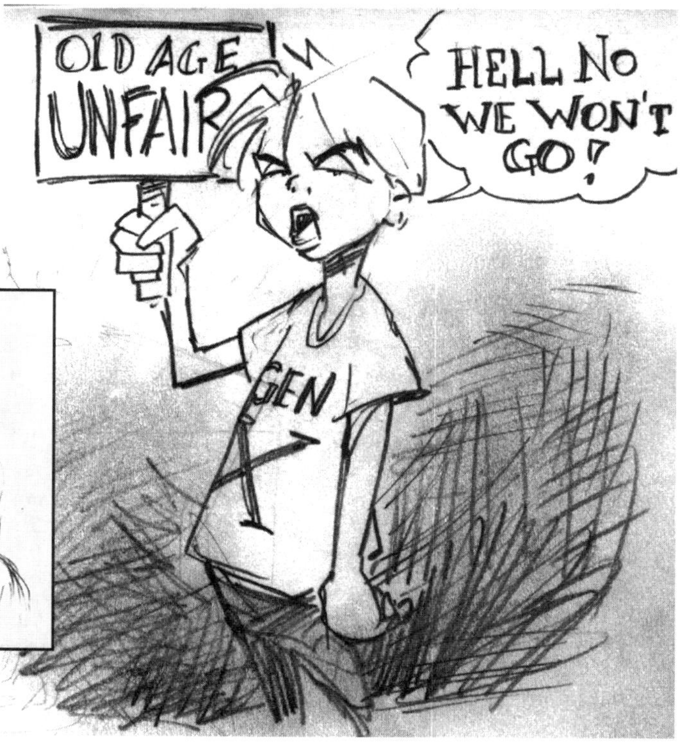
OLD AGE UNFAIR
HELL NO WE WON'T GO!
GEN X

# AVENGERS IN PARADISE

...a nifty idea from one of our distributors

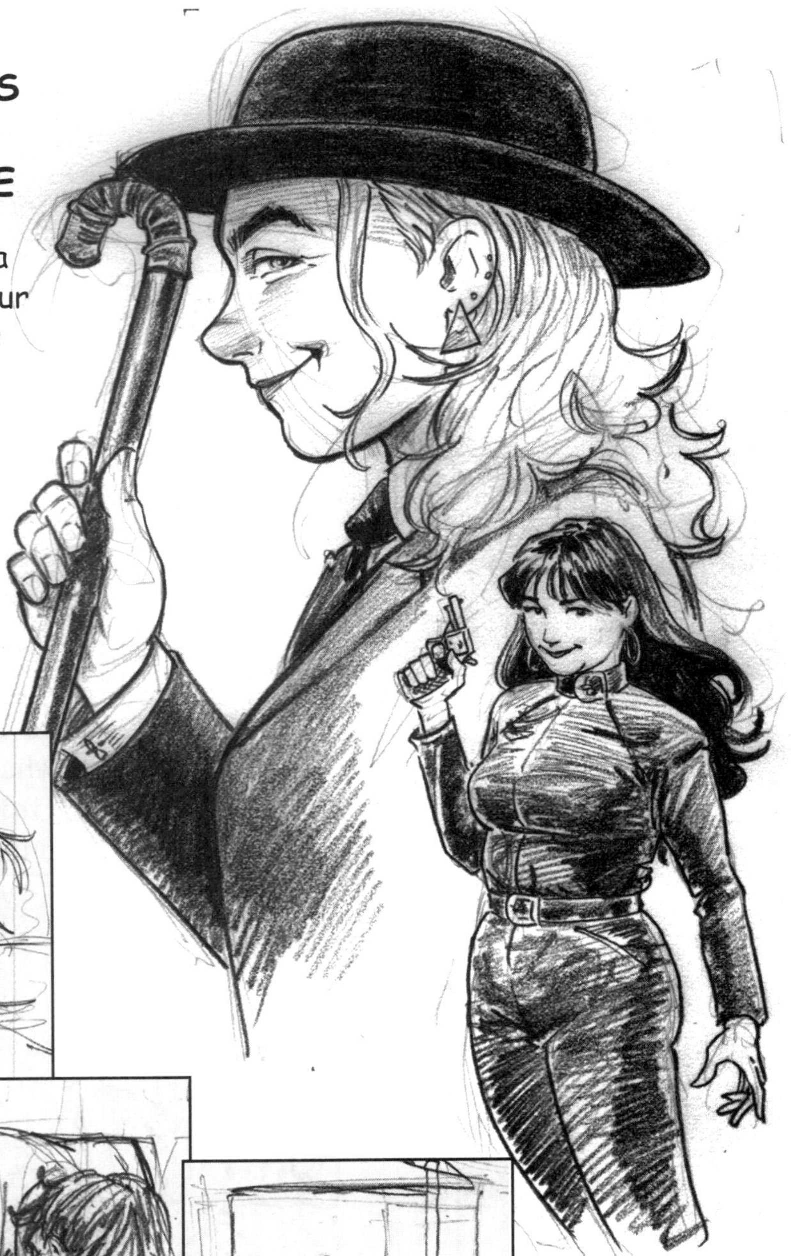

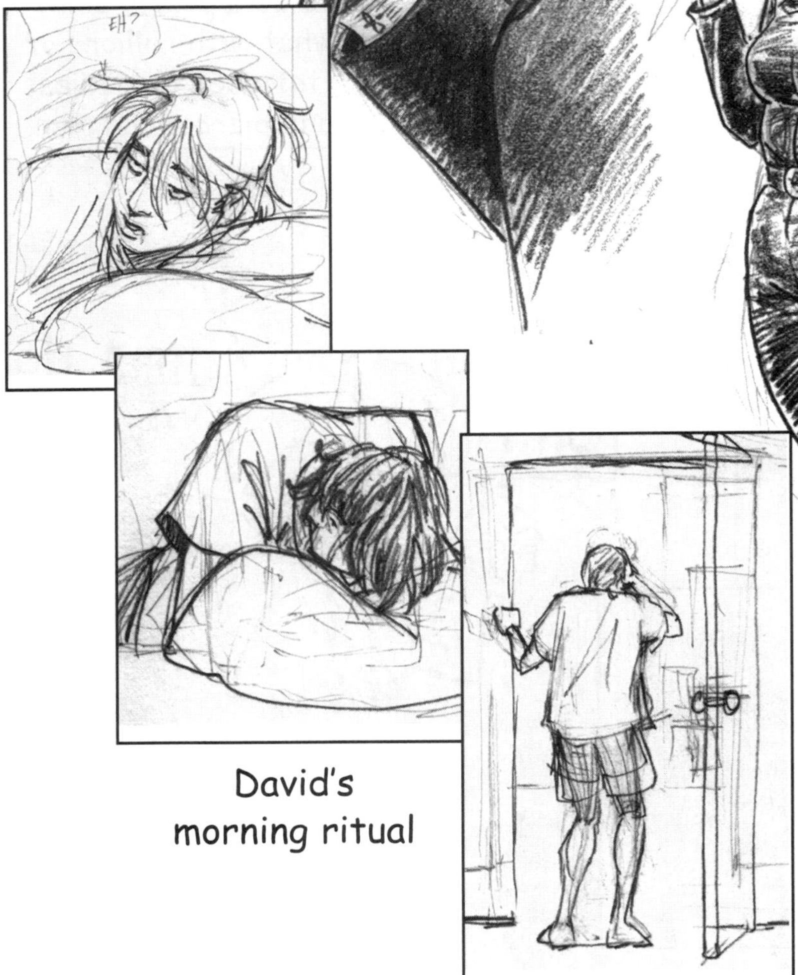
EH?

David's morning ritual

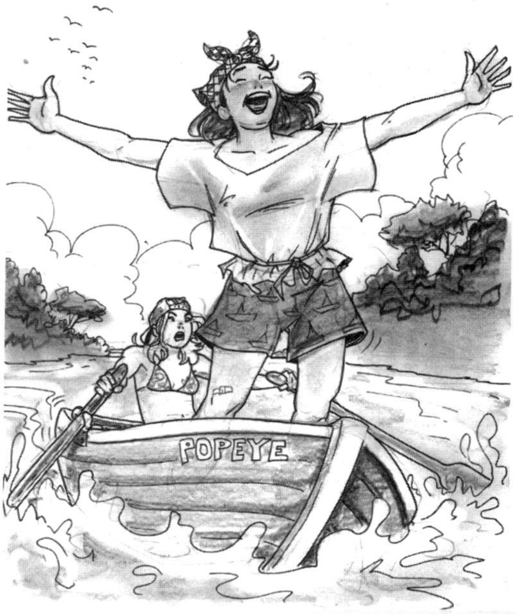
POPEYE

What bald men dream about

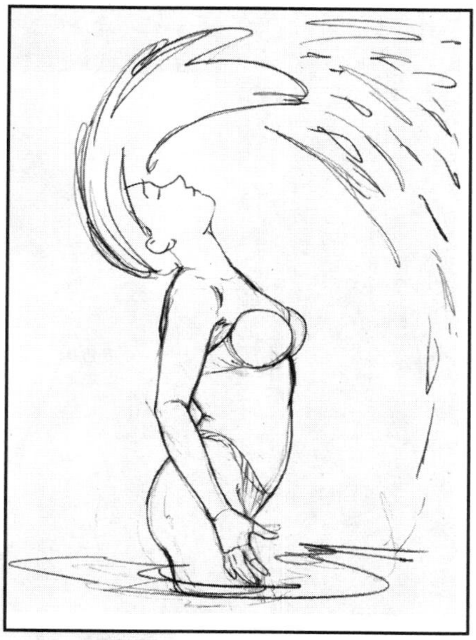

Why Francine never catches any fish — they really hate her version of Climb Every Mountain. Big show tunes girl, Francine, especially when you get her outside.

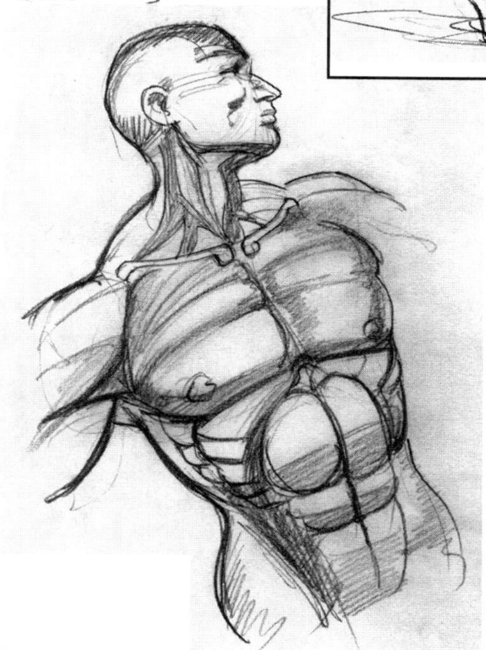

How can you draw Micky Mouse if you don't know what a skinned autopsy dude looks like? That was Da Vinci's attitude.

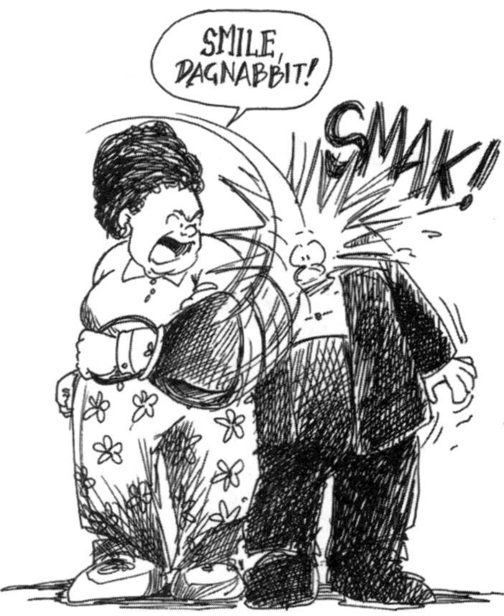
SMILE, DAGNABBIT!
SMAK!

This is legal in America.

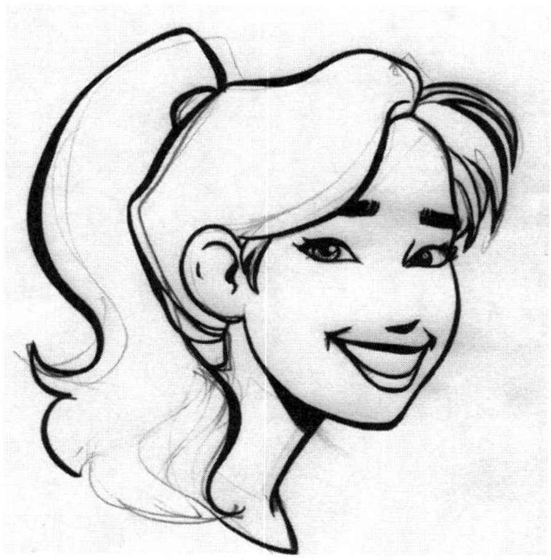

Snoopy In Paradise

For Sparky
1922 - 2000

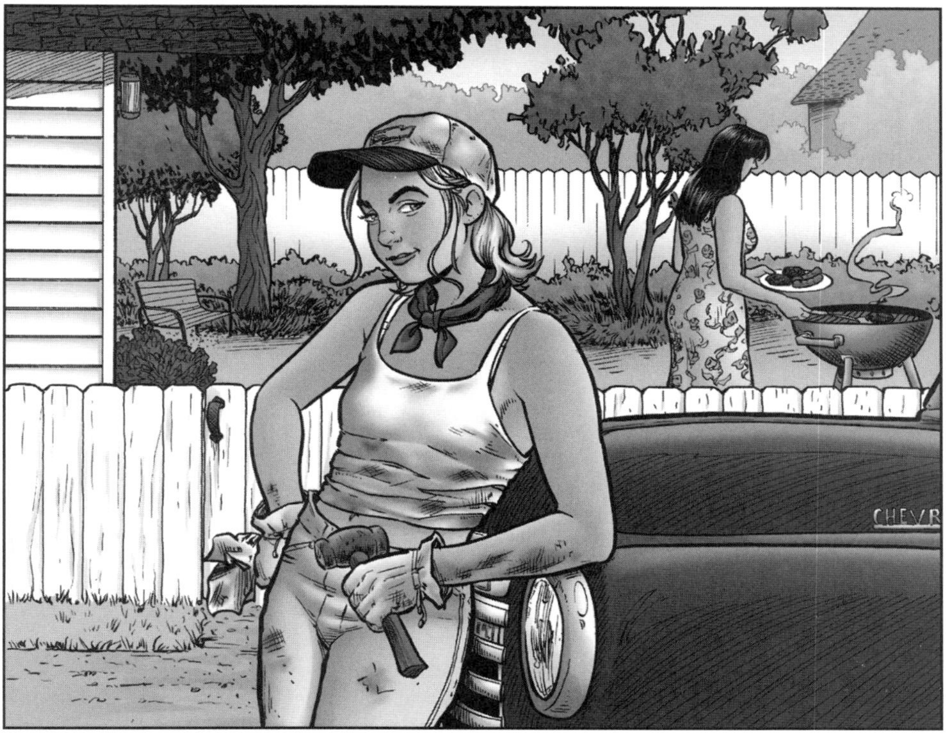
CHEVR

Acknowledgements

*Pretty Maids All In A Row* by Joe Walsh & Joe Vitale,
from the album *The Eagles: Hotel California*
©1976 Elektra/Asylum/Nonesuch Records

*Ssssh!* by Fleming and John, from their cd,
*The Way We Are* ©2000Fleming and John

For more Strangers In Paradise books go to:
www.StrangersInParadise.com
email: SIPNET@StrangersInParadise.com
write to: SIP, P. O. Box 271487, Houston, Texas 77277, USA.